HANDBOOKS

P9-CEC-145

7/08

MARYLAND
& DELAWARE

JOANNE MILLER

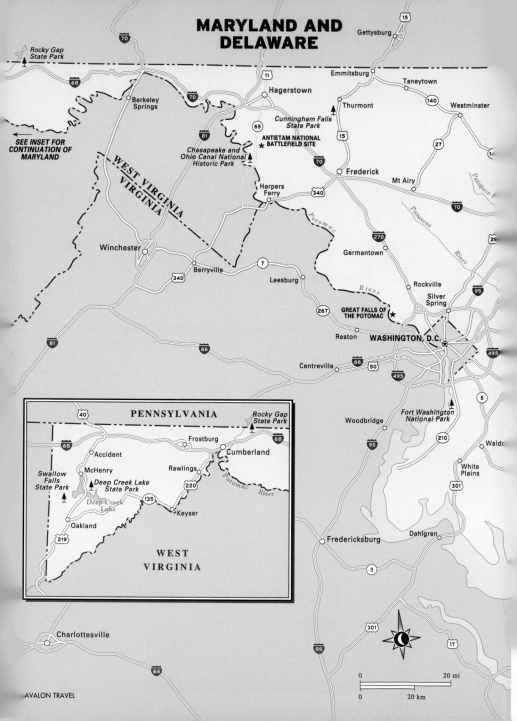

MARYLAND AND DELAWARE

Gettysburg

Rocky Gap
State Park

Berkeley
Springs

Emmitsburg

Taneytown

Hagerstown

Thurmont

Westminster

Cunningham Falls
State Park

SEE INSET FOR
CONTINUATION OF
MARYLAND

ANTIETAM NATIONAL
BATTLEFIELD SITE

Frederick

Mt Airy

WEST VIRGINIA
VIRGINIA

Chesapeake and
Ohio Canal National
Historic Park

Paropsco R

Harpers
Ferry

Patuxent

Winchester

Germantown

River

Berryville

Rockville

Leesburg

Silver
Spring

GREAT FALLS OF
THE POTOMAC

River

Reston

WASHINGTON, D.C.

Centreville

Fort Washington
National Park

SEE INSET FOR
CONTINUATION OF
MARYLAND

Woodbridge

Waldo

PENNSYLVANIA

Rocky Gap
State Park

White
Plains

Frostburg

Cumberland

Accident

McHenry

Rawlings

Swallow
Falls
State Park

Deep Creek Lake
State Park

Deep Creek
Lake

Potomac River

Keyser

Oakland

Fredericksburg

Dahlgren

WEST
VIRGINIA

Charlottesville

0   20 mi

AVALON TRAVEL

0   20 km

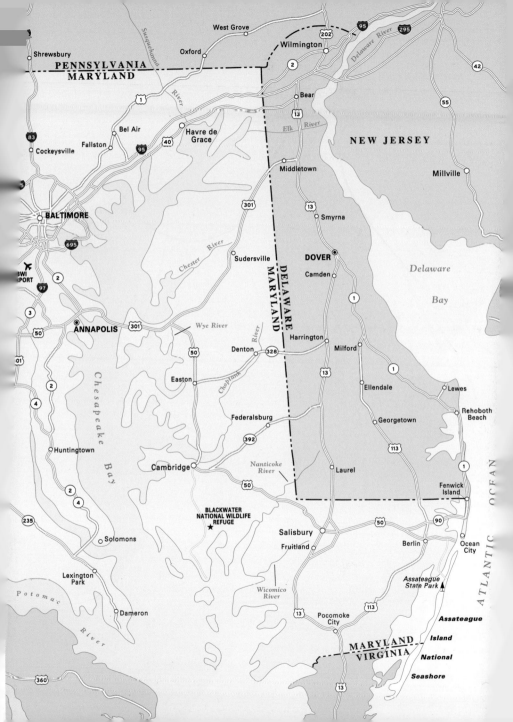

DISCOVER MARYLAND & DELAWARE

Sunlight on the bay is bewitching. This dancing light drew Native Americans to the shallow waters to gather food for their families. Hundreds of years later, Europeans, exhausted from the religious battles of the Reformation, saw heaven reflected on the gentle waves. The seat of this most wondrous of waters – *Terra Mariae*, Mary's land – was meant to welcome all who sought peace.

The mighty Chesapeake, and the land that caresses it, continue to enchant today. Spun out from the hub of the bay, Maryland offers sandy peninsulas, fertile upland, and cool mountains. Bounty was and is everywhere, from shellfish and other seafood to thousands of acres of cultivated fields and farms teeming with livestock. Glittering cities rise above the coastal plain. How can one place be so many things?

On the west side of the Chesapeake, great population centers stretch from Baltimore south to Washington, D.C. Annapolis, the

Baltimore Harbor and the National Aquarium at sunset

wonderfully preserved state capital, lies at the western terminus of the bay bridge, linking west and east shores. Bethesda and Silver Spring are two of the many suburban branches that spread from the city of Washington, but the appearance of overdevelopment is deceptive. Tracts of open land – including a vast wildlife refuge – refresh the landscape.

Surrounded by water, southern Maryland is the birthplace of the state. St. Mary's City was the first colony, and the winding waterways and farmlands are still as bucolic as they were in Lord Baltimore's day. Solomons Island is a lovely base for exploring the ancient Calvert Cliffs and the rest of this quiet countryside.

The Piedmont Plateau spreads across the western part of the state, growing bumpy and sweet with pine as it enters the Appalachian Mountains. Far removed from salt spray, the west is a land of peaceful

Chesapeake City, Maryland

orchards and small farms scaling into gentle mountains, a place of warm fruit pies and black-water lakes – a different world, not three hours away from the bustle of Baltimore's Inner Harbor.

On the northern boundaries of the bay, open land and forest set the stage for wineries and horse farms. Here, the population becomes increasingly dense as it reaches Baltimore City on the northwest side of the bay. The old tobacco port of Baltimore grew into an industrial power during the 1800s, and today it offers visitors a thousand pleasures: a world-class aquarium, art museums, and absolutely amazing food among them.

East of the Chesapeake, a wide spit of land forms the Delmarva (Delaware-Maryland-Virginia) Peninsula, with historic towns, low-lying farms, and fisheries. A chain of barrier islands runs along the lower part of the peninsula. Ocean City, Maryland, which lies at the southernmost end of one of these islands, is a renowned recreational surf-bathing and fishing resort. Nearby Assateague Island is a state and national preserve.

Delaware – so named because of its proximity to the river, which

Amish farm horses

in turn was named for Thomas West, Baron De La Warr, the first governor of Virginia – is flanked by Maryland to the south and west, and the Delaware River and Atlantic Ocean on the east. The state combines two radically different elements: urban industrialization and rural agriculture. It's rich, fascinating, and underappreciated, which makes it all the more appealing. Besides, how can you dislike a place where the state bird is a chicken? Not just any chicken, of course – it's the blue rock, a tough and tenacious type bred especially for fighting.

Delaware serves up a bounty of historical sites and places to play along its golden shores, including the charming colonial capital, New Castle, and Fort Delaware, a bit of the Civil War on Pea Patch Island. Bombay Hook, Prime Hook, and Chesapeake and Delaware Canal wildlife refuges, Delaware Seashore, and Cape Henlopen satisfy urges for outdoor recreation. Different versions of beach life are available at Rehoboth, Bethany, and Fenwick Island. Just bring a change of bathing suit for each.

Though Delaware is small in area, its importance in industry, banking, and technology far exceeds its size. Within its three counties

Easton Courthouse, Maryland

is everything a visitor could desire, from active outdoor recreation to the pleasures of a fine meal and luxurious guest quarters. Delaware is the quiet, skinny girl in the back of the schoolroom who goes on to become class valedictorian, moves to the big city, becomes a super-model, and makes a zillion dollars before she retires at 30 to start her own bank. Chances are, your credit cards are based in Delaware, thanks to its liberal interest laws. Half of America's Fortune 500 companies are based in the "Corporate Capital of the World," Wilmington. And there's no sales tax on purchases in Delaware.

Maryland and Delaware are beautiful places; nothing about them is austere. They are destined to answer your heart's desire, be it a silent and lonesome hike through pine woods or the mad whirl of a reel connecting with a big fish; canoes gliding on lakes of mirrored sky or salt spray peppering your face as your sailboat tacks into the wind. Or perhaps your dreams are man-made: crab cakes, crispy on the outside, creamy within, and impossibly tender fried chicken; or ornate jewels made for heiresses and three-story-high glass walls with sharks circling behind. If you can imagine it, you will find it here, dancing in the sunlight, heaven captured and shared.

New Castle, Delaware

Contents

MAP CONTENTS

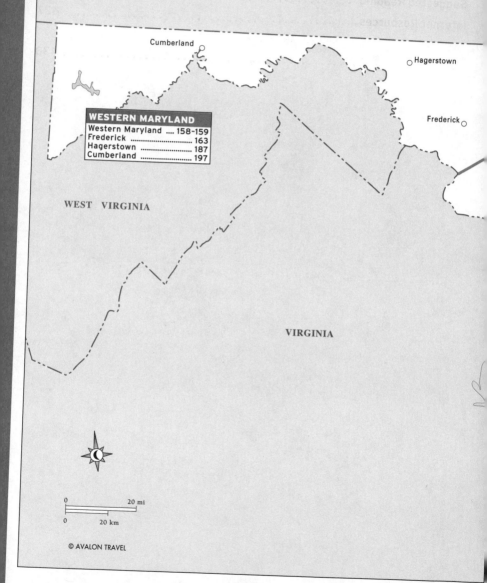

PENNSYLVANIA

Cumberland ○

○ Hagerstown

Frederick ○

WEST   VIRGINIA

VIRGINIA

0   20 mi

0   20 km

© AVALON TRAVEL

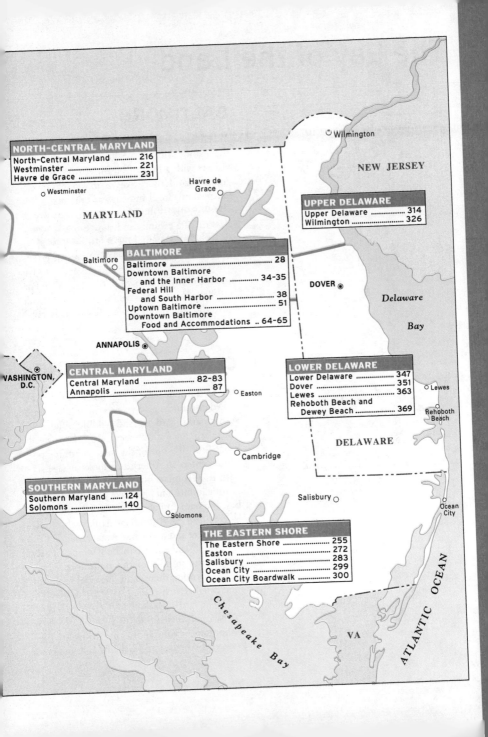

○ Westminster

Havre de Grace ○

MARYLAND

○ Wilmington

NEW JERSEY

Baltimore ○

DOVER ◉

Delaware

Bay

ANNAPOLIS ◉

WASHINGTON, D.C. ⊛

○ Easton

○ Lewes

○ Rehoboth Beach

DELAWARE

○ Cambridge

Salisbury ○

○ Solomons

○ Ocean City

Chesapeake Bay

VA

ATLANTIC OCEAN

The Lay of the Land

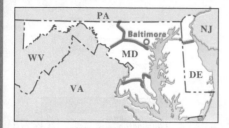

BALTIMORE

This former tobacco port grew into an industrial giant during the 1800s, and today it woos visitors with a host of pleasures from the past and present. History lives on in Ft. McHenry, where our national anthem was written; the National Aquarium in Baltimore offers world-class marine exhibits and shows; the Walters Art Museum, Baltimore Museum of Art, and Visionary Art Museum present extensive collections of modern and classic art. Delve into the idiosyncratic worlds of Edgar Allan Poe and Babe Ruth, visit a dental museum that will leave you smiling, or down a few beers in boisterous Fell's Point.

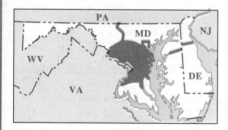

CENTRAL MARYLAND

This is the state's most populous area, where crowded suburbs give way to small towns and scenic parks, gardens, and wildlife refuges. If you're looking for architectural splendor, head to Annapolis, one of the most charming political centers in America. It looks a stage set, with its Georgian buildings, cobbled streets, historic homes and jewel-like placement on the Bay; the state capital of Maryland, home to the U.S. Naval Academy, enchants with a lively atmosphere and many fine restaurants.

Though the suburban belt wraps tightly around the middle of the Baltimore-Washington corridor, there's still plenty of room for rural delights such as the Patuxent National Wildlife Refuge, Seneca Creek State Park, and Brighton Dam Azalea Garden. If shopping is your sport, the "Miracle Mile" between Bethesda and Rockville is your arena.

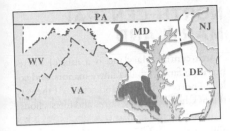

SOUTHERN MARYLAND

Plenty of diversions await anglers, boaters, and beachgoers on the rural shores of southern Maryland. Experience the past in the counties where Maryland was born. The fourth English settlement in North America, **St. Mary's City** (a National Historic Landmark) transports visitors to colonial times through excavations and reconstructions, and the **Potomac River Museum and St. Clement's Island** chronicle the first hesitant landing of English settlers. Fans of U.S. history will enjoy following in the footsteps of John Wilkes Booth on **The Assassin's Trail.** The 15-million-year-old fossils at **Calvert Cliffs State Park** offer a more ancient view. Back in the present, uncrowded villages and resorts such as **North Beach and Chesapeake Beach** provide just the right amount of quiet beauty combined with activities for a relaxing holiday.

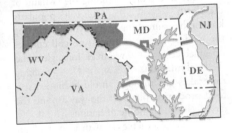

WESTERN MARYLAND

The city of **Frederick** has grown into one of Maryland's favorite destinations, as much for its historic past as its modern-day restaurants. Home to the **National Museum of Civil War Medicine** and the **Schifferstadt Architectural Museum,** Frederick serves as the gateway to both western Maryland and national memory. Pivotal Civil War sites **Antietam National Battlefield** and **Harper's Ferry National Historic Site** have become peaceful pilgrimage destinations. Outdoor enthusiasts should continue west through Amish farmland into the Allegheny Mountains, where beautiful black-water **Deep Creek Lake State Park** offers hiking, skiing, and canoeing. The west is well known for its bevy of parks: **Swallow Falls** and **Big Run** are popular among families for splashing in summer streams and snowshoeing along tree-shrouded paths in winter.

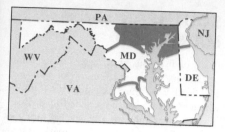

NORTH-CENTRAL MARYLAND

North-central Maryland is a mix of horse-breeding farms, rural country manors, and colonial ports both sleepy and active. At the very top of Chesapeake Bay, farms and forests house historic wineries such as Boordy Vineyards and Ladew Topiary Gardens, a superb private park and mansion. Havre de Grace is a popular getaway, notable for its Victorian mansions, fine restaurants (including Bomboy's — chocolate fanatics, take note) and signature little lighthouse. Lovely Chesapeake City rests on the western end of America's busiest canal. In Kent County, you'll also find some of the finest cycling routes in the country.

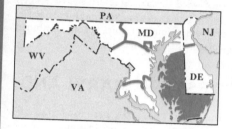

THE EASTERN SHORE

East across the Chesapeake Bay Bridge, you'll find thousands of miles of bay and ocean shoreline to explore, including the "Miami of the North" Ocean City. OC, as it's popularly known, has something for everyone, including the wildest variety of miniature golf courses imaginable. Crisfield was made for anglers, and the local museum's Port of Crisfield walking tour takes you through an old-fashioned seafood processing plant on the way around the city. Salisbury, home of famous Salisbury Pewter, is the local big city with a "zoo without borders" and the must-see Ward Museum of Wildfowl Art. Offshore, slow-paced Deal and Smith Islands offer a taste of the waterman's life, while native patched ponies roam freely on Assateague Island National Seashore.

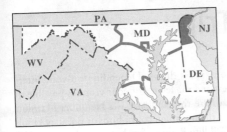

UPPER DELAWARE

The name DuPont is everywhere in the Brandywine Valley on the properties and superb gardens the family has bequeathed—**Winterthur, Hagley Mills,** and **Nemours Mansion** provide a glimpse of how the other half once lived. Enjoy the restaurants and museums, particularly the **Delaware History Center and Delaware Art Museum,** in the state's largest city, Wilmington. The historic town is experiencing a renaissance, with a revitalized riverfront and a thriving live theater scene. Watch the ships roll by in wonderfully preserved **New Castle,** the state's original capital and a living, breathing town that retains its colonial flavor with many historic buildings open to the public. **Fort Delaware State Park** on Pea Patch Island was used as a model prison during the Civil War and is now a wildlife sanctuary with historical reenactments; don't miss the firing of the cannon!

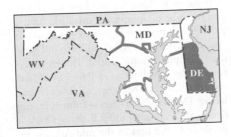

LOWER DELAWARE

Tour the Amish country around **Dover,** the state capital, or try your luck at the casinos or the track, **Dover Downs.** The **Air Mobility Command Museum** in Dover is a treat for flight fans, while lovers of sea and sand will want to head straight for the shore. Each resort town is unique, from the fine restaurants and small-town atmosphere of quiet **Lewes** to wide-open, bustling **Rehoboth Beach,** hard-partying **Dewey Beach,** and sedate **Bethany Beach. Cape Henlopen State Park** and **Delaware Seashore State Park** offer summer at its finest. And did I mention the shopping? The highway between Lewes and Rehoboth is mall central—with no sales tax. Happy holiday!

Planning Your Trip

Maryland truly has it all—fine museums, natural history collections, and a plethora of restaurants in Baltimore; hundreds of boating destinations and places to enjoy water sports on the Chesapeake, its tributaries, and Deep Creek Lake; and miles of trails, camping, and other outdoor recreation on the bay and in the mountains. The state also covers a lot of territory: Though it's possible to drive from the eastern boundary at Delaware to the western edge at West Virginia or around the Chesapeake Bay in a day, it makes much more sense to choose your delights. Fortunately, one of the best things about Maryland is that you can have breakfast in a Baltimore café and still get to a rustic campsite in time to rustle up lunch.

The type of experience you choose and the amount of time you have will determine your destination. Plan on at least one week for each area. The Maryland chapters are divided into contiguous areas, based around Baltimore (the primary airport hub). Seeking big-city sightseeing mixed with a more rural experience? Then Baltimore and north-central Maryland are for you. A trip combining urban pleasures and American history might include Baltimore and central Maryland. If you prefer the outdoors far from the bright lights, consider western Maryland or the Eastern Shore. If a sea-and-sand vacation is in order, try southern Maryland for its less crowded beaches, or Ocean City on the Eastern Shore, where the action is. Are Civil War sites on your agenda? Check out western and southern Maryland.

Delaware is as small as Maryland is big—but it's also mighty. The First State packs a lot of fun into three counties: everything from scenic hikes to sugary beaches to mansions belonging to the wealthiest families in America. You can drive from one end of Delaware to the other in about three hours, and accessibility is just one of its draws. Depending on your interest and the length of your visit, it's possible to admire the cupids at the Nemours Mansion in the morning, count birds at Bombay Hook Wildlife Refuge after lunch, and arrive at the beach by nightfall.

The Delaware chapters are arranged north–south into Upper and Lower Delaware. Plan on a week in each area to see all the sights. The northernmost county contains the major urban area in Delaware: Wilmington, an up-and-coming city with a small-town feel. The countryside surrounding Wilmington—the Brandywine Valley—is home to most of the northern area's attractions. Here you'll find three Dupont properties, all stunning must-sees for anyone interested in decorative arts and crafts.

If you're looking for outdoor recreation, you won't be disappointed; this little state is packed with parks, refuges and greenways. If you're a birder or a cyclist, you've found paradise. The pretty state capital, Dover, is surrounded by Amish farms in Lower Delaware; the coastline features large wildlife refuges. Lower Delaware's beaches—from jumping Rehoboth Beach to peaceful Bethany Beach—are some of the best in the mid-Atlantic region. This area offers nightlife aplenty, two state parks (Delaware Seashore State Park and Cape Henlopen State Park) for campers, and a fabulous tax-free group of malls for those who just can't stop shopping.

WHEN TO GO

Late summer in Maryland can seem almost tropical, so if your tolerance level for thick air is high, you'll enjoy all parts of the state. The west tends to be less humid than the areas surrounding Chesapeake Bay, and many city dwellers escape to the higher elevation of Deep Creek Lake during the warmest months. Generally, off-season (late fall, winter, early spring) in any part of Maryland will yield a bounty of discounts and package deals. Though anglers and hunters are limited to their seasons, others will find that the best times to visit are determined by destination.

Ocean City and the Atlantic shore are favorite spots for visitors from the chilliest days of May (the water is *cold*) all the way through mid-October. September/October is an especially lovely time to be there—the summer crowds are gone, the water is warm, many hotels offer discounts, and the sun continues to light up the beach all day. Long, romantic (and very private) walks on the beach are yours during the winter, when some of the best restaurants and businesses stay open for the local trade.

If active outdoor sports are on your list, summer is an ideal time to go west. Hiking, biking, and water sports on the C&O Canal path and Deep Creek Lake are all the more enjoyable in fine weather; since many vacation at the shore, this leaves the western trails free of huddled masses. This is also the area to catch a bit of fall color. Maryland's premier ski resort welcomes visitors in the winter—this is the prime area for all winter sports.

Autumn, winter, and spring are good times to visit Baltimore, as the crowds thin out and attractions continue to entice. Fresh seafood is at its peak in the fall and winter, and the city's many fine restaurants make the most of it.

The annual temperatures in Delaware mimic the Chesapeake Bay, though the winters tend to be more extreme. Most of the state's attractions are outside the urban area of Wilmington, and even there casual clothing is de rigueur. As summer humidity builds, it's a good idea to protect yourself from biting insects with lightweight, long pants and shirts. Mosquitoes are particularly pestiferous due to the preponderance of groundwater and marshes, but don't let the threat of a few bites stop you from enjoying Delaware's truly extraordinary outdoors.

WHAT TO TAKE

Temperatures in the winter months occasionally drop below zero, depending on where you are. In western Maryland and upper Delaware, expect the coldest weather and dress accordingly. For the rest of the state, take plenty of clothing that can be layered, and bring an umbrella. Summer is uniformly warm and humid; expect rain throughout the year. Shorts and T-shirts are common in both the rural areas and the cities. A common style of dress year-round is "sailing preppy"—short-sleeved knit shirts with collars, khaki or navy shorts or pants, and loafers or boat shoes. The look is Ralph Lauren/Talbot's/Lands' End.

If you're traveling by car, the interstates and large highways have frequent rest stops; however, if you plan to tour the back roads, take both toilet paper and snacks. The villages in the rural areas are few and far between, and there's no guarantee that stores will be present, let alone open, even during the day. For back-road touring, a map from a local gas station is a must, and a compass isn't a bad idea either.

Explore Maryland & Delaware

THE BEST OF MARYLAND & DELAWARE

Both states offer a wonderful variety of things to see and do. The urban areas host sophisticated museums and developed historical sites; the outlying countryside is a recreational smorgasbord. "The Best" stretches from the far west of Maryland to the Atlantic. This two-week tour starting and ending in Baltimore barely scratches the surface, but will give you a taste of the beauty and richness of this land of bays and rivers.

Day 1

Begin in Baltimore, taking in the incomparable **Walters Art Museum** (the best of the best) and the **National Aquarium**, then enjoy dinner in **Little Italy**.

Day 2

Drive south to **Annapolis**, strolling among the historic buildings, and take a tour of the handsome grounds of the **US Naval Academy**.

Day 3

Travel west to the site of one of the Civil War's bloodiest encounters, historic **Antietam Battlefield,** then head north to **Frederick** for dinner and an overnight stop.

Days 4-6

Continue west on old U.S. 40 to spend a few days exploring the black waters of beautiful **Deep Creek Lake** and its surrounding state parks, especially **Swallow Falls.**

Days 7-8

Return to central Maryland, stop off at magical **Ladew Topiary Gardens**, and overnight in **Havre de Grace**. Continue into Upper Delaware, visiting the DuPont Properties of **Hagley Mills** and **Winterthur**. Overnight in the historic town of **New Castle**.

Days 9-10

Head south to the Delaware Beaches, especially **Lewes,** and get some **tax-free shopping** in

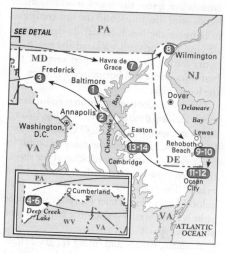

at the outlets. Camp near the sea in **Henlopen State Park** or **Delaware National Seashore Park.**

Days 11-12

Ocean City is the ultimate beach town—enjoy the surf, sand, and boardwalk, then continue south to **Assateague Island** to get a close-up view of those adorable wild ponies.

Days 13-14

Head back to **Baltimore** on U.S. 50, with a detour to the **Red Roost** in White Haven for all the crab you can eat. Overnight there or in the scenic shore towns of **Cambridge, Easton** or **St. Michaels.**

FIVE DAYS IN CHARM CITY

Baltimore appeals to a huge variety of interests. This whirlwind tour crams a lot into five days—take longer if you can, and enjoy all the fabulous restaurants in the outlying areas. The itinerary below concentrates on a few highlights. Take a water taxi between various sites on the harbor.

Day 1

No visit to Baltimore would be complete without a stop at **Fort McHenry,** the birthplace of our national anthem. While in the neighborhood, take in the **Baltimore Museum of Industry,** which cleverly displays the city's manufacturing history. Time for one more stop? Make it the **American Visionary Art Museum,** "outsider art" at its finest.

Day 2

If you're in the mood for a little workout, a run up the steps of the **Washington Monument** (designed by the same architect as the Washington Monument in D.C.) will leave you gasping. Nearby, the **Walters Art Museum** displays outstanding collections; and last, but certainly not least, stop in for a look at beautiful old **Penn Station,** a window into the past.

Day 3

The roundhouse at **B&O Railroad Museum** is a radiant monument to the iron horse, and who'd have thought the **Dr. Samuel D. Harris National Museum of Dentistry** has one of the most delightful collections in town? The **Babe Ruth Birthplace and Orioles Museum** is unstinting in its appreciation of the great American game.

Day 4

A world-class nature site, the **National Aquarium in Baltimore** is a must-see. **Port Discovery,** ostensibly for kids, will delight every member of the family.

Day 5

If you have the transportation, go up to Druid Park, enjoy the **Conservatory** and spend the rest of the day at the **Baltimore Zoo,** one of the best I've seen.

MARYLAND & DELAWARE FOR FAMILIES

Outdoors or indoors, there are countless recreational options for families looking to share fun. The destinations below offer something for all ages.

Baltimore

Must-sees include a day at the **Baltimore Zoo,** a ride on the water taxi to the **Baltimore Museum of Industry,** and a play date at especially-for-kids **Port Discovery.** No visit to Charm City would be complete without a day at **National Aquarium in Baltimore** (don't miss the porpoise show).

Eastern Shore

The biggest and best-known destination on the shore is **Ocean City,** with its fabulous beach, boardwalk, **Life-Saving Station Museum,** and a variety of amusement parks, miniature golf courses, shopping, and restaurants.

Upper Delaware

The **Delaware Museum of Natural History** is a little beauty, informative and fun. The **Delaware History Center** in downtown Wilmington is one of the best interactive history museums around.

AMERICAN HISTORY 101

Maryland and Delaware feature some of the earliest sites of European habitation on the East Coast. The entire area is rich in American history.

Baltimore

The War of 1812 comes alive at **Fort McHenry**, site of the "rockets' red glare" and the **Star-Spangled Banner Flag House and Museum**, where the gallant flag was created.

Central Maryland

Annapolis, the state capital, offers a tasty assortment of historic buildings, the **US Naval Academy** (the J.P. Jones crypt and chapel are gorgeous), and many shops and restaurants. History detectives won't want to miss the **Surratt House Museum** and **Dr. Samuel A. Mudd House Museum**, integral parts of the Abraham Lincoln assassination story. Follow the **Assassin's Trail** by car for a lovely tour of the area.

Southern Maryland

Explore Maryland's early colonial past at **St. Clement's Island-Potomac River Museum** and **Historic St. Mary's City**, then check out a combination of Civil War history and outdoor recreation at **Point Lookout State Park.**

Western Maryland

Head to **Antietam Battlefield**, and, if there's time, take a look around **Monocacy Battlefield** and the **Kennedy Farmhouse.** If Civil War sites are of particular interest, plan on an extra day and cross the border into **Harper's Ferry.**

Plan to spend at least one day in **Frederick**, stopping by the fascinating exhibits at the **National Museum of Civil War Medicine** and eating at one or two of many good restaurants.

Upper Delaware

Small towns with distinct personalities are one of the draws here. **New Castle** and **Odessa** both have different and special authentic historic districts.

THE GREAT OUTDOORS

Parks and wild areas are everywhere—you'll find one within a few miles of wherever you find yourself. Here are a few selected for their beauty and interest.

Central Maryland

There are plenty of outdoor recreation and scenic spots, including **Patuxent Research Refuge/National Wildlife Visitor Center** and **Accokeek National Colonial Farm**, which offers a glimpse of early Maryland.

Southern Maryland

Wander among ancient fossils at **Calvert Cliffs State Park.** If your interests are more contemporary, you'll appreciate the **Calvert Marine Museum**, with its restored lighthouse.

Western Maryland

The **C&O Canal National Historical Park** is one of the nation's exemplary recreation areas, though **Swallow Falls State Park** and **Deep Creek Lake** both offer plentiful activities and captivating scenery as well.

North-Central Maryland

Take in **Ladew Topiary Gardens**, a handsomely appointed private home converted to a museum and park, which features some of the most amusing plants on the planet. **Chestertown**, the cultural center of Kent County, is a perfect place to set up a home base while cycling the scenic roads through miles of agricultural land and marshes.

Eastern Shore

Looking for a little outdoor recreation? **Blackwater National Wildlife Refuge**, south of Cambridge, is a large inland waterway, and **Jane's Island State Park**, near Crisfield, is surrounded by the Chesapeake.

Upper Delaware

Take the ferry from Delaware City for a picnic and a day of historical fun: If you're seeking the great outdoors, **Fort Delaware** is a beautiful park, and the Civil War prison on the grounds displays a rare bit of well-preserved history.

Lower Delaware

Birders and other wildlife enthusiasts shouldn't miss **Bombay Hook National Wildlife Refuge;** and **Prime Hook National Wildlife Refuge** offers outdoor enthusiasts another opportunity to commune with nature and observe wildlife up close.

BALTIMORE

From its gracious Victorian days as the haunt of the upper crust to its current status as a renaissance city, Baltimore has seen good times and bad, but its robustness stems from the people who go home at night to a little place on a side street and settle in with a beer by the blue-white light of the tube. The industrial strength that kept the city alive through economic hard times has fallen upon hard times itself. As in many vital centers of American production, jobs have gone elsewhere. What remains, however, are the products of determination—the fruits of Baltimore's will to survive and prosper. Against all odds, it has become a magnet for visitors, a wonderful place full of things to see and do.

Like that other phoenix of a city, Pittsburgh, Baltimore is a city of neighborhoods.

Mount Vernon and Belvedere were society neighborhoods in center city; Fell's Point and Canton were port villages, as was Federal Hill. Highlandtown (pronounced HA-len-town) and Greektown were both villages east of the main part of town that have retained their individuality in spite of being swallowed up by the spread of the big city. All have particular charm, history, shopping, and great places to eat.

Plenty of money has remained in town. There are generously endowed art collections, state-of-the-art science and natural history museums, a fantastic zoo, and good restaurants too numerous to count. Baltimore has become a playground for families—what could be more endearing than that? And hon, the people are great.

© JOANNE MILLER

HIGHLIGHTS

◖ **National Aquarium in Baltimore:** Another world-class attraction; stand on walkways while stingrays swim beneath your feet and watch the feeding at a multistory shark tank (page 32).

◖ **Port Discovery:** Ostensibly for kids, this giant gym and game room will delight every member of the family (page 33).

◖ **American Visionary Art Museum:** An extraordinary display of artwork from "outsiders" – artists who are not formally taught – that will touch you deeply (page 37).

◖ **Fort McHenry:** The stars and stripes continue to wave over the battlements of the birthplace of our national anthem; the fort remains much the same as it did during the War of 1812 (page 39).

◖ **The Baltimore Museum of Industry:** Clever interactive displays show what built Baltimore, from umbrellas to Bromo Seltzer (page 40).

◖ **B&O Railroad Museum:** A radiant monument to the iron horse; engines and cars from all eras can be seen here, at the starting point of America's first railroad (page 41).

◖ **Babe Ruth Birthplace and Orioles Museum:** Unstinting in its appreciation of the great American game, this museum will delight sports nuts and fans of the Babe (page 41).

◖ **Dr. Samuel D. Harris National Museum of Dentistry:** This one will leave you smiling; it's one of the most delightful and original collections in the world. Don't miss George Washington's dentures! (page 43)

◖ **Walters Art Museum:** The best of the best – a well-rounded collection of superb paintings, statuary, jewelry, and Asian art (page 44).

◖ **Washington Monument:** If a little workout is in order, run up the steps of this, the original Washington Monument by the same architect who made the Washington D.C. version (page 45).

◖ **Baltimore Zoo:** One of the top animal collections in the country, this zoo has beautifully landscaped humane enclosures (page 52).

LOOK FOR ◖ TO FIND RECOMMENDED SIGHTS, ACTIVITIES, DINING, AND LODGING.

BALTIMORE

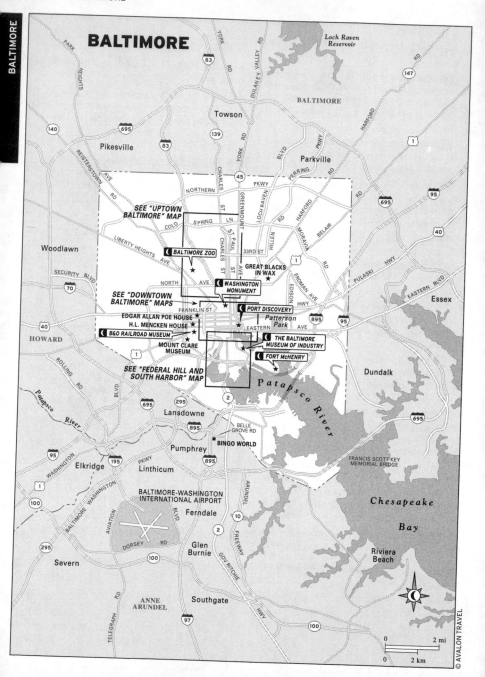

BALTIMORE

Loch Raven Reservoir

BALTIMORE

Towson

Pikesville

Parkville

Woodlawn

SEE "UPTOWN BALTIMORE" MAP

BALTIMORE ZOO ★

GREAT BLACKS IN WAX

SEE "DOWNTOWN BALTIMORE" MAPS

WASHINGTON MONUMENT

Patterson Park

PORT DISCOVERY

EDGAR ALLAN POE HOUSE ★
H.L. MENCKEN HOUSE ★

B&O RAILROAD MUSEUM

MOUNT CLARE MUSEUM

THE BALTIMORE MUSEUM OF INDUSTRY

FORT McHENRY

SEE "FEDERAL HILL AND SOUTH HARBOR" MAP

Essex

HOWARD

Dundalk

Patapsco River

Patapsco River

Lansdowne

BELLE GROVE RD

FRANCIS SCOTT KEY MEMORIAL BRIDGE

Pumphrey   BINGO WORLD

Elkridge   Linthicum

BALTIMORE-WASHINGTON INTERNATIONAL AIRPORT

Ferndale

Chesapeake

Bay

Severn

Glen Burnie

Riviera Beach

ANNE ARUNDEL

Southgate

© AVALON TRAVEL

0   2 mi

0   2 km

HISTORY

Charm City began life as a tobacco port founded early in the 18th century. Location is everything, and Baltimore is in the right place: on the Patapsco River fall line, where the river drops precipitously to the Chesapeake Bay. Baltimoreans used power generated by tumbling falls to water crops and turn mills. The city's strategic placement spurred its growth, and by the time of the American Revolution, it was already a thriving seaport.

During the Revolution, the city served as the seat of the Continental Congress while Philadelphia was under British siege in 1776–1777. The British took pleasure some years later in bombarding Fort McHenry during the War of 1812, inspiring a local lawyer to pen what was to become our national anthem. However, Baltimore's booming commerce wasn't threatened until the opening of the Erie Canal in 1825. Always on the ball, business interests in the city prompted construction of the first U.S. railroad here, the Baltimore and Ohio, begun in 1827.

The site of numerous riots between Southern and Northern sympathizers during the Civil War, Baltimore remained within the Union but under martial law throughout the war. During the latter half of the 19th century, the city was transformed from a mercantile to an industrial center. Baltimore built itself with the muscular biceps of the working man (and woman). In 1904, a fire destroyed most of the downtown business district, but recovery was rapid. The city's continued growth in the 20th century was due in large part to its port facilities, which expanded from the original all-purpose piers to the present 45 miles of developed waterfront.

Today, Baltimore—named for the baronial title of the Calvert family—is one of the busiest ports in the U.S. It handles more than 30 million tons of all types of cargo from around the world each year. Once the home of the famous *Baltimore Clipper* and a major shipbuilding industry, the city now hosts 126,700 residents who continue to work in maritime-related jobs. Baltimore is a wholesaling and manufacturing powerhouse, a workingman's town par excellence.

H. L. MENCKEN ON BALTIMORE

Baltimorean by birth and choice, Henry Louis Mencken was America's most prominent journalist, book reviewer, and political commentator in the early 20th century. His father (also known as H. L.) owned the Mencken Cigar Company of Baltimore, and the younger H. L. was seldom seen without a stogie in hand. A skeptic by nature, Mencken was sure of his opinions and wicked with his prose, and his writing often criticized the government and organized religion. Though he worked out of New York City, he chose to live in Baltimore for these reasons, outlined in *Happy Days* (New York: Alfred A. Knopf, 1940):

The city into which I was born in 1880 had a reputation all over for what the English, in their real-estate advertising, are fond of calling the amenities. So far as I have been able to discover by a labored search of contemporary travel-books, no literary tourist, however waspish he may have been about Washington, Niagara Falls, the prairies of the West, or even Boston and New York, ever gave Baltimore a bad notice. They all agree, often with lubricious gloats and gurgles (a) that its indigenous victualry was unsurpassed in the Republic, (b) that its native . . . females of all ages up to thirty-five were of incomparable pulchritude, and as amiable as they were lovely, and (c) that its home-life was spacious, charming, full of creature comforts, and highly conducive to the facile and orderly propagation of the species.

With industry comes innovation: In 1851, the first ice cream factory was built by Baltimore dairyman Jacob Fussell; in 1876, Johns Hopkins University was the first in the United States to be formed as a graduate study and research facility. And there are plenty of recognizable local names to drop: baseball hero Babe Ruth, muckraker Upton Sinclair, filmmaker John Waters, and musician Frank Zappa were all born here, and Oprah Winfrey started her talk show career in Baltimore. The local newspaper, the *Baltimore Sun,* has fostered multiple Pulitzer Prize winners. But as fascinating as its history might be, it's contemporary Baltimore that draws visitors.

ORIENTATION

The main streets of Downtown are Mulberry (east–west) and Charles (north–south). Baltimore is made up of dozens of small neighborhoods, many of which are exclusively residential. The **Inner Harbor,** roughly from the National Aquarium around to Federal Hill, is the site of most of the big hotels and shopping areas. Water taxis are easily caught from here to explore the rest of the city's attractions.

Federal Hill, southwest of the inner harbor, was an outlying village that has been absorbed by the city. This 30-block area has become an upscale haven of beautiful older homes, restaurants, and shops. Homes in the tree-lined residential area of Otterbein, just west of Federal Hill, were once available to homesteaders for $1 a year. Federal Hill is another good place to set up a base to check out Baltimore on foot or by water taxi.

South Harbor is anchored by Federal Hill on the west end and Ft. McHenry to the east— once heavily industrial, it's now a mix of industry and residential neighborhoods.

Several attractions bring visitors into **Downtown West,** including the Babe Ruth home and B&O Railroad Museum. This section of town is mostly urban, with a residential mix that gets rough around the edges a little farther west.

Mount Vernon, site of the Washington Tower and Walters Art Museum, and

Belvedere, east of Mount Vernon, were easily the most socially prominent neighborhoods in Baltimore during the 19th century, and they remain architecturally interesting. This neighborhood is several blocks from the harbor—a good walk along restaurant row (Charles St.).

Close to downtown on the east, another wonderful neighborhood that has preserved a distinct personality is **Little Italy,** extending from Pratt Street to President Street on the inner harbor. The restaurants are justly famous in the area.

Other neighborhoods that were once outlying villages have become tourist areas. One is **Fell's Point,** a shipbuilding and trading port east of the city. The streets are named after British places and people; row houses, predating the Civil War, were built for workers who labored in what was once Baltimore's deepest port. Today, Fell's Point offers visitors numerous shops, galleries, and restaurants. Walking tours of the neighborhood originate from the **visitors center** (808 S. Ann St., 410/675-6750).

Further east, **Canton** also retains many of its original structures, and some consider it the most authentic of old Baltimore neighborhoods. Homes in these neighborhoods are often sheathed in "formstone," a white or colored fake stone wall-covering sold as part of a widespread scam during the mid-1950s (characters in the film *Tin Men* are based on formstone salesmen). Both neighborhoods are on the harbor and offer easy access to downtown by water taxi. Fell's Point is a little livelier, and Canton a bit more quiet and residential. Both make good home bases for your Baltimore visit.

Continuing east on Eastern Avenue, drivers will pass through Highlandtown (site of many scenes in John Waters' movies) and under a rail bridge decorated with a blue and white "key" pattern that marks the beginning of **Greektown.** This ethnic enclave has held onto the shops and restaurants of the immigrants who settled there.

Uptown is the area just north of Mount Vernon. Nearby Bolton Hill, southwest of the Maryland Institute of Art, is another still fashionable area of 19th-century townhouses: F. Scott and Zelda Fitzgerald, radio star Gary Moore, and the Cone sisters all lived there. Farther north, Hampden was a New England–style mill town that has long since become part of the city. North of Hampden, Druid Hill Park and the city zoo are the big attractions. Since these neighborhoods are some distance from the harbor, they would require public transportation or a car to get downtown.

PLANNING YOUR TIME

To see everything worth seeing in Baltimore would take two weeks. Those with specific interests can pare that down to a leisurely three days—for instance, history buffs could take in **Fort McHenry**, the **Baltimore Civil War Museum**, and **The Star-Spangled Banner Flag House and Museum,** with time enough for dinners in little Italy and Fell's Point every night. Art aficionados could plan a short trip around the **Walters Art Museum, Baltimore Museum of Art,** and **American Visionary Art Museum.** But why limit yourself?

The best bet is to plan on at least a week and group your chosen activities by area, planning to see the most popular sights after noon, when they're least crowded. On the morning on the first day, orient yourself to the lay of the land by buying a **National Historic Seaport of Baltimore** ticket, taking two hours to walk around the **Maritime Museum** ships and lighthouse, with a vertical trip up to enjoy the view from the **Top of the World observation center** (the Historic Seaport ticket is your admission to the ships, tower, Museum of Industry, and water taxi). Then take a water taxi from the inner harbor to the port neighborhoods: Canton (good shopping and restaurants), Fell's Point (a maritime museum, more great restaurants, and a vibrant nightlife), and Federal Hill (fine restaurants and a nice neighborhood park). During your voyage, you would be wise to stop off at **The Baltimore Museum of Industry** (two–three hours).

On day two, get some exercise! Many visitors stick close to the inner harbor, so it's often crowded—but if you do the same, you'll miss a lot of what Baltimore is about. In the morning, take the **Mt. Vernon and Belvedere** walking tour (three hours); the older neighborhoods north of the inner harbor have a history and charm all their own. In the afternoon, head out by car or water taxi to **Fort McHenry** in south Baltimore (one hour plus transit time), returning via the **American Visionary Art Museum** (two hours) on the way back to dinner in Federal Hill.

Day three could include a trip west to the **B&O Railroad Museum** (two hours), **Edgar Allen Poe's gravesite** (30 minutes), a stop at the Lexington Market for lunch, and the **Babe Ruth Birthplace and Orioles Museum** (two hours) on the way to dinner. On day four, head north for a leisurely morning at the **Baltimore Zoo** (two–three hours), with lunch on the north end of town, perhaps at the **Baltimore Museum of Art** (two–three hours). Finish off the day at the **Dr. Samuel D. Harris National Museum of Dentistry** (two hours)—you'll remember to brush that night, guaranteed.

Day five could start with an energizing climb up the **Washington Monument** (one hour) followed by a tour of **Walters Art Museum** (two–three hours) and a late lunch on Charles Street. The afternoon is a good time to visit the **National Aquarium in Baltimore** (three hours). Day six starts out at **Port Discovery** (one hour–all day) the place for playful adults and families with children, followed by lunch on the waterfront, a visit to the **Baltimore Civil War Museum** (one hour), and a stop at the **The Star-Spangled Banner Flag House and Museum** (one hour). Day seven, depending on your level of energy and the amount of time you have in the area, could be spent visiting one or more of the dozens of other interesting sights listed in this chapter—churches, ethnic museums, history museums, natural history museums, historic houses, parks, and so on—cheering at a ball game, or taking the water taxi to different restaurants to eat your way around Baltimore.

If you have a car, it's best to stay on the outskirts of town and drive in—parking isn't difficult, except in the inner harbor. One way to avoid that problem is to drive to Canton, park in the free lot next to the water taxi stand, and take the water taxi around the inner harbor. A car will give you access to outer Baltimore, but it is a liability at inner harbor hotels, since overnight parking is expensive.

Without a car, it's easiest to stay close to the water in any of the small neighborhoods such as Fell's Point, Canton, or Federal Hill, or at one of the big hotels that ring the inner harbor. Water taxis will get you around the harbor, and land taxis (or your feet) will get you to the outer destinations.

Sights

If you plan on taking a water taxi around the harbor (highly recommended), Ed Kane's water taxis include a Letter of Marque with the price of an adult all-day ticket ($8). During the Revolution, such a letter authorized a ship to legally raid British commerce—basically, legalized piracy. The modern-day Letter of Marque allows ticket holders to "raid" participating merchants of Baltimore (including a few of the best sights) for discounts.

The **National Historic Seaport of Baltimore** (www.natlhistoricseaport.org) offers several discount ticket packages to groups of 10 or more. Packages include a few or all of Baltimore's premium sites around the harbor.

INNER HARBOR/DOWNTOWN

If you're interested in ships and maritime history, you would do well to check out **Sail Baltimore** (www.sailbaltimore.org), which provides free public access to a variety of vessels through its visiting ships program. Participating vessels come and go throughout the year, staying for anywhere from one day to several weeks, and open their decks to the public for free tours. Visitors can go onboard and tour the ships, interact with people from around the world, and learn about different cultures, navigation, geography, technology, and maritime history. An average of two dozen ships a year participate in the program, including international tall ships, military vessels, and educational and environmental ships.

◖ National Aquarium in Baltimore

By now, everyone has heard about the National Aquarium (Piers 3 and 4, 501 E. Pratt St., 410/576-3800, www.aqua.org). The aquarium is open 10 A.M.–8 P.M. Friday and 10 A.M.–5 P.M. Saturday–Thursday January–February and November–December, 9 A.M.–8 P.M. Friday and 9 A.M.–5 P.M. Saturday–Thursday March–June and September–October, 9 A.M.–8 P.M. daily July–August 19, and 9 A.M.–8 P.M. Friday and 9 A.M.–6 P.M. Saturday–Thursday August 20–August 31.

Visitors may purchase advance tickets online (with an additional fee) or at the aquarium, and tickets are also available from TicketMaster with an additional processing charge (410/481-SEAT in Baltimore, 800/551-SEAT outside the region). Admission charges for adults are $21.95, seniors $20.95, and children 3–11 $12.95. The information phone line listed above provides information about hours and bargain days.

The aquarium project started in 1970 as part of the inner harbor redevelopment, and has since become the crown jewel of the waterfront. The modern facility showcases sophisticated theme exhibits, including an outdoor seal pool; aqua environments "Mountains to the Sea," "Surviving through Adaptations," "North Atlantic to the Pacific," and "Open Ocean"; and a temperature-controlled "South American Rain Forest." There's been a lot of excitement over Spirit, Raven, and Maya, three dolphins born in 2001 and featured in performances of "Coastal Connections: Dolphins at Our Shores." There's a walkway over an extensive manta ray pool, and a spiraling walkway through a four-story aquarium, the Atlantic Coral Reef. Wetsuited divers swim around the

© JOANNE MILLER

Baltimore Harbor and the National Aquarium

tank during feeding times, which are posted in the main lobby.

The main building gives you the feeling of of of being underwater—a hypnotic effect guaranteed to leave you spacey (it has the same effect on the aquarium staff, or so they tell me). The central facility is linked by a walkway to a Marine Mammal Pavilion with a 1,300-seat amphitheater and a 1.2-million-gallon pool that features 30-minute presentations starring the aquarium's talented team of dolphins. The entire aquarium is state-of-the-art and an amazing experience—don't miss it. It's also very crowded. The best times to visit are during the fall and winter, and before 11 A.M. and after 3 P.M. There are services available for visitors with vision, hearing, and mobility special needs.

U.S.S. *Constellation* Museum

In 1853, just before steam propulsion was adopted as auxiliary power for all new warships, Constellation was the last all-sail ship built by the Navy, and the largest "sloop" built to that date (Pier 1, 301 E. Pratt St., 410/539-1797, www.constellation.org, 10 A.M.–5:30 P.M. daily April–Oct., 10 A.M.–4:30 P.M. daily Nov.–March, extended hours may be available June–Aug., $8.75 adults, $7.50 seniors, $4.75 children 6–14).

The beautiful ship did duty as an interceptor of slave ships off the mouth of the Congo River in 1859 and served in every major war until she was decommissioned in 1933. After that, she spent time as a "relief flagship" for the Navy before being restored and put on display in Baltimore. The ship offers interactive exhibits and a chronicle of its history.

◖ Port Discovery

If the short set hasn't run off enough energy touring the inner harbor, make sure you stop by this warehouse/play area, one block north of the aquarium (34 Market Place, also known as NationsBank Plaza, 410/727-8120, www.portdiscovery.org). If you go there first, you may never leave. This gigantic playroom was designed by Disney and offers hours of serious fun for all ages.

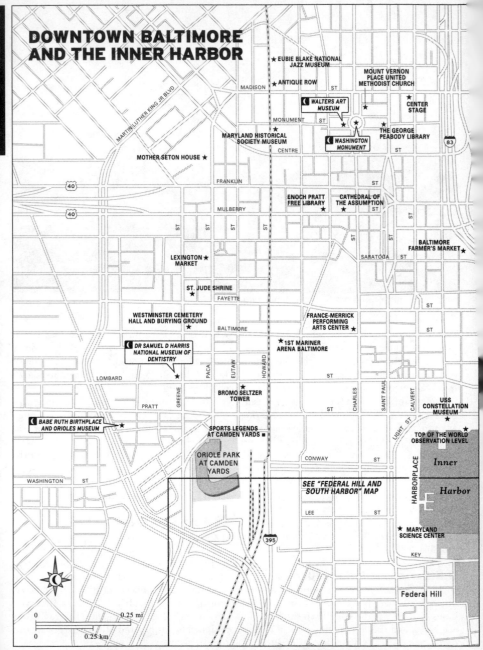

DOWNTOWN BALTIMORE AND THE INNER HARBOR

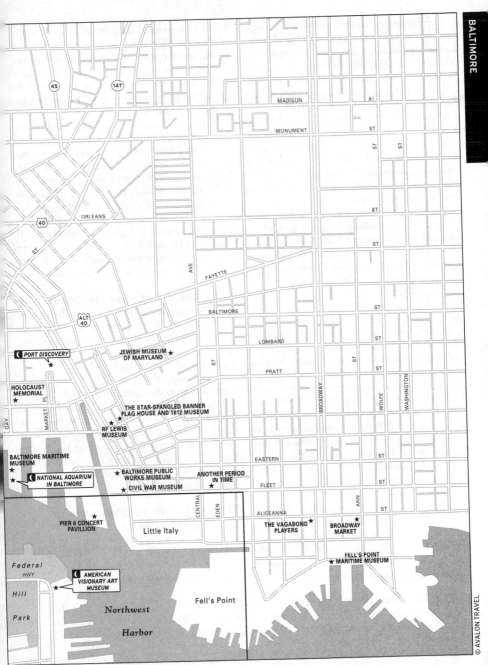

MADISON

MONUMENT

45   147

ST

ORLEANS

40

ST

FAYETTE

AVE

BALTIMORE   ST

ALT
40

LOMBARD

JEWISH MUSEUM ★
OF MARYLAND

☾ PORT DISCOVERY
★

ST

PRATT

HOLOCAUST
MEMORIAL
★

THE STAR-SPANGLED BANNER
★ FLAG HOUSE AND 1812 MUSEUM

BROADWAY

WOLFE

WASHINGTON

MARKET PL

GAY

RF LEWIS
★ MUSEUM

BALTIMORE MARITIME
MUSEUM
★

EASTERN   ST

★ BALTIMORE PUBLIC
WORKS MUSEUM   ANOTHER PERIOD
IN TIME

☾ NATIONAL AQUARIUM
★ IN BALTIMORE   ★ CIVIL WAR MUSEUM   ★   FLEET

CENTRAL

EDEN

ALICEANNA

ANN   ST

PIER 6 CONCERT
★ PAVILLION   Little Italy   THE VAGABOND ★
PLAYERS   BROADWAY
MARKET

Federal
HWY

☾ AMERICAN
★ VISIONARY ART
MUSEUM

FELL'S POINT
★ MARITIME MUSEUM

Hill

Park   Northwest

Fell's Point

Harbor

Port Discovery has different hours throughout the year. From Memorial Day through Labor Day, summer hours are 10 A.M.–5 P.M. Monday–Saturday and noon–5 P.M. Sunday. In July and August, enjoy special Friday Fun Nights—the museum is open until 8 P.M. September hours are 9:30 A.M.–4:30 P.M. Friday, 10 A.M.–5 P.M. Saturday, and noon–5 P.M. Sunday. October–May hours are 9:30 A.M.–4:30 P.M. Tuesday–Friday, 10 A.M.–5 P.M. Saturday, and noon–5 P.M. Sunday. The museum is closed on Thanksgiving and Christmas. Admission is $10.75 for ages 2–102 and free for kids under two.

Some of the exhibits, such as the three-story net/pipe/ramp climbing gym, are best left to kids and professional gymnasts. Other exhibits are meant to be shared by adults and kids: One special shadowy, mysterious exhibit consisted of figuring out a hieroglyphic message by putting together a puzzle of pot shards, pulling yourself across the "Nile" on a raft, and wandering around a dark maze inside a pyramid to find the secrets of the Pharaohs. Expect lots of creative learning, holograms, and other special effects—and lots of fun. There are play stations appropriate for all ages, including an area dedicated to an international version of Clifford, the big red dog. This is light years away from plunking the kids down in front of a video terminal. Adventurous adults without accompanying children can sneak in and play the day away. Highly recommended.

One special attraction at Port Discovery is the HiFlyer, a spherical, helium-filled balloon with an enclosed gondola that holds 20–30 passengers and transports them 450 feet up the air for a real bird's-eye view of the harbor in the afternoons and evenings. No fear of blowing away and ending up in the bay, however—the balloon is tethered by a steel cable. Call to see if the balloon is operational, as weather affects its availability.

Baltimore Maritime Museum

Dedicated to the preservation and celebration of four historic ships clustered near the Baltimore Aquarium (Piers 3 and 5, 410/396-3453, www .baltomaritimemuseum.org, 10 A.M.–6 P.M. daily Labor Day–Veteran's Day, 9 A.M.–5 P.M. the rest of the year, $8 general, $6 seniors, $4 children 6–14, under 6 free), this living museum gives visitors an opportunity to see what shipboard life is like. There are several very different vessels to choose from, and each ship provides detailed operating and historical information.

The U.S. Coast Guard Cutter *Taney* is the last surviving ship from the December 7, 1941, attack on Pearl Harbor. She served as a command ship at Okinawa, a fleet escort in the Atlantic and Mediterranean, and a medical ship in Vietnam, and she's the last ship afloat that participated in the search for Amelia Earhart.

The Lightship *Chesapeake*—so-called because her masthead light, foghorn, and bell helped guide mariners to safe harbor during storms—was built for strength in 1930. Her gigantic anchors held her on station during the worst of storms.

The Seven-Foot Knoll Lighthouse, built in 1855, marked the entrance to the Baltimore Harbor for 135 years before being moved to its current site on dry land. A recent renovation included new exhibits on lighthouse keeping and the history of Seven-Foot Knoll.

It's a creepy thrill to walk through what seems like an endless parade of tight little doors on the USS *Torsk,* a World War II submarine built in 1944. It holds the record for most dives, having submerged 11,884 times. Think about that when you're inspecting those tiny bunks. Not recommended for claustrophobics, the tour requires walking and climbing in some tight spaces.

Top of the World Observation Level and Museum

This imposing tower (World Trade Center, 401 E. Pratt St., 410/837-VIEW or 410/837-8439, 10 A.M.–9 P.M. daily Memorial Day–Labor Day, 10 A.M.–6 P.M. Wed.–Sun. Sept.–May, $5 adults, $4 seniors, $3 children 3–12) offers panoramic views of the city and well-designed displays of Baltimore history and cultural life. Architect I. M. Pei designed the World Trade Center as a showplace; an elevator takes you directly to the 27th floor.

Maryland Science Center

Maryland's oldest scientific institution (601 Light St., 410/685-5225, www.mdsci.org) is one of the oldest in the nation. It's open 10 A.M.–5 P.M. Tuesday–Friday, 10 A.M.–6 P.M. Saturday, and Sunday noon–5 P.M. from the second week in September to the third week in May. Hours the rest of the year are 10 A.M.–5 P.M. Monday–Friday, 10 A.M.–6 P.M. Saturday–Sunday. Admission prices are: museum only—adults $12, children 3–12 $8; IMAX theater only—$7.50 all; combination ticket to museum and theater—adults $15.50, children 3–12 $10.50.

Painter Charles Wilson Peale and a group of friends who shared an interest in the natural world, including Charles Carroll of Carrollton and J. H. Latrobe, met informally in 1797 and opened a natural history museum—of sorts. Visitors could examine a live rattlesnake, stuffed birds, wax figures of famous people, a kitten with one head and two bodies, and an assortment of sea life. Over time, the organization developed into the Maryland Academy of Science, and the unprecedented growth in scientific and technical knowledge during the 20th century expanded the mission and resources of the organization into its current form. From asteroids in the atrium to a math exhibit titled "Beyond Numbers," from the hands-on science arcade to "The Visible Human," the Science Center seeks to stimulate and cultivate awareness, interest, and understanding of the sciences in its diverse programs. In addition to its regular and featured exhibits, the center offers planetarium shows, an antique telescope/observatory on the roof, and an IMAX theater, all included in the single admission price.

FEDERAL HILL SOUTH
◖ American Visionary Art Museum

This sleek art museum (800 Key Hwy., 410/244-1900, www.avam.org, 10 A.M.–6 P.M. Tues.–Sun., $12 adults, $8 students and seniors) holds work "born of intuition and self-styled imagination… created by farmers,

housewives, mechanics, retired folk, the disabled, the homeless, as well as the occasional neurosurgeon—all inspired by the fire within." You'll not find any formal schools of work here. During one exhibit period, a 12-foot-tall sculpture of Baltimore movie diva Divine welcomed visitors to view art cars, 20-foot-tall whirligigs, matchstick altars, crayon paintings, homemade air balloons, and hundreds of other wondrous objects created by self-taught artists. The galleries will leave you delighted, and with a new respect for art as a means to express the inner lives of everyday people. The featured artists' personal stories are as interesting as their work. Richard Saholt, a World War II veteran diagnosed with schizophrenia, cured himself through his collages; Martin Ramirez's works on scraps of paper held together with spittle and mashed potatoes now sell in excess of $100,000; Frank Jones was a prisoner who drew visions of his own winged devils in houses to "contain them."

One recent exhibit featured the work of 73-year-old Paul Darmafall, known as the Baltimore Glassman. His painting/mosaics are created on scrap doors and other bits of wood; millions of bits of broken glass are his medium. The paintings transform litter into jeweled statements about the importance of fresh air, pride in America, and the evils of electricity. You may be inspired to create something of your own. Even the bathrooms are done up, the ceilings covered with thousands of tissue roses.

The museum restaurant, the Joy America café has its own following, and the gift shop is worth a stop. Parking can be challenging—there's a pay lot across the Key Highway in front of the Rusty Scupper restaurant, but there are often cheap metered spaces on the street behind the museum.

Mount Clare Museum

Located in Carroll Park (1500 Washington Blvd., 410/837-3262, www.mountclare.org, 10 A.M.–4 P.M. Tues.–Sat., $6 adults, $5 seniors, $4 children under 18), Mount Clare was the home of Charles Carroll, the Barrister—all

BALTIMORE

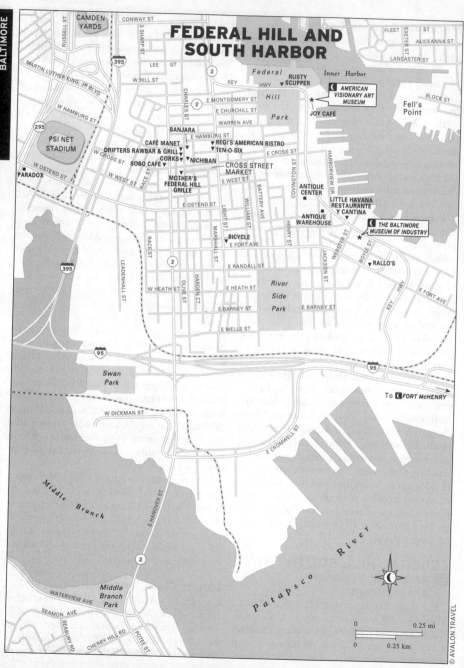

FEDERAL HILL AND SOUTH HARBOR

CAMDEN YARDS

CONWAY ST

FLEET ST
EXETER ST
ALICEANNA ST
LANCASTER ST

S SHARP ST
S CHARLES ST

MARTIN LUTHER KING, JR BLVD

RUSSELL ST

LEE ST
W HILL ST
KEY HWY

Federal
Hill
Park

Inner Harbor

RUSTY SCUPPER

AMERICAN VISIONARY ART MUSEUM

Fell's Point

BLOCK ST

E MONTGOMERY ST
E CHURCHILL ST
WARREN AVE

JOY CAFÉ

W HAMBURG ST

PSI NET STADIUM

BANJARA

E HAMBURG ST

CAFÉ MANET

REGI'S AMERICAN BISTRO
TEN-O-SIX

W OSTEND ST

PARADOX

DRIFTERS RAWBAR & GRILL
CORKS
SOBO CAFÉ

W CROSS ST

NICHIBAN

E CROSS ST

CROSS STREET MARKET

HARBORVIEW DR

W WEST ST

MOTHER'S FEDERAL HILL GRILLE

RACE ST

E WEST ST

COVINGTON ST

ANTIQUE CENTER

LITTLE HAVANA RESTAURANTE Y CANTINA

E OSTEND ST

LIGHT ST

WILLIAM AVE

BATTERY AVE

HENRY ST

ANTIQUE WAREHOUSE

THE BALTIMORE MUSEUM OF INDUSTRY

WEBSTER ST

BOYLE ST

BICYCLE
E FORT AVE

MARSHALL ST

JACKSON ST

RALLO'S

395

E RANDALL ST

W HEATH ST

HARDEN CT

E HEATH ST

River Side Park

KEY HWY

E FORT AVE

OLIVE ST

E BARNEY ST

E BARNEY ST

E WELLS ST

LEADENHALL ST

95

95

Swan Park

To ☾ FORT McHENRY

W DICKMAN ST

S HANOVER ST

E CROMWELL ST

Middle   Branch

Patapsco   River

2

Middle Branch Park

WATERVIEW AVE

SEAMON AVE

SEABURY RD

CHERRY HILL RD

POTEE ST

0   0.25 mi

0   0.25 km

© AVALON TRAVEL

THOSE CONFUSING CARROLLS

Though the name Charles Carroll of Carrollton is familiar to anyone interested in the Revolutionary War years, the number of historic homes with the name of Carroll attached may lead one to think that, like George Washington, Charles Carroll slept everywhere. In fact, each of the Carroll historic homes belonged to different relatives and different generations of the same family.

Charles Carroll (1660-1720), the Irish settler (C.C.I.S.) and family patriarch, was the first attorney general of Maryland. He left us without a home to visit in America. However, his son, Charles Carroll of Annapolis (C.C.O.A., 1702-1782), left us a lovely mansion in that town overlooking the harbor. His (C.C.O.A.'s) son was Charles Carroll of Carrollton (C.C.O.C., 1737-1832), the signer of the Declaration of Independence, who lived outside Buckeystown,

a property that remains private. Mount Clare, Baltimore home of Charles Carroll, Barrister (C.C.B.), a cousin and contemporary of C.C.O.C.'s – though from the Protestant side of the family – is now part of a public park.

C.C.O.C.'s son, Charles Carroll of Homewood (C.C.O.H., 1775-1825), built the Homewood house on what is now the campus of Johns Hopkins University with money received as a wedding gift from his dear old dad. Funds dried up, however, as junior continued to "improve" the property. Undaunted, C.C.O.H. and his wife, Harriet Chew, had several children, among them Charles Carroll of Doughoregan (C.C.O.D., also known as The Colonel, 1801-1862). Though descendants of the Carrolls continue to reside in Maryland, they now prefer to keep their homes to themselves.

Carrolls are distinguished by nicknames or place names, since there were so many of them. Tours are given on the hour 10 A.M.–3 P.M.

Once set on a bucolic hill far from the center of Baltimore, the house now adorns a sometimes seedy city park—but if you're interested in authentic furnishings and decor from the 1760s, this is a must-see. It's the only 18th-century museum house in Maryland to contain so many of the daily artifacts of life belonging to the builder of the house and used by the family. Many of the items were hunted down and reclaimed by the staff from repositories on the Eastern Shore, often from descendants of Mrs. Carroll (née Margaret Tilghman). Portraits of the Carrolls painted by Charles Wilson Peale in 1770–1771 hang in the house, and rotating exhibits—a recent one included ladies' fans from the period—add extra interest.

SOUTH HARBOR
◖ Fort McHenry

This historic military site (E. Fort Ave., 410/962-4290, www.nps.gov/fomc, 8 A.M.–

7:45 P.M. daily June–Labor Day, 8 A.M.–4:45 P.M. daily Labor Day–June) played an active role in our nation's history from 1776 through World War II. A $5 admission for visitors over age 16 is charged to enter the fort; access to the surrounding park grounds is free.

Water taxis operate to Fort McHenry 11 A.M.–5:00 P.M. Memorial Day–Labor Day (and during the off-season, weather permitting) from Landing 11 in Fell's Point. Visitors may transfer at Fell's Point, but must board any water taxi in the system no later than 3 P.M. to make the connection to the fort. Visitors may not park and board at the fort, and the last boat leaves the fort at 5 P.M., daily.

Built during the Revolutionary War, the earth-walled, star-shaped stronghold called Fort Whetstone was surrounded on three sides by water. Ships sailing into Baltimore would have to pass the fort first, and the site was far enough from Baltimore to provide protection without endangering the city.

The Revolutionary War ended without an attack on Baltimore. However, improvements to the fort continued. In 1798, French engineer

Jean Foncin was selected to plan a new fort. James McHenry, secretary of war under President George Washington, was instrumental in providing support for its construction. The fort was renamed in his honor.

The fort found lasting fame during the War of 1812. British naval vessels attacked in September 1814. For 25 hours, the British bombarded Fort McHenry from ships anchored in the Patapsco River. The fort's defenders held firm, and Baltimore was saved. It was during this bombardment that Francis Scott Key was inspired to pen the poem that became our national anthem.

During the Civil War, the fort's guns were turned toward the city. Union troops were stationed at Fort McHenry to keep Baltimore out of the hands of those who would have Maryland join the Southern rebellion. The fort also held political prisoners suspected of being Confederate sympathizers, often without trial. Following the Battle of Gettysburg in early July 1863, nearly 7,000 Confederate soldiers were detained in the fort.

Fort McHenry continued its military service to the country until July 20, 1912, when the last active garrison left the fort. From 1915 to 1917, Baltimore used the site as a popular city park and beach. In 1917, the U.S. Army once again occupied the site to establish a hospital for wounded veterans returning from World War I. It was the largest military hospital in the United States, with over 100 temporary buildings. Some of the earliest developments in the fields of reconstructive and neurosurgery were made there. When the war ended, the need for the hospital slowly diminished, and in 1925, the hospital buildings were torn down.

During that year, Fort McHenry was made a national park, and it was transferred to the care of the National Park Service in 1933. During World War II, the fort served as a Coast Guard Training Center for fire control and port defense. Fort McHenry was designated a National Monument and Historic Shrine in 1939. It is America's only Historic Shrine.

◖ The Baltimore Museum of Industry

This is one of my favorite places in the city, and I'm not alone—it was chosen as Baltimore's "Best Hands-On Museum for Kids" by *Baltimore Magazine* for several years running (1415 Key Hwy., 410/727-4808, www.thebmi.org, 10 A.M.–4 P.M. Tues.–Sat., 11 A.M.–4 P.M. Sun., adults $10, seniors/students/children $6).

Inside the converted oyster cannery that serves as the museum's home, workers have constructed an abbreviated version of Baltimore's industries: an oyster cannery, a print shop, a bank, a store, a movie theater, a garment factory, and more. Each of these "businesses" is put into action by a worker/guide who talks about the industry and its heyday. Often, visitors can join in, cranking out a handbill on the 1880 job press or making cans in the oyster company assembly line. In addition to the many live exhibits, there are plenty of colorful and informative displays on the companies and products that originated in Baltimore—many have become household names in America and beyond. "Born in Baltimore, raised

Fort McHenry

everywhere" was the slogan of Gans Brothers umbrellas—the city was the umbrella capital of America until the last factory of Polan, Katz and Co. (the first to introduce colored umbrellas) closed in 1981.

Also of interest is a wall of Baltimore "firsts"—the first gas lights, the first street lit by gas (not Light Street, as you might suppose, but Howard Street), straws and drinking cups produced by the Sweetheart Company, Black & Decker's cordless drill, Howard Head's aluminum skis, the first phone system, and, of course, Bromo Seltzer, created by Isaac Emerson in 1890 and named for a then active Italian volcano, Mt. Bromo. The "miracle cream" Noxzema debuted here in 1914, mixed up in a coffee pot in the backroom of Dr. Lloyd Bunting's pharmacy.

DOWNTOWN WEST
◖ B&O Railroad Museum

A must-see for rail and history enthusiasts, this museum (901 W. Pratt St., 410/752-2490, www.borail.org, 10 A.M.–4 P.M. Mon.–Fri., 10 A.M.–5 P.M. Sat., 11 A.M.–4 P.M. Sun., $14 adults, $12 seniors, $8 children 2–12) is one of the finest rail collections in America, as well as the home of the B&O rail roundhouse and Mount Clare Station. The first passenger trains in the New World headed west to Ellicott's Mills from here in 1830; America's first steam engine, the *Tom Thumb*, originated from here; and, in 1844, Mount Clare received Samuel F. B. Morse's famous telegraph message, "What hath God wrought?" from Washington, D.C. The museum features exhibits, replicas, and artifacts of railroading, including models and replicas from the "Fair of the Iron Horse" in 1927. It's hard to believe that almost 4 percent of the total population of America worked for the railroads in 1925. Even if railroad lore isn't one of your interests, stop by to take a look at the roundhouse. Originally constructed in 1884, it was rebuilt after a disastrous snowstorm in 2002 (with improvements to the original design). This magnificent building holds machines that ran the rails, from the earliest "grasshopper" locomotives to

the 320-ton monster steam engine *Allegheny*, and beyond to the diesel era. Early coach cars look like elegant little houses on wheels. The equipment is beautifully maintained, and the smell of wood, oil, and polish will transport you back to the days of coach travel. The outside yard features trains and more trains, and parking is safe and plentiful.

◖ Babe Ruth Birthplace and Orioles Museum

If you're looking for scandalous details of a hero's life, you won't find them at the Babe Ruth Birthplace and Orioles Museum (216 Emory St., 410/727-1539, www.baberuthmuseum.com, $6 adults, $4 seniors, $3 children). The museum is open 10 A.M.–6 P.M. daily April–October and until 7:30 P.M. on all Orioles home game days, and 10 A.M.–5 P.M. Tuesday–Sunday November–March. It covers the bats, the balls, and the legend—a sprightly film and artifacts chronicle the Babe's life and concentrate on his rough childhood, larger-than-life talents, and love for kids, but skim over his infamous excesses. But you leave feeling great about the Babe, and even more enthusiastic about the game. My question is, does "The Homer That Saved Little Johnny," in which Babe Ruth promised a severely ill boy that he would "knock a homer" for him against St. Louis in the 1926 World Series, count as a miracle? The Babe hit three homers, and Johnny recovered. If there ever was a patron saint of baseball, it would have to be George Herman Ruth. There's also historical information about the Orioles and rotating exhibits—one display addressed the historic Cuba-Orioles game.

Tickets may be purchased to both the Babe Ruth Birthplace and Sports Legends at Camden Yards (below) at either venue for $14 adults, $11 seniors, and $8 children.

Sports Legends at Camden Yards

Camden Station is the gateway to Oriole Park, the hometown field of the Baltimore Orioles (301 W. Camden St., 410/727-1539, www.baberuthmuseum.com, $10 adults,

THE BABE

When her birth time grew near, Katherine Ruth moved into the home of her father, Pius Schamberger, to escape the noise and congestion of the apartment above her husband's saloon a few blocks away. George Herman Ruth was born at 216 Emory Street in 1895. He grew up a product of a rough neighborhood – by the time he was seven, his parents deemed him incorrigible, and he was sent to St. Mary's Industrial School, a Catholic institution for orphans and delinquent boys.

At the age of 19, he had already established a reputation as the best young athlete in Baltimore, particularly when it came to baseball. The owner of the minor league Baltimore Orioles, Jack Dunn, signed Ruth to his first professional contract in 1914, and at the same time assumed Ruth's legal guardianship. Other team members called the rookie "Jack Dunn's baby," which the local press shortened to "Babe."

Threatened by financial ruin, Dunn sold Babe and several other players to the Boston Red Sox within the year. That same year, Ruth married his first wife, Helen, who would die tragically in a fire in 1929. Ruth played for the Red Sox for more than five seasons, becoming one of the American League's greatest left-handed pitchers. In 1916, he established a World Series record by pitching 29 consecutive scoreless innings in series play. In spite of his pitching ability, the Sox switched Ruth to the outfield so he would have more chances at bat.

In short order, Ruth established himself as a great home-run hitter. Traditional power hitters of the time were belting 8–12 homers per season, but Ruth doubled, then tripled those numbers – to a high of 60 home runs per season after he joined the New York Yankees in 1920. (Hank Aaron didn't manage to break the Babe's 714-hit career home run record until decades later.) Yankee Stadium was built to accommodate the huge crowds that came to see the Babe, and sportswriters dubbed it "The House That Ruth Built."

In the 1920s, Babe Ruth *was* baseball. The newspapers followed his giant appetites for food, drink, and social life, and he became an American icon, congratulated by presidents and adored by kids. He returned their affection, and the press worshipfully followed his visits to hospitals and interaction with his young fans. Ruth married his second wife, Claire, in 1929, and adopted her daughter by a previous marriage shortly after. In one newsreel, he told the press that Claire was going to be his new trainer and would watch out for him, but age and years of high living had taken their toll.

Babe Ruth retired from baseball in 1935, capitalizing on his fame to act (badly) in a few Hollywood films. He attempted to become the manager of a big-league ballclub; a desire that was blocked, he felt, by Major League owners. Nonetheless, he made appearances at ballparks around the country for the rest of his life. He died of throat cancer in 1948, and is buried in the Gates of Heaven Cemetery in Hawthorn, New York.

$8 seniors, $6.50 children). The museum is open 10 A.M.–6 P.M. daily April–October and until 7:30 P.M. on all Orioles home game days, and 10 A.M.–5 P.M. Tuesday–Sunday November–March.

Unused since the 1980s, the station building—once the grand terminus of the B&O Railroad—was in serious danger of substantial structural damage. The Babe Ruth Museum saved the building from destruction and now occupies the basement and first floor of the Station with 22,000 square feet of artifacts and interactive exhibits, creating one of the most spectacular sports museums in America.

This is an all-sports venue, covering achievements by Babe Ruth, the Sultan of Swat, Johnny Unitas, Ironman Cal Ripken Jr., "Human Vacuum Cleaner" Brooks Robinson, Wimbledon champ Pam Shriver, gold medalist Michael Phelps, and many other mega-achievers from the sports world. Exhibits range from "Curse of the Bambino" to "History of the Preakness."

Tickets may be purchased to both Sports

Legends at Camden Yards and the Babe Ruth Birthplace at either venue for $14 adults, $11 seniors, and $8 children.

◖ Dr. Samuel D. Harris National Museum of Dentistry

This peculiar institution (31 S. Greene St., 410/706-0600, www.dentalmuseum.org, 10 A.M.–4 P.M. Wed.–Sat., 1–4 P.M. Sun., $4.50 adults, $2.50 seniors and children older than 7) will leave you smiling beyond all expectations. The faint scent of clove oil in the lobby may bring back an unpleasant memory or two of being strapped to the chair, but that will be dispelled the minute you enter this clever, informative, and entertaining museum. Video games—including tooth jukeboxes that play silent film clips and old commercials ("You'll wonder where the yellow went...")—make learning fun for all ages. Changing exhibits, which recently included the amazing feats of "iron jaw" performers, a "Match the Smile to the Celebrity" game, and an array of fancy toothbrushes, might make you consider becoming a dentist. Kids may decide to take time out on tooth-shaped chairs while their elders inspect George Washington's authentic dentures. (Surprise! They're not made out of wood.) It's an appealing mix of gear, lore, and gadgets associated with dentistry and teeth. In case you're overwhelmed by oral angst, you can always petition St. Appolonia, patron saint of dentists and sufferers of dental pain. Don't forget to brush.

Bromo Seltzer Tower

This only-in-Baltimore sight is hard to miss at 21 South Eutaw Street, as its clock with four faces can be seen from much of the city. At one time, a giant, whirling blue Bromo Seltzer bottle capped the crenellated tower, but neighbors complained that the eerie blue light kept them awake at night. But at least they always knew the time.

Mencken and Poe Sites

Though it's now privately owned, the **H. L. Mencken House** (1524 Hollins St. on

Bromo Seltzer Tower

© JOANNE MILLER

Washington Sq.) deserves a nod and a smile as tribute to one of the most popular writers of the 20th century. The Friends of the Mencken House (www.menckenhouse.org) have vowed to preserve the home, which is under their protection. Their website contains contact information if you would like to arrange a visit.

The **Edgar Allan Poe House** (203 N. Amity St. 410/396-7932, noon–3:45 P.M. Wed.–Sat. Apr.–early Dec.), privately owned for years, has come under the purview of the city and is now open to the public. Call to confirm hours. Be aware that the neighborhood had slipped well past marginal into the nether regions, but is on its way up again. A visit to Poe's grave at the old **Westminster Hall and Burying Ground** (500 W. Baltimore St., 410/706-2072, 8 A.M.–dusk daily, free) might be in order. Visitors leave flowers, notes, pennies, and the occasional empty pint bottle on the grave of the famous author and his wife. The burying ground holds several historical figures of interest, including James McHenry, signer of the U.S. Constitution. The Gothic Revival church next to the

BALTIMORE

THE TELL-TALE HEART

Edgar Allan Poe lived in Baltimore from 1829 to 1836 and died here in 1849 at age 40. At the time of his death, he was relatively unknown and quite poor; he was buried in the back of an old cemetery (the western burying ground) on the edge of town, with barely a stone marking his grave.

Legend has it that years later, Baltimore's schoolchildren initiated a "Pennies for Poe" campaign through which they hoped to raise enough money to move Poe's grave to a more prominent location in the cemetery (now named Westminster) and mark it with a more worthy headstone. They couldn't collect the money they needed, but the city chipped in and helped them out. Now it's a tradition for visitors to the grave to leave pennies on the tombstone.

Every year since 1949, a mysterious stranger clad in a three-quarter-length black coat and fedora has visited the grave on Poe's birthday. The stranger places his hands on Poe's tombstone and appears to pray. A moment later he is gone, leaving three roses and a bottle of cognac. The three roses are thought to represent the poet, his wife, and her mother. All are buried in the tiny cemetery.

Edgar Allan Poe's grave

The identity of the mysterious stranger has remained a riddle since the ritual began. The original visitor carried on the tradition until 1993, when he left a cryptic note saying, "The torch will be passed."

---

burying ground no longer holds services and is maintained by the U.M. School of Law. It's periodically open for organ concerts—call for dates and times.

St. Jude Shrine

This church (Paca St. and Saratoga St., 410/685-6026, www.stjudeshrine.org) is dedicated to the Catholic patron saint of hopeless cases and lost causes, St. Jude Thaddeus. Though the body of St. Jude rests in St. Peter's in Rome, this small church was consecrated in 1917 and has been going strong ever since. The shrine is open 6:30 A.M.–4:30 P.M., Monday–Tuesday and Thursday–Friday, 6:30 A.M.–8:30 P.M. Wednesday, 7 A.M.–4:30 P.M. Saturday, and 7 A.M.–2 P.M. Sunday. Masses are held daily.

MT. VERNON
Walters Art Museum

When I first saw the name Walters Gallery, I pictured a little suite of rooms with paintings for sale and wondered what all the hoopla was about. After my first visit, I could see the hoopla was justified—the massive and well-chosen collections were expansive and outstanding. Now, after an extensive multi-million-dollar renovation that resulted in 39 newly configured and refurbished galleries, a new four-story glass entryway, more public spaces, and a new name, the Walters Art Museum (600 N. Charles St., 410/547-9000, www.thewalters.org) is better than ever. It's open 11 A.M.–5 P.M. Wednesday–Sunday, and until 8 P.M. on Friday. This is the best deal in town: Admission is free.

© JOANNE MILLER

Named for William Walters and his son Henry, the gallery consists of three very large connected buildings, significant in themselves for their outstanding architecture. But what's in them—the fruit of a half-century of conscious acquisition, one of the most generous acts of cultural philanthropy in American history—is mind-boggling. The directors of major American museums collectively held their breath when Henry Walters' will was read, only to find that he left his entire bequest, including buildings, to the city where he was born, "for the benefit of the public." The original palazzo and the more modern 1974 building hold selections from the "main" collection, covering 55 centuries from antiquities to modern art; and the third building, the Hackerman House Asian Art Gallery, displays the Oriental collection. A recent exhibition on 17th-century Dutch and Flemish paintings was titled "An Eye for Detail," a phrase that effectively sums up the ability of the Walters to pick the most astounding examples of period, style, and artwork. Absolutely everything in these galleries is the best example available—visitors can spend hours in a single gallery marveling at a Victorian brooch in the shape of a siren made from a single Mabe pearl, a Fabergé egg with a golden palace inside it, or a jeweled Tiffany iris. A gold and red-enamel watch with pearls for hours (it was meant for a blind person) is near a box by Bourcheron made from gold, rock crystal, and diamonds. The rich materials depict a bucolic scene on the box lid: a coach and horses speeding through the countryside.

It's almost beyond comprehension that items as diverse as the oldest surviving text by the mathematical genius Archimedes, Egyptian sculpture, Byzantine icons, paintings by Peter Paul Rubens, and Kabuki prints by Knish Horsed could be appreciated by, much less carefully collected by, a single father and son. Each item in this collection is to be savored and enjoyed. Don't miss it!

George Peabody Library

This magnificent building dates from the founding of the Peabody Institute in 1857, and is one of the most beautiful repositories of learning in the world. Though the books are non-circulating to the public, the library is open to visitors with a photo ID for viewing from the ground floor (17 E. Mount Vernon Pl., 410/659-8197, website: www.library.jhu .edu/infofor/visitors.html). The Peabody is now a part of Johns Hopkins University Sheridan Libraries; viewing hours during Fall and Spring semesters are Mon.-Sat. 8 A.M.– 10 P.M., Sunday 10 A.M.–3P.M. During the summer and in between semesters, it's open Mon.-Sat. 8 A.M.– 10 P.M., Sunday 1P.M.– 5P.M. free). Reflecting the scholarly interests of the 19th century, the library consists of a general reference collection on virtually every subject but law and medicine. The 255,000 volumes date from the 16th to the early 20th centuries.

George Peabody embodied the classic rags-to-riches story. Born to a poor family in Massachusetts, he became wealthy as an investment banker in England, and, as an investment, started a dry goods firm in Baltimore in 1814. Peabody financed the westward expansion of American railroads and, when he retired, sold his interest in the investment bank to his partners, J. P. Morgan and his father—the company eventually became the House of Morgan. In the years that followed, Peabody created museums of natural history, archaeology, and ethnology at Yale and Harvard, the Peabody Museum in Salem, Massachusetts, and a number of philanthropic foundations. Upon his death in 1869, he bequeathed the Peabody Institute and Library to Baltimore.

Even if you aren't here for the books, come inside to see the extraordinary architectural details of the building—the stack room contains five tiers of ornamental cast-iron balconies that rise upward to a skylight that forms the ceiling. You will, as one local writer predicted, say, "Wow."

◖ Washington Monument

Attention, athletes: The challenge is to make it up the spiraling 228 steps of the Washington Monument (609 Washington Pl., 410/396-1049, 9 A.M.–4 P.M. Wed.–Sun., $1) without clinging to the walls and gasping more than once. Baltimoreans are proud that this monument to the father of our country predates the D.C. model by decades. In fact, the architect, Robert Mills, honed his skills in Baltimore and went on to create the obelisk in the capital city. The most embarrassing thing about the monument is that sound carries throughout the tower better than a two-block phone connection, so everyone knows you're winded. The rewards at the top are bragging rights, great views, and several years' worth of graffiti (you can rest while you're reading). There's a little gallery with historic displays on the bottom floor.

Mount Vernon Place United Methodist Church

If a set painter were to design a church as the background for a Gothic romance, she would probably come up with something that looks like this (10 E. Mount Vernon Pl., 410/685-5290, call for tour times, donations accepted). This soaring green serpentine, gray stone, and red-painted church was built in 1874 on the spot where Francis Scott Key died some 30 years before. The inside is less ornate than the outside, but interior carvings and faux stonework carry on the high gothic theme of flowers, fruit and animals. The organ has nearly 4,000 pipes.

Basilica of the Assumption

Historically known as the mother church of Roman Catholicism in the United States (Cathedral St. and Mulberry St., 410/727-3565, www.baltimorebasilica.org, 8:30 A.M.–4:30 P.M. daily), this is the chief house of worship encompassing the vast Diocese of Baltimore, which once extended from Maine to Georgia and west to the Mississippi. The Basilica offers regularly scheduled tours at 9 A.M., 11 A.M., and 1 P.M. Monday–Saturday and at noon on Sunday. If you would like a Saturday tour, email seningen@baltimorebasilica.org to check availability, as weddings and baptisms are often scheduled on that day.

The building was initiated by the first U.S. archbishop, John Carroll (brother of Charles Carroll of Carrollton), who is buried in a crypt on the site. Benjamin Henry Latrobe, architect of the U.S. Capitol building in D.C., donated

Mount Vernon Place United Methodist Church

© JOANNE MILLER

the design. The cornerstone for the church was laid in 1806, but the war of 1812 delayed completion until the early 1920s. The importance of the stately basilica was underscored by visits from Pope John Paul II in 1995 and Mother Teresa in 1996. The building's central dome features a radiant portrait of Mary rising into heaven and the entire church is redolent of a century of frankincense.

Enoch Pratt Central Library

Enoch Pratt, a merchant banker who made his fortune in Maryland, gifted the city with an entire free library system, consisting of 26 branches and the Central Library (400 Cathedral St., 410/396-5430, www.pratt.lib.md.us, 10 A.M.–8 P.M. Mon.–Wed., 10 A.M.–5:30 P.M. Thurs., 10 A.M.–5 P.M. Fri.–Sat. year-round, also open 1–5 P.M. Sun. Oct.–May), which is the state library resource center. The central library is another historic building illuminated by a spectacular skylight. The Pratt libraries maintain several special collections. Among them are 5,500 volumes of the works of H. L.

Mencken, and 325 volumes and manuscripts of the works of Edgar Allan Poe. The children's reading room, with its fountain and fireplace, is a delightful place to visit for readings and other special events. Pratt books circulate to those with a local address and library card. The central library is also a good place to pick up free newspapers, neighborhood flyers, and bus schedules.

Eubie Blake National Jazz Museum and Cultural Center

A repository of memorabilia about the legendary ragtime and musical theater composer (847 N. Howard St., 410/225-3130, www.eubieblake.org), this museum also has displays on other jazz greats born in Baltimore, including Billie Holiday, Chick Webb, Cab Calloway. The gallery features new art exhibitions frequently, and provides instruction in visual and performing arts to the community. Regular hours are not established, so contact the museum directly for times and admission fees.

Mother Seton House

This small school and church house (600 N. Paca St., 410/523-3443, www.motherseton house.org, 1–3 P.M. Sat.–Sun., donations accepted) is the site of the original posting of American saint Elizabeth Seton when she committed to the Catholic Church and began her teaching career in western Maryland. There is a small chapel and the dwelling house used by the sisters of St. Joseph on the property.

LITTLE ITALY
Baltimore Civil War Museum

This little museum at the President Street Station (601 President St., 410/385-5188, www.mdhs .org/explore/baltcivilwar.html, 10 A.M.–5 P.M. daily) is best reached on foot after parking in the nearby industrial neighborhood—the roads are a bit confusing due to ongoing construction. Admission is $4 for adults, $3 for seniors and kids, and if you can dig up a Civil War veteran, he'll get in for free. Artifacts and pictures detailing Baltimore's history in the conflict are of particular interest; the President Street Station was the site of mob riots during the early part of the war. The displays are informative and well-put-together; it's a worthy stop for Civil War buffs. One panel tells the story of Henry "Box" Brown, a slave shipped from Richmond, Virginia, through Baltimore to Philadelphia, Pennsylvania, by abolitionist James A. Smith. Brown spent 26 hours in a crate. When it was opened, he sang, "I waited patiently for the lord, and he heard my prayer...." Smith tried to ship two more slaves, but was caught—he served eight years in prison.

The Star-Spangled Banner Flag House and Museum

This renovated site (844 E. Pratt St., 410/837-1793, www.flaghouse.org, 10 A.M.–4 P.M. Tues.–Sat., $7 adults, $6 seniors, $5 children) is the home of Ms. Mary Pickersgill, flag and banner maker. During the summer of 1813, the British threatened to attack Baltimore, and the defenses at Fort McHenry were subsequently strengthened. The commandant, Major George Armistead, ordered a flag "so large that the British will have no difficulty seeing it from a distance." Ms. Pickersgill, with the help of her mother, daughter, and two nieces, sewed the 30-by-34-foot flag—bigger than the house—by hand. They went to a neighborhood brewery to have room to spread out the blue field on which they placed 15 stars. For her services, Mary was paid $405.90 (the receipt is in the house), and the sturdy flag went on to stream gallantly below bombs bursting in air. The house contains furniture from the period, and the visitors center features a video about the War of 1812 and the flag. In the garden, there's a stone map of the United States with each state cut from stone native to that state.

Free street parking is available on a first come, first served basis on Albemarle Street beside the museum entrance. Get a free parking pass in the gift shop when you arrive.

Though the flag itself is displayed at the Smithsonian Institution in Washington, D.C., a highlight of the museum is the Great Flag Window, which is the same size, color, and design as the original flag.

A COLLISION HAS OCCURRED

Baltimore has the dubious distinction of being the site of the first blood spilled in the Civil War. Maryland was deeply torn: Though it was officially a Southern slave state below the Mason-Dixon Line, its strategic position surrounding the capital made it imperative that Maryland's loyalties remain with the Union. The citizens of Baltimore did not necessarily agree with this idea.

On April 19, 1861, four days after President Lincoln called for a muster of troops to defend Washington, a Massachusetts regiment reached Baltimore's President Street station by rail at around 10 A.M. The troops were to remain in the cars, which were to be hitched to horses and pulled several blocks west to the Camden station rails, where they would continue on to the capital. An angry pro-Southern mob attacked the train with paving stones and managed to halt the last two cars. Roughly 100 uniformed Union soldiers were forced to leave the cars and march through the mob of 3,000, which pelted them with rocks and eventually gunfire. Finally, their commander ordered them to load their rifles and protect themselves.

A short distance away, 10 companies of un-armed troops from Pennsylvania endured a two-hour assault trapped in rail cars, covering themselves as well as possible from the rain of stones and shattered window glass. The mob dragged trees and other debris across the tracks to prevent the troop trains from moving toward the capital. Eventually, the police – ambivalent about opposing such large numbers of rioters and possibly moved by Southern sympathies – managed to clear the tracks and free the trains. Three soldiers, eight rioters, and one bystander died in the confrontation.

Shortly afterward, the governor of Maryland, Thomas Hicks, and George Brown, mayor of Baltimore, wrote to the president: "Sir, A collision between the citizens and the Northern troops has taken place in Baltimore, and the excitement is fearful. Send no more troops here. We will endeavor to prevent all bloodshed."

President Lincoln, prizing Baltimore's strategic position, placed the city under martial law. A month later, Union troops built a fort and positioned cannons and gun emplacements on Federal Hill. Baltimore's citizens would not be permitted to collide with the federal government again for the duration of the war.

Reginald F. Lewis Museum of Maryland African American History and Culture

The East Coast's largest museum chronicling the history of African Americans, the Lewis Museum (830 E. Pratt St., 443/263-1800, www.africanamericanculture.org/museum; 10–5 Tues.–Sat., noon–5 Sunday, $8 adults, $6 seniors) houses artifacts and exhibits that cover 350 years of Maryland history. Inside, there's a genealogy center, theater, recording studio for oral history, gift shop, and café, in addition to the galleries.

Jewish Museum of Maryland

This special collection (15 Lloyd St., 410/732-6400, www.jewishmuseummd. org, noon–4 P.M. Tues.–Thurs. and Sun., $8 adults, $4 students, $3 children under 12) concentrates on preserving Maryland's Jewish history and culture through a collection of photographs, papers, and objects. This is no dry historical treatise, though—the rotating exhibits are interesting and well-designed. One recent exhibit focused on Jewish life in Maryland's small towns. The story of Jewish participation in the building of Baltimore is fascinating. Jewish families began to settle in Baltimore in the Fell's Point area early in the 19th century. By the 1840s, more than 1,000 lived on the eastern edge of the city. The Civil War brought a new prosperity, and wealthy Jewish businessmen built elegant homes and the stately Oheb Shalom temple on Eutaw Place. Lloyd Street Synagogue, the third-oldest standing synagogue in the country and the

© JOANNE MILLER

Jewish Museum of Maryland

pumping station, and it reveals the city's infrastructure through exhibits, video presentations, interactive computers (where visitors can build their own city), and "Streetscape"—an outdoor maze of drains, conduits, and pipes. Who'd have thought sewage could be so much fun?

FELL'S POINT
Fell's Point Maritime Museum
This block-long seafaring history trove is a cooperative venture between the Maryland Historical Society and the Society for the Preservation of Federal Hill and Fell's Point (1724 Thames St., 410/732-0278, 10 A.M.–5 P.M. Thurs.–Mon., $4 adults, $3 children 13–17, free for students with ID/seniors/children 12 and under. It displays artifacts and tells the story of those who earned their living on the water. Now a trendy residential neighborhood, Fell's Point was the site of Baltimore's first shipyard in the 1730s, as well as home to a thriving maritime industry through the mid-19th century.

UPTOWN/BOLTON HILL/ HAMPDEN
Baltimore Museum of Art
In the toney north end of town (N. Charles St. and 31st St., 410/396-7100, www.artbma .org, 11 A.M.–5 P.M. Wed.–Fri., 11 A.M.–6 P.M. Sat.–Sun., free), BMA is Maryland's largest art museum and the home of several notable collections given by philanthropic Baltimoreans, including the Cone sisters. Another outstanding site for art, this museum is free every day. The museum is open 11 A.M.–8 P.M. the first Thursday evening of each month, and tours, talks, live music, and hands-on workshops for kids are often on the menu.

A major renovation has recently reframed (literally) the Cone collection, and the Matisses and other works presented to the city by Dr. Claribel Cone and Miss Etta Cone remain at the heart of the museum's displays. In addition, the museum's west wing houses 16 galleries for the display of the permanent collection of post-1945 art (including a gallery of works by Andy Warhol). Two sculpture gardens showcase modern and contemporary sculpture, and three floors of the original

oldest in Maryland (1845), is next door to the museum, as is the B'nai Israel Synagogue, built in 1876. Call to arrange a guided tour. There is an excellent gift shop on the premises.

The **Holocaust Memorial,** at the intersection of Water, Gay, and Lombard Streets, is a sculptural reminder of World War II devastation and the hopes of new generations for a more tolerant future.

Baltimore Public Works Museum
This collection (751 Eastern Ave., 410/396-5565, www.baltimorepublicworksmuseum.org, 10 A.M.–4 P.M. Tues.–Sun., $3 adults, $2.50 seniors and students) is undeniably unique. If you've ever wondered how tunnels, roads, bridges, clean water, waste water, and recycling systems are created and maintained in a big city, this is your opportunity to learn. Baltimore is proud of its public works programs: The city pioneered the first gas streetlight (1816), the first earthen dam (at Druid Lake, 1875), and the formula for chlorinating water to prevent waterborne diseases. The museum is housed in a beautiful 1911

THE FIRST (ART) FAMILIES OF BALTIMORE

William Walters, born in 1819, claimed that he spent his first five dollars on an artist's view of Napoleon crossing the Alps. After shrewd investments made him a rich man, he continued to indulge his love of art, first collecting works by American painters of the New York School and the Chesapeake Bay. During the Civil War, Walters moved his family to Paris – his Southern loyalties made for an uncomfortable home and business life in Union Maryland. Abroad, he discovered Corot, Daumier, and the sculptor A. L. Barye. He also developed an appetite for oriental porcelain and other Asiana. Upon Walters' death in 1894, his son Henry expanded the collection; in 1902, he purchased the contents of the Accoramboni Palace in Rome, some 1,600 works, including dozens of sculptures from classical antiquity. Though Henry lived with his friends Pembroke and Sarah Jones in their residences in New York and Rhode Island – he married Sarah after her husband's death – he always shipped the goods to Baltimore. Henry Walters left the fabulous collection and its buildings to the city on his death in 1931. The Walters Art Museum remains one of the showplaces of Baltimore.

Dr. Claribel Cone and Miss Etta Cone were sisters, "spinsters," and members of a group of wealthy Jewish immigrant Baltimoreans who envisioned a museum of art for the city in 1914. Claribel hosted Baltimore's leading salon in the family's Eutaw Street apartments, regularly attended by Gertrude Stein and her brother Leo, who moved to Baltimore from San Francisco in 1892. The Cone sisters followed the Steins to Europe in 1903 and became acquainted with the avant-garde painters of the day. Thanks to Ms. Stein and her friends, the Cone's tastes were decidedly modern: They became major patrons of Picasso and Matisse, and collected Gauguin, Seurat, and others. Matisse became especially favored, and at the time of the sisters' deaths, they owned 42 of artist's paintings, 18 sculptures, and dozens of works on paper, including 250 items that illustrated his first book, *Poésies de Stéphane Mallarmé*. Picasso, however, fell out of the Cones' favor when he entered his cubist period. Etta, who survived her sister by 20 years, brought the collection up to 3,000 pieces, adding works by Cézanne and Van Gogh before her death in 1949. She bequeathed the entire collection, plus a substantial endowment for maintenance, to the fortunate Baltimore Museum of Art.

building present American painting and sculpture prior to 1900, decorative arts of the 18th through the 20th centuries, and period rooms from six historic Maryland houses. Whew! Of course, that's in addition to the art from Africa, the Americas, and Oceania; the Chinese ceramics; paintings by European masters; and collections of prints, drawings, and photographs. Whatever your artistic interest, you'll find it here. Gertrude's, an attractive indoor/outdoor restaurant inside the museum (see the *Food* section) is an excellent spot for a meal.

Maryland Historical Society Museum and Library

The broad-based collections here touch every part of Maryland's history (201 W. Monument St., 410/685-3750, www.mdhs.org,

10 A.M.–5 P.M. Wed.–Sun., $8 adults, $6 children 3–17 and seniors, $4 children 3–12, free the first Thurs. of the month). Interactive displays give the feel of a boat's pilot house, ship's chandlery, and a sailor's life in the 1880s; the Civil War is depicted in letters and photographs; and rooms are filled with displays of 20th-century fine and decorative arts. There are paintings by the Peales, a Claire McCardell Costume and Textile Gallery with changing exhibitions, an original draft of the poem that became our national anthem, and a gallery of sporting art. Families will appreciate the "history haversacks" for kids that contain a pack of parent-child pastimes, scavenger hunts, crafts, and other hands-on activities to be used during self-guided treks through the exhibitions.

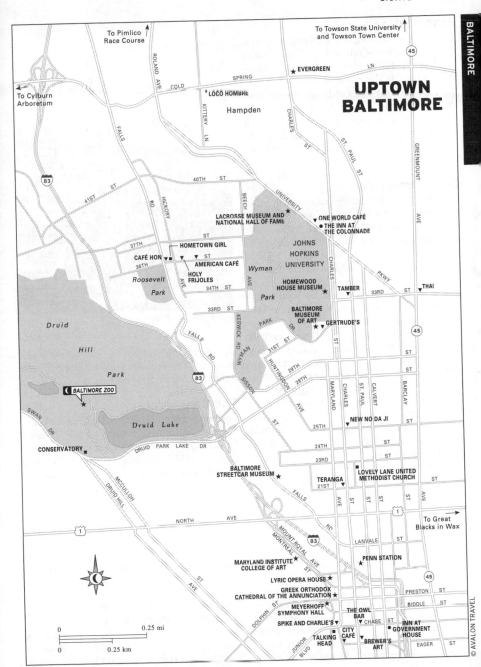

To Pimlico
Race Course

To Towson State University
and Towson Town Center

45

To Cylburn
Arboretum

ROLAND AVE

SPRING

GOLD

★ EVERGREEN

LN

★ LOCO HOMBRE

Hampden

KITTERY LN

CHARLES ST

ST PAUL ST

GREENMOUNT AVE

**UPTOWN
BALTIMORE**

FALLS

83

40TH ST

41ST ST

HICKORY RD

BEECH

UNIVERSITY

LACROSSE MUSEUM AND
NATIONAL HALL OF FAME ★

★ ONE WORLD CAFÉ
● THE INN AT
THE COLONNADE

37TH ST

HOMETOWN GIRL ▼

JOHNS
HOPKINS
UNIVERSITY

CHARLES ST

PKWY

CAFÉ HON ▼ ■ ST
36TH ▼
AMERICAN CAFÉ

HOLY
FRIJOLES

AVE

Wyman

Roosevelt
Park

34TH ST

Park

HOMEWOOD
HOUSE MUSEUM ★

TAMBER ▼

33RD ST ★ THAI

33RD ST

PARK DR

BALTIMORE MUSEUM
OF ART ★ GERTRUDE'S ▼

45

Druid

FALLS RD

KESWICK RD

MAN AVE

31ST ST

ST

Hill

29TH ST

Park

HUNTINGDON AVE

28TH

SISSON ST

MARYLAND

CHARLES

ST PAUL

CALVERT

BARCLAY

★ BALTIMORE ZOO

25TH ST

NEW NO DA JI ▼

Druid Lake

24TH ST

SWAN DR

23RD ST

CONSERVATORY ■

DRUID PARK LAKE DR

BALTIMORE
STREETCAR MUSEUM ★

FALLS

TERANGA ▼
21ST ST

■ LOVELY LANE UNITED
METHODIST CHURCH

ST

MCCULLOH

DRUID HILL AVE

NORTH AVE

1

MOUNT ROYAL AVE

83

LANVALE ST

1

To Great
Blacks in Wax

MONTREAL

PENN STATION

MARYLAND INSTITUTE ★
COLLEGE OF ART

45

ST

LYRIC OPERA HOUSE ★

PRESTON ST

GREEK ORTHODOX ★
CATHEDRAL OF THE ANNUNCIATION

BIDDLE ST

MEYERHOFF ★
SYMPHONY HALL

THE OWL
BAR

CHASE ST

INN AT
● GOVERNMENT
HOUSE

SPIKE AND CHARLIE'S ▼

DOLPHIN ST

JUNIOR

BLVD

■ CITY
CAFÉ

■
TALKING
HEAD

▼ BREWER'S
ART

EAGER ST

0   0.25 mi

0   0.25 km

© AVALON TRAVEL

Penn Station

This elegant building is still as engaging as it was in the heyday of railroads (1515 N. Charles St., 410/291-4261). This glistening glass-and-stone palace is the place to catch the train; there's also a great little candy store inside, with the city's best candy apples (cinnamon and caramel). Temporary parking out front makes it easy to pop in for a pit stop and a snack, and to check arrivals and departures on the clicking-clacking flip boards.

🄲 Baltimore Zoo

The aquarium is spectacular, but one of my other city favorites is the Baltimore Zoo (Druid Hill Park, 410/366-LION or 410/366-5466, www .baltimorezoo.org). Hours are 10 A.M.–4:30 P.M. Monday–Thursday and 10 A.M.–8 P.M. Friday–Saturday March–June, 10 A.M.–6 P.M. Friday–Saturday Memorial Day–Labor Day, and 10 A.M.–4:30 P.M. Friday–Saturday September–December. Adult admission is $15, seniors $12, and children 2–11 $10.

This beautifully landscaped park features more than 2,000 animals, including many threatened and endangered species. Cages are few: Many animals are kept in natural habitats, such as the boardwalk through the African veldt and the Maryland wilderness area. Healthy, active animals are showcased in numerous educational programs, and keepers hold regularly scheduled "encounters" to talk about everything from bees to polar bears throughout each day.

The zoo offers many special family-oriented events throughout the year: Puppet shows, camel rides, a climbing wall (the Siberian Summit), a little train (ZooChoo), and a carousel add extra fun for nominal charges. Kids receive a free Zoofari Adventure Guide, a brightly illustrated manual that turns learning about animals—with the help of Paco, the zoo's macaw mascot—into puzzles and games. The 180-acre grounds are extensive, and a tram is available for those who would rather ride than walk. There are four refreshment stands on the grounds, and two gift shops—an opportunity to pick up hippo-shaped poo perchers

The Conservatory

© JOANNE MILLER

(fertilizers) for your plants. This is one of the best zoos I've seen—a well-maintained, enlightened, happy place to visit.

The Conservatory

Located at Druid Hill Park (McCulloh St. and Gywnns Fall Pkwy., 10 A.M.–4 P.M. Thurs.–Sun., free) is a soaring Victorian glass "palace" created in 1888. The original Palm Court now has four greenhouses attached, and all are surrounded by outdoor gardens. Neglected for years, the conservatory has been renovated and filled with all types of exotic plants in discrete environments ranging from jungle to desert. The parks department has developed a series of special events-find an excellent month-to-month online guide at http://baltimorecity.gov/ government/recnparks/special_events.htm.

Lacrosse Museum and National Hall of Fame

What soccer is to most of the world, lacrosse is to the East Coast. The Lacrosse Museum and National Hall of Fame (113 W. University

THE LITTLE BROTHER OF WAR

French Jesuit missionaries in Canada and upstate New York recorded accounts of lacrosse (loosely translated, "a game played with a curved stick and ball") being played by the Huron in the 1630s. Though different forms of the game existed at the time of European encroachment, lacrosse was played by indigenous peoples throughout the Great Lakes and the eastern United States.

Lacrosse had a central role in Native American culture. Its origins are rooted in legend, and the game itself was surrounded with ceremony. Equipment and players were ritualistically prepared by a shaman, and team selection and victory were often considered to be supernaturally controlled. The game was used to vent aggression and territorial disputes between tribes, and the rituals to prepare the players were identical to those practiced in preparation for war – hence the Algonquin name for the sport, "Little Brother of War." Today, the game is still played by the Iroquois and tribes in the Southeast, and is often used for curative purposes.

The modern form of lacrosse, which employs a three-foot-long shaft ending in a crook and a large, flat, triangular webbed surface, was adapted from the New England tribes. A ball is passed between team members (who never touch it with their hands) and moved toward goals on either end of the field.

and male and female stars. Pro football veteran Jim Brown's picture graces the hall of fame: He played for Syracuse University in 1957. Lacrosse is played internationally, with world championship competitions every four years (the 2006 world championship was held in London, Ontario). America sports one of the best teams in the world; since 1982, the U.S. Team has won every world contest except 1998, when Canada took the title. The next world game will be played in Manchester, England.

Homewood House

A jewel on the campus of Johns Hopkins University (3400 N. Charles St., 410/516-5589, www.jhu.edu/hwdhouse, 11 A.M.–4 P.M. Tues.–Fri., noon–4 P.M. Sat.–Sun., $6 adults, $5 seniors, $3 students); this is the country home of Charles Carroll Jr., son of Charles Carroll of Carrollton (probably the most influential Carroll of them all). C. C. Sr. built the Federal-style house in 1801, and it's decorated with fine 18th- and 19th-century furnishings. All tours are guided and begin on the hour and half hour; the last tour starts at 3:30 P.M.

Bufano Sculpture Garden at Johns Hopkins University

In Dunning Park behind Mudd Hall (3400 N. Charles St.), this playful walk among the trees will raise your spirits, especially since each of the 10 pieces that sit alongside a meandering path under a grove of trees has been restored after years of neglect, following an attack by vandals. Bufano's work in this collection consists mostly of charming interpretations of animals in various types of stone, either singly or in groups, sometimes a mother and babies.

Evergreen

Evergreen (4545 N. Charles St., 410/516-0341, www.jhu.edu/evrgreen, 11 A.M.–4 P.M. Tues.–Fri., noon–4 P.M. Sat.–Sun., $6 adults, $5 seniors, $3 students) is maintained by Johns Hopkins University—no Carrolls here, though. The house is open for tours on the hour. The 48-room Italianate house on 26 acres was the residence of former ambassador John Work

Pkwy, 410/235-6882, www.lacrosse.org/museum, $3 adults, $2 children 5–15) celebrates the sport, from its origins as a stickball game played by Native Americans prior to European settlement to today's modern teams. The museum is open 10 A.M.–3 P.M. Monday–Friday June–January, 10 A.M.–3 P.M. Tuesday–Saturday February–May.

Home to USLacrosse national headquarters, an umbrella organization for lacrosse clubs across the nation, the museum displays the fast-moving game's history, equipment,

Garrett, who converted the gymnasium into a theater devised by famous Russian émigré Léon Bakst, a designer for Diaghilev and the Ballets Russe. The Garretts supported many of the arts of Baltimore in the 1920s–1930s, and the house reflects their interests and taste: a rare book library, Tiffany chandeliers, Japanese netsuke, and Chinese blue-and-white porcelain are all on display.

Cathedral of the Annunciation

This Greek Orthodox church (24 W. Preston St. at Maryland Ave., www.goannun.org) is a magnificent domed building enclosing gilded icons, ornate woodwork, and mosaics. Over the entrance, the Greek inscription reads "House of God, Gate of Heaven." Unlike many orthodox churches, this one has benches, so attendees can sit rather than stand during the service. Though the church is locked when not in use, stop by the office during the week 9 A.M.–5 P.M.and ask to be admitted. The cathedral sponsors an outstanding Greek festival annually in early November.

Lovely Lane United Methodist Church

The designer of this structure (2200 St. Paul St., 410/889-4458, www.lovelylane.net) was infamous New York architect Stanford White, who was shot to death by his lover's husband, causing a sensational trial in the early years of the 20th century—but that's another story. Guided tours are offered at noon on Sunday Labor Day–July 1, and 11 A.M. on Sunday July 1–Labor Day. Visitors are also welcome to visit on their own during church office hours (9 A.M.–3 P.M. weekdays), as scheduled events permit. Donations are appreciated. The massive, sturdy granite building is the mother church of American Methodism, and a museum on the premises exhibits historical materials related to the founding of the sect.

Meyerhoff Gallery/Maryland Institute College of Art

Rotating exhibitions at the Maryland Institute College of Art's Meyerhoff Gallery (1300 Mt. Royal Ave., 410/669-9200, 10 A.M.–5 P.M. Mon.–Sat., noon–5 P.M. Sun., free) provide a chance to look at the work of tomorrow's artists. Some of the work is extremely good, and the most varied show of the year, the Alumni Exhibition, features the work of hundreds of graduates of the school since its inception in the 1930s. The Alumni Exhibition is usually held in June.

Baltimore Streetcar Museum

The Baltimore Streetcar Museum (1901 Falls Rd., 410/547-0264, www.baltimorestreetcar .org, noon–5 P.M. Sat. June–Oct., noon–5 P.M. Sun. year-round; $8 adults, $3 seniors and children) is the result of the efforts of local volunteers to preserve an important part of the city's past. In 1859, Baltimore laid its first horse-powered rail transportation system; within a few years, electricity replaced horseflesh. The long-distance transportation provided by the colorful electrified trolleys made it possible for the busy seaport town to expand out from the harbor to create the many neighborhoods that characterize it today. In fact, the first successful commercial electric railway in the United States was the Baltimore–Hampden run, built in 1885. The museum chronicles the early days with an audiovisual presentation, *Trolley—The Car That Built Our Cities,* with pictorial displays of the town in the 1940s and 1950s, and of course, the railcars themselves. The yard and car house contain both unrestored and restored cars from every era of Baltimore's past. The museum also features an antique trolley for a rocking, clanging ride into history on a short rail trip. The "trolleymen" are all volunteers, dressed as authentic conductors—and they know everything about these early transportation systems you'll ever need to ask. The admission fee includes the museum exhibits, car house, and unlimited rides on the streetcar line.

Cylburn Arboretum

The mansion at this property (4915 Greenspring Ave., 410/367-2217, www.cylburn association.org) houses a small nature museum

the main drag of one of Baltimore's tougher neighborhoods—the good news is that it's the focal point of a revitalization movement. It's open 9 A.M.–6 P.M. Tuesday–Saturday and noon–6 P.M. Sunday January 15–Oct. 14, 9 A.M.–5 P.M. Tuesday–Saturday and noon–5 P.M. Sunday October 15–January 14, 10 A.M.–4 P.M. Monday February and July–August, and on Martin Luther King Jr. Day.

The museum is set up in an old theater. Though the displays don't even flirt with high-tech, the idea—of pride in the accomplishment and achievement of African Americans from ancient times to the present—is absolutely on target. Black heroines and heroes of every era are represented. A replica of a slave ship, similar to those that brought the ancestors of most American blacks to this continent, provides considerable food for thought in terms of understanding the courage, strength, and adaptability it takes to survive in a hostile world.

WALKS AND TOURS
Mount Vernon Place and Belvedere Walking Tour

In the last few hundred years, this still elegant but slightly worn section of Baltimore provided the stage for international romance, literary history, and proper etiquette, with a little muckraking thrown in.

The tour starts at 11 West Mulberry Street, built by John H. B. Latrobe around 1830. An engineer who practiced law, Latrobe represented the B&O Railroad and other big businesses in Baltimore. However, his wealth came from the invention of the Latrobe Stove, an enclosed fireplace he invented in order to keep his wife from retreating to her native Natchez, Mississippi, during Baltimore winters. As part of his civic duty, Latrobe judged a literary contest and awarded the first prize of $50 to the orphaned son of a local pioneer family, Edgar Allan Poe. The story, "A Ms. Found in a Bottle," was Poe's first published work. Within a few years, Poe became famous for his fiction—he invented both detective and horror genres with stories such as "Murders in the Rue Morgue," "The Pit and the Pendulum," and

© JOANNE MILLER

Cylburn Arboretum

and is surrounded by several gardens, including a heritage rose garden with species more than a century old. The grounds are open 6 A.M.–9 P.M. daily year-round, the mansion is open 7:30 A.M.–3:30 P.M. Monday–Friday, and the museum is open 1–3 P.M. Tuesday and Thursday and by arrangement. Admission is free. Jesse Tyson, a wealthy Baltimore industrialist, started to build Cylburn for his mother in 1863, but her death and the Civil War delayed completion until the 1880s. Tyson, then in his 60s, married a 19-year-old debutante, moved into the house, threw lavish parties, and established the gardens. Ever modest, he's quoted as saying, "I have the fairest wife, the fastest horses, and the finest house in Maryland." You can see for yourself.

National Great Blacks in Wax Museum

Great Blacks in Wax (1601–03 E. North Ave., 410/563-3404, www.ngbiwm.com, $9 adults, $8 seniors, $6 children 3–11) is on

"Masque of the Red Death." However, proper Baltimoreans found him "unstable as water," and employment opportunities were nil—a difficult situation for a young man who had secretly married his 13-year-old first cousin and was struggling to support both her and her mother. Poe lived in other cities (including Philadelphia), but came home to Baltimore in his later years, lived in a house on Amity Street, and is buried in Westminster Cemetery along with his wife.

Around the corner, the building that once occupied 417 North Charles Street was the birthplace of novelist Upton Sinclair; it was demolished in 1969. The son of a Baltimore "establishment" family, Sinclair shocked the world when he exposed the meatpacking industry in his celebrated 1906 work *The Jungle*. Sensitive to political corruption and social injustice, Sinclair wrote about venereal disease (*Damaged Goods*, 1913), Christian hypocrisy (*The Profits of Religion*, 1918), and the shortcomings of American journalism (*The Brass Check*, 1919). The author released some of his works himself when commercial publishers refused them, notably *Upton Sinclair Presents William Fox* (1933), which exposed financial chicanery in the film industry. In 1934, Sinclair ran as the Democratic candidate for governor of California on the EPIC (End Poverty in California) program. Narrowly defeated, he returned to writing, turning out 11 novels featuring protagonist Lanny Budd—confidant of international leaders, intimately involved in intrigues before and during both World Wars. The third novel in the series, *Dragon's Teeth* (1942), about Hitler's rise to power, won a Pulitzer Prize in 1943.

In Baltimore, one man threw away his crown for a wife, and another threw away his wife for a crown. Head north on Charles Street, make a left on Madison, and a right on Cathedral Street. Light from the Tiffany and Lafarge stained-glass windows of Emmanuel Episcopal Church at 811 Cathedral Street bathed the baptism of Wallis Warfield in 1896. Warfield later captured the heart of King Edward VIII. Farther up the street at the corner of Cathedral

and Read, the Medical Arts building sits on the site of Betsey Patterson Bonaparte's last home. Patterson married Jerome Bonaparte, the youngest brother of Napoleon, in 1803. Two years later, Napoleon had the marriage annulled so that Jerome could marry Catherine of Wurttemberg and become king of Westphalia. Jerome commanded an army in the invasion of Russia in 1812. After taking part in the Battle of Waterloo (1815), he fled France. He later returned and witnessed the establishment of the Second French Empire under his nephew Napoleon III. Betsey remained in Baltimore until her death.

Writer and journalist H. L. Mencken lived at 704 Cathedral Street with his wife, Sarah, from 1930 until her death after a long illness in 1935. Mencken was considered the most influential American editor, essayist, and social critic of the first half of the 20th century. He began his career as a reporter for the *Baltimore Morning Herald*, then, in 1905, became a controversial columnist for the *Baltimore Evening Sun*. One of his essays, "Puritanism as a Literary Force" (1917), interpreted Puritanism as the root of most American problems. "The Sahara of the Bozart" (1920) slammed southern culture and literature, which ironically helped inspire the southern literary renaissance of the 1920s and 1930s. Mencken's influence waned in the 1930s; he adamantly opposed Roosevelt's New Deal programs, and his acerbic style was better suited to more prosperous times. Mencken's most celebrated work includes essays collected in the six-volume *Prejudices* (1919–1927), as well as book- length musings on playwright George Bernard Shaw (1905), philosopher Friedrich Nietzsche (1908), and women (1917).

To the east, 14 East Chase Street was the home of a young lady who would become the social arbiter of polite society in America during the mid-20th century: Emily Post. A government agent once visited Post—whose book *Etiquette* was a national bestseller—in order to review her tax papers, and commented, "No woman has a right to make so much money."

A few blocks north and east, 212 East Biddle

Street housed Johns Hopkins medical student Gertrude Stein, daughter of a wealthy Pittsburgh family. Ms. Stein eventually gave up on medicine and began writing. One of her works, *Three Lives*, is set in Baltimore. Her experimental style prompted H. L. Mencken to remark, "She made English easier to write, and harder to read." After moving to Paris, Ms. Stein talked the Cone sisters from Baltimore into investing in Impressionist art, much of which is now in the Baltimore Museum of Art.

Stein's neighbor across the way at 215 East Biddle Street was none other than Wallis Warfield, all grown up. She wed her first husband in Christ Church on Chase and Paul Streets; they divorced a few years later. Edward VIII had already been crowned King of England in 1936 when he met Wallis Warfield Simpson. Political opposition to his marrying a divorcée forced him to abdicate later that year, though he retained the title of Duke of Windsor. He and Simpson wed in 1937 and lived in France until their deaths.

Guided Walks and Tours

The **Mount Vernon Cultural District** (217 N. Charles St., 410/244-1030, www.mvcd .org) sponsors free walks and historical talks throughout the year. In the past, visitors have been treated to a pre–Valentine's Day "Mount Vernon's Romantic Legacy" walking tour, featuring many of the sights above, including tales of locals Jerome Bonaparte and Betsy Patterson, the Duke and Duchess of Windsor, H. L. Mencken's short-lived marriage, and George Peabody's bad luck with women. Another tour is titled "The Great Book Hoof" and includes stops at the Peabody Institute and Library and tidbits about Mencken, Francis Scott Key, Mark Twain, F. Scott and Zelda Fitzgerald, Robert Frost, and filmmaker John Waters. The district also publishes self-guided walking tours of Mount Vernon, Belvedere, and Cathedral Hill that are fun and informative.

Ride the Ducks (Light St. Pavilion, 877/887-8225, www.baltimoreducks.com) gives tours aboard World War II–era amphibious vehicles, so visitors can see the city by land and by water. Built in 1945, the Army DUKW vehicles are big trucks with watertight hulls that travel on six wheels, then navigate the wet stuff with a rudder and marine propeller. This is a good introductory tour, as it covers several neighborhoods and hot spots, such as the Washington Monument and Edgar Allan Poe's gravesite.

Entertainment and Events

NIGHTLIFE

Baltimore has an active party scene. The Inner Harbor hotels and bars are always hopping at night and tend to be easy, safe destinations. Here are a few that stand out, plus some out-of-the-way places.

Pubs and Restaurant Bars

The Owl Bar (1 E. Chase St., 410/347-0888, 11:30 A.M.–2 A.M. Mon.–Sat., 11:30 A.M.–11 P.M. Sun.) is an evening meet-and-greet place with good pub food—reservations are necessary on the weekends. **Capitol City Brewing Company** (301 S. Light St., #93 Light Street Pavilion, 410/539-7468, www .capcitybrew.com, 11 A.M.–11 P.M. daily, bar open until 12:30 A.M.) has brews, food, and a great view of the harbor.

The Wharf Rat at Camden Yards (206 W. Pratt St., 410/244-8900, www.thewharf rat.com, 11:30 A.M.–2 A.M. daily) is a friendly English-style pub with full-service dining and an exhibition brewery.

Whitecap Tavern (110 S. Eutaw St., 410/962-0202, 2 P.M.–2 A.M. Mon.–Thurs., 11 A.M.–2 A.M. Fri.–Sun.) is a cozy bar/lounge open for lunch and dinner. It's in the Marriott Inner Harbor, across from Oriole Park at Pratt and Eutaw Streets.

Michener's Pub at the Sheraton (7032 Elm

Rd., 410/859-3300, 11 A.M.–2 A.M. daily) serves pub food in an intimate atmosphere (the restaurant, also named Michener's, is much more posh). It's closer to the airport than its downtown sister.

Jazz Bars

For a drink and post-dinner tête-à-tête, try the **Celebrities Lounge** at the Tremont Plaza Hotel (222 St. Paul Pl., 410/727-2222, 11:30 A.M.–3 P.M. and 5–11 P.M. Sun.–Thurs., 5 P.M.–midnight Fri.–Sat). Enjoy live jazz on Wednesday and Friday nights at **The Lobby Bar** in the Radisson Plaza Lord Baltimore (20 W. Baltimore St., 410/539-8400, 5 P.M.–1 A.M. Mon.–Thurs, 11:30 A.M.–1 P.M. Fri.–Sun.). My favorite intimate bar is the **Explorer's Lounge** in the Harbor Court Hotel (550 Light St., 410/234-0550, 11 A.M.–2 A.M. daily). The lounge has hand-painted African murals, aged cognacs, and live jazz.

North of town, the **Martini Bar** in the Crowne Plaza Baltimore North (2004 Greenspring Dr., Timonium, 410/252-7373, 3–10 P.M. daily) showcases a suave piano player during its Friday happy hour.

Social Bars

A couple of neighborhood bars offer different atmospheres: **Claddagh Pub** (2918 O'Donnell St., Canton, 410/522-4220, www.claddaghonline.com, 11 A.M.–2 A.M. Mon.–Fri., 9 A.M.–2 A.M. Sat.–Sun.) is an occasionally rowdy neighborhood Irish bar that serves breakfast 9 A.M.–1 P.M. on the weekends. **Mother's Federal Hill Grille** (1113 S. Charles St., Federal Hill, 410/244-8686) serves food as well as drink. It's open to the street, so the bar is a great place for people-watching and meeting. Hours are 11 A.M.–11 P.M. (bar closes at midnight) Monday, 11 A.M.–11 P.M. (bar closes at 2 A.M.) Tuesday–Thursday, 8 A.M.–11 P.M. (bar closes at 2 A.M.) Friday–Saturday, and 8 A.M.–10 P.M. (bar closes at 1 A.M.) Sunday.

Music and Dancing

The **Latin Palace** (509 S. Broadway St., Fell's Point, 410/522-6700, www.latinpalace.com,

4:30 P.M.–2 A.M. daily) plays hot rhythms from south of the border, plus a variety of other music. The club restaurant, Las Palmas, serves dinner 5–11 P.M. weekdays and 5 P.M.–midnight weekends. The dance club and bar are open 8 P.M.–2 A.M. Tuesday–Sunday, and there are salsa lessons 8–9:30 P.M. Wednesday–Saturday.

The best dance club in town is reputed to be the **Paradox** (1310 Russell St., 410/837-9110, www.thedox.com), not only for its roomy dance floors and retro look, but also for its mix of gay, straight, black, white, etc., patrons, mostly age 21 to early 30s. Days and hours are irregular (check the website), but expect action 11 P.M.–7 A.M. on Friday and Saturday nights.

The small but mighty **Talking Head** (203 Davis St., 410/962-5588, www.talkinghead club.com) is gaining a reputation as a hip place to hear live rock 'n' roll. Days and hours are irregular—contact the club for upcoming shows and times.

Comedy

The **Comedy Factory** (36 Light St., 410/ 547-7798, www.baltimorecomedyfactory .com), above Burke's Restaurant, features shows at 8 P.M. on Thursday, and at 8 P.M., 10 P.M., and midnight Friday and Saturday. There's a one-drink minimum; call for reservations and lineup. The **Power Plant Live!** (34 Market Place, 410/727-5483) showcases big names like Margaret Cho and Gary Owen.

THE ARTS
Performing Arts Venues

The newest space on the scene is the multimedia **Patterson Theater** (3134 Eastern Ave., Highlandtown, 410/276-1651, www.creative alliance.org). This historic movie theater with a rare marquee (it's vertical, with a five-part lighting sequence) closed in 1995 and reopened in 2003 as a "cultural factory" and home to the Creative Alliance, a community-based arts nonprofit. In its new incarnation, the brick structure houses a theater, two art galleries, eight live-work studios for artists, a film- and video-making center, a sidewalk café, and offices for the Creative Alliance. The Patterson offers workshops, life drawing sessions, critiques, and more for artists in all media. It also presents exhibitions of contemporary art, theater, performance art, cabaret, and live ethnic and experimental music, blues, and jazz, plus zydeco and tango dances with live bands. The theater will also be a locus for the screening of locally made films and videos.

The **Baltimore Center for the Performing Arts** (1 N. Charles St., 410/625-4230) is a nonprofit corporation dedicated to the presentation of theater, music, and dance in downtown Baltimore at the Morris A. Mechanic Theatre.

The **1st Mariner Arena Baltimore** (201 West Baltimore St., 410/347-2020, www.baltimore arena.com) hosts sporting events, *Stars on Ice*, Ringling Brothers and Barnum & Bailey Circus, WWF Wrestling, USHRA Motorsports events, and concerts.

Pier 6 Concert Pavilion (Pier 6, 731 Eastern Ave., no direct phone, www.piersixpavilion .com) presents pop, jazz, and classical concerts outdoors.

Classical Music and Opera

The **Baltimore Opera Company** (110 W. Mount Royal Ave., Ste. 306, 410/625-1600, www.baltimoreopera.com) produces fully staged grand operas featuring international singers, directors, and conductors at the **Lyric Opera House** (110 W. Mount Royal Ave., box office: 410/727-6000), a replica of Germany's Leipzig Music Hall. Operas are performed in the original language with English subtitles.

Meyerhoff Symphony Hall (1212 Cathedral St., 410/783-8100) presents the internationally acclaimed **Baltimore Symphony Orchestra** (www.baltimoresymphony.org), which offers a wide variety of classical, pops, and family concerts year-round.

Theater

The **Baltimore Theatre Alliance** (P.O. Box 10621, 410/662-9945, www.baltimoreperforms .org) is a nonprofit organization of over 40 theaters, managers, producers, directors, artists, technicians, and theatergoers dedicated to supporting and promoting theater in the greater Baltimore area. They're a great resource for the latest theater news.

The **France-Merrick Performing Arts Center** (in the old Hippodrome Theatre, 12 N. Eutaw St., 410/752-7444, www.france-merrick pac.com) presents Broadway musicals such as *Chicago* and *Wicked*.

Center Stage (700 N. Calvert St., 410/332-0033, www.centerstage.org) is the State Theater of Maryland and considered one of the top 10 regional theaters in the country.

Maryland Stage Company (1000 Hilltop Circle, 410/455-2917, www.umbc.edu/theatre) is a professional theater-troupe-in-residence, as well as a training ground for theater students at the University of Maryland.

The Vagabond Players (806 S. Broadway, 410/563-9135) presents Broadway plays such as *Death of a Salesman* and *Prelude to a Kiss* in Fell's Point.

FESTIVALS AND EVENTS

Baltimore's inner harbor (particularly Harborplace, 410/332-4191) has continual entertainment and sponsors many events during the year. Since event contact numbers frequently change, get in touch with the city's main visitor center (877-BALTIMORE/877-225-8466, www.baltimore.org) for the latest. The **Baltimore Fun Guide** (www.baltimorefun guide.com), an online publication of the Greater Baltimore Cultural Alliance (113 W. North Ave., 410/230-0200) lists hundreds of local events.

The **Harborplace Street Performers Auditions** take place mid- to late April in the Harborplace Amphitheatre—comedians, jugglers, and magicians perform to win a spot on the roster.

Right around Easter, **Bunny Bonanzoo** is one of the city's oldest and best loved Eastertide traditions, featuring a bunny hop and egg hunt, among other activities, at the wonderful Baltimore Zoo (410/366-5466).

The Merrie Month of May brings the

Preakness, second jewel in horse racing's Triple Crown. There's a parade with marching bands, floats, and equestrian units, and dozens of related events and parties. The race is held at Pimlico Race Course (410/542-9400).

From June through September, the city hosts several weekend festivals (877/225-8466, www.bop.org/events/bopaevents) celebrating its varied ethnic heritage. The festivals all feature food, music, and live entertainment, and include German, Ukrainian, Greek, and Latino cultures, among many others.

Artscape (877-225-8466, www.artscape .org) is Baltimore's free annual festival of literary, performing, and visual arts, with readings and performances throughout July. Three stages showcase more than 150 performers, arts programs, and exhibitions.

Every year in October, the Lexington Market presents its **Chocolate Festival** (410/685-6169), which lauds the seductive bean in all its forms. Tasting, music, games, and demonstrations round out the four-day celebration.

The city celebrates Turkey Day with a **Thanksgiving Day Parade** on Pratt Street with floats, marching bands, and even good old Santa making an early appearance.

Shopping

Antiques

Antique Row, on the 800 block of North Howard Street, is a loose compendium of different dealers. Most carry an eclectic mix of goods, many of exceptional quality. This area has been the center of Baltimore's antiques trade for a century. One shop, **Cross Keys Antiques** (801 N. Howard St.), is a good if somewhat pricey resource for European furniture, paintings, chandeliers, accessories, and garden furniture from the 17th through the 20th centuries.

In another part of town, more than 40 dealers display their wares in quaint shops and multi-dealer emporiums on the streets of Fell's Point.

The **Antique Center at Federal Hill** (1220 Key Hwy. at East Cross St.) is a renovated industrial building that houses 35 dealers of upscale antiques and fine art.

Antique Warehouse (1300 Jackson St. at Key Hwy.) also shows the wares of 35 dealers.

Another Period in Time (1708–1710 Fleet St.) offers collections by 14 dealers of clocks, lamps, jewelry, paintings, coins, furniture, advertising materials, and collectibles.

Second Chance, Inc. (1400–1600 Warner St., 410/385-1101, www.secondchanceinc.org) fills 100,000 square feet of warehouse space with architectural antiques (ironwork, tin ceilings), building materials (cabinet doors, tiles), furniture, and antique furnishings, all salvaged from existing buildings that are being demolished or acquired through dealers and companies (Ritz-Carlton held a furniture liquidation there). Second Chance employs and trains low-income Baltimoreans in the building trades.

Malls

Towson Town Center (825 Dulaney Valley Rd., U.S. 695—exit 27A, www.towsontown center.com) is the biggest shopping destination close to the city. It has 200 retailers, including H&M, Macy's, and Nordstrom Rack.

Harborplace (www.harborplace.com) and the **Gallery at Harborplace** are shopping/eating extravaganzas. The former consists of a series of buildings on the water at Light Street and Pratt Street, while the Gallery is on Pratt Street between Calvert and South Streets. The shopping areas comprise more than 100 dealers, such as Banana Republic, Coach, Godiva, and more, and there are dozens of eateries and snack shops and 16 sit-down restaurants and cafés (Capitol City Brewing Co., J. Paul's, Phillips Seafood Buffet, and more). It is possible to spend an entire week in Baltimore and never leave this three-block area, but hey, is that all you came for?

Specialty Shops

A great only-in-Baltimore spot, **Hometown Girl** (1001 W. 36th St., 410/662-4438, www .celebratebaltimore.com), in the Hampden neighborhood, features all things Baltimorean, from videos to painted screens. One T-shirt was printed with "Balmerese" translations of ordinary English phrases.

A People United (516 N. Charles St.) is the city's favorite place to pick up global artifacts and Asian furniture. Nearby **Nouveau** (519 N. Charles St., www.nouveaubaltimore.com) features contemporary goods for the home—and they have another, even larger shop in Canton at 2400 Boston Street.

A fun place to shop for a unique gift, **2910 on the Square** (2910 O'Donnell St., www.2910onthesquare.com) in Canton has an ever changing panoply of personal and home goods. While in Canton, stop at **Chesapeake Wine Company** (2400 Boston St. in the Can Company, 410/522-4556, www.chesapeake wine.com). The tasting bar is the best in the city, and you can pick up snacks at the deli in front.

For book lovers, the **Ivy Bookshop** (6080 Falls Rd.) is an independent that offers staff recommendations with a literary bent, and **Normals** (425 E. 31st St., www.normals.com) has an exceptional collection of used books and music.

Food Markets

Baltimore has a long history of local public markets. The following are very visitor-friendly and all good places to pick up fresh food or to-go items.

The "World-Famous" **Lexington Market** (400 W. Lexington St., www.lexingtonmarket .com, 8:30 A.M.–6 P.M. Mon.–Sat.) was established in 1782 and is America's oldest continuously operating market. There are at least 140 reasons to go there (there are that many shops and food stalls), not the least of which is Faidley's Seafood.

Among the other produce and to-go stalls at the Lexington are purveyors of meats, fresh fruits and vegetables, candies, pastries—just about anything you'd want to eat, and all at good prices. The market also features live entertainment on Saturdays—I saw Part Harmony a local a cappella group sweeter than the cookies surrounding them; and Big Cam and the Lifters sang '50s and '60s hits to celebrate the success of John Waters' film version of the musical *Hairspray.*

The **Broadway Market,** at Broadway and Fleet Streets in Fell's Point, is nearly as old as the Lexington, but much smaller—it feels like more of a neighborhood place. There are about 20 food stalls and a very popular diner counter where locals drop by for eggs and toast.

The **Cross Street Market,** at Cross and Charles Streets in Federal Hill, is another smaller neighborhood market with roughly 20 purveyors. You'll find Good 'N' Natural health foods not far from Baltimore's Best BBQ.

Trinacria's Grocery (406 N. Paca St.) is one of those places that would be easy to overlook if you didn't know about it. This little store, packed full of fine Italian imported goods and wines, supplies a number of restaurants in Little Italy and also offers tasty, inexpensive deli items.

A true open-air market, the **Baltimore Farmers Market** (in the shadow of the Jones Falls Expressway at Holliday and Saratoga Sts., 410/752-8632) operates from 8 A.M. until everything is sold out on Sunday mornings from late May through December. The **32nd St. Farmers Market** (www.32ndstreetmarket .org), on the 400 block of East 32nd Street, is a local favorite and open 7 A.M.–noon Saturday May–November. The **Highlandtown Farmers Market,** in the 3500 block of Bank Street at the corner of South Conkling and Bank Streets, takes place 8 A.M.–noon Saturday July–October.

Sports and Recreation

PARKS

Baltimore City Department of Recreation & Parks (410/396-7000, www.baltimorecity.gov/government/recnparks) is the place to call for information on the city's public parks. Three of note include **Druid Hill Park,** on Druid Park Lake Drive, the second largest urban park in America (Central Park in New York City is larger). Like Central Park, Druid Hill is dandy in the daytime, iffy at night. **Patterson Park,** at Eastern Avenue and Patterson Park Avenue, is a community park that covers a city block in a residential neighborhood. This is where the baseball teams meet and kids work hard at getting dizzy on the merry-go-round. There's a covered ice rink in winter, too. The park is in such good shape thanks to the local community, whose members have made it a priority. Local workers take a picnic lunch to **Federal Hill Park,** at Key Highway and Battery Avenue, to catch a breeze off the harbor in warm weather and enjoy the spectacular views.

Harborwalk Promenade

A paved pathway ideal for a stroll or jog, this urban trail is nearly eight miles long and extends all the way from Fort McHenry along Fort Avenue, then along the water past Fell's Point to Canton Waterfront Park. It's a fantastic way to get exercise and spend the day. Because of ongoing construction, the path may "disappear" at some points, but it's easy to find again.

SPECTATOR SPORTS
Horse Racing

The **Pimlico Race Course** (5201 Park Heights Ave., 410/542-9400, www.pimlico.com) hosts the Preakness, plus plenty of other racing action.

Team Sports

Oriole Park at Camden Yards (333 W. Camden St., 410/685-9800) is the home park of the **O's** (www.baltimore.orioles.mlb.com). The 2006 AFC Division champions, the **Baltimore**

Pimlico Race Course

© JOANNE MILLER

Ravens (410/261-7283, www.baltimore ravens.com), also play at Camden Yards in the newly named PSI Net Stadium (1101 Russell St.). The 1st Mariner Arena (201 W. Baltimore St., 410/347-2020) is where to see the hometown NPSL soccer team, the **Baltimore Blast**; the **Baltimore Bay Runners**, the IBL basketball team; and the **Baltimore Thunder** lacrosse team.

College lacrosse action is represented by the **Johns Hopkins Blue Jays**, who play at Homewood Field (Charles St. and University Pkwy., 410/516-8000).

Bingo

If your dreams of recreation are filled with rows of numbers, try **Bingo World** (4901 Belle Grove Rd., 800/992-9300, www.bingoworld.com). Games are played at 11:45 A.M., and 7:30 and 11:00 P.M. seven nights a week, plus 3:30 P.M. Fridays and Saturdays. And they're not far from downtown—call for free transportation.

Accommodations

Like most big cities, there are a few B&Bs here, but lodgings in Baltimore tend to be hotels on the expensive side. But most lodgings, especially hotels, are flexible about rates—meaning if they have too many rooms available, they may be willing to drop prices, and conversely will raise prices if room space is at a premium. Prices seldom change if you've booked the room in advance, although last-minute arrivals can sometimes find bargains (or no room at the inn). Rates vary by season (lowest rates are in the winter months, highest in summer), capacity, and day of the week. The following are a few personal picks, with top choices indicated.

INNER HARBOR
$250 and Up

The **Hyatt Regency Baltimore** (300 Light St., 410/528-1234 or 800/233-1234, www .baltimore.hyatt.com/hyatt/hotels/index .jsp, rooms $279–329, suites and waterview rooms at a higher rate) is in the ideal location for visitors who plan to spend most of their time in the area. One of the primary hotels on the water, the Hyatt offers plenty of amenities, including a fully equipped exercise facility, an outdoor pool, a sauna, tennis courts, and a jogging path. It's big—with 486 guestrooms, including 25 suites, two restaurants, and two lounges—and popular, so book well ahead. Like most Hyatts, this one has a six-

story glassed-in atrium and glass elevators. The views, even from the back rooms, are spectacular. The Hyatt also offers a club level for an extra charge, which includes continental breakfast, evening hors d'oeuvres, and cocktail service.

Leave the cutoffs at home if you're planning on staying at the ⟨ **Harbor Court Hotel** (550 Light St., 410/234-0550 or 800/824-0076, www.harborcourt.com; $309–432 standard room, $354–477 harbor view, $500–800 and up for suites). This place exudes serious glamour. Besides being the venue for two of the best restaurants in town, this hotel has won so many awards that it's embarrassing: #11 Hotel in the United States and #75 Best Destination in the World, "The Gold List" Best Places to Stay (all by *Condé Nast Traveler*); Four Diamond Awards from AAA and Mobil Travel Guide; Best in Baltimore, Zagats, etc. But is it really that good? Oh, yes. Rumor has it that oil sheiks have been known to reserve entire floors for their families when coming for various treatments at Johns Hopkins—apparently, the big and beautiful rooms just aren't big enough. Among the available TV channels is a very modest version of MTV in Arabic (you can watch it in the bathroom—all the rooms are equipped with a TV set—if bathing bores you).

Harbor Court aims for a grand English country house look, complete with swimming

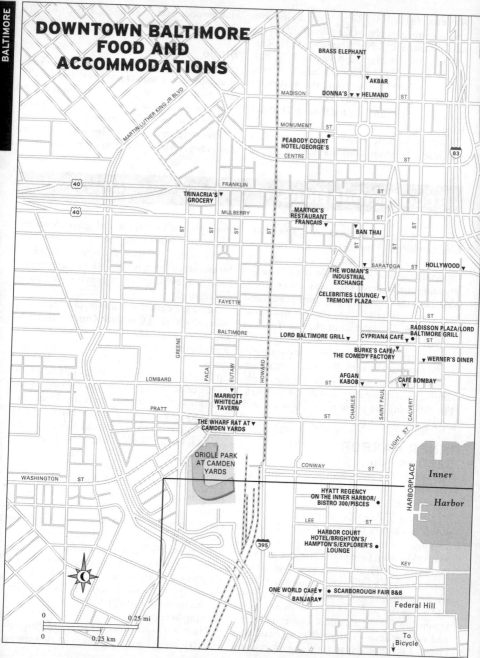

DOWNTOWN BALTIMORE FOOD AND ACCOMMODATIONS

BRASS ELEPHANT ▼

AKBAR ▼
DONNA'S ▼ ▼ HELMAND

MADISON ST

MONUMENT ST

PEABODY COURT HOTEL/GEORGE'S
CENTRE ST

83

FRANKLIN ST

TRINACRIA'S ▼ GROCERY

MULBERRY ST

MARTICK'S RESTAURANT FRANCAIS ▼
BAN THAI ▼

SARATOGA ST
HOLLYWOOD ▼

THE WOMAN'S INDUSTRIAL EXCHANGE ▼

CELEBRITIES LOUNGE/ TREMONT PLAZA ▼

FAYETTE ST

BALTIMORE ST
LORD BALTIMORE GRILL ▼
CYPRIANA CAFÉ ▼
RADISSON PLAZA/LORD BALTIMORE GRILL ●

BURKE'S CAFÉ/ THE COMEDY FACTORY ▼
WERNER'S DINER ▼

LOMBARD ST
AFGAN KABOB ▼
CAFÉ BOMBAY ▼

MARRIOTT WHITECAP TAVERN

PRATT ST

THE WHARF RAT AT CAMDEN YARDS ▼

GREENE ST
PACA ST
EUTAW ST
HOWARD ST
CHARLES ST
SAINT PAUL ST
CALVERT ST
LIGHT ST

ORIOLE PARK AT CAMDEN YARDS

WASHINGTON ST

CONWAY ST

HARBORPLACE

Inner
Harbor

HYATT REGENCY ON THE INNER HARBOR/ BISTRO 300/PISCES ●

LEE ST

395

HARBOR COURT HOTEL/BRIGHTON'S/ HAMPTON'S/EXPLORER'S LOUNGE ●

KEY

ONE WORLD CAFÉ ▼
BANJARA ▼
● SCARBOROUGH FAIR B&B

Federal Hill

To Bicycle

MARTIN LUTHER KING JR BLVD

40

40

0   0.25 mi

0   0.25 km

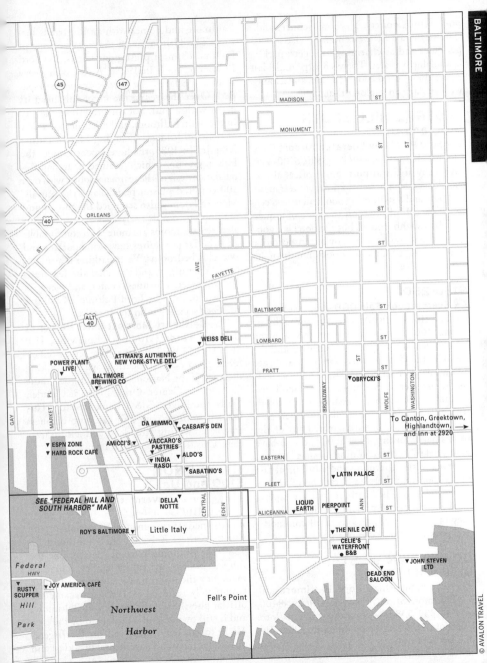

45 · 147

MADISON · ST

MONUMENT · ST

ST · ST

ST

ORLEANS · 40

ST

ST

ST

AVE · FAYETTE

BALTIMORE · ST

WEISS DELI · LOMBARD · ST

POWER PLANT LIVE!

ATTMAN'S AUTHENTIC NEW YORK-STYLE DELI

BALTIMORE BREWING CO · PRATT · ST · ST

ST

OBRYCKI'S

BROADWAY · WOLFE · WASHINGTON

GAY · PL · MARKET

DA MIMMO · CAESAR'S DEN

To Canton, Greektown, Highlandtown, and Inn at 2920 →

ESPN ZONE · HARD ROCK CAFÉ · AMICCI'S · VACCARO'S PASTRIES · INDIA RASOI · ALDO'S · EASTERN · ST

SABATINO'S · LATIN PALACE · ST

FLEET

SEE "FEDERAL HILL AND SOUTH HARBOR" MAP

DELLA NOTTE · CENTRAL · EDEN · ALICEANNA · LIQUID EARTH · PIERPOINT · ANN · ST

ROY'S BALTIMORE · Little Italy · THE NILE CAFÉ

CELIE'S WATERFRONT B&B

Federal · HWY

RUSTY SCUPPER · JOY AMERICA CAFÉ · JOHN STEVEN LTD

DEAD END SALOON

Hill · Park · Northwest · Fell's Point

Harbor

© AVALON TRAVEL

pool, tennis courts, a croquet court, and a state-of-the-art fitness center. Service is whisper-quiet and as charming as it gets; parking is available by valet. There's a large multi-language library off the lobby, a café, and a lounge with an African explorer theme.

FEDERAL HILL SOUTH
$100 and Up

The **Four Points by Sheraton Airport** (7032 Elm Rd., Baltimore, 410/859-3300, $100–200) isn't really at the airport, but it offers airport shuttle service, a better-than-decent restaurant and pub, and a swimming pool and fitness center. It's south of town on the edge of a questionable neighborhood, but the hotel is a good one—and if you have your own transportation or plan to take public transport into town, it's a smart choice.

$150-250

€ Scarborough Fair B&B (1 E. Montgomery St., 410/837-0010, www.scarborough-fair.com, $160–210) is my favorite B&B in the harbor area, since it's near everything, and the rooms in the Georgian-style brick building are a home away from home. That's quite a statement, considering the building was modified by innkeepers Ellen and Ashley Scarborough from offices into six tastefully furnished guestrooms, all with private baths. Four of the rooms have working fireplaces, and two have whirlpool tubs. In the dining room, a light tea is served in the afternoon and a full breakfast in the morning; there's a library on all things Maryland, too. The Scarboroughs are experts on the local area (especially restaurants), and they offer the most precious of all commodities, parking, at no extra charge.

DOWNTOWN WEST
$150 and Up

The **Radisson Plaza Lord Baltimore** (20 W. Baltimore St. at Hanover, 410/539-8400 or 800/333-3333, www.radisson.com/lord baltimore, $139–209 standard room, $264–314 one-bedroom queen suite, larger rooms and suites available) is in the middle of downtown

Baltimore and comes with an illustrious history. The Hilton was a makeover of one of Baltimore's most prestigious hotels, the Lord Baltimore, built in 1928 ("A Radio in Every Room," declared the *Baltimore Sun* newspaper). Over the years, the hotel enhanced its decor with a mural of the growth of the city in the main ballroom, and it has hosted a slew of political leaders, including Martin Luther King Jr., In 1985, the hotel opened under the Hilton gravure, which retained its Italian Renaissance design, the immense lobby with over 100 coffered plaster panels, and the murals. Mercifully, they also scrapped the tiny rooms, making one out of every two. As a result, the airy, elegant rooms are more than comfortable, and the largest suites have kitchenettes and two-plus bedrooms. Valet parking is available for $25 per night, and the hotel also features a fitness center, a business center, and plenty of package deals. The Lord Baltimore Grill (see the *Food* section) is on the premises.

The **Baltimore Marriott Inner Harbor at Camden Yards** (110 South Eutaw St., 410/962-0202 $139–350, depending on season) offers a good central location, within walking distance of the National Aquarium, Baltimore Convention Center, Orioles Park at Camden Yards, and Ravens M&T Bank Stadium. This hotel is nonsmoking and caters to business travelers, meeting attendees, and leisure travelers. Onsite parking is $22 a day.

MT. VERNON
$100 and Up

The **€ Inn at Government House** (1125 N. Calvert, 410/539-0566, $125–145) is a nicely refurbished 19th-century Victorian in the shabby-genteel Belvedere neighborhood. In 1889, the original mansion that became the inn was built by a wealthy banker, John Gilman, for a then astronomical sum of $40,000. Completely restored in 1985, it became the official guesthouse for the city of Baltimore, and is still owned and maintained by the city. All 19 rooms have baths and small refrigerators. Rates include a continental breakfast and free parking.

(Peabody Court–A Clarion Hotel (612 Cathedral St., 410/727-7101 or 800/292-5500, www.peabodycourthotel.com, $139–229 per room, discounts for online booking, seniors, and AAA members) is in a great location, on the west side of Mount Vernon Square Park. The narrow park surrounds the original Washington Monument and abuts the Walters Art Museum and the Peabody Institute. The hotel—Baltimore's oldest and best known—has a small, elegant lobby with a six-foot Baccarat chandelier and an in-house restaurant and bar, George's on Mount Vernon Square (see the *Food* section). Its 100-plus rooms have been updated with modern accoutrements and are very clean and pleasant. The Peabody Court has 24-hour valet parking service for an additional fee of $27 plus tax for overnight guests, and $17 plus tax for daily valet parking (the going rate)—but you can park safely overnight on the streets for free if you're up early in the morning to move the car. For more information on the Mount Vernon area, visit the Mount Vernon Cultural District website (www.mvcd.org).

FELL'S POINT
$150-250

It would be easy to miss the front door of **Celie's Waterfront Bed & Breakfast** (1714 Thames St., 410/522-2323 or 800/432-0184, www.celieswaterfront.com, $139–239), tucked as it is between shops, cafés, and watering holes on one of Fell's Point's main streets—it's actually across from the gloriously overdecorated police station that held a starring role on the old television series *Homicide*. Celie's is notable for two things: heavy security (no surprise there) and access to a satellite system that will either have you bopping while you iron (audio music channels) or watching TV programs you never thought you'd see (*I Love Lucy* meets the pansexual channel). Fell's Point is a delightful neighborhood, full of shops and cafés; and if you're into partying late, this is the place—Celie's is a grateful short stagger from anyplace in town. The six guestrooms are fully equipped with all the amenities and decorated in Baltimore eclectic. Some of the guestrooms have

fireplaces, others have whirlpool tubs, private balconies, or harbor views, and one room is completely accessible for travelers with disabilities. All have private baths. Overnight guests are treated to a continental breakfast in the morning, served in a dining room that opens onto a small garden.

CANTON EAST
$100-150

If you don't mind being several miles east of downtown, the **La Quinta Inn & Suites North,** formerly known as the Fairfield Inn (4 Philadelphia Court, Rosedale, 410/574-8100 $89–165) offers clean rooms with the usual amenities, a complimentary breakfast, and easy access to the local malls. The hotel is located close to U.S. 695.

$150-250

Debbie and David Schwartz renovated an old Canton bordello into the sleek and friendly **(Inn at 2920** (2920 Elliott St., 410/342-4450, www.theinnat2920.com, $155–255). David, a former corporate chef for a major hotel chain, rustles up a spectacular breakfast made from fresh local produce (special dietary needs are welcomed)—a perfect addition to the all-natural theme in decor and accoutrements. The inn was designed to be as allergen-free as possible, right down to the filtered air—but the five guestrooms, all with private bath, are far from sterile. Vintage pieces mix with earth colors, contemporary furniture, and pieces by local artists. Guests do have to climb stairs, but parking is free and plentiful, and good restaurants and bars are within easy walking distance.

UPTOWN/HAMPDEN
$100-150

Though it's on the northern border of Baltimore near the town of Towson, the **Sheraton North Hotel** (903 Dulaney Valley Rd., 410/321-7400, $92–175) is an upscale hotel for much less money. It has a swimming pool, fitness center, restaurant, and lounge—all the amenities you'd expect. Plus it's in a nice area, though several miles from downtown and the inner harbor.

℄ The Inn at the Colonnade (4 W. University Pkwy., 410/235-5400, www.colonnade baltimore.com, $129–170 standard room, larger rooms and suites available, discounts for online reservations made at http://doubletree1.hilton.com) is an elegant hotel owned by the Doubletree chain and located near Johns Hopkins. It looks like it would cost a great deal more, considering the neighborhood and the fact that it has all the amenities: swimming pool, sun decks, an exercise room, and a business center.

BWI AIRPORT
$125 and Up

Sleep Inn & Suites Airport (6055 Belle Grove Rd., Baltimore, 410/789-7223, $125–169) is five miles north of the airport and seven miles south of the inner harbor. This is a clean, pet-friendly hotel that offers free shuttle service to the airport and train station. In the morning, a complimentary continental breakfast is served, and free weekday newspapers are available. A restaurant is adjacent to the hotel, and the Sleep Inn also has laundry facilities, high-speed Internet access, an exercise room, and a parking area— all of which count if you're driving in.

Food

It won't take long to discover that Baltimore is Food Central for the Chesapeake Bay. I eat my way through town, from stand-up counters to the last word in elegant. You can get very, very fat here—everybody serves crab cakes, which, to my infinite despair, are not a diet food. The following restaurants—a sampling of the extraordinary variety and price range available—are listed by neighborhood, then by type of food, with the least expensive first. Restaurants can come and go with the tide; most of these have demonstrated a little staying power. Every one of the places below deserves kudos for one reason or another.

Specific hours of operation are given whenever possible, but you can safely assume that breakfast is generally served 8–10 A.M., lunch noon–2 P.M., and dinner 5–10 P.M. During the week, few kitchens serve beyond 9:30 P.M.

INNER HARBOR
Stopping off for a snack or meal in the Inner Harbor poses no problem other than choice. All the restaurants listed below are within a block or two of the water. There are several "name" chains in this area, and a few small but good surprises.

American
Looks like home to me: **Burke's Café** (36 Light St., 410/752-4189, www.burkescafe.com, 7 A.M.–2 A.M. daily, $10) is an old-fashioned bar-restaurant. Think giant onion rings and pan-fried chicken.

Bistro 300 (300 Light St., 410/528-1234, 6:30 A.M.–10 P.M. daily, $13–17), on the mezzanine of the Hyatt, serves breakfast, lunch, and dinner. It features the "please everybody" combination of pub grub and breakfast buffets.

Harborplace on Light Street is a massive collection of 40 eateries on two floors. The snack and takeout shops are open for lunch and dinner daily, including the **Capitol City Brewing Company** (410/539-7468, $14) for brews and burgers and **Phillips** (410/685-6600, $17), an outpost of the Ocean City seafood restaurant; there are places to sit cafeteria-style. For a snack or light meal, there's enough variety for everyone. Harborplace on Pratt Street has an assortment of sit-down restaurants; all are open daily for lunch and dinner.

The lights dim and restaurant chatter ceases as TV sets placed strategically throughout the **ESPN Zone** (601 E. Pratt St., 410/685-3776, lunch and dinner daily, $12) blare at eardrum-busting levels with the intro to another "sports moment" (usually an interview with a power sports personality). This testosterone-drenched, sports-themed restaurant caters to those who can't walk in the house without flipping on ESPN to check bowling scores. Megajocks and those who just like to watch will enjoy the constant sports reporting between the "moments"—it's possible to catch a soccer game in China, a tennis match at Wimbledon, and women's basketball from the local college, simply by swiveling your head. The rest of us come for the great burgers and fries. The food is good, if the hyperactivity level doesn't bother you (kids *love* it). An added dimension: There's a floor full of video games upstairs (bring lots of change), and plenty of sports memorabilia to gawk at.

If you'd rather boogie than bogey, there's always the **Hard Rock Café** (601 E. Pratt St., 410/347-7625, 11 A.M.–midnight Sun.–Thurs., 11 A.M.–2 A.M. Fri.–Sat., $13–20) next door. Both of these places can be very busy, so make it an early lunch or dinner.

Try the top-notch seafood and service at (**Pisces** (300 Light St., 410/605-2835, dinner Tues.–Sun., brunch 10 A.M.–2 P.M. Sun., $28). You'll enjoy gazing out over the inner harbor while sipping an excellent martini and diving into your seared tuna. Fortunately, the restaurant hasn't gotten smug about the view and started serving mediocre food—this has remained a favorite among locals and visitors alike.

Brighton's (550 Light St., 410/347-9750, breakfast daily, lunch, afternoon tea, and dinner Mon.–Sat., breakfast and lunch $8–25, dinner $29), in the Harbor Court Hotel, is the eatery that services hotel guests. Though this might relegate it to ordinary in some hotels, expect a lot here. The casual-dressy restaurant (much more relaxed than Hampton's) is four-star-rated, and the food and service are excellent. Breakfast in this gracious room is especially pleasant—suited businesspeople take morning meetings here. Brighton's also serves a formal tea with celebrated scones 3–5 P.M. Monday–Saturday. Use the valet parking at the hotel's entrance, as it's free with a validated ticket.

Continental
(**Hampton's** (Harbor Court Hotel, 550

Light St., 410/234-0550, dinner daily, champagne brunch 10:30 A.M.–2 P.M. Sun., $45) is a destination four-star restaurant where the elite meet to sample innovative American cuisine and an extensive, sophisticated wine list. "Elegant" is the word. A *Condé Nast Traveler* readers' poll called this restaurant number one in service and number two overall in the United States in the late '90s, and nothing has changed since then. The place has won so many awards—from Mobil Travel Guide's Four-Star Distinction to *Traveler's* Top 50 to the AAA Four Diamond Award—it's a foregone conclusion that you will dine well. Specialties include lobster flamed in Laphroaig Scotch whiskey, and lamb with cilantro gremolata and Grand Mariner, and each season brings a new menu. Reservations recommended, and a jacket is preferred but not required for gents.

International
If you're looking for something more exotic and a lot less expensive, walk a few blocks to **Cypriana Café** (120 E. Baltimore St., 410/837-7482, 7 A.M.–4 P.M. Mon.–Fri., $8), which serves up an extensive menu of traditional Greek dishes—lamb pita and crispy spinach pie are favorites. This is a to-go place, but there are tables outside to enjoy on warm and sunny days. The café also offers a good roster of vegetarian selections.

Another favorite in the cheap eats category of inner harbor restaurants: **Afghan Kabob** (37 S. Charles St., #C, 410/727-5511, $6). The appetizers (around $4 each) are enough to fill you up, and the grilled kebabs are cooked to perfection. It isn't fancy, but it's definitely a favorite with the weekday lunch crowd.

FEDERAL HILL
American
(**Regi's American Bistro** (1002 Light St., 410/539-7344, www.regisamericanbistro .com, 11 A.M.–midnight Mon.–Thurs., 11 A.M.–2 A.M. Fri., 10 A.M.–2 A.M. Sat., 10 A.M.–11 P.M. Sun., $11–24) calls itself "your friendly neighborhood bistro" and serves a sophisticated menu of pastas, salads, soups, crab cakes,

potato-encrusted beef, and sandwiches at decent prices. This is the kind of place you could probably eat at every day and still like it. Regi's serve a popular brunch menu on Saturday and Sunday, so call to make sure you can get in.

⟨ Mother's Federal Hill Grille (1113 S. Charles St., 410/244-8686, www.mothers grille.com, breakfast, lunch, and dinner daily, $7–25) is a hip bar with good, inexpensive breakfasts, sandwiches, soups, entrées, and salads. Entrées include pasta, beef, and, of course, crab and shrimp dishes. Mother's is known for its nightly specials, such as the Monday night prime rib for $11 and the Friday night "most entrées, $10" special. They have a small but good vegetarian selection, too. Be aware that this place becomes a bustling bar scene in the late evening.

SoBo (6–8 W. Cross St., 410/752-1518, lunch and dinner daily, $13–20) is an informal place with informal food: chicken pot pie, chili, macaroni and cheese, and burgers. The kids won't feel out of place here.

The menu at **Corks** (1026 S. Charles St., 410/752-3810, www.corksrestaurant.com, dinner daily, $16–29) is designed from the wine up, according to chef Jerry Pellegrino. This upscale neighborhood restaurant features nouvelle cuisine thoughtfully paired with one of the best wine lists in the city—all bottles are sold for only $11 over cost. The menu concentrates on seafood (grilled Pacific Salmon fillet with sloppy goat cheese polenta and wilted Swiss chard) and meat (orange and basil brined grilled pork chop with garlic mashed rutabaga and roasted red grapes, garlic, and ham). Reservations are wise.

Also recommended: **Drifter's Raw Bar** (1024 S. Charles St., 410/727-1355, www .driftersrawbar.com, 4–2 A.M. Mon.–Tues., noon–2 A.M. Wed.–Fri.–Sat., 2 P.M.–2 A.M. Sat.–Sun., $16) is in the former Bandaloops space, where the young and enthusiastic come for ursters (local slang for "oysters"), drinks from draft beers to exotic cocktails, and an expanded pub menu for lunch and dinner. The space is divided into two levels and three

bars, and restaurant stays open late when the Ravens play.

International

Café Manet (1020 S. Charles St., 410/837-7006, 9 A.M.–9 P.M. Mon.–Thurs., 9 A.M.–11 P.M. Fri.–Sat., under $18), was named by several people as an excellent restaurant for a casual lunch or dinner, though the hours are sometimes unreliable—call first. The prices and variety might make up for reliability. The chef creates whatever his mood dictates: Italian, French, Argentinean and Hungarian dishes have all appeared on the menu, including chicken Provençal, shepherd's pie, *pulpo a la gallega* (Galician-style octopus), and a variety of pastas. Desserts and a glass of house wine are both less than $5.

Banjara (1017 S. Charles St., 410/962-1554, lunch Tues.–Fri. and Sun., dinner daily, $11–24) is a favorite among the locals for its excellent East Indian cuisine and reasonable prices. Curries, tandoori, and biryanis made with chicken, lamb, and seafood are available, and Banjara has an extensive vegetarian menu as well. In case none of those tempt you, pizza is also served.

Nichiban (1035–1037 S. Charles St., 410/ 837-0818, http://angritt.com/nichiban, dinner Mon.–Sat., lunch 11:30 A.M.–2:30 P.M. Fri. only, $3–15) is a popular sushi bar packed with locals on weekend nights, kicking back with a tray of *tekka maki* and a cup of green tea.

Ten Oh Six (1006 Light St., 410/528-2146, dinner Tues.–Sun., $15) may look unimpressive from the street, but the Thai fusion menu continues to excel. Few menus include boar alongside drunken noodles and yum-beef salad.

Nouvelle Cuisine

⟨ Bicycle (1444 Light St., 410/234-1900, www.bicyclebistro.com, dinner daily, $25) remains one of the hottest restaurants in town. Diners choose from a menu featuring squeaky-fresh seafood and vegetables. The Balinese mahi-mahi and shrimp is seasoned in a garlic chili sauce and comes with baby spinach baked in phyllo over Shanghai noodles in creamy cilantro/walnut jalapeño pesto—it's complicated and delicious. The menu changes with the seasons.

SOUTH HARBOR
American
Rallo's (838 E. Fort Ave. at Lawrence St., 410/727-7067, 5:30 A.M.–7:30 P.M. Mon.–Sat., 7 A.M.–3 P.M. Sun., $5–10) is one of those places that's such a fixture, it's a water taxi stop (it opened in 1941). This tavern/diner serves inexpensive breakfasts and the kind of sandwiches you can usually only get at home: braunschweiger, meatball, hot dogs, and Italian cold cuts, to name a few. Don't forget that vitamin-packed liver-and-onion entrée—they also have breaded pork chops, veal parmesan, and other old favorites (entrées include two vegetables).

One very popular chain establishment in the inner harbor is **Rusty Scupper** (402 Key Hwy., 410/727-3678, lunch and dinner daily, lunch $14, dinner $19–35). The seafood is fresh, the wine list is good (lots of California vintages), and the servings are reliably big (including the desserts—one helping of the chocolate cake could serve five people). The view is one of the best in the inner harbor, and the bar offers a beautiful view of lights around the water.

Nouvelle Cuisine
The C **Joy America Café** (800 Key Hwy., in the American Visionary Art Museum across from the Rusty Scupper, 410/244-6500, 11 A.M.–10 P.M. Tues.–Sat., 11 A.M.–4 P.M. Sun., $20) gives cuisine a new look and an innovative twist on the ingredients. The silverware and plates are chosen for their amusement value, and the food pairings are fresh and unusual, with a pan-Latin theme. The menu, written out in handmade "books," keeps with the museum's theme of enhancing the everyday with fun. Joy America is brought to you by the owners of Spike and Charlie's.

International
Walking into **Little Havana Restaurante y Cantina** (1325 Key Hwy., 410/837-9903, www.littlehavana.com, 4:30 P.M.–midnight Mon.–Thurs., 11:30 A.M.–2 A.M. Fri.–Sat., 11 A.M.–midnight Sun., $11–24) is like stepping into an authentic Cuban restaurant/nightclub—a bar in the middle of the large, open room is surrounded by dark wood. Immediately after entering, you're seized with the urge to light up a cigar and mambo over to one of the tall, dimly lit booths. Seafood, chicken, and other meats are prepared in the Cuban tropical manner: pollo a la Castro, chorizo Habaña, and paella are on the menu. It has a late-night menu and open-air dining that overlooks the inner harbor when the weather is fine. The brunch is legendary, thanks to the bottomless bloody Marys and mimosas.

DOWNTOWN WEST
Many Baltimoreans refer to Charles Street as Restaurant Row, though some of the places mentioned here are a few blocks away. You can get anything you want, often at low prices. There are quite a few cafés that serve coffee and food—including **City Café** (1001 Cathedral St.), and **Donna's Coffee Bar and Café** (800 N. Charles St., with several branches)—and an endless array of international restaurants. The following is a mere sampling of what's available.

American
Check out the Lexington Market for takeout foods, especially C **Faidley's Seafood** (410/727-4898, www.faidleyscrabcakes.com, 9 A.M.–5 P.M. Mon.–Sat., top price $22). Several people told me that Faidley's had the best crab cakes in Baltimore (a pretty daunting challenge), but, after downing their Backfin Crab Cake sandwich ($11), I'd have to say Faidley's has the best stand-up, takeout, or ship-anywhere crab cake in the city. And Backfin is their second grade—all lump, at $16, is the top of the line. They serve several kinds of seafood: crab, shrimp, trout, oysters, and more, in platters, assortments, sandwiches, and soups. Be prepared to wait in line.

George's on Mt. Vernon Square (101 W. Monument St. at the Peabody Court/Clarion Hotel, 410/727-1314, breakfast, lunch, and

I SCREAM, YOU SCREAM

In the middle of the 19th century, a Baltimore dairyman named Jacob Fussell made daily rounds delivering milk. He stored the cream he was unable to sell on ice, and when he turned that extra product into ice cream, his customers raved. Soon Fussell stopped selling milk and devoted his dairy to the production of the sweet treat. In 1851, he opened the first ice cream factory in America, and soon started churning out the frozen favorite and delivering gallons of it up and down the East Coast. One of his old delivery trucks is on display at the Baltimore Museum of Industry.

dinner daily) has made a comeback as a place to enjoy a good glass of wine, a grilled scallop salad ($13), or a sandwich (around $10) from a menu that changes with the seasons. The setting is cozy: Deep burgundy walls, hardwood floors, and original marble tabletops provide a casual but elegant dining experience. It's a taste of old Baltimore and is convenient to the Walters Art Museum.

There's always a diner, and the **Hollywood Diner** (400 E. Saratoga St., 410/962-5379, 6 A.M.–4 P.M. daily, under $12) caters to the breakfast and lunch crowd with a classic menu that includes some vegetarian dishes. This place was used in the 1982 film *Diner*. The kitchen is staffed by an adult manager, but the Hollywood diner is now known as a place that helps adolescents with a history of delinquency learn job and life skills under the auspices of the Chesapeake Center for Youth Development—a fact reflected in its early closing hour.

Another diner of note is **Werner's** (231 Redwood St., 410/752-3335, 7 A.M.–midnight Mon.–Fri., under $12), which also served as a backdrop for the Hollywood magic—in *Tin Men* (1987) and *Liberty Heights* (1999).

Now here's a place! **◖ The Woman's Industrial Exchange** (333 N. Charles St., 410/685-4388, www.womansindustrialexchange

.org, breakfast and lunch Mon.–Fri., under $12) has a history as interesting as its name. After the Civil War, through the Depression, and up to today, neighborhood ladies in need of a few dollars could sell their handiwork through the exchange without suffering the embarrassment of public penury. A shop still sells craftwork in the front (the hand-crocheted christening dresses and hand-sewn children's clothes are excellent buys for the price and quality). In the back, a little restaurant serves chicken salad sandwiches, aspic, and bread pudding to generations of genteel ladies and neighborhood priests. The spick-and-span, checkered-tile floor and blue-uniformed waitresses make this a Baltimore exclusive.

Brewer's Art (1106 N. Charles St., 410/547-6925, www.belgianbeer.com, 4 P.M.–2 A.M. Mon.–Sat., 5 P.M.–2 A.M. Sunday, $18) draws a hip crowd to sample an international menu of beers, along with grilled tuna salad and updated pub food.

Lord Baltimore Grill (20 W. Baltimore St., 410/539-8400, breakfast, lunch, and dinner daily, lunch $9, dinner $25), in the Radisson Plaza Lord Baltimore, is cool, quiet, and just coming into its own as a fine restaurant. The menu is American, with an emphasis on steaks and chops for dinner.

Continental

The **Brass Elephant** (924 N. Charles St., 410/547-8480, dinner daily, $25) is another Baltimore favorite. Jack Elsby has been welcoming guests to his elegant townhouse since 1980. The food is contemporary continental—duck farfalle, tea-smoked quail, and filet mignon—and the wine list is quite good. The "tasting menu" is a satisfying choice if you can't decide on just one entrée. It's a bit dressy (jackets for gentlemen are appreciated, but not required).

Spike and Charlie's (1225 Cathedral St. at Preston, 410/752-8144, dinner Tues.–Sun., $29) was voted the "Best Place for Special Occasions" by *Baltimore Magazine* and has won *Wine Spectator's* Award of Excellence in the past.

A hometown favorite with a French accent, **Martick's Restaurant Français** (214 Mulberry St., 410/752-5155, dinner Tues.–Sat., $20) serves fabulous pâté, bouillabaisse, and chocolate bread pudding. Though Martick's was a "Best Restaurant" winner in *City Paper* in the past, diners either love it (citing a real Baltimore feel and personal service) or hate it (small portions and slow service).

International

Akbar (823 N. Charles St., 410/539-0944, www.akbar-restaurant.com, $12) serves an inexpensive northern Indian lunch buffet and a full dinner daily. It also features brunch on the weekends and has another branch south of town in Columbia.

Ban Thai (340 N. Charles St., 410/727-7971, www.banthai.us, lunch and dinner Mon.–Sat., $8–14) is the place for Thai, with very fresh food—the noodle dishes are justifiably popular—and attentive service.

(Helmand (806 N. Charles St., 410/752-0311, www.helmand.com, dinner daily, $18) created a market for Afghan cuisine and remains popular, especially for its *kaddo borawni* (spiced pumpkin) and pastries. Helmand also has an outstanding vegetarian menu.

LITTLE ITALY

Baltimore has one of the most authentic and wonderful Italian districts of any American city. The neighborhood is delightful to walk around in, and the food is incredible! Little Italy is bordered on the north by the old Jewish district, so there are a few fine delis, plus a couple of surprises: a Hawaiian fusion eatery and an East Indian old favorite.

Italian

Sabatino's (901 Fawn St., 410/727-9414, www.sabatinos.com, lunch and dinner until 2 A.M. daily, $13–28) opened in 1955 and serves a huge menu of classic Italian dishes—spaghetti with meatballs, rigatoni with pesto—in massive quantities. Going away hungry is not an option. The restaurant also makes a side dish, Spinach à la Ralph, that's

a meal in itself and so delicious, you'll dream about it.

If Sabatino's is classic, **(Aldo's** (306 S. High St., 410/727-0700, dinner daily, $25) is the Italy of Prada and Versace. The columned interior is as elegant as the tiny roast quail. The owner and executive chef, Aldo Vitale, designed much of the burnished, deeply carved woodwork in the foyer bar, as well as the sophisticated menu. His handsome sons, Alessandro and Sergio, guide visitors through the wine list and suggest the freshest choices of the day. Valet parking is available. Have a little goat cheese salad (it's so fresh that they must keep the goat in the cellar) and limonata (a potent lemon-flavored liquor).

I'll admit it, I'm addicted to **(Vaccaro's Pastries.** The original location (222 Albemarle St., 410/685-4905) serves food as well as cakes, pies, cannoli (filled and unfilled), classic Italian pastries, and housemade gelato (very rich ice cream) and granita (sorbet). Vaccaro's also makes serious cookies, with enough almond paste to cause immediate girth expansion. There are additional locations in Harborplace, Owings Mills, and the D.C. area.

Also recommended: **Amicci's** (231 S. High St., 410/528-1096, www.amiccis.com, lunch and dinner daily $9–22), which won a Best Italian Restaurant award in 2005, particularly for its garlicky jumbo shrimp served a variety of ways. It also offers a good vegetarian selection of Italian favorites. Other picks include **Caesar's Den** (223 S. High St., 410/547-0820, www.caesarsden.com, lunch and dinner daily $11–24), for the grilled meats and the black fettuccine with arugula; **Della Notte** (801 Eastern Ave., 410/837-5500, www.dellanotte.com, lunch and dinner daily, $15–35), for traditional Italian food, indoor/outdoor dining (there's a tree in the middle of the dining room), and parking(!); and **Da Mimmo** (217 S. High St., 410/727-6876, http://damimmo.com, lunch Mon.–Fri., dinner daily, $15–40), famous for its broiled veal chops alla Fiorentina, three-hour-long dinners and expense-account patrons. But it's pretty much impossible to get a bad meal anywhere in the area.

Jewish

Lombard Street, just north of Fell's Point, was the site of the first Jewish congregations in Baltimore, well before the 1900s. Once a thriving neighborhood, the district has seen better times, but two remaining delis keep the old food traditions alive. **Weiss Deli** (1127 E. Lombard St., 410/276-7910, 8:30 A.M.–4 P.M. Mon.–Sat., until 3 P.M. Sunday), "The Place with Real Good Taste," is a few feet away from the city's original temple. Fancy it's not, but piled-on pastrami doesn't get much cheaper. A butter-soaked bagel is less than a buck, and it's a good place to pick up cold cuts and picnic supplies ($6). The deli has table seating and takeout.

Attman's Authentic New York-Style Delicatessen (1019 E. Lombard St., 410/563-2666, www.attmansdeli.com, 8 A.M.–6:30 P.M. Mon.–Sat., 8 A.M.– 5P.M. Sun., lunch and dinner, $8) has been around since 1915 and is still everyone's favorite place for corned beef, pastrami, and the infamous hot-dog-and-baloney sandwich. You can hang out in the kibbutz room every day.

International/Fusion

Roy's Baltimore (720-B Aliceanna St., 410/659-0099, www.roysrestaurant.com, dinner daily, $15) is one of the many offshoots of celebrity chef Roy Yamaguchi's restaurant empire. It features his twists on classic French, Hawaiian, and Asian dishes such as crispy duck-cake appetizers and seared butterfish in misoyaki sauce. There's also a prix fixe menu offered daily.

Inexpensive and perennially popular, **India Rasoi** (411 S. High St., 410/385-4900, lunch and dinner Mon.–Thurs., dinner only Fri.–Sat.) features an East Indian lunch buffet for $8 and dinner entrées that average $13.

FELL'S POINT

This district is alive with pubs, bars, and small cafés, in addition to some fancy restaurants.

American/Seafood

A longtime resident of the city swore to me that **John Steven Ltd.** (1800 Thames St., 410/327-5561, 11 A.M.–11 P.M. Sun.–Thurs., 11 A.M.–midnight Fri.–Sat., lunch $25, dinner $32) is the king of crab cakes. The menu is eclectic: southwestern, sushi, and seafood. The bar is one of the most popular in town and open until 2 A.M. for the Fell's Point party crowd.

Another established restaurant in the point is Chef Nancy Longo's **Pierpoint** (1822 Aliceanna St., 410/675-2080, lunch Fri.–Sat., dinner Tues.–Sun., $18–39). The rumor is that Chef Longo prepares James Beard's favorite bouillabaisse, and bends a few traditions by smoking her crab cakes (they must be hard to keep lit) and serving barbecued duck egg rolls. Expect the freshest ingredients served in classic Maryland recipes.

The **Dead End Saloon** (935 Fell St., 410/732-3602, lunch and dinner Mon.–Sat., $11–24) is a rock 'n' roll sports bar; the testosterone gloom is tempered by cheerful plantings in front and bright light streaming in from the windows overlooking quiet Fell Street. It offers a full bar, daily lunch specials under $9, and good pub food at reasonable prices. This is a pleasant alternative to Fell's Point's more formal dining.

Obrycki's (1727 E. Pratt St., 410/732-6399, www.obryckis.com, $28) was recommended by the owner of an Italian restaurant as "the place we go when we don't want home cooking." Obrycki's is open for lunch and dinner daily in the summer, but closed mid-November to mid-March, so call ahead for hours. A few blocks east of Little Italy and north of Fell's Point, it's a colonial-style, newsprint-on-the-tables crab house, serving steamed hard-shells, crab cakes, crab soup, and crab marinara. A kids' menu is also available.

International/Vegetarian

For something a touch more exotic, **The Nile Café Egyptian Kitchen & Oven** (811 S. Broadway, 410/327-0005, lunch and dinner daily, $12) offers Middle Eastern/Egyptian cuisine, and—for that Cleopatra/Marc Antony connection—a variety of pizzas. There is a good selection of vegetarian items, and some foods can be make vegan on request.

Liquid Earth (1626 Aliceanna St., 410/276-6606, breakfast, lunch and dinner Mon.–Sat., breakfast and lunch Sun., under $11) is a deluxe juice bar that serves vegetarian and vegan sandwiches. The meatless muffaleta and submarine sandwiches get raves.

CANTON
American

For Sunday brunch, a local favorite is **The Morning Edition Café** (153 N. Patterson Park Ave., 410/732-5133, 9 A.M.–2:30 P.M. Fri., 8 A.M.–3 P.M. Sat., 9 A.M.–3 P.M. Sun., $3–15). Cranberry/apple/walnut pancakes and strawberry/hazelnut french toast are a few examples of what's available.

Another brunch favorite is the **Blue Moon Café** (1621 Aliceanna St., 410/522-3940, Mon.–Weds. 7 A.M.–3 P.M., Thurs.–Sat., 11 A.M.–3 A.M. Sun., $10). It serves big portions of the usual breakfast favorites—but try to come on a weekday, since this tiny place is often packed on the weekends, with an hour wait.

Helen's Garden Restaurant (2908 O'Donnell St., 410/276-2233, www.helens garden.com, lunch and dinner Tues.–Sat., brunch and dinner Sun., $19) is an upscale neighborhood place where you'll meet quite a few Cantonites over a bowl of fresh homemade soup or quesadilla platter if you sit at the friendly bar. The restaurant also has table seating and an excellent wine selection.

For a casual bar with great crack-'em-yourself crabs, try **Kelly's** (2106–08 Eastern Ave., 410/327-2312, lunch and dinner Weds.–Sun., $11–24). Crabs run $27–40 per dozen.

◖ **Birches Restaurant** (641 S. Montford Ave., 410/732-3000, dinner Mon.–Sat., $8–24) is a neighborhood favorite with a faithful following. Steak sandwiches, quesadillas, and mac-and-cheese sound ordinary, but in the hands of Birches' chefs, they shine with the addition of gourmet ingredients like perfectly rare and tender beef, Vermont cheddar, and Danish blue cheese.

International
Nacho Mamas (2940 O'Donnell St., 410/

675-0898, lunch and dinner daily, $12) is one of those bar/restaurants so full of character that it's both a nightlife spot and a place to chow down. You can get Natty Boh here (National Beer—once made in Baltimore, now out of North Carolina, but the same fizzy, light brew), and enjoy your tacos in the Elvis lounge, with images of the grand wiggler himself on the walls and overhead.

Tiburzi's Cafe (900 S. Kenwood, 410/327-8100, dinner daily, lunch Weds.–Fri. and Sun., $11–24) is a sleek addition to the suburban side of Canton. The menu features pastas and other Italian favorites.

◖ **DiPasquale's Deli** (3700 Gough St., 410/276-6787, www.dipasquales.com, 9 A.M.–6 P.M. Mon.–Sat., $8) serves up chicken parmesan and hot and cold subs that will take the chill off any winter day. The DiPasquale family started out in the Italian specialties business in the early 1900s, and the deli continues to make many of its own pastas and breads.

GREEKTOWN

This is the quintessential Greek neighborhood, with dozens of restaurants to prove it, across all price ranges. Not everything is Greek, however; one of the city's best and cheapest Tex-Mex restaurants is also in the neighborhood.

Mediterranean
◖ **Ikaros** (4805 Eastern Ave., 410/633-3750, lunch and dinner daily, $10–15) presents traditional Greek dishes—such as an excellent moussaka and sizable kebobs—served by a friendly staff. Just to give you some idea of Ikaros's staying power, it was voted Best Greek Restaurant for 19 consecutive years by *City Paper*. You can't go wrong here.

Samo's (600 S. Oldham St., 410/675-5292, lunch and dinner Mon.–Sat., $5–15) is famous for the garlic-spiked leg of lamb. Once just a hole in the wall, this popular and low-cost eatery has expanded and still offers great food at reasonable prices.

The **Acropolis** (4718 Eastern Ave., 410/675-3384, 11 A.M.–10 P.M. Mon.–Fri., 11 A.M.–11 P.M. Sat.–Sun., $8–18) features dishes such as braised lamb and moussaka, notable for their home-cooked style.

International

Habenero Grill (4701 Eastern Ave., 410/342-0937, www.habanerogrill.com, breakfast, lunch and dinner daily, until midnight Fri.–Sun., $5–10) combines Tex-Mex with a few Salvadoran dishes on its inexpensive menu. The appetizers are especially good.

UPTOWN

As you might expect of an area heavily populated by college students, the streets that surround the campus are a hotbed of international cheap eats, plus a couple of elegant places with exceptional food.

American

Café Hon (1002 W. 36th St., 410/243-1230, www.cafehon.ezsitemaster.com, brunch Sat.–Sun., lunch and dinner daily, breakfast $5.50, lunch $8, dinner $17) is at a neighborhood crossroads and serves meatloaf, burgers, roast beef with mashed potatoes, and all the other comforts of home.

Tamber's Nifty Fifties Dining (3327 St. Paul St., 410/243-5777, www.tambers restaurant.com, 10 A.M.–10 P.M. Mon.–Thurs., 9 A.M.–11 P.M. Fri.–Sat., 9 A.M.–10 P.M. Sun., $9–16) used to be an old-fashioned diner with the usual burgers and malts, but the owners have whipped up an additional Indian menu to broaden your horizons—aficionados claim it's the best Indian food in town. Tamber's has also renovated the upstairs into a bar and lounge, where you can order food from the restaurant while relaxing with a beer.

Gertrude's (10 Art Museum Dr., in the Baltimore Museum of Art, 410/889-3399, www.johnshields.com/restaurant/rest/gertrudes.html, lunch and dinner Tues.–Fri., dinner Sat.–Sun., brunch Sun., dinner $12–22) is the brainchild of TV celebrity John Shields, Mr. Maryland Cooking himself—in fact, you can catch him buzzing around the restaurant when off-duty from his show. The food ranges from good to great (seafood is a specialty), and the

setting couldn't be more beautiful—big windows face one of the museum's sculpture gardens, and patrons vie to dine al fresco in good weather. Sunday brunch is very popular and reservations are recommended.

☾ The Owl Bar in the Belvedere Hotel (1 E. Chase St., 410/347-0888, lunch and dinner Mon.-Sat. 11:30A.M.– 2 A.M., kitchen closes at midnight, Sunday 11:30A.M.– 11P.M.) is a cool place to have lunch, a late dinner, or drinks any time. The bar has been around since the hotel opened in 1903, though the owls perched above the bar didn't appear until Colonel Consolvo, the bar's owner 1917–1936, took over. Rumor says that the owl's eyes would blink when whiskey was available during Prohibition. These days, the fancy bar food (brick-oven pizzas, chicken Caesar salad, open-face prime rib sandwiches) are the draw, along with the romantic murals that grace the walls.

International

Holy Frijoles! (908 W. 36th St., 410/235-2326, lunch and dinner daily, 11:30 A.M.–midnight Mon.–Sat., until 10 P.M. Sun., under $10) does the Mexican thing in an informal and inexpensive setting. This is one of the favorite college hang-out spots, and the food is really good—Baltimoreans voted its burrito the best in town in 2006.

Loco Hombre (413 W. Cold Spring Ln., 410/889-2233, www.locohombre.com, 11 A.M.–10 P.M. Mon.–Thurs. and Sun., 11 A.M.–11 P.M. Fri.–Sat., $6–24) is another place to roll your beans, though the setting and menu are a lot fancier. Chicken mole plates, baby-back ribs, and tapas are also available.

Vegetarian

One World Cafe (100 W. University Pkwy., 410/235-5777, www.one-world-cafe.com, breakfast, lunch, and dinner daily, brunch Sat.–Sun., $6–13) was voted Baltimore's best vegetarian restaurant several years running. It offers organic whole foods, a juice bar, fresh smoothies, fancy coffee drinks, and a full liquor bar. What more could you ask?

Information and Services

TOURIST INFORMATION

The **Baltimore Area Convention and Visitors Association** (100 Light St., 12th Fl., Baltimore, MD 21202, 410/659-7300 or 877-BAL-TIMORE/877-227-8466), www.baltimore .org) will answer all your questions and send additional information as needed.

MEDIA
Newspapers

The daily sheet in town is the **Baltimore Sun,** with day and evening editions. The **Washington Post** is also good for general news and information on the gateway area between Baltimore and the capital.

Free Newspapers

The Baltimore Guide (a neighborhood paper that comes out every Wed.) and **City Paper** are local entertainment and arts guides. **Baltimore Quickguide** (www.cityspin.com/baltimore) gives pertinent visitor information in a nutshell. **WHERE Baltimore** (www.wheremagazine.com) is a similar publication from the same publisher that duplicates much of the basic information, but adds interesting articles.

Broadcast

Radio station **WBAL** (1090 AM) is a news and weather station, and **WYPR** (88.1 FM) is an affiliate of National Public Radio.

PERSONAL SAFETY

Downtown Baltimore—a few blocks away from the inner harbor—can be raucous and a little scary for visitors at night (unless you're from New York City, which case you'll find this town pretty tame). Paca and Howard Streets are filled with people hailing each other, laughter, and a nasty argument or two. Chances are you're a stranger, so it's probably a good idea to keep to the high-tourist-traffic areas. Though the downtown hotels encourage visitors to use their convenient (and expensive) valet parking, street parking in well-lit areas east of Charles Street remains reasonably safe (keep everything in the trunk).

Forty-five Downtown Public Safety Guides patrol the streets of Baltimore every day during daylight hours, serving as goodwill ambassadors and additional "eyes and ears" for the police. The guides are trained by representatives of the local hospitality industry to answer questions, give directions, and generally help visitors have a great experience while in town; they're also trained by the police to spot and report suspicious behavior. In addition, Downtown's Public Safety Guides provide Safety Escorts for anyone who would like extra peace of mind while walking to a car or bus, or waiting for a taxi after dark. Safety Escorts are available within the DMA District from 10 A.M. to 10:30 P.M. seven days a week. To request a Safety Escort, call 410/244-8778 during business hours or 410/802-9631 after hours.

In other parts of the city that attract tourists, the worst you'll likely encounter is a panhandler. Much of Baltimore is residential, but the economic spread is vast—and it changes quickly from block to block. The west side, northeast, and south side have some pretty heavy neighborhoods. Baltimore has one of the lowest incidences of crimes against visitors in cities of similar size. However, if you feel uncomfortable, always follow your instincts.

Getting There and Around

GETTING THERE
By Air
Baltimore/Washington Airport (BWI, www
.bwiairport.com) is 10 miles south of town. Lim-
ousines (410/519-0000, www.rmlimo.com, about
$40) are available, as well as a somewhat unre-
liable shuttle (800/776-0323, www.theairport
shuttle.com) that sometimes takes an hour to
make a 20-minute trip. Pickup at a specified
time can be iffy, depending on how many passengers are riding with you. The fare is $33 to
downtown, more for other destinations. Both
limos and the shuttle operate between the airport
and downtown hotels. Taxis are also available
((410/859-1100, $20–28 to the inner harbor).

The best deal by far from the airport to
downtown is by light rail (410/539-5000, www
.mtamaryland.com, 6 A.M.–11 P.M. Mon.–Fri.,
7 A.M.–11 P.M. Sat., 11 A.M.–7 P.M. Sun. and
holidays, only $1.60 each way). Call or check
the website for schedules and stops.

By Train
The **Amtrak** (800/USA-RAIL, www.amtrak
.com) train pulls into Baltimore at Penn Station from points east and west.

By Bus
Greyhound Bus Terminals (www.greyhound
.com) are at 2110 Haines Street downtown and
at the Best Western Hotel (5625 O'Donnell St.,
Baltimore Travel Plaza). Contact 800/231-2222
or ifsr@greyhound.com for ticket and schedule
information.

GETTING AROUND
By Car
BWI hosts most of the large rental car companies and a few smaller ones. Penn Station also
has a few car rental booths, and some rental
agencies will pick you up at other locations.
Some of the companies available are **Budget**
(410/859-0850), **Enterprise** (800/325-8007),
Hertz (410/850-7400 or 800/654-3131), and
Thrifty (410/850-7139).

The main route around the city is the Baltimore Beltway, a combination of U.S. 695, U.S.
95 and U.S. 895. The Jones Falls Expressway
is the main route on the west side of town,
and U.S. 40/Mulberry St./Franklin St. bisects
Downtown and Uptown, while Charles St.
runs north–south. Expect heavy commute traffic on all routes 7–10 A.M. and 5–7 P.M.

By Taxi
Yellow Transportation (410/685-1212) has
been in charge of the city's taxicabs, buses, lim-
ousines, 21-passenger mini-coaches, vans, and
trolleys since 1909. They also operate BWI's
SuperShuttle transportation between BWI
Airport and Baltimore's downtown area hotels
(800/258-3826, www.supershuttle.com/htm/
cities/bwi.htm). Price varies by destination,
and the company will only quote fees when
you book online or at the airport.

Cab companies proliferate—some of the
bigger ones are **City Cab** (410/566-6660),
Diamond (410/947-3333), and **Yellow** (410/
756-1096). In an effort to increase their knowledge of the city and the quality of personal
service, Baltimore's 2,500 cabbies can volunteer to receive eight hours apiece of hospitality training.

By Mass Transit
Baltimore's **MTA** (Mass Transit Administration, www.mtamaryland.com) is responsible
for buses, light rail, and the Metro subway system. Routes reach all parts of the town and
outlying areas. The fares for each system is
$1.60 (commuter route fares depend on des-
tination), exact change required. A $3.50 one-
day pass is good for unlimited use of all three
systems. For route maps, call 410/539-5000.

By Water
Ed Kane's Water Taxi (410/563-3901 or 800/
658-8947) is the best way to get around the
inner harbor and places within walking distance of the bay. Parking fees downtown are

stiff; a lot of people park in Fell's Point ($6 all day) or Canton Water Park (free) and take the water taxi from those stops downtown and back. The water taxi charges $8 adults, $4 children 10 and under for unlimited pickups all day; there are no tickets to carry. Captain Dennis, first mate Tom, or one of the other taxi pilots stamps your hand with a little picture of the boat. Thirteen boats serve 40 attractions. The fare also includes a Letter of Marque ticket that features dozens of discounts.

CENTRAL MARYLAND

Maryland's most populous area has more to offer visitors than miles of suburbs. Much of the western part of this area—bordered by the meandering Potomac River—is rural. In the central and eastern portions, small towns are linked by high-speed freeways and narrow two-lane roads. Treasures dot this landscape like wildflowers in a field—easy to miss if you're not looking.

The state's capital, Annapolis, is one of the most historic and delightful political centers in America. The town has retained its Federal-era authenticity while enlarging its appeal through inviting shops, good restaurants, and the attractions of the U.S. Naval Academy. Another small town, Ellicott City, once a summer retreat for Baltimore's middle classes, remains a charming place for a getaway.

Of the counties that make up central Maryland—Anne Arundel, Howard, Montgomery, and Prince George's—only the latter two abut Washington, D.C. However, the history, energy, and wealth that radiate from the nation's capital spread far beyond its invisible borders. Fortunately for visitors, many government agencies do research and business in Maryland, providing low- or no-cost opportunities to see programs of national significance in action. The Beltsville Agricultural Research Center, NASA/Goddard Space Flight Visitor Center, and Patuxent Research Refuge/National Wildlife Visitor Center are among the facilities that offer information and activities for visitors. The U.S. government is the largest employer in Maryland, and Rockville and Bethesda are two of the most visited areas in the state. The

© JOANNE MILLER

HIGHLIGHTS

◖ U.S. Naval Academy (USNA): The beautiful USNA campus includes the Navy Chapel, adorned with sailing ships and stained glass; the exquisite marble crypt of John Paul Jones; and a sprightly exhibit of model ships that will fascinate young and old alike (page 89).

◖ Blob's Park Biergarten: Try this place just because it's fun and authentic. Max Blob built a beer garden for his friends on his farm, and it became a combination German dinner and polka joint for all ages (page 97).

◖ Cryptologic Museum: There are exhibits on cracking codes and creating codes, plus information on the codes held within slave quilts and two Cray supercomputers – the great-granddaddy of all our desktops (page 100).

◖ Brighton Dam Azalea Garden: This springtime special began as a labor of love by one man, and is now recognized as one of Maryland's showplaces, (page 103).

◖ Clara Barton National Historic Site: A true heroine and world-renowned "Angel of the Battlefield" spent her last years here. The home looks much as it was in Barton's day, when simplicity and shared work were the ideal for the devoted community organizer (page 106).

◖ C&O Canal National Historic Park: The 184.5-mile Chesapeake & Ohio Canal National Historical Park trail officially begins at the tidewater lock near the Thompson Boat Center in Washington, D.C., but you can catch the flavor of it right here (page 110).

◖ Patuxent Research Refuge/National Wildlife Visitor Center: It's the oldest and one of the largest wildlife research centers in the United States and the world, filled with clever exhibits and well-informed personnel (page 113).

◖ College Park Aviation Museum: The airport that serves as home to this unusually sophisticated museum dedicated to flight (with full-size airplanes suspended from the ceiling) was established in 1909, when Wilbur Wright came to train two military officers to fly the U.S. government's first airplane (page 117).

◖ Accokeek Foundation/National Colonial Farm: The foundation grounds are home to a living-history mid-18th-century farm with rebuilt structures, where it's possible to experience the drifting sunlit pollen, quiet waters, and peaceful surroundings that the earliest settlers took for granted (page 118).

CENTRAL MARYLAND

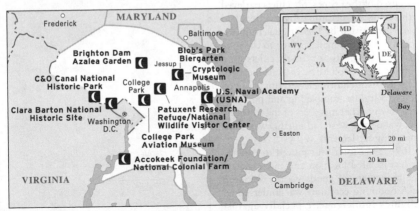

LOOK FOR ◖ TO FIND RECOMMENDED SIGHTS, ACTIVITIES, DINING, AND LODGING.

road from Rockville to Washington, D.C., is heavily trafficked and lined with shopping centers and restaurants. But there's history here as well, and within a short distance, the fields are heavy with winged creatures and delicate floating seeds in the summer, views of the broad Potomac in winter. Take time to explore.

HISTORY

In 1634, Leonard Calvert traveled up the Potomac in the *Dove* and negotiated with local Piscataway and Yoacomoco tribes for 30 square miles of land within the territory awarded to his family. The new settlement became the colonial capital of Maryland, St. Mary's. Farming, the production of tobacco as a profit-making crop, the plantation system, and the abundance of the countryside brought relative prosperity and growth to the early colony. Small groups of colonists struck out from St. Mary's, seeking planting and trading opportunities. By 1652, encroaching European settlements forced shore tribes to abandon their villages and move north into the territory of the Susquehannocks.

Throughout the mid-1600s, the Iroquois Confederation in southern New York state warred with the Susquehannocks, who moved south and west into central Maryland. During this time, a number of settlers in outlying areas were murdered, and Susquehannocks were accused of the crimes. Six chiefs parleyed with the colonists, claiming the murders had not been committed by the Susquehannocks. The chiefs produced medals given to them by Governor Calvert. Five of the six chiefs were slaughtered by the colonists, and one escaped. Outraged Susquehannock warriors moved south into Virginia, rampaging and pillaging colonial towns; other members of the tribe dispersed, wandering west and north, away from the spreading settlements.

In 1694, the capital was moved to Annapolis, a less isolated location and more central for the movement of goods via the shipping trade. A booming economy was underscored by religious intolerance, especially against Catholics. In spite of these difficulties, Maryland continued to grow richer, thanks to its

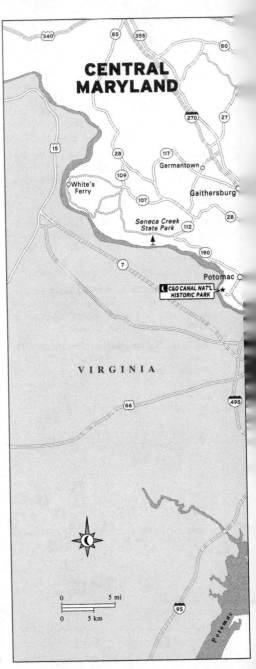

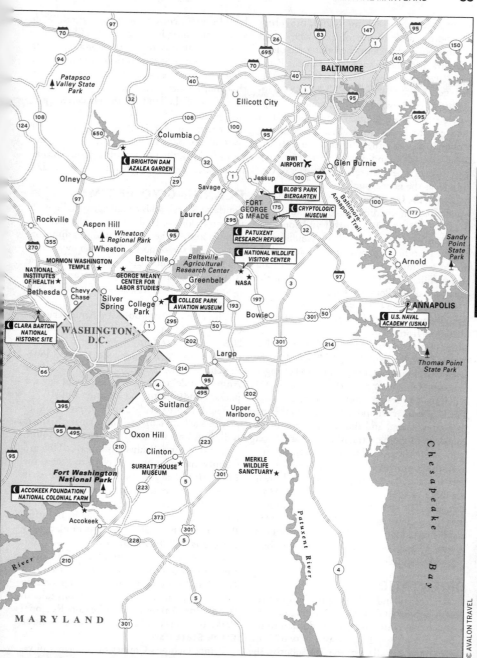

many waterways reaching inland, providing transport avenues to the tobacco, wheat, and produce farms that flourished alongside them. In central Maryland, surrounded by the Potomac River, rivers and streams seemed to flow with gold.

During the Revolution, most colonists supported freedom—but many who depended on the area's chief cash crop, tobacco, held strong economic ties with the mother country. In the late 1700s, Maryland deeded part of its territory to form a new "state," the District of Columbia, as the new capital.

During the Civil War, tobacco again played a major part in dividing the area. Though officially a Union state, central and southern Maryland largely supported the Confederacy because of its heavy dependence on slave labor. Blockade-runners routinely transported food and supplies to the Confederate army on the other side of the Potomac River.

From after the Civil War until the 1930s, steamboats remained the main source of transportation from Annapolis and Baltimore to various points around the bay. When the Potomac River Bridge (U.S. 301) opened in the late 1930s, the popular mode of travel changed to automobiles, their numbers increased by the building of highways throughout the counties. The U.S. military found several sites in the area that suited them, and thus became the major employers in south central Maryland as tobacco cultivation lost ground in the modern age.

With the growth of the U.S. government, the need for workers and suppliers exploded, creating miles of suburbs in every direction. However, just a few miles beyond the expansive cities that form the ring around Washington D.C. and the corridor between Washington and Baltimore, a rural landscape that could have been plucked from colonial days awaits visitors.

ORIENTATION

Central Maryland is largely made up of the heavily populated Baltimore–Washington D.C. corridor that clings to I-95, in addition to the suburbs that spread out from the two cities. Expanding east and west from the suburbs, the land becomes considerably more rural. Wide swaths of rolling hills separate small towns to the west, culminating in the Potomac River. East and south of the corridor, the towns are larger, but the greenswards become wider farther south. Chesapeake Bay forms the eastern boundary of the land. In the far eastern portion of central Maryland, Annapolis contributes greatly to Maryland's colonial charm. In spite of rampant development, several state parks and wildlife refuges bring natural beauty to this area, the beating heart of Maryland.

PLANNING YOUR TIME

Southern Maryland is equally divided between the attractions of civilization—chiefly in Annapolis and in the area around Washington, D.C.—and the opportunity to get away from it all. This chapter is divided by county: Anne Arundel, Howard, Montgomery, and Prince George's, each with its own set of interests worthy of a week's visit.

The city of **Annapolis** in Anne Arundel County could fill at least three days with the **U.S. Naval Academy** (two hours–all day), the authentic period architecture, good lodging choices and restaurants, and art. Greater Anne Arundel features two delightful day use parks, **Sandy Point** and **Thomas Point.**

The Ellicott City area of Howard County presents a day's diversion with its historic buildings and the **B&O Railroad Museum,** a must-see for rail fans. In Greater Howard County, one very unusual place to visit is the **Cryptologic Museum** (one–two hours), a haven for those interested in coding, decoding, and the general doings of the National Security Agency. If it's spring, swing by beautiful **Brighton Dam Azalea Gardens** or plan a day at **Patapsco Valley State Park.**

In Montgomery County, fans of horticulture will want to plan a day on the road. Visit **McCrillis Gardens** in Bethesda—a good stop for an early lunch. In the afternoon, take in **Brookside Gardens** in Wheaton Regional Park, or visit **White's Ferry and Seneca Creek State Park.**

Prince George's County offers plenty of variety. Don't miss the **Accockeek Foundation National Colonial Farm** (all day), one of the most beautiful rural areas in the state.

The triple crown of government agency facilities also deserves a visit—each will take the better part of a day, including transport. **Beltsville Agricultural Research Center** informs visitors of the latest developments in American agriculture, and families can immerse themselves in space lore at the **NASA/ Goddard Space Flight Center.** Due to increased security, both facilities require considerable planning ahead (at least a month) to make reservations. The **Patuxent Research Refuge** offers environmental and wildlife education, and the **College Park Aviation Museum** also deserves a stop.

FESTIVALS AND EVENTS

Phone numbers for events change frequently. The best places to check for updated information are the county tourism bureaus—contact information listed in this chapter.

January through April, the **Conservatory Spring Display and Sculpture Show** (301/ 962-1400) at Brookside Gardens in Wheaton cheers the winter-bare soul. Sculptures made by regional artists are displayed among the colorful flowering bulbs, annuals, perennials and shrubs.

Whatever the weather on Easter Sunday, steeplechase and horse racing make for an exciting day at the **Marlborough Hunt Races** (410/798-5040) at the Roedown Farm in Davidsonville, Anne Arundel County.

Gladiator meets *Private Ryan* in the annual **Marching Through Time** (301/464-5291) living history encampment at the Marietta Mansion in Glenn Dale (Prince George's County). More than 300 reenactors represent soldiers and others from Roman times to World War II. Food, craft, and hobby vendors are onsite, too.

The annual **Maryland Sheep & Wool Festival** (410/531-3647, www.sheepand wool.org) held during the first full weekend in May, will instruct you in "Rug Braiding" and "Hands-On Beginning Shepherd Skills," among dozens of other classes, exhibits, and

displays. It's held at the Howard County Fairgrounds in West Friendship.

The **Chesapeake Bay Bridge Walk** on Memorial Day gives participants a chance to enjoy views from the bridge during a 4.3-mile-long stroll.

Columbia Festival of the Arts (410/ 715-3044) in June is 10 days of performing arts at Lake Kittamaqundi in Columbia, including two weekends of free performances in addition to ticketed performances, workshops, and master classes. Past festivals have featured Branford Marsalis, Rick Danko, and many others.

While you're in town for music, don't miss **Jazzfest,** presented in partnership with the Festival of the Arts. Jazz greats Jimmy McGriff and Hank Crawford have performed at prior festivals, and events include concerts, workshops, and the "House of Jazz"—dinner and continuous live entertainment. Columbia sponsors events throughout the year.

Kunta Kinte, hero of Alex Haley's *Roots,* arrived on these shores on the auction block at Annapolis. In August, the spirit of Kunta Kinte is celebrated at the Anne Arundel County Fairgrounds, Route 178, Crownsville.

sailboat race on the Chesapeake

A host of performers celebrate the **Kunta Kinte Heritage Festival** (www.kuntakinte .org), a weekend of dance, food, and music.

Germantown, in Montgomery County, celebrates its heritage during **Oktoberfest** (www .germantownoktoberfest.org) with authentic food, crafts, and games, all to the tune of a German band. Other entertainment includes hot-air balloon races.

The nation's oldest and largest **Sailboat Show** (www.usboat.com) takes place in Annapolis in October. New sailboats, sailing accessories, equipment, and services are on display. There's also a **Powerboat Show** this month.

The **Maryland Million** is the state's celebration of a 250-year tradition of thoroughbred breeding and racing. A million dollars in purses are wagered on Maryland-sired horses, and other events such as a horse country tour, horse shows, and polo matches are on the roster. Festivities take place at Laurel Park track in Laurel.

GETTING THERE AND AROUND
By Air
The main airports serving central Maryland are **Baltimore-Washington International Airport** (BWI), south of Baltimore, and **Ronald Reagan Washington National** (DCA) and **Dulles International Airport** (IAD), both in Virginia south of Washington, D.C. All may offer commuter flights to the small commercial airport near Londontown, south of Annapolis—check the airport websites for details. All major car rental agencies are represented.

By Train
Amtrak (800/USA-RAIL, www.amtrak.com) runs trains to Baltimore, Washington, D.C., and New Carrollton (Annapolis).

By Bus
There's a **Greyhound/Trailways** terminal in Annapolis (800/231-2222, www.grey hound.com). Outside of Annapolis, there is no intra-city public transportation.

By Car
This is the most common way to travel around central Maryland. Major routes are I-95, I-270, U.S. 301, U.S. 50, Routes 1, 3, 4, 29, 97, and 295. I-495 (the beltway) circles Washington, D.C.

Annapolis

Annapolis has the highest concentration of Georgian-style buildings in the United States. In this "Athens of America," many of the homes were previously used only in winter, when government was in session. Nowadays, it's become a year-round draw for students of history and those who study fun.

Don't expect a dour history tour—Annapolis is one of the liveliest cities around. Colonial buildings on the streets hold art galleries, fashionable shops, and dozens of restaurants. Two diverse seats of higher learning, the US Naval Academy and St. John's College, provide more than a modicum of culture. The town's harbor and surrounding rivers teem with boats of all types. The local free paper is the *Bay Weekly* (www.bayweekly.com). This is an interesting place to visit—and a hard place to leave.

Maryland is the only colonial state in America that has preserved all the homes of its signers of the Declaration of Independence—and all are in Annapolis. Three of them—the William Paca House, the Charles Carroll House, and the **Chase-Lloyd House** (22 Maryland Ave., 410/263-2723, 2–4 P.M. Mon.–Sat. Mar.–Dec., $2)—are open to the public for tours. Only the first floor of the Chase-Lloyd House is available for public viewing (the other two floors of this Palladian-style mansion are occupied).

SIGHTS
William Paca House and Garden
The home of this Revolutionary War leader (186

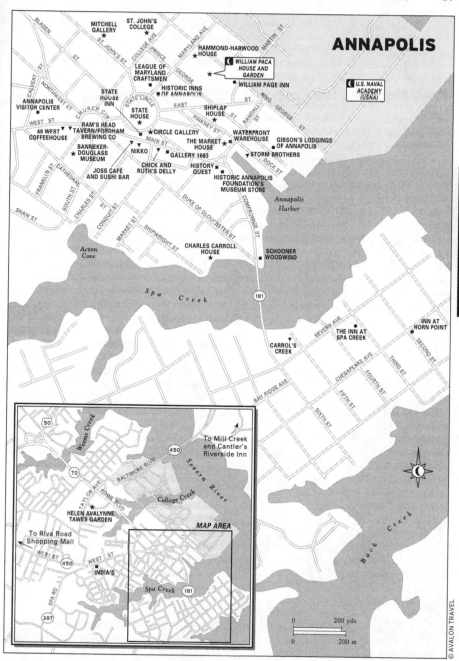

ANNAPOLIS

CENTRAL MARYLAND

Prince George St., 410/267-7619, house open 10 A.M.–5 P.M. Mon.–Sat. and noon–5 P.M. Sun. late March–Dec. 31, noon–5 P.M. Fri.–Sun. mid-Jan.–late March, tours on the hour and half hour, $8 house and garden, $5 garden only) was completed in 1765 and is the home of a three-term governor of Maryland and signer of the Declaration of Independence. The manor house and formal two-acre pleasure garden were restored and furnished to reflect the lives and interests of the attorney-patriot Paca, his family, his household (which included slaves), and his community. The house was all but obliterated when a hotel, Carvel Hall, was built around it and on top of the gardens in the early 20th century. After the hotel was dismantled, the original structure was lovingly restored. Only the stone boundaries of the gardens remained, under nine feet of landfill; they were brought back to life after restorers studied a portrait of Paca by Charles Wilson Peale that detailed the garden and its two-story summerhouse in the background. The restoration, with its Chinese Chippendale motifs inside and out,

is masterful, and the gardens are an authentic period delight.

The Charles Carroll House

A restoration in progress (107 Duke of Gloucester St., 410/269-1737, www.charlescarrollhouse.com, 10 A.M. 2 P.M. Sat., noon–4 P.M. Sun. June–Oct., $5), this building is the original home of three generations of Carrolls, including Charles Carroll, the settler and first attorney general of Maryland; his son, Charles Carroll of Annapolis; and his grandson, Charles Carroll of Carrollton, signer of the Declaration of Independence. Charles Carroll of Carrollton was considered the wealthiest man and the largest slaveholder in the colonies at the time of the Revolution. In 1828, he became president of the American Colonization Society, which sought to return freed slaves to Africa. The house features exhibits, tours, living history performances, and special events related to Maryland's 18th-century heritage.

The Hammond-Harwood House

Built in 1774 (19 Maryland Ave., 410/263-4683, www.hammondharwoodhouse.org), this home retains over 90 percent of its original building materials and was considered the finest example of Georgian architecture in colonial America. Hours are noon–5 P.M. Tuesday–Sunday April–October, and the house is also open for special events and on select weekends November–March. Guided tours take place on the hour. Admission is $6 for adults, $3 for children, and $5.50 for students (including college students).

The Hammond-Harwood house is deemed the masterwork of architect William Buckland, notable for its level of detail and ornately carved interior and exterior moldings. The house is furnished with mid-18th-century pieces and fine art, including a collection of portraits by the Peale family.

The Maryland State House

This lovely historic building (91 State Cir., 410/974-3400, 9 A.M.–5 P.M. Mon.–Fri.,

© JOANNE MILLER

Pinkney Street

10 A.M.–4 P.M. Sat.–Sun., free) is the oldest state capitol in continuous legislative use. The house has 30-minute tours at 11 A.M. and 3 P.M.

From November 26, 1782, to August 13, 1784, the Maryland State House served as the nation's capitol and meeting place for the Continental Congress; the Treaty of Paris was ratified here in 1784, ending the Revolutionary War. Exhibits and displays chronicle Maryland history, and one room is devoted to a mural of General George Washington resigning his commission as commander in chief of the Continental Army. Hoping to retire from public life, he emerged six years later as president. The walls are hung with several portraits by Charles Wilson Peale, including one of William Pitt, the English statesman who inspired early colonials to win back the forks of the Ohio (modern Pittsburgh) from the French during the French and Indian War. A photo ID is required to enter the State House, and all bags will be checked at security.

◖ U.S. Naval Academy (USNA)

Established in 1845, the USNA (121 Blake Rd., 410/263-6933, www.navyonline.com) is the undergraduate college of the United States Navy. Guided walking tours of the academy are offered 10 A.M.–3 P.M. Monday–Friday, 9:30 A.M.–3 P.M. Saturday, and 12:30–3 P.M. Sunday April–June; 10 A.M.–3 P.M. Monday–Saturday and 12:30–2:30 P.M. Sunday July–August; 10 A.M.–2:30 P.M. Monday–Saturday, and 12:30–2:30 P.M. Sunday December–March. Tours cost $8 for adults, less for seniors and students, and begin at the **Armel-Leftwich Visitor Center** (Gate 1, 52 King George St., 410/263-6933, 9 A.M.–5 P.M. Mar.–Dec., 9 A.M.–4 P.M. Jan.–Feb.).

Like all top colleges, the USNA accepts only the academic cream of the crop of high-school students, but they must also demonstrate physical prowess—fitness activities take up a minimum of two hours every day, in addition to a full academic course load. Polar explorer Rear Admiral Richard Byrd (class of 1912) was captain of the 1910 men's gymnastic team, and football player Roger Staubach (class of 1965) was a Heisman trophy winner before he turned pro. The class of 1980 was the first to accept women, and by 1998, 55 had graduated. This four-year college offers 19 majors, covers all costs, and pays a stipend to students. Graduates become Navy ensigns or Marine Corps second lieutenants, and are required to serve for five years.

The visitors center displays Freedom 7, the space capsule piloted by Rear Admiral Alan Shepard (class of 1945), and interactive exhibits that feature the history, requirements, and opportunities the academy offers. An excellent gift shop gives visitors the chance to purchase Navy- and Marine-logo-emblazoned merchandise while listening to tapes of the Navy band thumping out military marches.

Campus attractions include **Halsey Field House** and **Lejeune Physical Education Center,** two of several facilities used by midshipmen (students) for sports and physical training. Inside are an Olympic-size pool, diving

chapel and crypt of John Paul Jones at the USNA

complex, wrestling loft, and weight-training/conditioning area. The Athletic Hall of Fame, a collection of photographs of notable sportsmen and women, is on the second floor of Lejeune.

The **Navy chapel** and **crypt of John Paul Jones** (410/263-3601, 9 A.M.–4 P.M. Mon.–Sat., 1–4 P.M. Sun.) are must-sees. The chapel is more like a cathedral—soaring Tiffany windows soften the light, and the walls support carvings of ships, representing God watching over sailors. The public is invited to worship: Catholic services are held at 9 A.M. and Protestant services at 11 A.M. on Sundays.

The crypt of John Paul Jones lies underneath the chapel. Contrary to popular legend, Jones did not found the Navy, though he was responsible for many of its traditions. His senior officer, John Barry, is the Navy's founding father, and is buried in Philadelphia near Independence Hall. The crypt of John Paul Jones is meant to represent a burial at sea, and is one of the most beautiful funerary presentations in the world. The darkened room, guarded constantly by still-as-statues marines, is dramatically lit, and the coffin rises beneath a dome on waves of bronze and marble.

The **Statue of Tecumseh,** in Tecumseh Court, is a reproduction of the original ship figurehead that stands in the visitors center. Named in honor of the Shawnee chief, the statue represents the warrior spirit of midshipmen—during Commissioning Week (graduation), Alumni Weekend, and before all home football games (particularly the annual Army-Navy game), Tecumseh is painted and dressed in full war regalia.

In **Preble Hall** (9 A.M.–5 P.M. Mon.–Sat., 11 A.M.–5 P.M. Sun., free), the **U.S. Naval Academy Museum** contains more than 35,000 paintings, prints, and artifacts depicting naval history. The museum is closed for renovations until winter 2008–2009; call for availability. The **Rogers Ship Model Collection** in the basement of Preble Hall is another exceptional attraction. The gallery contains dozens of pristine miniature reproductions of warships from the 17th, 18th, and 19th centuries—some more than 250 years old—and models crafted from the bones of beef rations allowed French prisoners of war during their incarceration in England from 1756 to 1815. Some of the bone carvers became so successful that they remained in England after their release. Henry Huddleston Rogers, an American industrialist, bequeathed most of the models to the academy in 1935, and all are constructed with strict regard to scale, usually 0.25 inch to the foot. This is one of the best collections in the world, fascinating for kids and adults.

Once located in Preble Hall and now available online (www.usni.org/webstore), the **U.S. Naval Institute Bookstore** offers a selection of books and other items about the Navy, ship modeling, and related subjects, published by USNI Press.

In the entrance to **Bancroft Hall,** one of the largest single dormitories in the world, is **Memorial Hall,** a magnificent rotunda that honors graduates killed in action and midshipmen who died prior to graduation. Commodore Oliver Hazard Perry's famous "Don't Give Up the Ship" flag is displayed here.

Full dress parades are held in April, May, and September. Call 410/263-6933 for times and dates of these and other special events.

Museums

The small **Annapolis Maritime Museum** (133 Bay Shore Ave., 410/295-0104, www.annapolismaritimemuseum.org, 11 A.M.–4 P.M. Sat., 1–4 P.M. Sun., free) gives out free walking tour brochures, so visitors can roam and learn the history of Eastport. Across the bridge from Annapolis proper, Eastport began as a small farming community and became increasingly residential until, by 1868, the farms had all but disappeared. Boatyards were built in the late 19th century—John Trumpy & Sons moved to the town from New Jersey and built some of the grandest luxury motor-yachts on the water for presidents and kings. Eastport retains its maritime flavor, and the close-knit community "seceded" from Annapolis to become the Maritime Republic of Eastport when faced with the closure of the Spa Creek Bridge in 1998.

Banneker-Douglass Museum (84 Franklin

St., 410/974-2553, 10 A.M.–4 P.M. Tues.–Sat., free) features exhibits of African American art, historical artifacts, archives, rare books, and special collections. Other visiting times are available by appointment. Named for scientist Benjamin Banneker and abolitionist Frederick Douglass, it's housed in the 1876 Mt. Moriah AME Church building.

Gardens

You wouldn't expect to find a garden featuring Maryland's natural environments in the middle of an office complex, but **Helen Avalynne Tawes Garden** (Tawes State Office Bldg., Taylor Ave., 410/260-8189, dawn–dusk daily, free)

is full of surprises and a fun place to wander, featuring every environment found in the state. Park in one of the government building visitor spaces and enter through the Tawes building—there are a number of exhibits on wildlife, a small cafeteria, and gift shop inside the visitors center (Mon.–Fri. 9 A.M.–3 P.M.).

Galleries

Click on **Art in Annapolis** (www.artin annapolis.com) for a listing of galleries and art events in town.

The **Mitchell Gallery** (Mellon Hall, off St. John's St. on the campus of St. John's College, 410/626-2556, noon–5 P.M. Tues.–Sun.,

---

ST. JOHN'S LIBERTY TREE

The style of St. John's College varies greatly from Annapolis's other font of higher learning, the US Naval Academy. St. John's students study the "Great Books," beginning with Aristotle and ending with Nietzsche. Tuition is around $30,000 a year, and croquet is the only intercollegiate sport. Though both schools are steeped in tradition, St. John's recently lost one of its most prized, the Liberty Tree.

The 400-year-old tulip poplar that stood on St. John's campus in front of McDowell Hall was the last of the liberty trees, which served as rallying points for the Sons of Liberty. Pre-Revolutionary colonists used the poplar and trees like it as meeting places for fomenting rebellion against the British. There were once 13 liberty trees, one in each of the original colonies, and they became a potent Revolutionary War symbol. At least two were destroyed by British forces, and others were cut down or lost to disease or old age.

Winds from Hurricane Floyd fractured the trunk of the St. John's tree, which then endangered everything around it, according to a report by arborist Russell Carlson. It also suffered damage from lightning and earlier hurricanes over the years, and was largely held together by concrete and metal cables. In his report, Carlson said, "The entire tree now consists of a hollow shell of wood, sometimes

only two or three inches thick." He estimated that 85 percent of the wood was lost to decay, and he rejected the use of extensive internal or external mechanical supports. "It would be an obtrusive and ignominious life-support system for this grand old champion. Campers and wanderers, children and philosophers, vagrants and presidents have all stood in the shade of this ancient giant. But finally, it is time to say goodbye to our old friend." The college, which held its commencement under the tree for 200 years, decided to remove the tree.

In the spring of 1999, state officials arranged for cuttings to be taken from the tree, so clones could be produced and presented to the 49 other states. Several hundred people gathered in a solemn ceremony in late autumn of that year, as crews began cutting down the old poplar. Wreaths were laid at the base of the tree and at the base of its 100-year-old offspring, which stands a hundred yards away. "We all feel a great sense of sadness over the duty we must perform today," said college president Christopher Nelson.

After a bell tolled 13 times for each of the original colonies, crews went to work with chain saws. It took several days to bring down the whole tree, whose wood was used to make mementos for St. John's students and alumni.

7–8 P.M. Fri., free) is open to the public and often features museum-quality work by artists such as Rembrandt, Renoir, Calder, and Lipschitz. However, the gallery's purpose is to help students establish connections between the visual arts and liberal arts with exhibits of historical and regional interest, so exhibits are broad in scope and often include works by students.

Circle Gallery (18 State Cir., 410/268-4566, 11 A.M.–5 P.M. Tues.–Sun., free) displays original fine art in all media by local and regional artists. Featured works are by members of the Maryland Federation of Art, and many of them are stunning. The exhibits change monthly.

Gallery 1683 (151 Main St., 410/280-2140, www.gallery1683.com, 10 A.M.–5 P.M. Tues.–Sat. noon–5 P.M. Sun., free) shows a variety of artists using different media and approaches. Exhibitions change monthly and vary from shows devoted to the work of a single artist to group works. All the artists displayed here have won awards for achievement, and all focus on the beauty of Chesapeake Bay.

Other Historical Sights

Largely responsible for the preservation of the town, the Historic Annapolis Foundation (HAF, 800/603-4020 and 410/267-7619, www.annapolis.org) began as an effort to stop developers from pulling down colonial-era buildings in the 1950s. Properties were restored house-by-house with state and federal money, and each house that was sold came with an easement. The ongoing advisory group regulates everything visible from the street except the color of the houses (it's easy to pick out rebels in downtown Annapolis). In recent years, the group's function has shifted from regulation to education.

The foundation maintains a number of properties, among them the **Shiplap House** (18 Pinkney St.), built in 1715, one of the oldest houses in Annapolis. It has been restored as an 18th-century house and inn, and is the site of the HAF offices. Close by, the **Waterfront Warehouse** (4 Pinkney St., free) features a model of the Annapolis waterfront as it looked

in the 1750s. Pinkney Street is a joy in itself—it takes little imagination to picture its colonial days, since most of the rowhouse fronts are reminiscent of the period. Number 43 is typical of a house used to board troops for the Revolutionary War (open by appointment only, 800/603-4020 or 410/267-7619).

The HAF offers several audio-with-map walking tours, tours escorted by a colonial guide (more sprightly than you'd expect), and horse-drawn carriage tours. You can reserve on the foundation's website or at **HistoryQuest** (99 Main St., 10 A.M.–5 P.M. Mon.–Sat., 11 A.M.–5 P.M. Sun.), a building with quite a history of its own. Once a 1790s bakery, this restored structure contains two floors of artifacts and exhibits on the history of Maryland's capital. The ground floor features Fleming's Bake Shop, with local home-baked goods, vintage cookbooks and glassware, and a multitude of cooking tools, gadgets, and gifts.

SHOPPING

Main Street contains most of the trinket and clothing shops in Annapolis. One diverse and interesting shop is **Historic Annapolis Foundation's Museum Store** (77 Main St.). Maryland Avenue is also a fun place to stroll. Outside of town (Exit 22 off U.S. 50/301), the **Annapolis Harbour Center** (2512A Solomons Island Rd., 410/266-5857) is a mall with a nautical village theme that features more than 50 stores, including Ann Taylor Loft and Old Navy.

League of Maryland Craftsmen

This gallery/shop (216 Main St., 410/626-1277, www.artinannapolis.com/leagueofmaryland craftsmen, 10 A.M.–5:30 P.M. Mon.–Fri., 10 A.M.–6 P.M. Sat., noon–5:30 P.M. Sun.) features the work of more than 150 league members. The thorough jury process is evident in the quality of the merchandise—there's nothing made from kits or assembled from commercial components here. Wonderful glass, charming ceramics, and prints are a few of the finds. This is a good resource if you're looking for a special gift.

RECREATION
Walking Tours
Stop by the **Annapolis Visitors Center** (26 West St., 410/280-0445, www.visit-annapolis .org, 9 A.M.–5 P.M. daily), and take one of its hour-long history tours ($12.50) to orient yourself to the town and see some parts of it you might otherwise miss. The tour ends up at the Governor Ritchie Overlook, with panoramic views of the Naval Academy and city. **Discover Annapolis Tours** (410/626-6000, www.discover-annapolis. com) depart from the visitors center also.

The **Historic Annapolis Foundation** (18 Pinkney St., 410/267-7619, www.annapolis .org) offers several audio walking tours. One, the African-American Heritage Audio Walking Tour, explores the city through the diverse experiences of slaves (Kunta Kinte, a real person and hero of Alex Haley's book *Roots,* first landed here) and freemen who played a large part in the everyday life of Annapolis. The tours are available at **HAF's Museum Store** (77 Main St., 410/268-5576). There is a $10 charge to use the audio equipment.

© JOANNE MILLER

view of Annapolis from across the Severn River

Boat Tours
Some say the best way to see Annapolis is from the water, and **Watermark Cruises** (410/268-7601, www.watermarkcruises.com), based at City Dock, offers several options. Visitors can enjoy narrated cruises focusing on the ecology and scenery of the Severn River, or travel out on the bay to the Thomas Point Lighthouse.

ACCOMMODATIONS
Annapolis has dozens of B&Bs and historic inns, as well as larger hotel chains. One unusual option is to spend the night aboard a yacht in the harbor. Be warned: The prices in Annapolis are not for the faint of heart. Here are a few select lodgings.

$50-100
One of the least expensive lodgings in town, with the added benefit of being very close to breakfast (included in the price of lodging), is the **Scotlaur Inn** (165 Main St., 410/268-5665, www.scotlaurinn.com, $85–125). Ten basic, neatly furnished guestrooms with private baths are owned and operated by "Uncle Teddy," the zippy proprietor of Chick and Ruth's Delly. The inn is above the restaurant, so nourishment is just a short tumble down the stairs, 24/7.

$100-150
Gibson's Lodgings of Annapolis (110 Prince
George St., 410/268-5555, www.gibsons lodgings.com, Apr.–Nov., $139–249, $179 average) are actually three separate homes surrounding a courtyard parking lot (free parking). The two-story stucco Berman House has eight guestrooms sharing four baths, plus one guestroom with a private bath; it's also wheelchair-accessible. The Lauer House combines modern architecture with the style of earlier times and offers two suites, plus four rooms with private baths. The Patterson House features two guestrooms with private baths and four guestrooms sharing two baths, two parlors, and a formal dining room. This Georgian townhouse with a Victorian facade once served

I HEAR YOU CALLING ME

The Maryland Inn was built on the front part of a lot deeded to the Annapolis Town Drummer in 1772. The Town Drummer held a position unique to Maryland. His function was much like that of the Town Crier, except that he conveyed public information through a complex variety of drumbeats. In Annapolis, one of his tasks was to call the General Assembly to session. If a member failed to appear by the third drumroll, he was fined 100 pounds of tobacco. William Butterfield, who performed the tasks of the Town Drummer during the 1750s, was paid five pounds sterling per year for his efforts.

as home to Richard Hill, first naval officer of the port of Annapolis in 1681. All guests enjoy a full continental breakfast.

The **State House Inn** (25 State Cir., 410/990-0024, www.statehouseinn.com, $139–209) is also across from the colonial-era capitol building on State Circle—it sounds busy, but it's not, as everything in Annapolis remains on a horse-and-buggy scale. The completely renovated and updated inn is of the same period as the State House; each of the seven rooms has a private phone and TV, and a whirlpool bath, regular bath, or shower. All rooms are beautifully decorated in period style, and a continental breakfast is offered each morning in the parlor.

❰ **Historic Inns of Annapolis** (58 State Cir., 410/263-2641 or 800/847-8882, www.annapolisinns.com, $129–219) is made up of three 18th-century buildings. The Governor Calvert House (58 State Cir.) is the check-in point for all the facilities. This 54-room lodging was built for a colonial governor who wanted a short commute (the capitol is across the street). He was also quite an innovator. Archaeological research on the site uncovered a hypocaust, a heating system of Roman origins: a fire built in one end of a series of brick chan-

nels heated air that flowed under the buildings, warming floors and greenhouses. Other lodgings include the 26-room Robert Johnson House (23 State Cir.) and the 44-room Maryland Inn (16 Church Cir.). "Elegant" best describes the accommodations; all rooms have been carefully refurbished and upgraded (cable TV, free movies, and private baths are standard) and are individually decorated with period antiques. Airport transportation, laundry, and valet parking are available for an extra fee; there is no overnight parking in the immediate area. The historic inns are in the middle of the action—everything in Annapolis is a short stroll away. The **Treaty of Paris Restaurant** continues the upscale 18th-century theme—it's in the Maryland Inn (the inns also feature a pub, Drummer's Lot, and the King of France Tavern). Packages and discounts are available.

In Eastport, the **Inn at Horn Point** (100 Chesapeake Ave., 410/268-1126, www.inathornpoint.com, $139–239) is a 1902 Victorian converted into a four-guestroom, one-suite B&B. Each of the rooms—some named after famous yachts—has a private bath with clawfoot tub and shower, plus an Internet hookup. A full breakfast is served. Onsite parking is a plus; most attractions, restaurants, and nightlife are just a short stroll away. A water taxi stand is also a favored option, and you will find one within three blocks. Rates vary depending on season and room, and rates are based on a two-night stay.

$150-250

❰ **The Inn at Spa Creek** (417 Severn Ave., 410/263-8866 or toll-free 877/269-8866, www.innatspacreek.com, $160–250 Apr.–Dec., discounted rates Jan.–Mar.) is also over the bridge in the Eastport section of town. If you're a walker, you'll find the distance to downtown just right; parking is available, a plus in a small town with few and expensive options. The inn itself is unusual: It's a very modern, airy, bright building in a colonial haven. The interior calls to mind a great ship on the sea, and it's easy to imagine standing at the bow next to the railing on the upper deck (especially after a good, strong cup of coffee served a few steps away in the open kitchen). Three rooms, all with private baths, range from a spacious twin to a luxurious suite. The Garden View has a private entrance. Room rates include breakfast and are based on a two-night stay.

The **William Page Inn Bed & Breakfast** (8 Martin St., 410/626-1506, www.williampage inn.com, $140–250) is just two blocks from the waterfront, right near the Naval Academy. The 1908 building has been cheerfully renovated, and three of the bright, airy rooms have private baths, while two share a bath. Breakfast and free off-street parking are included in the room rate.

On the Water: The *Schooner Woodwind* (near the Marriott, 80 Compromise St., 410/263-7837, www.schooner-woodwind.com, $265) is a 74-foot wooden sailing schooner that offers four staterooms with two shared heads (toilets), plus an evening sail. The boat is available on Saturday night from the first weekend in May to the last weekend of September. Book ahead—the overnights often sell out early in the year.

FOOD
American
Annapolis has more places to eat than the food court at the Great Mall of America. Most are open every day, and some provide evening entertainment. Here are a few, tried and true.

Storm Brothers Ice Cream Factory (130 Dock St., 410/263-3376, www.stormbros.com, summer hours 11 A.M.–9 P.M. daily) has been around since 1977, started by a couple of ambitious young brothers and financed by the local auctioneer. This is the place to stop for a cool cone of locally made Moose Tracks or Muddy Sneakers ice cream (or both, what the heck), all at decent prices. Lick and look at the boats passing by.

49 West Coffeehouse (49 West St., 410/626-9796, www.49westcoffeehouse.com, 7:30 A.M.–midnight Sun.–Thurs., until 2 A.M. Fri.–Sat., $5–19) offers breakfast, lunch, and dinner, plus live music—classical to jazz—and a continually changing art exhibit. The light gourmet fare, full bar, and coffee and tea selection encourage lingering, as does the plethora of newspapers and books to enjoy.

Chick & Ruth's Delly (165 Main St., 410/269-6737, www.chickandruths .com, 6:30 A.M.–11:30 P.M. Sun.–Thurs., 6:30 A.M.–12:30 A.M. Fri.–Sat., $4–20) is a local institution. Chick and Ruth Levitt started a sandwich shop in 1965, and expanded the menu over the years to include breakfast, lunch, and dinner for both the early and late crowds. Many residents grew up on messy Delly pastrami sandwiches, and pictures of local and national celebrities decorate the walls. The specialty sandwiches are named for politicians: The "Robert Ehrlich" (former MD governor) is a crab-cake wrap with romaine for $8.99. Traditional Jewish deli foods anchor the menu, along with everything else that can be cooked in a hurry—the milkshakes are excellent. If you're real good, you'll get a visit from "Uncle Teddy," Levitt family scion, who began working behind the counter at age 10.

The Market House on City Dock, on the waterfront at the base of Main Street (25 Market Pl.), offers a number of options. Though the market house isn't big, it holds a lot of variety: a delicatessen, a sandwich shop, a raw bar, a fish market, a poultry seller, a pizza place, a fruit market, and an ice cream shop are among the purveyors. The market is open 9 A.M.–6 P.M. Monday–Thursday, 9 A.M.–7 P.M. Saturday and Sunday May–October; and 9 A.M.–6 P.M. daily November–April, except 9 A.M.–3 P.M. Tuesday.

One of my favorite places in Annapolis, the **Ram's Head Tavern/Fordham Brewing Co.** (33 West St., 410/268-4545, www.rams headtavern.com, lunch and dinner daily, brunch Sun., $6–22) features great, sophisticated pub food and brews. The shrimp dishes and hamburgers are equally good, and the dining area is divided into several rooms, so you never feel crowded, no matter how busy it gets. This is the home of the Fordham Brewing Company, and their excellent brews (produced with equipment imported from Germany) are featured among the 170 served. Part of the tavern is sectioned off for stage shows. Past performers include the Fabulous Thunderbirds blues band, the Dukes of Dixieland from New

Orleans, and comedian Kevin Meaney; ticket prices range from $10 to $40.

International

For something a little more exotic, try **Nikko** (189A Main St., 410/267-6688, lunch and dinner daily, lunch $5–9, dinner $11–22). It offers traditional dishes such as tempura and gyoza at good prices, but the main focus is on quick-grilled seafood and meats. As you would expect, the sushi is morning-port fresh. Good lunch specials are also available.

Joss Café and Sushi Bar (195 Main St., 410/263-4688, lunch and dinner daily) also serves traditional dishes such as tempura, teriyaki, sukiyaki, sushi, and sashimi, and you can wash it all down with sake and beer. Prices range from $3.50 for individual sushi to $22 for a full meal.

Farther down the road, **India's** (257 West St., 410/263-7900, www.indiasofannapolis .com, $8–23) serves tandoori (clay oven) specialties, curries, and a wide variety of East Indian foods. The $8.95 buffet lunch offered 11:30 a.m.–2:30 p.m. Monday–Friday is popular, and dinner is also available daily. The food is both tasty and authentic.

Seafood

The *Baltimore Sun, Baltimore Magazine,* and *Bon Appétit* all give **C̄ Carrol's Creek** (410 Severn Ave., Eastport, 410/263-8102, www.carrolscreek .com, lunch 11:30 a.m.–4 p.m. and dinner 5–10 p.m. Mon.–Sat., brunch 10 a.m.–1:30 p.m. and dinner 3–10 p.m. Sun., $25) high marks for seafood, grilled fish, steaks, and chops. In warm weather, the harbor view from the deck is peerless. The sea scallops in shredded phyllo dough on wilted spinach are especially good. The restaurant has its own parking lot.

Though it's not in Annapolis proper—it's on the other side of the Naval Academy bridge on Mill Creek, **Cantler's Riverside Inn** (458 Forest Beach Rd., 410/757-1311, www.cantlers .com, lunch and dinner daily, $7–30) is worthy of mention for the freshness and quality of its seafood. The main kitchen serves lunch from 11 a.m. and full dinners until 11 p.m.

weekdays, then continues to offer a limited menu until midnight on Friday and Saturday. Cantler's brings seafood in on its own boats; the hard-shell crabs compete with the view. Many patrons arrive by boat and berth for the evening in one of the local marinas.

INFORMATION

For further information on activities and attractions in Annapolis and Anne Arundel County, contact the **Annapolis and Anne Arundel County Conference and Visitors Bureau** (26 West St., Annapolis, MD 21401, 888/302-2852, www.visit-annapolis.org).

GETTING AROUND
By Car

Most parking meters in town accept coins for two hours, and meter maids are vigilant. City garages are open 24/7; $1.25 per hour up to eight hours. The two largest garages are Gotts Court on Calvert Street between West Street and North West Street, and Noah Hillman on Duke of Gloucester Street across from Market Street.

By Bus

Annapolis offers excellent public transit via **ARTMA** bus and trolley. Buses operate 6 a.m.–7 p.m. Monday–Saturday and limited routes 10 a.m.–6 p.m. Sunday. Buses travel around old town and out to the Riva Road shopping mall and other outlying points. Base fare is $1 (exact change), and transfers are free. Trolleys run 6:30 a.m.–8 p.m. Monday–Friday and 10 a.m.–6 p.m. weekends from the Stadium Parking Lot on Rowe Boulevard, and from the Gotts Court garage by the visitors center to downtown Annapolis. Bus and trolley fares and transfers are interchangeable.

By Water

Jiffy Water Taxi (410/263-0033 or VHF Ch. 68) originates from the city dock and makes various stops in the harbor. The taxi operates 9:30 a.m.–11 p.m. Monday–Thursday, 9:30 a.m.–1 a.m. Friday, 9 a.m.–1 a.m. Saturday, and 9 a.m.–11 p.m. Sunday mid-May–Labor Day. Rates are $2–4.50, depending on destination.

Greater Anne Arundel County

It's easy to think of Anne Arundel County as only Annapolis, but there are a few interesting places to visit outside the scenic state capital—especially if you love to exercise your mind by examining an archeological site, relax on the beach, knock back a knockwurst next to someone in lederhosen (let's polka!), or watch knights knock each other off horses. You'll need a car to get around, as these destinations are widely scattered within the county.

SIGHTS
London Town

This archeological site (839 Londontown Rd., Edgewater, 410/222-1919, www.historiclondontown.com, 10 A.M.–4 P.M. Tues.–Sat., noon–4 P.M. Sun., $7) was once an important tobacco-shipping center and served as the county seat 1684–1695. House tours are given hourly, and there's a museum shop on the premises.

After the town reached its zenith in the 1730s, shipping and industry began to move elsewhere. By the end of that century, little remained of London Town. Today, it's the largest archaeological investigation in the state. The site features the William Brown House, an elegant dwelling built in 1760, with an eight-acre woodland garden.

Parks and Trails

Sandy Point State Park (1100 East College Pkwy., 410/974-2149, $4) is a day-use park at the terminus of the William Preston Lane Jr. Memorial Bridge (the Bay Bridge), seven miles east of Annapolis off U.S. 50/301. The park is surrounded on three sides by water. Swimming, fishing, crabbing, boating, and wind-surfing are popular on the park's beaches, which have lifeguards on duty from Memorial Day to Labor Day. The park provides several launching ramps and a concession for bait and tackle; rowboats and motorboats are available for rent. Two trails and miles of waterfront are ideal for hiking and migratory bird viewing.

Thomas Point State Park, at the end of Thomas Point Road, is almost like a private club. Closed gates bar the way at the entry point of the park (they look locked, but they're not). The signs that say "permit required" refer to an annual parking permit limited to 60 per year for repeat users—usually anglers who come for a few of the rockfish (striped bass) that begin life in one of the 150 tributaries of the Chesapeake Bay. However, occasional day users who wish to picnic and enjoy the park's short trails and a view of Thomas Point's eight-sided lighthouse (a little more than one mile out in the bay)—probably the most photographed lighthouse in the bay, and the last to be officially manned—are not charged. Be warned: There are only a few parking spaces, and they are gone early in the day during the summer. The park closes at sunset.

The Baltimore-Annapolis Trail (www.dnr.state.md.us/greenways/b&a_trail.html), a 13.3-mile, 10-foot-wide paved trail, runs from Glen Burnie to Annapolis. Walkers, runners, bicyclists, and equestrians are all welcome to use the 2 percent–grade trail. In Glen Burnie, the northern terminus, the trail is accessed off I-97 (exit 15 to Dorsey Rd.). Turn right onto Route 648 (Baltimore-Annapolis Blvd.), then take the first right after the second traffic light. There is free parking in the garage above the theater. The southern terminus is in Arnold. Take Rte. 50 to exit 27 toward the Naval Academy. Parking is 0.1 mile along on the right, on Boulters Way. Call 410/222-6244 for a map and other access points on the trail.

◖ Blob's Park Biergarten

Dust off those short leather pants and prepare for some frivolous footwork (8024 Blob's Park Rd. at Rte. 175 and Washington Rd., Jessup, 410/799-0155, www.blobspark.com, 7 P.M.–midnight Fri.–Sat., 2–8 P.M. Sun.). This is a fun place to spend an evening, especially on the weekends, when singles and families hop and twirl to live polka bands. Blob's began in 1933, when Max Blob built a beer garden for his friends on his farm; family members continue to run the business, which expanded into a big new building in the mid-1970s. Blob's serves dinner nightly, and the fare is traditional German at traditional prices: sauerbraten and dumplings ($7.50), bockwurst, bratwurst, and knockwurst plates ($6.50 each), and sandwiches ($3.50 or less). Beer? Of course—more than 70 brands to choose from! The service isn't fancy and the seating is family-style, but the crowd (with many people dressed in Polish or German costumes) is happy. Plan to eat early on nights when the band plays—the kitchen closes around 8 P.M. to make way for some serious dancing. Now get out there and POLKA!

Medieval Times Dinner & Tournament

If you prefer your dinner served by wenches, try this place (7000 Arundel Mills Cir., at Arundel Mills Mall, Hanover, 888/935-6878, www.medievaltimes.com, dinner daily, $50 adults, $37 children ages 12 and under), an entertainment/dinner concept venue. The setting is the 11th century, and m'lord and his lady are served a four-course meal while knights on specially bred Andalusian horses joust and whack each other with swords, all in good fun. Reservations required.

Ellicott City

Ellicott City is a charming small town in Howard County, busy with visitors seeking relief from the steamy city during the warm months—and has been since H. L. Mencken's time. New shops mix with good restaurants and historic attractions to provide an afternoon's entertainment. Most of the addresses listed are on Main Street, which is about five blocks long. In spite of its size, the town has a parking fine system that can only be described as diligent. The Howard County Visitor Information Center (8267 Main St.) has an excellent flyer called "Smart Parking"—it might save you a buck or two—or visit www.ellicottcity.net/tourism/parking for current information.

SIGHTS
B&O Railroad Station Museum

The station (2711 Maryland Ave., 410/461-1945, www.ecborail.org, Weds.–Sun. 11 A.M.–4 P.M., $5 adults) will delight history and rail fans with its sound and light show featuring a 40-foot-long scale model of the first 13 miles of passenger railroad in the United States (from Baltimore to Ellicott City—making this the oldest standing station in America). In addition, a living history program presented by costumed docents takes place in the restored rooms of the 1830 building and 1927 caboose.

The museum presents special events throughout the year, such as the Holiday Model Train Exhibit, late November–January.

Patapsco Female Institute Historic Park

An active archaeological site (3691 Sarah's Ln., 410/465-8500, www.patapscofemale institute.org, 1–4 P.M. Sun. Apr.–Oct., $4 adults), Patapsco was one of the nation's first women's facilities that educated girls ages 12–18 in music, languages, history, and the sciences. The institute was founded in 1837 and became Maryland's most prestigious school for young ladies during the 1840s and 1850s. A key factor in the success of Patapsco was the appointment of Almira Hart Lincoln Phelps as principal. A liberated woman by the standards of any age, Ms. Phelps wrote textbooks on chemistry, biology, botany, physics, and geology for secondary schools and colleges, and turned a portion of the fortune she made back into the institute. She disdained an ordinary "finishing school" education and insisted that the institute prepare the girls to earn a living. The school continued until 1891, but competition from public schools, which were developed in the late 1860s, finally forced it to close.

Today, elevated walkways lead visitors

THE ROAD TO ELLICOTT CITY

Like other well-to-do Baltimoreans in the late 19th century, writer H. L. Mencken's family would spend the warm summer months in the vacation haven of Ellicott City – not only to escape the heat, but also to avoid the frequent urban infestations of yellow fever. Mencken remembers the journey to their holiday home in his childhood memoir, *Happy Days:*

From our house in Hollins Street to Ellicott City was but ten miles by the old National Pike, but the road had no surface save bare rock and there were four or five toll-gates and six or seven immense hills along the way, so no one ever drove it if the business could be avoided. One of the hills was so steep and so full of hair-pin bends that it was called the Devil's Elbow. A hay-wagon coming up would take half a day to cover the mile and a half from bottom to top, and sometimes a Conestoga wagon from Western Maryland (there were still plenty of them left in the 1880s) got stuck altogether, and had to be rescued by the plow-horses of the adjacent farmers. At intervals of a mile or so along the road there were old-time coaching inns, and they were still doing a brisk trade in 25-cent country dinners and 5-cent whiskey.

through the 8,000-square-foot granite Greek Revival structure, and the grounds are being redesigned as 19th-century formal gardens. The school is a short (but very steep) walk from Main Street in Ellicott City. Take Church Road from Main Street to the dead-end at Sarah's Lane; autos may turn left and park in the courthouse parking lot. The visitors center is in the pretty, renovated 1837 yellow building, Mount Ida, across from the courthouse. During open hours, two guided tours are available at 1:30 and 3 P.M. Admission includes a video tour of historic Mount Ida and a guided tour of the site. Patapsco hosts several events throughout the year, such as Victorian teas and period fashion shows. Call for more information.

Other Historic Sights

Thomas Isaac's Log Cabin, on the west end of the town's Main Street, is the oldest surviving structure in Ellicott City, built circa 1780 (410/313-1413, www.thomasisaaclogcabin.net, 1–6 P.M. Fri.–Sat., noon–5 P.M. Sun., free).

If touring historic buildings is among your interests, make sure to plan ahead and book visits (by appointment only) to the **Ellicott City Colored School** (excellent overview of Black American history in the county, 410/313-1428) and the **Ellicott City Fire Station** (artifacts from Ellicott City's fiery past, 410/313-1413).

SHOPPING

Ellicott City features dozens of shopping opportunities along Main Street, mainly for collectibles and antiques. **Retropolitan** (8006 Main St.), **Ellicott's Country Store** (8180 Main St.), and **Joan Eve** (8018 Main St.) are just a few. For multiple dealers in the same location, try **Antique Depot** (3720 Maryland Ave.).

Fine arts aren't left behind at **Galerie Elan** (8090 Main St.) and **Kushnir/Taylor Art Gallery** (8289 Main St.), a shop with branches in Washington, D.C., and New York, featuring paintings by American artists. **Oh My Word** (8191 Main St.) represents more than 42 calligraphers—visitors can have poems, sayings, and original writing custom-designed.

RECREATION

The Howard County Tourism Council Visitor Information Center (8267 Main St., Ellicott City, 410/313-1900 or 800/288-8747, www.visithowardcounty.com) gives "ghost tours" of Ellicott City on Friday and Saturday evenings April–November. Local shop owners reveal eyewitness accounts of recent spooky activity.

FOOD

Main Street and the surrounding streets are lined with plenty of cafés and eateries. Here are a few.

Cafés

A café with light meals, **《 Bean Hollow** (8059 Main St., 410/465-0233, breakfast and lunch daily, $4–15) is a good place to stop downtown. The café roasts its own coffee and offers 30 varieties.

American

The Tiber River Tavern (3733 Old Columbia Pike, 410/750-2002, www.tiberrivertavern.com, lunch and dinner daily, $15–28) is in an old stable just a short walk from Main (though it is uphill). The food is a combination of continental and American specializing in seafood, and the decor is charming. The bar is a popular spot at night.

Ellicott Mills Brewing Company (8303 Main St., 410/313-8141, www.ellicottmills brewing.com, lunch and dinner daily, open until 2 A.M. Fri.–Sat., $12) offers a spate of its own brews, strictly produced within the confines of the Bavarian purity law, *Reinheitsgebot,* established in 1516—the law states that all beer must be brewed from only four ingredients: water, malt, hops, and yeast. The brewmeister, Martin Virga, trained in Munich and attributes the quality of his beer to the low mineral content of local water. To accompany this excellent beer, chef Rick Winter creates an eclectic menu with such unusual features as wild boar in beer sauce, buffalo strip steak, and ven-

ison sausage. Yes, they have chicken salad, too. Brewery tours are available by appointment.

Though it's a few miles west of Ellicott City off Frederick Road, **The Crab Shanty** (3410 Plum Tree Dr., 410/465-9660, www.crab shanty.com, lunch Mon.–Fri. and dinner daily, brunch Sun., $12–30) has remained a popular choice for seafood lovers since 1981. The prices for crab and other seafood are reasonable, and specials are offered every night.

Alexandra's (in Turf Valley Resort, 2700 Turf Valley Rd., 410/465-1500, lunch and dinner Mon.–Sat., brunch and dinner Sun., $12–35) is also some distance from downtown Ellicott City—a few miles west of the Crab Shanty off U.S. 40. But if elegant dining is what you're looking for, this is the place. American dishes—steak, seafood, and poultry—with an international flair are served along with a view of the landscaped grounds.

For a more casual atmosphere in the same location, try **Terrace on the Green** (breakfast, lunch, and dinner, $6–18) for big sandwiches, soups, salads, and really good burgers.

Continental

《 Tersiguel's (8293 Main St., 410/465-4004, www.tersiguels.com, dinner daily, brunch Sun., $15–36) is a *rara avis*—an award-winning French country restaurant actually in the country. Regular entrées and a prix fixe menu are served at dinner nightly. Tersiguel's receives consistently high marks from visitors for both the food—which is local and fresh—and the service.

Greater Howard County

The bucolic, historic, and scientific meet in the outer ranges of the county, which includes a government site open to the public, beautiful parks and gardens, art, excellent restaurants, and shopping in an old mill site.

SIGHTS
《 Cryptologic Museum

Still have that Captain Marvel decoder ring?

Then the National Security Agency's museum (Colony 7 Rd. at intersection of Rtes. 295 and 32, Fort Meade exit off Rte. 32, 301/688-5849, www.nsa.gov/museum, 9 A.M.–4 P.M. Mon.– Fri., 10 A.M.–2 P.M., first and third Sat. each month, free) is for you. The displays are in a branch of the agency; inside exhibits discuss cracking and creating codes. There's a variety of exhibits, including information on the codes

held within slave quilts and two Cray supercomputers (the great-granddaddy of all our
desktops). Adjacent to the museum is the National Vigilance Park, which showcases two re-
connaissance aircraft used for secret missions:
the RU 8D represents the Army Airborne Sig
nal Intelligence contribution in Vietnam, and
the C-130 memorializes an Air Force aircraft
shot down over Soviet Armenia during the
Cold War.

Benjamin Banneker
Historical Park

This park is located just north of Ellicott
City on the original homestead of "the first
Negro Man of Science" (300 Oella Ave., Oella,
410/887-1081, Tues.–Sat. 10 A.M.–4 P.M., $3
donation appreciated). Benjamin Banneker's
grandmother was a maid in England who emigrated to Maryland as an indentured servant.
When she finished her seven years of bond-
age, she bought a farm along with two slaves
to help her work it; she eventually freed both
slaves and married one, Robert Bannaky. They
had several children, among them a daughter,
Mary. When Mary Bannaky grew up, she
bought a slave named Robert, married him,
and had several children, including Benjamin
in 1731. The family farm was known as "Bannaky Springs" due to the freshwater springs
on the land. Robert Bannaky (he took her last
name) used ditches and little dams to control
the water from the springs for irrigation, so
that crops flourished even in dry spells.

Benjamin's grandmother taught him and his
brothers to read. There was no school in the
area until a Quaker teacher came to live in the
Patapsco Valley. He set up a school for boys
that Benjamin attended (it was here that he
changed the spelling of his name to Banneker).
He learned to write and do simple arithmetic.

When Banneker was 21, he saw a patent
watch for the first time; he took the watch
apart and carved watch parts out of wood
to make a clock of his own, the first striking clock to be made completely in America.
Banneker's clock was so precise it struck every
hour, on the hour, for 40 years. After Bannek-

er's success with his wooden watch, he worked
as a watch-and-clock repairman and helped
Joseph Ellicott, one of the founders of Ellicott City, build a complex clock. They became
friends. Joseph and his brother George lent
Banneker books and scientific instruments,
and Banneker taught himself astronomy and
advanced mathematics.

After Banneker's parents died, they left him
the family farm. He built a "work cabin" with
a skylight on the property to study the stars and
make calculations, compiling information and
publishing the results in six almanacs. In 1791,
Major Andrew Ellicott, George Ellicott's cousin,
asked Banneker to help him survey the "Federal
Territory" (the section of Maryland proposed
for Washington, D.C.). Banneker and Ellicott
worked closely with the notoriously foul-tem-
pered architect in charge, Pierre L'Enfant, until
L'Enfant was suddenly dismissed from the project. When L'Enfant left, he took the partially
finished plans with him. Banneker re-created
the plans from memory and expanded them to
design the city. He continued to study and record his astronomical observations until he died
on October 26, 1806.

The historical park is composed of a museum building with artifacts and biographi-
cal material and a main gallery with changing
displays; in addition, trail guides lead walking
tours in the park's wooded 142 acres.

The African Art
Museum of Maryland

Dedicated to collecting, exhibiting, and preserving the art of Africa, this small museum/
gallery (5430 Vantage Point Rd., Columbia,
410/730-7105, www.africanartmuseum.org)
offers an excellent opportunity to enjoy the di-
versity of African art and culture in a pleasant
setting. Exhibits contain traditional art forms
such as masks, carvings, and shell work, but
Doris Ligon, the director, is equally interested
in modern African artists. Recently, the museum featured the colorful and ornate tapestries of Abdoulaye Kasse, master weaver from
Senegal, with a special appearance by the artist
(and his loom). Works by contemporary artists

reflect the sophistication and enormous variation found in one of the world's largest continents. This museum is a rare find.

SHOPPING
Savage Mill

This unusual shopping area (8600 Foundry St., Savage, 800/788-6455, 10 A.M.–6 P.M. Mon.–Wed., 10 A.M.–9 P.M. Thurs.–Sat., 11 A.M.–6 P.M. Sun.) started out as a textile mill complex in 1820. Today, it consists of nine remaining buildings that are used as an upscale marketplace with more than 50 specialty shops, art and craft studios, and dealers of high-quality antiques and collectibles. In addition, the nearby Manor House (built in 1840 for the mill's first manager) is maintained as a permanent decorators' showplace, highlighting items from the market's merchants. Rams Head Tavern of Annapolis has a branch in the mill. While you're in the area, take a look at the **Bollman Truss Railroad Bridge,** right next to the mill. It's one of only two iron semi-suspension bridges in the world. Built in 1869, it's now used as a footbridge spanning the Little Patuxent River.

Columbia Mall

Columbia is a planned community made up of one very large shopping area (10300 Little Patuxent Pkwy., 410/730-3300, www.themall incolumbia.com) and several "villages," each centered around a small shopping and restaurant complex. Columbia Mall has every major mall store, plus most of the smaller ones—there may be sales, but this isn't an outlet center. The area has plenty of restaurants, too.

RECREATION
Patapsco Valley State Park

Set in a largely undeveloped area along the Patapsco River, the park follows the narrow river valley a few miles west of Baltimore and runs the entire length of the city, from Liberty Heights Road in the north almost to the airport in the south. In an area consisting of one housing development after another, the relative wilderness comes as a welcome surprise.

Because the park covers so much territory, there are several park entrances. The Avalon–Glen Artney–Orange Grove area, the oldest developed area in the park, offers hiking, picnicking, equestrian trails, fishing, canoeing, and ball fields. It's located off Route 1 (exit 3); drive toward Elkridge and make a left on South Street, the first street after crossing the river. The park entrance is on the left. The Hilton area offers one of the park's camping facilities, in addition to hiking, picnicking, and a playfield; from I-695, take exit 13 (Frederick Rd.) through Catonsville to South Rolling Road. In 150 feet, turn left onto Hilton Avenue and follow it 1.5 miles to the park entrance on the right. Hollofield (exit 15 off I-695, to U.S. 40 west, approx. two miles to the park entrance on right) features a scenic overlook, picnicking, fishing, and family camping. Additional camping may be found at the McKeldin area, along with hiking and equestrian trails, picnicking, fishing, and a ballfield. To get there from I-695, take I-70 to Marriotsville Road (exit 83). The park entrance is about for miles along on the right. The Pickall area has 11 picnic pavilions, a scenic trail, ball fields, and a playground; to get there from I-695, take Security Boulevard (exit 17) 0.5 mile to North Rolling Road, then turn left. The park entrance is approximately 1.5 miles along on the left.

Overall, the park features six hiking trails, ranging in distance from 1.2–3 miles and in difficulty from mild to strenuous. Naturalists lead informative hikes during the warmer months, including an especially popular "light of the moon" walk several times a season. There is no charge for general park use, but the 73 campsites, operated from the first Friday in April to the last weekend in October, vary in price depending on amenities. Reservations may be made by calling 888/432-2267. The Maryland Department of Natural Resources now has an online reservation system (http://reservations .dnr.state.md.us). For more information on the park and trails, contact Patapsco Valley State Park (8020 Baltimore National Pike, Ellicott City, MD 21043, 410/461-5005). Trail maps may also be ordered online at www.easycart

.net/MarylandDepartmentofNaturalResources/ Central_Maryland_Trail_Guides.html.

C Brighton Dam Azalea Garden

Recognized as one of Maryland's springtime showplaces, this garden sits on five acres next to the Tridelphia Reservoir and Brighton Dam, on Brighton-Clarksville Road (off Rte. 650) on the Montgomery County/Howard County border (301/774-9124, dawn–dusk, free). The gardens began in 1949 as a labor of love by Raymond Bellamy, late chairman of the Washington Suburban Sanitary Commission (WSSC); maintenance and improvement have been provided over the years by WSSC personnel. Ten Oaks Nursery in Clarksville donated more than 300 plants to supplement cuttings, and the garden now contains 22,000 azaleas, hybrids, and other spring-blooming plants. The display is best in May and June.

Golf

Fairway Hills Golf Course (5100 Columbia Rd., Columbia, 410/730-1112) and **Timbers at Troy** (6100 Marshalee Dr., Eldridge, 410/313-4653) are both 18-hole public courses.

ACCOMMODATIONS
Turf Valley Resort

Though the resort (2700 Turf Valley Rd., 410/465-1500, www.turfvalley.com, rooms, suites, and villas $150–500) is technically in Ellicott City, it's actually much closer to U.S. 40. It's an indulgence, and a great one. The elegantly landscaped property covers 1,000 acres and encompasses a hotel and spa, two restaurants, three superb golf courses (totaling 54 holes), a driving range, indoor and outdoor pools with whirlpool and steam room, tennis courts, volleyball, basketball and shuffleboard courts, and individual housing units. One luxury suite in the hotel could house a huge extended family—they could probably all take a whirlpool in the tub at the same time, too. Less expansive rooms are also available. Guests might feel guilty at their good fortune if the staff weren't so pleasant and accommodating, the food in the restaurants so wonderful, and the feeling of enjoyment so complete.

The spa uses Aveda natural personal products, and the staff is highly trained. Herbal wraps, massages, and facials are among the simpler offerings. One of the most complex is the Silk Body Polish, which consists of lying face-down on a table while an attendant rubs salt and pre-chosen aromatherapy oils into your skin, then operates a "Swiss hose" (essentially a hose full of holes) and a series of nozzles above you to swirl warm water continuously on your back and legs. The effect is one of being able to breathe underwater while being carried through a whirlpool. Afterward, you can hear the blood racing through your body for several minutes, and you have the sensation that you've never felt better in your life. The spa offers packages.

Turf Valley is central Maryland's only getaway spa, and it's first-rate. Fortunately, the tariff for all this smooth fun is frequently made more accessible by packages and overnight specials, particularly in the off-season (Nov.–Mar.). Call the resort for details. AAA/AARP and other discounts are available.

Camping

In addition to camping at Patapsco Valley State Park, **Ramblin' Pines** (801 Hoods Mill Rd., Woodbine, 410/795-5161 or 800/550-8733, www.ramblinpined.com) offers a full-service campground with full hookup sites, 30- and 50-amp electric, pull-through, and tent sites. In addition, the park has rustic cabin rentals, an activities building, a game room, a launderette, a dump station, and a general store. Onsite are a swimming pool, a catch-and-return fishing pond, a miniature golf course, and other recreational activities. There is a two-day minimum stay on weekends, and discounts are available for AARP, AAA, GoodSam, and other RV club members.

FOOD
American

Located in a lovely historic manor house, **Kings Contrivance Restaurant** (10150 Shaker Dr.,

410/995-0500, www.thekingscontrivance.com, lunch Mon.–Fri., dinner daily, $12–30) serves a sophisticated American menu with dishes such as roasted duck breast with orange-ginger sauce and pepita-crusted salmon.

History and elegance are inextricably bound in the C **Elkridge Furnace Inn** (5745 Furnace Ave., Elkridge, 410/379-9336, www.elkridge furnaceinn.com, lunch Tues.–Fri., dinner Tues.–Sat., $13–30). Nestled on the Patapsco River, the inn was first established as a tavern in 1744. An iron-smelting furnace was added around 1750, and in 1810, the Ellicott brothers, James and Andrew, modernized the iron-smelting furnace and constructed an elegant home next to the existing tavern. The house and inn are set on 16 acres graced by beautiful linden, holly, and magnolia trees. Chef-owner Dan Wecker has garnered a passel of awards for his menu, including *Wine Spectator*'s Award of Excellence and a Zagat rating of "Extraordinary." Lunch might include roast leg of lamb with scalloped potatoes Dauphinoise, or seafood crêpes Nantua: shrimp, scallops, and crab meat wrapped in crêpes and topped with a lobster sauce. Dinner features supreme de volaille Micronesia: boneless, skinless breast of chicken stuffed with toasted macadamia nuts and arugula, served with a fresh fruit salsa and herbed risotto; and a filet de porc aux abricots: medallions of pork tenderloin with grilled apricots and a spiced rum demi-glace. The wine list is on a par with the food, and Sunday brunch has been added to the mix.

International

Bombay Peacock Grill (10005 Old Columbia Rd., Columbia, 410/381-7111, www.bombay grill.com/columbia, lunch and dinner daily, $8–16) features pan-Indian cuisine with many vegetarian choices. Tandoori mixed grill and chickpea curry are favorites. Over the years, this has expanded into a chain, but this location is the original.

Columbia is home to another exceptional East Indian restaurant, **Mango Grove** (6365B Dobbin Rd., Dobbin Center, 410/884-3426, www.themangogrove.com, lunch and dinner Weds.–Sun., $8–17). This one has the added quality of being exclusively vegetarian, with an emphasis on Ayurvedic principles (the ancient healing/balancing system of India). It specializes in hearty South Indian dishes (characterized as meat-and-potatoes without the meat) and has gained such a reputation that Baltimoreans will make the trip down for a meal. It also opened a non-vegetarian carryout and Indian grocery nearby at **Curry N Spice** (6476, Unit 4, Dobbin Sq.).

Hunan Manor (7091 Deepage Dr., Columbia, 410/381-1134, lunch and dinner daily, $13) features a lengthy menu and is reputed to have the best hot-and-sour soup in Maryland.

INFORMATION

For Howard County and Ellicott City, call or stop by the **Howard County Tourism Council Visitor Information Center** (8267 Main St., Ellicott City, 410/313-1900 or 800/288-8747, www.visithowardcounty.com).

GETTING AROUND

The best way to get around widespread Howard County is by car. Ellicott City is small and Columbia is fairly compact, but the rest of the county is inaccessible by any other means. I-95 and Route 1 run south from Baltimore. U.S. 29 is central, and Routes 97 and 32 are the north–south roads in the western half of the county. U.S. 40 and I-70 run east–west from Baltimore.

Montgomery County

Starting with Takoma Park, the first Washington, D.C., "suburban development," the towns and villages around the capital city have expanded exponentially and grown together into a boundary-confused mega-suburb that surrounds the capital for nearly 20 miles in every direction. A few of the towns in this capital gateway area—chiefly Bethesda and Rockville—have identifiable centers, though the boundaries between Bethesda, Chevy Chase, and Silver Spring have long since disappeared. Beyond the farthest reaches of commuter growth, the county is dotted with pretty little towns and villages separated by green farmlands. The western section of Montgomery County along the Potomac is downright rural—something of a surprise after the upmarket sprawl of the capital gateway.

THE PRICE OF BEING A HEROINE

Women who move beyond traditional roles – no matter how humanitarian – have always been treated ambivalently by American society. Clara Barton was born on Christmas Day in 1821 and brought up with a sense of duty to humanity, and, for the era, a liberal education. She worked as a teacher, starting one of the first free schools in New Jersey. During the Civil War, she felt compelled to join other members of the U.S. Sanitary Commission to work on the battlefields of Manassas, Antietam, Fredericksburg, and elsewhere, earning herself the sobriquet "Angel of the Battlefield." Barton was reputed to have said, "Men have worshipped war till it has cost a million times more than the whole earth is worth... Deck it as you will, war is Hell. Only the desire to soften some of its hardships and allay some of its miseries ever induced me to face its pestilent and unholy breath."

After the war, Barton continued her charitable work and began to speak out and express her opinions and convictions – particularly about the enfranchisement of former slaves and her support for the growing feminist movement. "I must have been born believing in the full right of women to all privileges and positions which nature and justice accord her common with other human beings. Perfectly equal rights – human rights," she wrote.

In 1868, debilitated by years of toil during the Civil War and the conflict between Barton's personal belief in the equality of women and her culture, she suffered a bout of "hysteria;" her doctors recommended travel abroad. She journeyed to Europe and heard about the Red Cross established by the Treaty of Geneva some years before. She worked with the organization during the Franco-Prussian War and became determined to bring the Red Cross to the United States. She was confounded by 10 years of poor health, as well as public and government apathy – but by 1882, the U.S. Senate ratified the Treaty of Geneva, establishing the Red Cross in the United States, with Clara Barton as its founder and president.

In the last 15 years of her life, Barton purchased a barn in then-rural Glen Echo and used the space for Red Cross personnel and storage. At the age of 76, she directed relief on the battlefields of Cuba during the Spanish-American War. At that time, a faction in the Red Cross pressed for her resignation – they considered her a charismatic figurehead when the changing world required hard business sense and organization. She retired under protest and converted the Glen Echo barn into a spartan home for herself. Though bitter about being ousted from the organization she worked so hard to create, Barton continued her life's work by establishing the National First Aid Association of America to encourage emergency preparedness on the community level. She died in her Glen Echo home, where "the moon seemed always to be shining," in 1912.

SIGHTS

◖ Clara Barton National Historic Site

The world-renowned "Angel of the Battlefield" spent her last years here (5801 Oxford Rd. at MacArthur Blvd., Glen Echo, 301/320-1410, www.nps.gov/clba, 10 A.M.–4 P.M. daily, by guided tour on the hour only, free). The home, converted from a Red Cross warehouse, is preserved much as it was in Barton's day, when simplicity and shared work were the ideal for Barton and her coworkers. A truly remarkable and courageous woman, Barton never trained in any medical profession. She was a schoolteacher and clerk who found her calling among the dying and wounded of the Civil War and went on to create the American branch of the Red Cross—an emergency care organization previously developed on the battlefields of Europe—to serve in peacetime disasters such as the Johnstown, Pennsylvania, flood of 1889.

Glen Echo Park

© JOANNE MILLER

Glen Echo Park

Long a shadow of its former self, Glen Echo Park (MacArthur Blvd. and Goldsboro Rd., Glen Echo, 301/492-6282) began as a chautauqua, a center where people could participate in science, art, and literature. In 1899, it was converted to a full-scale amusement park with rides and a ballroom where Glenn Miller played (the Spanish Ballroom is now open for dancing on the weekends year-round). Few vestiges of the gaily colored amusement park remain in the peeling buildings and crumbling bumper car pavilion, but Glen Echo is on its way to becoming, once again, a center for learning and the arts, now that it's become part of the National Park System. For starters, the park's stunning 1921 Dentzel-carved **wooden carousel** (10 A.M.–2 P.M. Wed.–Thurs. and noon–6 P.M. Sat.– May–Sept., 10 A.M.–2 P.M. Wed.–Fri. July–Aug.) has been refurbished by volunteers. Professionals in fields ranging from performing and visual arts to consumer-oriented topics are repairing and revitalizing the buildings and, in exchange, opening the facilities to the public for classes, demonstrations, and performances. The Crystal Studio houses an artisan glassblowing shop, **Glassworks** (301/229-4184), which produces exquisite bowls and goblets; visitors are afforded a rare opportunity to see glass blown directly from the furnace in a time-honored tradition (definitely the place to be on a cold day). Shops and demonstration areas are open at different times. The NPS office is open 9 A.M.–5 P.M. daily. Picnic areas are first come, first served. There is a charge for the carousel, shows, and dances, but entry to the park, the demonstrations, and parking are free.

F. Scott and Zelda Fitzgerald Burial Place

Francis Scott Key Fitzgerald (named for his illustrious ancestor) and his glamorous wife traveled the world while writing the novels and stories that would make them both famous. He was an icon of the Jazz Age and died in Hollywood, California, in 1940—so why is he buried in Rockville? Fitzgerald's father's family had been residents of the Rockville area since the early 1800s, and their prodigal son visited

© JOANNE MILLER

F. Scott and Zelda Fitzgerald grave

the area many times. His father and mother joined an assortment of ancestors buried in the cemetery of St. Mary's Catholic Church, the oldest in Rockville (1817). Fitzgerald chose the little burial ground as the final resting place for his wife and himself after attending his father's funeral in 1931. The grave is just behind the small church. In *Tender Is the Night* (1934), Fitzgerald describes his protagonist's feelings at the burial of his own father: "It was very friendly leaving him there with all his relations around him.... Good-bye my father—good-bye all my fathers."

Once on the edge of town, St. Mary's is now in the midst of heavily traveled major roads. The church and cemetery are at 500 Veirs Mill Road (Rtc. 586) at the intersection with Rockville Pikc (Rte. 355), which becomes Hungerford Drive at the same intersection.

If you're in the mood to explore another interesting cemetery in the Rockville area, go to **Aspen Hill Pet Cemetery** (13630 Georgia Ave., entrance on Aspen Hill Rd.). One of the oldest pet cemeteries in the country, it was founded in the 1920s. The circle-eyed pooch, Jiggs, from *Our Gang,* at least one dog owned by J. Edgar Hoover, and Lyndon B. Johnson's beagle were all buried or cremated here.

George Meany Center for Labor Studies and Memorial Archives Library

This center (10000 New Hampshire Ave./Rte. 650, Silver Spring, 301/431-5451, www.nlc .edu/archives, 8:30 a.m.–4 p.m. Mon.–Tues. and Fri., 7:30 a.m.–6 p.m. Wed.–Thurs., free) is a division of the AFL-CIO labor organization. It consists of a campus concentrating on the study of labor and a library open to the public. A big bronze sculpture portraying a beefy, cigar-waving George Meany is in the library lobby—a powerful portrayal of the former plumber and leader of the American labor movement for 55 years. He was awarded the 1963 Presidential Medal of Freedom for his human rights work with "the people's lobby." The library features an exhibit on the history of the labor movement and the lives of working people, and, in addition, houses thousands of books, pamphlets, and other source materials that illuminate the history of every labor organization from Actors Equity to the United Textile Workers of America. The library periodically prepares special bibliographies on topics such as "Women at Work and in the Labor Movement." Anything you ever wanted to know about work in America and the world is here. Materials may be borrowed through interlibrary loan.

National Institutes of Health (NIH)

Both the NIH (Cedar Ln., Bethesda, 301/496-4000, www.nih.gov/about/visitor, campus map available online) and its nearby **National Library of Medicine** (8600 Rockville Pike, Bethesda, 301/594-5983) are free to visit and have something to offer visitors.

Try not to let the entrance procedures put you off. The NIH, like all federal government facilities, has instituted security measures to ensure the safety of employees, patients, and visitors. The NIH Visitor Information Center is in

Building 45 (Natcher Conference Center, Room 1AS-13, 45 Center Dr., on the NIH campus). However, by the time you read this book, construction may have been completed on a new NIH Gateway Center for the Bethesda campus. It will provide a central location for registering and orienting visitors and provide additional parking spaces outside the secured perimeter of campus. The center will consist of three facilities: a visitor/guest registration and badging center (Building 66); an underground parking garage for 350 cars (MLP-11); and a visitor vehicle inspection station (Building 66A).

Parking is limited. Visitors may enter with cars from the Rockville Pike at South Drive (Metro), which is open 24 hours a day, or from Old Georgetown Road at Center Drive (used primarily for commercial vehicles and visitors) from 5 A.M. to 2 P.M. (inbound traffic only) and from 2 P.M. to 7 P.M. (inbound and outbound traffic).

All visitor vehicles, including taxicabs, hotel and airport shuttles, and delivery trucks and vans will be inspected before being allowed on campus. Visitors will be asked to show one form of identification (a government-issued photo ID: driver's license, passport, green card, etc.) and to state the purpose of their visit. Be sure to allow extra time for this procedure. Visitors may also be required to pass through a metal detector and have their bags, backpacks, or purses inspected or X-rayed as they enter buildings.

The visitors center is open Monday–Friday 8:30 A.M.–4:30 P.M., except on federal holidays. It conducts a free general overview of the NIH and a tour of the Mark Hatfield Clinical Research Center at 11:00 A.M. on Monday, Wednesday, and Friday (call 301/496-1776 to reserve a spot). A photographic exhibit, "Nobel Laureates of the NIH" is on display at the visitors center, along with information on the NIH's origins.

The **National Library of Medicine** features changing exhibits on medicine (reading room open to the public 8:30 A.M.–5 P.M. Mon.–Fri., 8:30 A.M.–2 P.M. Sat.). One recent exhibit focused on asthma and included a stellar list of overachievers who suffered from the illness, among them Pliny the Elder (Roman historian), John Calvin (religious reformer), Ludwig van Beethoven (composer), Marcel Proust (author), Edith Wharton (author), and Che Guevara (revolutionary).

McCrillis Gardens

This five-acre, beautifully landscaped public garden seems miles away from the suburban hustle of Bethesda, even though it's minutes from the main street (6910 Greentree Rd., Bethesda, 301/962-1455, 10 A.M.–sunset, free). The Brookside Gardens School of Botanical Art and Illustration is on the premises in the McCrillis home, and student works may be on display to visitors. On-street parking is limited, so get there early. Peak bloom is the first week of May.

William McCrillis was special assistant to the Secretary of the Interior under three presidents, starting with Franklin Delano Roosevelt. As a hobby, he bred and developed an impressive array of azaleas and other shade plants. He

Mormon Temple in Kensington

© JOANNE MILLER

© JOANNE MILLER

White's Ferry

Virginia. Now a little provisions store operates on the Maryland side, and it rents canoes by the hour for a quiet trip up the Potomac. They'll arrange a shuttle pick-up with 48-hour notice (call 301/349-5200 for more information). The area is verdant, quiet, and isolated; a park with a picnic area and a boat launch abuts the ferry slip. These are all owned by the store and charge a small fee for use. The day I visited, a church was holding services there: A single baritone led the group in Spanish hymns, and little boys in suits and girls with white kerchiefs over their hair played games on the grass.

SHOPPING
Shopping Areas
Judging from the number of options for shopping in Montgomery County, residents have a great deal of time and money on their hands. The 10-mile stretch of road between Bethesda and Rockville is known locally as the **"miracle mile."** It's lined with shopping centers for every taste and budget, from G Street Fabrics in the Mid-Pike Plaza (11800 Rockville Pike), to Lord & Taylor and Bloomingdale's in the White Flint Center (11301 Rockville Pike).

Similar to New York's Fifth Avenue, the shops in Chevy Chase on **Wisconsin Avenue** at Bradley Boulevard house the most sophisticated national and international purveyors of clothing, jewelry, and accessories (think Ralph Lauren and Armani).

Specialty shops can also be found in historic communities such as Burtonsville, Damascus, Germantown, Kensington, and Poolesville. These quaint towns have a corner on antiques, especially the community of Kensington.

and his wife donated their home and the surrounding acreage to Maryland in 1978.

Washington, D.C., Temple
The soaring architecture of this Mormon Temple (9900 Stoneybrook Dr., Kensington, 301/588-0650, free) can be seen for miles in the lower county area. Though the temple is not open to the public, the extensive formal gardens are, and the grounds and building are especially festive during the Christmas holidays.

White's Ferry
White's Ferry (Rte. 107 to White's Ferry Rd., Dickerson, 301/349-5200, open daily year-round, $4–8) has been in operation since the early 1800s, when it was the only ferry that crossed the Potomac. Today, the *Jubal Early* takes cars and visitors across the river 5 A.M.–11 P.M., much as the mule-driven barges did in the early days of the republic. During the Civil War, the ferry's namesake, General Jubal Early, along with Robert E. Lee and J. E. B. Stewart, used the ferry to clandestinely transport troops from

Food Shops
Butler's Orchard (22200 Davis Mill Rd., Germantown, 301/972-3299) offers all manner of fruits and vegetables in season, as well as events from May to December, including hayrides, pony rides, a straw mountain, and plenty of peaches.

The Montgomery County Department of Economic Development (Agricultural Services Division, 18410 Muncaster Rd., Derwood, MD

CENTRAL MARYLAND

20855, 301/590-2823) publishes an annual **Montgomery County Farm Directory** (available online at www.montgomerycountymd.gov and at local libraries). More than 48 farms open their doors to the public. Fresh produce is for sale, and other activities such as hayrides, demonstrations, and music are also planned.

One unusual place to pick up supplies in Bethesda is the **Montgomery Farms Women's Cooperative Market** (7155 Wisconsin Ave., Bethesda, 301/652-2291, 7 A.M.–3 P.M. Wed.–Sat. year-round), which includes a farmers market 9 A.M.–5 P.M. on Sunday. An anachronism among downtown Bethesda's skyscrapers and modern development, this aged wooden building houses an old-fashioned produce, meat, and poultry market. Weather permitting, there's also an outdoor flea market Friday–Sunday.

RECREATION
C&O Canal National Historic Park

This park extends all the way from Washington, D.C., to Cumberland in the far west of Maryland (local access: 1057 Thomas Jefferson St. NW, Washington, D.C., 210/653-5190; Great Falls Tavern visitors center, 11710 MacArthur Blvd. near Falls Rd./Rte. 189, Potomac, 301/767-3714; or 40 W. Potomac St., Brunswick, 301/834-7100, dawn–dusk). A $5 fee is charged to enter the park by car; cyclists and walkers pay $3. Summer is a very busy time for this park, so plan accordingly.

The 184.5-mile Chesapeake & Ohio Canal National Historical Park trail officially begins at the tidewater lock near the Thompson Boat Center (by the intersection of Virginia Ave. and Rock Creek Pkwy.) in Washington, D.C. The trail meanders along and catches the towpath further on (for the best mile-marker-by-mile-marker description of the canal and its history, see *The C&O Canal Companion,* listed in the *Suggested Reading* list at the back of the book). Great Falls Park is between mile 14 and mile 15 of the canal. The Great Falls of the Potomac were the largest impediment to navigation on the river. The successful six-lock bypass (lock 15, at mile 13.6, is the first; lock 20, mile 14.4 at Great Falls, is

the last) built there became a tourist attraction at the outset of construction in 1828. The Great Falls Tavern, built to house and feed visitors, still stands and now serves to disseminate information on the canal and the area. There are several footpaths in the park: The path near lock 17 (mile 14.1) leads to Olmstead Island and the Great Falls Overlook; another, the Billy Goat trail (begins at mile 12.7), runs between the canal and river, and is an excellent way to see the geographical layout of the area. The locks and weirs are all operational at Great Falls, and it's a good place to see how the canal operated in its heyday. The NPS keeps a stable of six to eight mules of the type used to pull the canal boats on the towpaths, with occasional demonstrations. You can see them at the Great Falls Tavern visitors center.

Seneca Creek State Park

This park (11950 Clopper Rd., Gaithersburg, 301/924-2127, open daily Apr.–Oct. for $2–3 per person, open daily Nov.–March for free) is a rural enclave on the west side of the county. Its 6,000-acre grounds and Clopper Lake offer hiking, biking, fishing, and canoeing. This park also has several areas designated for hunting during the appropriate season. Trails wind past a historic mill and stone quarry, and there's a Frisbee golf course and playground. This is a day-use park—no camping allowed.

Riley's Lockhouse (at lock 24/mile 22.7), on the C&O canal nearby, is the only original one left on the canal. It's at the end of Riley's Lock Road (on the Potomac), off River Road in the southernmost part of Seneca Creek State Park. The lockhouse is open to the public for tours 1–4 P.M. Saturday March–November.

Brookside Gardens

Located in Wheaton Regional Park (1800 Glenallan Ave., Wheaton, 301/962-1400, free), these gardens consist of 50 acres of display plantings, including a Japanese-style garden, a children's garden, and fragrance garden. There is also a conservatory for tropical plants. The gardens are open sunrise–sunset daily (except Christmas Day). The conservatory is open 10 A.M.–5 P.M., and the visitors center 9 A.M.–5 P.M. The gar-

MONTGOMERY COUNTY PUBLIC GOLF COURSES

Tournament golf is one of the most popular pastimes in Montgomery County. Home to the annual Kemper Open, the county hosted the U.S. Open and the Kemper back-to-back in 1997. These courses are open to the public:

FALLS ROAD – 18 HOLES
10800 Falls Rd., Potomac
301/299-5156

HAMPSHIRE GREENS – 18 HOLES
616 Firestone Dr., Ashton/Sandy Spring
301/476-7999

LAYTONSVILLE – 18 HOLES
7130 Dorsey Rd., Laytonsville
301/948-5288

LITTLE BENNETT – 18 HOLES
25900 Prescott Rd., Clarksburg
301/601-9209

**NEEDWOOD – 18 HOLES/
9 EXECUTIVE HOLES**
6724 Needwood Rd., Derwood
301/948-1075

NORTHWEST PARK – 27 HOLES
15701 Layhill Rd., Silver Spring
301/598-6100

POOLESVILLE – 18 HOLES
16601 W. Willard Rd., Poolesville
301/428-8143

RATTLEWOOD – 18 HOLES
13501 Penn Shop Rd., Mt. Airy
(Frederick County border)
301/607-9000

SLIGO CREEK PARK – 9 HOLES
9701 Sligo Creek Pkwy., Silver Spring
301/585-6006

**WHITE OAK GOLF COURSE –
9 HOLES**
10911 New Hampshire Ave., Silver Spring
301/593-6910

CENTRAL MARYLAND

dens are landscaped to offer horticultural interest throughout the year, with plants such as paperbark maple and Lenten rose in January, and hydrangeas and roses in June.

Greenbelt Park

This pretty urban park (6565 Greenbelt Rd., Greenbelt, MD 20770, 301/344-3944) offers walking, hiking, and jogging on more than 12 miles of trails, biking on paved areas, picnicking, and overnight camping. The 174-site family campground is open year-round for tent camping, truck campers, and travel trailers, and offers modern restrooms with showers, drinking water, tables, and fire grills.

American Film Institute (AFI) Silver Theatre and Cultural Center

The hot spot for movies and film entertainment in the area is the recently built Silver Theatre (8633 Colesville Rd., Silver Spring, 301/495-6720, www.afi.com). A branch of AFI Los Angeles, the three-screen film complex is anchored by the rehabilitation of the historic 1938 Silver Theatre and offers a year-round program of American and international cinema, in addition to an eclectic mix of festivals, premieres, on-stage guest appearances, and educational programs. One annual festival that's gaining national attention is SILVERDOCS (www.silverdocs.com), sponsored by AFI and the Discovery Channel. This competition selects the best documentaries from all over the world and screens them in June each year.

ACCOMMODATIONS

The heavily urbanized zone of Montgomery County—Bethesda, Rockville, Silver Spring, Gaithersburg, and nearby College Park (just

CENTRAL MARYLAND

over the line in Prince George's County)—offers dozens of chain hotels. The outlying rural areas feature additional hotels and a few B&Bs. Here are a few lodgings of note.

Bethesda Marriott

This hotel (5151 Pooks Hill Rd., 301/897-9400 or 800/228-9290, www.marriott.com, $119–279, depending on the season and room) is a particularly fine example of the chain—not unexpected, since this area is Marriott's home base. This one offers all the usual amenities, including two restaurants, a lounge, a health club, tennis courts, and an indoor/outdoor pool. It's especially convenient, as Pooks Hill Road is right off Route 355, far enough away from the urban centers to be pleasant, but right in the middle of everything. Weekend packages and discounts are available.

Longwood Manor Bed & Breakfast

A restored 1817 Georgian manor set on two acres of lush gardens, this B&B may look familiar (2900 DuBarry Ln., Brookeville, 301/774-1002, www.erols.com/longwood manor, $95–150). The building, six miles north of Washington, D.C., resembles Mt. Vernon—Thomas Jefferson was a houseguest. Rooms and suites have private baths, and there's a swimming pool.

Cherry Hill Park

A camping option in the area (9800 Cherry Hill Rd., College Park, 301/937-7116 or 800/801-6449, www.cherryhillpark.com, $40–80), Cherry Hill has sites for tents and RVs. It's open year-round and offers a pool, sauna, hot tub, and store in addition to electric, cable TV, water, and sewer hookups. Cherry Hill is at the junction of the U.S. 95/495 split. The Metro Bus stops by the campground to make getting around easy.

FOOD
Bethesda

This town has a reputation for exotic eateries mixed with mall quick-stops and high-end

restaurants. Those in search of sophisticated menus and exotic settings can stroll down Bethesda's **Restaurant Row.** Tucked within this eight-block neighborhood between Route 355 (Rockville Pike/Wisconsin Ave.) and Old Georgetown Road is a mix of traditional, seafood, and ethnic restaurants. European, Asian, Middle Eastern, Caribbean, and South American fare are all available in the shifting kaleidoscope of eateries.

One of the local favorites in the Restaurant Row neighborhood is **Rock Bottom Brewery** (7900 Norfolk Ave., Bethesda, 301/652-1311, 11 A.M.–1 A.M. daily, until 2 A.M. Fri.–Sat., $6–20). It's a popular place to stop for well-made, sophisticated pub food and brews. The brewmaster consistently wins awards for his specialties, Raccoon Red and Terrapin Alt.

At **BD's Mongolian Barbeque** (7201 Wisconsin Ave., Bethesda, 301/657-1080, www.bdsmongolianbarbeque.com, lunch and dinner, $6–16), you can create your own stir-fry from mounds of meats, poultry, seafood, and vegetables for a fixed price. The staff and atmosphere are friendly and casual; it has a full bar, too.

The Miracle Mile

Along the "miracle mile," the **Silver Diner** (11806 Rockville Pike, Rockville, 301/770-2828, breakfast, lunch, and dinner daily, $6–15) is a glorified version of the old-style diners made from converted dining cars. This oft-packed place is on the main road in front of a shopping center, the Mid-Pike Plaza.

Chevy Chase

Most of the eateries in the area (like those mentioned above) are chains. If you're feeling adventurous, take a stroll among the many locally owned restaurants along **Connecticut Avenue** (Rte. 185) south of Chevy Chase Circle. The 5500 block is ripe with a variety of eateries, including Greek, Mexican, and casual American options. Another possibility for good restaurant choices is the intersection of **Wisconsin Avenue NW (Rte. 395) and Western Avenue NW.** North of that intersection, Willard Avenue off Wisconsin has a few interesting places, too.

INFORMATION
Contact the **Montgomery County Visitor Information Center** (12900 Middlebrook Rd., Ste. 1400, Germantown, MD 20874, 301/916-0698 or 800/925-0880, www.cvb montco.com).

GETTING AROUND
Like most American counties, Montgomery is most conveniently traveled by car. However, the **Washington Metropolitan Area Transit Authority** (the Metro, www.wmata

.com) does have service lines throughout the gateway portion of the county, radiating out of Washington, D.C. The west red line crosses into the county at Friendship Heights and travels northwest through Bethesda past Rockville to Shady Grove; the east red line travels up through Silver Spring through Wheaton to Glenmont. The green line winds northeast through College Park and Greenbelt. All stations sell fare cards, and fares are based on when and where you travel, starting at $1.35. A $6.50 One-Day Pass (available at most stations) buys a full day of Metro rides and will get you most anywhere; it's also a great way to see all the attractions in D.C.

Prince George's County

Central Maryland offers a marvelous government-sponsored panoply of attractions that are free to the public: the Patuxent Research Refuge and National Wildlife Visitor Center, Beltsville Agricultural Research Center, and NASA/Goddard Space Flight Center.

SIGHTS
◖ Patuxent Research Refuge/ National Wildlife Visitor Center
This facility (10901 Scarlet Tanager Loop off Powder Mill Rd., Laurel, 301/497-5760, www .fws.gov/northeast/patuxent, visitors center and refuge open 10 A.M.–5:30 P.M. daily mid-Mar.–Oct., 10 A.M.–4:30 P.M. daily Nov.–mid-Mar., free) is so vast that airline pilots look for the pool of black marking the unlit refuge to sight their way to BWI Airport at night. Nearly 13,000 acres were carved from former military lands to create this sanctuary; Patuxent is the oldest and one of the largest wildlife research centers in the United States and the world.

Primarily used for wildlife and environmental research, the grounds include four miles of walking trails, plus half-hour guided electric tram tours through surrounding woods, fields, and wetlands on weekends from spring through fall (weekday tours may be arranged in advance).

The visitors center is particularly worthwhile. Visually dramatic dioramas on global and environmental issues, habitats, endangered species, and the techniques and tools of research scientists make up the largest part of the center. Gray wolves, whooping cranes, sea otters, and other creatures are frozen in time in their natural habitats. Another section of the center is set up as a viewing pod with spotting scopes, binoculars, and radio tracking equipment for visitors to observe wildlife through a large picture window overlooking part of the refuge. Free wildlife films are offered on weekends, and there's a gift shop. The staff is dedicated, knowledgeable, and unabashedly pro-wildlife. Considering the excellence of the displays and the opportunity for learning and appreciating the bounty of the planet alongside those who have made this study their lives, this is not a place you'd expect to enter for free—but it is. There is a nominal charge to ride the tram: $3 for adults, $1 for children 12 and under.

Beltsville Agricultural Research Center (BARC)
This research center has a similar purpose to that of Patuxent—to use current resources in the best way possible. The BARC National

CENTRAL MARYLAND

THE NATIONAL WILDLIFE REFUGE SYSTEM

Sponsored by the U.S. Fish and Wildlife Service, the refuge system is a diverse network of national public lands set aside for conservation of fish, wildlife, and plants – a total of more than 92 million acres of land and water. Though President Theodore Roosevelt established the first national refuge in 1903 (Florida's Pelican Island) to protect egrets, herons, and other endangered birds, J. Clark Salyer, a government official, is considered the "Father of the Refuge System." Representing the nascent refuge movement, Salyer began the process of placing land aside during the severe drought of the 1930s by driving around the country and buying critical wetland as waterfowl refuges. Several such refuges have been named for writers and artists associated with an appreciation of the natural world: Mark Twain, Rachel Carson, J. J. Audubon, and and "Ding" Darling, originator of the duck stamp. In 1997, a separate agency for refuges was created within the Department of the Interior (www.fws.gov/refuges/index.html). Of the 500 current refuges, nearly 400 protect or have reintroduced threatened and endangered species. Roughly 98 percent of the land in the refuge system is open to the public.

According to the "2006 National Survey of Fishing, Hunting, and Wildlife-Associated Recreation" published by the NWRS, 87 million US residents over age 16 enjoyed some recreational activity relating to fish and wildlife. Almost 34 million people spent time fishing and/ or hunting and 71 million people engaged in wildlife-watching activities such as observing, photographing, and/ or feeding wildlife. Hundreds of national wildlife refuges are located along the major waterfowl flyways. Patuxent, on the Atlantic flyway, is one of these stepping-stones, preserving the Eastern U.S. corridor so hundreds of bird species may survive their annual migration.

Visitor Center (Log Lodge Rd., follow signs on Powder Mill Rd./Rte. 212, Beltsville, 301/504-9403, www.ars.usda.gov/is/nvc, tours available 8 A.M.–4:30 P.M. Mon.–Fri. by reservation, free) is housed in a magnificent log structure built by the Civilian Conservation Corps during the Depression. It features an overview of the research done at the facility and an apiary with the queen bee marked in blue among millions of her workers (searching for her among the horde is a busy, buzzy version of *Where's Waldo?*). Guided tours of the agricultural center field laboratories and buildings are available at no charge by appointment only through the visitors center (write or call ahead).

This 7,000-acre U.S. Department of Agriculture facility is made up of 47 laboratories and management units on a working/experimental farm, and includes the U.S. National Arboretum some distance away in northeast Washington, D.C. (3501 New York Ave. NE, 202/245-2726).

The scope of the research done on the premises is extensive. Livestock and poultry studies include development of natural products as diet additives to increase disease resistance (and eliminate dependence on antibiotics); research on the Chesapeake Bay ecosystem revealed significant amounts of pesticides returning to land in rain and dust. Scientists developed two new American elm varieties resistant to the fungus that nearly eliminated the species in the 1930s, and other researchers developed DEXA, a method to measure bone density and body composition via radiation equivalent to a fraction of a dental X-ray. Also under way are studies on the most effective ways to recycle nutrients in manure, sustainable plant production through cover crops, and 100 percent recyclable packing "peanuts" (made from corn byproducts).

NASA/Goddard Space Flight Center

The home of acronyms, Goddard (GSFC, www.nasa.gov/centers/goddard) was established in 1959 as the National Aeronautics and

ROCKET SCIENTIST

Robert H. Goddard's experiments in rocket propulsion first came to the notice of the public in 1907 when a powder rocket misfired, producing an acrid cloud of smoke in the basement of the physics building at Worcester Polytechnic Institute where Goddard studied. Fortunately, he was not expelled. Goddard went on to teach physics at his alma mater, and later at Clark University, but his true life's work was invention.

He received two U.S. patents for rocket propulsion fuel and rocket structural developments, and, two days before the 1918 Armistice, created a prototype for the bazooka at the Aberdeen Proving Ground in Aberdeen, Maryland. His launching platform was a music rack. In 1926, Goddard built and tested the first rocket using liquid fuel in Auburn, Massachusetts. Though his discoveries at the time were as revolutionary as those of the Wright Brothers, they made little impression on government officials. Modest subsidies from the Smithsonian Institution and the Daniel Guggenheim Foundation made it possible for him to sustain a lifetime of research while teaching.

In 1920, when Goddard wrote of the possibility of a rocket reaching the moon, the press ridiculed his idea. After that incident, he was reported to have "reached firm convictions about the virtues of the press corps, which he held for the rest of his life." During World War II, Goddard helped develop practical jet-assisted takeoff and liquid propellant rocket

© JOANNE MILLER

NASA Space Capsule at Goddard

motors capable of variable thrust. Goddard's achievements received little notice until the dawn of the space age, when many of his ideas were used as the basis for modern technology. In September 1959, the 86th Congress authorized the issuance of a Congressional gold medal to honor Professor Robert H. Goddard, space-age pioneer.

Space Administration's (NASA's) first center devoted to the exploration of space. The visitors center (8800 Greenbelt Rd., Greenbelt, 301/286-9041, www.nasa.gov/centers/goddard/visitor/contactus) and neighboring gift shop are open by appointment only 10 A.M.–4 P.M. weekdays except major holidays; admission and all activities are free. The Goddard Center prefers reservations made at least one month in advance—this can be done online.

The facility continues to seek answers about the formation and substance of the universe, but is also dedicated to the study of earth as an environmental system and the development and use of cutting-edge technologies that impact the world. Started in response to the 1957 Soviet launch of *Sputnik,* GSFC grew from 160 researchers to nearly 12,000 in Greenbelt (there is another center in Wallops, Virginia). It's a thrilling way to introduce budding scientists to the real thing.

One of GSFC's first projects was OAO-2, the Orbiting Astronomical Observatory launched in 1968 to determine the properties of interstellar

DID SHE OR DIDN'T SHE?

Mary Elizabeth Surratt, a devout Catholic, had the misfortune to be married to a fervent supporter of the secessionist cause. During the Civil War, the tavern and post office operated by John Surratt Sr. in Surrattsville (now Clinton) became a hub of pro-South activities and a convenient stop for Confederate agents. In 1862, he died suddenly and left his wife with complicated debts, runaway slaves, and insistent creditors. Mary, her son John, and daughter Anna were forced to move to a house they had previously leased at 541 H Street in Washington, D.C. She intended to rent out the extra rooms to support herself and her family. By March 1865, seven boarders filled the house.

Meanwhile, John Wilkes Booth was formulating a plan to hold Abraham Lincoln hostage to force the exchange of Confederate prisoners. Booth was given a letter of introduction to sympathizers in Charles County, Maryland, where he met Dr. Samuel A. Mudd and Thomas Harbin, a Confederate secret service agent. Harbin counted among his associates a courier for the Confederate government, John Surratt Jr.

Dr. Mudd met Booth in Washington in December 1864, a meeting that included John Surratt Jr. Surratt then deeded to his mother all of his worldly goods and proceeded to help Booth round up an active group of kidnap conspirators. All of the conspirators met at Mrs.

Surratt's H Street boarding house at one time or another.

On March 15, 1865, Booth explored Ford's Theatre as a possible place for the abduction. On March 17, when he heard that Lincoln was going to attend a play in another location just outside the city, he mobilized his conspirators – but, Lincoln never showed up.

Booth then persuaded a few of his old cohorts to join him in his next scheme. Since it was obvious that the South was about to surrender, kidnapping would be futile. Booth insisted the only meaningful act would be the assassination of the president and his cabinet. John Surratt was not among the conspirators – he had left on assignment to Elmira, New York.

On April 10, Booth came to Mrs. Surratt's H Street home. That evening, she asked Louis Weichmann, one of her boarders, to take her out to the Surrattsville tavern the next day in order to settle a debt. Before they reached Surrattsville, they met John Lloyd, keeper of the tavern. She asked him to "get [the shooting irons] out ready – they would be wanted soon," according to his testimony. On April 14, 1865, Mrs. Surratt again asked her boarder to drive her to the tavern. "I must get those things of Booth's," she told him, and came back with a paper-wrapped package that she described as "glass." At the tavern, Mrs. Surratt gave John

dust and hot stars in the Milky Way. Numerous other projects followed, including the Hubble Space Telescope (HST), the first observation device designed to be serviced in space. The successor to HST is the much more powerful James Webb Space Telescope (JWST), a large, infrared-optimized space telescope scheduled for launch no earlier than June 2013. Several NASA satellites have been launched to study the ozone layer and map weather patterns, useful for predicting environmental damage and storms. Goddard researchers developed a new nonsurgical technique for detecting breast cancer (the Breast Biopsy System, or BBS). And

GSFC's Acousto-optic Imaging Spectrometer (AImS) was used by the Smithsonian in 1998 to identify and repair deterioration to the Star-Spangled Banner (the giant flag that flew over Fort McHenry in Baltimore in 1814, inspiring Francis Scott Key).

GSFC offers many programs to the public free of charge throughout the year. In the visitors center's 2,600-square-foot gallery, self-guided earth science exhibits, films, and hands-on activities are available to visitors by appointment. Occasionally, a host of model rockets are launched (visitors are welcome to bring their own). The center also offers special

Lloyd the package and told him to have the package, weapons, and some whiskey ready, and to give them to "whoever would call for them that night."

On the evening of April 14, Abraham Lincoln attended a performance at Ford's Theatre with his wife. A well-dressed gentleman – Booth – entered the theater by the rear door. He went up the stairs and to the box occupied by the president. Taking out a card, he gave it to the president's messenger, and immediately followed him into the box. As he entered, he fired, aiming at the president's head. One of the president's guests tried to stop Booth, but Booth stabbed him in the chest. Booth leaped down to the stage, shouting, "Sic semper tyrannis" ("Thus be it ever to tyrants"), the motto of Virginia. In a moment, he was gone.

Booth escaped with his co-conspirator David Herrold. Police went to Mrs. Surratt's house on April 17, arrested her, her daughter Anna, and several boarders. While the police were at the house, a young man dressed as a laborer came to the door – Mrs. Surratt denied knowing him. After being questioned by the police, he was arrested, and was later identified as Lewis "Paine" Powell, an occasional visitor at Mrs. Surratt's who had been identified as an attacker of Secretary of State Seward. Three days later, another conspirator, George Atze-

rodt, was captured near Middleburg, Maryland. On April 14, he had stayed at the Kirkwood House, Washington, where Vice President Johnson was lodging. A revolver was found there, along with some bowie knives and evidence of his complicity with Booth. Apparently, he had lost his nerve.

The conspirators in custody were tried in Washington by a military court. Four of them – Herrold (captured in Virginia), Atzerodt, Powell, and Mrs. Surratt – were hung. Mrs. Surratt insisted on her innocence to the end, and Powell said, "She might have known something was going on, but did not know what."

Her defenders portrayed her as a religious woman, a good mother, and a person in the wrong place at the wrong time – but her boarder Louis Weichmann wrote, "I don't believe that Mrs. Surratt was an innocent woman." Though Mrs. Surratt was reputed to have considered Weichmann as a son, his statements at the trial were the most damning.

Mrs. Surratt's son John escaped to Canada after the assassination. In the spring of 1866, Surratt was arrested in Italy, but he escaped and fled to Egypt, where he was once again arrested. John Surratt was brought to trial in a civil court, and the proceedings ended with a hung jury. He was set free and never indicted again.

programs for children, such as "Rockets, Rockets, Rockets!" (basic rocketry, an alternative to blowing up the garage with the Jr. Science Lab Kit) and "Stars in the Sky" (create your own constellation). Children's programs must be booked at least two months in advance due to space limitations (or should I say mass/volume limitations?). Call 301/286-9041 to verify event schedules and make reservations.

[College Park Aviation Museum

This airy, modern museum (1985 Corporal Frank Scott Dr., off Paint Branch Pkwy., College Park, 301/864-6029, www.pgparks.com/

places/historic/cpam, 10 A.M.–5 P.M. daily, $4 adults) is set on the world's oldest continuously operating airport. The airport was established in 1909 when Wilbur Wright came to train two military officers to fly the U.S. government's first airplane; in fact, an audio-animatronic Wright greets museum visitors. He stands next to the stopwatch and other artifacts Wright used and tells about the airfield's early years.

The 27,000-square-foot glass-and-brick museum was designed by the same architectural team that produced the Smithsonian's National Air and Space Museum. The display area features a rare 1911 Wright B Aeroplane, a 1918 Curtiss Jenny, and others suspended in midflight like insects in amber. Other rooms offer interactive exhibits: a wind tunnel, a map with headphones so visitors can hear local air traffic communication, a flight simulator, and more. An onsite aviation library offers research opportunities (call 301/864-6029 for more information). The museum sponsors many programs throughout the year, such as model-making workshops, Air Career Night (with speakers who examine the past, present, and future of aviation), and the annual AirFair held in September.

Surratt House Museum

Built on a crossroads and operated as a tavern before and during the Civil War, this was the home of Mary Elizabeth Surratt, convicted conspirator in the assassination of President Abraham Lincoln (see the sidebar "Did She or Didn't She?" in this chapter). The well-preserved house (9118 Brandywine Rd., Clinton, 301/868-1121, www.surratt.org, noon–4 P.M. Thurs.–Fri. and 11 A.M.–3 P.M. Sat.–Sun. mid-Jan.–mid-Dec., $3 adults) looks much as it did during the 1860s, with the table set for visitors and the post office/tavern ready to dispense mail and whiskey. The upper floor remains open to show the concealment space that held the "shooting irons" used to confirm Mrs. Surratt's guilt and cause her to be the first woman executed by the federal government. The town of Clinton was once called Surrattsville; the name was changed after Mrs. Surratt's hanging.

Take the "Assassin's Trail" tour outlined in the *Southern Maryland* chapter and find out more about Mary Surratt, her tavern, and the events that took place after the assassination of Abraham Lincoln. Though Prince George's County and Southern Maryland were generally pro-Confederacy, and the Surratt tavern a well-known meeting place for Southern sympathizers, historians continue to argue whether Mrs. Surratt was a pawn in a plot hatched by her son and his friend John Wilkes Booth.

Belair Mansion and Stable Museum

Built in 1745, the mansion (12207 Tulip Grove Dr., Bowie, 301/809-3089, www.cityofbowie .org/museum, noon–4 P.M. Wed.–Sun., free) was the Georgian plantation house of Samuel Ogle, Provincial Governor of Maryland. Enlarged in 1914 by the New York architectural firm of Delano and Aldrich, the mansion was also the home of William Woodward, a famous horseman in the first half of the 20th century. Restored to its former glory, the house reflects its occupants in artwork and furnishings. Governor Samuel Ogle's paintings of the Four Seasons, a gift from Lord Baltimore, Proprietor of the Colony of Maryland, hang in the hall. Later works include privately issued prints of the famous Belair Stud Thoroughbred racehorses and a 1932 bronze of Triple Crown winner Gallant Fox.

Belair Stable (2835 Belair Dr., 301/809-3089, noon–4 P.M. Wed.–Sun., free) was part of the famous "Belair Stud," one of America's premier racing stables from 1930 to 1960, home to Gallant Fox and Omaha, father-and-son winners of the Triple Crown; Nashua, "Horse of the Year" in 1955; and many other well-known racehorses. Until its closing in 1957, Belair was the oldest continually operated racing horse farm in the United States. The stable has been restored and is open as a museum, with displays on thoroughbred history and bloodlines, racing silks, and trophies, a carriage collection, and the 1923 stablemaster's apartment.

◖ Accokeek Foundation/ National Colonial Farm

Although the property (3400 Bryan Point Rd., Accokeek (uh-CO-keek), 301/283-2113, ext. 15, www.accokeek.org) is a bit out of the way, it's definitely worth visitng for the destination itself and the verdant land that surrounds it. The grounds and visitors center are open 10 A.M.–4 P.M. Tuesday–Sunday March 15–December 15, and 10 A.M.–4 P.M. om weekends only mid-December–mid-March Admission is $3. The grounds are home to a mid-18th-century farm with rebuilt structures, as well as the Ecosystem Farm, a modern experimental organic vegetable farm. A guided tour of the Ecosystem Farm is offered at 11 A.M. on Saturday and Sunday. Because of the farm's isolation, it's possible to experience the drifting sunlit pollen, quiet waters, and peaceful surroundings that the earliest settlers took for granted (in between endless chores). Today, flyovers from BWI periodically violate the silence, but the occasional interference is a minor consideration.

The view of Washington's Mount Vernon across the Potomac continues to be magical, thanks to the Accokeek Foundation's 1961 creation (in partnership with the National Park Service) of Piscataway Park (301/283-2113, dawn–dusk daily, free). The park stretches for six miles from Piscataway Creek to Marshall Hall on the Potomac River. It features a public fishing pier, two boardwalks over fresh water tidal wetlands, and a variety of nature trails, meadows, and woodland areas, each with unique features. A solitary walk around the grounds will leave you enchanted.

Montpelier Mansion and Cultural Arts Center

This lovely architectural gem (9652 Muirkirk Road, Laurel, 301/953-1993, http://www.pgparks.com/places/artsfac/mac.html) is a true Georgian beauty. Public tours of the mansion are available on the hour noon–3 P.M. Sunday–Thursday Mar.–Nov. and 1–2 P.M. Sunday December–February. Admission is $3. The mansion, completed in 1783, hosted both George Washington and Abigail Adams, wife of President John Adams (traveling separately, we assume). Mrs. Adams described the estate as a "Large, Handsome, Elegant House, where I was received with what we might term true English Hospitality." The nearby cultural arts center houses three galleries and studios with working artists, and it sponsors exhibits and art events throughout the year.

Marietta Mansion

This modest, federal-style brick house (5626 Bell Station Rd., Glenn Dale, 301/464-5291, 11 A.M.–3 P.M. Fri., noon–4 P.M. Sat.–Sun., $3) was home to Gabriel Duvall, Associate Justice of the United States Supreme Court 1811–1834. In the early 1830s, Duvall became guardian of his grandchildren and built a two-story addition. Marietta is situated on 25 acres of lawn, and the house is furnished to reflect the period of the Duvall family's occupancy. Of the many outbuildings that originally supported the 650-acre estate, only the law office and root cellar remain.

Marietta is operated by a division of the Parks Department. The property is home to the Prince George's County Historical Society and the Frederick S. DeMarr Library of County History.

RECREATION
Old Town Laurel Walking Tour

Established as a mill town in the mid-1800s, Laurel continues to be the hub of a busy, populous area. Unlike most towns, however, Laurel's Old Town, along Main Street from U.S. 1 (Baltimore Ave.) to 9th Street, retained many of its historic buildings, including the brick, stone, and stucco mill company workers' houses, an old electric car station made into a saloon (Oliver's), and the pharmacy, built in 1871. Stop by the Laurel Museum (817 Main St., 301/725-7975, www.laurelhistory.org, free), the town's oldest mill worker's house (1840) for a map and schedule of tours. It's open 10 A.M.–2 P.M. Wednesday and Friday and noon–4 P.M. Sunday.

Six Flags America

This is one of the more than 30 mega–theme parks owned by Premier Parks (Rte. 214, Largo, 301/249-1500, www.sixflags.com). Day admission to the more than 100 rides, water park, shows, and play activities (excluding Go-Karts and the Rock Climbing Wall) is $49.99 for adults, $34.99 for kids 54 inches and under, and free for kids ages three and under. The website offers preseason discounts. Parking is additional. Six Flags is open April 12–October 31, weather permitting, with some blackout dates; the water park is open from the third weekend in May to

Labor Day weekend. Closing time varies (as late as 10 P.M. on July and Aug. weekends), but the park always opens at 10 A.M.

Premier poured in more than $40 million to develop the old Adventure World site in 1999. Much of the sweet, old, occasionally run-down amusement park feel has been exchanged for a slick, racy cartoon theme park that, judging from the crowd, appeals to urban teens and young families. It managed to keep the best (two wooden roller coasters, one of which, the Wild One, is rated among the top five in the world by coaster aficionados) while adding high-speed thrill rides—The Joker's Jinx, The Bat Wing, Superman Ride of Steel, and Two-Face twister roller coasters among them. Also new is a revamped section for smaller kids, Looney Tunes Movie Town; several live musical entertainments (Bugs Bunny stars in one); and a stunt show. An elaborate water park, game arcade, and all the fair food you'd ever want are also on the premises.

Fort Washington National Park

This pleasant park on the Potomac (13551 Fort Washington Rd., Fort Washington, 301/763-4600, 8 A.M.–dusk daily, $3) surrounds an authentic 19th-century fort. Fort Warburton, as it was originally known, was built in 1809 after the Treaty of Paris. British/American hostilities continued after the United States was formed, and the fort was built to protect the new nation's capital. Its effectiveness came into question, however, when the British sailed up the Patuxent River to the east and marched overland to Washington, D.C., sacking the city in 1814. Fort Warburton/Washington was blown up by the American commander to keep it from falling into enemy hands. In 1815, Secretary of War James Monroe hired Pierre L'Enfant, a temperamental architect from Washington, to redesign the fort. He was fired less than a year later (what a résumé he must have had), and the fort was periodically ignored and upgraded over the years, serving in some military capacity until 1939, when it was transferred to the Department of the Interior. After a short stint as a military facility during World War II, the fort was converted into a public park in 1946.

Merkle Wildlife Sanctuary

The sanctuary (11704 Fenno Rd., Upper Marlboro, 301/888-1410, visitors center 10 A.M.–4 P.M. Sat.–Sun., sanctuary trails 7 A.M.–sunset daily, $2–3 per vehicle) offers a visitors center with captive live animals, exhibits, and demonstration gardens, four hiking trails of varying difficulty (ranging from 0.75 mile to 2.8 miles), and a spectacular drive-through route.

Edgar Merkle, founder of Merkle Press in Washington, D.C., and an ardent conservationist, arranged to gift and sell portions of his 400-acre farm to the state of Maryland with the stipulation that the area would continue to be managed as a refuge. The refuge now encompasses more than 1,600 acres, and is one of several that make up the Patuxent Agricultural Demonstration Project, created to improve water quality on the river.

One of the best features of the sanctuary is its Critical Area Driving Tour (CADT), a one-way, seven-mile loop with pullouts and observation towers. The road passes through several different ecosystems, with excellent opportunities to enjoy wildlife sightings. Fall highlights include Canada goose breeding season; midsummer is rife with riparian activity; and each spring, a bounty of colorful wildflowers bloom in fields and marshes. The CADT is open to cars 10 A.M.–3 P.M. Sunday year-round. It's open 7 A.M.–sunset daily January–September for horseback riders, hikers, and bikers only—the best way to be part of the landscape. The tour begins at Patuxent River Park off Croom Road. For safety's sake, horses are prohibited on the CADT bridge, so all horseback riding must begin and end at Merkle Wildlife Sanctuary boundaries.

Equine Attractions

Prince George's Equestrian Center (14900 Pennsylvania Ave., Upper Marlboro, 301/952-7908), part of the Show Place Arena, features a heavy schedule of dressage, hunter/

jumper, and breed horse shows from May through August. **Rosecroft Raceway** (6336 Rosecroft Dr., Ft. Washington, 301/567-4400) features harness racing May–August. **Laurel Park Race Track** (Racetrack Rd. off Rte. 198, Laurel, 301/725-0400, www.laurelpark.com) features thoroughbred racing, including the historic half-million-dollar February sprint races.

ACCOMMODATIONS

Colony South Hotel (7401 Surratt's Rd., Clinton, 301/856-4500 or 800/537-1147, $149–229) is a good option for lodging in an area that's slim on options other than chain hotels. The Colony has been around awhile, a fact that's easy to discern if you wander onto one of the "smoking" floors; however, the entire hotel has been upgraded to attract a more distinguished clientele, and it does. The rooms are updated and attractive, and amenities include a fitness center, an indoor pool, tennis courts, and an outdoor walking/jogging trail. There's a small takeout café near the lobby, and the **Wayfarer Restaurant** serves a continental breakfast ($8), an Italian-American menu for lunch ($12), and dinner ($19) daily, as well as brunch on Sunday. The **Decoy Lounge** is the local hot spot. The hotel offers discounts for AAA, AARP, and military members.

FOOD

The C **Bay 'n' Surf** (14411 Baltimore Ave./U.S. 1, Laurel, 301/776-7021, www.baynsurf.com, lunch Mon.–Fri. $12, dinner daily $21) is one of those places you'd whiz right by unless you knew how good the food was. Though it offers beef and chicken dishes, this restaurant is known for its fresh seafood platters. A good bet is the Chesapeake Bayshore Lunch: backfin crab cake with fries, cole slaw, and a cup of the celebrated crab soup for $10.95. Everything on the menu is available for carryout.

94th Aero Squadron Restaurant (5240 Paint Branch Pkwy., College Park, 301/699-9400, daily, lunch $8, dinner $20) is a delightful theme restaurant overlooking the historic College Park Airport. With the atmosphere of a European WWII bistro, it features warm decor, artifacts, and a lawn full of vintage warplanes. It also offers a popular brunch on Sunday.

INFORMATION

Prince George's County Conference & Visitors Bureau (9200 Basil Ct., Ste. 101, Largo, MD 20774, 301/925-8300 or 888/925-8300, www.goprincegeorgescounty.com) can fill you in on events and attractions in the area.

CENTRAL MARYLAND

SOUTHERN MARYLAND

The corridor between Baltimore and Washington, D.C. is heavily trafficked and lined with shopping centers, restaurants, and suburban pleasures and pastimes, but the shores of the Chesapeake retain some of the early wild flavor of the area. Within a short distance of highways and housing developments, the fields are heavy with winged creatures and delicate floating seeds in the summer, and views of the bay and broad Potomac, which embraces the west and south sides of southern Maryland, in winter.

Southern Maryland used to be one of the least populated areas in the state. Though it still looks like wide-open space to visitors, this once rural area is being discovered by D.C. dwellers in search of better housing. The slow development of the southern counties from colonial times to the present made superhighways unnecessary, however, so the suburbanization of southern Maryland will take a while.

Today, the area around Washington has become densely populated, but the lower counties remain largely rural, with small pockets of population concentration. It's an angler's paradise: 80 percent of all rockfish caught in the Potomac River are caught between the Route 301 bridge and St. Clements Island. As the Potomac River widens into the Chesapeake Bay, visitors have the opportunity to view some of the state's historic sites. In Calvert County, boaters, anglers, and beachgoers can all enjoy themselves in uncrowded resorts and villages. Until far more city dwellers from both Baltimore and Washington flock to southern Maryland, this is a wonderful place to enjoy a quiet vacation.

HIGHLIGHTS

◖ The Assassin's Trail: This 50-plus-mile road trip roughly follows the route of John Wilkes Booth's escape after he assassinated President Lincoln during the last days of the Civil War. New roads have covered the old, and paths have been altered, but with the exception of the dense urban sprawl reaching from Washington, D.C., to Clinton, much of the countryside remains as it was in 1865 (page 134).

◖ Calvert Marine Museum: This lively venue covers every aspect of life in the waters of Chesapeake Bay, from the fossilized remains of a "megatooth" Miocene shark to an authentic lighthouse decorated as if it were still inhabited by the keeper and his family. There's an indoor 15-tank "estuarium" that displays local water creatures, and river otters entertain the crowds (page 138).

◖ Annemarie Garden on St. John: A magical combination of wilderness and sophisticated site-specific sculpture, the garden borders St. John Creek, and the shady green groves of trees that cover the land make for a peaceful commune with nature. Visitors wander on paths that visit each of the art-themed "rooms" in this exceptional public space (page 138).

◖ Calvert Cliffs State Park: The chalky, fossil-filled Calvert Cliffs were formed more than 15 million years ago, when a warm and shallow sea covered all of southern Maryland. Six hundred species of fossils, including calcified shark teeth and various mollusk shells, are visible on the cliffs. The cliffs are a rare sight and offer plenty of recreational opportunities, including 13 miles of foot trails (page 144).

◖ Historic St. Mary's City: This well-preserved town keeps the whole family engaged with its combination of living history and bucolic surroundings – and its proximity to two of the best restaurants in the area. St. Mary's City was the colonial capital of Maryland, the first permanent settlement established by Lord Baltimore in 1634, and the fourth English settlement in North America (page 118).

◖ Point Lookout State Park: This scenic multi-use recreational area on the southern tip of Maryland was one of three manors owned by Leonard Calvert, the state's first governor. The park features exhibits on the area's Civil War role as a prison, and also hosts a swimming beach, a fishing pier, a boat ramp, boat and canoe rentals, and tent and cabin camping facilities (page 150).

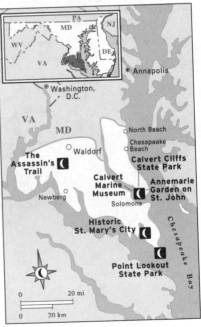

LOOK FOR **◖** TO FIND RECOMMENDED SIGHTS, ACTIVITIES, DINING, AND LODGING.

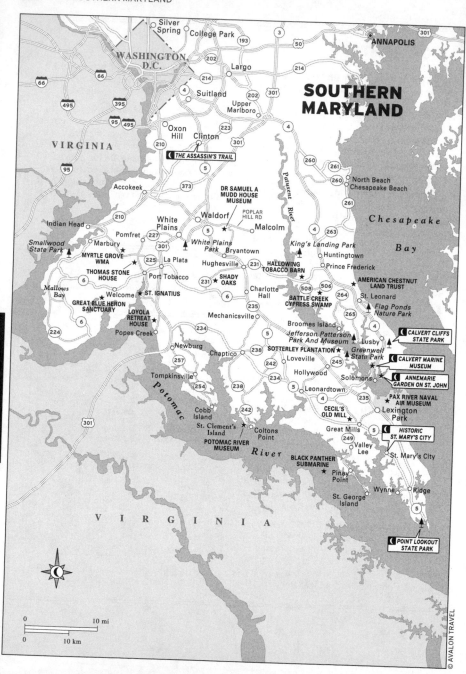

© AVALON TRAVEL

HISTORY

The south counties are the birthplace of Maryland as a Euro-American entity, but the area was populated by Native Americans and their predecessors for centuries. The earliest people came to southern Maryland's shores to harvest the natural abundance of the Patuxent River (also known as the "Pax" River) and Chesapeake Bay as early as 5000 B.C. Ample evidence of their lives—oyster shells and native species of corn in storage pits—has been found on the Jefferson Patterson Park archaeological site in Calvert County. Objects from the site have been carbon dated to A.D. 1450, and other evidence places shore dwellers in the area from 600 B.C. to A.D. 1500. In St. Mary's City, archaeologists found signs of occupation as early as 7000 B.C. More recently (4000 B.C.), the area was home to a large number of tribal groups: the Piscataway, Yoacomoco, Mattaponi, Doegs, Choptank, and Patuxent.

Two small ships, the *Ark* and *Dove,* under the command of Leonard Calvert, landed on St. Clement's Island on March 25, 1634. The settlers had seen the fires of the native Yoacomoco on the shore, and they feared a massacre. But the Native Americans proved friendly, and Calvert bartered land to build St. Mary's City, the first capital of the colony. In 1694, the capital was moved to Annapolis.

Originally established with religious tolerance in mind—especially for Catholics, like the Calverts—the colony became a battleground as the European Reformation spread to the New World. Protestant Reformists sacked St. Mary's and other villages in 1658; they captured two priests and sent them back to England as prisoners. Even after the Reformation wound down, Catholics found it difficult to practice their religion openly.

During the Revolution, most colonists supported freedom—St. Mary's refused to allow a ship bearing British-taxed tea to land—however, many who depended on the area's chief cash crop, tobacco, held strong economic ties with the mother country.

During the Civil War, tobacco again played

© JOANNE MILLER

Amish farm horses

a major part in dividing area residents. Though officially a Union state, southern Maryland was almost entirely in support of the Confederacy because of its heavy dependence on slave labor. Blockade-runners from the lower counties routinely transported food and supplies to the Confederate army on the other side of the Potomac River. After assassinating President Lincoln in Washington, D.C., John Wilkes Booth and his companion David Herrold (or Herold—*Harper's Weekly*, during its Civil War reportage, used the double "r" version) escaped through southern Maryland and on to Virginia.

From after the Civil War until the 1930s, steamboats remained the main source of transportation. When the Potomac River Bridge (U.S. 301) opened in the late 1930s, the popular mode of travel changed to automobiles, their numbers increased by the convenience of highways built throughout the counties. The U.S. military found several sites in the counties that suited them, and they became the major employers in southern Maryland as tobacco cultivation lost ground in the modern age.

With its foundation of rich soil surrounded by water, the southland has always been a land of bounty. Today, farms separate the small housing divisions and highways, and watermen continue to make their living from the Chesapeake. Though the Potomac River has seen its share of misuse and pollution, even that waterway is making a comeback under the enlightened care of local government and those who dwell near it.

ORIENTATION

Two long "necks" (bodies of land separated by wide rivers) make up the eastern part of southern Maryland on the Chesapeake Bay. The upper neck is Calvert County, and the lower neck consists of two large counties, St. Mary's and Charles. The Potomac—quite wide at this point—separates the southernmost points from the state of Virginia. This area of Maryland is mostly rural, with small towns and the occasional suburb dotting the landscape. The largest town is La Plata (la PLAY-ta), in Charles

County. The gentle hills are often covered with pines and deciduous trees, separating wide swaths of agricultural land. Because southern Maryland is surrounded on three sides by water, this is boating and fishing country, too.

The main north–south arteries are Route 4, from Washington D.C. to the length of Calvert County, crossing the Patuxent River and curving west into St. Mary's; and Rtes. 5 and 235, which run directly from Washington, D.C., to the tip of St. Mary's County. U.S. 301/Route 3 is the main road from Baltimore through Charles County, crossing the Potomac River into Virginia. Smaller routes lace the counties from east to west, chiefly Route 6.

PLANNING YOUR TIME

Southern Maryland lets you get away from it all and learn something at the same time. If you're interested in the Civil War, you may enjoy following the **Assassin's Trail,** a 50-mile one- or two-day road trip that follows the escape route of John Wilkes Booth, the assassin of President Abraham Lincoln. The trip starts in Washington, D.C., and visits the **Surratt House Museum** (one hour) and the **Samuel A. Mudd House Museum** (one hour), among other sites.

The rural south is popular with bicycle riders—the land is flat, scenic, and not heavily traveled, except on the major roads. A 24-mile one- or two-day route detailed here is the **Scenic Loop to Cobb Island.** The tourism divisions of the various counties have published a well-researched, award-winning map that features routes all over the area, highlighting scenic spots and resources for cyclists. Ask for a free *Southern Maryland Bicycle Map* from any of the county information sources listed in the *Information* sections of this chapter.

Journey south a little more than two hours from Baltimore by car, and you'll be in the southernmost part of the lower counties on the Chesapeake Bay. Plan three days in Solomons, using the town as a base. Take one day to visit the attractions there—**Calvert Marine Museum** (two hours) and peaceful, art-filled **Annemarie Garden on St. John** (two hours)—and the other two to laze on the white sands of the **Twin Beaches** (Chesapeake Beach and North Beach) or walk the trails of **Calvert Cliffs State Park** (one hour—all day) or one of the other uncrowded parks. Camping is also a pleasant option in this part of Maryland. Another two to three days can be spent based in and enjoying **Historic St. Mary's City** (two hours—all day), Point Lookout State Park, and Piney Point Park. The roads in this area are wonderful to drive or bike on, and the waterways are also justly famous.

FESTIVALS AND EVENTS

Many states are issuing new area codes for growing counties, and southern Maryland is a prime example. If you reach a phone number that has been disconnected, try the local county tourism bureau; they often have up-to-the-minute information on festivals and events. Southern Maryland Online (www.somd.com/calendar) also features many local events.

Three of Maryland's six tobacco warehouses are in Charles County, and mid-March–April is tobacco auction time in Hughesville. Visitors are welcome to watch the action as auctioneers, buyers, and sellers amble down the aisles of elbow-high tobacco.

In April, Jefferson Patterson Park in St. Leonard is a lovely place to enjoy the **Celtic Festival of Southern Maryland** (410/257-9003 or 443/404-7319). Music and historic reenactments, bagpipes, highland dancing, and athletic competitions are among the entertainment.

During the **Annual Piscataway Indian Festival and Pow Wow** (16816 Country Ln., Waldorf, 301/372-1932, www.piscataway indians.org) in late May or early June, several tribes celebrate their heritage. Visitors can check out native regalia, crafts, food, drinks, songs, and dances.

The **Annual Southern Maryland Quilt & Needlework Show** (301/373-2280 or 800/681-0850) in May benefits Sotterley Plantation in Hollywood. Visitors can enjoy the juried handiwork and spend the afternoon picnicking near the Patuxent River and exploring the craft booths.

The **John Wilkes Booth Escape Route Tour** (301/868-1121) gives participants the chance to follow the trail of President Lincoln's assassin in considerably more comfort than Booth himself. Tours take place in spring and fall on an air-conditioned bus, sponsored by the Surratt House Museum. The tours sell out early, so reserve a space well ahead.

Fireworks? The Navy Surface Warfare Center (301/743-5574) has a shell or two—some consider its **Fourth of July celebration** to be the best in southern Maryland. It's held in the Village Green Park in Indian Head.

In September, the **St. Mary's County Fair** (St. Mary's County Fairgrounds, Leonardtown, 301/475-2256) features an antique tractor pull, carnival, crafts, live entertainment, a "Masters of the Chainsaw" review, and rides.

Also in September, the **Charles County Fair,** (301/932-1234) in La Plata will fill your day with farm animals, displays of all kinds, demonstrations, pig races, and carnival food (FYI, pigs do not race to the carnival food—but it's not a bad idea).

During the holidays, Historic St. Mary's City presents a number of events, including an **Open House and Community Concert** (240/895-4990 or 800/762-1634) in the Old State House and an evening of feasting and madrigals.

Solomons is also done up for the holidays; during the second week in December, the streets are lit by candlelight, and the shops are open late; a lighted boat parade takes place on the weekend. Nearby **Annemarie Garden** is also festively lit.

GETTING THERE AND AROUND
By Air

The main airports serving southern Maryland are the **Baltimore-Washington International Airport** (BWI), south of Baltimore, and **Ronald Reagan Washington National** (DCA) and **Dulles International Airport** (IAD), both in Virginia, south of Washington, D.C. All three may offer commuter flights to the small commercial airport near Londontown, south of Annapolis—check online or call for details. All major car rental agencies are represented at these airports.

By Bus

There's a **Greyhound/Trailways** terminal in Annapolis (800/231-2222, www.greyhound .com). Outside of Annapolis, there is no intracity public transportation.

By Train

Amtrak (800/USA-RAIL, www.amtrak.com) runs trains to Baltimore, Washington, D.C., and New Carrollton (Annapolis).

By Car

This is the easiest and most convenient way to travel around southern Maryland. Because the bay inundates most of the area, major routes run north–south: U.S. 301, Rtes. 4 and 5, Route 210, and Route 235. U.S. 495 is the ring road around Washington, D.C.

Western Calvert County and Charles County

The broad Potomac is the western boundary of southern Maryland. The suburbs spread out from Washington and thin out in Charles County, which is not so much sprawling as diffused. The largest population concentration on this side of southern Maryland is around the Charles County seat in La Plata. U.S. 301 runs through the town and leads up to it in either direction with a series of shopping centers and fast-food joints. The remainder of the county is doggedly rural. Long, flat, two-lane roads make traveling the backcountry easy by car or bike.

SIGHTS
Surratt House Museum

This was the home of Mary Elizabeth Surratt, convicted conspirator in the assassination of President Abraham Lincoln. The well-preserved house (9118 Brandywine Rd., Clinton, 301/868-1121, www.surratt.org, 11 A.M.–3 P.M. Thurs.–Fri. and noon–4 P.M. Sat.–Sun. mid-Jan.–mid-Dec., $3 adults) looks much as it did during the 1860s, with the table set for visitors and the post office/tavern ready to dispense mail and whiskey. The upper floor remains open to show the concealment space that held the "shooting irons" used to confirm Mrs. Surratt's guilt and cause her to be the first woman executed by the federal government. The town of Clinton was once called Surratts-

ville; the name was changed after Mrs. Surratt's hanging.

Though Prince George's County and Southern Maryland were generally pro-Confederacy, and the Surratt tavern a well-known meeting place for Southern sympathizers, historians continue to argue about whether Mrs. Surratt was a pawn in a plot hatched by her son and his friend John Wilkes Booth. The house/museum features rotating period displays throughout the year, and it's the home base of the John Wilkes Booth Escape Route Tours every April and September. The 12-hour bus tour visits the roads and houses used by Booth (most of which are intact). Call or visit the museum website for current prices and reservations on the tour. They often sell out in the first few weeks of availability (no reservations before mid-Jan. for the spring tours and mid-June for the fall tours).

Dr. Samuel A. Mudd House Museum

The Mudd plantation, set on 10 acres, is one of the few houses in Maryland that has remained in the same family since original settlement by Thomas Mudd in the mid-1600s (3725 Dr. Samuel Mudd Rd., Waldorf, 301/274-9358, noon–4 P.M. Sat.–Sun. and 11 A.M.–3 P.M. Wed. Apr.–mid-Nov., $5 adults). Dr. Samuel Mudd, born in 1833 to a wealthy, slave-own-

© JOANNE MILLER

Dr. Samuel A. Mudd House Museum

ing family, took over the plantation upon his marriage. He was a 32-year-old country doctor and the father of four when President Lincoln was assassinated. John Wilkes Booth and his companion, David Herrold, made their way to Mudd's home at 4 A.M. the morning after the assassination. Although he was reputed to have met Booth on at least three prior occasions, Dr. Mudd said he did not recognize his patient, and that the two used the names "Tyson" and "Henston." Dr. Mudd set Booth's broken leg and sheltered them until 2 P.M. later in the day.

During the trial of the conspirators that followed, Dr. Mudd was indicted, although he continued to protest his innocence. One of the conspirators, Mr. O'Loughlin (suspected of an attempt on General Grant's life), Dr. Mudd, and two others implicated in helping Booth escape all received life sentences. Mudd was sent to Fort Jefferson prison in Dry Tortugas Island, Florida, in 1865. An attempted escape that year failed, and Dr. Mudd was reassigned to the prison's carpentry shop. Another attempt

was successful, but Mudd was recaptured and sent back to the prison. In the summer of 1867, yellow fever broke out on the island. After the prison's physician died, Mudd took a heroic role in caring for the sick and came down with the disease himself, though he survived. Because of his outstanding efforts, all noncommissioned officers and soldiers on the island signed a petition to the government in support of Dr. Mudd. His wife continually wrote letters to President Andrew Johnson seeking her husband's release. He was pardoned on February 8, 1869. He returned home, fathered five more children, partially regained his medical practice, and lived a quiet life on his farm until his death from pneumonia in 1883. He was buried in the St. Mary's cemetery next to the Bryantown church, where he reputedly first met Booth in 1864.

Proponents insist that Mudd was never an accomplice to Booth, though others—including several well-regarded historians—claim the two men had met some time before, and that Mudd knew exactly what he was doing.

© JOANNE MILLER

old plank barn, Charles County

After the Civil War, journalist George Alfred Townsend interviewed Confederate secret agent Thomas Harbin, who confirmed meeting with Mudd and Booth at the Bryantown Tavern, a story never quoted by present-day defenders of Dr. Mudd. Dr. Mudd's grandson, Dr. Richard Mudd of Saginaw, Michigan, worked tirelessly to clear his grandfather's name of any complicity. He filed a petition in the United States District Court for the District of Columbia bringing suit against the Secretary of the Army, Togo West, et al., ordering the Archivist of the United States to "…correct the records in his possession by showing that Dr. (Samuel A.) Mudd's conviction was set aside pursuant to action taken under 10 U.S.C. sec. 1552." In March 2000, Army Assistant Secretary Patrick T. Henry rejected an appeal to overturn the 1865 conviction. Henry said his decision was based on a narrow question— whether a military court had jurisdiction to try Samuel Mudd, who was a civilian. He stated, "I find that the charges against Dr. Mudd constituted a military offense, rendering Dr. Mudd

accountable for his conduct to military authorities." Others, including a U.S. district judge, have ordered the army to reconsider the conviction, and Dr. Mudd's champions have included several former presidents, Jimmy Carter and Ronald Reagan among them.

In that light, visitors loudly proclaiming Dr. Mudd's conspiratorial guilt will get run out of the Mudd house on a splintered rail (wear thick pants if you plan to picket). There's also a gift shop on the property.

Smallwood State Park

General Smallwood Retreat House (U.S. 1, Marbury, 301/743-7613, 1–5 P.M. daily May– Oct.) is named for a Colonial Army general and former governor of Maryland. The original home of General Smallwood, decorated with 18th-century furniture, is open to the public, and a colonial tobacco barn has been re-created on the premises.

The house is part of Smallwood State Park, which features hiking trails in Mattawoman Natural Area (named for the Mattawoman Indians, who had a fort and town here in 1670), picnic sites, and the 50-slip Sweden Point Marina. The concession store rents rowboats, motorboats, canoes, and paddleboats. Fishing is a popular pastime at the park, which hosts a number of bass fishing tournaments each year. The 300 foot fishing pier, shores of the Potomac River, and Mattawoman Creek are home to several varieties of catfish, herring, pickerel, bluegill, croaker, carp, pumpkinseed, rockfish, crappie, and perch. Wading and swimming are not permitted. Smallwood offers 15 campsites and four mini-cabins by reservation, and is open to the public year-round. A $3 entrance fee per person is charged April–October on weekends and holidays; the remainder of the year, the fee is $3 per vehicle.

A welcome addition to Smallwood State Park is **Mattawoman Creek Art Center** (301/743-5159, www.mattawomanart.org, 11 A.M.–4 P.M. Fri.–Sun., free), a two-gallery space that presents changing exhibits of regional, national, and international art. The art center evolved from a virtually forgotten century-old farmhouse into a complex that combines art and nature. The studio spaces of several working artists are also on the premises, and the organization offers classes and workshops.

Port Tobacco Historic District

The former town of Port Tobacco, at Route 6 and Chapel Point Road, is the site of one of Maryland's oldest communities, originally an Indian village known as Potobac. Captain John Smith dropped by in 1608. A few of the original buildings have been reconstructed: the courthouse and a small museum (301/934-4313, 11 A.M.–4 P.M. Sat.–Mon. April–Oct.); and a one-room school (301/934-8836 11 A.M.–4 P.M. Sat.–Sun. Apr.–Oct., 11 A.M.–4 P.M. Sat.–Mon. June–Aug.).

Once a busy colonial shipping port, the

SLAVERY

In the early days of the colony, slave ships from England, Holland, and New England carried black Africans from the Ivory Coast to the Caribbean (the Middle Passage). The few slaves brought to Maryland came from ports there, in the West Indies. By 1700, slavery had become a way of life in Maryland, and slave ships sailed directly up the Chesapeake to dozens of small ports.

Slavers picked up their human cargo from factors in Africa who kept barracoons (warehouses where prisoners were stored until sold). The barracoons were kept full by slatees, chiefs of inland tribes, who staged kidnapping raids on other tribes. The raids increased in frequency as the sale of captives proved more and more profitable. Their victims would be chained together and branded with the slaver's company symbol. Narrow, fast slave ships packed their unwilling passengers tightly next to each other or spoon fashion, one behind the other. Often, nearly half the captives didn't survive the voyage.

Survival had value. Bought by a planter on consignment, a slave who survived three years in the fields was considered acclimatized and brought three times his original price. At first, black Africans were held on the same basis as indentured whites – released after a few years' service. But by 1663, slavery-for-life codes were recognized as law, and blacks were hanged for causing – or even being accused of – the death of their masters. Runaways were often beaten and sometimes maimed.

In spite of the immoral and brutish practice of keeping slaves, colonists continued to import them and profit from their unpaid labor. In 1712, estimates of the slave population stood at roughly 8,000 out of a total of 46,000 Maryland residents – sizable, though far less than neighboring Virginia. The percentage of slaves in the state actually dropped by the middle of the next century, but planters in southern Maryland and the Eastern Shore depended entirely on slave labor for economic survival. As a result, it was in their best interests to support the Confederacy during the Civil War.

TOBACCO BURNS

Tobacco was a perilous way to make a living. Though it was the main commercial crop of colonial planters in Maryland, the financial risks it posed were enormous. After the uncertainties of weather, soil depletion (tobacco leaches nutrients from the soil much more quickly than other crops), insects, and disease, the planter also had to pay for losses in transporting his crop by sea to the London market. If the tobacco was damaged by seawater, rotted from sitting in damp holds, or got misplaced at sea, the planter took the full loss.

Tobacco stalks with attached leaves were harvested in autumn, and overwintered in a tobacco barn – allowed to cure, dry out, and mellow. The following spring, leaves were stripped from their stalks and gathered into a "hand," made up of eight or 10 leaves from one plant. Hands were then compressed into a straight-sided, barrel-like container called a hogshead, which measured between five and six feet tall and roughly five feet in diameter. A packed hogshead weighed around 950 pounds.

Most Maryland planters grew Oronoco, a variety that wasn't "stemmed," or heavily veined, like Sweet Scented, the main variety of Virginia. As a result, it was lighter by weight. Since English taxes were levied by hogshead rather than by weight, "Maryland" (Oronoco) tobacco was taxed more heavily than "Virginia" (Sweet Scented), a constant source of protest. Maryland planters remedied this discrepancy by making their hogsheads somewhat larger than the standard size. A number of planters also packed their hogsheads with "trash" – stems, leaves, and other unusable filler – giving Maryland tobacco a reputation for questionable quality.

After being sealed, a hogshead was turned on its side, attached by poles to a team of horses, and rolled down to the warehouse at the nearest wharf – these "rolling roads" were the origin of many of today's roads. The hogsheads were then packed into the holds of British ships (Maryland was forbidden to trade with any other country), along with smaller quantities of "loose leaf" from smaller growers, and shipped to England, where it was sold and distributed to other countries – particularly France and Holland, where Oronoco tobacco was popular. Consignment firms, such as Bridges and Company, that handled the transport of tobacco grew wealthy as agents for planters, shipping and selling the leaf (for a percentage) to the English market. After the crop was sold, the consignment firm would pick up items such as cloth and books ordered by the planter and ship them back by return vessel – charging the planter for freight expenses and services rendered.

By the early part of the 18th century, the old consignment system had begun to fail, and planters could take greater profits with less risk. However, European buyers hesitated to purchase any colonial tobacco because so much trash was being shipped in the hogsheads. A severe depression in the tobacco market caused Virginia to enact an inspection law that raised both the quality and reputation of its leaf, but Maryland lagged behind for some years, losing much of its market.

In 1758, an agent named John Stevenson bought 1,000 barrels of wheat and some flour and sent them to New York aboard the *Sharp*. The profits from this voyage caused a sensation among farmers in Maryland. Many planters on the Eastern Shore abandoned tobacco and planted wheat, and Maryland's agricultural future set out on a different course.

Today, however, tobacco remains a cash crop for many farmers in southern Maryland. Visitors may attend tobacco auctions held in the spring in Hughesville.

settlement faded away as the land around it failed under the duress of tobacco farming, combined with the move of the county seat to nearby La Plata. At the time, La Plata boasted some railroad siding, a telegraph station, and little else. A special election was held in 1892 to determine whether the courthouse should remain at Port Tobacco or be moved to La Plata. Port Tobacco won, but less than three months later, its courthouse burned to the ground—but not before the county records had been carefully removed. No one was ever prosecuted, and the courthouse and county seat went to La Plata. Then the Port Tobacco River silted over, leaving the town high and dry.

Further down Chapel Point Road is **St. Ignatius,** the oldest Catholic Church in America. It sits high on a hill above Chapel Point, overlooking the confluence of the Port Tobacco River and the Potomac. The graveyard, dating from 1860, spills down the hill to the road below. The priests' cemetery alongside the church dates from 1794. The colonial cemetery was located near the river shore, but most of the tombstones were destroyed when Union soldiers camped there and used them for target practice. There is ongoing controversy over future use of the land below the church—the riverfront offers prime development property, but local interests have so far quashed the project. The church, founded in 1641 by Father Andrew White, continues to serve as a house of worship. If the church is open, go inside to see and appreciate the kneeling pads in the pews; parishioners have lovingly decorated many with crewelwork. The old wooden tabernacle on the altar is made of mahogany from Santo Domingo, and the needlework on and in it was done by Carmelite nuns before 1830. The window above the entrance of the church commemorates the baptism of the Piscataway chief and his wife, who were converted to Catholicism by Fr. White. When he sailed with Leonard Calvert aboard the *Ark,* Fr. White brought a relic of the True Cross with him—it is still kept in the church.

Not far west from old Port Tobacco is the **Thomas Stone House National Historic**

Site (6655 Rose Hill Rd., 301/392-1776, 9 A.M.–5 P.M. daily Memorial Day–Labor Day, Wed.–Sun. the remainder of the year, free), the country home of a lawyer and signer of the Declaration of Independence. Stone and his wife died within months of each other in 1787, leaving their children to be cared for by his relatives. The mansion stayed in the family until 1936 and remained intact until swept by fire in 1977. The National Park Service restored the property and now offers mansion tours, exhibits, an orientation video, picnic sites, and walking trails. The park is five miles west of U.S. 301 on Rose Hill Road between Rtes. 6 and 225.

The Stone House supports a number of special events throughout the year, such as an annual Southern Maryland Heritage Day in June, and outdoor concerts. Call the number above for specifics.

Pomfret

African Americans have a long—and not always willing—history in Charles County. Through the Civil War, the entire tobacco economy was made possible by slave labor. Segregation—voluntary and otherwise—caused African Americans to create their own communities. One that continues today is Pomfret, and the church that services the community there has achieved some recognition as a lively place of faith. The **African-American Heritage Society** (7485 Crain Hwy., La Plata, 301/609-9099) chronicles the black experience in southern Maryland. Since it's run largely by volunteers, it's necessary to call and make an appointment to see the collection.

Loyola Retreat House

If your travels have left you ready for respite, try some quiet time at Loyola (Pope's Creek Rd., Pope's Creek, 301/934-8862). This Jesuit country retreat, on 235 acres of woodsy bluffs overlooking the Potomac, is no yuppie spa. The surroundings are lush, but the accommodations—with meal plans—are modest and inexpensive. There are 75 single rooms with half bath (toilet and sink) in the

SOUTHERN MARYLAND

main building (showers down the hall) and a lounge with fireplace for conviviality. The premises are often used for silent retreats; the Catholic order of St. Ignatius Loyola focuses on deepening one's faith and commitment to justice. This is an excellent place to leave the world behind and spend time in renewal and introspection. Private retreats (completely on your own) or directed retreats (that include a daily meeting for spiritual counseling) are available for varying lengths of time. Call for more information.

Piscataway Indian Museum

The museum (16816 Country Ln., Waldorf, 301/782-2224, www.piscatawayindians.org/museum, 11 A.M.–4 P.M. Sun., donation) is operated by the Maryland Indian Heritage Society. A modern take on the traditional longhouse, the museum displays replicas of living quarters and artifacts of the many tribes that flourished in the area; they also feature information on tribes from other parts of America. The museum is dedicated to Native American ancestors and the retention of indigenous culture. There's a gift shop/trading post with native-made crafts on the premises. One of the best times to visit is during the June Pow-Wow or during the Fall Festival, the third week in September.

DRIVING TOURS
◖ The Assassin's Trail

This 50-plus-mile road trip roughly follows the route of John Wilkes Booth's escape after he assassinated President Lincoln during the last days of the Civil War. New roads have covered the old, and paths have been altered, but with the exception of the dense urban sprawl reaching from Washington, D.C., to Clinton, much of the countryside is as it was in 1865. Some sites are privately owned—please don't disturb the residents—and are so noted. All distances are approximate.

John Wilkes Booth spent considerable time in two Washington, D.C., residences: the Pedersen House (516 10th St. NW) and Mary Surratt's boarding house (604 H St. NW). The tale of his escape begins at Ford's Theatre (511 10th St. NW). Go south on 10th Avenue, then turn left (east) on Pennsylvania Avenue across the John Philip Sousa Bridge. On the edge of Washington, D.C., Pennsylvania Avenue becomes Route 4.

Immediately after the assassination, Booth and Herrold hurried from Ford's Theatre, crossed the Potomac River on horseback, and rode 12 miles through Prince George's County, Maryland, to the Surratt house and tavern, 9110 Brandywine Rd., Clinton, to pick up guns and supplies. About one mile after crossing the Sousa Bridge, take Branch Avenue (Rte. 5) south. At 4.75 miles, look for Route 337 (Allentown Road), and turn left (west). After a few hundred yards, make a left (south) onto Old Branch Road, which parallels Route 5. Follow Old Branch for 2.66 miles until it crosses Woodyard Road in Clinton—the Surratt House is just south of the crossroads. After visiting the museum, continue south (Old Branch becomes Brandywine Road) for a little over four miles. The road branches to the left (east) and becomes Floral Park Road, which leads directly to U.S. 301/Route 5.

Suffering from a broken leg sustained during his escape from Ford's Theatre, Booth proceeded with his companion to Charles County. They crossed into Charles County on the Old Washington Road, and then proceeded to Dr. Samuel Mudd's house (about 12 miles). Continue south on U.S. 301 about three miles to Mattawoman/Beantown Road (Rte. 205), and continue south 2.5 miles until it dead-ends on Poplar Hill Road. Make a left (east) 2.3 miles on Poplar Hill Road to Dr. Samuel Mudd Road; the Mudd farm is less than half a mile along on the left. There, Dr. Mudd set Booth's leg and Booth and Herrold rested for several hours.

Before the assassination, Booth met with Southern sympathizers at Bryantown Tavern. After leaving the Mudd farm, turn right on Dr. Samuel Mudd Road, go 1.5 miles (south), then turn right on Bryantown Road (Rte. 232). Go three miles, cross Route 5 (Leonardtown

Road)—Bryantown Road becomes Oliver's Shop Road/Route 232—and immediately turn right onto Trotter Road (west). The tavern, the second house on the right, is now privately owned. St. Mary's Catholic Church is one mile south of Trotter Road on Oliver's Shop Road, on the east side.

After leaving Dr. Mudd's home, Booth and Herrold tried to rent a carriage, but were unsuccessful. They continued on horseback and during the next week were seen in the vicinity of Zekiah Swamp. From St. Mary's Church, turn left (south) onto Oliver's Shop Road and travel four miles to Route 6 (stay right at the Y). Turn right (west) on Route 6 (Charles St./New Market Rd.). In a little less than a mile, you'll see the sign for Zekiah Swamp. (If you'd like to see the Zekiah Swamp Natural Environment Area, turn left on Penns Hill Road—it's 4.5 miles to the south, a nine-mile round-trip). Continue on Route 6 for roughly three miles and turn left (south) on Bel Alton-Newtown Road. After two miles, you'll come to a plaque on the right for Rich Hill, the home of Samuel Cox, in Bel Alton (privately owned—the house can't be seen until you pass the plaque). Booth and Herrold hid in the thick woods on Cox's farm for several days while Union troops sought them nearby.

Continue on Bel Alton Road about one mile, crossing the railroad tracks; make an immediate left (south) onto Wills Street. Another Confederate sympathizer suspected of sheltering Booth and Herrold owned the Collis House (now private) at 9185 Wills Street. At the southern end of the street is a pine thicket where the conspirators also hid out.

Return to Bel Alton Road and turn left (west). It dead-ends at Crain Highway/U.S. 301. Take this road south about 1.33 miles to Pope's Creek Road. Turn right on Pope's Creek. On the right side of the road, about a mile south, is Huckleberry Cottage, home of a Confederate agent, Thomas A. Jones, who also helped to shelter Booth and Herrold. The cottage is on the grounds of the Loyola Retreat House. Jones supplied the boat that ferried the conspirators to Virginia from Dent's Meadow (about 1.8 miles north of Pope's Creek) on the night of April 21, 1865. Follow Pope's Creek Road about three miles around until it dead-ends at Edgehill Road. Turn left on Edgehill for 1.3 miles to Crain Highway. Turn left on Crain and cross the Harry Nice Memorial Bridge ($1.50 toll) into Virginia.

After crossing the Potomac, you can drive by a couple of homes that sheltered Booth and Herrold. All are privately owned. Turn left at the first traffic light onto Potomac Drive (Rte. 614). Quesenberry house is at the end of Potomac Drive at Ferry Dock Road. Backtrack on Potomac Drive to Route 206 (Dahlgren Road) and turn left, eventually crossing U.S. 301 and driving past Route 218. Go about 1.5 miles and turn left into the Cleydael housing development; turn right at Old Peppermill Road and look for the Cleydael House, second house on the right (an old white frame house with a porch and black shutters). Backtrack out of the Cleydael development, turn left on Route 206, and go about a mile. Turn left on Route 611 (Eden Dr.) and go about two miles, then turn right on U.S. 301 (known here as the James Madison Highway). In the village of Port Royal, turn left on Caroline Street. The Peyton House, now dilapidated, is on the right corner of Caroline and King Streets.

Leaving Port Royal, turn right on King Street, then right on Middle Street, then left on U.S. 301. The plaque for Garrett farm is only 2.5 miles south of Port Royal, but it's in the northbound lane of U.S. 301, so it's best to travel south to Bowling Green and double back. Continue south from Port Royal on U.S. 301 to the 301 South/Business exit into Bowling Green. Turn left at the light onto Main Street; go about 0.4 mile and stop when you see DeJarnette and Beale Insurance Agency on the left. That's the former site of Star Hotel, where Willie Jett stayed (he lead cavalry into Garrett farm). Backtrack to U.S. 301 and turn north toward Port Royal. Travel about nine miles (you'll pass a sign for Peumansend Creek), and look carefully on the right side of the road for the plaque designating the former site of

Garrett farm, where the law finally caught up with Booth.

Scenic Loop to Cobb Island

This approximately 24-mile round-trip leaves suburban congestion behind and coasts into the low country to Cobb Island; it's ideal for bicycles as well as cars. The lightly traveled, paved roads reveal glimpses of plantation homes, many from the mid-18th century and most privately owned. Start on Route 257 (Rock Point Road) past the intersection of U.S. 301 at Newburg. Follow Route 257 all the way down to Route 254, then to the island. Cobb Island itself is mainly residential, with a couple of older seafood restaurants. For the return trip, consider taking Mt. Victoria Road (the road branches off at Tompkinsville in the south and rejoins Rock Point Road at Newburg).

SHOPPING

Though any town of any size in Charles County has one or two antiques shops, the crossroads of Hughesville is a hub of collectible commerce. Don't be concerned about the lack of street numbers. Technically, all the shops listed are in the 8300s, but though few have addresses on them, the buildings are among the main features of Hughesville—there's no danger of zipping past. The local favorite, **Hughesville Bargain Barn 1 and 2** (Rte. 5 south and Leonardtown Rd., 301/934-8580, White Barn open year-round, Red Barn open noon–5 P.M. Sat.–Sun. May–Feb.), is made up of two converted tobacco auction barns that house more than 70 shops with permanent and transient dealers of antiques and collectibles. The barn features everything from local crafts to old farm tools, cast-offs, and treasures.

Waldorf, near the intersection of Routes 5 and 925, is another antiques hot spot with **Memory Lane Antiques & Collectibles** and **Our Heritage House,** among others.

The **Indian Head Flea Market** (Rte. 210, Indian Head) is held every Saturday May–October. From July–October, local farmers stop by with pickup trucks of local produce.

RECREATION
Golf

In the southern part of the county, **Swan Point Golf Course** (11550 Swan Point Blvd., Swan Point, 301/259-0047, www.swanpointgolf.com) offers the public a championship 18-hole course in a beautiful setting. Designed by Bob Cupp, senior designer for Jack Nicklaus, the course is tucked into a private 904-acre waterfront community where the focus is on appreciation of nature and golf, naturally. A marina is attached to the property.

Part of the public White Plains Park in the northern part of the county, **White Plains Golf Course** (1015 St. Charles Pkwy., Waldorf, 310/645-1300) features an 18-hole course, putting green, and practice areas. The

BOAT TRIP ON THE STYX

For more than two centuries, boats of all descriptions were the main – and often only – form of transportation that connected the widespread plantations and settlements of southern Maryland. All of the rivers in the southern counties, plus the Chesapeake itself, were traversed by some sort of vessel. The *Express* was one of several packet boats – a vessel that made scheduled stops carrying passengers and mail – up the Potomac River from ports on Chesapeake Bay. One of the *Express*'s stops was Cross Manor, home of Captain Randolph Jones and his family. During a heavy storm, Capt. Jones was sitting in his parlor one evening entertaining friends when they heard a knock at the door. The captain looked out the window and saw his wife motioning him toward the door. But when he opened it, no one was there.

Within a few hours, he learned that the *Express* had gone down in the Chesapeake, and his wife, a passenger aboard the vessel, drowned at the very time that he had seen her through the window of their home.

park also has six lighted tennis courts open April 1–October 31.

Biking

Charles County has at least three excellent **bicycle loop trips** that cover various types of scenery and terrain, from farmland to riverfront. See any county information source for a map of all southern Maryland routes.

Bird-Watching

Great blue herons—the county bird—return to pair up, reinforce their nests, and lay eggs during Valentine's Day week at **Nanjemoy Creek Great Blue Heron Sanctuary.** The herons have been returning to the site since the 1940s; the rookery grew from around 100 nests to more than 700 in 2003. The sheer volume of their droppings, combined with beaver activity, has thinned out enough trees to make the birds expand their nesting area beyond the 273-acre Nature Conservancy sanctuary. The conservancy is planning to expand its holdings to further protect the birds and the headwaters of Nanjemoy Creek. The birds stay on the sanctuary until their young are fledged in July. Birders will find good spotting places at the ends of the roads that front the waters of Nanjemoy Creek: Benny Gray Point Road, Bluff Point Road, Tayloes Neck Road, and Walter's Landing Road.

Fishing and Hunting

Mallows Bay, on the western border of Charles County on the Potomac River, is a veritable graveyard of ships, with vessels dating from the American Revolution to 1920. The U.S. Shipping Board Emergency Fleet sent 235 wooden ships that had carried troops and supplies to Europe during World War I here to be salvaged and sunk. Many of them have literally become islands, and they provide some of the best bass fishing grounds on the East Coast.

Myrtle Grove Game Refuge, half a mile north of Ripley on Route 225, was developed for the purpose of propagating game, which it does very well. Anglers will appreciate the year-round riches of Myrtle Grove Lake, and hunters can pursue a range of game from white-tailed deer to wild turkeys. An eight-station firearms shooting range is open for use by permit every day except during deer season. Permits can be obtained from the Myrtle Grove Work Center (310/743-5161) or any DNR Regional Service Center.

ACCOMMODATIONS AND FOOD

You can find chain hotels such as Best Western, Days Inn, and Howard Johnson's (aka Hojos) in either La Plata or Waldorf. Here are a few other options:

Shady Oaks of Serenity (7490 Serenity Dr., Bryantown, 301/932-8864 or 800/597-0924, $85–135) is a modern adaptation of Georgian architecture, set in a development of stately homes. The peaceful country that surrounds this B&B offers visitors a pleasant alternative to the motels that line busy U.S. 301 near La Plata. Kathy and Gene Kazimer are wonderful hosts very helpful, referring visitors to needed services and giving directions through the vast rural spaces of this county. Each of the comfortable rooms has a TV and bath, and a suite is available for larger families. Shady Oaks also has meeting space for groups up to 25. A continental breakfast is included.

Goose Bay Marina and Campground (9365 Goose Bay Ln., Welcome, 301/932-0885, www.goosebaymarina.com) offers 90 RV and tent sites, plus 250 boat slip rentals. Limited tent camping is also available in Smallwood State Park.

Capt. Billy's Crab House & Restaurant (11495 Popes Creek Rd., Newburg, 301/932-4323, www.captbillys.com, lunch and dinner Tues.–Sun., $5–30) has been in business since the end of World War II. The food is good and the menu extensive, offering frybaskets for around $13 and fancier entrées for market price—for example, a broiled seafood platter runs $29. You'll also find traditional Maryland fare like crab meat in garlic butter, oysters casino, and fried chicken. Though the mailing address is in Newburg, Popes Creek Road is off U.S. 301 roughly nine miles south of La Plata.

Capt. John's Crab House (16215 Cobb Island, 301/259-2315, www.cjcrab.com, breakfast, lunch, and dinner daily year-round) serves up simple and inexpensive breakfasts (under $9), but dinner entrées such as lobster tails, combo platters, and prime rib can run up to $30. The restaurant also features daily specials and an extensive takeout menu for anyone who doesn't have time to lounge around enjoying the great view from the dining room windows.

INFORMATION

For a packet of information and answers to any questions you might have, contact **Charles County Tourism** (P.O. Box 2150, La Plata, MD 20646, 301/645-0558 or 800/766-3386, www.explorecharlescomd.com).

Solomons

Solomons, a tiny enclave of homes, restaurants, shops, and lodgings, was actually an island until about 1868. At that time, Isaac Solomon, who developed oyster canning in Baltimore, purchased "Sandy Island" and built a processing plant at the northern end. The channel that separated the mainland from the island was gradually filled in with oyster shells until only a ditch remained. A small bridge near the Waterman's Memorial Park connects the island to the mainland, and the area is known collectively as Solomons. A riverwalk along the water extends from the park to the island neck, affording strollers an opportunity to enjoy the bay and the shops and restaurants that line the principal street, Solomons Island Road (Rte. 2).

SIGHTS

◖ Calvert Marine Museum

One of the most fun things to see and do in Solomons (14200 Solomons Island Rd., 410/326-2042, www.calvertmarinemuseum.com, 10 A.M.–5 P.M. daily, $7 adults), this museum covers the maritime history and life of the river and bay. One exhibit features the fossilized remains of local ancient inhabitants, including the extinct "megatooth" white shark of the Miocene age. There's an indoor 15-tank "estuarium" that displays local water creatures, and river otters entertain adults and children alike.

A boardwalk extends into the marsh for active exploration. Visitors can clamber up ladder-like stairs to an authentic screw-pile lighthouse, the Drum Point light. The inside is decorated as it would have been when a lighthouse keeper and his family were in residence. The boathouse is full of log canoes, skiffs, scrapes, and other examples of small craft used on the Chesapeake.

Every day June–August (12:30–4:30 P.M.), and on weekends in May and September (10 A.M.–noon and 1–4:30 P.M.), the museum runs shuttle buses to the Cove Point Lighthouse at the end of Cove Point Road, a spot great for viewing the Chesapeake. Since the lighthouse is still in active use, access may be limited.

The museum also operates the J. C. Lore Oyster House, half a mile south of the main museum, which is dedicated to information about the boom and decline of the region's commercial seafood industries. It's open during same hours that the Cove Point Lighthouse shuttle runs (see above).

Museumgoers also have the opportunity to cruise around Solomons Harbor and the Patuxent River aboard the *Wm. B. Tennison,* an 1899 nine-log bugeye. Cruises are available at 2 P.M. Wednesday–Sunday May–October, and an additional 12:30 P.M. cruise is offered weekends July–August. The fee is $7 for adults.

◖ Annemarie Garden on St. John

Memory is a form of renewal. It offers a second chance.

– Jane Rosen-Queralt, *A Survivor's Map*

Annemarie Garden on St. John (two miles north of Solomons on Dowell Rd.,

KEEPER OF LIGHTS

One of the world's earliest warning lights was also one of the seven wonders of the ancient world: the lighthouse of Alexandria, Egypt. Built around 280 B.C., it towered 450 feet above the harbor. The light within was an open flame. At the time, bonfires on promontories were the rule and the only protection available to ship captains on stormy nights – until the glass lantern room was invented and first installed in England's Eddystone Light. Candles replaced open fires, and mirrors placed in huge wooden bowls served as crude reflectors.

Born near the cusp of the 18th and 19th centuries, Frenchman Augustin Fresnel was a slow learner who could barely read by the age of eight. However, he led a secret life away from school – his friends called him "the genius" for his ability to modify their toys to go faster, higher, and longer. As an adult, Fresnel applied his talents to optics and produced the most important breakthrough in distance warning lights in 2,000 years.

In 1822, Fresnel, working with several glassmakers, produced a combination of prism shapes that gathered and intensified light and projected it outward. The lens looked like a giant glass beehive, with a light at the center. The apparatus came in eight "orders": the largest (First Order) nearly 12 feet in height, with concentric rings of glass prisms above and below to bend the light into a narrow beam. The first Fresnel lens, installed in the Cardovan Tower lighthouse on the Gironde River in France, was visible a remarkable 20 miles away. Fresnel lenses quickly spread all over Europe.

Despite the clear superiority of Fresnel lenses, America clung to the weak lights that protected U.S. coasts; the French export was too expensive, the government declared. Finally, a reshuffling of the government's Lighthouse Board in 1852 brought in eminent scientists and mariners, who began distribut-

Calvert Marine Museum Lighthouse

© JOANNE MILLER

ing the Fresnel lens to most U.S. lighthouses. Fresnel's theories of light form the basis of modern optics, and his lenses are still used in distance lights. The principle behind his lighthouse lens is also used in automobile headlights and the flashing lights on police and emergency vehicles.

Southern Maryland is home to several of the Chesapeake Bay's lighthouses, all automated or removed from service: Cove Point (1828, tours given by Calvert Marine Museum), Drum Point (1854, rebuilt on the grounds of Calvert Marine Museum), Point Lookout (1830, now a Naval training station in Point Lookout State Park), and Piney Point Lighthouse (1836, in Piney Point Park). Most of the lighthouses in the bay were equipped with a Fresnel lens.

410/326-4640, www.annmariegarden.org, 9 A.M.–5 P.M. daily, free except for special events) is a magical combination of wilderness and sophisticated site-specific sculpture, including the lyrical quote above, which is part of an assembly on an elevated walkway. St. John refers to the creek that runs through the back of the property, and the shady green groves of trees that cover the land make for peaceful communing with nature.

After buying the garden as an investment property in 1960, Francis Koenig decided to keep the 30-acre parcel as it was and named it for his wife. "Everything I have built in my life will someday be taken down. The Annemarie Garden will always remain," he said.

You can't miss the entrance on Dowell Road: Artists Peter King and Marni Jaime of Pensacola, Florida, constructed two enormous walls covered with eight tons of ceramics that bracket iron gates. The sculpture inside is as varied as you can imagine. *Tribute to the Oyster Tonger,* by Antonio Mendez, is a formal fountain that's irresistible to children in the summer; in some seasons, you can glimpse giant tin fish floating through the trees. A pathway winds through the groves, with stops at various "rooms" containing works by nationally famous sculptors. Two more installations of note are *The Council Ring,* by B. Amore and Woody Dorsey, a beautifully constructed ring of granite council chairs; and the *Generations Room,* by Jerome Meadows, symbolizing the generational cycle of plants and man. Art exhibitions are held in the garden gallery, and the garden sponsors special events throughout the year, including Garden in Lights (during the holiday season) and Artsfest, with over 250 performing and visual artists, plus food and spirits. Call the number above for dates. Be sure to stop by the restroom—it's a beautiful surprise, and all the work inside was donated.

ACCOMMODATIONS

There are several B&Bs on the island, including the ones featured here. The Holiday Inn is on the mainland part of Solomons, just be-

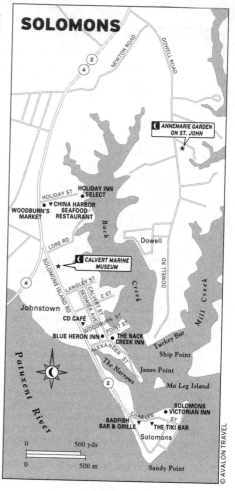

fore the island bridge. All accommodations are within easy walking distance of attractions (except Annemarie Garden, which is a short drive out of town).

Holiday Inn Select (155 Holiday Dr., P.O. Box 1099, Solomons, 410/326-6311 or 800/356-2009, $99–140) would be just another Holiday Inn if it weren't for the spectacular views from the waterside rooms, the Hospitality Harbor Marina (where you can dock your boat for a fee), and the outdoor courtyard and bar, the Afterdeck. All the amenities are in place: Rooms range from basic sleeping quarters with a coffee maker, an ironing board, and cable TV to suites with whirlpool baths and kitchenettes. A health club, tennis courts, and an outdoor pool are also on the premises. Since Holiday Inn offers many deals and packages, you'll see lots of kids here, as well as businesspeople.

Solomons Victorian Inn (125 Charles St., 410/326-4811, www.solomonsvictorian inn.com, $100–255) looks out over Solomons Harbor from the southernmost part of the island. The inn features five rooms in the main house, all with private bath, plus a third-floor suite. In addition, the carriage house offers two rooms with private entrances, views, and whirlpool tubs. The decor reflects the era, and a full breakfast is served in a delightfully bright sunroom.

◖ **The Back Creek Inn** (Alexander Ln. and Calvert St., 410/326-2022, www.bb online.com/md/backcreek, $105–220) is in the residential section of Solomons and looks out onto the tree-lined banks of Back Creek. The 1880 home is decorated in contemporary style and offers four rooms, two suites, and a cottage, all with private bath, cable TV, and a full country breakfast. It also has a private pier, and bicycles are available for guest use.

The Blue Heron (14614 Calvert St., 410/326-2707, www.blueheronbandb.com, $155–225) has a modern flavor and beautiful water views. A deep-water dock is available for boaters. Two rooms and two suites have private baths. One of the innkeepers is a Cordon Bleu–trained chef, so expect gourmet breakfasts; special-rate packages include several cooking/eating classes. A two-night stay is required.

FOOD

The main road in Solomons runs north–south—when the road narrows so you can see the water within 50 feet on both sides, you've reached the neck. If you get lost (unlikely), ask anyone. Two landmarks on the neck, the Lighthouse Inn, and Bowen's Inn (established in the

1800s), as well as a nearby condominium, were completely destroyed by fire in 2006. The fire was reputedly caused by a carelessly tossed cigarette butt and fueled by high winds.

The **CD Cafe** (14350 Solomons Island Rd., 410/326-3877, www.cdcafe.info, lunch and dinner daily, $9–18) is a local favorite for reliable chow. The big Bistro Burger ($9) with salad is served all day, and the entrees have a modern twist (New York strip steak with a mango-chipotle drizzle, $24).

The ◖ **Lighthouse Inn** (14636 Solomons Island Rd. at the neck, 410/326-2444, www .lighthouse-inn.com) was the premier restaurant in town before the fire, known not only for its excellent seafood, but also for its view of the water and dockage. Rebuilding has been slow but determined. The owners are planning an updated architectural design, and, as of this writing, intend to keep the same menu. Along with seafood dishes such as the mariner's platter ($27) and seafood Naples ($17), the menu also featured Santa Fe chicken and mixed grill. There is no current plan to replace Bowen's Inn.

Woodburn's Market (Solomons Island Rd./Rte. 2, Patuxent Plaza, 410/326-3284, 7 A.M.–9 P.M. Mon.–Sat., 8 A.M.–7 P.M. Sun.) isn't a restaurant but an upscale gourmet market that sells ingredients and takeout food from a sushi bar, pizza bar, pastry shop, and more.

Also in Patuxent Plaza, **China Harbor Seafood Restaurant** (13958 Solomons Island Rd., 410/326-0700, www.chinaharborrestaurant .com, lunch and dinner daily, $9) offers fresh seafood specialties, as well as mild Cantonese-style duck, pork, and vegetable dishes.

Nightlife

Badfish Dock Bar & Grille (120 Charles St., Solomons, 410/394-0110, www.thebadfish.net, dinner Tues.–Sun., $20), formerly known as Harbor Sounds, is Solomons' party place, with a Cajun/American menu, daily food or drink specials, a full bar, and live music on the weekends. It's part of the Harbor Island Marina (105 Charles St., 410/326-3441, www.harborisland marina.biz), a popular stop for boaters.

The Tiki Bar (Solomons Island Rd. past the neck, 410/326-4075, www.tikibarsolomons .com, 4 P.M.–1 A.M. Mon.–Thurs., 2 P.M.–2 A.M. Sat., noon–1 A.M. Sun., closed early Oct.–late April) is a venerable night spot, a little grass shack lit by tiki torches night and day. The Tiki Barn features dozens of varieties of cigars and other tobacco products.

Twin Beaches

Today, the "Twin Beaches" are quiet waterfront residential communities that cater to boaters and bathers, but it was not always so. Chesapeake Beach was the terminus of the Chesapeake Beach Railway, and a grand resort and boardwalk opened there in 1900. Adjacent North Beach grew as a neighboring cottage community. In 1930, the railway closed operations, and the amusements were moved inland; the park was finally closed in 1972. A boardwalk runs along Route 261, paralleling the communities and offering a mile of beachfront to sun seekers. Parking is available all along the boardwalk on Bay Street.

SIGHTS
Chesapeake Beach Railway Museum
The Chesapeake Beach Railway Museum (Mears Ave. and C St., Chesapeake Beach, 410/257-3892, www.cbrm.org, 1–4 p.m. daily May–Sept., 1–4 p.m. Sat–Sun. Apr. and Oct., free) features memorabilia from the beach's glorious past as a resort and amusement park.

Chesapeake Beach Water Park
The family-friendly Chesapeake Beach Water Park (Rte. 261 and Gordon Stinnett Ave., 301/855-3803, 11 a.m.–8 p.m. Sat.–Sun. Memorial Day–June 10, 11 a.m.–8 p.m. daily June 10–first day of school, 11 a.m.–8 p.m. Sat.–Sun. Aug. 19–Labor Day) is a good place for kids to cool off on hot summer days. Admission ranges $6–20, depending on day, size, and residency (the closer your home address, the cheaper it is). It features eight slides (including one with wheelchair access), lap lanes,

a children's activity pool, a separate "diaper" pool for the littlest swimmers, a 12-foot floating alligator, a 12-foot floating sea serpent, a giant crab, a seashell slide, and a slow river. An adult must accompany children under 13. It's owned and operated by the citizens of Chesapeake Beach.

FOOD
Beach Cove (8416 Bayside Rd., Chesapeake Beach, 301/855-0025, www.beachcoverestaurant.com, lunch and dinner daily, lunch $9, dinner $8–29) is a casual restaurant with an outside deck that looks out over the bay. Beach Cove offers poultry, meat, seafood, and pasta dishes, as well as a full bar, and it features live music on Wednesday, Friday, and Saturday.

The **Rod 'N' Reel** (Rte. 261 and Mears Ave., Chesapeake Beach, 301/855-8351, 11 A.M.–10 P.M. Mon.–Fri., 8 A.M.–10 P.M. Sat., 8 A.M.–9 P.M. Sun., $13–30) is a big seafood restaurant that serves up its own catch of the day. Rod 'N' Reel also rents out space on its boats for fishing parties; call 800/233-2080 for more information. In 2004–2005, the Rod 'N' Reel expanded into a resort with rooms, a salon, and a spa, and the owners added two more restaurants, **Smokey Joe's Grill** (barbeque, breakfast, lunch, and dinner, $10) and the **Boardwalk Café** (casual American, lunch and dinner, $9).

The **Thursday's Bar & Grill** (7th St. and Bay Ave. at the end of the boardwalk, North Beach, 410/286-8695, www.nbeachmd.com/thursdays, lunch and dinner daily, lunch $7, dinner $15) looks a bit like a tavern, but offers a lively menu that includes seafood classics, prime rib, and chicken.

Greater Calvert County

Calvert County combines ripe farmland with watery entertainment on its narrow peninsula. Solomons is the most developed town, though Prince Frederick is the county seat. Much of the county produces plentiful fruits and vegetables in season, and the Calvert County Agriculture Commission lists a wide variety of products for sale, from goats to gourds to daylilies. Visit the commission's website (www.calvertag.org) and type in "farm tour" for the latest updates. You can also get a brochure through the **Calvert County Visitors Center** (410/257-5381 or 410/326-6027, www.ecalvert.com/content/tourism/visitorsguide).

SIGHTS
Jefferson Patterson Park and Museum

This innovatively used property (10515 Mackall Rd., St. Leonard, 410/586-8500, www.jefpat .org, 10 A.M.–5 P.M. Wed.–Sun. Apr. 15–Oct. 15, free) is named for one of its owners, a former ambassador and son of the founder of the National Cash Register Company. His wife, Mary "Marvin" Breckinridge Patterson, was the granddaughter of B. F. Goodrich, and—prior to marrying the ambassador—was also a freelance photojournalist of some repute. She once rode a bicycle in northern Finland to capture pictures of an arctic Lapp colony, and she was the first female CBS broadcaster in Europe, sharing the spotlight with her old friend Edward R. Murrow. The Pattersons used "Point Farm" as a retreat and laboratory for modern methods of agriculture. After Mr. Patterson's death in 1977, Mrs. Patterson continued to live occasionally at the farm; in 1983, she donated the property to the state of Maryland, under the stewardship of the Maryland Historical Trust.

The property is now home to the Maryland Archaeological Conservation Laboratory (MAC), a state-of-the-art research, conservation, and collections facility for archaeological finds from all over Maryland, and the Academy of Natural Sciences Estuarine Research Center. MAC's library is open to the public on a non-lending basis 9 A.M.–5 P.M Monday–Friday. Visitors can see archaeology in action on the property by strolling down the one-mile Riverside Trail. The 0.8-mile Woodland Trail affords the opportunity to enjoy local flora and fauna, and the 0.75-mile Shoreline Loop explores a section of the Patuxent River shoreline. The Academy of Natural Sciences offers a self-guided 0.25-mile BayScapes walk from its parking lot at 10454 Mackall Road.

The visitors center houses a permanent exhibit, "12,000 Years in the Chesapeake." The park sponsors many special events throughout the year, including a Celtic Festival and Highland Gathering in April, an African American Family Community Day in May, a War of 1812 Tavern Night and Reenactment of the Battle of St. Leonard in September, and other events throughout the season; call 410/586-8501 for

Amish farm haystacks

more information. To get there, take Route 4 south, then turn right (west) on Route 264 three miles south of Prince Frederick. Follow Route 264 for two miles, then turn left on Route 265 (south) for six miles.

Calvert Cliffs State Park

The most prominent physical feature of the Chesapeake's western shore is in **Calvert Cliffs State Park** (14 miles south of Prince Frederick on Route 2/4 in Lusby, Calvert Cliffs State Park, c/o Smallwood State Park, 2750 Sweden Point Rd., Marbury, MD 20658, 301/743-7613, day use only). Stretching 30 miles along the coast of Calvert County, the cliffs were formed more than 15 million years ago, when a warm and shallow sea covered all of southern Maryland. The land became uplifted at the end of the last ice age, exposing more than 600 species of fossils in the cliffs, including calcified shark teeth and various mollusk shells.

The park features 13 miles of foot trails; a two-mile hike from the parking lot leads visitors to the open beach and fossil-hunting area (visitors may keep what they find). Because the cliffs are unstable, fossil-hunting is not permitted close to the cliff bottoms. Bicyclists and equestrians are restricted to specific trails, and some trails are closed during hunting season (hunting is permitted in the park). A one-acre pond is stocked with freshwater fish, and a playground is available. Camping is for youth groups only. There is a $5 charge for vehicles to enter the park. Follow signs from Route 2/4 to reach the park entrance.

Other Parks and Scenic Spots

Southern Maryland has little "islands" of ecosystems, and **Battle Creek Cypress Swamp** (Gray's Rd., Prince Frederick, 410/535-5327, Nature Center hours 8:30 A.M.–4:30 P.M. daily, free) is one of them. One of the north-

---

NUCLEAR POWER IN CALVERT CLIFFS

The fossil-filled bluffs of southern Maryland are home to the past and the present. The state's one and only nuclear facility, Calvert Cliffs Nuclear Plant, lies just north of Calvert Cliffs State Park. Only 380 acres of the 2,100-acre site are used for the plant, and the rest is maintained in a natural state.

For a simple example of how nuclear power works, first picture the results: When you turn on a light switch at home, electrical current flows from the wall connector through the wire and into the light bulb. When you turn the switch off, the current remains (which is why it's a bad idea to stick your finger in a wall socket), pumped through miles of wires from the source, the energy plant. At the plant, electricity is produced and stored in a generator, which is powered by the spinning motion of giant fans, or turbines. The turbines may be driven by water, wind, or steam: Nuclear energy produces steam. Unlike the burning action necessary to convert carbon-based sources to heat to turn water into steam, nu-

clear energy relies on fission – the splitting of uranium atoms – to generate heat.

U.S. nuclear power plants come in two varieties: pressurized water reactors and boiling water reactors. Calvert Cliffs is a pressurized reactor plant. The reactor, in which the nuclear core is seated, heats pressurized water (called primary coolant) in a closed system. Another closed system filled with water (secondary coolant) flows around the ultra-hot primary coolant pipes and becomes steam, which then drives a turbine.

Prior to September 11, 2001, the Calvert Cliffs facility was open for tours and featured informative displays and a pleasant picnic area. Now, as with all U.S. plants, it's under heavy security and closed to the public until further notice. This plant was the first U.S. facility to have its license extended, in 1999, for another 20 years of use – and it has one of the most outstanding safety and production records in the nation. Calvert Cliffs supplies much of the energy used in central Maryland.

ernmost occurring stands of bald cypress trees in America, this swamp/sanctuary features a small interactive museum where visitors can see a rare albino snapping turtle and wander on walkways above the water. Most of the bald cypress trees here are 75–100 years old, though the trees can live for 2,000 years. The trail can be walked in 15 minutes, and among the jutting "knees" (projections from the tree roots that help to anchor the conifers) are remnants of moonshine stills that operated during Prohibition. The Nature Conservancy acquired this unique property in 1957, and you'll feel you've stepped into a land far removed from the Chesapeake shore. To get there from Route 301, turn to Route 4 south and continue through Prince Frederick. Turn right (west) onto Sixes Road (Rte. 506), look for the sign, and turn left (south) on Gray's Road. The sanctuary is about 0.25 mile south on the right (west) side of the road.

If your taste runs to chestnut rather than cypress, take a walk around the **American Chestnut Land Trust** (Scientists Cliffs Rd., Port Republic, 410/586-1570, dawn–dusk daily). This 810-acre ecological preserve is home to one of the state's largest living American chestnut trees. Leave your car at the gate and explore the 12 miles of wooded trails.

One of the prettiest beaches in the area can be found at **Flag Ponds Nature Park** (10 miles south of Prince Frederick, 410/535-5327, 9 A.M.–6 P.M. daily Memorial Day–Labor Day, weekends only April–May and Sept.–Oct., closed the rest of the year). There is a fee to park: $5, or $7 if your plates are out of the county. The park is named for the blue flag iris and other wildflowers that bloom from early spring to autumn. A half-mile trail leads to the boardwalk and beach; there is a parking area closer to the beach for those who might have difficulty walking. On the way to the white sands, visitors will pass an old fisherman's shanty, one of three left over from the days when the area supported a major fishing industry. There's a wide-open vista of Calvert Cliffs to the south. Visitors occasionally see one-inch blue balls wash up on the beach. They're used

walkway at Flag Ponds Nature Park

© JOANNE MILLER

to clean the condenser tubes at Calvert Cliffs Nuclear Power Plant—most are trapped in the system, but a few escape into the bay, providing a strange juxtaposition with shark vertebrae and other natural flotsam. Yucca, a plant most people associate with the desert, also blooms freely among the dunes and pines in May. Several short (less than one mile) trails loop around three small ponds on the park property.

King's Landing Park (west of Huntingtown on the Patuxent River, 410/535-2661, 8:30 A.M.–8 P.M. daily Memorial Day–Labor Day, 8:30 A.M.–4:30 P.M. Mon.–Fri. and 8:30 A.M.–6 P.M. Sat.–Sun. the rest of the year, free) features a 200-foot fishing pier and a great place for kayakers and canoeists to access the river. Walking trails lead through mature hardwood forests, and a boardwalk overlooks marshes along Cocktown Creek.

The **Port Republic School Number 7** (Broomes Island Rd./Rte. 264, 410/586-0232 or 410/586-0482, 2–4 P.M. Sun. only June–Aug., free) is a restored 19th-century one-room schoolhouse on the grounds of Christ Church.

Schoolhouses like this one ordinarily held up to 30 students in grades ranging from kindergarten to 12th—all held in check by one harried teacher.

The **Hallowing Point Park Tobacco Barn** (4755 Hallowing Point Rd. off Rte. 231, Prince Frederick, 410/535-1600, ext. 2225, 9 A.M.–5 P.M. daily, free) was built around the time of the Civil War, and now holds exhibits on the history of the Calvert County tobacco industry and the process of raising tobacco. The barn is set in a pretty park near the Patuxent River.

SHOPPING

Calvert Country Market (Rte. 4, Prince Frederick Shopping Center, 98 S. Solomons Island Rd., 410/414-9669, www.calvertcountrymarket.com, open daily except Mon.) features locally grown fresh produce, area seafood, and local crafts—an old-fashioned indoor market.

The **Chesapeake Market Place** (5015 St. Leonard Rd., 0.25 mile east on Calvert Beach Rd. from the intersection of Route 4 and Calvert Beach Rd., St. Leonard, 410/586-3725, www.chesapeakemarketplace.com, Wed.–Sun.) is an indoor market with 100 antiques and collectible shops. Resurrected from an old lumberyard in the 1990s, it hosts popular auctions on Wednesday and Friday nights.

Much of the county produces fruits and vegetables in season; the Calvert County Agriculture Commission lists a wide variety of products for sale, from goats to gourds to daylilies. Visit www.calvertag.org and type in "farm tour" for the latest updates.

RECREATION
Fishing

Did you say fishing? Calvert County is well equipped to furnish visitors with anything that has to do with water sports. **Solomons Charter Captains Association** (800/450-1775, www.fishsolomons.com) will hook you up with a fishing charter. Solomons Charter Boats cleans your fish and gives out B.Y.O.C. (Bring Your Own Catch) tickets, good at several participating restaurants that will cook the catch to order. Two other sources for head boats

are **Chesapeake Beach Fishing Charters** (301/855-4655 or toll-free 866/532-9246, www.chesapeakefishingcharters.com) and **Rod 'N' Reel** (Chesapeake Beach, 800/233-2080, www.rodnreelinc.com).

If you'd prefer to go your own way, try **Solomons Boat Rental** (410/326-4060 or 800/535-2628, www.boat-rent.net) for powerboats, or **Bills Boat Rental** (Broomes Island, 410/586-3599) for skiffs, canoes, sailboats, and windsurfers.

Golf

The **Chesapeake Hills Golf Club** (11352 H. G. Truman Rd., Lusby, 410/326-4653, www.chesapeakehills.com) is a traditional par 72 course, with a putting green, a practice sand trap, and driving range.

Twin Shields Golf Club (2425 Roarty Rd., Dunkirk, 410/257-7800 or 301/855-7670, www.twinshields.com) is a par 70 course offering 18 holes, a driving range, and teaching and putting greens.

ACCOMMODATIONS AND CAMPING

The **Cliff House** (156 Windcliff Rd., Prince Frederick, 410/535-4839, www.bbonline.com/md/cliffhouse, $120) is a private home overlooking the Chesapeake Bay, with water access for fishing. A single suite with a queen-sized bed and full bath are available to guests with children older than 12. Breakfast is included.

Breezy Point Beach (Breezy Point Rd., Chesapeake Beach, 410/535-0259), a combination public beach and campground, is run by the county. The beach features a swimming area, picnic facilities, a playground, bathhouses, and a 300-foot fishing and crabbing pier. It's open 6 A.M.–sunset May 1–October 31, and a fee of $6 per adult and $4 per child is charged. Camping facilities are available May 1–October 31 and include water and sewage. Depending on the site, seasonal fees range from $1,850–2,550, but monthly camping ($380) and daily camping ($30) are also available. To get there, take Route 260 east toward Chesapeake Beach. Turn right (south) on Route 261. Go five miles and turn left (east) at the green sign that says "Breezy Point." Follow the road one mile to the campground.

Breezy Point Cabins (5230 Breezy Point Rd., 410/535-4356) features six cabins next to the beach. Rates are $375 per week and $1,300 per month.

Patuxent Camp Sites (4770 Williams Wharf Rd., St. Leonard, 410/586-9880, $35) is open year-round, but shuts down a few of its 125 campsites in winter. Water and electricity, full bath facilities, a boat ramp, and a 100-foot pier are provided. Reserve early for a good site by the water.

FOOD

One of my favorite places to eat in the county used to require a drive out to the end of Broome's Island Road: 【 **Stoney's Seafood House** (Broome's Island, 410/586-1888, www.stoneysseafoodhouse.com, lunch and dinner daily spring–fall, call for hours, $8–30). Outdoor tables look out over the rural harbor, filled with the comings and goings of small boats (there's indoor seating, too). It's a great place to enjoy crab cakes, chowder, and oyster sandwiches at good prices. The tables are set with the traditional newspaper, a roll of paper towels, and cracking implements if crabs are what you seek (it also serves salads, burgers, and other fare). The good news is that Stoney's has added a location in Prince Frederick (Fox Run Shopping Center, 545 N. Solomons Island Rd., 410/586-1888, lunch and dinner daily) that's open year-round.

Vera's White Sands Restaurant (1200 White Sands Dr., Lusby, 410/586-1182, www.veraswhitesandsbeachclub.com, dinner only, $13–30) is in a class by itself. The eponymous and legendary Vera Freeman created the tiki-torch decor and ran the place for many years. In 2006, she retired and the name and restaurant were taken over by her neighbors, Steve Stanley and Lisa Del Rico. Though they've renovated the place from top to bottom and brought in an experienced chef and crew, the decor will still have you humming "Bali Hai." The new owners have created a brand new beach, boat ramp, and docks; there are also plans for live music and a veranda for dancing. The menu isn't restricted to conch and blowfish—it's continental, and there's a full bar. Bring the boat, as Vera's provides a dock.

A popular hangout for local families is **Adam's, the Place for Ribs** (220 Solomons Island Rd., Prince Frederick, 410/586-0001, lunch and dinner daily, lunch $9, dinner $16). In addition to barbecued ribs, chicken, and shrimp, the menu also includes broiled steaks, sandwiches, salads, and children's options. Adam's has a full bar, and there's often a wait for a table on Saturday night.

INFORMATION

Calvert County (Prince Frederick, MD 20678, 410/535-4585 or 800/331-9771, www.ecalvert.com/content/tourism/visitorsguide) has a visitors center at 14175 South Solomons Island Road (410/326-6027). It's the place to go for maps and information on destinations in that area. **Solomons** has its own website at www.sba.solomons.md.us.

Southern Maryland/This Is Living (P.O. Box 2154, Leonardtown, MD 20650, 301/475-0044, somdthisisliving.somd.com) is a full-color, glossy publication focused on the southern Maryland region. Designed for residents as well as visitors, this magazine features information on activities and sites in Calvert, Charles, and St. Mary's Counties. Emphasis is on new and historical homes, gardening, history, and historical sites, in addition to special editions on antiquing, dining out, what to do, and where to go.

St. Mary's County

The shoreline of St. Mary's County looks as convoluted as the average primate brain. Narrow roads crisscross the land and terminate at points on the water—a great place to drive or bike with no destination in mind. Since there's so much farmland, people are used to driving distances to get a crab dinner or enjoy a little history. But the distances aren't intimidating, and the scenery is priceless.

SIGHTS
◖ Historic St. Mary's City

This reconstructed town (Rosecroft Rd. off Rte. 5, 301/862-0990 or 800/762-1634, www .stmaryscity.org) was the colonial capital of Maryland, the first permanent settlement established by Lord Baltimore in 1634, and the fourth English settlement in North America. Entrance fees are $10 adults, $8 seniors, $6 students, and $3.50 children 3–12.

Winter: The Shop at Farthing's Ordinary and Museum grounds are open are open 10 A.M.–5 P.M. Wednesday–Sunday late November–late December and Januray–March. No charge to visitors.

Spring: All facilities are open 10 A.M.–5 P.M. Tuesday–Saturday mid-March–mid-June, including living history exhibits. On Sunday, the living history exhibits are closed, but the visitors center, exhibit hall, Shop at Farthing's Ordinary, and museum grounds remain open.

Summer: All facilities are open 10 A.M.–5 P.M. Wednesday–Sunday mid-June–mid-September, including living history exhibits.

Fall: All facilities are open 10 A.M.–5 P.M. Tuesday–Saturday mid-September–November. On Sunday, the living history exhibits are closed, but admission is reduced and the visitors center, exhibit hall, Shop at Farthing's Ordinary, and museum grounds remain open.

Archaeologists are excavating more than 150 structures on 20 sites in an 832-acre

the *Maryland Dove* docked at Old St. Mary's

© JOANNE MILLER

A VERY LITIGIOUS WOMAN

In 1638, Margaret Brent emigrated from England with her sister, Mary, and settled on St. Mary's town lands, naming their 70-acre farm "Sister's Freehold." Both Margaret and Mary remained single – this proved to be extremely freeing, since married women were not allowed to own property or bring actions in court. Margaret frequently lent money to other colonists, readily going to court to collect overdue payments. In fact, her name appears so often in early court documents – 124 times in eight years – that the American Bar Association's Commission on Women in the Profession named its Women Lawyers of Achievement Award after her. Most of Margaret's cases involved property disputes and debts. She had no formal legal training, but then there were no lawyers in Maryland. Everyone argued their own cases before the provincial court or appointed "attorneys in fact" to act for them. Because of Margaret's success in her own cases, others probably asked that she speak on their behalf.

She became a close friend of the Catholic governor, Leonard Calvert. As religious hostilities spilled over to the New World, Protestant renegades ransacked Maryland's few colonial outposts in 1645, including St. Mary's City. When the colony was retaken in 1647, Leonard Calvert, dying, appointed Margaret sole executrix of his estate, bidding her to "Take all and pay all." After his death, hired mercenaries threatened to wreak havoc if they were not paid. Calvert's personal estate was poor in everything but land – he was also responsible for land and cattle belonging to his brother, Cecil, in England. When Leonard died, the provincial court granted Margaret power of attorney over Cecil's properties until he could name another – a process that would take many months. Under English law, Margaret could not sell anything, and therefore could not pay the soldiers. Margaret approached a meeting of the Assembly and asked for permission to vote twice as a member, not only for herself, but also as attorney for the Calvert estate. Since women were not allowed to vote in the Assembly at all, she probably hoped to persuade them to allow her to sell Cecil Calvert's cattle. Permission was denied.

Margaret sold the cattle, anyway, paid the mercenaries, and saved the colony. Unfortunately, Cecil didn't see it that way. In Margaret's defense, the Assembly wrote, "We do Verily Believe and in Conscience report that it was better for the Collonys safety at that time in her hands then in any mans else in the whole Province after your Brothers death for the Soldiers would never have treated any other with that Civility and respect and though they were even ready at several times to run into mutiny yet she still pacified them."

Lord Baltimore (Cecil's more glamorous alter ego) refused to be mollified, railing against Margaret and her siblings. Around 1650, the Brents bought extensive property in Virginia and moved there. Margaret kept out of the court system and died at her plantation, named Peace, in 1671.

---

area; meanwhile, the entire preserve is open to the public as an outdoor museum, complete with costumed interpreters. Much of the acreage is a rural preserve of shoreline, fields, forests, and wetlands, providing a variety of habitats for wildlife watchers. The effect is a kinder, gentler—and authentically low-key—Williamsburg.

Your first stop should be the visitors center, which features an exhibit called "Once the Metropolis of Maryland." The exhibit traces the story of Maryland's first capital from its English roots in the 1630s through its demise at the end of the 17th century, then its subsequent rebirth as a major archaeological project and outdoor museum in the later 20th century. Significant artifacts found at the site are on display, coupled with stories of discovery and the interpretation of these finds, as well as descriptions of how the work of historians and archaeologists comes together to describe the past. While you're there, pick up a list of daily highlights to learn when various demonstrations (17th-century navigation aboard the *Maryland Dove*, the plantation walking tour, etc.) are given. A walking trail leads to the Woodland Indian Hamlet, an exhibit with re-created *witchotts* (wood and bark dwellings) that interprets 17th-century contact between European settlers and the Yoacomoco inhabitants. The founding site of the Roman Catholic Church in the English colonies can be seen in Chapel Field. Visitors can view the cross-shaped brick foundations where the 1667 Brick Chapel is being reconstructed using 17th-century materials and techniques.

Town Center, the heart of the colonial capital, is being re-created as research on the original structures is completed. Visitors can explore an "ordinary" (a combined tavern/inn), learn about colonial commerce at Cordea's Hope, and see a mock trial at the State House of 1676. The State House of 1676 is a re-creation of an imposing brick structure, among the first public buildings in Maryland. Nearby, a plaque honors Mathias de Sousa, the first Marylander of African descent, who came aboard the *Ark* when the ship explored St. Mary's River in 1634. The home of Maryland's first governor, Leonard Calvert, and other colonial buildings are marked with ghost frames today; in time, they too will be rebuilt.

The Shop at Farthing's Ordinary features unusual items inspired by history and nature, and also serves refreshments. One of the most fascinating re-creations of the period is in the river below: an authentic working square-rigged ship, the *Maryland Dove*. Historic St. Mary's City also has a working farm, the Godiah Spray Tobacco Plantation; costumed interpreters portray the Spray family and their indentured servants as they act out the everyday life of early Tidewater farmers. The Brome-Howard Inn is adjacent to the property.

Historic St. Mary's City sponsors special events throughout the season, including the Maritime Heritage Festival in June; the Tidewater Archaeology Dig in July, which encourages visitors to participate in archaeological excavations; and Woodland Indian Discovery Day in September, a hands-on exploration of Native American culture and skills. Interpretive signage and an audio tour are available, in addition to costumed interpreters.

◖ Point Lookout State Park

This scenic multi-use recreational area (end of Rte. 5, Scotland, 301/872-5688, 8 A.M.–sunset daily, $3–6 entrance fee) was one of three manors owned by Leonard Calvert, first governor of Maryland. The park is open year-round, but the visitors center is seasonal (daily Apr.–Oct., closed Tues. and Thurs. Nov.–Mar.).

When the Civil War started, Point Lookout was a popular summer resort with a hotel, beach cottages, a wharf, and a lighthouse. As the war raged on, the resort failed, and the Union leased the property for use as an army hospital. By 1863, the hospital was used to hold Confederate sympathizers from Maryland. Soon after the Battle of Gettysburg, construction began on a camp capable of holding 10,000 prisoners of war, to be named Camp Hoffman. By 1864, over 20,000 imprisoned enlisted men crowded the camp. Disease, contamination, and freezing conditions killed nearly 4,000 prisoners out of the total of 52,000 held there over the years. Those that survived were sent home at war's end, and by 1865, the camp was deserted.

The state took over in 1965 and turned the 1,046-acre property into a park. The visitors center features exhibits on the area's Civil War past. The park contains the partially reconstructed remains of Fort Lincoln, the last of the original Civil War structures. The park features a swimming beach, 400-foot fishing pier, boat ramp, and canoe, motorboat, and rowboat rentals, plus 143 tent sites (26 have full RV hook-ups), six camper cabins, a cottage, camp store, and self-service laundry. Reservations are required.

Visitors may drive to the end of the park's main road to see the fenced and gated Point Lookout lighthouse (in summer, the park may charge a day-use fee). It's maintained by the Coast Guard, and the Point Lookout Lighthouse Preservation Society (www .pllps.org) has information on visiting hours. The light had three female keepers between 1830 and 1869. Perhaps it was their ghostly presence, among others, sensed by paranormal researchers during the 1990s, when they claimed to have recorded 24 different "voices" in the lighthouse.

Other Parks and Scenic Spots

Piney Point Lighthouse and Park (Lighthouse Rd., Piney Point, 301/769-2222, open daily, $3) sits at the end of a road lined with beach houses. The colony, though not fancy, comes complete with individual private cabanas on the beach across the road from the homes. The area was a popular getaway for American presidents, beginning with James Madison.

The Piney Point Lighthouse, a classic light tower, was constructed in 1836, when it held a fixed beacon light that was visible from more than 11 miles away. Today, it's one of only four such towers in existence on the Potomac River.

Piney Point Lighthouse

A pleasant six-acre park with boardwalk and beach access surrounds the lighthouse, and a small, separate, nearby museum chronicles local history. During a mid-June visit, the park was animated by a small group of squealing kids and their adult supervisor (and no one else) popping in and out of the water.

A **"Black Panther" German submarine** lies one mile from the lighthouse; the U-boat, coated with black rubber that made it invisible to the sonar of the day, was captured at the end of World War II and intentionally sunk off the coast after being tested by the Navy. It has become Maryland's first underwater park: the U-1105 is accessible by boat and may be explored by divers. For information regarding recreational diving on the U-1105, contact the Maryland State Underwater Archaeologist (410/514-7662) or the St. Clement's Museum (301/769-2222).

With a little imagination, it's easy to picture the view of the Patuxent River from the windows and gardens of **Sotterley Plantation** (Rte. 245/Sotterley Rd., Hollywood, 301/373-2280 or 800/681-0850, www .sotterley.com, grounds open 10 A.M.–4 P.M. Mon.–Sat., noon–4 P.M. Sun. year-round, manor house open 10 A.M.–4 P.M. Tues.–Sun. May–Oct.) as it was in 1710, the year this manor house was built. Sotterley was once a thriving tobacco plantation and a colonial port of entry, and the house and adjacent outbuildings are superbly preserved. Older than Mount Vernon or Monticello, it has been home to governors and gamblers alike. A guided mansion tour with a self-guided grounds tour costs $8 adults, $5 children ages 6–12; the self-guided grounds tour is available year-round on its own for $2. Sotterley also sponsors events throughout the year, including Ghost Tours in October and an annual Southern Maryland Quilt and Needlework Show in May.

Not far from Sotterley is **Greenwell State Park** (Steerhorn Neck Rd., Hollywood, c/o Greenwell Foundation, 301/373-9775, day use only, free). This 596-acre park is on the Patuxent River. The Greenwell family donated part of the property to the state for use as a public

beach at Piney Point

© JOANNE MILLER

park, with particular emphasis on access for the disabled. The state bought the adjacent acreage, and the park now offers several miles of marked foot trails, fishing, picnicking, swimming, and beach boat launches.

Other Attractions

St. Clement's Island-Potomac River Museum (Bayview Rd., end of Rte. 242—follow signs, Colton's Point, 301/769-2222, 9 A.M.–5 P.M. Mon.–Fri. and noon–5 P.M. Sat.–Sun. Mar. 25–Sept. 30, noon–4 P.M. Wed.–Sun. Oct. 1–Mar. 24, $3) celebrates the landing of the first Maryland colonists in 1634, as well as their Catholic faith. Though it's a bit out of the way, the museum is worth visiting for its interesting displays and murals on the history of Maryland. The setting is also beautiful, with St. Clement's Island, the original landing place, not far offshore. The island has shrunk somewhat since Jesuit priest Andrew White first said mass there for the small, ocean-weary band that disembarked from the *Ark* and the *Dove;* wave action of

the Chesapeake has eaten away at the shoreline for nearly 400 years, shaving 400 acres down to 40 acres. Today, however, the island is a state park with hiking trails, exhibit panels, and picnic facilities. A water taxi departs from the museum to the island at 12:30 P.M. on weekends May–October and returns at 2:15 P.M.; there's also a later trip that leaves at 2:30 P.M. and returns at 3:45 P.M. There is an additional charge to take the water taxi to the island.

The **Pax River Naval Air Museum** (22156 Three Notch Rd., Lexington Park, 301/ 863-7418, www.paxmuseum.com, 10 A.M.– 5 P.M. Tues.–Sun., free) is the only museum in the country dedicated to Naval aviation. The grounds feature aircraft from different eras, and exhibits inside the museum illustrate testing and evaluation of aircraft systems and components. The museum has a nifty model shop on the premises. It's just outside the main gate of the Patuxent River Naval Air Station; a guided tour may be arranged by calling the number above.

BEFORE BLAIR WITCH

The Blair Witch Project, an independent film that swept America in 1999, was filmed near the town of Burkittsville, not far from South Mountain. However, Maryland's interest in witches began much earlier. The concept of ordinary people being "bewitched" was born centuries ago, and all it took to convict a neighbor of having unsavory friends was the testimony of two witnesses of "good and honest report." One suspicious activity might be witnessing the teen next door as she "entertained a familiar spirit and had conference with in the likeness of some visible creature" ("Here, Spot, come get the stick. Don't you want the stick? Come and get it!").

Maryland remained relatively low on the point-and-burn scale, as compared to say, Salem, Massachusetts. Bad luck aboard the *Charity of London,* bound for St. Mary's City in 1654, was blamed on the demonic congress of one Mary Lee. The captain (perhaps fully aware that the boat's leakage problems were due to neglect) opted to put the ship ashore in Bermuda. On the way there, unfortunately, the crew tied Ms. Lee to the capstan, extracted a "confession," and promptly hung her.

Not all those accused of witchcraft were women – John Cowman was convicted in 1674 for "enchantment upon the body of Elizabeth Goodale," but was granted a reprieve after a guided tour of the gallows. Rebecca Fowler of St. Mary's City wasn't so fortunate. Many Marylanders were accused of being accursed, but she retains the distinction of being the only one actually hung, in 1685. Apparently she and the "Divell" caused several people in the community to fall ill.

In 1702, Charles Kilburn complained that when he met one Katherine Prout on the path, she would abuse and threaten him, specifically stating that she hoped he would "languish to death." Though charges of witchcraft were dropped, the court fined Ms. Prout for "misbehavior in her Saucy Language and abusing this Court." Kilburn was back in court two months later, suing Prout for slander for calling him a "foresworn rogue." Prout was ordered to pay the highly sensitive Kilburn a token sixpence, then forced to pay court costs of 1,101 pounds of tobacco. It seems the judge was the real foresworn rogue.

Ms. Prout, apparently finding court procedure to her liking, sued another woman for slander and theft of molasses and "New England Capons" (mackerel) from her cellar. Prout won this one (to the tune of three pounds sterling), and never ventured before the bench again.

The last formal witchcraft case was heard in Annapolis in 1712. Virtue Violl ("spinster") of Talbot County rendered her neighbor speechless after causing her to pine. Ms. Violl pleaded not guilty and was excused.

SHOPPING

Cecil's Old Mill (Indian Bridge Rd. off Rte. 5, Great Mills, 301/994-1510, Thurs.–Sun. Mar.–Oct. and daily Nov. 1–Dec. 24) is full of the work of local artists and craftspeople at great prices. Much of it is country-style (cows and chickens are popular subjects), but this is really worth a stop.

Leonardtown has a number of antiques shops on Fenwick Street and Washington Street, including **Antiques on the Square** (Washington St.), a multi-dealer shop with a bit of everything. Also check out the **Maryland Antiques Center** (26005 Pt. Lookout Rd., Leonardtown, 301/475-1960, www.paxp.com/mac), which has more than 30 dealers and a tea shop inside. Both are open daily.

Deep in the heart of Mennonite farm country, the roads around **Loveville** are dotted with roadside stands and nurseries from June through November.

There's an **Amish Farmers Market and Auction** every Wednesday and Saturday–Sunday year-round during daylight hours (30030 Three Notch Rd., Charlotte Hall). The market features fresh produce and more than 100 stalls selling crafts, antiques, and pastries.

RECREATION
Charter Fishing

The fishing season in St. Mary's starts in late April and runs through December. Blue fish, striped bass (rockfish), sea trout, flounder, white perch, hard head (croaker), Norfolk spot, Spanish mackerel, black sea bass, and channel bass are commonly caught. Most of the charter boats run out of Ridge. Here's a sampling: Capt. Greg Madjeski (48415 Wynne Rd., 301/872-4215), Capt. Greg Drury (16390 Fishermen Wy., 301/872-4455), Capt. Gary Sacks (48862 Curley's Rd., 301/872-5506), Capt. Bruce Scheible, who provides the raw material for Schieble's—see the *Food* section (48342 Wynne Rd., 301/872-5185), Capt. Bob Holden (43785 Blake Creek Rd., Leonardtown, 301/994-0269), Capt. Butch Cornelius (St. Georges Island, 301/872-9585), and Capt. Steve Owens (P.O. Box 176, St. Mary's City, 301/737-4286).

Golf

Breton Bay (21935 Society Hill Rd., Leonardtown, 301/475-2300) is a par 72 course reputed to be great for the long driver. **Wicomico Shores** (35794 Aviation Yacht Club Rd., Mechanicsville, 301/884-4601) is an 18-hole course overlooking the Wicomico River.

Spectator Sports/Speedways

Not all that moves is wet. **Maryland International Raceway** (27861 Budds Creek Rd., Mechanicsville, 301/884-9833 or 301/449-RACE/301-449-7223, www.mirdrag.com) and **Potomac Speedway** (27963 Budds Creek Rd., Mechanicsville, 301/884-4200) present drag racing and stock car racing March–November.

ACCOMODATIONS AND CAMPING

The elegant **【 Brome-Howard House Inn** (18281 Rosecroft Rd., St. Mary's City, 301/866-0656, http://bromehowardinn.com, $125–185) once sat squarely in the middle of "downtown"—it was built by a physician and tobacco plantation owner, John Brome,

in about 1840. The property passed through many hands until it became part of Historic St. Mary's City. Because the house was considerably newer than the 17th-century period on which the town focuses, the commission in charge of development decided to move the house and its outbuildings to a bluff overlooking the St. Mary's River, where it remains today. A young couple from the Washington, D.C., area, Lisa and Michael Kelley, have made it their goal to turn the building into a world-class restaurant and lodging. The house features five large bedrooms, two (a suite) with shared bath, three with private bath; three have fireplaces, and two have water views. A five-mile walking trail winds along river beaches and shady woods to St. Mary's City. An excellent full breakfast is included.

A fun place to get away from it all with the family, **Camp Merryelande Vacation Cottages** (15914 Camp Merryelande Rd., Piney Point, 800/383-1073, www.campmd.com) offers six fully furnished cottages and bunkhouses on the beach of St. Mary's River. There are also tent sites and showers on the property, and it's open year-round. Cottage rates run $115/night, $675/week up to $425/night, $1895/week May–Oct. 31, depending on size (cottages sleep from 4–24). Rates are discounted by 25 percent the remainder of the year.

FOOD

The restaurant at the **【 Brome-Howard Inn** is open to the public for dinner Thursday–Sunday ($19), and brunch is also served on Sunday. Chef Michael's food is innovative and sophisticated without being pretentious. The filet mignon and breast of duck are highly recommended.

The reputation of **【 Café des Artistes** (41655 Fenwick St., Leonardtown, 301/997-0500, www.cafedesartistes.ws, lunch Tues.–Fri., dinner Tues.–Sat., noon–8 P.M. Sun., lunch $13, dinner $20) has spread far and wide. Karleen and Loic Jaffres have created a continental atmosphere with a menu to match—classic dishes such as chicken Cordon Bleu and beef Wellington share the spotlight with crab cakes and grilled Norwegian salmon. The food is exceptional, as are the prix fixe dinners ($19.95) and senior specials. There's often music on the weekends. Save room for dessert, and definitely make reservations.

Locals swear that once you've tasted Julie's fried fish at **Scheible's Crabpot Restaurant** (at Scheible's Motel, 48342 Wynne Rd., 301/872-5185, Ridge, lunch and dinner daily, $25 and under), you'll be a deep-fried convert. It's a dive with lots of local color and ultra-fresh seafood; Bruce Scheible is lifelong waterman, so the fish are truly right off the boat.

Evans Seafood (16688 Piney Point Rd., Piney Point, 301/994-9944, lunch and dinner from noon daily, lunch $9, dinner $20) is one of the county's premier restaurants. The menu includes seafood, steaks, and stuffed ham; the restaurant has pleasant water views. The upper deck is open at noon daily, the downstairs opens at 3 P.M.

Bert's Restaurant and '50s Drive-In (28760 Three Notch Rd., Mechanicsville, 301/884-3837, lunch and dinner daily, $8) is a St. Mary's County landmark. The front door looks like a jukebox, and there's 1950s memorabilia galore. The menu includes sandwiches, pizza, full-course dinners, and soft and hand-dipped ice cream.

INFORMATION

For further information on St. Mary's destinations, contact **St. Mary's Travel & Tourism** (P.O. Box 653, 23115 Leonard Hall Dr., Leonardtown, MD 20650). The welcome center is at 37575 Charlotte Hall School Road in Charlotte Hall (301/884-7059, www.co.saint-marys .md.us/tourism).

SOUTHERN MARYLAND

WESTERN MARYLAND

One warm midsummer evening a few years ago, a small group gathered in front of the Piper farmhouse, on the edge of Antietam battlefield. As Venus pierced the fading sky, the nearby field of ripening corn blazed with lightning bugs, all rising at once to the heavens—"like the souls of all the boys who died here," said one. The American Civil War is more than a memory to those who live in western Maryland; the area provides a landscape where the spirits of Native Americans, patriots, volunteers, pioneers, farmers, and industrialists reside, at peace among the villages and cornfields, tufted hills and black-water lakes. This long arm of land stretches out to those who seek a slower, more relaxed pace, with plenty of enticements such as shopping, antiquing, history quests, and outdoor recreation.

West of Hagerstown, farmlands tended by descendants of the first Anabaptist settlers spread over ridges and valleys; the hilly terrain then convolutes into the peaks of the Allegheny Mountains. The forefathers of these toilers of the earth often used the alternative spelling "Allegany" in naming towns and counties along the way. The mountain range, which stretches diagonally east–west across Pennsylvania, continues south through western Maryland, and provides rugged forests, fast-moving streams, and wide lakes for lovers of outdoor recreation. This is wild Maryland, ideal for hikers, bikers, water sports enthusiasts, and those who enjoy winter sports, hunting, and fishing.

Though western Maryland is the shy sister of the rest of the state, it's far from undiscovered. Frederick, a sophisticated and

© JOANNE MILLER

HIGHLIGHTS

☾ Mount Olivet Cemetery: One of several interesting stops in the lovely old town of Frederick, Mount Olivet is the resting place of several historical celebrities (page 165).

☾ National Museum of Civil War Medicine: This museum is dedicated to all the women and men who innovated during the Civil War to bring medicine out of the dark ages (page 165).

☾ National Shrine of St. Elizabeth Ann Seton: This is the site of a beautiful basilica dedicated to America's first Catholic saint (page 168).

☾ Scenic Tour of Covered Bridges: Maryland has three covered-bridge beauties in this area (page 171).

☾ Harpers Ferry National Historical Park: Harpers Ferry National Park spans the Potomac and Shenandoah Rivers – and a century of history. The park consists of the entire town and fort, and the setting on the rapids couldn't be more scenic (page 176).

☾ Antietam National Battlefield: This striking monument is preserved in memory of those who died on the bloodiest day of fighting in the Civil War (page 177).

☾ Washington County Museum of Fine Arts: Sitting peacefully by the lake in Hagerstown's City Park, this small, graceful museum maintains a remarkable collection of top-quality American paintings (page 188).

☾ C&O Canal National Historical Park: The towpath of the former Chesapeake and Ohio Canal features a number of campgrounds along its 184-mile length (page 191).

☾ Thrasher Carriage Museum: One of the top five collections in the country, the carriages on display here are upper-middle-class rigs built between 1880 and 1910 (page 199).

☾ Swallow Falls State Park: Breathtaking scenery and swimming opportunities make this one of the most popular recreational areas in Garrett County (page 206).

☾ Deep Creek Lake State Park: Maryland's largest lake is a deep-hued beauty offering plenty of recreation year-round (page 207).

LOOK FOR ☾ TO FIND RECOMMENDED SIGHTS, ACTIVITIES, DINING, AND LODGING.

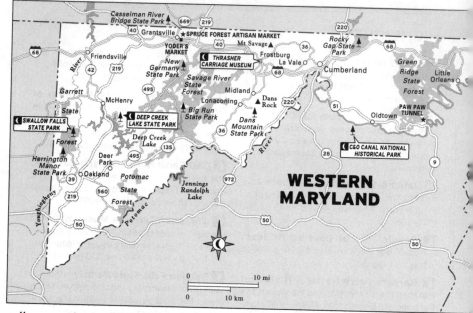

well-preserved colonial/Civil War–era town with upscale shops and restaurants, is western Maryland's gateway. After a day in Frederick, you might be tempted to peruse the windows of real estate offices in the hope of snagging a trim brick rowhouse at a good price—the city is a welcoming place to visit and to live. Deep Creek Lake, in the far southwest, is surrounded by fancy vacation homes fronted by expensive watercraft. It's the getaway area of choice for many Washingtonians, Baltimoreans, and even Pittsburghers—the area's cool mountains and stunning water vistas are just isolated enough that they'll never be overrun. Like the lake, western Maryland's still waters run deep.

HISTORY

Humans have been associated with this rich land for thousands of years. Prehistoric nomadic hunters and gatherers, followed by tribes of Native Americans, roamed through the western mountains but left little record of their presence. By the middle of the 17th century, the fierce Iroquois Confederacy (a six-tribe brotherhood consisting of the Cayuga, Mohawk, Oneida, Onondaga, Seneca, and Tuscarora nations) claimed western Pennsylvania and Maryland to the south, using the area to expand their hunting territory. They permitted Lenni Lenape (Delaware) and Shawnee—escaping European encroachment in Delaware and Maryland—to populate the then empty territory. Beginning in the 1700s, European pioneers trickled into the region and eked out an existence using the area's abundant natural resources.

Hagerstown was settled in 1737, Frederick (named for the Prince of Wales) in 1745. About the same time, Thomas Cresap, a settler from Yorkshire, England, moved to the wild frontier west of Hagerstown to Shawnee Old Town (now Oldtown), where he built a fortified house and made a living farming, trading, and raising cattle. Though Cresap's name isn't widely known outside the state's history books, he was involved with every major event that shaped western Maryland and the young colonies, and his life represents those tough and resilient settlers of the west. Shawnee Old Town was on the Great War Road between the Iroquois Six Nations of New York and their enemies, the

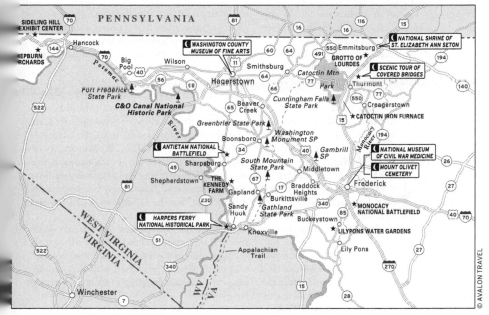

Cherokee of North Carolina. Passing white traders and Indian war parties alike stopped at Cresap's for food and rest; they dubbed him "Big Spoon." He was so familiar with the region that he was asked to determine a boundary dispute between Virginia and Maryland: the location of the "First Fountain" of the Potomac, the headwaters that would serve as the western boundary of Maryland.

In 1750, Cumberland, west of Oldtown in the Allegheny Mountains, was nothing more than a storehouse and trading post for the Ohio Company, a group of wealthy Virginia planters and London merchants who wished to keep the Ohio Valley (present-day Pittsburgh and the convolution of the Allegheny, Monongahela, and Ohio Rivers) away from the French, who held Canada and northwestern Pennsylvania.

During the 18th century, European settlement was curtailed for many years west of Frederick due to the French and Indian War and Pontiac's Rebellion. After nearly 80 years of relative peace, however, the Civil War had a devastating effect within the triangle formed by Frederick, Harpers Ferry, and Hagerstown.

Several sites—now protected and lacking the plastic fanfare that sometimes surrounds such areas—allow visitors to contemplate the price exacted from this nation in its fight to determine the true meaning of individual rights. One angle of the triangle can be stretched out a few miles north past Frederick and Emmitsburg, Maryland, into Gettysburg, Pennsylvania—the northernmost point reached by the Confederate Army.

In 1859, native Marylander and radical abolitionist John Brown gathered a group of like-minded men around him in Kennedyville, Maryland, to plot the takeover of Harpers Ferry. His goal was to capture the military encampment there, free local slaves, and start his own revolutionary army. Though Brown ultimately failed, many saw him as a martyr to the cause of antislavery. As the controversy over personal and states' rights deepened, several Southern slaveholding states seceded from the Union, forming the Confederate States of America. Former Union general Robert E. Lee was chosen to command the outmanned, outgunned Confederate States Army and won several early victories against the Union. He moved his troops into Maryland, in the hope of winning over the border state.

Lee's troops were overwhelmed by Union forces on South Mountain, and he commanded all troops to reassemble outside the village of Sharpsburg, near the Shepardstown crossing. During the next few days, both sides sustained heavy casualties during the battle of Antietam; Lee withdrew across the Potomac. Within a year, he marched north again through Maryland to meet defeat at Gettysburg. Lee retreated to Virginia, then sent part of his army north toward Washington, D.C. They defeated Union recruits at Monocacy, but were unable to take the Union capital. Within a few months, Lee surrendered at the Appomattox courthouse, and the war was over.

Western Maryland, particularly Cumberland, was rich in the natural resources that powered the Industrial Revolution after the Civil War. Coal, iron, and glass were all manufactured with the assistance of the free-flowing Potomac River. Later, the C&O Canal ferried tons of coal to the mouth of the Chesapeake to be used to power oceangoing ships. But even as it was being built, the canal was overtaken by the swift railroad, rendering it obsolete. Cumberland remained a boomtown through the early part of the 20th century, when America's industrial base again changed. Coal, iron, and steel were either not in demand or more easily produced elsewhere. Western Maryland began to revert to its former forested glory, and the farms that had been the backbone of the economy for so long continued to reap their bountiful harvests. Though agriculture remains the economic mainstay of western Maryland, tourism, with an emphasis on history and outdoor recreation, has become the new focus.

ORIENTATION

From east to west, the population grows more sparse and farmland more evident. Frederick has been discovered; within an hour of Baltimore, this once sleepy village has become a destination, and is easily the best launching point for any exploration of Civil War sites or the many state parks in the area. There's still plenty of open space here to enjoy, but if you're after something approximating wilderness—this *is* America, after all—take Horace Greeley's advice and "Go west!"

The ideal way to see the western part of western Maryland is on U.S. 40, the old national toll road. I-68 runs parallel with the old road, but whisks drivers along at subsonic speed, so that the heavy forest that lines the road becomes a purple-green blur. The old road, two-lane and often deserted, winds through the expansive farm country and gentle mountains, giving glimpses of businesses that started up during the "See the U.S.A. in your Chevrolet" era.

Once in the Deep Creek Lake area, you've reached one of Maryland's finest all-season outdoor destinations. It's loaded with large and small parks interspersed with fine restaurants and upscale lodgings—truly something for everyone.

PLANNING YOUR TIME

Western Maryland lends itself to three distinct types of holidays: Civil War sites, outdoor pleasures, and general interest. A combination of interests would best be served by highlights from each of the following:

Civil War history enthusiasts could plan to spend at least one week, starting with a visit to **Mount Olivet Cemetery** (one hour) and the **National Museum of Civil War Medicine** (two hours) in Frederick. Take advantage of the many sophisticated restaurants and charming downtown while there. Then move on to the sites of **The Kennedy Farm** (30 min plus travel time), **Antietam National Battlefield** (one day), and **Harpers Ferry National Historical Park** (one day). These are just the must-sees—many other interesting sites are listed in this chapter as well.

For those who crave active recreation or simply the great outdoors, opportunities are limited only by time (plan on at least a week). Exploring the **C&O Canal National Historical Park** could take a day or two by car, and a month on foot. In the far west, **Swallow Falls State**

Park and Deep Creek Lake State Park are two of many beautiful all-season parks where you can enjoy water sports, winter sports, and just plain lazing around. The Deep Creek Lake area is also home to exceptional camping, other lodging, and restaurants.

Interested in sightseeing? The west has plenty, all of which would take at least one week to see: the **National Shrine of St. Elizabeth Ann Seton** (one hour) is a beautiful basilica in gorgeous country. Get a feel for the area during a **Scenic Tour of Covered Bridges** (one day), and shop 'til you drop at the **Route 65 Flea Market** (two hours). Art lovers won't want to miss the **Washington County Museum of Fine Arts** (one–two hours) in Hagerstown, and a little farther down the road, the **Thrasher Carriage Museum** (one–two hours) combines beauty and practicality. If possible, continue west on the old National Road (U.S. 40) past **Sidling Hill** to Garrett County and the Amish farm country—scenic and delightful.

FESTIVALS AND EVENTS

The Tourism Council of Frederick (800/999-3613, www.fredericktourism.org) has additional information on upcoming events.

In late April, the **Farm Museum Spring Festival** (Rose Hill Manor Park, 1611 N. Market St., Frederick, 301/600-1650) includes demonstrations, a manor house tour and hands-on crafts, activities and games for children at the Children's Museum and a tractor pull, music, animals, hayrides, food, and more at the Farm Museum.

Fort Frederick State Park (301/842-2155, www.friendsoffortfrederick.org) sponsors several events throughout the year, including a public competitive black-powder shoot for muzzleloaders only.

Sharpsburg (Washington County, www.washingtoncounty.com) is home to the oldest **Memorial Day parade** in America, a tradition started after the Civil War to honor returning veterans. The parade is followed by a ceremony in the National Cemetery.

The **American Indian Inter-Tribal Cultural Organization Pow-Wow** (301/604-3533) is held annually in Frederick between August and October, featuring traditional singing, dancing, crafts, and food.

July brings the annual **Fiddler's and Banjo Contest** in Friendsville (Garrett County), sponsored by the local Lions Club. Spontaneous clogging appreciated!

In September, **The Great Frederick Fair** (301/663-5895) features livestock, exhibits, entertainment, and a carnival.

Also in September, the **Western Maryland Street Rod Round-Up** (301/697-0142) in Cumberland features more than 1,000 pre-1949 cars and trucks.

One of the best places to enjoy fall color in Maryland is on a **Fall Color Hayride** (301/334-9180) in Herrington Manor State Park near Oakland. The wagons take in the state forest and adjoining country roads.

In October, cakewalkin' in western Maryland: Hagerstown hosts its own version of the **Alsatia Mummer's Parade** (301/739-2044), an event with 150 units, bands, and floats.

On December 1, Antietam National Battlefield in Sharpsburg sets out 23,110 luminaries along a 4.5-mile route to honor Civil War soldiers killed and wounded during the three days of battle there. The **Memorial Illumination** (301/432-5124) has been an annual event for more than a decade.

During the **Festival of Lights** (301/600-2489) in mid-December, carolers stroll through downtown Frederick to City Hall for an evening of festive music.

GETTING THERE AND AROUND
By Car

Car travel is by far the easiest way to get around, especially when touring the Civil War battle sites. Most of the state parks and forests in Garrett County are only accessible by car. The main east–west arteries that run through western Maryland are I-70 from Baltimore to Hancock and I-68 from Hancock to the Maryland border. Both of these four-lane speedways roughly parallel the old National Road, U.S.

© JOANNE MILLER

hitching a ride Amish-style

40, a much slower, smaller (two-lane), and more scenic route. In Frederick County, I-270 runs north from Washington, D.C., to Frederick; in Garrett County, U.S. 219 is the main north–south route.

By Bus

Greyhound buses run to Frederick, Hagerstown, Cumberland, Oakland, and points in between from many major cities. Routes, scheduling information, and prices can be obtained by calling 800/231-2222.

By Train

The only passenger train that touches the western region is Amtrak's Capitol Limited out of Washington, D.C. It stops in Rockville, Maryland; Harpers Ferry; and Martinsburg (on the West Virginia side of the Potomac); then arrives in Cumberland on its way to Pittsburgh. Call 800/USA-RAIL (800/872-7725) or visit www.amtrak.com for timetables and prices.

Frederick and Vicinity

Frederick played a significant role in America's history, and the town continues to cherish and build on those memories. One Frederick resident, Dr. John Tyler, gained fame before the Civil War as the first American ophthalmologist to successfully perform cataract removal; the physician lived and worked at 108 West Church Street. In front of his home, he placed a statue of his faithful and beloved dog, Guess. In 1862, Confederate troops passing through the town commandeered Guess, apparently with the intention of melting him down into bullets. The iron dog was found intact some time later near the battlefield at Antietam. Today, Guess continues to stand vigil at Dr. Tyler's former front door, a reminder of the town's active past.

Frederick is a delight not only for its historical value, but also for the excellent variety of contemporary shops, restaurants, and activities available to visitors. Most of Frederick's attractions are within walking distance of the

center of town, so it's easy to park your car along one of the residential streets and walk in. The town is laid out in a simple grid, with the central intersection at Market (north–south) and Patrick (east–west) Streets.

Frederick is surrounded by farmlands, forests, and mountains—an ideal situation for those who want outdoor recreation along with sophisticated small-town pleasures. There are several good parks and a number of unusual sites in the area, including the Basilica of Elizabeth Ann Seton, America's first Catholic saint.

SIGHTS
Schifferstadt
Architectural Museum

This simple sandstone-block building (1110 Rosemont Ave., Frederick, 301/668-6088, www.frederickcountylandmarksfoundation .org, noon–4 P.M. Thurs.–Sun. Apr.–Oct., $3) sits at the end of the city park; in addi-

WESTERN MARYLAND

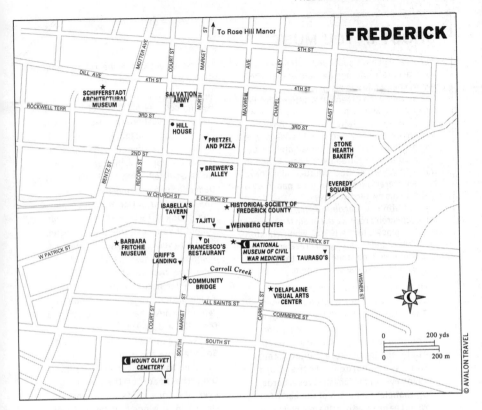

FREDERICK

To Rose Hill Manor

DILL AVE
ROCKWELL TERR
★ SCHIFFERSTADT ARCHITECTURAL MUSEUM
■ SALVATION ARMY
● HILL HOUSE
▼ PRETZEL AND PIZZA
STONE HEARTH BAKERY
▼ BREWER'S ALLEY
EVEREDY SQUARE
ISABELLA'S TAVERN
★ HISTORICAL SOCIETY OF FREDERICK COUNTY
▼ TAJITU
■ WEINBERG CENTER
★ BARBARA FRITCHIE MUSEUM
GRIFF'S LANDING ▼
▼ DI FRANCESCO'S RESTAURANT
◀ NATIONAL MUSEUM OF CIVIL WAR MEDICINE
▼ TAURASO'S
Carroll Creek
★ COMMUNITY BRIDGE
★ DELAPLAINE VISUAL ARTS CENTER
◀ MOUNT OLIVET CEMETERY

4TH ST · 3RD ST · 2ND ST · W CHURCH ST · E CHURCH ST · E PATRICK ST · W PATRICK ST · ALL SAINTS ST · COMMERCE ST · SOUTH ST · 5TH ST · 4TH ST · 3RD ST · 2ND ST

BENTZ ST · RECORD ST · COURT ST · MARKET ST · MOTTER AVE · COURT ST · MARKET ST · NORTH ST · MAXWELL · CHAPEL · EAST ST · WISNER ST · SOUTH ST

0   200 yds
0   200 m

© AVALON TRAVEL

tion to the museum, the grounds afford excellent picnic sites and strolling paths. Inside the two-story structure, wood, pottery, and iron implements illustrate the daily lives of the German immigrant farmers who populated the area in the early days of the colony. Schifferstadt is the oldest known house in Frederick still standing; the cast-iron stove, dated 1756, is inscribed in German: "Where your treasure is, there is also your heart." In summer, the kitchen garden in back is fragrant with rosemary and other culinary herbs. There's a small gift shop off the main building.

Barbara Fritchie Home and Museum

The Fritchie Museum (154 W. Patrick St., 301/698-0630, 10 A.M.–4 P.M. Mon. and Thurs.–Sat. Apr.–Sept., 10 A.M.–4 P.M. Sat. and 1–4 P.M. Sun. Oct.–Nov., $2) celebrates the life of an original assertive woman. Fritchie delivered a fiery fist-shaking to a column of Confederate troops when they tried to shoot out her 34-star Union flag on their way through Frederick. Whether the story is true or a bloom of a poet's imagination (see the sidebar "Shoot If You Must" in this chapter), Barbara Fritchie herself was quite a gal. She married when she was 40—late in life for a woman of her time—settling down with (literally) the boy next door; he was 28 and son of her saloonkeeper neighbors. She outlived him by 14 years and was 95 when she defied Jackson's troops, proof that you can get away with almost anything if you live long enough. The cozy two-story house/museum contains

SHOOT IF YOU MUST

Barbara Fritchie's supposed outspokenness with armed Confederate soldiers in 1862 earned her a place in history, thanks to abolitionist poet John Greenleaf Whittier. Whittier, who lived in Massachusetts, heard Fritchie's story some months after the event took place and wrote a piece on it, using lavish poetic license. Published almost immediately, it became an instant hit and was republished in *Harper's Weekly* in 1866. Whittier might have had a different impression if he had known that Fritchie owned two slaves.

In addition to becoming *the* choice for schoolchildren's recitals, the poem found favor in other places. In the 1930s, when Winston Churchill visited the area with President Franklin D. Roosevelt, he stood outside the Fritchie house and recited the entire poem:

> Up from the meadows rich with corn,
> Clear in the cool September morn,
> The clustered spires of Frederick stand
> Green-walled by the hills of Maryland.
> Round about them orchards sweep,
> Apple and peach tree fruited deep,
> Fair as a garden of the Lord
> To the eyes of the famished rebel horde.
> On that pleasant morn of the early fall
> When Lee marched over the mountain-wall
> Over the mountains winding down,
> Horse and foot, into Frederick-town.
> Forty flags with their silver stars,
> Forty flags with their crimson bars,
> Flapped in the morning wind: the sun
> Of noon looked down, and saw not one.
> Up rose old Barbara Fritchie then,
> Bowed with her four score years and ten
> Bravest of all in Frederick-town
> She took up the flag the men hauled down
> In her attic window the staff she set,
> To show that one heart was loyal yet.
> Up the street came the rebel tread,
> Stonewall Jackson riding ahead.
> Under his slouched hat left and right
> He glanced: the old flag met his sight.
> "Halt" – the dust-brown ranks stood fast,
> "Fire" – out blazed the rifle blast.
> It shivered the window, pane and sash:
> It rent the banner with seam and gash.
> Quick as it fell, from the broken staff
> Dame Barbara snatched the silken scarf.
> She leaned far out on the window-sill,
> And shook it forth with a royal will.
> "Shoot if you must, this old gray head,
> But spare your country's flag," she said.
> A shade of sadness, a blush of shame,
> Over the face of the leader came.
> The nobler nature within him stirred
> To life at that woman's deed and word;
> "Who touches a hair on yon gray head
> Dies like a dog! March on!" he said.
> All day long through Frederick's streets,
> Sounded the tread of marching feet.
> All day long that free flag tost,
> Over the heads of the rebel host.
> Ever its torn folds rose and fell
> On the loyal winds that loved it well.
> And through the hill gaps sunset light,
> Shone over it with a warm good-night.
> Barbara Fritchie's work is o'er.
> And the rebel rides on his raids no more.
> Honor to her! and let a tear
> Fall, for her sake, on Stonewall's bier.
> Over Barbara Fritchie's grave,
> Flag of freedom and Union, wave!
> Peace and order and beauty draw
> Round the symbol of light and law
> And ever the stars above look down
> On thy stars below in Frederick-town.

many items owned or made by the Fritchie family, including doll clothes sewn by Barbara for her niece.

◖ Mount Olivet Cemetery

Mount Olivet (515 S. Market St., 301/662 1164, dawn–dusk daily, free) is the resting place of several historical celebrities, including the first Gray Panther, Barbara Fritchie, and Francis Scott Key, who grew up in the area and penned "The Star-Spangled Banner." Key's memorial is the first thing visitors see when driving into Mount Olivet—his bronze likeness gestures limply toward Old Glory, flying a few feet away. (Shouldn't he be more excited? However, considering Key was held on a prison ship for some hours before he emerged into the rockets' red glare, perhaps the statue is historically accurate.) Barbara Fritchie gets her own flag and a triangular boulder. Thomas Johnson, the first governor of Maryland, is just west of Fritchie (follow the signs).

Most interesting, however, may be the Civil War monuments and Confederate soldiers' graves built on the northwest side of the cemetery nearly 20 years after the Battle of Antietam. A small black granite stone under a willow memorializes children who died in the conflict: the nameless drummer boys and 13-year-olds who fought for both sides. The Confederate Soldiers' Monument, a tall granite obelisk under a circle-of-13-stars flag, was erected by the Ladies Monumental Association of Frederick County in 1880. During the war, few Southern families had the ways or means to bring home the bodies of their loved ones. Consequently, rebel soldiers were often buried in mass graves. At the bequest of sympathetic Northerners like the Ladies of Frederick, Confederate soldiers' remains were extracted from common graves on the battlefields of Antietam, Monocacy, and elsewhere, identified as well as could be done, and properly buried.

Along the fence near the monument, named and unknown soldiers are remembered with plain headstones. One of the graves belongs to George Boatwright, who is perhaps still waiting to hear a "Yes!" to his proposal of marriage

from his beloved Mattie (see the sidebar "The Ballad of George and Mattie" in this chapter). The Confederate Soldiers' Monument bears these words: "Soldiers rest, thy sleep the sleep that knows no waking / Dream of battled fields no more / Days of danger, nights of waking / Their praises will be sung in some yet unmoulded tongue / Far on in summers that we shall not see. Honor to the Brave."

The Catoctin Iron Furnace

Part of Cunningham Falls State Park (dawn–dusk, free), the furnace is three miles south of the town of Thurmont on Route 806. This intact iron furnace operated from 1776 until 1903 and was once part of a booming industrial complex and community. Before he was elected, Maryland's ubiquitous first governor, Thomas Johnson, owned and operated the furnace with his brothers; they supplied 100 tons of shells used by revolutionary forces at Yorktown.

◖ National Museum of Civil War Medicine

Frederick played a central role in the Civil War for more than four years: three Confederate invasions, 38 skirmishes, and three major battles (South Mountain, Antietam, and Monocacy). The museum (48 E. Patrick St., 301/695-1864, www.civilwarmed.org, 10 A.M.–5 P.M. Mon.–Sat. and 11 A.M.–5 P.M. Sun. mid-Mar.–mid-Nov., closes at 4 P.M. mid-Nov.–mid-Mar., closed Dec. 24–Jan. 2 and most national holidays, $6.50 adults) is dedicated to all the women and men who brought medicine out of the dark ages, fueled by the imperatives of the War Between the States.

Dental surgeon Dr. Gordon Damman began collecting Civil War memorabilia in high school. The 3,000 artifacts in his collection—including a medical chest made by Dr. E. R. Squibb, who invented numerous medical instruments and later founded Squibb Pharmaceuticals—became the basis for this museum. The historic building that houses the museum was an embalming station for the dead from Antietam in 1862.

THE CIVIL WAR: FREDERICK

Union troops within Maryland's borders repeatedly fought the Confederate Army in its attempts to capture Washington, D.C., and Philadelphia, the two Federal centers of power nearest Confederate territory. As a result, three major battles were fought in this triangle, the "crossroads of the Confederacy" – and it all started in Frederick.

Confederate Army leader Major General Robert E. Lee wrote to rebel President Jefferson Davis in early August 1862: "The present seems to be the most propitious time since the commencement of the war for the Confederate Army to enter Maryland." Lee knew that Maryland was deeply divided and possibly ripe for secession; once the state joined the Confederacy, Washington could no longer be the Federal capital. On September 2, Lee, Stonewall Jackson, General D. H. Hill and 60,000 troops began a rapid march north to Frederick, arriving a few days later. Lee exhorted the people of Frederick and all Marylanders to join his army.

According to the editors of *Harper's Weekly Magazine* (1866), "This prospect was not alluring to those to whom war had presented itself as a gay holiday show. When the theoretical secessionists of Maryland saw their liberators, officers as well as men, barefoot, ragged, and filthy, they looked upon them with hardly concealed aversion. Yet that ragged and begrimed army was as brave a body of soldiers as the world ever saw. The enthusiasm of the Maryland secessionists exhausted itself in a few women secretly sewing clothing for the army, and in presenting to Jackson a magnificent horse, which threw him the first time he mounted it."

Union General McClellan was by then aware of Lee's presence and had begun to advance his troops toward Frederick. Characteristically, McClellan estimated Southern troops at twice their strength, while just as mistakenly, Lee estimated Northern troops as far fewer than their actual number of nearly 120,000 – three to one.

While in Frederick, Lee decided that winning Harpers Ferry and the 12,500 raw Union troops who held it was crucial to Confederate victory; the Potomac crossing was his supply line. In a decision that altered the course of the battles that followed, Lee divided his forces into several groups. He sent his generals out from Frederick by different routes: Longstreet's troops went northwest to Hagerstown for money and supplies, while Hill's men were ordered southwest to Boonsboro for the same purpose. A group of men led by General Walker was sent first to destroy the canal aqueduct at Monocacy Creek, then to Harpers Ferry. Another contingent left Frederick on September 10, marching directly to Harpers Ferry. By September 15, Federal forces there surrendered with little resistance.

South Mountain runs roughly north–south, starting in the vicinity of York, Pennsylvania, and ending at the Potomac River near Harpers Ferry. It's crossed east–west by two large gaps (Turner's and Crampton's) and one small gap (Fox). Lee left a rear guard in Frederick and began a leisurely march with the remainder of his troops down the west side of South Mountain, planning to meet the others at the ferry crossing. McClellan's men occupied and skirmished with Lee's rear-guard forces on September 12 in Frederick.

Thanks to a stunning piece of luck – Lee's battle plans found wrapped around three tobacco butts left as trash in his encampment – McClellan anticipated that he could throw the Union Army between Lee's divided forces and "cut the enemy in two, and beat him in detail." The Confederates learned that McClellan's men were moving to Turner's Gap, and 28,000 of Lee's troops were spread over a distance of 25 miles. He hurriedly recalled Hill and Longstreet, whose only hope was to delay the Union advance for a day while the scattered divisions could reunite.

WESTERN MARYLAND

The museum does an admirable job of chronicling the lives of those who served in the war as soldiers, as well as those who healed them. The well-displayed collection features the Union coat of Louis Razinski, assistant surgeon of the 36th New York Volunteers, who later became surgeon to the 54th Massachusetts, the famous black regiment featured in the film *Glory*. Videos and displays tell of members of the fledgling nursing profession, such as Clara Barton, founder of the Red Cross—as she tended a man on the battlefield of Antietam, a bullet passed through her sleeve and killed the soldier she nursed. *Little Women* author Louisa May Alcott also volunteered to help the wounded. She wrote: "The sight of several stretchers, each with the legless, armless, or desperately wounded occupants, admonished me that I was there to work, not to wonder or weep."

Because of the vast number of surviving disabled, the Civil War was responsible for many developments in prosthetic devices and plastic surgery. These treatments were in their infancy, and, as the museum's video illustrates, the end result was meant to replace function with little thought to aesthetics. Several fine videos, along with authentic medical and period paraphernalia and an interesting layout, make this small museum a must-see for medical professionals and anyone interested in the human side of the Civil War.

The Historical Society of Frederick County

One of the oldest historical societies in Maryland (24 E. Church St., 301/663-1188, guided tours 10 A.M.–4 P.M. Mon.–Sat., $3 adults), the society was founded in 1888 to commemorate native son Francis Scott Key and Key's brother-in-law, Roger Brooke Taney. Both men practiced law in Frederick, and Taney went on to become Chief Justice of the U.S. Supreme Court; he handed down the unfortunate decision on the Dred Scott case prior to the Civil War (in short, "Once a slave, always a slave"). Judge Taney's home on Bentz Street in Frederick is owned by the society and is open for tours during the same hours ($4 admission includes both sites).

caution sign in Western Farm Country

Church Street, lined with genteel mansions, was the "millionaire's row" of Frederick. The current three-story home of the historical society was built in the 1820s by local physician Dr. John Baltzell, and later served as a home for female orphans. The building displays furnishings and art of the early 1800s, including portraits of prominent Frederick County residents, glassware, dolls, and an exceptional array of tall case clocks (Frederick was the clock capital of the colonies in the late 18th century). An excellent small shop is attached to the main building.

Delaplaine Visual Arts Center

National and regional exhibitions encompassing all aspects of visual arts, including drawing, painting, crafts, photography, and large installations, are featured at the Center (40 S. Carroll St. on Carroll Creek, 301/698-0656, www.delaplaine.org, 9 A.M.–5 P.M. Mon.–Sat., 1–4 P.M. Sun., free). The Mountain City Mill building that houses the center was once a whiskey rectifying house, then a flour mill. The bridge that crosses Carroll Creek next

© JOANNE MILLER

WESTERN MARYLAND

THE AMERICAN LOOK

In the 1950s, *Life* magazine listed a Frederick woman, Claire McCardell, as one of the 100 most important Americans of the 20th century. Her name may be unfamiliar now except to dedicated followers of fashion, but McCardell was a clothing designer who radically altered the way American women dress based on her own reaction to lifestyle changes following World War I. What clothing manufacturers needed to do, she said, was make clothes a woman could get into without the help of a maid, and care for without a laundress. In other words, it was time to make independent clothes for independent working gals.

McCardell explained, "[I've always] designed things I've needed myself. It just turns out that other people need them, too." She left Frederick in 1932 and went to work for Townley Frocks in New York City, staying with the company until her death in 1958. In an era when clothing designers weren't name brands, McCardell's ideas influenced every American designer who came after her. Leotards and ballet slippers for everyday wear, the "separates" concept, and wool jersey suits are a few of her innovations that still turn up on fashion runways year after year.

which appear to be carved in the rock. The website for this project (http://bridge.skyline. net) was named one of the top 10 arts sites on the Web by America Online.

Rose Hill Manor Park

This lovely historic building and the grounds surrounding it (1611 N. Market St., 301/600-1646, www.rosehillmuseum.com, tours available 10 A.M.–4 P.M. Mon.–Sat. and 1–4 P.M. Sun. Apr.–Oct., 10 A.M.–1 P.M. Sat. and 1–4 P.M. Sun. in Nov., $5 adults, $4 children 3–17) was the home of Thomas Johnson, first elected governor of Maryland, from 1794 until his death in 1819. Johnson nominated his good friend George Washington to be commander-in-chief of the Continental Army. Today, the 43-acre park and manor are a "touch-and-see" museum that provides glimpses into 19th-century life.

The first floor of the manor houses the Children's Museum. Guided by costumed docents, children can make stitches on a quilt, card wool, and play with replica toys, kitchen tools, and costumes. The upper floors of the manor exhibit historic furnishings, including a study where Governor Johnson might have worked.

The outlying structures include an icehouse with 13-foot stone walls, a log cabin with furnishings similar to the original, a blacksmith shop, and early American garden and orchard. Also on the grounds are a Carriage Museum with more than 25 restored vehicles ranging from an Amish-style buggy to an elaborate 12-passenger carriage; and a Farm Museum featuring hundreds of farm implements, a bank barn, and a dairy barn.

◖ National Shrine of St. Elizabeth Ann Seton

The site of the basilica dedicated to America's first Catholic saint (333 S. Seton Ave., Emmitsburg, 301/447-6606, www.emmitsburg. net/setonshrine—saints have websites these days) includes a museum, historic buildings, and the mortuary chapel where Elizabeth Ann Seton was interred. The museum and historic buildings are open 10 A.M.–4:30 P.M. daily (but

to the arts center is worth a moment. Visitors standing near the creek just outside the Barbara Fritchie house often look up and down Carroll Creek for the **Community Bridge,** an arts project sponsored by the citizens of Frederick. Most see an old stone bridge a block away on Carroll Street. "It must work," said one of the guides at the Fritchie house, "That's the bridge." Made of solid concrete, the bridge has been masterfully painted by trompe l'oeil muralist William M. Cochran, whose angels appear on walls all around Frederick, to resemble ancient stonework. It features a number of sponsored "stones" with sheaves of wheat, angels, spirals, and other abstract designs, all of

closed Mon. Nov. 1–Apr. 1) and closed New Year's Day, Easter, Thanksgiving, Christmas, and the last two weeks of January. The Basilica is open 10 A.M.–4:30 P.M. daily. Admission is free.

Mother Seton, who converted to Catholicism and served as a teaching sister in the early 1800s, was recognized as a saint by that church in 1959. Catholic saints are required not only to have led virtuous lives, but also to have been responsible for four verifiable miracles.

Mother Seton practiced her faith and educated local inhabitants in the Emmitsburg area. She also established Sisters of Charity, a community that later merged with a similar group of nuns in France to become Daughters of Charity, a communal religious order. Their informational brochure states, "We... pray, work, and live together in order to bear witness to Christ, and to strengthen one another for the service of the poor." Daughters of Charity dedicate their lives to the improvement of health care and education in severely depressed areas.

The museum presents a straightforward telling of how an ordinary widow with several children rediscovered her spirituality, acted upon her faith, and became revered. The basilica, a church that contains a saint's relics (mortal remains), demands a visit to view the beautiful statuary, stained glass, marble, and glasswork within. Worshipers are often in the basilica praying at all times of day, but it's permissible to quietly walk the perimeter of the church. (The urns on either side of the entry contain water that's been blessed by a priest. Catholics will touch it and make the sign of the cross on themselves to signify entry into a holy place.) The parklike grounds contain historic buildings used by Mother Seton and her community, as well as the Mortuary Chapel where her remains were buried before she was canonized.

Grotto of Lourdes

Though the grotto and its grounds (west of Rte. 15 about two miles south of Emmitsburg—look for signs on the highway for the turnoff and follow signs along the road, free) may strike some as an affected manifestation of personal religious beliefs, many Catholic faithful make a pilgrimage to this spot, which grants indulgences. The Catholic church recognizes heaven, hell, and purgatory; the last of these is a sort of pleasant waiting room for heaven, where one works off minor sins over time. A pilgrimage to the grotto, with appropriate prayers, grants an indulgence to the pilgrim (i.e., less time to serve in purgatory). The grotto is a simulacrum of the original in France, in which the Virgin Mary appeared to a young girl, Bernadette Soubirous, 18 times. Bernadette was later canonized.

The grotto is built near the site of old Mt. St. Mary's, the church in which Saint Elizabeth Ann Seton worshiped. The grounds also include a small chapel and beautifully crafted stations of the cross (the story of the end of Jesus of Nazareth's life from his condemnation to his being laid in the sepulcher), religious mosaics, and numerous sculptures of other Catholic saints. A campanile topped with an enormous gilded statue of the Virgin Mary stands in place of the long-destroyed church. The statue is visible from Route 15 for several miles.

ENTERTAINMENT

The **Weinberg Center** (the former Tivoli Theater, 20 W. Patrick, 301/228-2828, www.weinberg center.org) is now a center for all kinds of performing arts, such as musicals, musical performances, and children's theater.

SHOPPING
Downtown Frederick

This part of town is made for strolling, and the intersection of Patrick and Market Streets is a good place to start. North Market is lined with collectibles shops, antiques stores, galleries, and craft shops. A local candy maker, the **Candy Kitchen** (specializing in handmade chocolates, 301/698-0442), is on the east side of North Market between Church and Patrick Streets. **Third Street** starting with the Salvation Army store (301 W. 3rd St.) and moving east, has a plethora of less organized (and often cheaper) shops.

Frederick has dozens of antique dealers. **Cannon Hill Place** (on S. Carroll St. at Commerce St. between South St. and E. All Saints, 301/695-9304, 9 A.M.–5 P.M. daily) is an old warehouse with lots of antiques and collectibles for sale by multiple dealers; there's also a café inside. **Antique Station** (194 Thomas Johnson Dr., north of downtown off Motter Ave./Oppossumtown Pike, 301/695-0888, 10 A.M.–6 P.M. Thurs.–Tues.) features more than 140 dealers.

Lilypons Water Gardens

Eight miles south of Frederick off Route 85 (6800 Lilypons Rd., Buckeystown, 800/999-5459), Lilypons features acres of lilies and lotus blossoms, fountains, and goldfish. This commercial enterprise is a fine place to walk even if you're not looking to furnish your own pond. The water gardens are in bloom Memorial Day–Labor Day, and the grounds are open March–October. It's free to enter, and Lilypons sponsors several special events in season.

Malls

Everedy Square is the site of Talbots and other boutiques; **Shab Row,** a renovated group of rowhouses, features more shops and the **Frederick Coffee Company** (100 N. East St.), an espresso bar and café. Everedy Square was once the factory headquarters of the Everedy (battery) Company, and the brick paved buildings along Shab Row were the original homes of Frederick's earliest citizens. Both are on North East Street between East 2nd and East Patrick Streets.

The 60-shop **Frederick Towne Mall** is home to the larger national retailers such as JCPenney and Bon-Ton, and a 10-screen cinema. It's on U.S. 40, just west of Frederick.

Country Markets and Orchards

McCutcheon Apple Products (13 S. Wisner St., 301/662-3261) has a factory store at this location that sells sweet cider, apples, preserves, honey, pickles, and more. **Mr. Natural's,** a fruit

baskets of apples from the orchards of Frederick

© JOANNE MILLER

stand and nursery on U.S. 15 at the intersection of Route 806, offers a variety of goods year-round, delivered with a dose of grinning sunshine from the curly-tressed Mr. Natural himself. **Pryor's Orchard** (13841-B Pryor Rd.) 0.5 mile west of Thurmont on Route 77, is open mid-June to mid-November selling seasonal fruits (peaches, apples, pears, plums, cherries), vegetables, nuts, honey, and ready-made goods.

SPORTS AND RECREATION
Baseball

The **Frederick Keys** (301/662-0013, www .frederickkeys.com) a farm team of the Baltimore Orioles, are big with baseball fans in Frederick and elsewhere. Not only do they hold the *Oh* during the singing of "The Star-Spangled Banner" out of respect for the Orioles, but the crowd also "shakes its keys" during the seventh-inning stretch. The Keys play at Harry Grove Stadium, a small open-air field with stadium seating just beyond Olivet Cemetery on South Market Street.

Outdoor Recreation

Most state parks, forests, and national parks offer some sort of overnight facility, though types and prices vary by park. Each park office will have current information and maps.

◖ Scenic Tour of Covered Bridges

The hunt for king-post trusses—covered bridges constructed with a sidewall consisting of a triangle reinforced with upright timbers—never ends! Maryland has considerably fewer covered bridges than Pennsylvania, but these three are beauties, and the roads through them are surrounded by green spears of corn and flowing wheat in summer, frost-cracked trees and long views in the winter. There's also an intimate, secluded park for a picnic, and this tour is suitable for both cars and reasonably fit bike riders: The terrain consists of soft rolling hills and long straightaways. The off-road loop from the Roddy Road exit off U.S. 15 is just under 22 miles. All distances are approximate.

From the junction of Route 140 and U.S.

15 in Emmitsburg, travel 3.9 miles south to the Roddy Road exit (bikers may want to start here). Turn left (east) on Roddy Road. One mile south, you'll pass through the Roddy Road covered bridge. Continue south 1.2 miles to the intersection with Route 77. Continue south on Route 77 for 0.33 mile; look for signs for Graceham. Turn left (east) on Route 77, passing through the lovely village of Graceham to Old Frederick Road (about two miles from the intersection). Turn right (south). Within a few hundred feet, you'll pass through Loy's Station covered bridge. The little park south of the bridge is an ideal place for a rest stop and picnic.

Continue south on Old Frederick Road to Creagerstown (2.3 miles from Rte. 77). At the intersection of Route 550 and Old Frederick Road in Creagerstown, continue on Old Frederick Road 4.1 miles south to Utica Road. Turn right on Utica Road (west) and pass through Utica Mills covered bridge within a few hundred feet. Utica Road, 1.25 miles long, dead-ends at Route 805. A left turn (south) for one

covered bridge near Frederick

© JOANNE MILLER

mile leads back to U.S. 15—central Frederick is less than five miles south on U.S. 15, and Emmitsburg is 12.5 miles north.

To return to the Roddy Road exit off U.S. 15 without taking the highway, turn right (north) on Route 805 through Lewiston to Route 806/Black's Mill Road (two miles). Turn left on Route 806—you'll pass the Catoctin Furnace on your left—into the town of Thurmont (3.9 miles). In Thurmont, take Route 77 east (0.8 miles) to Roddy Road and retrace your path back through the covered bridge to U.S. 15 (north, 2.2 miles).

Cunningham Falls State Park

A popular 5,000-acre recreation area in the Catoctin Mountains, this park is the site of Cunningham Falls, Maryland's highest waterfall. The 78-foot cascade shoulders its way through a rocky gorge and may be reached from four of eight hiking trails. Cunningham Falls State Park (park office at 14039 Catoctin Hollow Rd., Thurmont, 301/271-7574) is split into two parts: the Houck Area (where the falls are) and the Manor Area.

Because it's so close to Frederick, the park gets very crowded on warm weekends—camping reservations are a must. The 44 acres of Hunting Creek Lake offers swimming, boating, and fishing. Picnicking and hiking are also popular pastimes. Modern camping facilities are available in both areas of the park. There is a camp store, dump station, food and beverage outlet, and picnic shelters. Biking is prohibited on all trails, and pets on a leash are permitted only in the wildlands area of the park.

Hiking: Two of the park's eight trails are rated easy or easy-to-moderate: the 0.25-mile Catoctin Furnace Trail and the 0.5-mile Lower Trail (this is the shortest route to the falls). The strenuous, 27-mile Catoctin Trail is the most challenging, though park personnel rate all the other trails (ranging in length 0.75 mile–7.5 miles) as strenuous. A wheelchair-accessible, 300-yard trail to the falls may be accessed from Route 77 (opposite side of the road from the Falls Nature Trail).

Hunting and Fishing: Hunting is allowed on 3,500 acres of undeveloped wildlands within the forest. Call the main park number for a brochure with specifics. Disabled hunters can hunt in a special area by reservation. A current Maryland fishing license is required for all anglers over 15 years old. Little Hunting Creek in the Manor Area and Big Hunting Creek on Route 77 are catch-and-release trout streams limited to artificial fly-fishing only. In Hunting Creek Lake, anglers can fish for trout, bass, bluegill, sunfish, crappie, and catfish. Fishing facilities for wheelchair users include a fishing pier located by the boat ramp. The Maryland Freshwater Sportfishing Guide has information on applicable creel and size limits.

Swimming: Swimming is permitted in three designated areas of Hunting Creek Lake. Lifeguards are on duty Memorial Day to Labor Day.

Water Sports: The use of power boats, aquacycles, canoes, rowboats, and flat-water canoes (kayaks) are allowed on Hunting Creek Lake during the summer. Private launching is available for a fee at Catoctin Hollow Road ramp for watercraft, including those with one-horsepower-or-less electric motors only (gasoline motors are prohibited). In the summer season, canoes and rowboats may be rented at the boathouse.

Overnight Facilities: The Houck Area has 149 sites, including nine camper cabins. The Manor Area has 31 campsites. Site reservations are necessary Memorial Day–Labor Day, and are available at 888/432-2267 or http://reservations.dnr.state.md.us.

Getting There: The park is in the Catoctin Mountains, roughly 15 miles north of Frederick. The Manor Area is off U.S. 15, and the Houck Area is three miles west of Thurmont, off Route 77, on Catoctin Hollow Road. Follow signs to the parking areas.

Catoctin Mountain National Park

Operated by the National Park Service, this outdoor recreation area (6602 Foxville Rd., Thurmont, 301/663-9388) is right across Route 77 from the Houck Area of Cunningham Falls State Park. Catoctin has two family campgrounds, a group camping area, and cabins for individuals and groups, plus hiking trails and a number of special programs—including an orienteering overview, a cross-country skiing seminar, and nature walks. The Blue Blazes whiskey still, part of a larger Prohibition-era operation, is on the park grounds. Reminiscent of those used by farmers during the Whiskey Rebellion of the 1790s, the still offers information on whiskey-making.

Campsites and cabins are open mid-April to mid-November. The park begins taking reservations for the WPA-built cabins in January (301/271-3140); campsites are first-come, first-served, and begin filling up by Friday afternoons during the warm months (for more information on campsites, call 301/663-9388). There are several hike-in Adirondack Shelters (your basic lean-to) available at no charge year-round, with a permit from the park office.

Gambrill State Park

Northwest of Frederick off U.S. 40, Gambrill (c/o Cunningham Falls State Park, 301/271-7574) is primarily a day-use park with some improved campsites. The main feature of this park is its scenic vistas of the Catoctin mountains and surrounding valleys. The 1,600-foot summit of High Knob offers panoramic views of the Frederick City Municipal Forest to the north; Crampton's Gap, Middletown, and Monocacy Valleys to the southwest; and South Mountain to the southeast. In the 1930s and 1940s, many of the park's structures were built of native timbers and stone by Civilian Conservation Corps members.

Picnicking: The High Knob Area offers three picnic shelters and a lodge-style stone shelter, the Tea Room. These units are available for rental from April through October (call the number listed above).

Overnight Facilities: The Rock Run Area has 32 campsites, available Memorial Day to Labor Day on a first-come, first-served basis. There are also four camper cabins on site, which may be reserved at 888/432-2267 or http://reservations.dnr.state.md.us. The day-use area is free.

Getting There: The park is six miles northwest of Frederick, south of Cunningham Falls State Park. The park is accessed from U.S. 40 via Gambrill Park Road.

ACCOMMODATIONS

At **⟨ Hill House B&B** (12 W. 3rd St., 301/682-4111, www.itlink.com/hillhouse/1, $105–150), Mrs. Damian Branson makes the creamiest grits accompanied by the sweetest fried tomatoes on the planet. Of course, that's only one part of a stay (and part of a breakfast) at this charming B&B. Hill House is within convenient walking distance of downtown Frederick's shops and restaurants. Damian and her husband, Taylor, moved up from southern Maryland and bought and renovated this three-story row house in 1996. The unique decor of each guestroom reflects their interests: Chesapeake, Victorian, Mexican folkart modern, and Frederick Federal. There are three spacious rooms, each with private bath. In addition, the top floor is a suite of rooms, including a kitchen; it's ideal for longer stays, and guests can watch the fireworks after the local ballgame from the bathroom window (the Frederick Keys, a farm team of the Orioles, play at Harry Grove Stadium on the edge of town). The common rooms of the house are warm, welcoming, and especially pretty during the winter holidays. The Bransons are connected to Frederick's happenings and give great information on places to go and things to do. Corporate clients and long stays receive discounts on room rates.

The **Inn at Buckeystown** (3521 Buckeystown Pike/Rte. 85, Buckeystown, 301/874-5755 or 800/272-1190, www.innatbuckeys town.com, $115–175) features five guestrooms with private baths and five rooms with shared baths. The inn occupies a beautifully restored 1897 mansion, complete with three fireplaces and crystal chandeliers in a Nationally Registered Historic Village with pre-revolutionary and Civil War roots. The village is near the Monocacy River, close to a number of Civil War sites. The inn is also known for its dinners, teas, and Murder Mystery nights.

The Cozy (103 Frederick Rd./Rte. 806, Thurmont, 301/271-4301 www.cozyvillage .com, $60–165), near the Catoctin Mountains, features 17 rooms and suites named after U.S. presidents (the Clinton Room features a king-sized bed and a corner mirrored Jacuzzi) and press agencies. All have private baths, and some have kitchenettes or microwaves. The famous Cozy breakfast is served to guests, or you can eat at the dinner buffet and roll yourself to your room later.

FOOD
Snacks and Delis
Pretzel and Pizza Creations (210 N. Market St., 301/694-9299, breakfast, lunch and dinner daily, $4–18) proves that creativity and pretzel dough were made for each other—they have everything from sweet cinnamon to hot Cajun. The chicken calzone is a favorite, with other great cheap snacks under $5.

Beef 'N' Buns 'N' Paradise (near the Frederick County airport on 1201 E Patrick St., 301/631-0188, lunch and dinner Mon.–Sat.) produces the ultimate sloppy burger, cheesesteaks, and great fries. Once a seasonal quickstop, the restaurant may soon be kept open all year.

The **Stone Hearth Bakery** (138 N. East St., 301/662-2338) is the spot for fresh breads and other baked goods.

Italian
A classic spaghetti-and-meatballs Italian restaurant, **di Francesco's** (26 N. Market St., 301/695-5499, lunch Mon.–Sat., dinner daily, $10–19) has been a local favorite for years. Consistently delicious, it serves several types of pasta, as well as meat and poultry.

◖ **Tauraso's** (6 N. East St., 301/663-6600, www.taurasos.com, 11:30 A.M.–10 P.M. Mon.–Thurs., 11:30 A.M.–11 P.M. Fri.–Sat., $9–20) is a hip Italian spot. The menu features seafood with a nouvelle twist and a wide variety of pizzas, served in both formal and casual dining areas, plus a great fireplace to sit by in winter. This place attracts a fashionable crowd.

International
Serving Spanish tapas (little dishes), **Isabella's Tavern & Tapas Bar** (44 N. Market St., 301/698-8922, isabellas-tavern.com, lunch Tues.–Fri., dinner Tues.–Sun., plates average $6), has a good wine list and plenty of specials during the week, such as a three-tapas special for $11 on Friday nights before 6:30 P.M.

Tajitu (7 and 9 E. Patrick St., 301/631-6800, www.tajitu.com, 11 A.M.–10 P.M. Tues.–Sun, $9–18) is located in the former Snow White Hamburger Grill building (Tajitu has a Snow White Grill Museum, so the fairy tale lives on in Hagerstown). The cuisine is Ethiopian, with dishes such as doro wott (chicken stew) and tibs (pan-fried bits of beef with vegetables) with injera bread. Tajitu also has a fine vegetarian selection. Diners may sit at traditional tables and chairs or on pillows for Ethiopian-style seating in the rear of the restaurant.

Culinary Landmarks
The Shamrock (7701 Fitzgerald Dr., off Rte. 15, Thurmont, 301/271-2912, www.shamrock restaurant.com, 11 A.M.–10 P.M. Mon.–Sat., noon–9 P.M. Sun., $9–25) mixes casual dining with goofy entertainment, such as potato-peeling contests for patrons. The restaurant is known for its excellent fried shad roe, a Maryland specialty, as well as steaks, corned beef, and seafood. It offers weekend and holiday specials.

The Shamrock is near another local party spot: **The Cozy** (103 Frederick Rd./Rte. 806, Thurmont, 301/271-4301 www.cozyvillage .com, lunch and dinner daily, weekend breakfast buffet, lunch $7.50, dinner $10–15, buffet $7), which has fed visitors since 1929. The Cozy is famous for its buffets: Monday and Tuesday have the eight-entrée evening buffet (plus grilled steak Wed.–Thurs.), Friday and Saturday have the 19-entrée buffet, Sunday has the 10-entrée dinner buffet, there's an 8-entrée lunch buffet Monday–Friday, and then a country breakfast on Saturday—all at incredible prices. Whew!

Local Favorites

◖ **Hagan's Tavern** (5018 Old National Pike/ Rte. 40A, Braddock Heights, 301/371-9189, lunch 11:30 A.M.–3 P.M. Tues.–Sun., dinner 5–9 P.M. Tues.–Thurs., 4–10 P.M. Fri.–Sat., and 4–9 P.M. Sun., $8–25) is housed in a restored 1790 stone tavern and features an American menu in a colonial atmosphere. Period-style artwork and costumed staff add to the fun. Several people have rated the tavern as having the best food in the county, and the servers are top-notch.

Dutch's Daughter (581 Himes Ave., 301/668-9500, www.dutchsdaughter.com, lunch and dinner daily, Sun. brunch, $9–35) is reputed to have the best crab cakes in Frederick, and is the winner of several "Best of Frederick" awards. The owner, Eileen Gideon, began the restaurant with her sister 20 years ago in a VFW club. The name "Dutch's Daughter" is in honor of their father, Fred "Dutch" Onderdonk. Her sister left the business, and Eileen chose to pursue the dream of one day owning her own building. The current "Dutch's Daughter," a multi-room mansion, was built in March 2000. The restaurant is southwest of the main part of town off Route 15.

Breweries and Nightlife

◖ At **Brewer's Alley** (124 N. Market St., 301/631-0089, www.brewers-alley.com, lunch and dinner daily, $6–23), you'll find delicious appetizers (wood-fired soft pretzels with spicy Creole cheese), a broad southwestern/Cajun pub menu with lots of lighter dishes, and a knockout beer sampler—excellent hefeweizen and pale gold ale are crowd pleasers. In central Frederick, Brewer's Alley also offers a children's menu and its own root beer on draft.

Griff's Landing (43 S. Market St., Frederick, 301/694-8696, daily) serves a sophisticated pub menu, including a raw bar, but is better known as a meet-and-greet (make that "meat") bar with live entertainment (usually local bands) on the weekends.

INFORMATION

The **Tourism Council of Frederick County** (19 E. Church St., Frederick, MD 21701, 301/228-2888 or 800/999-3613, www.frederick tourism.org) has details on events and things to do in the area. A fancy new visitors center is in the works at East South Street.

Crossroads of the Civil War

It is well that war is so terrible, or we should grow too fond of it.

– Robert E. Lee, after the battle of Fredericksburg, 1862

CIVIL WAR HISTORICAL SITES

During the Civil War, the area of Maryland roughly between Hagerstown, Frederick, and Harpers Ferry was one of the most trafficked pieces of territory in the United States. Maryland, a deeply divided border state, vividly illustrated the phrase commonly associated with the Civil War—brother fighting against brother. Though the war ended with Lee's surrender at the Appomattox courthouse, it grew from a spark set in 1859.

In the summer of that year, radical abolitionist John Brown rented a small farmhouse north of Harpers Ferry, from which he rallied volunteers to his incendiary cause and planned a raid that would, he hoped, begin a slave revolution similar to the one that had recently taken place in Haiti.

The Kennedy Farm

This farm, also known as Samples Manor (2406 Chestnut Grove Rd., Sharpsburg, in the area formerly known as Kennedyville, 301/432-2666), was the leased summer dwelling of "Isaac Smith and family": aka John Brown, his daughter, his daughter-in-law, and three of his sons. Though privately owned, the farmhouse has been restored to its 1859 appearance. The grounds

the Kennedy Farm and John Brown farmhouse

© JOANNE MILLER

are open most days, and there is an automated information terminal on the upper balcony. Tours may be booked by emailing captain@johnbrown.org or calling 301/652-2857 or 301/977-3599.

In the 1850s, Dr. Booth Kennedy purchased the farm and frequently leased it to a church group, the Brethren. The "Smiths" stayed in the small log-and-wattle structure (leasing it from Kennedy's trustee for $35) from late spring to autumn of 1859, keeping to themselves, much to the chagrin of their curious neighbors. Though the two girls came and went frequently, the other dwellers within the house were well hidden during the day—12 white men and five black men, in addition to John Brown and his sons. Brown sent the women home in early October, just before the planned raid on Harpers Ferry.

◖ Harpers Ferry National Historical Park

Harpers Ferry National Park spans the Potomac and Shenandoah Rivers, and is shared by Maryland, West Virginia, and Virginia. The town of Harpers Ferry, at the confluence of the two rivers, is accessed via I-340, in West Virginia, and is definitely worth several hours of a visitor's time (contact the park by writing to Superintendent, P.O. Box 65, Harpers Ferry, WV 25425, 304/535-6029, www.nps .gov/hafe, 8 A.M.–5 P.M. daily, $6 per vehicle, $4 per person on foot).

In 1747, a Philadelphia millwright, Robert Harper, bought out the original German settlers and established an improved ferry service and several local industries. By October 1859, Harpers Ferry was a bustling town of nearly 3,000, 150 of whom were free blacks, with an equal number of slaves. The town was accessed by both the Baltimore and Ohio Railroad and the Chesapeake and Ohio Canal. The town's major business—and the main interest of John Brown and his followers—was the U.S. Armory. The armory consisted of 20 brick structures along the Potomac River, two arsenal buildings where thousands of finished weapons were stored, and the U.S. Rifle Factory.

It was Brown's intention to seize the 100,000 weapons at the arsenal and to flee to the nearby Blue Ridge Mountains, establishing a base for the slave-guerrilla war that he predicted would ensue. His 21-man "Provincial Army of the United States" crossed the railroad bridge from Maryland into Harpers Ferry on the evening of October 16, 1859, and seized the armory and several other buildings. Local militia and a contingent of marines under the command of Lt. Col. Robert E. Lee (among them Abraham Lincoln's future assassin, John Wilkes Booth) fought Brown's raiders for 36 hours, killing or capturing almost all the men, including Brown, who held out to the last in the armory fire-engine house. Found guilty of treason, Brown was hanged in December 1859. The attack on Harpers Ferry inflamed both North and South and led to secession of the Southern states over their right to allow slave ownership, followed by the bombing of Fort Sumter by Federal troops in 1861—the start of the Civil War.

Harpers Ferry continued to play a significant role for both sides for the duration of the Civil War; the town changed hands eight times between 1861 and 1865. On April 18, 1861, less than 24 hours after Virginia seceded from the Union, Federal soldiers set fire to the Harpers Ferry armory and arsenal to keep them out of Confederate hands. However, Confederate forces managed to douse the flames and send the remaining weapon-making machinery south to be used in their cause. When the Confederates abandoned the town two months later, they burned most of the factory buildings and blew up the railroad bridge that John Brown and his men had crossed in their failed attempt to capture arms. The ruins, however, became the foundation of a hopeful future. Storer College, an integrated school, was founded on the grounds of the armory just after the Civil War.

Harpers Ferry National Historical Park contains not only the town of Harpers Ferry, with its many restored buildings and cemetery, but also a number of hiking trails that trace paths taken by Union and Confederate troops: Maryland Heights, Loudoun Heights, Bolivar Heights, and Schoolhouse Ridge.

🄲 Antietam National Battlefield

Antietam Battlefield (Rte. 65, 0.7 mile north of Sharpsburg, contact the site by writing to Superintendent, Box 158, Sharpsburg, MD 21782, 301/432-5124, dawn–dusk daily, closed Thanksgiving, Christmas, and New Year's Day, $4) is preserved as a monument to those who died in the bloodiest day of fighting in the Civil War. During a single 20-minute segment of the battle, both sides suffered a total of 2,000 casualties. Six generals suffered mortal wounds.

Lee soon had news of victory at Harpers Ferry, but little had changed: The Union troops now camped in Pleasant Valley continued to present a barrier between him and his reinforcement troops at the crossing. Lee retreated the night of September 14 and took up positions between the Potomac and Antietam Creek in the small farming community of Sharpsburg. The scattered parts of his army joined him in Sharpsburg, taking a strong defensive position by the morning of September 17. Lee's forces numbered around 36,000 infantry and artillerymen—little more than half the original force.

Union general McClellan's plan was to strike north, middle, and south on the battlefield. The editors of *Harper's Weekly,* Guernsey and Alden, commented in 1866, "Every thing pointed to the one conclusion, that the whole Union force should be thrown at the earliest moment upon the Confederates. That this was to be done on the morning of the 17th was the decision, as understood by [Union general] Hooker, to whom the initiative was assigned." And so General Hooker's troops attacked Confederates in the woods near Dunker's Church, on the north end of the battlefield. (Dunker is a corruption of the German word *tunker* or *tunken,* meaning "to dip" and denoting a full-immersion baptism.) The Dunkers were a group of pacifists originally from Germantown, outside of Philadelphia; they were among the first settlers on Antietam Creek. The church that bears their name was built in 1853.

Burnside Bridge, Antietam Battlefield

After several hours of fighting, General Hooker fell mortally wounded, and the battle turned, due to the Southern artillery's 80 large guns. Shattered, Hooker's troops fled, and the battle went to the Confederates. However, they were unaware of their own victory and fell back.

Union forces pressed the Confederate center, and Lee threw the majority of his troops into that confrontation, withdrawing men from the woods to the north and south. The Confederate troops were overwhelmed by wave after wave of Union artillery, but managed to break the Union line. Two of General Hill's brigades clung desperately to a sunken road. By nightfall, troops of both sides occupied almost the same positions as they had that morning. One Union captain, Oliver Wendell Holmes Jr., fought with the 20th Massachusetts Volunteer Infantry and was wounded in the neck during the battle. He survived, returned home, and became a renowned U.S. Supreme Court Justice.

Lee had fewer than 2,500 soldiers left to defend the southern portion of the battlefield, a stone bridge over Antietam Creek. Union General Burnside, with 14,000 men under his command, had been ordered to take the bridge at 8 that morning. For an unknown reason, he hesitated to attack until 4 P.M. By then, Confederate forces at the bridge had been relocated, except for 500 Georgia riflemen under the command of an officer named Toombs. When Burnside did decide to take the bridge, he sent one group of soldiers after another into direct sniper fire—easy pickings for the Georgia riflemen, who were hidden in the forested heights on the other side. After Toombs' men had withdrawn to the defense of the Confederate center, Burnside's men crossed the easily fordable stream without opposition. In one of those ironic twists of history, the bridge is named after the man who sent hundreds to their deaths.

Though Dunker's Church was damaged in the first day's battle, it still provided necessary shelter and a modicum of peace. During a brief truce on the 18th, soldiers from both armies used the church as a field hospital; they spoke

THE ADVERSARIES

ROBERT E. LEE, COMMANDER, CONFEDERATE ARMY

Robert E. Lee, son of one of the founding families of Virginia, graduated from West Point with the highest honors of his class. Shortly thereafter, he married George Washington's step-granddaughter, and entered the A-list social crowd in Washington. For the next 30 years, he served the United States Army, capturing John Brown at Harpers Ferry.

Prior to the Civil War, Lee was dismayed by extremists on both sides, but his primary allegiance was to Virginia. The day after that state seceded in April 1861, Lee resigned his commission. At age 55, he chose to abandon everything he had worked for, his professional rank, and his private fortune. against the advice of his old friend General Scott, commander of the Union Army. In June, Lee accepted command of the Confederate States Army in Virginia, a position he held until the end of the conflict. Four years later, he surrendered the remnants of his army to Union Commander U. S. Grant, the successor of the man who urged him not to resign.

Critics of Lee complain that he was too genteel, that his politeness sometimes obscured quick, total obedience to his orders; while others felt he entrusted too much discretion to subordinates who were not up to the responsibility. Despite these weaknesses, many historians maintain that Lee was the most capable commander of the Civil War.

After the defeat of the South, Robert E. Lee served as a symbol of courage in defeat. He became president of Washington College (now Washington and Lee University) in Lexington, Virginia, and devoted himself to education and helping rebuild the South.

GEORGE B. MCCLELLAN, COMMANDER, UNION ARMY

Early in the war, the Union began to examine its forces: Who could transform these boy volunteers into an army? President Lincoln singled out General George B. "Little Mack" McClellan, who had won a series of encounters in rapid succession and was becoming increasingly popular with public. "Another quality, more characteristic of McClellan than of any other general," gushed *Harper's Magazine*, "... was his extraordinary capability of creating enthusiasm in his army." This praise was not a just a simple, frank outburst of admiration, but a mark of personal sympathy and fervent devotion.

President Lincoln saw McClellan as a political choice who would be likely to conciliate the South if it were possible; in addition, his popularity would unite the North. What Lincoln hadn't foreseen was that his own approach to warfare differed radically from those of Little Mack. Upon his appointment, McClellan set about reorganizing the army. Lincoln and his cabinet, meanwhile, set out to micromanage McClellan's movements, creating a situation where McClellan's strategies were frequently at odds with Lincoln's.

After Antietam, Abraham Lincoln heard that Lee's army was close to the Maryland border. He wrote to McClellan, insisting on pursuit and destruction, and McClellan demanded reinforcements and supplies. Lincoln countered that the Army of the South had little or none of what McClellan requested, yet they continued to resist in an annoyingly adept fashion.

On November 7, McClellan was relieved of command and replaced by Major General Burnside. The command would pass through many more hands before the war was over. In 1864, McClellan ran unsuccessfully against Lincoln for president of the United States.

---

freely of their homes and families, fully expecting to sight each other over rifles the next day. That battle never took place. In the darkness of night on September 18, the rebels slipped away, crossing the Potomac at Shepherdstown, foiling McClellan's plans to renew the battle on September 19. After the battle damage was repaired, the Dunkers continued to hold services in the small white church for several more decades.

Total forces engaged by the Union numbered nearly 58,000; by the Confederacy, 38,000. Though losses to both sides were close

THE BALLAD OF GEORGE AND MATTIE

George Boatwright, a young man from Toombsboro, Georgia, enlisted in May 1862 as an artillery soldier in the Confederate Army. He left behind a 13-year-old girl of slight acquaintance, Miss Martha Jane Burrows. George began a hesitant correspondence with "Miss Mattie": "It is the case with a majority of soldiers, to have some one to correspond with them, and knowing no better subject I solicited yours." Miss Mattie responded by asking why he wasn't writing to his girlfriend instead, and George replied, "you accuse me of being in possession of that almost indispensable article – [a] sweetheart. For I was not aware that I had one, but if such is the case, I appeal to you to inform me who she is, who has condescended to allow me to claim her, or who has thought enough of me to claim me."

Over the next year, they continued to write to each other whenever the machinations of war permitted – often missing each other's replies. George suffered through bouts of the "chills" (dysentery), and reported in July 1863 that "the coast service is so monotonous that I have nothing of interest to write." The situation had changed by October of that year, however: "I have been disappointed in procuring a furlough. Some of our company have... went home and over stayed their time, and our officers are refusing to grant furloughs at all now." George finally secured one day's leave in November and spent it with his family, returning to his battalion the next morning – his letters to Mattie begged her forgiveness for his inability to call on her. She assured him that she understood.

In January 1864, George was moved to write, "I hope you will excuse my boldness; for I am prompted by the purest of motives to speak thus: love you know is the first law of our nature and...the assurence you have given me of your willingness to correspond with me has caused a new era to dawn upon me.... I feel that life possesses a charm worth living for." He proposed to run the blockade around Savannah the following Saturday in order to see her. He carried out his promise and found her absent from home (she never received his letter); he was arrested by his fellow soldiers for disobeying orders, and remained under guard for some months. He wrote, "This is the first time I have been arrested since the war begun, and had I have known the good of it...it is the easiest position I have found.... I think when I get out of this I will run the blockade again."

By the time of his letter on April 30, 1864, both George and the war had changed. He had been moved from artillery to infantry: "In the

---

to equal on the north and center battlegrounds, Burnside's excessive losses brought the total of Union dead and wounded (but not missing) to 14,200; the Confederates parallel total was about 12,500. The Battle of Antietam (or Sharpsburg, as it's known in the South) was considered a draw, but it put a temporary end to Lee's plans to invade the North. However, he would enter the Maryland crossroads once again in less than a year.

The Antietam visitors center (on Rte. 65) displays Civil War relics and offers an interpretive film on the battle. A small store in the visitors center sells or rents an inexpensive and excellent audiotape auto tour of the battle. Since the battlefield is kept much as a shrine, car touring, bicycling, and walking are allowed, but picnicking and other recreational activities are not. Monuments to various regiments are scattered throughout the area, including one to the Zouaves, French colonial soldiers who fought for the Federal Army. There is a $3 charge to enter the park.

Pry House Museum

On the grounds of Antietam National Battlefield (301/416-2395, 11 A.M.–5 P.M. daily in summer, $2), this historic home and former field hospital is an extension of the National Museum of Civil War Medicine in Frederick. Exhibits include information on the Pry House and a re-creation of an operating theater, dis-

whole of our tramp, according to my memorandum, we marched upwards of one thousand miles. We captured and hung a great many deserters and bush-whackers and had a good time generally." Then, by the end of May: "We marched through Gen. Beauregards battlefield between Petersburg and Richmond, and from the appearance of it, the fight must have been a desperate one. There was an immens quantity of blood upon the field, though the bodies were all intered."

In late June 1864, George was dispatched under General Jubal Early in an attempt to draw Grant's troops away from the certain destruction of the remaining rebel army. Before he left Richmond, George wrote to Mattie: "Thees words are my hearts pure sentiments... they are words that I have longed to speak. I must say that you feel nearer to me than any one I have ever met with, and to seal what I am now saying, will you consent to be my Mattie?... Pleas answer my question in your next [letter], as my fate either for weal or woe depends on your answer." He added, "I scarcely have time to sleep any atal. I have been on the front line for several days.... Our boys equiped themselves very well with blankets, oil clothes, and canteens [for our march to Maryland]."

General Early's troops crossed the Potomac, extorting money from Maryland towns whenever possible, moving toward Washington, D.C., the federal capital. On July 9, Union general Lew Wallace's raw recruits met the enemy at Monocacy Junction. Though the Union took the worst of it during several hours of fighting, George Boatwright was mortally wounded. He died four days later and was buried in a mass grave. Decades after the war's end, George's remains were identified and reinterred at Frederick's Mount Olivet cemetery, plot number 243, along the north wall.

It's unknown when Mattie learned of George's fate, but she kept his letters until her death in 1932. She remained unmarried for 30 years, then wed a much older man. They were childless. Mattie helped raise her sister's children, and one of them, Jane Lucille Pope, was given the letters. When she passed away, the letters were found by Ms. Pope's daughter, who recognized their significance. With her husband, she traced George Boatwright to Monocacy.

Many thanks to Cathy Beeler of the National Park Service for sharing George's letters and the bittersweet romance of George and Mattie.

---

playing objects relating to the care of wounded and the effects on the civilian population in the area. Abraham Lincoln visited the house two weeks after the battle.

Antietam Cemetery

On Route 34 in the town of Sharpsburg, the cemetery is open dawn to dusk daily. Since so many soldiers died during the battle, burial was haphazard, often in shallow graves with little or no identification. By 1864, many of the graves surrounding Sharpsburg were becoming exposed. The state purchased an 11-acre burial site, and the arduous task of exhuming the dead began. In the years following the Battle of Antietam, two local men, Aaron Good

and Joseph Gill, were instrumental in finding the old burial sites and helping to identify the dead through letters, receipts, diaries, photographs, and marks on belts or cartridge boxes. Despite their efforts, 38 percent of the dead remain unknown. Their graves comprise the greater part of Antietam Cemetery. There is no charge to walk about the grounds.

Because the South was unable to raise funds to exhume their dead, and because bitterness continued after the war's end, no Confederate soldiers are buried here. Charitable organizations—often made up of Northern women—paid to have remains of 2,800 rebels (60 percent unknown) buried in three cemeteries: Mount Olivet Cemetery in Frederick, Washington

Confederate Cemetery in Hagerstown (now known as Mount Rose), and Elmwood Cemetery in Shepherdstown, West Virginia.

Monocacy National Battlefield

Monocacy (4801 Urbana Pike, Frederick, MD 21701-7307, 301/662-3515, open daily, free) was the final attempt of Southern troops to bring the war to the North.

In June 1864, Robert E. Lee withdrew his Army of Northern Virginia from the Confederate capital at Richmond to Petersburg, pursued by Union General Ulysses S. Grant. Grant had pulled all able-bodied forces from Washington, D.C., in the hope of defeating Lee and ending the war. Lee, desperate to draw Federal forces away from his army, ordered Lt. General Jubal Early to take a third of the Confederate forces, raid Harpers Ferry for supplies, then cross the Potomac at Sharpsburg. Early's goal was a last-ditch attempt to invade Washington, D.C. His men advanced through Hagerstown and Frederick, extorting $20,000 from the former and $200,000 from the latter.

Grant dispatched troops to meet the Confederate forces well before they arrived at the capital, but until they could reach Early's troops, the only Federal soldiers available to engage the rebels were a group of 2,300 raw recruits quartered in Baltimore under Major General Lew Wallace. Wallace, who would become famous in later years as author of the novel *Ben-Hur,* rushed his men west to Monocacy Junction, the meeting point of four major transportation routes: the Georgetown Pike to Washington, the National Road to Baltimore, the Monocacy River, and the Baltimore & Ohio Railroad. Wallace planned to stretch his little force along the river to protect as many of these transportation centers as possible. He knew he and his men would provide a delaying action at best; Confederate troops outnumbered him five to one.

On July 9, 5,800 of Grant's troops arrived to reinforce the battle, but by the afternoon, they were overrun by the superior Confederate forces. Roughly 1,300 Union troops were killed, captured, or wounded, while Early lost nearly 900 men.

Early continued his march to the capital and stood before the earthworks of Fort Stevens two days later, but one day too late: Grant's reinforcements had already arrived there to defend it. Had Early not been forced to lose a day at Monocacy, the Union capital might have been in Confederate hands. Though Early was successful in drawing troops away from Lee's fleeing forces, the taking of Washington was not possible; the rebel army withdrew to Virginia. Though the Confederates returned to western Maryland for raiding skirmishes, Monocacy marked the last major CSA offensive in the state.

The Gambrill Mill (4801 Urbana Pike/ Rte. 355), which was used as a field hospital during the battle (Wallace commented, "The place appeared well-selected for the purpose, its one inconvenience being that it was under fire"), houses a visitors center and is the base of walking and driving tours of the battlefield. From Memorial Day to Labor Day, it's open 8 A.M.–4:30 P.M. daily From Labor Day to Memorial Day, it's open 8 A.M.–4:30 P.M. Wednesday–Sunday.

OTHER POINTS OF INTEREST
Boonsboro Museum of History

This tiny, eclectic museum (113 N. Main St., 301/432-6969, 1–5 P.M. Sun. May–Sept. or by appointment, $3) is a treasure trove not only of Civil War relics, but also of history in general. Owner Doug Bast started collecting historical memorabilia when he was eight years old and never stopped. The museum contains numerous unusual Civil War artifacts, such as bullets carved by idle soldiers into tiny flowers, dice, buttons, and animals; a pike used by John Brown's raiders; an original order by Stonewall Jackson; and personal items of Confederate officer Henry Kydd Douglas. A diary written by the son of Harriet Beecher Stowe (she authored *Uncle Tom's Cabin*) is also part of the museum collection: Stowe searched for her son and located him after the battle of Antietam. He survived the war, but later died mysteriously as he set out for California by ship.

The walls are covered with weaponry from around the world; cabinets burst with ceramics and glass, including China trade porcelain of 1790, Depression glass from the 1930s, and examples of local Bell pottery. There's even a copy of *Martyr's Mirror*, the first book printed in 1748 by members of the Ephrata Cloister in central Pennsylvania, and a mourning bouquet made from human hair. The museum's exhibits change according to what has been lent out to surrounding museums. The array of items in the rooms can be dazzling and bewildering. Tell Doug your interests when you go in, and he'll show you around.

Crystal Grottoes Cavern

For those who need a troglodyte fix, Crystal Grottoes (19821 Shepherdstown Pike, Boonsboro, 301/432-6336, www.goodearthgraphics .com/showcave/md/crystal, 9 A.M.–6 P.M. daily Apr.–Oct., 11 A.M.–4 P.M. Sat.–Sun. Nov.–Mar., $10) is the place to go. Crystal Grottoes is about one mile west of Boonsboro. The limestone cavern features a large variety of formations and an easy set of dry walkways to follow. The tour is escorted and takes about 40 minutes.

RECREATION

Most state parks, forests, and national parks in greater Frederick County and adjoining Washington County offer some sort of overnight facility, though types and prices vary by park. Each park office will have current information and maps.

Greenbrier State Park

This Appalachian Mountain park (21843 National Pike, Boonsboro, MD 21713-9535, 301/791-4767, day use $3) is a multi-use facility featuring a 42-acre man-made lake and beach. Hiking trails, including a portion of the Appalachian Trail, meander through all types of wildlife habitats. The Appalachians are one of oldest mountain ranges, and Greenbrier's rocky outcroppings show much of the earth's

geologic history. Picnicking, two playgrounds, a visitors center, interpretive programs, and a nature study are also available.

Water Sports: Swimming, canoeing, and boating are all in the park. A boat rental and boat launch area is near the lake.

Fishing and Hunting: The freshwater lake is stocked with trout, largemouth bass, and bluegill. All Maryland fishing laws apply, and a Maryland Angler's License is required for all anglers age 16 years or older. Fishing with live minnow bait is not permitted. Hunting is permitted in designated areas of the park in season.

Winter Sports: Cross-country skiing on the park's hiking trails is permitted.

Overnight Facilities: There are 165 campsites (888/432- 2267 or http://reservations.dnr .state.md.us for reservations) offering conveniently located bathhouses with hot showers. Each campsite is equipped with a table, grill, and parking area. Forty sites have electric hookups. In addition, there is a camp store, dump station, and food and beverage concession.

Getting There: The park is approximately 10 miles east of Hagerstown on U.S. 40, and is also accessible via I-70 from the Myersville, Beaver Creek, or Hagerstown exits.

South Mountain State Park

An 8,039-acre site (c/o Greenbrier State Park, 21843 National Pike, Boonsboro, MD 21713, 301/791-4767), South Mountain attracts hikers year-round—40 miles of the Appalachian Trail pass through it. The park also features campfire programs, picnic shelters, and a playground. South Mountain, a ridge composed largely of quartzite, rises from 200 feet above sea level by the Potomac River to nearly 2,000 feet at Penn-Mar, almost 40 miles north. It posed a formidable obstacle to the early settlers until "Braddock's Road" (the National Road/U.S. 40)was completed, thereby opening the west to settlement.

Hiking: The Appalachian Trail follows South Mountain with numerous side trails. There are scenic overlooks within a short hike of the trailheads on Route 40, Weverton Cliff, Gathland, Route 17, or at Penn-Mar and High Rock.

THE BATTLE OF SOUTH MOUNTAIN

Though no official battlefield exists to commemorate South Mountain, a detailed map of the battle sites and car tour maps may be picked up at the visitors center in Gathland State Park.

Turner's Gap was the main Union objective because the National Road, which passed through it, led to Boonsboro and Hagerstown. Lee's lost orders indicated to McClellan that he would find pieces of the divided Confederate Army in those areas. Mountain House, a wayside tavern still in operation (now the South Mountain Inn), was a key landmark in the gap. The first action occurred at Fox's Gap, just south of Turner's Gap. Union troops coming from the east tried to round the right flank of the main Confederate forces posted at Turner's Gap. General Hill, who commanded the troops at Turner's Gap, dispatched General Samuel Garland's brigade south to meet the Union flank attack. Garland's men fought with Jacob Cox's Kanawha Division of the Union IX Corps on the eastern slope. Two future U.S. presidents served with the Kanawha Division: Lieutenant-Colonel Rutherford B. Hayes (who was wounded) and Commissary Sergeant William B. McKinley (who went on to dish up chow at Antietam). Hill's rebel troops fought Union forces for most of the day of September 14, trying to secure Turner's Gap. His reinforcements, lead by Longstreet, arrived late in the afternoon.

Farther south, at Crampton's Gap, Confederate General Franklin's troops left Harpers Ferry to try to hold the pass, which was quickly overrun by Union forces. The main thrust of Franklin's assault on Crampton's Gap came from the fields east of Gathland State Park. Confederate artillery at Brownsville Gap, a mile to the south, raked the Union ranks. The Union forces pushed the Confederates up the slope, through the gap, and into Pleasant Valley on the other side of the mountain.

The third phase of the battle began late in the day with a combined Union assault on both Fox's and Turner's Gaps. Union forces succeeded in securing Hagerstown Road north of Turner's Gap, but the determined

Gathland State Park

Confederates held on to the main prize, Turner's Gap. It was only a matter of time before the superior number of Union troops succeeded in taking the gap; General Lee ordered Hill to withdraw late in the evening, ending the Battle of South Mountain.

By the night of September 14, McClellan's army had possession of the three passes. Had he pushed on quickly, the Union general might have attacked Lee's army before it was reunited. McClellan's failure to advance is considered to be one of the greatest missed opportunities in American history, as well as one of the leading causes of his eventual dismissal as leader of the Union Army. Lee sent word to his scattered troops to join him near the village of Sharpsburg. It was there that the final and bloodiest battle in the Crossroads was fought: Antietam.

Of the 28,000 Union soldiers engaged in the Battle of South Mountain, 1,800 were reported killed, wounded, or missing. Of the 18,000 Confederates, 2,800 were lost. The nearby hamlet of Burkittsville received and treated wounded troops from both sides at the two churches on Main Street after the battle.

Winter Sports: Cross-country skiing is available on most trails.

Overnight Facilities: Backpackers are permitted to camp in any of the trail shelters or at the Dahlgren Backpackers' Camp.

Getting There: The South Mountain range and park covers considerable territory. Contact Greenbrier State Park for information on facility locations.

Washington Monument State Park

Four miles east of Boonsboro and 1.5 miles north of Alternate Route 40 on Monument Road, this park is named for the first U.S. monument erected to George Washington (c/o Greenbrier State Park, 21843 National Pike, Boonsboro, MD 21713, 301/791-4767). In 1755, British General Edward Braddock traveled through western Maryland with young George, a surveyor. They laid out a road that could be used by British soldiers to advance to the forks of the Ohio and capture the territory from the French during the French and Indian War. In 1827, the citizens of Boonsboro dedicated a rugged stone tower to the first president. During the Civil War, the tower was used as a signal station.

The Appalachian Trail winds through the park and passes the base of the monument, and there are additional hiking trails on the property. The park offers a visitors center, picnic shelters, playing fields, a playground, and campfire programs. The Cumberland Valley is a migratory bird flyway, providing excellent opportunities for birders in the spring and autumn. An annual hawk and eagle count is made by ornithologists at the monument. Cross-country skiing is a popular winter activity. Camping is limited to organized youth groups by reservation only.

The Appalachian Trail

Conceived in 1921 by private citizens and maintained today by volunteers, the trail winds 2,167 miles through 14 states from Springer Mountain, Georgia, to Mount Katahdin, Maine. It consists of a well-marked, narrow path with occasional overnight shelters and privies. Maryland has 37.5 miles of the interstate hiking trail, much of which runs along the east side of South Mountain from Harpers Ferry northeast toward the Pennsylvania border. For specifics on Maryland's portion of the trail, contact The Appalachian Trail Conference (P.O. Box 807, Harpers Ferry, WV 25425, 304/535-6331, www.dnr.state.md.us/publiclands/at).

SHOPPING

◖ **Route 65 Flea Market** (7445 Sharpsburg Pike, Boonsboro), a large livestock-shed-turned-collectibles-market, is on Route 65 about six miles north of Sharpsburg. Many dealers have booths there, and local farmers bring in their produce on the weekends. During the warm months, it's open 10 A.M.–6 P.M. on weekdays and 7 A.M.–6 P.M. on weekends.

Though tiny, **Turn the Page Bookstore & Café** (18 N. Main St., Boonsboro, 301/432-4588, www.ttpbooks.com) will satisfy your needs for caffeine and information. You might spot romance maven Nora Roberts there, visiting with the owner, her husband. The celebrated author of dozens of romance novels lives nearby with her family in rural Maryland.

Because of restrictions engendered by its proximity to the Antietam battlefield, the village of Sharpsburg has remained largely undeveloped. However, **Shepardstown,** on the West Virginia border (less than three miles west of Sharpsburg over the Potomac bridge on Rte. 34), has seen a renaissance, and is filled with interesting cafés, restaurants, and shops. Many visitors to Antietam cross the river to dine there.

ACCOMMODATIONS

AYH Harpers Ferry Lodge 19123 (Sandy Hook Rd., Knoxville, MD 21758, 301/834-7652, www.hihostels.com, Apr.–mid-Nov., $20–45) is the least expensive stay in this area. Private rooms and parking are available. Since the Harpers Ferry area is also a popular kayak, canoe, and tubing spot, make reservations well in advance. The hostel is open for groups by reservation only November–March.

One option in the Antietam area is the **Jacob Rohrbach Inn** (138 W. Main St., Sharpsburg, 301/432-5079 or 877/839-4242, www.jacob-rohrbach-inn.com, $104–185). Built around 1800 by Capt. Joseph Chapline, Revolutionary War patriot, the inn is a shining example of Federal- period architecture updated with modern conveniences. Jacob Rohrbach lost his life defending the property against horse thieves claiming to be Mosby's men on July 4, 1864. The building was appropriated and used as a hospital to care for the wounded following the battle of Antietam. Five guestrooms all come with private baths and gourmet breakfast.

The **Inn at Antietam** (220 East Main St., Sharpsburg, 301/432-6601, www.innat antietam.com, $120–185) in downtown Sharpsburg is an elegant Victorian with a view of the Blue Ridge Mountains. Each room is cleverly and uniquely decorated (the General Burnside Smokehouse Suite is about as country as it gets, with grand plaid-covered armchairs and a fireplace big enough to roast a hog). Innkeepers Charles and Bob are experts on the area and can recommend the best local tours and dining. The inn includes five suites and a penthouse, all with private baths and extra amenities such as fireplaces and wet bars. No pets or children younger than six, please, and the inn is closed in January.

FOOD

Battleview Market (5331 Sharpsburg Pike, 301/432-2676), a combination convenience store and deli on Route 65 between Sharpsburg and Antietam battlefield, serves up the best breakfasts and hoagies around. Prices average less than $10, and the market is open for three meals daily.

Some sort of trading post has existed on the site of the **Old South Mountain Inn** since 1732 (6132 Old National Pike/U.S. 40A, Boonsboro, 301/432-6155, www.oldsouthmountaininn .com, Sat. lunch, Sun. brunch, dinner Tues.– Sun., $23), but it wasn't until after 1765 that the stone house here was built as a family home by Robert Turner, the man for whom Turner's Gap is named. By 1790, it was a full-fledged inn, and remained so through the Civil War—it was the headquarters of Confederate officer D. H. Hill during the battle of South Mountain. In 1876, it was purchased by author, lecturer, and philanthropist Madeline Vinton Dahlgren, who built the stone chapel across the road. In 1925, the stone house was returned to its original purpose and renamed the Old South Mountain Inn. The menu is American: prime rib, beef Wellington, chicken, and seafood. A cozy bar, the President's Lounge, features pictures signed by Washington, D.C., bigwigs. The wine list offers California, French, German, and Italian vintages, as well as products from local vineyards.

INFORMATION

Since the battlefields are spread over two counties, information may be requested from the **Tourism Council of Frederick County** (19 E. Church St., Frederick, MD 21701, 301/ 228-2888 or 800/999-3613, www.frederick tourism.org), and **Hagerstown/Washington County Convention and Visitors Bureau** (16 Public Sq., Hagerstown, MD 21740, 888/ 257-2600, www.marylandmemories.org).

Hagerstown and Vicinity

As a slaveholding county in a federally held state during the Civil War, this peaceful farming town became the scene of considerable strife between Southern and Northern sympathizers. Like Frederick, Hagerstown was held for ransom by Confederate general Jubal Early; however, the demanded amount of $20,000 (not $200,000, as in Frederick) was suspected to be due to a clerk's error. The rebels got their $20,000 and didn't bombard the town.

Today, Hagerstown has returned to its quiet existence. The loudest roar to be heard is from stock cars at the Hagerstown Speedway, several miles west of the city. However, its heritage as a rich and long-established center between the Eastern cities and lands to the west is still

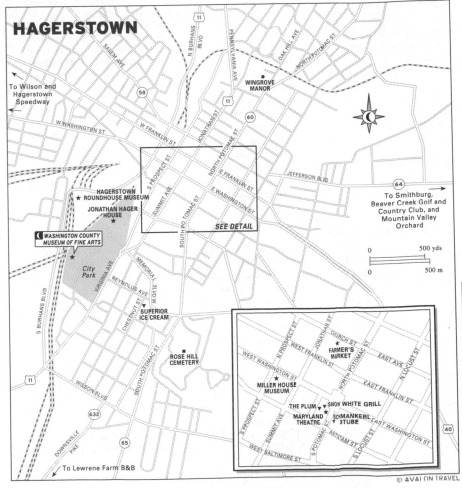

WESTERN MARYLAND

demonstrated by its exceptional art museum and historical sites.

SIGHTS
Hager House

The immaculately preserved Hager House (110 Key St., 301/739-8393, www.hagerhouse.org) is adjacent to the Washington County Museum of Fine Arts in Hagerstown's beautiful city park, off Prospect Street (U.S. 11). It's open 10 A.M.–4 P.M. Tuesday–Saturday and 2–5 P.M. Sunday April–December, closed January–March and the last week of November–first week of December (to prepare for the traditional German Christmas celebration). Admission is $3 adults, $2 seniors, and $1 children 6–12.

Jonathan Hager migrated from Germany in 1736, settling in the wilderness of western Maryland. In 1739, he built a three-and-a-half-story uncut fieldstone house for his new bride; the 22-inch-wide walls provided ample shelter from hostile elements, both natural and human. The home was taken over and restored inside and out to its colonial glory by the Washington County Historical Society. A museum featuring artifacts from the life of Jonathan Hager and his family is on the grounds next to the house.

Rose Hill Cemetery

Rose Hill Cemetery (600 S. Potomac St., 301/739-3630, free) is one of the sites where 2,447 unknown and 241 known rebel soldiers were reburied. The remains were gathered from mass graves at South Mountain, Antietam, Gettysburg, and Hagerstown. The large circular gravesite, known originally as Washington Cemetery, is surmounted by a granite monument; it's on the north side of Rose Hill Cemetery. When the gate is closed, Washington Cemetery is visible from South Potomac Street.

Miller House Museum

This two-story townhouse (135 W. Washington St., 301/797-8782, 1–4 P.M. Wed.–Sat. Apr.–Dec., $5 adults) was built in the early 1800s and serves as the headquarters and research library of the Washington County His-

THE ROAD TO GETTYSBURG

Maryland was once again invaded in June 1863, prior to the Battle of Gettysburg. Lee's troops had been making raids into Pennsylvania, hoping unsuccessfully to draw and divide Union forces. He resolved to make a serious invasion by his whole army. His troops crossed the Potomac at Williamsport and Shepardstown – cut off from their supply system, they were ordered to live off the country. Lee ordered that supplies should be extorted in an orderly manner: First, upon formal requisitions, payment being tendered in Confederate notes; if these were declined, certificates were to be given showing the amount and value of the property taken (a sort of IOU); and if these were refused, the required supplies were to be seized. The latter was the most common form of acquisition. Towns with few assets were literally held hostage and burned if they were unable to pay. The army marched on to Pennsylvania, engaged the Union Army during the three-day Battle of Gettysburg, and returned to Virginia once again.

torical Society. Once the home of a prosperous attorney, the Miller house is adorned with a "hanging staircase" (spiral stairs with no visible support), and fireplace hearths made of local puddingstone marble. The home contains several excellent period collections: More than 260 dolls, representing all major doll manufacturers of 19th-century Europe, are on display; and 200-plus clocks, including Hagerstown- and Frederick-made tall case clocks may be seen. The rooms of the house are furnished in 1820s style. The garden in back of the house has been replanted with old varieties of roses, herbs, fruits and vegetables.

⬧ Washington County Museum of Fine Arts

Sitting peacefully by the lake in Hagerstown's City Park, this small, graceful museum (City

Park at Prospect St./U.S. 11 and Memorial Blvd., 301/739-5727, www.washcomuseum.org, 9 A.M.–5 P.M. Tues.–Fri., 9 A.M.–4 P.M. Sat., 1–5 P.M. Sun., free) is a hidden gem in an unexpected setting. The museum maintains a remarkable collection of top-quality American paintings, drawings, prints, and sculpture from the 18th century to the present, as well as outstanding examples of glassware, ceramics, and furniture. Each intimate room is dedicated to a style or era, and the works in it are thoughtfully displayed. To stroll into the cool marble foyer on a hot day, then to take in each of the gallery rooms, enjoying post-colonial-era portraits by members of the Peale family, art moderne sculpture from the 1920s, and contemporary photography and abstract works, is to enjoy a visual feast. The art is inspiring, and there's no cost to view it. This museum is so exceptional that it has earned a well-deserved accreditation from the American Association of Museums, an honor extended to fewer than 10 percent of museums in the United States.

Hagerstown Roundhouse Museum

Though the real roundhouse no longer exists, this quirky collection (300 S. Burhans Blvd., 301/739-4665, www.roundhouse.org, 1–5 P.M. Fri.–Sun., $4) documents the history of the Western Maryland Railroad and six others that made Hagerstown the "Hub

---

A SEPARATE COUNTRY

The promise of abundant crops, especially in the long valley that unrolls south from Hagerstown to the Potomac River, attracted the first non-English settlers to Maryland. By the late 18th century, space was becoming increasingly rare in Pennsylvania and Virginia. The new settlers, seeking relief from religious intolerance and English persecution, recognized the possibilities of the mountain valleys. The west became the stronghold of independent freeholders, farmers who supported separation from Britain, remaining largely loyal to the North during the Civil War. Hagerstown and the rest of the west retain much of their rural flavor – although according to Frances Trollope, quite pleasantly changed from colonial days.

Ms. Trollope spent three and a half years in America, ostensibly to escape financial embarrassment in England. Upon her return she penned *Domestic Manners of the Americans*, a singularly snooty and bad-tempered look at the winners of the British-Colonial War. America-bashing was big in the old country; the book was a success and saved the Trollope family from economic ruin. In the section titled "Western Maryland, Summer 1830, Family Life and Domestic Arrangements of Small Landowners," Trollope wrote:

"We were invited to take tea with this family, and readily consented to do so. The furniture of the room was one heavy huge table, and about six wooden chairs. When we arrived the lady . . . vehemently urged us to be seated, and then retired into the closet-chamber above mentioned, whence she continued to address to us from behind the door with all kinds of "genteel country visiting talk," and at length emerged upon us in a smart new dress.

Her female slave set out the great table, and placed upon it cups of the very coarsest blue ware, a little brown sugar in one and a tiny drop of milk in another, no butter, though the lady assured us she had a "deary" and two cows. Instead of butter, she "hoped we would fix a little relish with our crackers," in ancient English, eat salt meat and dry biscuits. Such was the fare, and for guests that certainly were intended to be honoured.

I could not help recalling the delicious repasts which I remembered to have enjoyed at little dairy farms in England."

City." Displays include pictures, lights, lanterns, bells, whistles, and tools; a railroad library; railroad layouts; and a gift shop with railroad-related items. The special holiday show, "Trains of Christmas" (Nov. 24–Feb. 25) features an "O" scale snow scene layout on four levels with steam and diesel trains by Lionel, MTH, Williams, Weaver, and others. If you'd like to see a real steam locomotive, the museum sponsors a scenic train excursion to view the changing leaves every October. Or you could drop by the City Park and see the engine 202 steam locomotive and several cabooses (cabeese?). Make sure you call before you come—the museum is run by volunteers and isn't always open.

The Maryland Theatre

This performance space (21–27 S. Potomac St., 301/790-3500, www.mdtheatre.org) is a charmingly restored Victorian jewel. The Maryland Symphony often plays here, and there are performances and theatrical productions every week of the year. Built in 1915, the theatre was destroyed in the late 1970s by fire, but is completely restored today. If you saw the Shirley MacLaine/Nicolas Cage film *Guarding Tess,* you'll recognize the ornate interior instantly.

SHOPPING
Beaver Creek Antique Market

One hundred and fifty dealers show their antique and collectible wares at this massive covered market (20202 National Pike/U.S. 40, Hagerstown, 301/739-8075, www.beavercreekantiques.com, 9 A.M.–5 P.M. Thurs.–Tues.), and there are also several seasonal flea markets during the year.

Farmers Markets

The bustling and very authentic **█ Hagerstown City Farmers Market** (25 W. Church St., 301/739-8577, ext. 183, www.hagerstownmarket.org, 5 A.M.–noon Sat.) features a range of local produce, baked goods, an Asian market, and meats from surrounding farms. There's also a crafts area.

Many local Amish and Mennonite farmers sell here. Much of the produce sells out before 9:30 A.M., so it pays to get there early for the best selection. If you miss the market, there's always breakfast or a pork-chop sandwich for a few bucks at Karen's Country Kitchen, inside the market. Established in the late 1700s, the old Hagerstown Marketplace is still going strong.

Mountain Valley Orchard (22541 Jefferson Blvd./Rte. 64, Smithsburg, 301/824-2089) is one of several farm stores on Route 64, east of Hagerstown, near the crossroads of Route 66 (Mapleville Rd.). During the summer, the area's abundant produce—peaches, apples, plums—is sold at tasty prices.

Seven miles east of Hagerstown, **Clopper's Orchards** (23334 Fruit Tree Dr., Smithsburg, 301/824-7106) sells fresh-picked fruit. During the summer and fall, they send their own strawberries, black cherries, and peaches to a small dairy in Waynesboro, Pennsylvania, where it's transformed into custom-made ice cream and delivered back to the farm for sale. This is ambrosia and sells out quickly—but if they're temporarily out of stock, they also have traditional ice cream in plenty of flavors.

RECREATION
Hagerstown Speedway (15112 National Pike/U.S. 40, Hagerstown, 301/582-0640, www.hagerstownspeedway.com) caters to all types of auto racing, though stock cars are a specialty. Used primarily by local racers, the speedway began with a small track in the early 1950s and has become a premier draw for dirt racing fans. You'll hear the roar emanating from about five miles west of Hagerstown. Call for scheduled events and tickets. Self-contained units may camp for free on the Speedway grounds.

Beaver Creek Golf & Country Club (9535 Mapleville Rd./Rte. 66, Hagerstown, 301/733-5152, www.beavercreekcc.com), six miles east of Hagerstown near the village of Beaver Creek, features a challenging 18 holes, driving range, and restaurant. A PGA pro is on duty.

ACCOMMODATIONS

There are a number of chain hotels in the area, including **Hampton Inn-Hagerstown** (1716 Dual Hwy., Hagerstown, 301/739-6100), **Sleep Inn** (18216 Colonel Douglas Dr., Hagerstown, 301/766-9449), and **Comfort Inn** (50 Pine Dr., Greencastle, PA, 717/597-8164).

Situated in an upscale section of Hagerstown, **Wingrove Manor** (635 Oak Hill Ave., 301/797-7769, www.wingrovemanor.com, $145–160) is gracefully decorated to reflect its Victorian-era Greek Revival origins. Close to central Hagerstown, the manor features three rooms (one may be shared with an additional small room for a larger family), each with a large private bath; a home-cooked continental breakfast is served in the morning. Wingrove has been featured in *Elegant Living* magazine.

FOOD

At the **Snow White Grill** (12 S. Potomac St., Hagerstown, 301/739-7002), customers lurk about, peering out of their overcoats as if the lure of tiny burgers were somehow pornographic. Order two or three teensy "deluxes" (two inches square) with fried onion, tomato, lettuce, pickles, and mayo for $2 each; the burgers are really tasty and made fresh to order. Fries are $2.25.

A pleasant and inexpensive café, **The Plum** (6 Rochester Place, 301/791-1717, 7:30 A.M. to 2:30 P.M. Mon.–Fri., $8) dishes up pastries, soups, salads, and sandwiches downtown in an alley off West Washington between Summit and Potomac Streets.

On a hot night, the sidewalks surrounding **Superior Ice Cream** 500 (500 Chestnut St., 301/790-0650, $2) are filled with happy lickers. A Hagerstown institution for many years, Superior offers a variety of ice cream flavors, plus treats such as sundaes and dipped cones.

Schmankerl Stube (58 S. Potomac St., Hagerstown, 301/797-3354, www.schmankerl stube.com, lunch and dinner Tues.–Sun., $9–28), a Hagerstown favorite since 1988, is a Bavarian restaurant that serves specialties like Bavarian bratwurst with sauerkraut and spatzle (potato dumplings with meat gravy) or potato salad and vegetables ($16). Sample one of several German beers on draft, and enjoy outside dining in the biergarten during fine weather.

INFORMATION

Hagerstown/Washington County Convention and Visitors Bureau (16 Public Sq., Hagerstown, MD 21740, 301/791-3246 or 888/257-2600, www.marylandmemories.org) is the place to contact for more information.

Orchard Country and the C&O Canal

Rocky farms and orchards spread benignly to the west in Maryland's former frontier. Many side roads offer verdant views of the land as it begins to roll toward the Allegheny Mountains. The 184.5-mile-long C&O Canal, which was reconstructed into a hiking/biking path along the Potomac River, is an extraordinary example of intelligent reuse of unproductive space. Best known in the western part of the state, its overnight parks, miles of well-maintained bikeways, and wildlife-rich scenery beckon a much wider audience of adventurers. The canal's eastern terminus is in Georgetown, north of Washington, D.C.; Williamsport is roughly

halfway, and the western terminus (marked by a park and museums) is in Cumberland.

HISTORIC PARKS
◖ C&O Canal National Historical Park

The towpath of the former Chesapeake and Ohio Canal, this park (1850 Dual Hwy., Ste. 100, Hagerstown, MD 21740, 301/739-4200) features campgrounds roughly every 5–6 miles along its 184 miles; towns, hotels, and places to stock up on food in the sparsely populated west are more erratic. *The C&O Travel Companion* by Mike High (see *Suggested Reading* at

CANAL FEVER

The Chesapeake and Ohio Canal had its beginnings in the late 1700s, when the new nation sought pathways through the Alleghenies to the rich forks of the Ohio. Thomas Jefferson, among others, was convinced that the Potomac River was the route they sought. George Washington, who held land in the Ohio Valley, headed a group formed to navigate the river; the Patowmack Company sought to remove obstacles in the waterway and to skirt several of the falls that impeded navigation. Washington's tenure was interrupted by an eight-year stint as president of the fledgling United States. He died before the first leg of the canal, from Georgetown to Williamsport, was completed.

By 1825, canal fever had seized the eastern states. In New York, the Erie Canal was fast on its way to completion, and a group of influential Marylanders, including Francis Scott Key and George C. Washington (grand-nephew of the former president), pressed for government support for a canal from Georgetown to the rivers of Pittsburgh. In spite of its enormous cost of $22 million, the project got underway in 1828. Fourteen years later, the canal had reached the town of Hancock, roughly halfway, and funds had petered out. Worse, the Baltimore and Ohio Railroad had already bypassed the terminus of the canal and had reached the city of Cumberland. Maryland waived its lien on the canal, and construction was completed in 1850. Due to its ability to ship coal from the fields west of Cumberland south to the nation's capital, the canal could compete with the railroad. The Civil War raised canal revenues significantly, and the waterway continued to operate for an additional 15 years before it was finally rendered inoperative by two massive floods. It was then purchased and shut down by its rival, the B&O Railroad, around 1890.

Though the railroad kept the canal operating on a minor level, another flood in 1924 caused it to cease operations. During the Depression, the canal was sold to the U.S. government and turned into a Civilian Conservation Corps project. Another flood in 1942 destroyed all hope of restoring the canal to commercial usefulness. In 1954, under threat of turning the canal's towpaths into a highway, Supreme Court Justice William O. Douglas invited editors from the *Washington Post* to walk with him on the towpath, in the hopes of turning the canal site into a protected area. He succeeded in raising American consciousness of the value of the site, but it wasn't until 1971 that President Richard Nixon designated the C&O Canal a national park.

the back of the book) is an indispensable tool for anyone planning to travel part or all of the canal. In addition to food and lodging information, it lists canal specifics, such as where the locks are and where to find canal boats.

The Chesapeake and Ohio Canal was the focal point of an apocalyptic dam proposal that would have flooded massive portions of the Potomac Valley after World War II. It was also considered for conversion to a driving parkway in the 1950s. In 1954, Supreme Court Justice William O. Douglas invited the editors of the pro-dam, pro-power-company *Washington Post* to join him on a walking tour of the towpath. A sizable group started out near Cumberland, but only nine hiked the whole way to George-town; nonetheless, it brought the need for conservation of the area to public attention. It wasn't until 1971 that President Nixon designated the entire length of the canal a national historic park. Today, the C&O Canal offers one of the greatest recreational opportunities in America.

One way to travel all or most of the canal (allow five days by bicycle, up to three weeks on foot) is to take Amtrak's Capitol Limited (from Pittsburgh, Philadelphia, Baltimore, Washington, D.C., or New York, 800/USA-RAIL or 800/872-7725) or a Greyhound bus to Cumberland, and begin the journey there, ending at either Hancock (50 miles), Williamsport (100 miles), or Georgetown (184 miles) and returning via public transportation. Amtrak does not have baggage handling in Cumberland and other quick stops, so bikers may need to look at alternatives to bringing bikes on Amtrak.

Visitors centers are in Georgetown, Washington, D.C.; Great Falls, Maryland (both offer canal boat rides); and Williamsport, Hancock, and Cumberland, Maryland.

Traveling by Car: Most of the canal is inaccessible to cars, though drive-in camping, picnic areas, and canoe launch sites along the canal are available at McCoy's Ferry, Fifteenmile Creek, Little Orleans, and Spring Gap. All campsites, including hiker/biker campsites, are primitive. There is a paved road to Little Orleans campground in Green Ridge State Park (I-68/U.S. 40, exit 68), but beware! State maps often show the road as completely paved from Little Orleans to Paw Paw Tunnel—in reality, it's paved only to Little Orleans (halfway to the tunnel), then becomes a narrow, rutted, unmarked dirt road marked by hunting camps occasionally manned by questionable quasi-military personnel. Not a great place to ask for directions; stay on the asphalt.

A feat of industrial-era engineering, **Paw Paw Tunnel** is a 3,118-foot-long brick-lined passage carrying the towpath through a mountain. It was constructed over a period of 14 years. The tunnel is accessible from Route 51 east from Cumberland. Parking is available 0.5 mile from the tunnel entrance; it's a short and pleasant walk to the tunnel. The Tunnel Hill trail, which rises 362 feet over the top of the tunnel, affords great views of Green Ridge State Park, one of the largest in Maryland. The Purslane Run overnight campground is roughly 0.5 mile south of the parking lot on the trail, south of Route 51 on the Maryland side of the Potomac. Route 51 parallels the Potomac River on its way to Cumberland, passing through historic Oldtown, the farthest outpost of the frontier during colonial days.

Traveling by Bicycle: This is the favorite method of transportation for many visitors to the canal, permitting a relatively fast pace but affording opportunities to explore some of the canal's side interests as well. The road

is mixed gravel, so hybrid or offroad tires, a patch kit and inner tube, and panniers for supplies are necessary. If you'd rather go with a group, two resources are **Bike and the Like** (1 Houndstooth Ct., Owings Mills, MD 21117, 410/960-6572 or 877/776-6572, www.bike andthelike.com) and **Potomac Pedalers Touring Club** (PPTC Business Office, 10378 Democracy Ln., Ste. A, Fairfax, VA 22030, 703/691-8733, www.bikepptc.org).

Traveling by Foot: Though most campsites are placed conveniently, there are two expanses where the sites are farther than eight miles apart: between Georgetown and Swain's Lock (17 miles) and Bald Eagle Island and Huckleberry Hill (12 miles, near Brunswick, Maryland). A sturdy backpack with supplies (including sufficient water for two days) is necessary. The **C&O Canal Association** (P.O. Box 366, Glen Echo, MD 20812, 301/983-0825, www.candocanal.org) occasionally sponsors group hikes.

Traveling by Kayak or Canoe: Seeing the canal by water is limited to those areas that remain filled. The most popular of these is the 23-mile stretch between Georgetown and Seneca. There are also short segments at Big Pool, Little Pool (near Hancock), and a stretch between Oldtown and Town Creek. Boating on some sections of the Potomac River itself is considered hazardous, especially east of Harpers Ferry. Canoe launch sites on the Potomac are located throughout the park, with the westernmost site at Spring Gap. **Thompson Boat Center** (2900 Virginia Ave. NW, Washington, D.C., 202/333-9543, www.thompsonboatcenter .com), **Blue Ridge Outfitters** (66 Koonce Rd., Harpers Ferry, WV, 304/725-3444), and **Tom's Run Outfitters** (16210 Fairview Rd., Hagerstown, MD 21740, 301/733-0058, tom srunoutfitters.net) all offer rentals, advice, and some escorted trips.

Fort Frederick State Park

Fort Fred, as it's known locally (11100 Fort Frederick Rd., Big Pool, MD 21711, 301/842-2155), was the site of Maryland's major frontier defense during the French and

Indian War, built after the defeat of British general Braddock (1754–1763). The fort's gates are open 8 A.M.–sunset daily April–October, 8 A.M.–sunset weekdays and 10 A.M.–sunset weekends November–March. The grounds are free, but there is an admission charge to tour the fort: $3 adults and $2 kids 6–12.

The diamond-shaped corners on the rectangular fort were engineered to permit crossfire against invaders. Families within a radius of 10 miles would flee to the fort during Indian attacks. Those outside 10 miles would attempt to fortify a central home in their area—hence all the villages with "Fort" in front of their names. The fort was a prisoner-of-war camp during the Revolution, and the Union's defense against Confederate raiders during the Civil War. Fort Fred's massive stone surrounding walls and two barracks have been restored to their 1758 appearance; two-thirds of the fort's stone walls are original. History displays are set up in the fort, barracks, and nearby visitor center, and costumed interpreters are available for more information. Military reenactments, campfire programs, and other special events are held frequently. Fort Fred became Maryland's first state park in 1922. The grounds adjoin the Potomac River; the Chesapeake and Ohio Canal passes alongside. Big Pool, part of the original canal system, is a large body of captured water popular with canoeists and boaters. The serene setting is particularly pleasant for a picnic and a stroll. There are two museums on the property: the visitor center displays soldiers' regalia from different eras and related park history, and a Civilian Conservation Corps museum features the CCC's role in restoration. Captain Wort's Sutler Shop sells souvenirs and food.

Hiking: The park offers two short interpretive trails and the C&O Canal towpath for hikers and joggers.

Water Sports: There is no boat launch into the Potomac River at Fort Frederick, but boats may be launched at nearby McCoy's Ferry or Four Locks. There is a boat ramp for launch into Big Pool in the park; canoes and rowboats are available for rental from Captain Wort's Sutler Shop in the summer.

Fishing: Angling is popular on both the Potomac River and Big Pool. A Maryland license is required for all anglers over 15 years of age.

Winter Sports: Cross-country skiing is allowed on the fort's extensive grounds.

Overnight Facilities: From the first Friday in April to the last Sunday in October, visitors may rent one of 29 tent sites for a fee in the Riverfront campground; restrooms, picnic tables, and grills are nearby. Sites are first-come, first-served. Call 888/432-2267 or visit http://reservations.dnr.state.md.us for reservations.

Getting There: Fort Frederick State Park is in the Cumberland Valley, 18 miles west of Hagerstown and one mile south of I-70 near Big Pool, Route 56, exit 12. Bear right at the Y for the visitors center, where a 25-minute orientation film is shown on request. Bear left to get to the fort. Both U.S. 40 and Route 56 (exit 18 off I-70) are only slightly longer and much more scenic.

OTHER PARKS AND SCENIC SPOTS

Most state parks, forests, and national parks offer some sort of overnight facility, though types and prices vary by park. Each park office will have current information and maps.

Western Maryland Rail Trail

Located 0.5 mile west of Fort Frederick, this 23-mile paved path follows the former Western Maryland Railway line. The Rails to Trails Conservancy recently chose the Western Maryland Rail Trail as one of the top 12 trails in the United States for viewing fall foliage (peak foliage season in Western Maryland begins mid-October). The Western Maryland Rail Trail can be accessed from I-70, from either exit 12 (Big Pool, across from the post office), or exit 3 (Hancock, travel west on Route 144 1.4 miles, then turn left into the trail parking lot).

Green Ridge State Forest

This expanse of pines and hardwoods (28700 Headquarters Dr. NE, Flintstone, MD 21530-9525, 301/478-3124) stretches across the mountains of western Maryland and occupies

44,000 acres. The forest, once privately owned, cleared, and planted, was touted as "the largest apple orchard in the universe." When the orchard proprietor went bankrupt in 1918, the state Department of Forestry stepped in and began to restore Green Ridge to its original environment. Much of the forest remains wild, laced by dirt roads and trails, dotted with hunting lodges. Since conditions are primitive, stop by the forest headquarters, exit 64 south off U.S. 68, for a map of trails and campsites.

Fishing and Hunting: Popular fishing areas include the Potomac River, White Sulphur and Orchard Ponds, Town Creek, Fifteenmile Creek, and Sideling Hill Creek. Maryland Angler's License required. Hunting is the largest single recreational activity in the vast forest; wild turkey, grouse, squirrel, and deer are plentiful. All types of hunting are permitted during designated seasons.

Hiking: Twenty-four miles of trails over narrow ridges and forest streams pass by several overlooks for spectacular views of the surrounding mountains. The trails connect with the C&O towpath for an extended hike of 43 miles.

Biking: The forest offers a permanent 12-mile mountain bike trail. For intermediate–advanced riders, this challenging trail has steady climbs and fast downhills; four easy outs have been located throughout the trail, which offers weary riders a more moderate ride back to the trailhead.

Canoeing: Call the Green Ridge Headquarters for guided trip information on the Potomac River.

Horseback Riding: Equestrians are allowed in most areas of the forest. Two campsites are designated for horses, their riders, and their equipment.

Offroad Vehicles: The forest has designated 18 miles of trail for unregistered motorcycles, four-wheelers, and snowmobiles; a permit is required (call the park for more information).

Overnight Facilities: Green Ridge features 100 primitive single campsites and eight primitive group sites scattered all over the forest. The sites are filled on a first-come, first-served basis, and there is a charge for their use. Per-

Sideling Hill

mits must be obtained from the Green Ridge State Forest headquarters.

Getting There: Green Ridge State Forest is in eastern Allegany County, about 22 miles east of Cumberland (exit 64 on I-68).

Sideling Hill Exhibit Center

The narrowest point in Maryland is roughly three miles west of Hancock on I-68. Until the 1980s, the only way around Sideling Hill, a massive stone conformation, was U.S. 40. Engineers blasted Sideling Hill to cut a straight path for I-68, exposing geological formations formed 360 million years ago. The visitor center features exhibits on geology, focusing on the three kinds of rock that make up our planet: igneous (formed from the cooling of molten material—granite is an example), metamorphic (formed by intense pressure, heat, or chemical change, such as marble), and sedimentary (particles carried by wind or water that settle and become compacted). Sedimentary rock covers 80 percent of the earth's surface, and a bridge across the freeway outside the visitor center permits excellent views of the folded and twisted layers of sedimentary rock that make up Sideling Hill. A scope is available on the south side of the bridge; it may be focused on the nearby Mason-Dixon line as it marches east. The center is free and open 9 A.M.–5 P.M. year-round. Call 301/842-2155 for information.

ACCOMMODATIONS AND FOOD

In Hancock, near the Western Maryland Rail Trail, the **1828 Trail Inn** (10 W. Main St., Hancock, 301/678-7227, $115–125) was named for the year that rail and canal builders vied with one another to open up commerce to the Ohio River Valley. Two suites and a room all have private baths; one suite has a private entrance. The Trail Inn is simply decorated and unfussy.

🍴 **Weavers** (77 W. Main St., Hancock, 301/678-6346, 11 A.M.–8 P.M. Mon.–Thurs., 7 A.M.–8 P.M. Fri.–Sun.) is a pleasant little restaurant that has been in business since the late 1950s. Entrées average $9 (sandwiches around $5) and the Maryland crab soup (tomato-based, buttery, not spicy) is the best I've had. It's definitely worth a stop off the interstate. Weaver's has its own fresh salad bar and an outrageous bakery with tempting pies and cookies. Hancock has to be the inexpensive diner

capital of Maryland. **Park-N-Dine** (189 E. Main St., Hancock, 301/678-5242, breakfast, lunch, and dinner daily, $8) has been around since 1946 serving up pancakes and BLTs to hungry travelers. Where else can you get a white-meat turkey dinner for $9?

Hepburn Orchards (557 E. Main St./Rte. 144. Hancock, 800/227-7087, www.hepburns.com), a big warehouse at the Route 144 turnoff of I-68, sells plants and souvenirs, but the big draws are the produce (especially peaches) and the homemade pies and cookies. Behind the register, you can see the bake room where pies are lined up to be wrapped for sale. Prices are inexpensive, and the baked goods are excellent.

INFORMATION

Maryland's wasp waist divides this area into two counties. **Hagerstown/Washington County Convention & Visitors Bureau** (16 Public Square, Hagerstown, MD 21740, 301/791-3246 OR 888/257-2600, www.marylandmemories.org) has information on the eastern part, and the **Allegany County Visitors Bureau** (800/425-2067, www.mdmountainside.com) can help you out with the west. The **Hancock Chamber of Commerce** (126 W. High St., Hancock, MD 21750, 301/678-5900, www.hancockmd.com) can fill you in on happenings there.

Cumberland and Vicinity

Cumberland, with 24,000 residents, is Maryland's largest city in the west, and was once its industrial epicenter. A 12-foot-wide seam of bituminous coal was discovered under Big Savage Mountain and Dan's Mountain in 1810, changing the area from a sleepy frontier town to a major player. Cunard Line steamships demanded high-quality Cumberland coal, and the C&O Canal and B&O Railroad became profitable hauling the fuel to market. The creeks ran yellow with sulfurous mining byproducts until oil replaced coal in the early

1900s and Cumberland and its environs reverted to their green and settled heritage. Now, as the terminus of the C&O Canal and departure route for scenic trips through the Alleghenies, all of western Allegany County is finding new life through tourism.

On the county's eastern boundary, Frostburg, a quiet college town surrounded by farmland, already has its share of excitement: during July and August, Frostburg is overwhelmed by big guys in tights when the Washington Redskins come to town for training. Year-round,

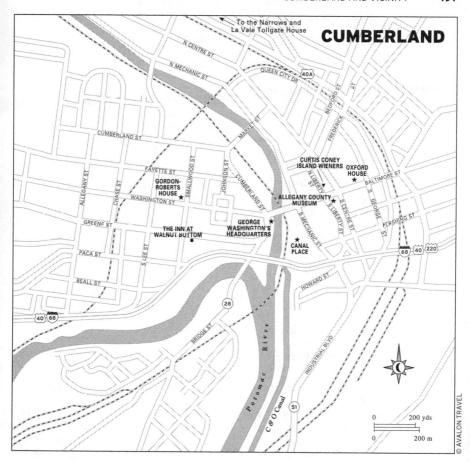

To the Narrows and
La Vale Tollgate House

CUMBERLAND

© AVALON TRAVEL

WESTERN MARYLAND

Frostburg is the home of one of the premier collections of horse-drawn carriages in the United States.

Scenic Drive

From Cumberland, take U.S. 40 through the narrows to Route 35/36. Head north on this road as the sparse suburbs give way to farmland. Turn west on Route 36 at Corriganville, and you'll follow the route of the Maryland Scenic Railroad through rolling hills reminiscent of Ireland and Scotland. At Mount Savage, turn south toward Frostburg. On the south side of Mount Savage, turn southeast on Route 638

toward Clarysville. When you reach U.S. 40, a right turn (west) leads to Frostburg, a right on Alternate U.S. 40 returns to Cumberland past the LaVale Tollgate House.

SIGHTS
Canal Place

Bordered by Baltimore Street, Mechanic Street, Route 51 (Industrial Blvd. S.) and the Potomac River, Canal Place (13 Canal St., 301/724-3655 or 800/989-9394, www.canalplace.org) encompasses the terminus of the C&O Canal and much of downtown Cumberland, and features a number of attractions. Its development

A WALKING TOUR OF GRAND HOMES

Washington Street was the path of realized dreams in Cumberland. Created by the city's wealthy and influential during its heyday, the structures are of a uniformly high architectural quality. All were constructed during the last half of the 19th century.

But the area now known as Washington Street had a much earlier use. Fort Cumberland, built by the British in the 1750s, was the last major outpost of civilization during the French and Indian War. The fort fell to ruin before the onset of the American Revolution. A century later, the massive Emmanuel Episcopal Church (16 Washington St.) was built on the site of the fort. The church features three Tiffany stained-glass windows in its English Country Gothic embrace. Nearby, at 30 Washington Street, the Allegany County Court House, built in 1893, is in Richardsonian Romanesque style, patterned after the Allegheny Court House – one of H. H. Richardson's masterworks – in Pittsburgh.

Continuing up the hill (and respecting the fact that all these homes are privately owned), visitors can appreciate an architectural mélange of early Victorian styles such as Greek Revival (number 104, built in 1841 for Judge Thomas Perry, a member of the House of Representatives), numbers 110 and 112, Greek Revival-Italianate (originally occupied respectively by a coal magnate and a hardware and saddlery entrepreneur), and Second Empire (108 Washington St., built for William Walsh, who also served in the House of Representatives). Bishop James E. Walsh, who was held prisoner in Red China for 10 years, was born in this house. Number 201 was built in 1846 by Southern sympathizer and banker William Sprigg. During the Civil War, the family was taken into custody and the building was used to house Union officers.

Joseph Shriver, a local banker and engineer on the C&O Canal and National Road, advanced pay for a regiment of Union soldiers during the Civil War when it was not forthcoming from the government. He built his Italianate home (300 Washington St.) in the 1860s. Sargent Shriver, philanthropist and Kennedy in-law, is a descendant.

A Colonial Revival built in 1890 (400 Washington St.) was constructed for Bayse Roberts, manager of the Electric Company and

began in the mid-1990s, and culminates with the rewatering of the terminus of the canal in Cumberland.

Western Maryland Railway Station, a magnificent four-story 1913 brick and wood train station, has been restored to full use and serves as the departure point of the **Western Maryland Scenic Railroad** (310/759-4400 or 800/872-4650, www.wmsr.com). WMSR sightseeing trains leave for round-trips to Frostburg on a regular basis; the trips are especially popular in the autumn. The station also houses the C&O Canal National Historical Park's Cumberland Visitor Center, several administrative offices, a gift shop, and a restaurant.

The Shops at Canal Place features a gift shop, fine arts gallery, seafood restaurant, a candy shop, coffee shop, ice cream parlor, toy shop, tour service, and gift shop.

A full-scale canal boat replica, **The Cumberland** offers guided tours of the living quarters, hay house, and stable aboard a typical canal barge. Tours are available on the weekends from May through October.

The **Trestle Walk/Promenade and Crescent Lawn** are worth a stroll. Trestle Walk is a pedestrian walkway that links the railway station with the C&O Canal and the Potomac River. Crescent Lawn is a recreational area/public park on the canal boat basin.

Allegany County Museum

A walk through this collection (81 Baltimore St., Lila Building, Cumberland, 301/777-7200, 10 A.M.–4 P.M. Tues.–Sun. May–Dec., $2) is a passage through Cumberland's past and present: Kelly Springfield tires, Old German Beer, Westvaco Paper, and thriving coal and

the Street Car Company of Cumberland in the early 1900s. One of the later owners of 403 Washington (built in 1862) was Mrs. Doub, wife of a local judge; she was remembered as "a quite colorful person" who would sit in the middle of Washington Street, easel poised and paints in hand, forcing cars to detour around her. The Doubs acquired the property in 1914. Number 408 was built in the 1870s for Daniel Annan, a descendant of the Revolutionary War general and member of the Continental Congress. A variation of Queen Anne and Colonial Revival, the home at 412 Washington Street was built for W. C. Devecmon, descendant of Pierre d'Evequemont, French aristocrat and cousin of Louis XVI. The five-story house has a 30-by-40-foot living room that was once the ballroom.

The house at 501 Washington Street was designed in the Queen Anne style and built in 1890 for Judge Hunter Boyd, chief judge of the Fourth Judicial Circuit of Maryland and an honorary pallbearer at Confederate General Robert E. Lee's funeral. Will Lowdermilk, the founder of the *Daily Transcript* (the first daily newspaper in Cumberland), built an Italian-

ate home in 1860 at 527 Washington Street. He was appointed postmaster of Cumberland by President Grant, served for eight years, then moved to Washington, D.C., in 1878 and opened the venerable Lowdermilk's Book Store. The McKaig Mansion (528 Washington St.) was built in Colonial Revival style in 1880 by Merwin McKaig, an industrialist with interests in the McKaig Foundry, Cumberland Steel, Liberty Trust, and other businesses. McKaig had only one descendant, William, who married but was childless. When William McKaig died, he left millions to a scholarship fund for promising students in the name of his wife, Lalitta Nash McKaig; he left the mansion and all his material possessions to his housekeeper. The property was never occupied again.

A pamphlet with descriptions of architectural details that includes several other houses on Washington Street is available from the Allegany County Convention & Visitors Bureau (Western Maryland Station Visitor Center, 13 Canal St., Cumberland, MD 21501, 301/777-5905). Ask for "Cumberland's Victorian District."

---

glass industries made Cumberland the queen city, the second-largest manufacturing city in Maryland, after Baltimore. Cumberland sits on a vein of high-quality quartz silica, and local glass factories produced a pure blue glass of the highest quality. Examples of housewares produced by myriad small glass manufacturers are displayed, along with other Cumberland memorabilia and industrial artifacts.

🏛 Thrasher Carriage Museum

I never thought I'd lust after horse-drawn conveyances, but the fabulously restored collection at this museum in the college town of Frostburg (about 10 miles west of Cumberland) changed my conception (19 Depot St., Frostburg, 301/689-3380, www.thrashercarriage.com., 10 A.M.–4 P.M. Wed.–Sat. and noon–3 P.M. Sun. March–Dec., by appointment only Jan.–

Feb., $4 adults). One of the top five collections in the country, the carriages on display are upper-middle-class rigs built between 1880–1910. All types of carriages are represented, including sedate and elegant ladies' carriages, racing rigs, and passenger vehicles. The collection also displays several models of historic interest: Theodore Roosevelt's green landau (a five-glass model—five windows—made by Cunningham, a true luxury item at $2,000 when purchased new in 1850); the basket-seat park phaeton used to convey Gerald Ford's daughter in his inaugural parade; and winter sleighs owned by the Vanderbilt family. There's also an unusual Park Drag, a private coach almost as big as a stagecoach, used to chauffeur a host and his friends to picnic sites and events, and to serve as a grandstand for the guests.

Several of the vehicles have been used in

A COACH AND FOUR

A century ago, the road was shared by horse-drawn vehicles that were equivalent to today's Mercedes, Porsches, Saabs, Mack trucks, and economy run-abouts – all priced accordingly. In the United States, the horse-and-buggy days lasted primarily from 1723 to 1920, with maximum use of the buggy for transportation between 1890 and 1910.

Though carriages were common in the wealthier regions of the American colonies, most carriages were made in Europe and imported at significant expense. Soon after independence, Congress banned the importation of completed carriages. American carriage building began to thrive in the 1790s. By the 1850s, the carriage industry in America had grown into big business; in the year 1900, as many as 907,500 pleasure vehicles were built.

American design also came into its own: The Rockaway was the first model that covered the driver outside the carriage – in European models, driver-servants were subject to the vagaries of weather. Early carriages had candle lamps in the front, used to show the position of the carriage on the road rather than for the purpose of lighting the way, and dozens of models were available, including sleek racing rigs; wicker, tub-shaped "governess" carts for driving the children about (as seen in *Gone with the Wind*); and lower, slower ladies' carriages with high fronts. It was considered unseemly for ladies to view a horse's natural functions, and totally out of the question for them to drive behind stallions (perhaps Victorian gentlemen chafed at the comparison).

Sensitivity aside, carriages were expensive. A custom-made Brewster was the equivalent of a Mercedes today – in fact, the Mercedes Motor Company eventually bought Brewster. An average model carriage cost $1,250 in 1906, and the price rose with added amenities and size.

One popular larger model, the buckboard, might be thought of as the first pickup truck. The term "buckboard," used so generically in movie westerns, actually refers to a type of suspension system that was invented to stabilize the carriage. The wide-bodied wagons named for their suspension system were widely used by most farm families in the years prior to the 20th century.

Some elements of carriage design survived unchanged: Wheels remained "dished" – slightly concave – for stability, a style directly descended from predecessors in ancient China. The width of the wheel had much to do with the load carried; the wheels of delivery wagons were considerably wider than those of two-seater carriages. The Kelly Springfield Company invented the rubber tire, a major advancement in comfort and durability, in the 1890s.

Carriage driving is an acquired skill, especially when handling teams of two, four (the famous "four-in-hand"), and up to eight horses. Some of the nation's most prestigious horse shows, such as the Devon horse show in southeast Pennsylvania, have display and competitive carriage driving events. Two organizations list upcoming events, and are a font of information on carriages and driving: the Carriage Association of America (3915 Jay Trump Rd., Lexington, KY 40511, 859/231-0971, www.caa online.com) and the American Driving Society (1837 Ludden Dr. Ste. B120, Cross Plains, WI 53528, 608/237-7382, www.americandriving society.org).

period films, including *Harry and Walter Go to New York* and *Pudd'nhead Wilson*. The museum is across from the Western Maryland Scenic Railroad Depot (tour trains stop here) in Frostburg.

Gordon-Roberts House

Built in 1867 for Judge Josiah Gordon, this handsome brick townhouse (218 Washington St., Cumberland, 301/777-8678, tours on the hour 10 A.M.–4 P.M. Tues.–Sat., $4 adults) was rescued from disrepair by the Allegany Historical Society and turned into a fine example of period architecture and furnishings. The Gordon-Roberts House features a Victorian gift shop and candlelight tours in December.

Collections include clothing, hats, and fans; Civil War relics; B&O Railroad china; hand-blown Allegany County glass, and some unusual pieces of furniture, such as the courting sofa in the parlor (two seats facing each other side-by-side) and the "hunter's cabinet" in the hallway (decorated with life-size wooden carvings of captured game). An oil painting of Lover's Leap, in the narrows west of Cumberland, hangs near the dining room. All the rooms of the house display regularly rotated collections.

There's a very cute tour especially for kids, the Victoria Mouse House Tour. Children help Victoria Mouse (the Gordon-Roberts House puppet) gather items to pack for a trip, pictured on a handout and scattered throughout the museum.

George Washington's Headquarters

In 1755, as a young colonel attached to General Braddock's troops, George Washington began his active military career in this one-room cabin. The cabin, in Riverside Park on Greene Street, Cumberland, is the only remaining structure left of Fort Cumberland, a depot and rallying point of the French and Indian War and later Indian hostilities. Washington returned many times to Fort Cumberland, including a visit in 1794 to inspect troops gathered to suppress the Whiskey Rebellion (the first tax revolt in the new nation) in Pennsylvania. At one time, Cumberland was named "Washington Town," the primary city in "Washington County" (now Allegany County). For those interested in the history and dimensions of the old fort, a walking trail that includes 28 narrative plaques begins in the tiny Heritage Park on the corner of Canal and Baltimore Streets.

La Vale Tollgate House

For a weird juxtaposition of the old and new, pay a visit to the La Vale Tollgate House (14302 National Hwy./U.S. 40A, La Vale, 301/729-3047, free). This toll collector's booth was the first to operate daily on the nation's

© JOANNE MILLER

a tribute to George Washington

first road to the west; a horse and rider had to spend $0.04 to pass through, and another $0.06 if accompanied by a score of sheep or hogs. The tollgate house is easy to miss among the plastic signs, car lots, and modern, boxy buildings on the highway—it's 0.1 mile west of the intersection of U.S. 40 and Route 53 on the south side of the road. The tollbooth is open 1:30–4:30 P.M. Saturday–Sunday May–August, and Sunday only in September.

RECREATION
Rocky Gap State Park

Once a little-used state park, a portion of Rocky Gap has undergone a glamorous face-lift to become a fancy golf resort for business meetings and vacationers (Rocky Gap State Park, 12500 Pleasant Valley Rd., Flintstone, MD 21530, 301/777-2139). It's on I-68, six miles east of Cumberland.

The state park portion of Rocky Gap features amenities similar to Maryland's other parks. A large camping area with 278 campsites is equipped with electricity and showers and some electric hookups. There are also camper cabins. Camping reservations for May 1–September 30 must be made by calling 888/432-2267. The park's main attraction is 243-acre Lake Habeeb, with three swimming areas, bathhouses, boat launch, boat rental and launch, and other concessions.

Dan's Mountain State Park

Dan's Mountain (c/o Rocky Gap State Park, 12500 Pleasant Valley Rd., Flintstone, 301/722-1480) is a day-use facility offering 481 acres of rugged terrain, a fishing pond, hiking, picnicking, and swimming in an Olympic-size pool with a water slide. There's also a recycled tire playground. To get there, take exit 34 off I-68 and travel south on Route 36 for approximately nine miles.

Dan's Rock Overlook affords a panoramic view of the surrounding region from a height of 2,898 feet, and is well worth the three-mile detour from the main road. Though it's still an infamous party place for Frostburg State students (the graffiti may teach you a few new tricks), the view is too good not to share. The county has built a series of steps to the top, for those who find the charms of bouldering less than obvious. To get there, look for Paradise Avenue on the east side of the road, 1,000 feet north on Route 36 from the intersection of Rtes. 936 and 36, north of the village of Midland. Once on Paradise Avenue, follow signs to Dan's Rock Overlook. In summer, the sides of the road are lined with blue chicory.

While visiting Dan's Mountain or the Overlook, take a few minutes to head south on Route 36 to the small town of **Lonaconing.** The town park has a well-preserved iron furnace, the first successful coke-fired furnace in America, in operation from 1839 to 1856. A bronze marker honors a local hero: one of the greatest left-handed pitchers of all time, Robert Moses (Lefty) Grove. A member of the Baseball Hall of Fame, Lefty Grove was born in Lonaconing in 1900, and pitched for Philadelphia and Boston from 1925–1941. In his six years as a player for Baltimore in the International League, he won 108 games and lost only 36. Lefty, where are you when we need you?!

The Narrows

Discovered after the road over Wills Mountain had been built by General Braddock, the Narrows became the route of the National Toll Road (U.S. 40A) in 1833. The Narrows is a scenic pass that twists its way through 1,000-foot-high rock walls west of Cumberland. On the north side of the road, looming over the Fruit Bowl farm stand, is the surreally high granite outface of **Lover's Leap.** Many places claim to be the original Lover's Leap, right down to the story of the Indian maiden and young settler who were not allowed to marry; one glance up at this craggy jumping spot, though, and you just might believe.

SHOPPING
Downtown Cumberland

The four-block area roughly bordered by Frederick, South Mechanic, Pershing/West Union, and South George Streets has been reborn as a comfortable stroll for shoppers, dotted with fountains and pedestrian walkways. The area, particularly along the Baltimore Street promenade, features many fine examples of late-19th-century commercial architecture. The former Lazarus department store (55 Baltimore St.) now contains antique and collectible wares from 100 dealers, and similar shops are interspersed with alfresco cafés, hot dog shops, bookstores, and a C. G. Murphy Variety Store (138 Baltimore St.). The latter is surfaced with "secret recipe" white enameled brick manufactured in nearby Mount Savage.

A detailed walking tour of downtown Cumberland, which has been designated an Arts and Entertainment District by the state of Maryland, is available courtesy of the Downtown Cumberland Business Association from the Allegany County Convention & Visitors Bureau. The tour also includes adjacent historic residential areas.

ACCOMMODATIONS
Rocky Gap Lodge & Golf Resort

This massive lodge (16701 Lakeview Rd. NE, Flintstone, 301/784-8400 or 800/724-0828, high season $219–619, Dec.–March $149–519) sits on Lake Habeeb, which offers swimming, boating, snorkeling, and fishing; the 18-hole Jack Nicklaus Signature golf course is also a big draw. The six-story modern lodge (described by Jim Yenckel in his *Great Getaways* newsletter as "sleek... bedecked in rustic looking wood and stone like a Marriott in a coonskin hat") is reminiscent of lodges at the Grand Canyon or Yosemite. It offers a variety of rooms and a spate of activities for all members of the family, from an indoor/outdoor swimming pool to campfire programs to rappelling to scuba diving. The resort also features a Bar & Grill and a formal dining room, the Lakeside (breakfast, lunch, and dinner daily, dinner entrées average $22).

Failinger's Hotel Gunter

Originally opened as the Hotel Gladstone in 1896, the historic old building has seen more than one major renovation (11 W. Main St., Frostburg, 301/689-6511, www.failingershotel gunter.com, $64–90). William Gunter took over in 1903 and turned the marginally successful resort hotel into a hotel/jail/gamecock-fighting arena/speakeasy. In 1986, the Failinger family renovated the dilapidated building (all those irritable chickens!), turning the basement into a historical mini-museum and the floors above into 16 small, functional hotel rooms. The basement area still holds the original jail, gamecock fighting arena and coal furnace, plus a replica of an underground coal mine. Artifacts found in the hotel during the renovation line the basement hallway, including original restaurant menus from 1907, baby clothes, and assorted bottles and newspapers.

The Inn at Walnut Bottom

◖ **The Inn** (120 Greene St., Cumberland, 301/777-0003 or 800/286-9718, www.iwbinfo .com, $112–162) links two houses—the 1820 Cowden House and the 1890 Dent House (Julia Dent was the bride of President Ulysses S. Grant)—built on the site of a grove of wild walnut trees. The current setting, though still on the outskirts of Cumberland, is distinctly urban, and innkeepers Grant Irvin and Kirsten Hansen have modernized eight rooms

to provide spacious accommodations with private baths, telephones, televisions, and all the other comforts of home. Two additional rooms share a bath, and two-bedroom family suites are available. The inn offers mountain bikes at no charge for guests who wish to explore the city and the C&O Canal towpath. Kirsten, who is a native of Denmark, trained for three years in Copenhagen and is certified in relaxation therapy; guests have the opportunity to experience *Afspaending*, a combination of massage, stretches, and mild exercise.

The Castle Bed and Breakfast

Around 1840, the Union Mining Company based in Mount Savage wanted to attract a medical doctor to the town; the solution was to build a fine home and invite a physician to nest in it. According to records, one Doctor Thompson took over the property, an American Gothic fantasy made of local limestone, and served the miners of the company and their families for the next 30 years.

Early in the 20th century, an eccentric inventor from Scotland, Andrew Ramsey, purchased the home and modified some of its architectural features. Perhaps because of the area's similarities to his birthplace, Ramsey altered the structure to resemble Castle Craig. Ramsey's trump card had been his invention of a one-step (normally a two- or three-step) process for glazing brick; he set up a kiln in Mount Savage. The company prospered, and Ramsey's work is in evidence all over the surrounding area, including commercial buildings on Baltimore Street and the train depot in Cumberland. Ramsey's glazed bricks still shine in the courtyard of his castle. The root cellar is lined with another of Ramsey's products: porcelain toilet bowls and tanks, which make excellent storage bins.

The Scotsman jealously guarded his secret process, but though he was an exceptional inventor, his business skills were no match for the Great Depression. He declared bankruptcy in 1929 and left the area. His secret glazing process died with him some years later. The castle became, briefly, a dance hall, a casino, and, possibly, a brothel. As the countryside healed from the ravages of industry and became as lush as the highlands, the castle fell into disrepair.

In 1984, the building was revamped into the ([**Castle Bed and Breakfast** (15925 Mt. Savage Rd., Mt. Savage, 301/264-4645, www.castlebandb.com, $135–195). Lavishly decorated, all five bedrooms feature a private bath. A full breakfast is served in the dining room or on the porches in good weather, and the property itself is surrounded by 1.5 acres of landscaped gardens. The castle, designated a National Historic Landmark, is a favorite for weddings and special events. It's less than a mile south of the village of Mount Savage on Route 36, a scenic eight-mile drive from Frostburg.

FOOD
Oxford House
Ms. Jaye Miller, former chef at the Swedish Embassy in Washington, D.C., makes the ([**Oxford House Restaurant** (129 Baltimore St., Cumberland, 301/777-7101, www.oxfordhouserestaurant.com, $22) one of the best places to eat in the area. It serves dinner 5–9 P.M. Monday–Saturday (service until 9:30 P.M. Fri.–Sat.) Crab Remick (crab, bacon, and tarragon served in an artichoke bottom) is a unique appetizer, and the entrées are equally delicious. The salads are perfectly balanced, and the desserts (like crushed meringues in frozen cream with lingonberries) leave happy memories. There's also a pub on the premises with a tapas menu.

Au Petit Paris
A little bit of elegance in the Wild West (86 East Main St., Frostburg, 301/689-8946, www.aupetitparis.com, dinner Tues.–Sat., $24), Au Petit Paris is rumored to be the best restaurant in Frostburg. In operation since 1960,

it serves a standard French menu in what can only be termed a "Frostburg French" setting—much too nice for Paris, and not quite country French. Louis St. Marie learned classic cooking from his French Air Force buddies in Amarillo, Texas, fell in love with the food and the intricate preparation process, and made it the family business.

Princess Restaurant
Serving good diner food with cheery service and great prices, the ([**Princess** (12 W. Main St., Frostburg, 301/689-1680, Mon.–Sat., breakfast $5, lunch $6, dinner $9) is the best casual place to eat in town. George Pappas Sr. began the business in 1939, and his family continues to run it. In the 1950s, President Harry Truman and his wife, Bess, passed through and sat in the third mirrored booth from the door. There are still Seeburg Consolettes at each booth.

Cafés and Takeouts
Curtis Coney Island Wieners (35 N. Liberty St., Cumberland, 301/759-9707) puts on the dog: It's been serving its famous wieners since 1918 with mustard, Coney Island secret sauce, and onions.

The **Tombstone Café** (60 E. Main St., Frostburg, 301/689-5254, $5) has coffee your way, plus salads and sandwiches.

Eastern Express (109–111 E. Main St., Frostburg, 301/689-5370, lunch and dinner, late hours, $9) satisfies that occasional need for something different with Americanized Chinese food (they deliver until after midnight on weekends).

INFORMATION
Contact the **Allegany County Visitors Bureau** (800/425-2067, www.mdmountainside.com).

Garrett County

Garrett County is justifiably famous for its recreational opportunities: More than 80,000 acres of the county's 648 square miles are dedicated to public parks, state forests, and open space. In fact, Garrett College (301/387-3044, www.garrettcollege.edu) and the Department of Natural Resources offer adventure sports courses with more than 50 choices in camping, mountain biking, rock-climbing, skiing, whitewater paddling, orienteering, swift water rescue, and many other activities.

The northern part of the county provides farmland for Amish and Mennonite settlers. The Grantsville area offers a quiet alternative to active outdoor recreation; a bulk store and crafts village provide a peaceful afternoon's diversion.

GARRETT COUNTY HISTORICAL MUSEUM

This small museum (107 S. 2nd St., Oakland, 301/334-3226, 11 A.M.–4 P.M. Mon.–Sat. in summer, 11 A.M.–4 P.M. Thurs.–Sat. in winter, free) chronicles the history of Garrett County through its artifacts. There are several pictures of those famous outdoorsmen and fishing buddies Henry Ford, Thomas Edison, Harvey Firestone, and President Warren G. Harding during one of their camping trips to Swallow Falls in 1919. So much for the separation of government and industry.

STATE PARKS AND FORESTS

Garrett County's state parks are usually equipped with picnic shelters and playgrounds, a variety of day- and extended-use recreational facilities, and overnight facilities. Some, such as Herrington Manor, have furnished cabins available year-round.

Because so much public land stretches over the county, hiking and other trails often stretch beyond the boundaries of parks. Get specific information by contacting individual parks.

Many state parks are within state forests, land set aside for both recreational and commercial use. State forests differ from parks in that they cover territory that is privately owned, and they usually offer primitive camping sites but very few other amenities. Trails and roads in the state forests are often, but not always, multi-use.

Casselman River Bridge State Park

Casselman Bridge (c/o New Germany State Park, 349 Headquarters Ln., Grantsville, MD 21536, 301/895-5453) is east of Grantsville on U.S. 40. The 80-foot stone arch bridge was constructed in 1813 as part of the old National Road. At the time, it was the largest of its kind in the world. The bridge is open to foot traffic and anglers, but offers no other recreation or overnight facilities.

New Germany State Park

A small park with a 13-acre lake, New Germany (349 Headquarters Ln., Grantsville, MD 21536, 301/895-5453, www.dnr.state.md.us/publiclands/western/newgermany.html) is popular during summer, offering a multi-use beach, picnicking, and camping. The park is five miles southeast of Grantsville—take exit 24 off I-68 on New Germany Road. There is a $2–3 service charge per person for the day-use area. Visitors enjoy hiking and campfire programs in the warmer months and cross-country skiing in the winter.

This park lies within the boundaries of Savage River State Forest. The lake was formed in the mid-19th century when Poplar Lick Run was dammed for sawmill and gristmill operation.

Hiking: Approximately four miles of the Meadow Mountain trail (the entire trail is 11 miles) run through the park. The trail is accessible from the parking lot.

Skiing: Ski rentals and lessons are available in the park through Allegany Expeditions (800/819-5170). The ski concession is in the Recreation Hall and is open when ski conditions are acceptable weekends and holidays

8:30 A.M.–5 P.M. Weekday rentals are available by appointment. Current ski conditions are available at www.garrettchamber.com/skireport.php.

Water Sports: A boat launch and rowboat rental are available on the lake.

Overnight Facilities: There is a camp store and dump station, and 39 individual campsites close to modern bathhouses with hot-water showers. Tent campsites are available Memorial Day–Labor Day on a first-come, first-served basis. The park offers 11 full-service cabins by reservation; all are furnished and equipped with electricity, bathrooms with showers, bedding, fireplaces, and kitchens. One cabin is equipped for the handicapped. The cabins are available year-round. Call 888/432-2267 or visit the park's website for camping reservations.

Big Run State Park

Big Run is a popular base camp for outdoor lovers intent on fishing, camping, hiking, or hunting. Picnicking and a playground are also available; the day-use area is free. The park (c/o New Germany State Park, 349 Headquarters Ln., Grantsville, MD 21536, 301/895-5453, www.dnr.state.md.us/publiclands/western/bigrun.html) covers 300 acres at the mouth of the Savage River Reservoir and is surrounded by the acreage of Savage River State Forest. The park is 16 miles from exit 24 off I-68, south of New Germany State Park on New Germany Road.

Hiking: Big Run contains the trailhead for the six-mile Monroe Run hiking trail.

Water Sports: The park offers a boat launch, fishing, and flat-water canoeing.

Overnight Facilities: Big Run State Park offers rustic camping year-round with 30 unimproved campsites and a youth group camping area. Contact New Germany State Park (see previous listing) for reservations.

◖ Swallow Falls State Park

One of the most popular recreational areas in Garrett County due to its breathtaking scenery and swimming/sunbathing opportunities, Swallow Falls (c/o Herrington Manor State Park, 222 Herrington Ln., Oakland, MD 21550, 301/387-6938, www.dnr.state.md.us/publiclands/western/swallowfalls.html) was named for the great flocks of cliff swallows that nested in the surrounding rock faces during pioneer days. The park is nine miles northwest of Oakland, on the Herrington Manor–Swallow Falls Road. It is four miles beyond the entrance to Herrington Manor State Park and three miles east of the West Virginia state line. The Youghiogheny (yuk-a-GAY-nee) River flows along the park's borders, passing through shaded rocky gorges and creating waterfalls, rippling rapids, and many sun-and-swim spots where visitors can play turtle. Picnic shelters and a playground are located near the parking lot; a day-use fee of $3 is collected during the summer season.

One of the features of the park is Muddy Creek Falls, a crashing 63-foot waterfall a short hike away from the parking lot. Swallow Falls is also home to an ancient stand of tall native hemlocks.

Hiking: The park contains a 1.5-mile loop trail that parallels the river, and is also part of the Garrett Trail System that starts north of Herrington Manor State Park and ends nine miles later at the Snaggy Mountain Road multiuse trail.

Overnight Facilities: The park features 65 campsites equipped with modern washhouses, laundry tubs, showers, and sanitary facilities. Most of the year, half can be booked by reservation and the other half are first-come, first-served. From Memorial Day to Labor Day, all require reservations. Campsites for those who wish to bring their pets are available, but pets must remain at the site (call for details). Pets are permitted in the surrounding areas of Potomac/Garrett State Forests; during the off-season (Labor Day–Memorial Day), pets are allowed in the day-use areas of Swallow Falls as long as they are on a leash. There is a two night minimum stay for weekends and a three night minimum stay for holiday weekends. Call 888/432-2267 or visit the park's website for camping reservations. Three camper cabins are also available by reservation (call the park office at 301/334-9180).

Herrington Manor State Park

This recreational area (222 Herrington Ln., Oakland, MD 21550, 301/334-9180, www .dnr.state.md.us/publiclands/western/her-ringtonmanor.html) features a 53-acre lake, tennis courts, a ball field, a volleyball area, picnic shelters, and a food and gift concession. The park is five miles northwest of Oakland on Route 20.

Hiking: The park offers 10 miles of looped trails of varying difficulty. The park office on Herrington Lane distributes trail maps.

Water Sports: The lake is stocked with trout. A swimming beach and boat rental concession operate in the summer.

Winter Sports: The boat rental concession rents cross-country skis during the winter for use on the park's trail system.

Overnight Facilities: Twenty furnished cabins, complete with electricity, bathrooms, kitchens, bedding, and tableware, are available by reservation on a weekly basis Memorial Day–Labor Day. For the rest of the year, the cabins are available on a one- and two-day basis. The park's cabins make it a year-round destination, but be sure to make reservations well in advance by calling 888/432-2267 or visiting the park's website.

◖ Deep Creek Lake State Park

Maryland's largest lake is the biggest draw in Garrett County. The park (898 State Park Rd., Swanton, MD 21561, 301/387-4111, www.dnr .state.md.us/publiclands/western/deepcree-klake.html) is 10 miles northeast of Oakland on the east side of Deep Creek Lake, two miles east of Thayerville, off U.S. 219. Most of the land around Deep Creek Lake was privately owned until 2000, when much of the buffer area was purchased by the state.

Park headquarters are at the intersection of Brant and State Park Roads and open during business hours Monday–Friday. Several picnic areas offer excellent views of the lake with easy access to the beach and other facilities, and evening campfire programs, talks on the natural and cultural resources of the park, and ranger-led hikes are available throughout the year.

Deep Creek Lake lies west of the Allegheny Front and the Eastern Continental Divide on a large plateau known as the Tablelands or Allegheny Highlands. Because of its mountainous setting, the region experiences unique weather. Long winters may bring more than 200 inches of snow, and the greening of spring sometimes does not occur until mid-May. Summer brings warm days and cool nights, and autumn comes alive with blasts of color in early October with clear, crisp days and cold evenings.

Deep Creek Lake came into being as part of a hydroelectric project constructed on Deep Creek in the 1920s by the Youghiogheny Hydroelectric Company. The park is the site of the historic Brant coal mine and homesite, where a restored mine entrance preserves a typical drift—or "adit"—mine. The mine was worked for several years by the Brant family and supplied bituminous coal for local heating and blacksmithing.

Once the site of massive deforesting, more than 95 percent of the park has been regenerated into a mature northern hardwood forest. Oaks and hickories are now the dominant species. Black bear, wild turkey, bobcat, and white-tailed deer have grown in numbers over the past decades as habitat has been preserved and managed; squirrel, chipmunk, raccoon, skunk, and opossum are frequently seen. The park is also home to numerous plant species, some rare, found on the forest floor.

Hiking: The Meadow Mountain section of the park offers nine miles of trails for hiking. Trails range from moderate to difficult. A trail guide is available at Park Headquarters and at the various trailheads for a small donation. Pets are allowed on trails and must be kept on a leash.

Fishing and Hunting: Fishing for trout, walleye, bass, and yellow perch is generally good on the lake (trout is stocked). Two wheelchair-accessible fishing docks are available at the park's boating facility.

Hunting is permitted in the park's backcountry areas during regular hunting seasons. The hunting areas are posted, and applicable regulations, including license requirements, apply.

Water Sports: The park includes approximately one mile of shoreline on the lake, and offers swimming, fishing, and boat launching. Lifeguards are on duty at the park's beach during the summer months. The boat launch facility is open most of the year except when weather or ice prohibit access. A limited number of rowboats are available for rental through the campground office.

Overnight Facilities: Meadow Mountain campground has 112 campsites that are available by reservation from spring through fall. Each site is located near heated restroom facilities complete with hot showers. Several disabled-access campsites are available by reservation. Electric hookups are available at 25 sites, and a dump station is onsite for self-contained units. The maximum stay is two weeks. Pets are permitted in certain designated loops. Call 888/432-2267 or visit the park's website for camping reservations.

Garrett State Forest

Acquired by the state of Maryland in 1906, Garrett State Forest (1431 Potomac Camp Rd., Oakland, 301/334-2038, www.dnr.state .md.us/publiclands/western/garrett.html) was the first site in the present public lands system. It's five miles northwest of Oakland, off U.S. 219. The 8,000-acre terrain consists of mountain forests—red oak, white oak, scarlet oak, black cherry, hickory, red maple, white pine, and hemlock—streams, and valleys. Visitors can glimpse beaver ponds and cranberry bogs along the streams, as well as many other wildlife species. Additional information and a map of the forest may be obtained by calling the headquarters.

Hiking: Garrett State Forest and Potomac State Forest share the Potomac River Trail System (10.5 miles), the Garrett Trail System (9 miles), and Backbone Mountain Trail System (8 miles).

Overnight Facilities: Garrett State Forest and Potomac State Forest share four campgrounds: Piney Mountain Campground (Piney Mountain Road, near Friendsville), Wallman Campground (Wallman Road, near Oakland), Lost Land Run (Lost Land Road), and Snaggy Mountain Camping Area (Snaggy Mountain Road). Most sites are first-come, first-served; primitive shelter sites and group sites may be reserved. Call the park office or visit the forest's website for detailed information on campsites.

Potomac State Forest

The highest point in any Maryland State Forest—Backbone Mountain, 3,220 feet—is within the boundaries of this 11,535-acre forest (1431 Potomac Camp Rd., Oakland, 301/334-2038, www.dnr.state.md.us/public lands/western/potomacforest.html). The forest is in southeastern Garrett County, off Route 135, between the towns of Oakland and Westernport, bordering the Potomac River. Another high point in the forest is the rock outcropping near the intersection of Route 135 and Walnut Bottom Road, which overlooks a portion of Potomac State Forest, Savage River State Forest, and Crabtree Creek. The headwaters of the Potomac River are also on state forest land. Additional information and a map of the forest can be obtained by calling forest headquarters or visiting its website. Potomac State Forest is known for excellent trout fishing.

Hiking: Potomac River State Forest and Garrett State Forest share three trail systems, listed under Garrett County State Forest.

Overnight Facilities: Potomac State Forest and Garrett State Forest share four campgrounds. Call the park office or visit the forest's website for detailed information.

Savage River State Forest

At 52,812 acres, this wilderness area (Savage River State Forest, 127 Headquarters Ln., Grantsville, MD 21536, 301/895-5759, www .dnr.state.md.us/publiclands/western/savage-river.html) is the largest facility in the state forest and park system. The state forest is in central and eastern Garrett County, off I-68. Its northern hardwood forest preserves a strategic watershed in Garrett County. About 2,700 acres of the forest have been designated as Big Savage Wildland, an unimproved area.

Hiking: The forest encompasses all or part of Meadow Mountain Trail System (11 miles), Margroff Plantation Trail System (7.5 miles), Negro Mountain Trail System (8 miles), Monroe Run (6 miles), and Big Savage Mountain Trail System (17 miles). A backpacking permit may be obtained at the Savage River office to backpack and camp in the state forest.

Biking: Mountain bikes are allowed on all hiking trails except for Monroe Run and Big Savage. Visitors can ride non-motorized bikes on many of the trails and roads in the state forest but are asked to exercise extreme caution, especially on blind curves.

Hunting: Hunting is allowed in most areas of the state forest in season. Hunters must be licensed. The state forest offers two miles of handicapped hunter access roads that are open throughout the hunting season. These roads can be distinguished by the "Vehicle Access by Special Permit Only" sign at the road entrance. To use these roads, hunters must have a valid permit in their possession and a Permit Display Card on their vehicle. Permit applications may be obtained from the Wildlife Regional Service Center (3 Pershing St., Room 110, Cumberland, MD 21502, 301/777-2136).

Water Sports: A boat launch is available, and the waterways offer both flat-water and white-water canoeing. Anglers must have a current license.

Winter Sports: The forest offers cross-country skiing and snowmobiling. Snowmobile and off-road vehicle (ORV) operators must have a current Department of Natural Resources (DNR) ORV sticker, available at the state forest headquarters. Trail maps are available at the park office for all trails, including 10 miles of cross-country ski trails.

Overnight Facilities: The forest offers 52 primitive sites on a first-come, first-served basis.

SHOPPING
Local Crafts
Spruce Forest Artisan Village (177 Caselman Rd., 301/895-3332, www.spruceforest .org, 10 A.M.–5 P.M. mid-May–Oct. 31) is made up of a group of historic buildings, some original to the site, others brought from as far away as Salisbury, Pennsylvania, and reconstructed on the property. The village is the realized dream of local resident Alta Schrock, who, while working as a teacher several decades ago, wanted to showcase crafts made by people in the surrounding mountains. At first, she drove from place to place in the area to pick up the handwork, selling the goods in a small shop. The buildings are set up as historical displays with interpreters (such as Compton School and Miller House), or house a select group of artisans demonstrating their crafts.

At various times, visitors can see working blacksmiths, soap makers, weavers, potters, woodcarvers, and others. Lynn Lais, whose subtle glazed ceramics are sold all over the United States, is based here, as is Gary Yoder, three-time winner of the World Champion Award for his radiantly alive and beautifully composed carved wooden birds. Yoder carved his first bird at Penn Alps as an 11-year-old, and continues to teach classes as artist-in-residence there during the summer. These days, his art is in such demand that he works by commission only, and the wait is one year. Many of the artisans sell their work on the premises.

The **Penn Alps Craft Shop,** inside the Penn Alps restaurant next to Spruce Forest (125 Caselman Rd., Grantsville, 301/895-5985, www .pennalps.com) features the cream of handmade goods from artists and craftspeople associated with Spruce Forest, plus a small amount of work of equal quality from other areas. This is a spectacular place to buy one-of-a-kind gifts. Handmade quilts, tiny blown-glass birds, silk-screened paper goods, honey from local apiaries, wooden furniture, and metal chimes are a few of the offerings.

Country Stores
People drive 50 miles to shop at **Yoder's Market,** a plentifully stocked bulk market attached to Yoder's butchery, about one mile north of the intersection of U.S. 40 and Springs Road (Rte. 669). Cereals, candy, flour, pastas,

dairy (butter in blocks), produce—everything you'd expect from a good Amish/Mennonite market. The store sells quality meats, as you'd expect, and the prices are good on everything. Yoder's has no phone and is closed on Sunday.

Other Shops

Since it serves a large influx of seasonal visitors, **Book Mark'et** (111 S. 2nd St., Oakland, 301/334-8778) stocks many of the latest popular titles, plus regional information. It's a comfortable place to browse, sit, and read, too. It has added a selection of antiques and collectibles on the mezzanine.

Though you won't be swept off your feet by volume ("Ten Antique Dealers Under One Roof"), the **Grantsville Antique Center** (located in Casselman Ventures, Main St., Grantsville, 301/895-5737) is a fun place to wander while in town. The building also contains a gift shop, a quilt materials store, and a thrift shop. The Antique Center and other shops are housed in the former elementary school, across from the Casselman Motel—you can't miss it. It's closed on Sunday.

You *might* be overwhelmed by **Englander's Antique Mall** (247 N. Second St. and Alder St., Oakland, 301/533-0000). It offers 6,000 square feet of antiques, jewelry, china, furniture, handcrafted toys and more. One of the best parts: Englander's has an original ice cream soda fountain parlor in operation.

RECREATION
Golf

In addition to an 18-hole golf course at Wisp (resort information under *Skiing,* below), the **Oakland Golf Club** (433 N. Bradley Lane, Oakland, 301/334-3883, www.golfatoakland.com) offers an 18-hole course in a country club setting complete with restaurant and lounge.

Horseback Riding

There are several stables in the Deep Creek Lake area. One that's been around since 1970 offers hayrides, camping, and lessons as well as horseback riding: **Western Trails Riding Stables**

(4009 Mayhew Inn Rd. off Rte. 219, Oakland, 301/387-6155, www.westerntrails.net).

Skiing

Wisp Resort (290 Marsh Hill Rd., McHenry, MD 21541, 301/387-4911, www.skiwisp.com) is a four-season vacation destination on Deep Creek Lake. In winter, 90 percent of the resort's skiable terrain is equipped for snowmaking and night skiing. Slopes are 20 percent beginner, 50 percent intermediate, and 30 percent advanced, and two triple and three double chairlifts carry skiers and snowboarders to 23 slopes totaling 14 miles of runs. Rentals, lessons, and programs for children are available. A tubing park features seven tubing lanes with two surface tows—it allows non-skiers to enjoy schussing down the slopes, albeit from a lower perspective.

During the warm months, the ski trails are used for hiking and mountain biking. Wisp also features an 18-hole terraced golf course and a resort hotel with pool and restaurants.

Watercraft on Deep Creek Lake

Boat and watercraft rental places abound around the lake. The **Aquatic Center** (634 Deep Creek Dr., McHenry, 301/387-8233, www.aquatic-center.com) rents water motorcycles and jet boats. **Crystal Waters** at Will O' the Wisp Resort (20160 Garrett Hwy./Rte. 219, 301/387-5515) rents ski boats, pontoon boats, fishing boats, pedal boats, canoes, and water-ski equipment.

White-Water Rafting

The Allegheny Mountains that uplift southwest Pennsylvania, western Maryland, and West Virginia are home to challenging white-water rafting. Two companies, both just over the border in Ohiopyle (uh-HI-a-pile), Pennsylvania, offer raft trips in the area: **Mountain Streams & Trails** (800/723-8669, www.mtstreams.com) and **White Water Adventurers** (800/992-7238, www.wwaraft.com). **Precision Rafting** in Friendsville, MD (301/746-5290 or 800/477-3723, www.precisionrafting.com) teaches kayaking in addition to leading white-water float trips.

ACCOMMODATIONS
Bed-and-Breakfasts

Stonebow Inn (146 Casselman Rd., Grantsville, 301/895-4250 or 800/272-4090, www.stonebowinn.com, $135–195), an adjunct to the art and crafts colony of Spruce Village, is an elegant Victorian B&B with additional guest quarters in its outbuildings. The home was built in 1870 by the Stantons, who owned and operated the nearby mill for five generations. Each of the inn's seven spacious rooms and two cottages is uniquely decorated and has all modern amenities, including thick terrycloth robes, a private bath, cable television, and access to a sauna; an old-fashioned rear porch looks over several acres of riverfront paths. Bicycles are available for guests to explore the surrounding Amish farmlands. Spruce Village is literally a few steps away, as are the Penn Alps restaurant and crafts store, where a complimentary breakfast is served to guests of the Elliot House in the morning. Rates vary depending on room, day, and season.

Few trappings remain to let guests know that ◖ **Carmel Cove Inn Bed & Breakfast** was once a Carmelite monastery (Glendale Rd., Deep Creek Lake, 301/387-0067, www.carmelcoveinn.com, $175–195). A short walk through the woods leads to Carmel Cove's dock, where guests may use a canoe to paddle out into the black waters of Deep Creek Lake. A tennis court, hot tub, billiards, bicycles, and sundeck add to the options. A full and delicious breakfast is served in the sky-lighted dining room; a large common room stocked with snacks and the daily papers offers pleasant diversion. All rooms have private baths, and some have decks and/or fireplaces. Carmel Cove is set among two acres of tranquil woods. In the winter, it provides snowshoe and cross-country equipment.

Inns

◖ **The Casselman Inn** (Main St., Grantsville, 301/895-5055, www.thecasselman.com, $39–83) was built in 1824 to serve travelers on the National Road, and the local handmade bricks and hand-hewn timbers and boards evident all over the hotel attest to the origins of the former Drover's Inn. The Casselman is owned and operated by a Mennonite family, the Millers, who comment in their brochure, "We believe that the finer things of life just dare not be lost in the rush of our modern day." The rooms in both the hotel and modern motor inn are cozy and clean, with the furniture either antique or handcrafted by members of the local community—or by the Millers themselves. If you're looking for an inexpensive stay in the area, the Casselman is the best choice. This historic inn features four rooms with private baths ($58–83), and all 40 of the modern motor inn's rooms have a private bath, television, and telephone ($39–70). A restaurant is also onsite.

◖ **Deer Park Inn** (65 Hotel Rd., Deer Park, 301/334-2308, www.deerparkinn.com, $125–145), a beautiful 17-room Victorian "cottage," was once part of the extensive Deer Park Resort. Built by prominent Baltimore architect Josiah Pennington in 1889, the home is now on the National Register of Historic Places. Deer Park's three spacious guestrooms will pull visitors back into the leisurely days of carriage rides and "taking the waters." The authentic decor is enhanced by Sandy Fontaine's beautiful arrangements of local wildflowers: bee balm, goldenrod, and Queen Anne's lace brighten every room in midsummer. Sandy's husband, Pascal, works his inimitable magic with breakfast: the omelettes, Cointreau and fruit in a melon shell basket, and plum preserves the color and clarity of garnets are almost worth the trip by themselves. Two rooms have private baths, and one room has a bath down the hall. All weekend reservations during the summer months require a minimum of two days.

Resort Hotels, Condos, and Motels

The **Wisp Resort Hotel** (Wisp Resort, 296 Marsh Hill Rd., McHenry, 301/387-4911, www.skiwisp.com) offers 67 guestrooms and 102 two-room suites that overlook the ski slopes and golf course. Wisp also owns or manages the following properties:

DEER PARK

Well before the Civil War, executives from the Baltimore and Ohio Railroad dreamed up a luxury resort where they and their friends could meet and relax. The war delayed construction, but the site – Deer Park – was completed in 1873. It had everything a wealthy patron would want: bucolic surroundings, an elegant hotel featuring rooms with baths and electric lights, an elevator, Turkish baths, separate bathing pools for men and women, an 18-hole golf course, tennis courts, bowling alleys, a complete livery service, and, of course, separate quarters for the servants. Guests were driven the short distance to the hotel from the depot by carriage.

By 1881, the resort had become so popular that additional "cottages" (two- and three-story vacation homes) were added for the use of guests. Other cottages were privately built and owned by employees and associates of the railroad, including the elegant three-story Victorian that is now the Deer Park Inn. Its architect, Josiah Pennington, designed several local homes. His style was unusual for the time, incorporating tile fireplaces, large, airy rooms with many windows, and wide verandas. All these features were innovative, considering the prevailing dark, velvet-draped style of decoration that characterized the era.

President Grover Cleveland and his bride, Frances Folsom, spent their honeymoon in another of Deer Park's cottages – it's still standing but is privately owned, as are the few remnants of the grand vacation destination. With the advent of the automobile, the hotel lost its exclusivity and fell out of fashion. In the 1940s, the grounds were purchased, and the hotel and several outbuildings were torn down and sold for lumber.

Today, Deer Park exists as a small residential village – but the name maintains a national presence. One of the draws of the original resort was its water, sourced in nearby Boiling Spring. The spring supplied the water for the hotel, and it was also bottled

Deer Park Inn

and served in the dining cars of the B&O Railroad. Boiling Spring has stayed in commercial operation and is now owned by Nestle. Flying Scot Sailboats, nationally distributed 19-foot daysailers, are manufactured on the dry land of Deer Park. A family-owned business since its inception, Flying Scots are not only popular on Deep Creek Lake (there are roughly 200 of them plying the dark waters), but may also be seen in waterways around the world – more than 5,000 of the lightweight watercraft have been distributed.

Deer Park Spring Water and Flying Scot continue to make the name of Deer Park known. But the once elegant Victorian playground of Deer Park lies within the memories of its villagers and beneath the wildflowers that blanket the open fields around the remaining cottages.

Will O' the Wisp (20160 Garrett Hwy., Oakland, 888/590-7283, www.willothewisp.com, $76–136 per day, $480–900 per week) features rustic cottages with one bedroom, a kitchen, and a living/dining room. There are also condominiums available, with prices varying according to size, day, and season.

Lake Breez Motel (20160 Garrett Hwy., Oakland, 301/387-5503 ext. 2206, www.deepcreeklakebreezmotel.com, May–Oct., $68–101) offers rooms with lake or garden views, an indoor pool, whirlpools and sauna, an exercise room and a game room, and a sandy beach with docking facilities

FOOD
Diners and Family-Style Restaurants

◖ **Casselman Restaurant,** located in the hotel (Main St., Grantsville, 301/895-5266, 7 A.M.–8 P.M. Mon.–Thurs., until 9 P.M. on Sat., closed Sun. except for inn guests) serves simple, American, meat-and-potatoes dishes and excellent baked goods at very reasonable prices (breakfast $4, lunch $5, dinner $9).

Next to Spruce Village, **Penn Alps** (125 Casselman Rd., 301/895-5985, www.pennalps.com, breakfast, lunch, and dinner daily, special dinner buffets Wed. and Fri.–Sun., $3–19) features an all-American menu with a few German specialties, such as pork loin and sauerkraut. May through August, Penn Alps sponsors concerts of both classical and traditional American music.

Canoe on the Run (2622 Deep Creek Dr., McHenry, 301/387-5933, breakfast, lunch and dinner daily, $5–12) is an upscale café that offers casual indoor/outdoor dining. It's open early for coffee drinks and morning treats, and midday and early evening for panini/sandwiches, soups, simple entrées, and salads.

◖ **Lakeside Creamery** (20282 Garrett Hwy, Oakland, 301/387-2580, www.lakesidecreamery.com) is home to award-winning specialty flavors such as chocolate raspberry truffle, apple pie, and even vanilla—cited by the National Ice Cream and Yogurt Retailers Association. The fudge and chocolate Muddy Creek Sundae will power a few trips around the lake, freestyle.

Continental

◖ **Deer Park Inn** (65 Hotel Rd., Deer Park, 301/334-2308, www.deerparkinn.com, dinner Mon.–Sat. in summer, Thurs.–Sat. in winter, lunch by special reservation only, $22) is the best place to eat dinner in Garrett County, bar none. This is not a well-kept secret, however—in spite of an 11-mile drive from Deep Creek Lake or Oakland, the small dining room was full of neatly casual diners on a Thursday night. Don't worry about not being seated—they have another dining room—but reservations are a good idea on weekends. Charging prices ($18 average) that challenge the ordinary steak and seafood restaurants around Deep Creek Lake, Chef Pascal Fontaine, formerly executive chef at the Westin Washington, D.C., trained at the Culinary Institute of Paris. He starts with locally grown and raised ingredients and produces marvelous food with a French accent: warm Vidalia onion tart on greens; homemade pâté with port sauce; honey-glazed braised duck legs with orange-and-green-peppercorn sauce; rabbit with basil and tomato confit (very popular); topped off with peach crisp with vanilla ice cream.

Cornish Manor (830 Memorial Dr., Oakland, 301/334-6499, lunch and dinner Mon.–Sat. $8–22), a pleasantly revamped Victorian home, is a lovely stop for lunch, dinner, or a drink. The intimate bar is cozy and casual with a European feel, and the screened porch with a view of the surrounding old trees is a favorite on summer days.

INFORMATION
Find out everything you need to know about Garrett County by contacting the **Garrett County Chamber of Commerce** (15 Visitors Center Dr., McHenry, MD 21541, 301/387-4386, www.visitdeepcreek.com).

NORTH-CENTRAL MARYLAND

The counties of north-central Maryland embrace the Chesapeake Bay like a gilded frame above a silver mirror. In addition to freshwater and bay fishing, this is the place to come for cycling. The neat, quiet towns of the western and eastern portions could have inspired Norman Rockwell.

Carroll County in the west is a golden spread of farms, carrying out the legacy of the German settlers who brought their hopes packed in solid chests from the old country during the first years of the colonies.

North of Baltimore, urban sprawl quickly fades into pine-covered hills. Baltimore County continues to be an eclectic mix of upscale rural country manors and small towns, largely residential. The majority of Maryland's wineries are here in the sunny north, in addition to many of the state's top horse-breeding farms.

Harford and Cecil Counties combine bucolic scenery with high-speed highways; dreamlike parks embrace the Susquehanna River. Colonial ports, both sleepy and active, provide plenty of attractions for visitors. Chesapeake City is, after all, the western terminus of the busiest canal in America. This gentle countryside is spiced with a pinch of ballplayer (Aberdeen is Cal Ripken's hometown) and a pound of heavy metal (the U.S. Government Ordnance Museum, also in Aberdeen).

Kent County is an in-crowd destination for sailors, boaters, and watermen. Rock Hall and Chestertown offer historic charm and plenty of good places to eat.

HISTORY

The Upper Bay, particularly around the shores of the Susquehanna River, had been populated

© JOANNE MILLER

HIGHLIGHTS

◖ Carroll County Farm Museum: A great place to explore in this rural county, the museum demonstrates the self-sufficiency necessary for survival during the days when farm families worked their land, produced their own food, soap, and household goods, and spun wool into yarn for clothing and house linens (page 220).

◖ Ladew Topiary Gardens: These are some of the best gardens in the United States – where else can you see a foxhunt (including fox, hounds and riders), all made out of boxwood? The swan hedges surround a beautiful collection of plantings: Something is always in bloom. The manor house, filled with hunt mementos, is a delight (page 227).

◖ Boordy Vineyards: No trip to the Upper Bay would be complete without a visit to Maryland's historic vintners – some of the oldest in the United States. A leisurely tasting combined with a scenic tour of the area is a real treat (page 228).

◖ Havre de Grace Decoy Museum: This museum displays waterfowl decoys as American folk art and chronicles bird migrations, hunting, and the lives of upper Chesapeake Bay watermen. In addition to the collections, a research library complete with works on types of decoys, carving, waterfowl, and the environment is one of the most extensive ever assembled (page 232).

◖ U.S. Army Ordnance Museum: Tanks a lot! Plus every type of defused weapon and device from the U.S. and other countries. Run by a branch of the armed forces dealing with the supply and storage of weapons, the park outside the building is filled with rows of military rolling stock, and the inside of the museum informs visitors about the role and development of artillery and equipment used in connection with it (page 235).

◖ Kent County Driving Tour: This tour starts in Chestertown and passes through historic and scenic areas of Kent County, including the oldest Episcopal Church in Maryland, Chesapeake Farms, a wildlife management demonstration area, and Eastern Neck Island National Wildlife Refuge (page 250).

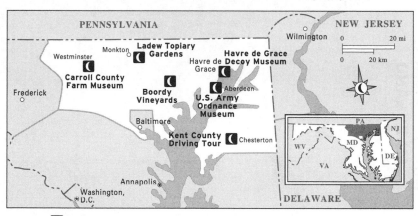

LOOK FOR ◖ TO FIND RECOMMENDED SIGHTS, ACTIVITIES, DINING, AND LODGING.

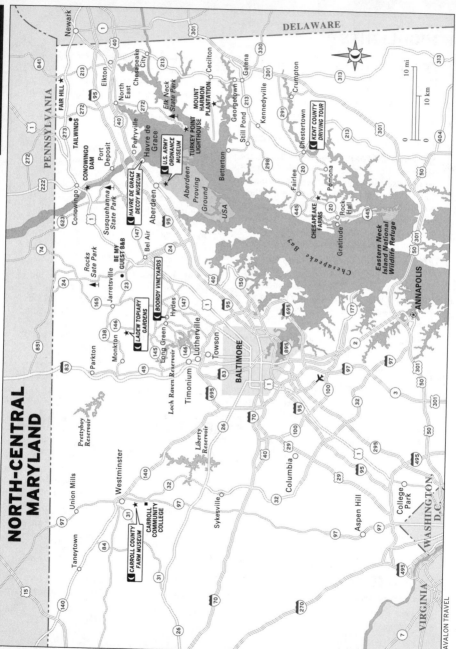

NORTH-CENTRAL MARYLAND

NORTH-CENTRAL MARYLAND

DELAWARE

PENNSYLVANIA

VIRGINIA

WASHINGTON, D.C.

BALTIMORE

ANNAPOLIS

Chesapeake Bay

Newark

FAIR HILL

TAILWINDS

CONOWINGO DAM

Conowingo

Port Deposit

Elkton

North East

Chesapeake City

Cecilton

Galena

Georgetown

Kennedyville

Crumpton

KENT COUNTY DRIVING TOUR

Chestertown

Still Pond

Betterton

Fairlee

Pomona

Rock Hall

CHESAPEAKE FARMS

Gratitude

Eastern Neck Island National Wildlife Refuge

MOUNT HARMON PLANTATION

Elk Neck State Park

TURKEY POINT LIGHTHOUSE

Perryville

Havre de Grace

U.S. ARMY ORDNANCE MUSEUM

HAVRE DE GRACE DECOY MUSEUM

Aberdeen

Aberdeen Proving Ground

USA

Susquehanna State Park

Rocks State Park

BE MY GUEST B&B

Jarrettsville

Bel Air

BOORDY VINEYARDS

LADEW TOPIARY GARDENS

Monkton

Hydes

Long Green

Lutherville

Timonium

Towson

Parkton

Loch Raven Reservoir

Prettyboy Reservoir

Union Mills

Westminster

CARROLL COUNTY FARM MUSEUM

CARROLL COMMUNITY COLLEGE

Taneytown

Sykesville

Liberty Reservoir

Columbia

Aspen Hill

College Park

10 mi

10 km

© AVALON TRAVEL

FOR SALE: ASSASSIN'S HOUSE, NEEDS TLC

Tudor Hall, the childhood home of John Wilkes Booth, assassin of Abraham Lincoln, is a graceful Gothic style house at the end of a tree-shaded cul-de-sac in Bel Air, Maryland. Also famous as the birthplace of Shakespearean theater in the United States, the home sits on eight acres, surrounded by hickory, beech, spruce, oak, and magnolia trees.

The house was built in 1847 by Junius Brutus Booth, a renowned Shakespearean actor who moved to Maryland from his native England. Both his sons, John and Edwin, became noted actors. After John assassinated President Lincoln in 1865, Junius Booth lost the property. Ownership changed hands over the years, until Howard and Dorothy Fox purchased Tudor Hall in 1968.

The Foxes played host to small theatrical productions and converted the home into a museum, but they were forced to let the property run down because of mounting financial trouble. The Foxes died within weeks of each other in 1999, both without a will. Their heirs decided to sell Tudor Hall.

Harford Community College trustees and others keen on preserving Tudor Hall worried that it would be torn down. The home is listed on the National Register of Historic Places, but there is no legal prohibition against razing it.

Tudor Hall's fate attracted interest from Hollywood: Actors Hal Holbrook and Stacy Keach joined a nonprofit group called the Preservation Association for Tudor Hall, and both pledged to help restore the property if Harford Community College bought it. Keach performed at the college to raise money to preserve the Booth property. "Are we going to allow it to become a condominium? It's sacrilege," he said.

In October 1999, the property was sold at auction for $415,000 to a local couple who planned to make it their residence. "We're disappointed that the Shakespearean history programs cannot be built at the home site," Harford College president Claudia Chiesi said after the auction. Stacy Keach added, "Hopefully, this wonderful couple will have an interest in preserving the legacy of the Booth family."

Unsettled by the weight of renovations, the new owners put the property on the market in 2006. Harford County purchased Tudor Hall and is in the process of gathering funds to restore it.

by native tribes such as the Conowingo and Susquehannoks since prehistory. As colonials began moving north from Annapolis and Baltimore and south from Pennsylvania, the first peoples moved west. Carroll County, west of the bay, was resettled by farmers and their families, hungry for land—many had worked off years of indentured servitude. They plowed the rocky, hilly ground away from the shore to establish tobacco and sustenance farms. The bay counties were repopulated by European watermen and hunters who reaped the incredible bounty of the northern Chesapeake, selling the surplus to the cities. The area was a major supplier of seafood and wild game—particularly birds, as the bay has long been a major migratory flyway.

The area was isolated and sparsely populated. The Revolution made relatively little impact on the lives of the families who had settled there, though the Susquehanna River/Chesapeake Bay confluence was a crucial transport area during colonial times—the British destroyed Havre de Grace, the town at the river's mouth, during the War of 1812.

During the Civil War, Confederate raiding parties periodically resupplied themselves at the expense of towns in Carroll County. A small skirmish at the village of Westminster yielded a major result: Rebel troops were delayed on their journey to Gettysburg, perhaps changing the outcome of that pivotal battle.

The most infamous man of that time—John Wilkes Booth—grew up in a pleasant manor house in Bel Air, about 20 miles north of Baltimore. His father, famed British actor Junius Brutus Booth, built the tree-shaded property to raise his two sons. He staged Shakespeare's plays in the manor hall.

Boats were traditionally the most common mode of transportation in the upper bay. As automobiles became more common, expanding roads created suburbs in a wide ring around Baltimore, and U.S. 40—the National Road established in the early years of the United States—became a throughway from Philadelphia to Baltimore. In spite of major routes passing through the area, it remains rural within a few miles of the whizzing cars, home to villages that have changed little for a century.

ORIENTATION

North-central Maryland is draped over the top of the Chesapeake Bay, and the area ranges from the golden farms and rural environs of the wild west in Carroll County through the suburban wilds of northern Baltimore to the open marshland and small towns of the upper Eastern Shore. The west is ideal for long picnics and fresh produce from farm markets during the warm months; heading east, the territory above Baltimore lends itself to wine tasting, and the upper Eastern Shore above the Chesapeake Bay Bridge is an area that begs the participation of cyclists— long, narrow, mostly untrammeled roads slice through whispering wheat fields to weave along miles of glittering bay and marshland. In addition to cycling, north-central Maryland is the place to come for freshwater and bay fishing.

The area is divided by the Susquehanna River, source of nearly half of the fresh water that flows into the Chesapeake. The water is least brackish here in the north, hospitable to freshwater fish and flora and fauna that thrive on the clear waters.

PLANNING YOUR TIME

North of the Chesapeake Bay Bridge, the Upper Bay offers a convenient getaway from the big cities in the Philadelphia–Washington, D.C. corridor. Plan on a week to give yourself plenty of time to overnight in each of the major destinations, or make day trips from Baltimore for a series of fresh experiences.

Westminster in Carroll County is a pleasant change from the bustle of city life. Though the village has grown considerably over the years, the town center still retains a historic feel. This is a good place for an overnight at one of the lovely inns, perhaps combined with the wine festival in September or a bit of shopping at the farmers markets. To really take in the rural experience, visit the **Carroll County Farm Museum** (two hours).

In Baltimore County, the **Ladew Topiary Gardens** (two–three hours plus travel time) is one of my favorite places in the Upper Bay. The outstanding topiary displays will please adults and children alike. And if the fruit of the vine interests you, no trip to the Upper Bay would be complete without a trip to Maryland's **wineries**—plan a picnic with a winery visit.

In Harford County, the **Havre de Grace Decoy Museum** (three hours) is only one of the attractions of **Havre de Grace;** others include a sweet stop at **Bomboy's** and a sunset view of the **Concord Point Lighthouse.** Drive to Aberdeen to see the unusual tank park and weapons on view at the **U.S. Army Ordnance Museum** (two–three hours), and include the **Ripkin Museum** if you're a Ripkin family or Orioles fan (one hour). Plan on two or more days in the area.

Cross over one of the graceful bridges that span the Susquehanna River and stop in **North East** to enjoy the **Upper Bay Museum** (one hour), genteel accommodations, and a good seafood dinner. It's especially festive around the winter holidays. While in the area, take in **Fair Hill Nature and Environmental Center** (take all day if you like horseback riding) and **Elk Neck State Park** and **Turkey Point Lighthouse** (three hours–all day). Plan on two days here, depending on your outdoor recreation interests.

Drive south to view the busy Chesapeake Canal and spend the night in **Chesapeake City.** Enjoy a sophisticated dinner at **Bayard House** and a leisurely breakfast while walking around this lovely little village.

The **Kent County Driving Tour** (two–three hours), **Chestertown,** and the village of **Rock Hall** will provide vistas of the some of the most beautiful scenery and delightful history of the

Upper Bay. If time permits, schedule a ride on the **Schooner Sultana** in advance—it's a once-in-a-lifetime experience. If cycling interests you, this is the place for it. Allow time to walk around both towns, just enjoying the architecture and small-town atmosphere. Plan on two to three days here.

FESTIVALS AND EVENTS

Many events and festivals list a volunteer's phone number as the main contact, and those are prone to change from year to year. When in doubt, contact the county visitors bureau.

Considered the oldest and most difficult steeplechase race in the country, the **Maryland Hunt Cup Race** (National Steeplechase Association, 410/392-0700) takes place in Glyndon, north of Baltimore, in late April.

In sympathy with Boston, Chestertown residents boarded the British brigantine *Geddes* in 1774 and dumped its tea shipment into the Chester River. The **Chestertown Tea Party Festival** (410/778-0416) in May features a colonial parade, music, food, boat rides, historical reenactments and a "Toss the Tory" event.

Once known as the marriage capital of the world for its lack of barriers to getting hitched in a hurry, Elkton celebrates **National Marriage Day** (www.elktonalliance.org) in June with an outdoor wedding and opportunities to make and renew vows.

In late June, take in the **Anniversary of the Civil War Battle of Westminster–Corbit's Charge** (410/848-9000) in Westminster, which includes a Civil War encampment, demonstrations, and a Benfield Brass Band concert, plus exhibits, living history, music, walking tours, and a commemoration ceremony.

No fish story, Rock Hall's annual **Rockfish Tournament** (410/269-6622) in June or July offers a $10,000 first prize for the best striper.

More than 300 juried artists and craftspeople display their wares at the **Havre de Grace Art Show** (410/939-9342) in August at Tydings Memorial Park.

September brings **The Maryland Wine Festival** (410/386-3880 or 800/654-4645) to the Carroll County Farm Museum in West-minster. Taste Maryland wines, attend wine seminars, and enjoy stage entertainment, crafts, and food.

In November, the **Annual Seafood Festival** (410/939-1525) at Tydings Park in Havre de Grace features free entertainment, a charity raffle, artisans, crafters, and of course, seafood!

Ladew Topiary Garden's **Christmas Open House** (410/557-9570) in December features the Manor House festively decorated by volunteers and garden clubs in honor of the holiday season. Greens, arrangements, and gifts are for sale.

GETTING THERE AND AROUND
By Air

There are regional airports in the vicinity of Elkton and Webster that offer a limited number of commuter flights. Baltimore-Washington International (BWI) is the major airport in the area.

By Train

An **Amtrak** train (800/USA-RAIL or 800/872-7245, www.amtrak.com) is available to Aberdeen.

By Bus

Greyhound Bus service (800/229-9424, www.greyhound.com) is available to Aberdeen. For intra-city transit, Harford County is served by **Harford County Transit** (410/612-1621 or 410/838-2562, www.harfordcountymd.gov/services/transportation). Caroline, Dorchester, Kent, Talbot and Queen Anne's counties are served by **Maryland Upper Shore Transit** (MUST, 866/330-6878, www.mustbus.info). Generally, exact fare of $1–2 is required.

By Car

This is the easiest and most convenient way to get around this part of Maryland. I-695 is the circle route around Baltimore. Radiating out from the city, Route 149 is a direct road to Westminster; I-83 is a straight north–south route through Baltimore County; I-95, U.S. 1, and U.S. 40 all head east; and Route 213 is the major north–south road in Cecil and Kent Counties.

Westminster and Carroll County

Carroll County remains determinedly untouched by urban encroachment. Westminster is the largest town, distinguished by a college and a healthy helping of history. The rolling hills of the Piedmont glow green in the evening light, much as they did when this area served as a crossroads for movement of both Northern and Southern troops during the Civil War. One modern change has done more for the town's growth and level of sophistication than any other: Westminster is now the off-season training site for the Baltimore Ravens.

SIGHTS

◖ Carroll County Farm Museum

In 1837, Carroll County built an almshouse that provided work and shelter for indigent men and women; they lived in separate quarters in the main house and an adjoining building. The almshouse stayed in operation as a self-sufficient working farm until 1965. The original almshouse building has been remade into a typical 19th-century farmer's home, and the property has been reborn as the Carroll County Farm Museum (500 S. Center St., Westminster, 410/386-3880, www.carrollcountyfarm

---

SPOOKY CARROLL COUNTY

Carroll County – and Westminster in particular – is so pretty, many visitors are loath to leave. Sometimes, however, their extended stays aren't brought about by a love of the rolling farm country. The old Odd Fellows Hall (140 East Main St.), which served as a barracks during the Civil War, had one such resident. During the 1800s, the hall served as a local theater and venue for traveling performers. The town's businesspeople, farmers, and their families would gather on Saturday night to enjoy an evening of comedy, music, or drama. One traveling jokester was Marshall Buell of Alabama. Dressed in a shabby outfit, Buell kept up a topical monologue, liberally laced with jokes about President Grant and other government officials. Some Grant supporters were not amused and expressed their displeasure by throwing a rock onto the stage. A second rock struck Buell in the neck. Shaken, Buell quickly finished his performance and exited the stage. Refusing the sheriff's offer of protection in the jail overnight, Buell explained he'd be on his way to Hagerstown for his next performance. As he saddled his horse in the darkness behind the hall, Marshall Buell was attacked. He was discovered lifeless, his throat slit ear to ear. Soon after, the town drunk reported seeing a "spirit-like" figure gesturing dramatically and mouthing a wordless monologue in back of the hall. No one believed him – except those who visited the theater the following Saturday night. There, they witnessed the ghost of Marshall Buell, still expounding – silently – on the defects of the president and his cabinet. Wonder what he'd have to say about the current administration?

The **Carroll County Historical Society and Visitors Center** now occupies 210 East Main Street, the Kimmey House. During the mid-1800s, it was the home of Dr. George Colgate, who expanded his home to create office space for his medical practice. This small-town doctor had many loyal patients, and it was not uncommon for his waiting room to be full to overflowing. Though most visitors to the house these days come to the historical society's administrative offices or library, occasionally personnel meet up with one of Dr. Collgate's ghostly patients, still waiting to see the doctor after 150 years. And you thought your insurance program was bad!

Stop by the visitors center for a copy of the *Ghost Walk* brochure (one of several walking tours offered), which features many more haunts in town. The **Carroll County Public Library** (410/848-4250) also offers guided Ghost Walks in the fall.

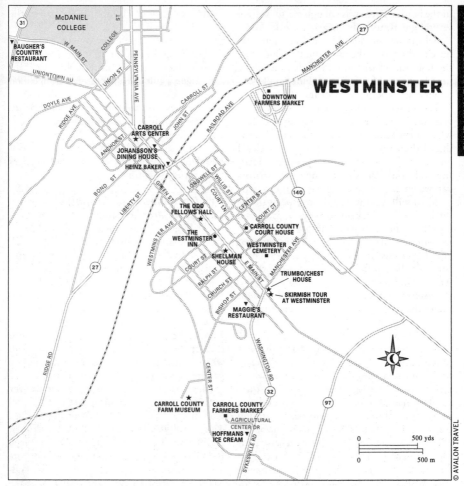

© AVALON TRAVEL

museum.org, 10 A.M.–4 P.M. Tues.–Fri. and noon–5 P.M. Sat.–Sun. July–Aug., Sat.–Sun. only first weekend in May–October 29, $5 adults, $3 ages 7–18 and 60 and better).

The farmhouse offers a treasure trove of Victorian antiques, many of which were donated by Carroll County families. One of the most interesting aspects of the farmhouse was the pioneering use of power generated by gas from fecal matter—a form of recycling that we could probably benefit from today. Workers filled the

1,000-gallon metal tank on the north side of the building approximately 90 percent full of water. To this they added manure—chicken, pig, human, and cow. This was mixed to the consistency of pea soup, with about 7 percent solids to 93 percent water. The tank was tightly closed. In a couple of days, gas was formed by the action of bacteria. The gas was roughly 60 percent methane and 35 percent carbon dioxide. Very little pressure was built up, so the gas had to be pumped to the light fixture system in the house. There was enough gas to operate several gas fixtures for nearly a week. Additional gas was produced by adding more manure to the top of the tank and drawing away the liquid from the bottom of the tank—the liquid was used for fertilizer. This simple system was used between 1850 and 1900.

The museum shows the self-sufficiency that was necessary for survival during the days when farm families worked their land, produced their own food, soap, and household goods, and spun wool into yarn for clothing and house linens. On the farm, visitors can watch artisans demonstrate period crafts; children will want to pay their respects to the ducks, horses, chickens, turkeys, pigs, goats, and lambs on the surrounding grounds. The museum tells the story of each farm animal and the purpose it served during the 19th century, whether for field labor, food, or clothing. Another kid-pleaser is the two-headed calf in the veterinarian's room, though adults might prefer the display of "tramp art," constructed from tiny bits of wood and glue by transients passing through the almshouse.

The County Farm Museum has numerous outbuildings beyond the farmhouse. There's a one-room schoolhouse, a springhouse where jars of food were kept cool, a general store, smokehouse, broom shop, garden, saddlery, blacksmith shop, and wagon shed, among others. The general store, reminiscent of the 1800s, sells items made by museum craftspeople, souvenirs, and old-fashioned candies. Among the carriages and sleighs in the wagon shed is the buggy that made the rounds for the first rural mail delivery service in America, begun in Carroll County. On the original route between Westminster and Uniontown, 2,700 pieces of mail were delivered, in addition to a pig and two live chickens, over the years. Though we take mail service for granted, many of the locals objected to rural mail delivery because it interfered with regular trips to town to pick up mail and socialize. Another fascinating piece of Americana in the carriage shed is an 18-foot bobsled; when launched from the hill on the west side of town, the sled could

reach a velocity of 70 mph on its way to the east side of town.

The Carroll County Farm Museum has several events during the year. In June, the Deer Creek Fiddlers' Convention features a day of dobros and banjos; a guitarist and bluegrass competition draws some of the best musicians in the region. Antique cars, steam engines, and home-cooked food star in early September during Steam Show Days. The third weekend in September is reserved for the Maryland Wine Festival, when Maryland's wineries offer tastes of their vintages and a variety of cuisines to sample.

Art Galleries and Exhibits

The **Esther Prangley Rice Gallery,** in Peterson Hall on the campus of McDaniel College, is a free fine-art museum hosting local, regional, and national artists along with faculty and students. Hours are concurrent with school days—call 410/827-2595 for more information.

The **Carroll Arts Center** (91 W. Main St., 410/848-7272, www.carr.org/arts, 10 A.M.–4 P.M. Mon.–Wed. and Fri.–Sat., 10 A.M.–8 P.M. Thurs., free) is in a renovated 1937 art deco theater. It includes a 263-seat audience hall where concerts, lectures, films, and plays are presented, as well as a large art gallery.

More art is on display at the **Scott Center for Fine and Performing Arts** at Carroll Community College (1601 Washington Rd., 410/386-8000, 9 A.M.–8 P.M. Mon.–Thurs. and 9 A.M.–3 P.M. Fri.–Sat. Sept.–May, free). Exhibits generally focus on county and state artists. Also on campus, the Great Hall Gallery under expansive cathedral ceilings, and the intimate Langdon Family Gallery. Hours vary, so call to confirm availability.

Skirmish at Westminster Tour

On June 27, 1863, General J. E. B. Stuart crossed the Potomac into Maryland with three brigades of Confederate cavalry, numbering nearly 6,000 men. He was on his way north to rendezvous with General Jubal Early. The next day, Stuart learned of the approach from Washington of a large Union wagon train. He succeeded in intercepting 125 supply wagons and their contents south of Carroll County. The poorly equipped Confederate forces welcomed the supplies; however, the wagon train and prisoners slowed the marching pace of the cavalry to a shuffle.

Moving on a parallel path west of the Confederates, Union major general John Sedgwick's Sixth Corps (a total of 18,000 men) marched north through Carroll County towns, passing through New Windsor and Uniontown, a few miles west of Westminster, on June 29 and 30. There, some of the men, including Captain David Acheson, wrote to their families: "All look anxiously for news from Pennsylvania. I hope this is but the beginning of the final defeat of the rebs." Acheson died in Gettysburg, three days later.

Continuing on his way north, Stuart moved to cut off communications between Washington and the Army of the Potomac. His men tore up tracks of the B&O Railroad at Hoods Mill and Sykesville and set fire to two small bridges, one of them at Piney Run, all in the southern part of Carroll County. A cotton factory was raided, and the Confederate soldiers used the belts from the factory's machinery to replace the soles of their boots.

Stuart approached Westminster on June 29. Shortly before noon, units of the First Delaware Cavalry, commanded by Major Napoleon B. Knight, with Captain Charles Corbit and Lieutenant Caleb Churchman as company commanders, arrived in Westminster to guard the rail and road junction in the town. They numbered less than 100 men. They joined a detachment of the 150th New York Infantry—numbering fewer than 20—who had already occupied Westminster as a provost guard for several months. The **Odd Fellows Hall** (140 E. Main St., built in 1854, now the Opera Printing Company) served as headquarters for the 16-man detachment of the New York Infantry.

Reports of approaching Confederates were brought to the Union troops by a doctor visiting a patient in the country. Union Major Knight was incapacitated—rumored to be drunk. In his absence, Captain Corbit immediately gathered his men and led a charge through the streets of Westminster toward the Washington Road. They expected to meet a small unit of Confederates, but instead found themselves confronting the front ranks of Stuart's veteran cavalry. A fierce skirmish ensued, and the little unit of Union forces was quickly overpowered; many were captured, including Corbit and Churchman. Knight escaped to Baltimore to give a stirring account of an encounter he had never seen.

The historical marker commemorating **Corbit's Charge** is on the corner of East Main Street and Washington Road. The **Trumbo/Chest House** (ca. 1830, 297 E. Main St.) was in the line of fire of the charging Confederate cavalrymen on the Washington Road to East Main Street. The side of this home has bullet marks from the battle. **Carroll County Court House** (101 N. Court St.), built in 1838, had a large Union flag flying from the cupola. The flag was torn down and carried away by Stuart's men following the engagement. Thirteen ladies of the town of Westminster had sewn the flag and signed their names on the stars. As Stuart's men marched through the town, they passed the **Shellman House** (206 E. Main St.). There, little Mary Shellman shouted "Johnny Red Coat" as General Stuart passed by. He dismounted and told her that her punishment for allegiance to the Union would be a kiss—he pecked her cheek, remounted, and rode on.

During the skirmish, two were killed, 11 were wounded, and a few managed to make their escape down Reisterstown Road, pursued by Confederates. Local physicians and citizens cared for the wounded on both sides in improvised hospitals in Westminster. The **Crouse House** (built in 1850, 325 E. Main St.) was used as a temporary hospital. The Westminster Cemetery on North Church Street was the site of the Union Meeting House used as a hospital. Local physicians treated the wounded of both sides here. The site is marked by an iron urn near the flagpole.

That night Stuart's five-mile-long column bivouacked along the Littlestown Pike between Westminster and Union Mills. The clash on the edge of town between General J. E. B. Stuart's cavalry and a small unit of the Delaware cavalry slowed the progress of the advancing Confederates. Instead of proceeding immediately into Pennsylvania to warn General Robert E. Lee about advancing Union troops, Stuart's cavalry was delayed long enough to spend the night in the Westminster area. Confederate brigadier general Fitz Lee slept in the orchard at the Shriver Homestead; men and horses rested for the first time since crossing into Maryland on June 27. General Stuart slept in Westminster and joined his troops in Union Mills early the next morning. The outcome of Gettysburg might have been different if Stuart had arrived before July 2.

Union Mills Homestead

The homestead (3111 Littlestown Pike, Union Mills, 410/848-2288, www.unionmills.org) is the family home of the Shrivers (Sargent Shriver, philanthropist, politician, and Kennedy in-law is a prominent relative, as is Maria Shriver, journalist and wife of movie star/politician Arnold Schwarzenegger), and both house and mill are open to the public for guided tours ($4). The property is maintained by volunteers, so make sure hours are accurate before you go. As of this writing, the house and mill are open 10 A.M.–4 P.M. Tuesday–Friday and noon–4 P.M. Saturday–Sunday June 1–September 1. During May and September, the house and mill are open noon–4 P.M. Saturday–Sunday only.

The homestead was first claimed in 1797, when brothers David and Andrew Shriver purchased a large tract of land along Big Pipe Creek. The waterway provided an excellent source of power for milling, the valley was good, fertile farmland, and the surrounding rolling hills contained heavy stands of black oak that could furnish tanbark for processing hides.

Soon the brothers constructed a gristmill, a tannery, and sawmill. The businesses were given the name Union Mills because of the partnership of the two brothers and their various enterprises. Andrew's strong support of Thomas Jefferson earned the homestead a post office; later a general store was added, and the

---

SPURNING "NORTHERN SCUM"

In the summer of 1862, the South was energized by its many victories over the superior numbers and weaponry of the North. Having freed Virginia from Northern troops – and, more significantly, once again having acquired the productive Valley of the Shenandoah for Confederate supplies – General Robert E. Lee turned his campaign northward to the border state of Maryland. At that time, Richmond, Virginia, was being flooded with refugees and Southern sympathizers from Maryland who claimed that they had been held in the Union by force, and that most citizens of that state were waiting for an opportunity to be free to join the South. A popular song at the time (and now the Maryland state anthem) stated this position:

> The despot's heel is on thy shore Maryland! My Maryland! His touch is on thy temple door, Maryland! My Maryland!

> Avenge the patriotic gore that flecked the streets of Baltimore, And be the Battle-queen of yore, Maryland! My Maryland!

> I hear the distant thunder hum, Maryland! My Maryland! The Old Line's bugle, fife, and drum, Maryland! My Maryland!

> She is not dead, nor deaf, nor dumb, Huzzah! she spurns the Northern scum, She breathes, she burns, she'll come, she'll come, Maryland! My Maryland!

---

homestead became a thriving crossroads settlement. For a time, the original house was opened as a stagecoach inn, which accommodated both Washington Irving and John James Audubon as overnight guests.

The original double house built for David

and Andrew Shriver is now the center of the present-day main house. As Andrew's family expanded, so did the house, growing from six rooms to 23.

Until the mid-1960s, the homestead was continuously occupied by different generations of Andrew Shriver's descendants. The house is filled with a wide range of original family furnishings from the 1700s to the 1900s—a room will often blend the styles of federal, antebellum, and late Victorian periods. Andrew Shriver was a great admirer of Thomas Jefferson and copied his front balcony from Jefferson's home at Monticello; Supreme Court Justice Roger Brooke Taney and attorney/poet Francis Scott Key both delivered speeches from this "Jefferson balcony."

Union Mills' most fascinating piece of history took place during the Civil War. The Shriver family—much like the rest of the state of Maryland—suffered divided loyalties. Andrew Shriver's family supported the Union, while directly across the road, his brother William Shriver's family supported the Confederacy. Each family had sons in the respective armies. Just before the battle of Gettysburg, on June 29, 1863, J. E. B. Stuart's Confederate cavalry rode into the homestead orchard around midnight. The family awoke to the sight of horses and soldiers filling the yard and surrounding the house. William Shriver's family fed the hungry soldiers flapjacks; the young men grabbed them off the griddle before they were cooked. When morning broke, the rebel cavalry departed toward Hanover, Pennsylvania, with T. Herbert Shriver as their guide. William Shriver entertained the Confederate officers at breakfast, and J. E. B. Stuart charmed the gathered Shriver family by singing, "If you want to be a bully boy, jine the cavalry."

Shortly after the Confederates left, the Union soldiers arrived. Major General George Syke's Fifth Infantry Corps camped in the surrounding fields, and Andrew Shriver's main house became headquarters for the Union division commander. The daughters sang and danced with Union soldiers in a room off the front hall that has been referred to ever since as the "dancing hall." These soldiers also departed for Gettysburg. For the next four days, the windows rattled from the cannon fire of the Battle of Gettysburg while the families awaited the outcome.

After the war, the homestead returned to its prosperous business enterprises. As time passed, modern factories replaced small family businesses and the Shriver family moved on. Today, the gristmill represents an excellent example of a working mill, with the wooden water wheel, gears, parts, and frame painstakingly re-created. Rye, whole wheat, buckwheat, and two kinds of cornmeal are ground in the mill and offered for sale. Union Mills Homestead has several special events throughout the year, chiefly the Annual Flower and Plant Market on the first weekend in May, and the Corn Roast Festival the first Saturday in August, which features a fried chicken dinner and all the roasted corn you can eat.

Backcountry Driving/Biking Tour

This 24-mile round-trip route takes you past a variety of terrains common to Carroll County. The route is moderately hilly and has a short stretch of dirt road that may be difficult for both cars and bikes in wet weather. Fourteen miles of the trip—the first and last segments—are on main roads, though traffic is light. The Carroll County Visitors Center (see the *Westminster and Carroll County Information* section) offers a variety of bike routes that cover the county. All distances in the following tour are approximate.

The route starts at the juncture of Main Street and Pennsylvania Avenue in downtown Westminster. Head directly north on Pennsylvania Avenue (which becomes Littlestown Pike) for seven miles until you reach the settlement of Union Mills. Continue on the Pike for 0.6 miles, then turn left (south) on Murkle Road for two miles. Turn right (west) on Stone Road, continue for 3.3 miles. Turn left (south) on Robert Arthur Road (this 0.9-mile connector road is gravel-covered, but in good shape). It dead-ends on Mayberry Road. Drive south on Mayberry Road 1.5 miles to Old Taney-town Road; jog to the left on Taneytown Road and continue south on Clear View Road for 1.6 miles. Turn left (south) on Trevanion Road for 1.5 miles to Uniontown. Uniontown remains much as it was at the beginning of the 20th century. Turn left (east) on Union-town Road and return six miles to downtown Westminster.

SHOPPING

Carroll County has two farm markets of note. The **Carroll County Farmers Market** (700 Agriculture Center Dr., 410/848-7748, 8 A.M.–1 P.M. Sat. mid-June–early Sept. and mid-Nov.–mid-Dec.) originated in 1971 as an outlet for farmers to sell locally grown produce. Free weekly demonstrations—including cooking, basketry, flower arranging, craft lessons, and sell-ing tips—are scheduled each Saturday through-out the summer. The market is free to enter and operates in enclosed buildings in a smoke-free environment. Fresh produce, baked goods, crafts, ceramics, baskets, jewelry, tole-painted items, wood items, furniture, quilts, and more are for sale. Special markets are planned for Eas-ter and Christmas. The farmers market is held at the Agricultural Center overlooking the Carroll County Farm Museum.

The **Downtown Westminster Farmers Market** (Conaway Parking Lot, Railroad Ave./Rte. 27 and Emerald Hill Lane, Westminster, 410/848-5294, 8 A.M.–noon) is held every Sat-urday from the first Saturday in June through the fourth Saturday in October. This is a "pro-ducers-only" market of fresh fruits and vegeta-bles, baked goods, plants, and honey.

Westminster Antique Mall (433 Hahn Rd., Westminster, www.westminsterantique mall.com) has goods from more than 165 deal-ers in the complex.

ACCOMMODATIONS

It's difficult to recognize **The Westminster Inn** (5 S. Center St., Westminster, 410/876-2893, www.westminsterinn.com, $115–160) for the schoolhouse it once was. The building went up in 1899, and though memories of chalk dust may still cling to some corners, it has been transformed into one of Maryland's most el-egant and romantic bed-and-breakfast inns. Each of the guestrooms is decorated in tradi-tional style, with a queen-size bed and private hot tub. The inn offers 12 guestrooms and one suite, each with private bath and complimen-tary breakfast. Guests also have complimen-tary use of a fitness club with a pool, aerobics classes, and weight equipment next door.

Deluxe in every way, **Antrim 1844 Country Inn** (30 Trevanion Rd., Taney-town, 410/756-6812 or 800/858-1844, www .antrim1844.com, $160–400) is one of the county's most beautiful getaways. In the main house (the mansion), nine guestrooms have been restored and redone with antiques, fire-places, canopy feather beds, and marble baths or double whirlpool tubs with panoramic views of the surrounding countryside. Twenty ad-ditional guestrooms are located in the out-buildings—each has its own fireplace and is furnished with a different theme, such as "The Ice House," with the atmosphere of an English cottage set in formal gardens, and "The Barn," with two rooms, each with its own private deck overlooking woods and a brook.

A formal breakfast is served around 9:30, often featuring the house specialty, Belgian waffles. Antrim also offers a dinner menu and special events throughout the year.

FOOD

Heinz Bakery (40–42 N. Main St., Westmin-ster) is highly recommended for baked goods of all types. There's a parking lot next to the building for quick stops.

A great place for home-style cooking, ◖ **Baugher's Country Restaurant** (289 W. Main St., Westminster, 410/848-7413, www .baughers.com, breakfast, lunch and dinner daily, $2–18) offers produce and a bakery in the front of the shop, and country breakfasts and dinners such as turkey and stuffing and meatloaf and mashed potatoes. Fresh fruit pies are the house specialty (you can have a slice topped with ice cream). Baugher's also has a farm (1236 Baugher Rd., Westminster,

410/857-0111) that's open for pick-your-own from May through September.

Johansson's Dining House (4 W. Main St., Westminster, 410/876-0101, www.johan ssonsdininghouse.com, 11 A.M.–10 P.M. Sun.–Thurs., 11 A.M.–midnight Fri.–Sat., $14) is the kind of place where a diner can sink into a big leather chair and watch the world go by. The restaurant serves a tasty, sophisticated menu of soups and salads, big burgers, and specials such as veal Oscar, chicken marsala, and a variety of fresh seafood. Lunch entrées average $8, with burgers, salads, and sandwiches slightly less. The large dining room is accessed through the bar, which may be packed and smoky at happy hour and beyond, but don't miss the chance to see the old-fashioned paddle fan whirling away above the heads of the crowd. Johansson's brews its own beer to accompany the hearty food.

Maggie's Restaurant (310 E. Green St., Westminster, 410/848-1441, www.maggies westminster.com, lunch and dinner daily, $9–18) is a popular local place, and the casual American menu is well prepared. The cozy pub features happy hour 3–6 P.M. Monday–Friday, with drinks and entrées discounted 25 percent.

For dessert, head out to **Hoffmans' Ice Cream** (934 Washington Rd., Westminster, 410/857-0824, www.hoffmansicecream.com, open daily) for some strawberry cheesecake, peanut butter ripple, or one of a dozen other flavors of handmade ice cream. It also has a little deli on the premises for an inexpensive snack or sandwich.

INFORMATION

The Carroll County visitors center (210 E. Main St., Westminster, 410/848-1388 or 800/272-1933, www.carr.org/tourism) has a wealth of information on the area, including a fine series of walking tours of the various towns, driving tours of Civil War sites, and an excellent series of bike tours for all levels of fitness.

Baltimore County

There is no doubt that Baltimore is moving north. Boundaries between the towns that once surrounded the city are disappearing, but the northern part of the county remains wooded, softened with open farmland. The winery business is still nascent in Maryland, though this area boasts one of America's pioneer vintners. Almost all of Maryland's wineries are clustered in the north-central counties.

SIGHTS
Ladew Topiary Gardens

This manor house with extensive formal landscaping (3535 Jarrettsville Pike, Monkton, 410/557-9466, www.ladew gardens.com, 10 A.M.–4 P.M. Mon.–Fri. and 10:30 A.M.–5 P.M. Sat.–Sun. Apr.–Oct., $13 house, nature walk, and gardens, $10 garden only) was created by Harvey S. Ladew, who had two abiding interests: fox hunting and gar-

dening. The small piece of Eden Mr. Ladew created has been deemed "the most outstanding topiary garden in America" by the Garden Club of America, and his home charmingly reflects his interests in horses and hounds.

Though many visitors are drawn to the outstanding topiary displays, especially the bounding fox and hounds on the front lawn and the swan hedge in back of the manor house, the house itself is not to be missed. Mr. Ladew's collection of ceramics, silver, and paintings portray clever foxes, noble horses, and eager hounds—and the framed photographs that decorate the house testify to his friendships with American and British notables, including the Duke and Duchess of Windsor. The rooms are elegant but comfortable, and the oval library, which has been highlighted in several architectural publications, has a secret swinging panel that leads to a card room in a separate building nearby.

HORSE COUNTRY

The Preakness is part of a long equine tradition in the mid-Atlantic. Since colonial days, Marylanders have always appreciated fine horseflesh in motion.

Modern fox hunting is thought to have originated in Maryland. Early-17th-century settlers were more involved in the necessities of hunting for food, but as they became more comfortable with their new home, necessity evolved into sport. Foxhounds – dogs specially bred for a speedy run over rough terrain – turned into a valuable commodity in the state. Riders followed the baying hounds and fox, testing their horsemanship and mounts to the utmost; a good long run was the goal. A hunter's horse was prized for stamina, rather than great jumping ability, though leaping rooks and rail fences was expected.

Early hunts easily lasted a week, spaced out by overnight visits to the homes of friends and participants. Fox hunting was considered a sport for gentlemen. Horse racing, on the other hand, was for everyone.

Returning tobacco ships brought Arabians and near eastern horses, imported to be interbred with English and European stock already in the colonies. Race meets were established on the peninsulas between rivers, and they began to attract the elite, including Colonel George Washington of the Virginia militia. Jockey clubs – exclusive groups of breeders and bettors – were formed at Marlboro, Chestertown, Annapolis, Port Tobacco, Leonardtown, and other ports on both shores of the state. Many towns have a Race Street – either the location of the actual track, or the road to it.

The gardens are laid out in more than 20 separate areas with different themes, sometimes based on color—such as the pink garden or the yellow garden, with its pagoda—or built around a sculpture like the *Temple of Venus* or a unique horticultural item like the golden rain tree. Some part of the garden is in bloom spring through fall; azaleas and tulips are followed by irises, hydrangea, and chrysanthemums. In addition, the property offers a 1.5-mile nature walk through the fields and woods. Though the gardens and house require a special trip, this is a destination not to be missed for anyone who admires a casual country-gentry style and a thoughtfully designed garden that reflects years of planning and care.

The Fire Museum of Maryland

This large building, though a bit hard to find at the back of a parking lot (1301 York Rd., Lutherville, 410/321-7500, 1–5 P.M. Sat. May and Sept.–Dec., 1–5 P.M. Tues.–Sat. June–Aug., $8), warehouses and displays a spiffy restored collection of more than 50 hand-drawn, horse-drawn, and self-propelled fire engines and other fire-fighting apparatus.

Weekday tours are available by appointment. The collection represents manufacturers as early as 1822 up to 1957 from several states, Massachusetts to Tennessee.

The museum was opened in 1971 as a private, nonprofit corporation by Stephen Heaver and his eldest son, Stephen Jr. The quality and breadth of the collection make this one of the finest fire-fighting equipment museums in the United States. The rigs are spit-shined by a staff of dedicated volunteers. Special exhibits include a fire alarm telegraph network, a display of fire company badges, a uniform collection, and information about Baltimore's high-pressure pumping system. This collection is a treat if you enjoy fire-fighting memorabilia and appreciate technological design and development.

The museum is located behind the multistory Heaver Plaza Office Building, one block north of exit 26B (Lutherville) off I-695 (the Baltimore Beltway).

◖ Boordy Vineyards

At Boordy Vineyards (12820 Long Green Pike, Hydes, 410/592-5015, www.boordy.com,

10 A.M.–5 P.M. Mon.–Sat. and 1–5 P.M. Sun.), 85 percent of all wines produced are crushed from their own grapes—a rarity in this area. Tours are given daily. In addition to its northern Maryland property, Boordy also owns vineyards on South Mountain in western Maryland near Burkittsville. Boordy is one of America's pioneer vineyards, and its founder, Philip Wagner, is credited as one of a handful of winemakers who revived a crippled industry.

During the Prohibition years of 1917–1933, untended vineyards and the loss of knowledge of high-quality winemaking came close to destroying America's wine industry. When Wagner published *American Wines and How to Make Them* in 1933, it was thought to be the only available book of its kind in the English language. During Prohibition, Phillip Wagner learned of the vidal blanc grape, which was the basis for a significant portion of the wines of France, yet largely unknown to the American public. On a tour of duty in Europe as a war correspondent for the *Baltimore Sun* a few years later, he and his wife, Jocelyn, collected the vines and brought them back to Maryland. The first vidal blanc vine in the United States was brought wrapped in a wet towel in Jocelyn's toilet case. This variety, which has superior disease resistance, made a well-balanced wine; it's now widely planted throughout the eastern United States. The Wagners set out their vines and began making quantities of wine.

In 1965, Boordy Vineyards pioneered the *sur lie* process in America, where wine is "left on the lees" (the crushed grapes and seeds, or lees, remain in the wine tank) for a brief period to add flavor, aroma, and complexity. The practice is common in California wineries today. Boordy's fame was greatly enhanced by Philip Wagner's reputation as an author on the subject of American winemaking. His classic, *Grapes Into Wine,* has been repeatedly revised and reprinted over the decades.

The R. B. Deford family, longtime friends of the Wagners and grape growers for Boordy Vineyards for many years, took over the Boordy name in 1980 and moved operations to their farm north of Baltimore. Rob Deford, who received formal training in enology at the University of California at Davis, set a new course for Boordy. He updated much of the equipment, adding new French and American oak barrels for aging. With the introduction of the three-time gold-medal-winning Boordy Nouveau in 1981, Rob Deford became the first Maryland vintner to successfully produce and market quality early-release wines.

Today, the winery continues to garner accolades from the wine world: Its 2000 reisling was named dessert wine of the year, and Tom Burns was named Winemaker of the Year by Maryland's wineries. Boordy's original three standard table wines white, red, and rosé have expanded to include varietals, port, and champagne. Special events and concerts are held frequently on the property; call for details.

Woodhall Wine Cellars (17912 York Rd., Parkton, 410/357-8644, www.woodhallwinecellars.com, 11 A.M.–5 P.M. Mon.–Fri, 10 A.M.–5 P.M. Sat., noon–5 P.M. Sun.) is another ambitious winery north of Baltimore. Boordy and Woodhall are the two oldest wineries in Maryland. Tours and tastings include barrel samples of various wines on request. Founded in 1983, Woodhall is a small, family-owned operation producing a full range of table wines, including dry, sweet, and dessert styles. Wines are further segmented into three groups: inexpensive everyday wines, midpriced premium wines, and complex "super varietals." Like many French wines, a number of Woodhall wines are blended from different sources or different varietals. The exceptions include a Vineyard Reserve cabernet sauvignon from Copernica Vineyards in northern Maryland, a seyval, and a riesling.

In the last few years, the three varietals above have been selected as best-of-show wines at the Maryland Governor's Cup Wine Judging. Woodhall's riesling was selected by the Goddard Space Center as one of three "40th Anniversary" wines; Maryland Public Television selected Woodhall's cabernet sauvignon as its "30th Anniversary" wine; and Woodhall's seyval was the "Aquarium White" of the National Aquarium in Baltimore.

The annual Harvest Winefest weekend

draws over 1,000 people during October to watch and participate in the Woodhall harvest, in addition to enjoying an afternoon of music, crafts, food, and wine. Woodhall features other special events throughout the year.

RECREATION
Gunpowder Falls State Park
This day-use park (2813 Jerusalem Road, Kingsville, Harford County, 410/592-2897, www.dnr.state.md.us/publiclands/central/gunpowder.html)—nearly 18,000 acres in Harford and Baltimore Counties—has a number of unconnected sections. They include the **Hereford Area,** along York Road in Parkton; the 21-mile **Northern Central Railroad (NCR) Trail,** which extends from Ashland to the Pennsylvania line; the **Central Area,** which extends from Baldwin to Days Cove and includes the historic village of Jerusalem; the **Hammerman Area,** which is located in Chase near the intersection of Eastern Avenue and Grace Quarters Road and offers a swimming beach on the Gunpowder River; and **Dundee Creek Marina,** also located in Chase, which offers boat launching, rowboat rental, fuel, and a marina store. In all, there are more than 100 miles of trails. Maps are available at the park office on the park's website.

The park was created to protect the stream valleys of Big and Little Gunpowder Falls and the Gunpowder River. Because of its length, the park's topography ranges from tidal marshes and wetlands to steep, rugged slopes. It features excellent trout fishing and other freshwater and tidal fishing areas. Leashed pets are welcome in all areas of the park except Hammerman.

Though mostly day-use, the park offers two camper cabins in the Hammerman area, plus a unique home away from home: the Mill Pond Cottage in the Hereford Wildlands. It features all the domestic comforts, including two bedrooms and a sleep sofa, a full kitchen, one and a half baths, washer and dryer, and a fireplace. The cottage runs $200 a night—book well in advance by calling the park headquarters (410/592-2897).

Getting There: Hammerman: From I-95, take exit 67A for MD-43 east (White Marsh Blvd.). Follow 43 to MD-40 east. Turn right at the first light onto Ebenezer Road and follow it for 4.5 miles. The park entrance will be on your left.

Monkton Station: From I-83 north, take exit 27 and turn right on Mount Carmel Road. Turn right on York Road and make a quick left onto Monkton Road. Follow it until it crosses the NCR Trail. Monkton Station will be on your left. Parking is limited.

Jerusalem Mill (park headquarters): From I-95, take exit 74 for MD-152 west (Mountain Rd.). Follow Mountain Road toward Fallston and turn left onto Jerusalem Road. Jerusalem Mill will be on your left after 1.1 miles. Parking is in the lot on the right, just before the mill.

Hampton National Historic Site
This elegant mansion north of Baltimore (535 Hampton Ln., Towson, MD 21286, 410/823-1309, daily) is set within 62 acres of parkland. Mansion tours start on the hour 9 A.M.–4 P.M. A quick stroll will show off the wonderful formal gardens; a longer walk will reveal other buildings and hidden treasures.

ACCOMMODATIONS AND FOOD
Chain hotels and restaurants dominate the landscape north of Baltimore until the suburbs thin out north of Timonium. Then you're in the country. It was an area favored by native peoples, and became a well-traveled route by the colonials and Victorians. The village of Monkton offers both food and lodging to weary travelers away from the big city.

The **Manor Tavern** (15819 Old York Rd., Monkton, 410/771-8155, www.themanor tavern.com, lunch and dinner daily, brunch on Sunday, $9–22) takes up where Slade's Inn leaves off. Formerly a stable for the original Slade's Tavern, the site has been transformed into an elegant restaurant. Food from the dining menu—including cream of asparagus and crab soup served in a bread bowl ($7.25) and the Manor burger ($7.50)—may also be ordered at the cozy booths in the lounge. In fine weather, there's an outside terrace and sunroom.

Havre de Grace

"Harbor of Grace" sits at the mouth of the Susquehanna River, a location that was explored by Captain John Smith in the mid-17th century. (However, recent sources claim that Victor Hernandez, a Spaniard, beat John Smith by a good 75 years, exploring the Upper Bay in 1588.) A ferry crossing was established at the mouth of the Susquehanna in 1695. The area was not chartered as a city until 1783, when it was a bustling town of seven houses. The city grew, and the old Post Road—now U.S. 40—was alive with stagecoaches traveling between Baltimore and Philadelphia; Havre De Grace narrowly missed (by one vote) becoming the nation's capital. The small port continued to grow, but in 1813, the British attacked the town and most of the structures were destroyed or damaged.

The Susquehanna & Tidewater Canal was completed in 1840 and opened all of central Pennsylvania to two-way trade between Philadelphia and Baltimore. The 45-mile canal ran from Havre de Grace to Wrightsville, Pennsylvania; the mule-drawn canal boats had to be raised a total of 233 feet through the use of 29 lift walks. The canal boats moved about 3 mph, and a trip took two days. The Susquehanna & Tidewater Canal enjoyed its most profitable years around 1870. It shut down, a victim of railroad competition, in 1900.

Fishing and boat-building added to the transport of grain and lumber as a source of income. After the Civil War, coal and the canning industry brought new money into the economy. In the 20th century, tourism accounted for the city's continued growth. A thoroughbred racetrack opened in 1912; direct trains from Philadelphia and New York to the Havre de Grace track were filled with racing fans that had come to see Whirlaway and other major competitors in the 1940s. The track closed in the 1950s, a victim of political maneuvering. By that time, the commercial market for waterfowl was long gone as well, though sport waterfowl hunting continued to be an attraction that lured many to the city.

Though the canal and racetrack are memories, there are more than 130 structures within the city limits that are of historic significance, and the town is deemed a National Historic District. Havre de Grace is a popular destination for a quiet overnight getaway from Baltimore or Philadelphia.

HAVRE DE GRACE

SUSQUEHANNA MUSEUM OF HAVRE DE GRACE AT THE LOCKHOUSE

ERIE ST
ONTARIO ST
OTSEGO ST
Susquehanna River
KEN'S/OLD CHESAPEAKE HOTEL
FRANKLIN ST
TIDEWATER GRILLE
GREEN ST
LA CLE D'OR
PENNINGTON AVE
SENECA CANNERY ANTIQUES
JUNIATA
ADAMS
CONGRESS AVE
BOURBON ST
SPENCER-SILVER MANSION
FOUNTAIN ST
GIRARD ST
VANDIVER INN
BOMBOY'S
REVOLUTION ST
STOKES
UNION
WASHINGTON
MARKET
LEWIS ST
ALLIANCE ST
CONCORD POINT LIGHTHOUSE
LAFAYETTE ST
CURRIER HOUSE B&B
GILES ST
HAVRE DE GRACE DECOY MUSEUM
HAVRE DE GRACE MARITIME MUSEUM
COMMERCE ST
CHESAPEAKE DR
Millard E Tydings Memorial Park
Boardwalk
SKIPJACK MARTHA LEWIS
Park
Island
0 200 yds
0 200 m

© AVALON TRAVEL

SIGHTS
◖ Havre de Grace Decoy Museum

This local museum (215 Giles St., 410/939-3739, www.decoymuseum.com, 10:30 A.M.–4:30 P.M. Mon.–Sat., noon–4 P.M. Sun., $6) documents and interprets waterfowl decoys as an art form and chronicles the art and use of decoys on the upper Chesapeake Bay. Annual special events include the Decoy & Wildlife Art Festival held the first weekend in May. The collection is one of the finest ever assembled. An extensive research library complete with works on types of decoys, carving, waterfowl, and the environment is available by appointment. There's a fine museum gift shop with a selection of working and art decoys, reference books, and other waterfowl-related items. On many weekends, contemporary decoy carvers from the Chesapeake Bay exhibit and demonstrate their craft.

Decoys were originally made for one purpose: to lure waterfowl for hunters. The early decoys were not fancy—sometimes little more than crudely carved blocks of wood. Each maker had his own ideas of what ducks and other waterfowl looked like, and made his decoys accordingly. The museum follows the development of decoy carving from a purely practical endeavor to a form of American folk art. In addition, the museum chronicles the history of waterfowl hunting in the upper Chesapeake. An abundance of ducks during spring and fall migrations was the primary draw for visitors into the area in the early 20th century. Overhunting and changing environments eventually caused the duck population to fall off radically, which led to a ban on hunting; the museum's display on the development of boats, guns, duck calls, a re-creation of a carving shop, and related items recalls an earlier time.

Susquehanna Museum of Havre de Grace at the Lockhouse

The lockhouse building is in a small park at the end of Conesteo Street (410/939-5780, www.lockhousemuseum.org, 1–5 P.M. Thurs.–Mon., donations accepted). The museum consists of the locktender's house, constructed about 1840, which served as both the office

Susquehanna Museum of Havre de Grace

© JOANNE MILLER

Concord Point Lighthouse

© JOANNE MILLER

Concord Point lighthouse, at the juncture of the Susquehanna River and Chesapeake Bay, was in continuous operation for over 150 years. Near the lighthouse is a small cannon used in the defense of Havre de Grace when the British burned and sacked the town in 1813.

Martha Lewis Skipjack

Early in the 20th century, V-bottom, double-sail boats known as skipjacks were a common sight on the Chesapeake Bay. Today, these working dredge boats that once made up the Chesapeake Bay oyster fleet are few. The *Martha Lewis* (410/939-0015, www.skipjackmarthalewis.org), docked at the end of Commerce Street off Tydings Park, is one of the last to fish commercially under sail in the United States. The skipjack, which is maintained by the Chesapeake Heritage Conservancy, offers several options for coming aboard, including a five-hour discovery classroom, an afternoon tea under sail (skipjacks are *very* steady), sailing classes, and an opportunity to work with a dredge crew hauling oysters June–November, weather permitting; check for hours of operation.

Havre de Grace Maritime Museum

At the mouth of the Susquehanna River on the Chesapeake Bay, this museum (100 Lafayette St., 410/939-4800, www.hdgmaritimemuseum.org, 11 A.M.–5 P.M. Mon., Wed., Fri.–Sun. Sept.–May, 11 A.M.–5 P.M. daily June–Aug., $2) tells the story of this region's rich maritime heritage through educational exhibits. The museum supports programs such as the Chesapeake Wooden Boat Builders School and the Susquehanna Flats Environmental Center, and a lecture, concert and film series.

SHOPPING

The first few blocks of **Washington and St. John Streets** offer a variety of low-key boutiques and antique shops. Book lovers will enjoy **Washington Street Books and Antiques** (131 N. Washington St., 410/939-6215, www.washingtonstreetbooks.com), a compendium of new and used books, crystals, incense, and so on. **Courtyard Bookshop** (313 St. John St.,

for the Susquehanna & Tidewater Canal and the home of the locktender and his family—a portrait of the last locktender, painted in 1889, hangs in the parlor. The lower floor consists of a restored office, parlor, rear office, kitchen, and gift shop. The second floor features a historical display room; a short video on the history of the canal is available for viewing. Just in front of the house is the outlet lock, and over it is a reconstruction of the original pivot bridge that was opened and closed by hand to permit the passage of boats.

Concord Point Lighthouse

Located at the foot of Lafayette Street, this tower (410/939-9040, 1–5 P.M. Sat.–Sun. May–Oct., free) is the most photographed and painted subject in the city. Built in 1827, it was one of eight lighthouses in the northern bay and was part of an effort to improve the flow of goods down the Susquehanna River from Philadelphia to Baltimore. The construction of these structures coincided with the opening of the Chesapeake & Delaware Canal. The

410/939-5150) specializes in used, out-of-print, and antiquarian books. **Seneca Cannery Antiques** (201 St. John St., 410/942-0701), houses multiple dealers specializing in furniture, jewelry, and glassware. The least formal antiques stores are on Market Street between Bourbon and Congress Streets.

ACCOMMODATIONS

The **Vandiver Inn** (301 S. Union Ave., 410/939-5200 or 800/245-1655, www.vandiverinn.com, $109–149 mansion, $129–149 Kent Guest House, $109–149 Murphy Guest House), consists of three separate structures that are among the most extensively restored buildings in Havre de Grace. Dating from 1886, the original building—the mansion—had fallen into disrepair; the current owners found, repurchased, and reinstalled the original stained-glass windows that had been removed from the house. In addition to overnight accommodations, the Vandiver Inn also offers special candlelit dinners by reservation on selected Fridays. All nine guestrooms in the mansion have private baths (though one is not in the room itself), and all are furnished in an understated Victorian style. The Kent and Murphy Guest Houses are adjacent to the mansion and provide an additional eight rooms with private bath.

The **Spencer-Silver Mansion** (200 S. Union Ave., 410/939-1485 or 800/780-1485, www.spencersilvermansion.com, $80–150) is another of Havre de Grace's large historic houses, and the only Victorian stone mansion in the city. The structure was embellished with a two-story bay window, tower, gables, a dormer, and a variety of other architectural effects when it was built in 1896 for merchant and foundry owner John Spencer. Later, Charles Silver, a local cannery owner, purchased the house. The mansion offers two rooms with private baths, two rooms that share a bath, and a carriage house with whirlpool bath and working fireplace. Children are welcome.

Also recommended is the **Currier House Bed and Breakfast** (800 S. Market St., 410/939-7886, www.currier-bb.com, $95–135). Members of the Currier family lived in Cecil and Kent Counties from 1648, and Matthew Currier moved into the house named after him in 1861. The house has been enlarged and modernized since then and now offers four guestrooms, all with private bath.

La Cle D'or Guesthouse (226 N. Union Ave., 410/939-6562 or 888/HUG-GUEST, www.lacledorguesthouse.com, $110–135) is housed in the historic 1868 Henry Harrison Hopkins House (this is the family home of Johns Hopkins of medical fame). The interior and two suites are decorated in post–Civil War period style, and filled with marvelous antiques.

FOOD

One of my favorite places in Havre de Grace is **Bomboy's** (329 Market St., 410/939-2924, www.bomboyscandy.com, candy store open 10 A.M.–6 P.M. Tues.–Sat. and noon–5 P.M. Sun., closed Mon. year-round, ice cream store open noon–9 P.M. Tues.–Fri., 1–9 P.M. Sat.–Sun. May–mid-Oct.). This family business makes a celebrated brand of homemade ice cream and has a steady flow of local traffic through its old-fashioned ice cream parlor. They keep 28 flavors in stock at all times and develop their own specialties, such as Hokey-Pokey (chocolate malt ice cream with chunks of chocolate fudge). Bomboy's also makes amazing homemade chocolates—visitors can order online if they just can't get enough.

The **Tidewater Grille** (on the water, 300 Franklin St., 410/939-3313, lunch and dinner daily, lunch $12, dinner $25) is appreciated by visitors and locals alike. The menu features the ubiquitous crab cakes, plus filet mignon, prime rib, pasta, and chicken.

Ken's Steak and Rib House in the old Chesapeake Hotel (400 North Union Ave., 410/939-5440, www.oldchesapeakehotel.com, lunch and dinner daily, entrees $9–27) is part bar/part eating establishment serving American pub food and specializing in smoked baby back ribs. Lunch fare includes tuna steak sandwiches, fried oyster sandwiches, burgers, and salads. Dinner entrées include beef, veal, lamb, seafood, and those famous ribs. As the evening wears on, the dining room may get a little smoky.

Greater Harford County

Though some visitors to Harford County never get beyond the boundaries of I-95 on their way to Philadelphia or Baltimore, this area is home to several scenic small towns with plenty of amenities, several verdant parks, and borders the busiest canal in America—the Chesapeake and Delaware Canal, stretching from the Delaware River below Wilmington to pretty Chesapeake City in Cecil County. Ladew Topiary Gardens is legendary among those who appreciate fine gardens, and they offer a little bit of England in the Maryland countryside. For a unique experience, stop by the U.S. Army Ordnance Museum in Aberdeen.

SIGHTS
Ripken Museum
The partial contents of this museum, temporarily in Ripken Stadium, are the embodiment of Ripken mania—for Orioles fanatics, this is a tiny slice of baseball heaven (Long Dr. off Rte. 22/Churchville Rd., Aberdeen, 410/273-2525, www.ripkenmuseum.com, call Jay Moskowitz at 410/297-9292 to see the display). Photographs, World Series memorabilia, and artifacts tell the story of the Ripken empire, beginning with father Cal Sr. and continuing with his two sons, Cal Jr. and Billy. All three worked for the Orioles in 1987: Cal Sr. managed the team, and his sons were the heavy hitters. The museum brings the whole family into the act, though—according to one of the photographs, the boys' sister Elly had the best batting average of them all in adolescence. The new home of the museum will be on the grounds of the Ripken Youth Baseball Academy in Aberdeen, and will also feature a film about Cal Jr.'s life and a video on his famous consecutive game streak that broke Lou Gehrig's record in 1995. Call 410/273-2525 or visit www.ripkenmuseum.com for an update on the museum's progress.

◖ U.S. Army Ordnance Museum
Combat fans, this weapons warehouse (Aberdeen Proving Ground, Aberdeen, 410/

U.S. Army Ordnance Museum

© JOANNE MILLER

278-3602, http://ordmusfound.org, 9 A.M.–4:45 P.M. daily, donations accepted) contains enough cannons, machine guns, fuses, bombs, and handguns (all inactive and under glass) to arm the most violent Hollywood film. Among the thousands of pieces of ordnance on display are a veritable Divided Nations of weapons from Japan, Russia, and Vietnam, among others. Oddly, the overall impression is not of mass destruction, but rather a fascination with the technical aspects and machined precision of each piece. There is a beauty in these dormant weapons. On the mezzanine, a 58-pound body armor suit worn by EOD (Explosive Ordnance Disposal) personnel is on display next to a panel explaining bomb disarmament via fuse removal—not a career for the wimpy. To see the displays, visitors must stop at the Maryland Avenue Gate on Route 715 and show a driver's license with a picture and car registration for a day pass.

One less aggressive display asks the question, "What has the Ordnance Corps done for you?" and provides several answers. ENIAC, the Electronic Numerical Integrator and Computer, developed by the Ordnance Corps, is the great-granddaddy of all modern computers. The Ordnance Corps also developed miniaturization by creating a tiny radio transmitter that would fit into the fuse of an artillery projectile—the forerunner of today's portable radios and hearing aids. America's ubiquitous sport utility vehicles evolved from the Ordnance Corps' World War II Jeep. The U.S. Army Ordnance Corps dates to the early days of the American Revolution, when, in 1775, the Continental Congress appointed a "Commissary General of the artillery stores" to provide necessary ordnance material. The Ordnance Corps' "Flaming Bomb" insignia, the oldest military insignia in the U.S. Army, was adopted in 1832.

The U.S. Army Ordnance collection came into being in 1918, when the Westervelt Board met in France and determined a need to evaluate the use of artillery during World War I in order to make recommendations concerning future policies. The Ordnance Corps collected all types of artillery, bullets, and gas masks to study and evaluate. Over time, the museum's collection expanded from artillery equipment to include small arms, military vehicles, aircraft bombs, fire-control equipment, and armored fighting vehicles. In 1942, a foreign materiel section was established.

Though the collection was nearly liquidated after the Vietnam War, a group of local citizens formed a foundation to save it, and built and donated the museum's current home. Its current mission is to collect, preserve, and account for historically significant weapons that relate to the history of the U.S. Army Ordnance Corps and the evolution and development of American military ordnance materiel from the Colonial period in America to the present.

The Ordnance Museum is surrounded by a large park (open daily during daylight hours) filled with more than 225 tanks and assault vehicles. It's a great place for a stroll and to exercise your imagination, whether in the form of memories or thankful thoughts that these behemoths are at rest. Whatever your feelings about weapons, the U.S. Army Ordnance Museum offers a unique opportunity to view a collection that can be found nowhere else in the world.

Steppingstone Museum

This privately owned and operated museum on the Susquehanna State Park grounds features rural farm exhibits dated 1880–1920 (461 Quaker Bottom Rd., 410/939-2299, www.steppingstonemuseum.org, 1–5 P.M. weekends May–Sept., $2). Call or check the website for information on special events.

RECREATION
Susquehanna State Park/ Rocks State Park

A woodsy getaway, these adjacent parks (3318 Rocks Chrome Rd., Jarrettsville, 410/557-7994, 9 A.M.–sunset daily) offer visitors 3,600 acres of activities. Rocks State Park maintains the park office for both Rocks and Susquehanna State Parks. The campground is open May 1– September 30, and some portions of the parks are closed in the winter months.

Susquehanna Park is three miles northwest of Havre de Grace. From I-95, take exit 89 for Route 155. Proceed west on Route 155 to Route 161. Turn right (north) on Route 161, then right (east) on Rock Run Road. Follow Rock Run Road to the park office.

The parks are in the Susquehanna River Valley and have considerable river frontage on the Susquehanna River and Deer Creek. Susquehanna State Park encompasses two smaller recreational areas: **Palmer State Park,** a 486-acre primitive area, runs along Deer Creek off Forge Hill Road; and a timber management area, the **Stony Demonstration Forest,** has several miles of primitive hiking trails.

Overnight Facilities: Restrooms and hot showers are available at each of the two campground loops. The park offers 69 campsites, and a fee is charged on a per-night/per-site basis. The campground is open May 1–

September 30. Reservations can be made by calling 888/432-2267.

Historic Area Walking Tour: The visitors center at the end of Rock Run Road in Susquehanna State Park contains several historic buildings. The **Rock Run Gristmill** (1–4 P.M. weekends May 1–Labor Day) was built in 1794. The **Rock Run House** is a stone manor built by James Archer before the Civil War. Archer was a brigadier general in the U.S. Army who resigned to join the Confederacy. He was wounded and captured at Gettysburg on July 1, 1863, and died shortly after being exchanged. The house is partially restored and contains furnishings and antiques from the era. It's open on summer weekends for tours. Reservations can be made by calling 410/557-7994. The **Toll House** was built for the toll collector who annexed fees to use the bridge that crossed the Susquehanna River at Rock Run. The bridge was destroyed in 1856 by ice floes during the great freeze that year. The Toll House now displays information on forestry and is the main information center at Susquehanna State Park.

Conowingo Dam Driving Tour

This approximately 38-mile tour begins at the intersection of Route 22 and I-95 north of Aberdeen, passing through farm country, forest, and river towns. The Conowingo Dam was built as a W.P.A. project during the Depression, and it's easy to see the art deco roots of its design when approaching it on old U.S. 1. The dam is open for tours by appointment; the visitors center (410/457-5011) is open 10 A.M.–4 P.M. Monday–Friday.

Drive north on Route 22 for approximately five miles to the village of **Churchville.** Turn right (east) on Route 155 and continue through wooded and rolling farmland to Route 161. Turn left on Route 161 (north); you'll pass one of the entrances to **Susquehanna State Park** on this road, so, if you'd like to stop for a picnic, this would be a good place to do it. Otherwise, continue north on Route 161 to the village of **Darlington.** At the intersection of U.S. 1, turn right (east) and cross the

Susquehanna River on the Conowingo Dam. On the other side of the dam (you're now in Cecil County), turn right on Route 222 (south) and drive through **Port Deposit,** a working-class village that grew from a mill and ferry built around 1725. In the 1800s, Port Deposit was a booming shipping center, and plans are afoot to revitalize it. There is a casual little museum here (**Paw Paw Museum,** 98 N. Main, 410/378-3086), with household items and letters from the Civil War, but hours are intermittent—if you're interested, make sure to call ahead. Continue to follow Route 222 south to I-95. From here, you can return west to your original starting point, or continue on to the village of **North East.**

Fishing

The Susquehanna River offers excellent fishing opportunities for striped bass, large- and smallmouth bass, perch, catfish, shad, walleye, carp, and bluegills. This portion of the Susquehanna River is a saltwater fishing area, and a bass sport license is needed.

Boating

A boat launch facility is accessible 24 hours a day at Lapidum Landing, at the south end of Susquehanna State Park off Lapidum Road. There is a fee to use the boat launch, and the area is equipped with restrooms and boat-trailer parking.

Hiking

Susquehanna and Rocks State Parks have nine marked trails ranging from 0.9 mile to three miles in length. Difficulties vary, and each trail offers a unique view of the terrain. The **Ivy Branch Trail,** an easy-to-moderate two-mile trail, crosses farm fields; while the **Deer Creek Trail,** a moderate-to-difficult 2.1-mile trail, has magnificent views of giant trees.

Picnicking and Swimming

The **Deer Creek** picnic area is on Deer Creek at the northern end of Susquehanna State Park and may be reached from the historic area by Stafford Road, which runs parallel to the Susquehanna

A BRIDGE OF ICE

For some years, the Philadelphia, Wilmington & Baltimore (PW&B) Railroad tried to get permission from Maryland's State Legislature to build a bridge across the mouth of the Susquehanna River. The bridge would not only extend the railroad's reach, but would also release it from financial dependence on ferries and riverboats. Politics were not the only obstacle: Swirling currents, unpredictable depths, and winter ice all made the project a risky one. "The big freeze" in the winter of 1853 provided a perfect solution to the PW&B's problems. The mouth of the Susquehanna and much of northern Chesapeake Bay froze solid. Boat traffic came to a standstill, and the railroad attempted to push its bridge once more through the legislature. The sole opposition came from the village of Port Deposit, which claimed a structure across the mouth of the river would not only hinder navigation when the ice finally dissipated, but would also obstruct the passage of broken ice into the Chesapeake, causing water to back up and flood the town. A compromise was finally reached, with the railroad agreeing to build a branch line into Port Deposit. Yard by yard, a wooden bridge was built, using the ice as a base. When the $1.5 million project neared completion, a tornado struck on July 25, 1866, blowing most of "the great engineering feat" into the bay. Rebuilding started immediately, and the completed bridge spanned the distance between Havre de Grace and Perryville. In November 1866, the bridge opened to traffic, creating an uninterrupted train route from Philadelphia to Washington for the first time in history.

River. Deer Creek is popular for tubing, swimming, and canoeing, though there are no lifeguards. It's also a freshwater fishing area.

ACCOMMODATIONS

Out of town and in the quiet countryside, **Be My Guest B&B** (2414 Rocks Rd., Forest Hill, 410/838-8943, $110–155) is surrounded by gardens and features made-to-order breakfasts and massages by appointment. The Victorian house has two rooms with private bath. The former blacksmith's shop next door provides extra lodging with full bath.

Near the freeway outside of Havre de Grace, the **Clarion Hotel Aberdeen** (980 Hospitality Way, Aberdeen, 410/273-6300 or 800/346-3612, $89–169) and nearby **Holiday Inn Aberdeen–Chesapeake House** (1007 Beards Hill Rd., Aberdeen, 410/272-8100, same rates) are safe bets for a functional, low-priced room. Both have been renovated, and before the renovation did allow pets. Call to see if that's still in effect.

INFORMATION

Contact the the **Harford County Office of Tourism** (1250 Bulle Rock Pkwy., Havre de Grace, MD 21078, 410/939-6631 or 888/554-4695, www.harfordmd.com). **Havre de Grace** also has its own visitors center and tourism commission (450 Pennington Ave., P.O. Box 339, Havre de Grace, MD 21078, 410/939-2100 or 800/851-7756, www.hdgtourism.com).

Chesapeake City

This small town packs some serious appeal. Crossing over the massive and graceful Chesapeake and Delaware Bridge that spans the mouth of the C&D Canal, the rooftops appear much as they did 100 years ago, when the village grew to serve the needs of the busy canal. The canal is still in operation today, and Chesapeake City has become a "boutique town," with inviting shops and excellent restaurants. Attractions are located in the historic district of South Chesapeake City, on the south side of the bridge, unless otherwise indicated.

CHESAPEAKE AND DELAWARE CANAL MUSEUM

The C&D Canal Museum (410/885-5622, 8 A.M.–4 P.M. Mon.–Fri., free) is set in the canal's original pumphouse in a park next to a public marina. There are picnic tables available to enjoy the beautiful view of the canal, bridge, and 30-foot replica of the Bethel Bridge Lighthouse, one of many wooden lighthouses in use before 1927. The museum tells the story of the C&D Canal from its beginnings in the 17th century to its present use as the busiest canal in the United States. Working models of locks and the original power plant for the giant water wheel that pumped water to raise water levels in the canal locks are on display. Follow Second Street south of town until you see a sign on the left for U.S. Army Corps of Engineers; follow that road to the parking lot.

SHOPPING

The two "downtown" blocks of Bohemia Avenue are where you'll find the **Back Creek General Store** (a place for antiques and cards), **Canal Artworks, McKeown Art Gallery,** and other shops offering a day's diversion. The street ends in the **Pell Garden,** a small public space with a beautiful view of the canal. The **Bohemia Café & Bakery,** a block away at Second and George Streets, is a good stop for breakfast treats or a cup of

© JOANNE MILLER

Chesapeake City

AMERICA'S BUSIEST CANAL

© JOANNE MILLER

Chesapeake Bridge, Chesapeake City

America's busiest canal – and the third most heavily trafficked in the world – the Chesapeake and Delaware Canal is 14 miles long, 450 feet wide, and 35 feet deep. It connects the Delaware River with the Chesapeake Bay and the Port of Baltimore. The eastern terminus is at Reedy Point in Delaware.

In the mid-1600s, a Dutch envoy and mapmaker, Augustine Herman, proposed the building of a waterway to connect the two bodies of water. The canal would reduce the water route between Philadelphia and Baltimore by nearly 300 miles. More than a century passed. In the mid-1760s, surveys were taken, but construction on a waterway was not begun until 1804. Over the next 20 years, the canal suffered a number of setbacks, and construction waxed and waned with the amount of available money. In 1824, canal construction resumed, using the labor of more than 2,000 men who dug and hauled dirt from the ditch by hand, working with picks and shovels for an average daily wage of $0.75. The waterway was finally open for business in 1829, one of the most expensive canal projects of its time (though not because of workers' wages).

Mule and horse teams pulled freight and passenger barges, schooners, and sloops through the canal. Lumber, grain, farm products, fish – everything needed for daily life – made its way between the big cities.

Loss of water from the locks was a problem early on. As boats passed through at Chesapeake City, the equivalent of a full lock of water drained into the lower-lying portion of the canal. This made it necessary to devise a means of lifting water back into the upper part of the project. A steam pump was purchased in 1837 to raise water from Back Creek, and a steam engine and large water wheel were installed at the pump house in Chesapeake City (now the C&D Canal Museum). The water wheel, powered by steam, remained in continuous use through the mid-1920s.

In 1919, the canal was purchased by the federal government and designated part of the Intra-Coastal Waterway. The eastern entrance, originally at Delaware City, Delaware, was relocated south to Reedy Point, and all locks were removed as the waterway was converted to a sea-level operation at 12 feet deep and 90 feet wide. In the years that followed, ships collided with bridges and traffic strained the canal's capacity, necessitating constant improvements; the canal has been periodically widened and deepened.

Today's canal is electronically controlled and carries 40 percent of all ship traffic in and out of the Port of Baltimore. A U.S. Coast Guard–certified pilot – a sailor with special knowledge of the areas he or she covers – steers vessels engaged in foreign trade through the canal, Delaware River, and Chesapeake Bay. Traveling east to west, a Delaware River and Bay pilot boards the ship as it passes through Lewes, Delaware, and guides the vessel up the Bay and into the canal through to Chesapeake City. The changing of the pilots takes place at Chesapeake City, as a private launch maneuvers alongside the vessel and a Maryland pilot climbs aboard via the ship's gangway, Jacob's ladder, or port entrance. The new pilot takes over and continues the ship's transit into the Chesapeake Bay to Baltimore or Annapolis.

coffee (410/885-3066, breakfast and lunch daily, dinner Thurs.–Sat., $4–18).

ACCOMMODATIONS

The following inns are open year-round

The **Ship Watch Inn** (401 1st St., 410/885-5300, www.shipwatchinn.com) is right on the water. It offers eight rooms with private bath for $155–195, and there's also a suite for $155–245.

The **Inn on the Canal** (104 Bohemia Ave., 410/885-5995, http://innatthecanal.com, $95–125 room with private bath, $175–225 suite) features seven guestrooms and a three-room suite, all with big tubs for a luxurious bath, and views of the city, canal, and basin.

The appropriately named **Blue Max Inn** (300 Bohemia Ave., 410/885-2781, www.bluemaxinn.com, $95–220 room, $175–250 suite) is a big blue Victorian a block up from the water. It offers seven rooms with private baths and two suites.

The restored **Old Wharf Cottage** (next to Bayard House, 11 Bohemia Ave., S. Chesapeake City, 410/885-5040, www.bayardhouse.com/cottage, $110–160) is a real charmer for a family, a romantic getaway, or two couples. It features a full kitchen and sofa bed on the first floor, and a bedroom on the second floor with a balcony overlooking the canal. A continental breakfast is provided.

FOOD

The Bayard House (11 Bohemia Ave., S. Chesapeake City, 410/885-5040, www.bayardhouse.com, lunch and dinner daily, lunch $18, dinner $28) serves sophisticated cuisine that will knock the socks off any gourmet. The ingredients aren't unusual—crab, rockfish, breast of duck—but the treatment and presentation are top-notch. The view helps, too: Windows open out onto the busy and varied boat traffic of the canal, and it's especially beautiful at sunset, when the boats are lit and the water becomes blue-purple. In warm weather, the patio outside is open to guests. I tried a dish unique to Maryland here: cooked fish roe. Nothing like caviar, it had the taste and texture of a pork/fresh-fish sausage. I'm a lifelong fan.

Schaefer's Canal House (208 Bank St., north side of the C&D Bridge, 410/885-2200, breakfast, lunch, and dinner daily, lunch $10–15, dinner $20–36) is an old fixture of North Chesapeake City. During the summer, it opens at 8 A.M. for breakfast and the kitchen closes down at 10 P.M. (9 P.M. Sun.). There's a seafood buffet for dinner on Thursday, and on Sunday, brunch is served 10 A.M.–3 P.M. It features an Eastern Shore menu, with plenty of seafood, chicken, and beef choices, as well as Austrian specialties. Weather permitting, there's an outdoor deck.

North East

North East is a charming village that once had a very tough reputation. However, the rowdies have been gone for more than a decade; nowadays, visitors come to North East to enjoy its excellent restaurants, a variety of shops, and the proximity to Elk Neck State Park and Turkey Point Lighthouse.

North East has a number of historic buildings, including **St. Mary Anne's Episcopal Church** (315 S. Main St., 410/287-5522), originally built in 1706, destroyed by fire, and rebuilt during the colonial era. The church retains much of its original exterior, and for special services continues to use a Bible and Book of Common Prayer presented in 1718 by Queen Anne of England. Services are at 8 A.M. and 10:30 A.M. on Sunday. Another historic building houses the Upper Bay Museum.

UPPER BAY MUSEUM

This collection (end of Walnut St. in the town park, 410/287-2675, noon–4 P.M. Wed.–Sun. and by appointment, $5) is sheltered in a structure built in 1880, originally a fish house where the daily catch was stored and sold. The Upper Chesapeake Bay enjoys a rich history of water-related industry and commerce. It's the site of the famed Susquehanna flats, one of the nation's finest hunting spots for waterfowl—in the past, the area attracted highly visible sportsmen such as J. P. Morgan and Grover Cleveland. Wildfowl hunting was once primarily a commercial venture, but now it's an exclusively recreational sport.

The heritage of both the commercial and recreational hunter is preserved by the Upper Bay Museum. It features an extensive collection of hunting, boating, and fishing artifacts native to the Upper Chesapeake. Commercial hunting was outlawed at the beginning of the 20th century due to diminishing populations of waterfowl; however, many watermen continued to make their living by attracting waterfowl within the range of their guns. Of particular interest are the outlawed gunning rigs and sculling oars used by bushwhackers to insure near soundless movement of the hunter's skiff. The museum exhibits a rare punt gun that was outlawed in 1918. The massive shotgun, primarily a tool of market hunters, often weighed over 100 pounds and measured 12 feet in length, nearly as long as the boat that held it—a hunter didn't aim the gun, he aimed the boat.

In spite of what may look like a waterfowl wipeout celebration, the museum is dedicated to the propagation and conservation of waterfowl and upland game, and to the improvement of their environments. It only makes sense; without prey, there are no hunters. The museum also features a fine collection of carved decoys, antique marine engines, and miniatures depicting the vessels of the Chesapeake Bay.

SHOPPING

Route 272 runs through the center of town, and most of the shops and restaurants are on the southern side, aka Main Street. A few of shops of note are **Main Street Books** (112 S. Main St., 410/287-2007), an eclectic bookstore, and a gift shop called **Where Butterflies Bloom** (32 S. Main St., 410/287-2975).

© JOANNE MILLER

boats racing on the Chesapeake

One of North East's unusual shops is the **Day Basket Factory** (714 S. Main St., 410/287-6100, www.daybasketfactory.com). The factory was started shortly after the end of the Civil War in 1876, when brothers Edward and Samuel Day came to North East from Massachusetts. They had been supplying the Southern market with baskets for picking cotton, and decided to ply their trade in North East both to save on shipping costs and because of the abundant supply of white oak, the best wood for basket-making. Baskets are still made in the back of the factory by local craftsmen, and a range of shapes and sizes are available for sale.

RECREATION

J&W Charers (410/287-7216) and **Mike Benjamin Charters** (410/287-5490) run head boats on the upper Chesapeake out of North East.

ACCOMMODATIONS

Tailwinds Farm (41 Tailwinds Ln., North East, 410/658-8187, www.fairwindsstables.com,

$90) offers guests canopied beds in a Victorian home on a working horse farm. Kids can visit the farm animals and help gather eggs from the henhouse. After a hearty breakfast, guests may choose to take a riding lesson or travel 10 minutes down the road to Fair Hill Natural Resources Management Area for a trail ride or a carriage ride with the innkeepers, the Dawsons. Stall rentals ($25) are available for horse owners who prefer to bring their own (no canopy bed for the equine guest, but a lovely bag of oats makes up for it). Tailwinds offers many programs for children and families throughout the year in this particularly beautiful setting.

A hybrid of a country inn and a standard hotel, the **Crystal Inn** (1 Center Dr., exit 100 off Route 272, 410/287-7100 or 800/631-3803, $64–169) offers the amenities of a hotel, such as a pool, fitness center, and cable TV, combined with the smaller size, free local telephone calls, and continental breakfast of an inn. The Crystal Inn is quiet, clean, and popular with families; it offers a number of specials throughout the year. Discounts are available for AAA and AARP cardholders.

Sunset at the **North Bay Bed and Breakfast** (9 Sunset Dr., 410/287-5948, http://northbayinc.com, $65–95 shared bath, $125 private bath) is the best time of day—unless you count breakfast. Guests often take a bottle of wine and two borrowed wine glasses down to the Adirondack chairs at the end of the lawn to watch the Chesapeake turn gold. This beautiful and stylish home, a long green lawn away from the headwaters of the Chesapeake Bay, is popular with visitors year-round. The upper floor guestrooms offer a view of the bird-filled forest or the Chesapeake; four rooms share two baths, or a private bath is available at extra cost. Hosts Bob and Pam Appleton also offer custom packages that include a half- or full-day sail on their beautiful 50-foot Gulfstar yacht, *Journey*. Pam, a former customer service manager, makes a formidable breakfast, and Bob, in addition to being a Coast Guard–licensed captain and sailing instructor, still works as a corporate trainer and motivator. A few miles south of North East off Hances Point Road, quiet country surroundings and warm hospitality make this B&B a special place to stay with reasonable rates. Children are welcome with forewarning, but Dusty, the resident kitty, requests no pets.

FOOD

Woody's Crab House (29 S. Main St., 410/287-3541, www.woodyscrabhouse.com, 11:30 A.M.–9 P.M. Sun.–Thurs., 11:30 A.M.–10 P.M. Fri.–Sat., entrees $16) is definitely the hot spot in North East. The restaurant offers every kind of sea creature that can be found in the Chesapeake, and a few more from out of town, like Alaskan king crab legs and Prince Edward Island mussels. Where else can you find a steamed sack of 50 shrimp for $17? They even have a vegetarian sack with steamed carrots, broccoli, corn on the cob, and more for $9. Meat eaters need not fear— burgers and chicken are also on the menu, plus a good selection of draft and bottled beers and wines. Kids will love the roasted peanuts served as appetizers; shells just get swept away on the floor along with errant bits of crab shell. The website is a hoot, by the way—especially if you're not a crab. For a sweet finish, Woody's also owns the ice cream shop next door.

Greater Cecil County

The land/water connection deepens in Cecil County. Two villages whose livelihood was indelibly linked to the north bay marshes and the flora and fauna of the area are the main attraction here, in addition to two exceptionally beautiful parks.

One fascinating tidbit about Cecil County revolves around Elkton's famous marriage industry that flourished in the 1920s and '30s. Unlike the surrounding areas, Elkton demanded no waiting period and no blood tests for prospective brides and grooms—sort of an eastern Las Vegas. Though the law changed in 1938, ballplayers Babe Ruth and Willie Mays, singer Billie Holiday, Bert Lahr (the cowardly lion in *The Wizard of Oz*), and John and Martha Mitchell of Watergate fame were all married in this small town (though not to each other, with the exception of the Mitchells). One wedding chapel still remains open for business, in case you have the urge to merge.

SIGHTS
Fair Hill Natural Resource Management Area
If you've seen the film *Beloved,* starring Oprah Winfrey and Thandie Newton, you'll know why this 5,600-acre partially developed day-use park is so popular with area residents (intersection of Rtes. 273 and 213, Elkton, 410/398-1246, $3–4 per vehicle). Besides providing ethereal scenery for that film, which was set in the mid-19th century, Fair Hill features 80 miles of trails winding among woods, rolling hills, and streams; the routes are shared by bikers, hikers, and equestrians. It is unspoiled and uncrowded. Many of the county's outdoor events take place here, such as the annual steeplechase races, Highland Gathering Scottish Games, and the Cecil County Fair. A stable that offers trail rides, carriage rides, hayrides, and pony rides is inside the entrance to the park on Route 273; it may be reached directly by calling 410/620-3883.

Both of Cecil County's covered bridges are in close proximity to Fair Hill. Gilpin's Falls Bridge is alongside Route 272 north of I-95, and Foxcatcher Farm Covered Bridge over Big Elk Creek (Tawes Dr.) is in the park itself.

Elk Neck State Park and Turkey Point Lighthouse
Lush forest covers 2,200 acres at the tip of a peninsula crowned by the **Turkey Point Lighthouse,** one of the bay's oldest in continuous operation. The park, at the end of Route 272 (410/287-5333, day use $3–4, more for camping) offers a sandy beach for swimming, boat rentals, a snack bar, gift shop, miniature golf, and 10 miles of hiking trails. The lighthouse can be reached by one of the trails; it stands on a bluff 100 feet above the Northeast River and Elk River, which flow together to form the Upper Chesapeake Bay. There are facilities for trailers and motor homes, tent sites, and rustic cabins for rent (888/432-2267 or http://reservations.dnr.state.md.us for reservations).

The state park is set in the **Elk Neck Forest,** 3,500 acres that feature hiking, and shooting and archery ranges.

Mount Harmon Plantation
This beautiful plantation may be out of the way (Mount Harmon Rd., off Grove Neck Rd./Rte. 282, 410/275-8819, www.mountharmon.org, 10 A.M.–3 P.M. Thurs.–Sun. May–Oct., $8) sitting as it does on an inlet of the Sassafras River on the southern border of Cecil County. But if your time and their hours coincide, it's worth the effort. From a historical point of view, this 1730 manor house and outbuildings atop an isolated knoll give a genuine picture of country life in colonial times. Visitors may tour the manor house, outside kitchen, gardens and tobacco prize house.

INFORMATION
The county's **Office of Tourism** is at One Seahawk Drive, Suite 114, in North East (800/232-4595, www.seececil.org). You can order a number of free brochures through the website, including a farm tour and event calendar.

Chestertown

Many people come to Chestertown to attend Washington College, a four-year institution that once had a reputation as a major party school, and many never leave. As a result, Chestertown has all the attractions of a big college town in a verdant, rural setting.

Chestertown was founded in 1706 and became an important port of entry in colonial times. Merchants who made their fortunes in foreign trade in the 18th and 19th centuries built several of the stately homes on Water Street. A driving/walking tour that details the history of Kent County and Chestertown may be picked up at the Kent County Visitors Center (122 North Cross St.).

THE SCHOONER *SULTANA*

The *Sultana,* an exact replica of a 200-year-old schooner, was initially conceived as a private cargo schooner in 1767 and later used by the British Royal Navy to patrol the Chesapeake, Delaware, and Narrangansett Bays. Opened in late 2002, **Sultana Projects** (mailing address: P.O. Box 524, Chestertown, MD 21620, physical address: 105 S. Cross St., 410/778-5954, www.sultanaprojects.org) is an interactive educational center open to the public. *Sultana* is one of the most thoroughly documented American-built vessels from the colonial period. Her lines, logbooks, crew lists, and correspondence have all survived intact to the present day. The *Sultana's* home port is Chestertown, but she may be found in sister ports on the Chesapeake Bay from the spring through the fall. Her mission is to provide hands-on educational experiences in colonial history and environmental science.

Late April–early November, visitors may sail aboard the ship on a two-hour or longer cruise (call 410/778-5954 for reservations, $50–15). The last day of the season in November is the downrigging weekend, when a bevy of tall ships visit Chestertown.

SHOPPING

High Street between Mill and Queen Streets and Cannon Street between Cross and Mill Streets are the main shopping areas in town. Antiques stores, art galleries, handmade-furniture studios, and handcrafted-sweater shops are among the businesses that make this area a true downtown. Goods for sale feature everything from whole foods (**Chestertown Natural Foods,** next to the free parking lot on Cannon St. between Queen and Cross Sts.) to literature (**The Compleat Bookseller** at the corner of High Sand Cross Sts.). A few other favorites are **Twigs & Teacups** (111 S. Cross St.), a sort of hip general store and contemporary emporium, and **Cornucopia** (112 Cross St.), a shop filled with luxurious bath items and housewares.

Chestertown Antique Mall (400 High St., Chestertown, www.chestertownantiquemall .com, 410/778-9006) is a browser's treasure trove. It contains quilts, sporting goods, American folk art, collectibles and much more.

ACCOMMODATIONS

Built in 1860 as a plantation house, the **Brampton Inn** (25227 Chestertown Rd., 410/778-1860 or 866/305-1860, www.brampton inn.com, $195–295) still retains nearly all of its original luxurious details, including plaster ceiling medallions and a three-and-a-half-story walnut and ash central staircase that wends among floors made of Georgia pine. Brampton has 10 large rooms, all with private baths. Most have a wood-burning fireplace ready to be lit during cold winter days. The manor house features a formal guest parlor and a family room with TV, VCR, and games. The 35 acres of grounds just outside of town provide a quiet place to stroll, and when the grove of Princess Pawlinia trees are in full purple bloom, it's hard to imagine a more beautiful setting. A full breakfast is served in the dining room, and afternoon tea with fresh coffee, tea, homemade muffins, cakes, and cookies is offered to each guest. The surroundings are elegant yet comfortable; innkeepers Michael and Danielle Hanscom and their friendly, helpful staff make this a very special place to stay. The guest book is filled with glowing comments

BAD-LUCK LOYALISTS

By the time the British engaged the Continental Army outside Philadelphia in 1776, scores of pro-British loyalists had been driven from their homes by colonial revolutionaries. A group of loyalists on the Eastern Shore of Maryland fled to British-occupied Philadelphia. Commissioned in 1777 as the First Battalion of Maryland Loyalists, led by former Kent County plantation owner Lieutenant Colonel James Chalmers, the soldiers evacuated the city in June 1778, ahead of the British army. While the British rear guard clashed with Washington's army in the Battle of Monmouth a short time later, the Marylanders were a full day's march in front. No military glory awaited them – as part of the advance guard, they had little to do except wait for the rear guard to finish battling the Colonialists and catch up.

After a short stint on Long Island, they were shipped off to Pensacola, Florida, to fight the Spanish. After a five-week siege by Spanish forces in the spring of 1781 (and an equally grueling bout of smallpox), the British and Provincial regiments at Fort George were forced to surrender. The Marylanders had proven courageous, executing a successful bayonet charge on one of the Spanish redoubts. This brief encounter would be their last taste of battle.

They sat out the rest of the war in New York. As with most loyalists, the United States offered no place for them, and they were forced to pack up and leave for Nova Scotia. When their transport ship set out for Saint John in September 1783, less than 100 of the original 300 members of the regiment were aboard. The rest had deserted or died of smallpox.

The transport ship struck a reef near the shore of Nova Scotia. Half the Maryland Loyalists and their families drowned. The survivors were brought to Saint John to face the approaching Canadian winter without clothing, blankets, or weapons. The tiny group of 50 Marylanders received their land grants (known as Block 1) along the northern shore of the St. John River. Some, like Captain Caleb Jones, former sheriff of Somerset County, Maryland, did quite well for themselves: Within four years, he purchased several adjoining lots from men who had been soldiers in his company. The rest faded into history.

from couples who honeymooned here and returned year after year.

In downtown Chestertown, the **White Swan Tavern** (231 High St., 410/778-2300, www .whiteswantavern.com, $140–210) offers a very different lodging experience. The restoration of the building began in 1978 with an archaeological dig, uncovering the site's use as a tannery prior to 1733 and as a tavern after 1793. The property was restored to its late-1800s appearance, and the four rooms and two suites are decorated in an updated colonial style with full baths.

Another attractive alternative is the **Widow's Walk Inn** (402 High St., 410/778-6455 or 888/778-6455, www.chestertown.com/widow, $85–150), a charming restored Victorian that offers two suites, one room with private bath, and two rooms with shared bath. The covered porches that surround the house are a perfect place for a cup of tea and good book on a warm summer day.

FOOD

Play It Again Sam (108 S. Cross St., 410/ 778-2688, 7 a.m.–5:30 p.m. Mon.–Sat., 9 a.m.– 4 p.m. Sun.) is the place for morning coffee, a light lunch, or a sweet anytime of day.

For a casual lunch or dinner for ages 21 and up, try **Andy's** (337 High St., 410/ 778-6779, www.andys-ctown.com, lunch 11:30 a.m.–2:30 p.m. Mon.–Sat., dinner from 5 p.m. Mon.–Sat., bar until 1 a.m. Fri.–Sat., $6). Visitors walk through a tavern to a large dining room in back filled with living-room furniture. Andy's features live music after 9 p.m. and a good pub menu with great burgers.

Blue Heron Café (236 Cannon St., 410/ 778-0188, lunch and dinner Mon.–Sat., lunch $10, dinner $20) is acknowledged as the best in town by many locals. The menu features crabs, chicken, rack of lamb, and jambalaya. Another favorite is the **Imperial Hotel** (208 High St., 410/778-5000, lunch and dinner Tues.–Sat., brunch Sun), featuring a similar menu, and prices as the Blue Heron.

O'Connor's Pub & Restaurant (844 High St., 410/810-3338, 11 A.M.–2 A.M. Mon.–Fri., noon–2 A.M. Sat.–Sun., lunch $7, dinner $18) is always hopping. It serves up steak, chicken, and fish dishes, all with an Irish twist.

ENTERTAINMENT

The **Prince Theatre** (210 High St., 410/810-2060, www.princetheatre.org) was built in 1926 as a vaudeville theater and movie house. The theater has been carefully restored and now presents an exciting range of musical acts, films, live theater, poetry readings, and many other events.

Cruising Chestertown by foot is a popular endeavor. If you'd prefer to go on your own, ask for the **Walking Tour of Historic Chestertown** from the Kent County Visitors Center. Download an architectural/historical walking tour of Chestertown from www.chestertown.com/places/tour. A driving tour of local farms is available as a PDF download from www.kentcounty.com/attractions/farmtour/farmtour.htm

Rock Hall

Rock Hall is one of the last watermen's villages along the north Eastern Shore. In the summer, its streets are crowded with boaters who've stopped off for a meal and the lively social life that the little town offers. The big annual event in Rock Hall is the Rockfish Tournament in June, and festivities continue through July Fourth to the Party on the Bay in August and FallFest in September.

SIGHTS
Waterman's Museum

This collection (20880 Rock Hall Ave., 410/778-6697, 8 A.M.–5 P.M. daily) is dedicated to preserving the history of Chesapeake Bay watermen. A two-room shanty holds a collection of models, equipment, and photographs that tell a sweet history of a hard industry. Entry to the museum is free, but you must stop in next door at the Ditty Bag store at Haven Harbor Marina Office to get the key.

Tolchester Beach Revisited Museum

Tucked away in Oyster Court off of Main Street in Rock Hall (see the *Shopping* section, 410/778-5347, 11 A.M.–3 P.M. Sat.–Sun., donation requested), this little local museum presents and preserves the history of the Tolchester Beach Amusement Park 1877–1962. Tolchester Beach was once one of the most popular resorts along the shores of the Chesapeake Bay, drawing hundreds of vacationers by steamboat. The museum contains more than 300 photos, relics, and other memorabilia recalling the bygone era of the popular bayside park.

SHOPPING

Sharp and Main Streets are the shopping stroll in Rock Hall, featuring a number of antique and clothing dealer. **Oyster Court,** a little village of craft shops off Main Street behind the Mainstay Theatre, contains a natural scent and soap shop, wood carver's shop, gift shops, and others.

RECREATION

Sailing and Powerboat Charters: Rent a craft for a half day, a full day, weekend, or longer. Charter boats are available from several locations in Rock Hall, including **Gratitude Yachting Center** (410/639-7111) and the **Sailing Emporium** (410/778-1342, www.sailingemporium.com/charters).

Fishing Charters: Several boats are available for charter. Four sources to contact are **Captain Manley** (410/639-7420),

NORTH-CENTRAL MARYLAND

Captain Jetton (410/639-7127), Captain Ritchie (410/708-7751), and Captain Simn (410/639-2966).

Equipment Rentals: Swan Haven (20950 Rock Hall Ave., Rock Hall, 410/639-2527, kayak, canoe, boats, bicycles), and Chester River Kayak Adventures (5758 Main St., Rock Hall, 410/639-2001, group or individual rentals, guided environmental tours) are local resources.

ACCOMMODATIONS

Swan Haven (20950 Rock Hall Ave., 410/639-2527, www.swanhaven.com, $100–188) overlooks Swan Creek and Rock Hall's many marinas. This Victorian "cottage" was built in 1898 and served at different times as a hospital and a private home. Visitors can enjoy a nap in the hammock or spend the evening relaxing on the bench out on the pier. Swan Haven offers bicycle, boat, and windsurfer rentals to its guests; sailing, fishing, and crabbing can be done nearby. Each of the 10 rooms has a private bath and cable TV.

The Bay Breeze Inn (5758 Main St., 410/639-2061, www.baybreezeinn.com room $95–130, carriage house $150) dates from the 1920s and is in the middle of Rock Hall's revitalized Main Street area. Two of the five rooms share a bath, the other three have private baths, and a separate carriage house is available. The inn offers kayak tours and special stay-and-play packages.

Moonlight Bay Inn & Marina (6002 Lawton Ave., 410/639-2660, www.moonlightbayinn.com, $134–179) offers 10 rooms, all with private bath, along with a 50-slip marina with bathrooms, a picnic area, and barbecues. Dorothy and Bob Santangelo renovated the 150-year-old house from a deteriorated wreck in 1992 and now offer one of the prettiest lodgings around, with a great view of the sunset.

FOOD

◖ Durding's Ice Cream (Sharp and Main Sts., 410/778-7957, 10 A.M.–8 P.M. Mon.–Tues. and Thurs., 10 A.M.–9 P.M. Fri.–Sat., 10 A.M.–7 P.M. Sun., closed Wed.) is the ultimate old-fashioned soda fountain and corner store. The original store was built just after the Civil War by the founder of Sharp and Dohme Pharmaceuticals (now Merck Pharmaceuticals). Mr. Alpheus Phineas Sharp and his wife retired to Rock Hall and eventually sold the shop to the Durdings. The pressed-tin ceiling, brass lamps, and wooden telephone booth complement the marble and stainless steel soda fountain counter—you don't see many of these around anymore.

The Bay Wolf (21270 Rock Hall Ave., 410/639-2000, noon–9 P.M. Sun.–Thurs., noon–10 P.M. Fri.–Sat., lunch $7, dinner $15) serves Eastern Shore cuisine and a few German dishes such as sauerbraten. The emphasis—no surprise—is on seafood.

Pruitt's Swan Point Inn (Coleman Rd. and Rock Hall Ave./Rte. 20, 410/639-2500, lunch and dinner Wed.–Sun., lunch $9, dinner $20) offers a menu of Cajun and Creole specialties and seafood. Diners can also spend the night at the inn.

Greater Kent County

The word "typical," as in Kent is a typical tidewater county, implies ordinary—but Kent County is anything but. In fact, many of the roads traveled in Kent County, called Chesapeake Country, are part of a recent designation as a National Scenic Byway. This is the only National Scenic Byway in the state. Kent County's portion of this Byway is Route 213 from the Chester River Bridge to Georgetown and the Sassafras River. Route 20 from Chestertown to Rock Hall also shares this honor, as well as Route 445 from Rock Hall to Eastern Neck National Wildlife Refuge.

The long, flat roads invite cyclists, the marshes are exceptional bird-watching territory, and the towns of Chestertown and Rock

Hall each offer visitors unique charm. This is a very beautiful place—it's no wonder so many visitors come here and decide to stay.

SIGHTS
Chesapeake Farms Agricultural and Wildlife Management Area

The 3,300 acres of Chesapeake Farms (Ricauds Branch/Langford Rd., 410/778-8400, www.dupont.com/ag/chesapeakefarms, free) are dedicated to the development, evaluation, and demonstration of advanced agricultural practices and wildlife management techniques. The farms are owned by a subsidiary of the Du-Pont company and are open to the public daily year-round by self-guided car tour. A brochure that directs visitors through the area is available online, at the Kent County Visitors Center in Chestertown, and at the headquarters just inside the entrance to Chesapeake Farms. The brochure discusses the use of various types of plantings and terrain that are demonstrated on the property; one of the field areas is heavily planted in sunflowers, reminiscent of a Van Gogh painting, in full bloom during July and August. Though visitors may spend as much time as they like touring the farms, they must remain in their cars, as their presence disturbs the natural movement of wildlife.

Chesapeake Farms experiments with various types of integrated pest management, as-needed pesticide use, and balanced wildlife/crop ratios. Birds and mammals are abundant on the property, and the migratory waterfowl rest area near the farm headquarters is a popular spot in the spring and fall.

Eastern Neck National Wildlife Refuge

Europeans settled Eastern Neck Island in the 1660s. Joseph Wickes built a mansion on the island, raised tobacco and other crops, and exported them on ships built at the family shipyard. Between 1800 and 1900, the original parcels of land were divided up into small family farms and a fishing village. The Chester

---

"THERE WAS SO MANY, THE SKY TURNED DARK"

This quote, ascribed to a waterman during the heyday of wildfowl hunting, describes the incredible bounty of ducks and other water birds that drew hunters to the marshes of the Chesapeake during the latter part of the 19th century. The upper bay and Susquehanna flats have evolved from a waterfowl center for the commercial trade – Philadelphia restaurants and hotels were a major market – to their current roles as playgrounds for private hunters. Decoy carvers such as P. Madison Mitchell, who plied his trade during the 1940s, have become celebrities.

By 1900, duck populations were decimated and the first national laws to protect them were established. Duck stamps, beautiful works of art in and of themselves, were sold as hunter's permits in an attempt to limit their numbers; this worked to some extent but not entirely. The new laws were difficult to enforce, and market hunters largely ignored them.

Prior to 1935, hunters scattered corn as bait and tied live geese and ducks near their blinds to draw wild birds. This practice was outlawed, as were sink boxes, bathtub-like boats in which the hunter sat, camouflaged. The sink box had wood-and-canvas panels fixed to each side, studded with decoys. Commercial hunters then used bushwhack boats, propelled by a single oar in the back to make as little noise as possible in the water. They often traveled in darkness (night hunting has been illegal since 1930). Today, hunters use duck calls and body booting, a method suitable only for the rugged – a hunter sits on a decoy rig in the water in a wet suit behind a one-dimensional painted decoy big enough to hide him.

Though overhunting depleted the waterfowl population prior to the 20th century, the greatest threat to wildlife now is depletion of wetlands habitat due to overpopulation in all areas of the Chesapeake Bay.

River Steam Boat Company operated a wharf that was served by steamships from Baltimore and other ports. During and after the 1920s, wealthy hunters were attracted to the area's concentration of waterfowl and bought portions of the island for hunting retreats. In the 1950s, a developer acquired a large tract and was preparing to turn it into 293 small houses when the U.S. Fish and Wildlife Service responded to the local outcry and purchased the entire island.

Eastern Neck National Wildlife Refuge (1730 Eastern Neck Rd., Rock Hall, 410/639-7056, dawn–dusk daily, free) includes a variety of habitats, including 1,000 acres of brackish tidal marsh, 600 acres of cropland, 500 acres of forest, 100 acres of grassland, and 40 acres of open water impoundments. Three threatened and/or endangered species, 243 species of birds, and a variety of mammals, amphibians, and reptiles inhabit the island. October through mid-March is the best time to see migratory waterfowl—the refuge staff has documented 40,000 waterfowl during peak periods and 32 different species have been reported, including Canada geese, tundra swans, and several species of ducks, including mallards, black ducks, and buffleheads. Songbird northern migration peaks late April–early May, and many species such as woodcocks, eagles, and bluebirds fledge during this period.

In addition to providing a sanctuary for the threatened southern bald eagle, the refuge is home to the endangered Delmarva fox squirrel. This species once lived throughout the Delmarva Peninsula and into southern Pennsylvania and New Jersey, though now it exists only in portions of four counties on the Eastern Shore of Maryland.

Six miles of roads and trails, including three wildlife trails and a butterfly trail with a handicapped-accessible observation deck featuring a panoramic view of the Chesapeake Bay may be reached from Route 445 in Rock Hall. At the Ingleside Recreation area on the west side of the refuge, there are facilities for crabbing and car-top boat launching from May 1–September 30. Picnic tables and grills are nearby. Bogle's Wharf is on the east side of the refuge and offers trailer boat-launching facilities for those with county permits (not available at the refuge office). Anglers like to cast off from the bridge that spans that Eastern Neck Narrows.

If you're going to hike the trails in this area, make sure you are mosquito- and tick-protected. During a bad infestation year, the grasses along the wooded marsh trails are perfect tick hangouts.

◖ Kent County Driving Tour

This 100-plus-mile drive covers Kent County from one end to the other and can be easily broken up into shorter segments, using Chestertown as a pivot point. Distances are approximate, though the roads are easy to see and clearly marked. Kent County's back roads are quite flat and seldom traveled—ideal for bikers and leisurely drivers.

The tour starts in Chestertown: Take Route 289 (Quaker Neck Rd.) five miles south from the city of Chestertown to the village of **Pomona.** In Pomona, turn north on Brices Mill Road—in about one mile, it becomes Ricauds Branch–Langford Road. This road was one of the nation's first turnpikes. In a little over two miles, you'll see **St. Paul's Episcopal Church** on the right. Erected in 1713, it's the oldest Episcopal Church in Maryland and contains the grave of actress Tallulah Bankhead, as well as that of colonial settler Daniel Coley, whose footstone admonishes: "Behold & see now here I lye; As you are so once was I."

Return to Ricauds Branch–Langford Road and continue west to Route 20. You'll pass **Chesapeake Farms,** a wildlife management demonstration area open to the public, on the left. Turn left (south) on Route 20 for six miles; continue to the town of **Rock Hall;** this scenic little village offers a number of attractions. You might also want to take Route 445 south approximately 10 miles to **Eastern Neck Island National Wildlife Refuge.**

After exploring Rock Hall, head north on Route. 445 about 10 miles to the intersection of Route 21. Continue nearly straight across the intersection; you're now on Bayshore Road, which curves around east to the village of

Fairlee (10 miles). Turn north on Route 298, travel 10 miles, and look for Cooper's Road on the left (north). Take this small two-lane road a little over six miles until it dead-ends, then turn right (east) to intercept Route 292. Turn left (north) to reach **Betterton** and Betterton Beach. You can see Aberdeen Proving Grounds across Chesapeake Bay from here.

Drive south five miles from Betterton on Route 292 to the town of **Still Pond.** The contemporary name is a corruption of "Steele's Pone," Steele being an early settler and "pone" meaning "favorite" in Elizabethan English. In 1908, the first enfranchised women in Maryland exercised their right to vote in Still Pond. Continue east about a mile on Route 566; keep an eye out for Bloomfield Road on the left. Take the small two-lane road north four miles to the intersection of Route 448. Turn left (north), and **Turner's Creek Wilderness Area** will be on the left.

Turn around and take Route 448 south five miles to the intersection of U.S. 213 in **Kennedyville.** Turn right on U.S. 213 to return to Chestertown (11 miles).

SHOPPING

One of the most mind-blowing sales in the world takes place in the vicinity of Kent County. **Dixon's Furniture Auction** (Rte. 544 at Rte. 290, Crumpton, on the border of Queen Anne's County, 410/928-3006) occurs every Wednesday except during Christmas week. It offers a mountain of goods of every quality and description in three "areas"—good, better, and best—with base prices gauged accordingly, from $15 up. A real live auctioneer goes over the merchandise piece by piece (better not be in a hurry if the plates you plan to bid on are on table #60).

Galena (Rte. 213 north of Chestertown) is home to several antiques, gift, and collectibles shops. **Galena Antiques Center** (N. Main St., 410/648-5781) is a multi-dealer co-op.

RECREATION

Kent County, flat as morning toast and liberally spread with a rich jam of quiet, scenic two-lane roads, is modestly famous for its **bicycle touring.** To celebrate this bounty, the Kent County Tourism Development Office (410/778-0416, tourism@kentcounty.com) offers several bike tours of varying length and complexity. The office can also give information on other popular dry-land entertainment, such as **hunting** and **sporting clays.**

Since the county is famed for its waterways as well as its roadways, **boat charters and rentals** abound, along with kayaks and other water toys. Many charters and equipment rental companies are in Rock Hall, but others exist as well; the tourism development office can provide an up-to-date list of all available charters and their points of origin.

ACCOMMODATIONS

The **Kitty Knight House** (Rte. 213, Georgetown, on the Sassafras River, 410/648-5200, www.kittyknight.com, $95–160) offers a healthy helping of history alongside its restaurants and lodgings. Kitty Knight moved away from her prominent Cecil County family, and in 1775 purchased the brick home that became the basis of the Kitty Knight House Inn. In May 1813, the British were burning and shelling agricultural ports that supported the American cause along the Eastern Chesapeake. Admiral Sir George Cockburn led British troops up the Sassafras River to set Georgetown aflame. Kitty, determined to defy the British and save her house, sat on the doorstep in spite of threats, orders to leave, and several attempts to set fire to the house. In the end, she prevailed, and her house was one of few spared. Forty years later, she was buried at the old Bohemia Church in Cecil County, and—proud of her single status to the end— insisted that her tombstone read "Miss Catherine Knight."

The Kitty Knight House Restaurant prides itself on serving fresh local meat, seafood, and vegetables, and will cook to order. The inn features a main dining room with a view of Georgetown Harbor. Dinner entrées average $19. Also on the premises: the more casual (and less expensive) Admiral Cockburn

Tavern. For overnight guests, each of the 11 rooms is equipped with a private bath and cable TV; the rooms vary in size and view.

Great Oak Manor (10568 Cliff Rd., 410/778-5943 or 800/504-3098, www.greatoak.com, $140–285) is a magnificent old Georgian country manor house eight miles from downtown Chestertown. It features 12 guestrooms with phones and private bath. Five of the rooms have working fireplaces, and the manor is next to a nine-hole golf course at Great Oak Landing.

FOOD

For an inexpensive snack, lunch, or light dinner, try **Procolinos Pizza** (Kent Plaza shopping center, Rte. 213, just north of Chestertown, 410/778-5900, 10 A.M.–10 P.M. daily, $10).

Village Bakery and Cafe (119D Main St., Galena, 410/648-6400, breakfast and lunch Tues.–Sat., brunch Sun., $6) offers a variety of fresh baked goods and sandwiches. On Sunday, the all-you-can-eat brunch buffet is very popular.

The Kennedyville Inn (11986 Augustine Herman Hwy./Rte. 213, Kennedyville, 410/348-2400, www.kennedyvilleinn.com, dinner Wed.–Sun., $12–24) has a reputation for innovative and excellent food. Its menu features emu with orange and ginger, and chicken breast with scallion pancakes and curry sauce.

GETTING AROUND

Transportation has never been easier or more fun (especially for those who come by water), thanks to the **Rock Hall Trolley Company** (410/639-7996 or VHF channel 71, www.rockhalltrolleys.com), offering regular trolley runs to and from and within Rock Hall and Chestertown. Trolley stops and times may be found at the Kent County Visitors Center or online. Unlimited daily use fares within towns are $3, the Rock Hall and Chestertown run costs $5, and babes in arms are free.

INFORMATION

Stop by the **Kent County Visitors Center** (122 North Cross St. at Rte. 213, Chestertown) for information and local brochures. For a free information packet, contact the **Kent County Tourism Development Office** (400 High St., Chestertown, 410/778-0416, www.kentcounty.com).

THE EASTERN SHORE

Maryland's Eastern Shore—also known as the upper Delmarva (DELaware, MARyland, and VirginiA) Peninsula—is bordered on the east by the Atlantic Ocean and Delaware Bay, and on the west by the mighty Chesapeake. If water views are what you're after, you'll achieve nirvana here. The peninsula has more than 7,000 miles of shoreline, hundreds of rivers, and thousands of acres of salt marshes—the Chesapeake is, after all, the largest inland estuary in the world. Several Wildlife Management areas touch the bay, including Blackwater, Fishing Bay, Ellis Bay, Deal Island, South Marsh Island north of Smith Island, and Cedar Island—all favored roosting places on the Atlantic flyway.

The bay is rich with opportunities for water recreation and is justly popular with boaters as well as landlubbers. From the Virginia border to the Bay Bridge, much of the southern central peninsula and northern part of Queen Anne's County that comprise Maryland's Eastern Shore continue to host small communities and vast farmland. A few cities—primarily Salisbury—have become more urbanized, though the population remains small.

Ocean City is a state unto itself. Once a spit of farmland, the area is now a playground for beach lovers, more like Miami than Maryland. However, there's plenty of fun to be found all over the Eastern Shore, whether you're seeking a quiet getaway or a social whirl.

HISTORY

For 11,000 years, the Eastern Shore was home to those who quietly farmed, hunted, and

© JOANNE MILLER

HIGHLIGHTS

◖ Chesapeake Bay Maritime Museum: Anyone interested in maritime history must visit this museum in St. Michaels which features more than 20 buildings of interactive exhibits on more than 18 acres; you'll find information on boat building, historic boats, decoys, and Chesapeake Bay life. Several historic vessels, such as the skipjack *Rosie Parks* and the log-bottom Bugeye *Edna E. Lockwood*, are docked on the waterfront (page 265).

◖ Islands and Towns Tour: This driving tour is a feast for the eyes. Travelers journey on a scenic route around the best of the area, starting in the attractive town of Cambridge and winding on back roads through Blackwater National Refuge, the watermen's community of Hooper's Island, and a variety of villages and buildings raised during European settlement – including Old Trinity Church on Taylor's Island, built between 1675 and 1690 (page 279).

◖ Ward Museum of Wildfowl Art: Visitors have to remind themselves that they are looking at carved and painted wood, not wild birds in flight. The work is extraordinary, as you might expect from the premier collection of wildfowl art in the world. The museum examines the history and heritage of the art, from antique working decoys to contemporary carvings (page 283).

◖ Gov. J. Millard Tawes Historical Museum: Set in the ultimate waterman's town and built on decades of oyster shells, the Governor J. Millard Tawes Historical Museum offers an intimate portrait of life in a port town. Guided walking tours are available from the Port of Crisfield (page 288).

◖ Ocean City Boardwalk: Stretching from the inlet north past 27th Street, the boardwalk functions as a chronological history of this fishing village/resort. The oldest and most active part of the boardwalk is between the inlet on South 1st Street and 8th Street, which includes the informative Ocean City Life-Saving Station Museum. People-watching, shops, all sorts of food concessions and rides and games make up a great place to spend a day or week (page 299).

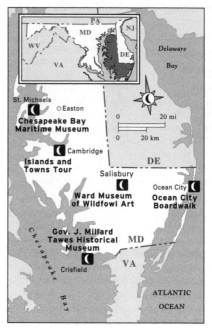

LOOK FOR ◖ TO FIND RECOMMENDED SIGHTS, ACTIVITIES, DINING, AND LODGING.

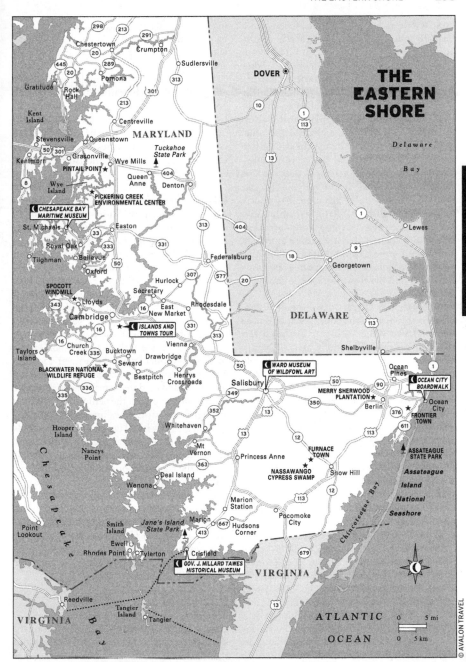

exploited the rich resources of the Chesapeake. Captain John Smith met the peaceful Algonquin-speaking Ozinies in what was to become Queen Anne's County in 1608 or 1609. Some 25 years later, William Claiborne established a trading fort on Kent Island—the first settlement in the state. Claiborne claimed that the territory belonged to Virginia; Lord Calvert insisted it was his, and the Ozinies and other natives left the area to escape the din of battle. Calvert won out, and British settlers followed the rivers and shorelines to clear the land for tobacco planting. In the early 1600s, one pound of the leaf could fetch more than double an average English sharecropper's annual income. Tobacco as a cash crop was so prevalent by the 18th century that it was used as money, and prices for most commodities were quoted in pounds of tobacco. Plantations grew along the rivers, and the rivers were the highways of the time.

Queen Anne's County was formally established in 1708, with the county seat at Queen Anne's Town (Queenstown). Within a few years, it was moved up the Corsica River to Centreville, which has the oldest courthouse in continuous use in Maryland (built in 1792).

By 1760, transatlantic tobacco trade prices were fluctuating wildly; many planters shifted to the blue-chip agricultural product of grain. The haphazard tobacco fields gave way to today's broad, orderly fields, and linked the Eastern Shore to northern markets, chiefly Philadelphia. Merchants from that area invested in local mills, including the Wye Mill, in order to control production and prices. Market towns like Centreville grew to reflect the bustling trade activity, and by 1820, 80 percent of arable land was under cultivation.

The industrial revolution brought steam power, and farm machinery increased productivity. At the same time, steam replaced sail and opened regional markets on the Chesapeake and Delaware Bays for produce, oysters, and fish. Steamboats plied the rivers of the Eastern Shore, and linked small towns with the outside world. Railroad lines were built throughout the region in the 1870s, and fishing and oyster-

ing boomed. Kent Narrows and Kent Island became important seafood processing centers, with as many as 12 packing houses operating at one time.

By the 1920s, steamboats themselves were obsolete, replaced by railroads. And the iron horse gave way to iron horsepower—automobiles—by the 1950s. Lifestyles remained slow on the Eastern Shore until 1952, when the completion of the first Chesapeake Bay Bridge ushered in rapid business, industrial, and real estate development.

ORIENTATION

Maryland's Eastern Shore covers a lot of (marshy) ground. Chesapeake Bay inundates the land, dividing it into hundreds of small bays and inlets. Rivers thread the entire peninsula, giving it the best of fresh- and salt-water environments. The main route, U.S. 50, crosses the Bay Bridge, slides down the coast to Cambridge, then hikes straight away east to Ocean City. U.S. 13 hops out of Delaware near Salisbury and runs south all the way to Crisfield.

The western side of the peninsula holds many smaller towns, all of which are attractive to boaters and landsmen for their antiques, rural surroundings, and outdoor recreation opportunities. In the southern part of the peninsula, Crisfield is an angler's paradise. The "interior"—including the villages of White Haven, Pocomoke, Snow Hill, and Berlin—is separated by wide swaths of farmland, streams and rivers. Salisbury, the "big city" of the Eastern Shore is a good place to base if you choose to spend your time in between the more populous areas, and want to explore the roads less traveled.

On the farthest reaches of Maryland's Eastern Shore, Ocean City becomes *the* big city only in the summer. It's made for family vacations and every rendition of beach life, from luxurious to casual beach bum.

PLANNING YOUR TIME

Whether you're coming up U.S. 13 from Virginia or traveling south on U.S. 50 from the Bay Bridge, the Eastern Shore of Maryland is a place to be savored slowly. You'll need a week to 10 days to appreciate the counties that make up the quintessential Tidewater—longer if you intend to take advantage of the fine cycling routes, particularly in Dorchester, Talbot, and Queen Anne's Counties. All of these areas are accessible by boat. Ocean City is the biggest and best-known destination on the Eastern Shore. It requires a week of your time just to work on your tan and your kite-flying skills.

As a first or last stop in contrast to the faster pace of Baltimore, plan a day in Queen Anne's County at **Wye and Environs,** including **Wye Mill,** a hike on **Wye Island,** and a snack pack from **Orrell's Maryland Beaten Biscuits** for a fillip of Eastern Shore ease. Stay in nearby **Queen Anne.** You can take the beautiful Tidewater farms, gentle pace of life, and quiet countryside home with you, at least in memory.

Though it's a tourist town, **St. Michaels,** in Talbot County, features the **Chesapeake Bay Maritime Museum,** a couple of hours of interest to anyone who loves the bay and boats. Make sure to visit the other towns in the area, particularly charming **Oxford** and **Easton** (stay for dinner). Two to three days in the area should give you plenty of time to see this well-loved part of the bay, and lodging and restaurant opportunities are plentiful.

Head south to Dorchester County, using **Cambridge** as a base for the **Islands and Towns Tour** (three hours of travel time) that includes **Blackwater National Wildlife Refuge.** This is also a good opportunity to enjoy the restaurant, spa, and golf course at the **Hyatt Regency.** Plan on at least two days here.

Schedule another two to three days in **Salisbury,** Wicomico County, for the **Ward Museum of Wildfowl Art** (two–three hours), the **Salisbury Zoo** (one hour), and the **Whitehaven Loop** (two hours of travel time), with dinner at the **Red Roost** and possibly an overnight in quiet **Whitehaven.**

In Somerset County, a stop in **Crisfield** should take two to three days—for the **Port of Crisfield Escorted Walking Tour** at the **Gov. J. Millard Tawes Historical Museum** (two hours) and a little fishing and shopping, while enjoying the beaches and trails of **Jane's**

Island State Park. Camping is particularly attractive here.

Worcester County's biggest attraction is **Ocean City,** a major destination. A week or more should be planned for laying around on the beach, playing miniature golf, eating seafood ad infinitum, and exploring the surrounding area. Day trips could include a trip down to Snow Hill and **Furnace Town** for a little history (two hours) and a canoe trip through peaceful marshlands (day-long). **Assateague Island** is an all-day must-see, if only for the adorable ponies.

FESTIVALS AND EVENTS

Ocean City holds events year-round in its convention center, including a big boat show in February. Many events are handled by individuals, so the listed phone numbers may not be accurate—call the local convention and visitors bureau at 800/OC-OCEAN (800/626-2326) for an updated list. St. Michaels Business Association (800/808-7622, www.stmichaelsmd .org) sponsors events around all major holidays, especially Halloween and Christmas.

In late March or early April, the prestigious **Ward World Championship Wildfowl Carving Competition** (Salisbury, 410/742-4988), held since 1970, includes a weekend of activities.

Get those arms in shape for the **Nanticoke River Canoe and Kayak Race,** an 8.1-mile course from Mardela Springs to Vienna at the end of April. This is the first in five races that make up the Delmarva Circuit.

The first week in May, **Spring Fest** (800/ 626-2326) is the "official" opening weekend of Ocean City. Four days of activities include entertainment, arts, crafts and food. The end of September or beginning of October is the official "closing" of the beach, and **Sunfest** is the four-day party that ends the summer with a bang.

The **Annual Antique & Classic Boat Festival** (410/745-2916), held at the Chesapeake Bay Maritime Museum in St. Michaels, features more than 100 classic boats and automobiles in a judged show. There are also seminars and special exhibits, free with admission.

In July, the **Tuckahoe Steam and Gas Show** (410/822-9868) in Easton features the huffing and puffing of a variety of antique steam engines, gas engines, blacksmith displays, a museum, a horse pull, and an auction.

The annual **Thunder on the Narrows** (http://kentnarrowsracing.com), in Kent Narrows, features hydroplane and speed skiff racing in August.

Also in August, Ocean City's **White Marlin Open** (800/626-2326, www.whitemarlinopen .com) offers cash prizes of $850,000, with more than 250 boats competing for record-setting catches of white marlin, blue marlin, wahoo, tuna, and shark.

The Annual Skipjack Races & Festival (410/784-2811 or 800/521-9189, www.skipjack .net/races) is held Labor Day weekend in September on Deal Island. Food, arts and crafts, and family activities are offered.

The **Pemberton Colonial Fair** (410/742-1741), held outside Salisbury, combines 18th-century games, performances (including period dancing, and dressage and other horse events), and booths in an authentic country manor house and grounds.

Olde Princess Anne Days (800/521-9189, www.visitsomerset.com/events) have been held since the late 1950s and remain as popular as ever. The historic house and garden tour and colonial fair takes place over two days in October.

Furnace Town, near Snow Hill, hosts the **Chesapeake Celtic Festival** (410/632-2032) in October. It features music, dancing, sheepherding, a medieval encampment, and food and crafts vendors.

In November, the **Waterfowl Festival** (www .waterfowlfestival.org) takes over the town of Easton (the streets are closed and decorated). This is one of the biggest events on the Eastern Shore, featuring art, sculpture, duck stamps, crafts, demonstrations, food, music, and more.

Ocean City sponsors a big **Christmas Parade** (410/524-9000) each year, featuring floats, bands, motorcycles, and all relevant Clauses.

GETTING THERE AND AROUND
By Air
Commuter airlines service the Salisbury airport from Baltimore and Washington, D.C., but that remains the only air access other than small planes. There is a small airport in Ocean City, and **regional airports** on Kent Island and in Easton and Cambridge, as well as in the vicinity of Salisbury and Crisfield. Commuter flights are available from BWI in Baltimore and all major airports in the Washington, D.C., area.

By Bus
Greyhound Bus (800/229-9424, www.grey hound.com) service is available to Stevensville (Kent Island), Easton, St. Michaels, Cambridge, Salisbury, Crisfield, Princess Anne, and Ocean City, with limited service to Vienna.

For local intra-city transportation, **Shore Transit** (443/260-2300, www.shoretransit .org) offers limited regional routes in Somerset, Wicomico, Dorchester, and Worcester Counties on Maryland's lower Eastern Shore. Caroline, Dorchester, Kent, Talbot and Queen Anne's Counties are served by **Maryland Upper Shore Transit** (MUST, 866/330-6878, www.mustbus.info).Generally, the exact fare of $1–2 is required.

By Car
Main car access to the Delmarva Peninsula from the west is the Bay Bridge, U.S. 50, which reaches all the way to Ocean City. The area is very spread out—for sightseeing, a car is really the only option. U.S. 13, which begins in Delaware, is the main north–south route. Other roads are generally well-maintained two-lane blacktop.

Wye Island and Vicinity

The area around the Wye River came to the attention of many Americans in the 1990s as the site of a series of peace talks between Israeli and Palestinian leaders hosted by President Clinton. The talks took place in a private plantation home on Wye Island.

SIGHTS
Wye Island NRMA
The entire island is designated a Natural Resource Management Area. Located at the end of Carmichael Road, Wye Island consists of a number of private homes in a scenic jewel of a rustic setting. There are turnoffs on the single road where visitors may park their cars and walk tree-lined lanes filled with songbirds, including the rare indigo bunting. The state of Maryland purchased the 2,450-acre island in the 1970s, when the original 13 farms were in danger of being broken up for development.

Village of Wye
The village, on Route 662, is home to the **Wye Grist Mill** (14296 Old Wye Mills Rd./Rte. 662, 410/827-3850, 10 A.M.–4 P.M. Thurs.–Sun. mid-Apr.–early Nov., $2), one of the earliest and most authentic industrial sites in Maryland. On the first and third Saturday of the month, volunteers demonstrate the traditional stone grinding process.

A mill has been operating on the site for more than 300 years. In fact, the milling operations were significant enough that the Maryland General Assembly of 1706 created Queen Anne's County using the mill as a reference point. In 1956, the mill and one acre were deeded by the state to Preservation Maryland. Today, the mill grinds Eastern Shore corn and wheat and Pennsylvania buckwheat by the traditional stone method using water power only, and visitors may purchase the flours. The small mill is a perfectly preserved example of colonial era technology, right down to the conduit pipes made of boards battened together. A video and exhibit chronicle the Eastern Shore's role in the

A LONG WAY FROM HAVANA

In April 2000, Wye Island became another sort of refuge. Elian Gonzalez, along with his father, stepmother, and baby half-brother, moved to a two-story white farmhouse on the grounds of the secluded Wye River Conference Center, the 1,100-acre estate that was home to one of the state's first governors, William Paca. The conference center, 70 miles east of Washington, is perhaps best known as the site of the Middle East peace negotiations in 1996 and 1998. The Gonzalez family was awaiting court action on whether the six-year-old boy should be granted an asylum hearing or be allowed to return with his father to his birthplace.

Elian was a survivor of a shipload of Cuban refugees that sank off the coast of Florida, and became a cause célèbre when relatives in the Miami Cuban community insisted that he stay in the United States rather than return home to his father and Castro's Cuba.

Before being moved to Wye Island, Elian's Cuban family had been staying at Andrews Air Force Base since their arrival in the United States. To reunite the family, Elian was forcibly removed from the home of his Miami relatives.

One neighbor said he didn't think Elian's visit caused nearly the commotion of the 1998 peace talks, when Secret Service agents shut down the road leading to the estate. "That's the only time we had security that high, when the president was here," said Kevin Compton, operations manager at Pintail Point Farm. "There's constantly stuff going on down there that requires security, but we don't ever feel it."

Elian returned to Cuba with his father at the end of June 2000.

19th-century agricultural boom. Each year, on the Saturday nearest June 26, Wye Mill hosts a harvest craft fair.

The 96-foot tall **Wye Oak,** south of the grist mill in the village, was a sight to behold. The tree had been around since 1540—it pushed up out of the ground barely 50 years after Columbus reputedly set foot on American soil. When Europeans first explored the upper regions of the Chesapeake Bay, this white oak was already fully mature. In 1909, the tree was recorded as the largest white oak specimen in the eastern United States—it was 32 feet in circumference, with a crown spread of 119 feet. Windfall was a continual threat to the old timer; over 100 cables intertwined throughout the crown to prevent the stiff limbs from snapping during high winds. In 2002, the Wye Oak lost its final battle with the elements and came down. Seedlings were planted at Mount Vernon and in 29-acre Wye Oak State Park behind the tree prior to its fall. Near the site of the old tree, a small brick building, **Wye School,** may have also been used as a plantation office or dwelling. Just down the road is the still-active **Old Wye Church,** built in 1717 and restored in the 1940s.

RECREATION
Pintail Point at
The River Plantation

On the way to Wye Island (511 Pintail Point Ln., Queenstown, 410/827-7029, www.pintail point.com), Pintail Point is a sort of Disneyland for sportsmen. The property has the look of a very wealthy private retreat and offers deluxe lodging (see the *Accommodations* section in this chapter) and extensive fishing, hunting, and sporting clay activities. Guests may take any of a number of fly-fishing classes, from casting to fly-tying, and may fish in the freshwater ponds on the property or take one of several charters out on the Chesapeake. Hunters can pursue deer, wild duck, sea duck, and dove hunting in season, or take advantage of Pintail's hunting preserve. Guests may bring their own dogs, or select one from the facility's kennels. Those more interested in sport shooting—golf with a gun—enjoy Pintail's

22-station shooting clay range. The "Cast and Blast" package features a half day of charter boat fishing, lunch, and a round of 50 targets on the sporting clay course. All equipment may be rented. The River Plantation also manages Hunters Oak Golf Club (500 Amberly Lane, Queenstown, 800/697-1777), for those who prefer the traditional game.

ACCOMMODATIONS AND FOOD

◖ **Pintail Point** (511 Pintail Point Ln., Queenstown, 410/827-7065, $185–500) offers guests several sporting activities and beautiful accommodations. Because of the isolated rural setting, visitors who have no interest in sports can still enjoy a quiet retreat. There are two bed-and-breakfast locations on the property. A 1936 English Tudor, the Manor House, is surrounded by gardens and walking paths along the Wye River. Three rooms, one suite, and a cottage, all with private baths, are available. Irishtown, an early-1900s farmhouse with three bedrooms and two baths, rents at $500 per night for the entire house.

A visit to Wye wouldn't be complete without a stop at **Orrell's Maryland Beaten Biscuits** (Rte. 662 next to the Old Wye Church, 410/822-2065, www.beatenbiscuits .bizland.com). Hot biscuits are available at the shop 9 A.M.–1 P.M. every Tuesday and Wednesday, and Orrell's might be open at other times—call if you're in the area. If you've never had a beaten biscuit, the first bite might be a shock: Even fresh out of the oven, the exterior is more reminiscent of granite than flour and water. The inside, however, is as tender and light as goose down. "Beaten," to me, means pummeled with a spoon—these biscuits date back to the plantation era, when leavening was in short supply and the term "beaten" was literal. Some cooks used a hammer, some the back of an axe—at Orrell's, the preferred instrument is a baseball bat. One old recipe states, "Beat 30 minutes for family and 45 for company." As you might expect, everyone at Orrell's is very mellow. Ruth Orrell began the biscuit business in 1935 using her mother's recipe, and the little bakery employs many of the neighboring women, who sit around the table in flowered aprons chatting and pinching off dough into biscuit-sized balls. Nothing settles an upset stomach faster, and odd as they may seem at first bite ("Should I eat it or skip it across the lake?"), they definitely grow on you. Ruth has a hefty business shipping biscuits all over the country. Call her or log onto her website and she'll send you a dozen or more of regular, honey, cheese, cayenne and cheese, or flat.

Greater Queen Anne's County

This county, which includes the Bay Bridge, Kent Island, and the gateway to the Eastern Shore, remains largely farmland, with a few small towns and commercial centers.

SIGHTS
Horsehead Wetlands Center
The center, administered by the Wildfowl Trust of North America (Perry Corner Rd., Grasonville, 410/827-6694, 9 A.M.–5 P.M. daily except major holidays, $5 adults, $4 seniors, $2 kids 18 and under) is composed of six distinct wetland habitats in 500 acres.

The Wildfowl Trust was established in 1979 by a group of conservationists who modeled it after similar organizations in the United Kingdom. The Grasonville property's original purpose was waterfowl research, though it's now used to study migratory behavior and patterns, and serves as an education and information center. Migrating birds pass through the property seasonally, and a captive population of waterfowl and raptors is kept on the property—many are birds that were injured in the wild and were unable to survive on their own, such as a blind owl and an eagle with an injured wing. The center offers an environmental science camp and other educational programs throughout the year. Four easy trails, all less than a mile, lead visitors through differing habitats and gardens. Several ponds and lakes are home to turtles and other amphibians, and the surrounding marshes support wildflowers and butterflies. A visitors center offers information on the wide variety of birds that pass through the area, and also has a small, well-stocked gift shop.

Queen Anne's Museum of Eastern Shore Life
This small museum (126 Dulin Clark Rd., Centreville, 410/758-8641) displays artifacts, household furnishings, and farmers' and watermen's gear from the past and present. Exhibits focus on rural life on the Eastern Shore. This is one of several historic sites administered by the Historic Sites Consortium of Queen Anne's County (888/400-7787). Others include the Tucker House, Wright's Chance, and the county courthouse in Centreville; the Cray House, old post office, and train depot in Stevensville; the colonial courthouse in Queenstown; Dudley's Chapel and the train station in Sudlersville; the Wye grist mill; and the Church Hill theater. If local history interests you, order an excellent free brochure, "Explore Our History and Heritage," by contacting the Historic Sites consortium (410/604-2100 or 888/400-7787, hsc@historicqac.org) with your name and address. You can also get one from the Office of Tourism (425 Piney Narrows Rd., 410/604-2100, www.qac.org/depts/tourism).

SHOPPING
Chesapeake Outlet Village (Rte. 301, Queenstown) will satisfy your needs for a quick outlet-shopping fix on the Eastern Shore. All the standards are there: Mikasa, Jones New York, Dansk, and more. Most shops are open daily.

Chesapeake Antique Center (www.chesapeakeantiques.com, open daily), adjacent to the Chesapeake Outlet Village on Route 301, is a multi-dealer antiques marketplace with a little of everything.

Though it's on the border of Queen Anne's

and Kent Counties, **Dixon's Furniture Auction** (intersection of Rte. 544 and Rte. 290, Crumpton, 410/928-3006) is worth a special trip. A public auction takes place every Wednesday. It offers a mountain of goods of every quality and description in three "areas"— good, better, and best, with base prices gauged accordingly, from $15 up. A live auctioneer goes over the merchandise piece by piece and tends to move fast, but be prepared to wait if the merchandise you want sits on the tables farthest from the front.

Kent Fort Farm (135 Eastern Ln., Stevensville, 410/643-1650, 9 A.M.–5 P.M. Wed. and Fri.–Sat., 10 A.M.–4 P.M. Sun. early summer–fall, weekends only in Oct.) is a great place to take the kids. It offers a variety of pick-your-own fruit. There's an annual peach festival the first Saturday in August, and a pumpkin patch on October weekends. Please note: This is a cash-only business.

RECREATION
Tuckahoe State Park

Tuckahoe Creek runs through the length of this park (13070 Crouse Mill Rd., Queen Anne, 410/820-1668). A lake offers boating and fishing, and the Adkins Arboretum encompasses 500 acres of park land and almost three miles of surfaced walkways leading through the tagged native species of trees and shrubs. The park offers scenic hiking, biking and equestrian trails, flat water canoeing, Visitors take advantage of numerous seasonal activities, such as bird watching and guided walks. Pets are allowed in the family camping area and most of the park, except the lake area, as long as they remain on a leash.

Boating and Canoeing: Canoeing at Tuckahoe is a popular activity on both the 60-acre lake and the creek because of the park's abundant wildlife. Visitors share space with bald eagles, ospreys, and great blue herons; beavers and muskrats have surprised visitors by swimming past their canoes. Tuckahoe is full of pockets of secluded beauty, some accessible only by canoe. Canoes, kayaks, and paddle boats may be rented for a daily fee. Guided canoe trips on

both the lake and the Tuckahoe Creek are offered throughout the year by the park naturalist. Gasoline motor use is prohibited.

Hiking, Biking, and Horses: Tuckahoe boasts 20 miles of excellent hiking, biking, and equestrian trails, such as the Tuckahoe Valley Trail, a self-guided Natural Trail, the Physical Fitness Trail, and the Lake Trail.

Camping: The park offers 51 single-family sites, 33 with electric hookups, and a central bathhouse. In addition, there's a youth group camping area with four sites, each site accommodating up to 30 people with a central bathhouse with showers and toilet facilities. Four camper (rustic) cabins are available; each cabin sleeps four and is equipped with a ceiling fan, electricity, and air conditioning, but no running water. Call 888/432-2267 for reservations.

Getting There: Tuckahoe State Park is located approximately 35 miles east of the Bay Bridge, just off Route 404. Travel east on Route 50/301 across the Bay Bridge. Route 50/301 splits; bear to the right on Route 50. Make a left at the intersection of Routes 50 and 404. Go approximately eight miles to the intersection of Routes 404 and 480. Make a left on Route 480. Eveland Road is on your immediate left. Once on Eveland Road, follow the directional signs.

ACCOMMODATIONS

◖ **Kent Manor Inn** (500 Kent Manor Dr., Rte. 8 south, Stevensville, Kent Island, 410/643-5757 or 800/820-4511, www.kentmanor.com, $180–265) was established on one of the oldest tracts of land in Maryland, dating back to 1651. The main section of the current hotel was built in 1820. More than 226 acres of the original farm surround the manor house, and all rooms in the gracious (and completely modernized) inn have a water view, private bath, and telephone. Kent Manor Inn has been designated a "Historic Hotel of America" by the National Trust for Historic Preservation. The elegant building, with its expansive lawns and gardens, is frequently a site for weddings. The inn also offers formal lunch and dinner in their first floor dining room; in summer, the windows look out on the lawns and inlet, and in winter, the Victorian fireplaces fill the space with warmth and light. The dining room is open to the public.

Stillwater Inn Bed & Breakfast (7109 2nd Ave., Queenstown, 410/827-9362, $125) is a stroll away from Queenstown Creek. This charming, airy, country-style B&B was built in 1904 for a local doctor, and sometimes served as the vestry of Wye parish before becoming a bed-and-breakfast. Both of the guestrooms have a private bath. The innkeepers, Kevin and Linda Vasbinder, serve a full country breakfast in the morning (included in room rate); Kevin's library may contain every fantasy book ever written, and it's tempting to sink into a world of sword and sorcery. Guests will enjoy the lovely private garden in the warmer months. It's a good idea to get directions from the innkeepers, as many of the streets of Queenstown were modified from narrow alleys and don't necessarily connect in a logical way. The old town area seems a million miles away from busy Route 301, though it's less than one mile.

FOOD
Quick and Cheap
Though the Kent Narrows and surrounding area are famous for big seafood restaurants, there are a few inexpensive places to eat that are quite good. Anyone who's crossed the bridge more than once knows **(Holly's** (five miles east of the bridge on Rte. 50 in Grasonville, 410/827-8711, 7 A.M.–9:30 P.M. daily, $7–18). This Eastern Shore institution is a restaurant and motel, opened by the Ewing family in 1955. Judging from the decor and the prices, Holly's remains firmly in the '50s; you'll barely have time to name more than a few states and their capitals (the placemats quiz your geographical knowledge) before your fried chicken special arrives. Even if your U.S. geography is rusty (where exactly is Missouri?), the food will make you feel smart. Real milkshakes and whole apple dumplings star on the diner-style menu, and most salads and sandwiches run under $7.

Chesapeake Chicken & Rockin' Ribs (on the north side of Rte. 50 at 101 Hissey Rd., seven miles east of the bridge, 410/827-0030, lunch and dinner daily) is a locally owned barbecue joint with tasty platters. Chicken with two sides is under $11, ribs and two sides are $15. You can eat in the cheerful dining room or get everything to go—party platters that serve up to 40 people are a specialty. It also offers excellent chicken soup and salads.

Bob's Mini Mart & Deli (102 Clay Dr., Queenstown, 410/827-8780, 5:30 A.M.–8 P.M. Mon.–Sat., $5 and under) isn't fancy, but the sandwiches, subs, and salads are good, and everything is prepared to order. The prices rival fast food. Yes, it's in a gas station, but there's a separate sit-down dining area. This is the place where the locals eat, and it's often very crowded around lunchtime.

Seafood
The large seafood eateries on Kent Island on the east end of the bridge range in quality and price. **Annie's** (500 Kent Narrows Way, 410/827-7103, lunch and dinner daily, salads and sandwiches $8, dinner $22) doesn't specialize—the menu is several pages long and includes all the local seafood dishes (steamed clams, crab cakes), Angus beef, sandwiches, salads, and Italian specialties (a local favorite). This is a big, casual place, with big plates—not gourmet, but perfect for the hearty eater who wants a lot of choices. Reservations are accepted.

(The Narrows (3023 Kent Narrows Way S., Grasonville, 410/827-8113, www.thenarrows restaurant.com, lunch and dinner daily, $10–27) has an elegant feel without being stuffy, and the menu is sophisticated and well prepared. Lunch features items such as a steak-and-brie sandwich and pecan-crusted catfish, and dinner offers grilled chicken Oscar and filet mignon with broiled crab cakes, among other dishes. It also serves light suppers—a petite version of regular menu items for a few dollars less. Reservations are recommended.

Drive a few miles down Kent Island on Route 8, and you'll come to Kentmorr Road, which leads to a planned development built around a private airport. Many of the homes

© JOANNE MILLER

crabs packed for shipping

have airplanes parked nearby, and at the end of the road, you'll find **Kentmorr** (910 Kentmorr Rd., Stevensville, 410/643-2263, www.kent morr.com, 11:30 A.M.–9 P.M. daily, $7–25), an upscale neighborhood restaurant with spectacular views and a broad menu. Though the place is out of the way, it's very popular. The menu features steamed crabs, a raw bar, prepared seafood dishes, chicken and beef, and soups, pasta, and salads. The chef will barbecue your choice of meat, and prime rib is a specialty. The Sunday breakfast buffet is a local favorite. Dinner choices include chicken, steak with crab cake, and steamed crabs (market price).

INFORMATION

Questions about Queen Anne's can be answered by the **Queen Anne's County Office of Tourism** (425 Piney Narrows Rd., Chester, MD 21619, 410/604-2100, www.qac.org/depts/tourism). You can order a visitors guide online.

St. Michaels

Founded in 1677, this county was once a haven for shipbuilders, privateers, and blockade-runners. St. Michaels prides itself on civic cooperation during the War of 1812. When British marines converged for a night attack on the town's shipyards in 1813, the forewarned residents doused their lights and hung lanterns in trees and masts, drawing fire away from the town—only one house was hit. Shortly after, Frederick Douglass—born near Tuckahoe Creek—lived as a slave in St. Michaels in 1830. He taught at a clandestine school for blacks here, then escaped to freedom in 1836.

These days, the town is a destination for pleasure boaters and yachts flying international colors. *Power & Motoryacht Magazine* named St.

Michaels as one of America's favorite anchorages, out of 12 including Desolation Sound in British Columbia and Bimini in the Bahamas. During the summer, the town is bustling, though the action slows down markedly by October.

SIGHTS
⟨ Chesapeake Bay Maritime Museum

This sprawling enterprise (end of Mill St., Navy Point, 410/745-2916, www.cbmm.org, 10 A.M.–5 P.M. daily spring and autumn, until 6 P.M. in summer, until 4 P.M. in winter, $10 adults, $9 seniors, $5 children ages 6–17) is one of Maryland's top cultural attractions, and a major attraction on the Eastern Shore.

Twenty-three buildings contain interactive exhibits on boat building, historic boats, decoys, and Chesapeake Bay life. The museum spreads over 18 acres, and several historic vessels, such as the skipjack *Rosie Parks* and the log-bottom bugeye *Edna E. Lockwood,* are docked on the waterfront. The Hooper Strait Lighthouse, a fully restored 1879 screwpile wooden structure, is one of the most popular exhibits. Visitors can climb the narrow stairs, visit the living quarters, and see the Fresnel lens that surrounds the light on the top deck—it's the second largest size ever made. The octagonal lighthouse was moved from its former location several miles out in Chesapeake Bay when it was scheduled for destruction in the mid-1960s. The museum offers families overnight stays in the lighthouse during the summer.

On Tuesdays and Thursdays, the workshops are busy with the sounds of volunteers (more than 300 of them) repairing and maintaining the museum's all-wood boat collection. Much of the wood—mostly white cedar—is donated.

The museum sponsors a number of special events throughout the year. Of note are the Arts Festival, Antique and Classic Boat Festival (see *Festivals and Events* in this chapter), and an Antique and Classic Boat Festival in June, the largest of its kind. This event displays boats (from 80-foot yachts to 15-foot working skiffs), models, books, and boat races. The museum shop is well stocked with toys, souvenirs, and books about boats and Chesapeake Bay life.

THE EASTERN SHORE

© JOANNE MILLER

skipjack at Chesapeake Bay Maritime Museum

LOG CANOES AND SKIPJACKS

Water transport on the Chesapeake was developed to meet a number of needs, from swift transportation to food gathering. Most of the bay and the many rivers that feed it are quite shallow (less than 10 feet). Wind-powered watercraft with shallow drafts were a necessity, and working boats also needed to be speed-controlled. The typical Chesapeake working vessel is wide, shallow, and heavy.

Log canoes were modified from the common form of Native American transportation, burned and hollowed-out logs. Builders lashed together several of these logs to form a hull, then placed decking over the logs and built up planks from the sides. Three- and five-log canoes were common. An unusual nine-log canoe is restored at the Maritime Museum in St. Michaels, which also sponsors log canoe races throughout the summer. Log canoes built for working watermen were sometimes referred to as bugeyes, thought to be a corruption of "buckie" or "pungie," the Scottish word for oyster in colonial times.

Skipjacks are broad, shallow-draft sailing vessels made especially for oystering. Their slow and steady pace permitted watermen to drag a 12- to 15-foot-long set of "tongs" behind the boat and pull the mollusks off the bottom.

SHOPPING

Talbot Street, the main street in town, is lined with antiques and collectible shops, clothing stores, bookstores, and every imaginable outlet for spending money. Many of the shops are open only during the high season, roughly mid-April to November. Of note are the **Mind's Eye** (205 S. Talbot, 410/745-2023), a contemporary crafts gallery, and **Chesapeake Trading Co.** (102 S. Talbot St., 410/745-9797) a good place to find all things Chesapeake.

RECREATION

Landlubbers can get two-wheeled transportation courtesy of **St. Michaels Town Dock Marina** (305 Mulberry St., 410/745-2400). The marina rents single bicycles.

Tours

The glass-enclosed 65-foot *Patriot* cruises the Miles River, and during the one-hour outing, covers Talbot County history and Chesapeake lore (410/745-3100, www.patriotcruises.com). There's a snack and booze bar on board. You can catch the boat at 11 A.M., 12:30 P.M., 2:30 P.M., and 4 P.M. daily April–November. Captain Dave points out clammers, crabbers, and stately homes. It's docked next to the Maritime Museum, and ticket prices are $10 for adults, $4.50 for kids under 12.

Ed Farley welcomes visitors aboard his skipjack *H. M. Krentz* (410/745-6080, www.oystercatcher.com) for a two-hour sail mid-April–October ($30). Captain Farley, a working waterman, gives a lively commentary about life in and around the Chesapeake.

Dockside Express Land & Sea Tours of St. Michaels (P.O. Box 122, Tilghman, 888/312-7847, www.docksidexpress.com, $10 per person, by advance reservation only) features costumed guides who escort visitors for a one-hour walk around St. Michaels. The tour focuses on local history.

And, if a steady equestrian pace is appealing, try a horse-drawn carriage ride from **Chesapeake Carriage Company** (9072 New Rd., 410/745-4011); reservations are required.

ACCOMMODATIONS

St. Michaels has dozens of inns and B&Bs, as you might expect from a summer tourist mecca. Lodgings on the main street, Talbot, cost less but experience fairly constant traffic until the wee hours during the summer.

$100-150

The Parsonage Inn (210 N. Talbot St., 410/745-5519 or 800/394-5519, www.parsonage-inn.com, $100–195) suffers slightly from a location problem, but makes up for it with lovely brick Victorian architecture and pretty rooms.

The former owner, Dr. Henry Dodson, established the local brickyard in 1877 and built the house to show off different patterns in 1883. All eight rooms have private baths and include breakfast. Three rooms feature fireplaces.

The **George Brooks House** (24500 Rolles Range Rd., 410/745-0999, www.georgebrooks house.com, $95–225) earned the Historical Society of Talbot County's Heritage Award for best historic renovation. This 1908 Gothic Revival Victorian is named for its builder, an African American entrepreneur and author on race relations whose successful business ventures provided this home and care for his 11 orphaned nieces and nephews. Each of six bedrooms features a private bath, hand-carved mahogany furniture, and Waverly fabrics on the bed and windows. The seven-acre property also has formal gardens and an outdoor pool. Rooms include a gourmet breakfast. .

$150-250

Two historic properties were restored and joined to create **Five Gables Inn & Spa** (202 N. Talbot

---

LEGAL PIRACY

Too small and poor to equip a proper navy that could seriously threaten the Royal Navy during the War of 1812, the U.S. government relied on Yankee ingenuity. Congress encouraged ship owners, especially those of American merchant vessels designed to be fast on American waterways, to enlist their assets in the fight. American merchant vessels built in the colonies were designed to be fast and maneuverable on American waterways. Ships built in Fell's Point, Baltimore, were especially suitable – topsail schooners later dubbed Baltimore clippers. The experienced seamen who sailed them were not at all interested in giving up their lucrative positions to become government employees.

In order to ensure the participation of these merchant seamen, who were not interested in leaving their lucrative positions to become government employees, Congress gave private ships the legal right to attack and seize enemy vessels, and to keep a percentage of the spoils. Two types of commissions were authorized: The first was for privateers, whose sole mission was to seize enemy shipping; the other was letters of marque, which permitted the captain to engage in trade when possible and privateering when the opportunity arose.

During the 30 months that followed, civilian privateers captured so many ships and so much valuable cargo that British merchants brought pressure on their government to end the war. Baltimore alone docked 122 private armed vessels, and St. Michaels was another popular berth for privateers.

Each privateer captain was required to keep a journal and turn it over to the customs collector at his U.S. port of entry. Failure to do so resulted in a $1,000 fine and revocation of commission. In spite of the danger to their livelihood, some crossed the line into piracy. Captain Alexander Thompson of the *Midas* burned and sacked a plantation in Royal Island, Bahamas. Not long after the *Midas* put into port in North Carolina, news of the raid quickly reached President Monroe. Thompson was censured and lost his commission; he published a poetic rejoinder in the newspaper, which included these words:

> To lend a hand in time of need When Britain she did burn Our Towns in every Part with speed. Determined to avenge the Cause I thought I would support the Laws And pay him [the British King] in his Kind.
>
> [signed] The subject of the foregoing nonsense you may find at the sign of the 3 Living Squirrels, Fells Point Baltimore

A peace treaty signed on Christmas Eve 1814 ended Captain Thompson's censure – privateering was no longer allowed. He received his share of the considerable spoils he brought in and went on to command several trading vessels. He continued to reside at the Three Living Squirrels until his death in 1829.

St., 410/745-0100 or 877/466-0100, www.five gables.com, $150–425). It offers lodging and Aveda spa treatments, including herbal baths and massage. Spa services are additional, and spa package specials are available throughout the year.

Hambleton Inn (202 Cherry St., 410/745-3350 or 866/745-3350, www.hambletoninn.com, Apr.–Nov. $145–275, Dec.–Mar. $184–265) offers five rooms with private bath in a lovely 1860 Victorian. The inn is in the middle of St. Michaels, but is a quiet two blocks away from the main street, on the water. It's open year-round, and a dock slip is available for a nominal fee. Enclosed porches decorated with seasoned wicker furniture look out on the harbor.

Aida's Victoriana Inn (205 Cherry St., 410/745-3368 or 888/316-1282, www.victoriana inn.com, $149–279) is across the street from the Hambleton, with very similar ambience and facilities. It also offers seven rooms with full bath, and one room is pet-friendly.

$250 and Up

The fanciest place in town, the **(Inn at Perry Cabin** (308 Watkins Ln., 410/745-2200 or 800/722-2949, www.perrycabin.com, $330–770), was originally the dwelling place of Samuel Hambleton, aide-de-camp to Commodore Oliver Hazard Perry in the War of 1812. When Hambleton retired to St. Michaels in 1816, he designed the north wing of the manor house to resemble Perry's cabin on the flagship *Niagara*—the ship that won the battle of Lake Erie. The property changed hands several times, and in 1989, the Greek Revival–style inn and surrounding property was bought and renovated by Sir Bernard Ashley (husband of Laura Ashley of chintz-and-prints fame). The inn features 78 guestrooms and suites, dockage, a heated indoor pool, health complex, helicopter access, and conference center, all set in protected wetlands and carefully tended gardens; the ambience is a cross between an upper-crust English country house and a top-level American hotel. There's even a snooker room and a secret passage in the library. Each of the rooms is spacious and varied in layout and feeling, individually decorated with antiques and compatible mod-

ern amenities in a simple, sleek style. Many have fireplaces and telescopes for viewing marsh wildlife. Expensive? Oh, yes. But prices include a full breakfast and afternoon tea in the inn's exceptional restaurant, and guests receive full value—the rooms and service are superb, and the inn is far enough from downtown St. Michaels to be a peaceful retreat, yet close enough to be easily accessible.

FOOD

An inexpensive place for breakfast, lunch, and dinner, **Chesapeake Cove** (204 S. Talbot, 410/745-3300, 11 A.M.–4 P.M. Mon.–Tues., 11 A.M.–8 P.M. Wed.–Fri., 8 A.M.–8 P.M. Sat., 8 A.M.–6 P.M. Sun., $8–20) is often crowded with locals.

Acme Markets (114 S. Talbot, 410/745-9819, 7 A.M.–9 P.M. daily) is a good place to pick up picnic fixings and household items.

A former clam-shucking shack, the **Crab Claw** (304 Mill St., Navy Point next to the Maritime Museum, 410/745-2900, www.the crabclaw.com, lunch and dinner daily Mar.–Nov., $20) is reputed to have the best steamed crab around, and it serves crab in every other conceivable form, too.

The **(Sherwood's Landing** (in the Inn at Perry Cabin, 308 Watkins Ln., breakfast, lunch, tea, and dinner daily, breakfast $11, lunch $20, dinner $32, reservations required for dinner) is a wonderful splurge served in a chandelier-lit dining room. The menu and wine list reflect the continental leanings of Chef Mark Salter, who trained in Germany, Switzerland, and France before coming to Sir Bernard Ashley's Llangoed Hall Inn in Wales. The food is sophisticated and delicious—how about sweet chili–glazed veal short ribs and grilled jumbo shrimp on sautéed French beans with parsnip hash cake and crispy butternut squash chips ($34)?

INFORMATION

For local tourist information in St. Michaels, contact the **St. Michaels Business Association** (P.O. Box 1221, St. Michaels, MD 21663, 410/745-0411 or 800/808-7622, www.stmichaelsmd.org).

Tilghman Island

Pittsburgh Post-Gazette writer Jayne Clark once noted, "If St. Michaels appears perfectly coiffed, then its neighboring community of Tilghman Island hasn't shaved in a few days." Eighty percent of the 750 people who call Tilghman (TIL-man) home make their living as watermen. Of the 10–15 working skipjacks that remain in service on the Chesapeake, eight are moored on the island, in Dogwood Harbor. Several of these, along with larger boats, are available for charter.

RECREATION
Tours and Charter Boats

Wade Murphy (410/886-2176 or 410/829-3976) takes guests for two-hour pleasure cruises ($30) aboard the oldest skipjack under sail, the **Rebecca T. Ruark.** The *Rebecca* was built in 1886 and refuses to give in to age; she's won local skipjack races nine out of 10 times.

Captain Mike Richards (410/886-2215 or 800/690-5080, www.chesapeakelights.com) takes visitors out on the motor-powered **Sharpe's Island** for a cruise around five lighthouses on the Chesapeake Bay ($65) or a sunset cruise ($50). Longer trips are available by reservation. The captain also offers full- and half-day Chesapeake Lights Tours, a look at some or all of the bay's 10 lighthouses. Captain Chris Richards (800/690-5080) offers visitors a champagne sunset sail on the 45-foot 1935 Bay Ketch, **Lady Patty.**

Captain Bill Fish (yes!) operates **Nancy Ellen,** a bay boat finished off to yacht standards, and equipped with light tackle and fly fishing equipment.

ACCOMMODATIONS AND FOOD

Originally constructed in the 1920s as a fishing camp for vacationing anglers trying their luck at the Eastern Shore, the two-story **Sinclair House** (5718 Black Walnut Point Rd. 410/886-2147 or 888/859-2147, www.sinclairhouse.biz, $119–129) was converted into the island's first B&B and remains a historic landmark on Tilghman Island. Sinclair House's innkeepers have lived and worked around the world. Monica, from Peru, met Jake in Guinea-Bissau, West Africa, where she served as an international officer with UNICEF and he was on diplomatic assignment to the U.S. Embassy. During their travels, both innkeepers were avid collectors of local art and handicrafts. Sinclair House now displays their eclectic treasures. Each of the four guestrooms (all have private baths) has a theme: African, Indonesian, Moroccan, and Peruvian. The inn closes during the winter.

Black Walnut Point Inn (end of Black Walnut Rd., 410/886-2452, www.blackwalnut point.com, $120–225) has four rooms in the main building and a cottage, all with private baths, tennis courts, and a pool on 57 acres. Rates at this upscale private resort on the tip of Tilghman Island require a two-night minimum on weekends.

The **Lazyjack Inn** (5907 Tilghman Island Rd., off Dogwood Harbor, 410/886-2215 or 800/690-5080, www.lazyjackinn,com, $129–176) is as quiet and tranquil as it gets. The 160-year-old house offers four rooms, each with private bath, and each with a special feature, such as a water view, fireplace, or private entrance. Mike and Carol Richards make a sumptuous breakfast to greet you in the sunny dining room overlooking the harbor. Mike also operates the *Lady Patty.*

The **◖ Bay Hundred** (6178 Tilghman Rd., 410/886-2126, lunch and dinner daily, $10–29), just north of the Knapps Narrows Bridge, is a casual place with great views and good food. Owner Fanoula Sullivan brings sophistication to the usual seafood-restaurant menu, featuring filet Chesapeake (beef mignon in bacon, topped with crabmeat) and salmon Rockefeller (grilled, topped with fresh sautéed spinach). The menu is broad and eclectic; reservations are essential.

INFORMATION

For updated local tourist information on Tilghman Island, visit www.tilghmanisland.com and click on "Welcome to Tilghman Island."

Oxford

Judging strictly from its decelerated pace of life, Oxford is tough to peg as one of two ports of entry for all of colonial Maryland (the other was Anne Arundel, later known as Annapolis). Before the Revolution, Oxford was a booming shipping and trade town; after the loss of British ships and the subsequent trade, the town dwindled. Following the Civil War, Oxford entered into a new period of prosperity thanks to the railroad and increasing national markets for local oysters. With the diminution of the oyster beds in the early 1900s, Oxford once again tightened down. Today, the town is mainly a home for watermen and a sleepy getaway for visitors—there's not a lot to do in Oxford, and most people like it that way.

Oxford Custom House

SIGHTS
The Oxford Bellevue Ferry
The ferry (410/745-9023, www.oxfordbellevue ferry.com) has been in business since 1683, making it the oldest privately run ferry service in America. It crosses the Tred Avon River (0.75 mile), making 25–30 trips a day, and has counted Paul Newman and the prime minister of Madagascar among its passengers. The ferry runs 9 A.M.–sunset daily March 1–November. Drive or walk aboard: walk-on passengers pay $2, car and driver pay $8 one-way or $12 round-trip.

Oxford Historic Homes
Oxford has a number of buildings rich in the history of recent centuries. Most are private residences, so please enjoy them from the outside. **Oxford Custom House** (N. Morris St. and the Strand) created in 1976, is an exact replica of the first Federal Custom House built by Jeremiah Banning, the first Federal Collector of Customs. It's open weekends from April through late autumn. The **Academy House** (Bratt Mansion, 205 N. Morris St.) was the officers' residence for the Maryland Military Academy from 1848 to 1855. **Barnaby House** (212 N. Morris St.) was built in the 1770s by local captain Richard Barnaby. The **Grapevine House** (309 N. Morris St.) was built in 1798; the grapevine in front of the house was brought to Oxford from the Isle of Jersey in 1810.

Byberry and Calico are two houses moved to the grounds of **Cutts & Case** boatworks (306 Tilghman St.) in the 1930s. Byberry is Oxford's oldest house, dating from 1695. The original structure is a typical early Oxford cottage. Calico, a Tudor-style cottage, was built in the early 1700s. Cutts & Case is a family-owned business world-renowned for classic yacht design, construction, and restoration. Even those unfamiliar with wooden boats will recognize the shop's crossed-flags logo. The smell of shaved cedar fills the workshops, and beautiful wooden boats in all stages of restoration line the pier behind the buildings.

ACCOMMODATIONS AND FOOD
◖ The **Robert Morris Inn** (314 N. Morris St. and the Strand, 410/226-5111 or

888/823-4012, www.robertmorrisinn.com, breakfast and lunch daily, dinner Thurs.–Mon. Apr.–Nov.) dates back to 1710, when it was put together by ships' carpenters—evident in the wooden pegged paneling in the formal dining room. Robert Morris Jr. ran the Oxford-based shipping business started by his father; the endeavor was so successful, Morris was able to lend large sums of money to finance the colonies' fight against Britain. He counted George Washington as a friend, and, after warming up his pen hand writing checks to the Continental Congress, became a signer of the Declaration of Independence, the Articles of Confederation, and the U.S. Constitution. From April to November (and some winter weekends), the inn offers simply decorated bed-and-breakfast rooms in the main building (private baths, $110–290). The establishment is celebrated for its traditional Chesapeake seafood and fine dining—more casual in the back tavern and formal in the front dining room ($25). Author James Michener, who spent considerable time here researching his book *Chesapeake,* claims the inn's crab cakes are the best: "Raise a glass of beer in memory of an old-timer who enjoyed the place very much," he said.

Robert Morris Inn also owns the **Sandaway Lodge,** a rambling Victorian half a block away on a private beach (many rooms have enclosed porches, $140–290). Since the Sandaway is used frequently for weddings, the leafy interior of the gigantic weeping beech tree on the grounds has seen its share of tipsy wedding guests.

Combsberry (4837 Evergreen Rd., 410/226-5353, www.combsberry.com, $250–395) is just plain gorgeous, one of the premier historic homes on the Eastern Shore. The land was purchased in 1718 for 21,000 pounds of tobacco and 50 pounds of silver; the plantation's whitewashed brick manor house was built in 1730. After years of desultory care, the property was purchased by a group of investors for quick turnaround. Fortunately for visitors, the real estate market took a dive, and two of the partners, Mahmood and Ann Shariff, were reluctant to part with the property. They bought out their associates and restored the crumbling relic into an elegant, artistic guest house. Breakfast is served either in the formal dining room or in the country kitchen that overlooks the nine-acre grounds dotted with majestic magnolia and willow trees and informal gardens. Four guestrooms are in the main house, and two more are in a newly built carriage house. All have private baths and water views, and are decorated in English country style.

Also recommended in Oxford is the **Pier St. Restaurant and Marina** (W. Pier St., 410/226-5171, 11:30 A.M.–9 P.M. daily, $10 lunch, $20 dinner, closed during the winter), which serves an American menu strong on seafood.

INFORMATION

For local tourist information in Oxford, contact the **Oxford Business Association** (410/745-9023, www.portofoxford.com).

Easton

Easton almost has the look of a movie set—a handsome little town with unique, locally owned shops, an exceptional art museum, and carefully maintained homes. The county seat, Easton has been awarded the ongoing "Main Street" designation; and in 2000, it received recognition for excellence in the area of downtown revitalization set by the Maryland Main Street Program and the National Trust for Historic Preservation's National Main Street Center. If anything, it has more to offer visitors than ever. The message board at St. Andrew's Anglican Church in town advertises, "Broken hearts mended." What more could you ask?

SIGHTS
Academy of the Arts

The academy (106 South St., 410/822-2787,

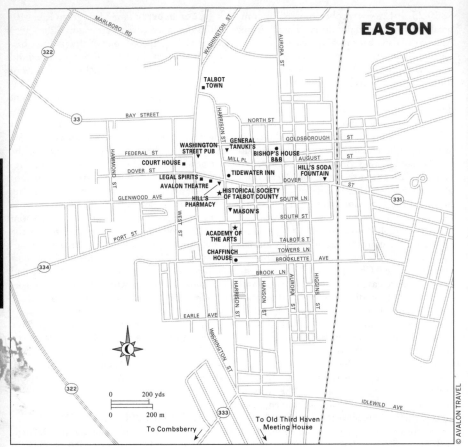

EASTON

www.art-academy.org, 10 A.M.–4 P.M. Mon.–Sat., open until 8 P.M. Tues.–Thurs., closed Aug., $3 adults, $2 children over 12) is a modern space in an old building.

The facade is a restored 1820s schoolhouse, but the inside is all space and light. The academy serves two main purposes: a public arts program with sunny, well-equipped workshops, and a display space for professionally curated exhibits. The quality of any display space reflects its curators, and the hardworking staff at the academy chooses extremely well. The museum often partners with the National Gallery of Art in Washington, D.C., and was the recipient of the Grover Batts Collection, 178 important works from artists such as Thomas Hart Benton and Rockwell Kent. Though the emphasis is on work by Eastern Shore residents, exhibitions include pieces by internationally acclaimed artists. A past exhibit focused on master Russian Impressionist Nikolai Timkov and his contemporaries. This work, though not widely known, was exceptional in every way. The permanent collection includes works by James McNeil Whistler, Grant Wood, Leonard Basking, and other notables.

Old Third Haven Meeting House

In 1682, a small group of Quakers took

© JOANNE MILLER

Easton Courthouse

two years to build what is now known as the meeting house (405 S. Washington St., 410/822-0293). The white clapboard building, still in use, is the oldest religious structure in the United States and the earliest dated building in Maryland. The meeting house stands in an open grove of trees at the end of a lane (look for the small sign on the west side of the street). It's almost always open, and in summer, you may see the resident family of fat woodchucks scurrying about. William Penn was among the prominent Quakers who sat in the simple wooden pews to worship; George Fox, founder of the Religious Society of Friends (Quakers) sent books to this meeting, establishing the first public library in the province. All are welcome to attend a meeting any Sunday at 10 A.M. (the brick building next to the meeting house is used in the winter).

ENTERTAINMENT AND RECREATION
Historical Society Tours

The Society (25 S. Washington St., 410/822-0773, www.hstc.org) offers several walking tours of the town to acquaint visitors with its many historic buildings. The South Washington Street offices house a permanent exhibit of local history (10 A.M.–4 P.M. Mon.–Sat., free) and operates **Tharpe Antiques & Decorative Arts** (30 S. Washington St.) as a museum shop. The Historical Society's "The Craftsmen and the Collector Tour" is a 45-minute guided tour of three houses that represent each of the three centuries since the founding of Talbot County in 1662—"Ending of Controversie" is a faithful reproduction of the 1670 home of Quaker Wenlock Christison. The Joseph Neall House was the residence and shop of a Quaker craftsman of the late 18th century, and the James Neall House (1810) was built in the federal style for a family of 11, plus retainers.

The Historical Society also offers a Frederick Douglass Driving Tour that includes 14 sites connected to the abolitionist, including his birthplace. Ask for a brochure at the offices or by phone.

Avalon Theatre

The theater (40 East Dover St., 410/822-7299,

THE EASTERN SHORE

www.avalontheatre.com) presents lively year-round entertainment, including movies, choirs, musicians from the Caribbean and New Orleans, and ornate displays (one year, model trains and railroad lore filled the space at Christmas). The real star, though, is the restored art deco theater itself, with its state-of-the-art sound and lighting systems. Call for the schedule.

Pickering Creek Audubon Center

This is a private sanctuary operated by the Audubon Society (11450 Audubon Ln., 410/822-4903, www.pickeringcreek.org, 8:30 A.M.–5 P.M. Mon.–Fri., 10 A.M.–4 P.M. Sat., donations appreciated). The buildings are closed on Sunday, but the grounds are open to visitors. The property—the home of a Matapeake Indian village prior to European colonization—features more than 100 acres of hardwood forest, including old-growth oak, beech, and hickory, and 270 acres under low-impact cultivation (an organic community garden). Additional acreage is in conservation easements, buffer strips, wildlife plantings (where local farmers plant a certain portion of the land in feed for wildlife), and a nature preserve. There's a mile of shoreline, and fresh and brackish marshes on the Wye River. The thrust here is on education, and the center offers numerous opportunities to enjoy the outdoors and learn. Evening canoe trips, forest ecology walks, herb workshops, and sea kayaking are a few of the one- and two-day programs that take place throughout the warmer months.

There's a nature walk, and the sanctuary is studded with more than 40 bluebird boxes—as you might expect of the Audubon Society, this is an excellent bird-watching location. To get there, take Route 662 north from Easton (this runs parallel with U.S. 50) past the Easton Airport. Follow the signs: Turn left at Sharp Road (west), and veer right at the Y. Turn right (north) to Presquille Road, then right on Audubon Lane.

SHOPPING

Harrison Street in Easton is the site of several antiques and collectibles shops. Contemporary crafts and clothing shops also line the street. **Talbot Town** (218 N. Washington St.), a small in-town mall, features a Talbots (no relation) and several upscale home decorating shops. **Courthouse Square Shops** line a pass-through from Harrison Street to Washington Street; of note is **Rowens Stationery Store,** featuring local-interest books as well as bestsellers.

There are several antique shops and multi-dealer shops in the 7700 and 7800 blocks of **Ocean Gateway** (Rte. 50). **Foxwell's** (7793 Ocean Gateway) and **Camelot Antiques** (7871 Ocean Gateway) are representative. The **Wood Duck** (8374 Ocean Gateway) is a gallery featuring decoys, carvings, limited editions, and original artwork. Also check out **Sullivan's Antiques Warehouse** (28272 St. Michaels Rd./Rte. 33).

A favorite **"nameless" store** is at the intersection of Royal Oak Road and Bellevue Ferry Road. Two old buildings stand across from one another—one has furniture piled end over end, and the other has everything else. Great prices and great fun.

ACCOMMODATIONS

The **Tidewater Inn** (101 E. Dover St., 410/822-1300 or 800/237-8775, www.tidewaterinn.com, room $109–269, suite $300) combines the intimate feel of a B&B with the amenities of a large hotel. Once a haunt of camouflage-coated goose hunters, the inn caters to upscale customers today (the goose hunters are still there, but now they dress for dinner). It's not as formal as it sounds, but leave the muddy boots and dogs outside. They're tough on the carpet and mahogany antiques in the lobby—and they'll wreak havoc in the pool. This is the best "modern" hotel in the area. It offers special-rate packages throughout the year, and there's a sophisticated restaurant on the premises (brunch 10 A.M.–4 P.M. Sat.–Sun., lunch 11 A.M.–4 P.M. Mon. and Thurs.–Fri., dinner 4 P.M.–10 P.M. Thurs.–Mon., $9–30). The **Decanter Wine Room** features more than 2,000 wine selections.

If an 1893 Queen Anne Victorian is more to your taste, try **Chaffinch House** (132 S.

Harrison St., 410/822-5074 or 800/861-5074, $140–180). All of the rooms have private baths and are decorated in period style.

Also recommended is the **Bishop's House B&B** (214 Goldsborough St., 410/820-7290 or 800/223-7290, www.bishophouse.com, $180–190).

FOOD

⟨ Mason's (22 S. Harrison St., 410/822-3204, www.masonsgourmet.com, lunch and dinner daily, $8–32) is a charming place to stop for a delicious gourmet lunch or dinner (try the rockfish tournado stuffed with local crab, $28), followed by handmade chocolates. It was noted by *Wine Spectator* magazine as one of the "best restaurants in the world for wine lovers."

Hill's Soda Fountain, in Hill's Drug Stores (32 E. Dover St., 410/822-2666, store open 8 A.M.–7 P.M. Mon.–Sat., fountain open 8 A.M.–4 P.M. Mon.–Fri., 8 A.M.–3 P.M. Sat., closed Sun., $7) is the real thing. You'll find malts and burgers, tuna sandwiches, and chips.

General Tanuki's (25 Goldsborough St., 410/819-0707, lunch, and dinner Mon.–Sat., dinner Sun., $9–25) features an eclectic menu with a pan-Asian influence. Lunch sandwiches include the "Thanksgiving": smoked turkey and wild mushroom stuffing with orange chili sauce on marble rye ($10), and the dinner menu features Hawaiian pizzas ($10) and Thai mussels ($19).

Legal Spirits Tavern (42 East Dover St., 410/820-0765, lunch and dinner daily, lunch $9, dinner $22) offers Eastern Shore cuisine—cream of crab soup is a specialty—complete with copious desserts.

One of the local happening hot spots at night is the **Washington Street Pub,** across from the courthouse (20 N. Washington, 410/822-9011, www.wstpub.com, lunch and dinner daily, $7–18). It has a raw bar and 19 of the coldest beers in town on tap.

INFORMATION

For updates on Easton, contact the **Easton Business Management Association** (410/822-0065, www.eastonmd.org).

Greater Talbot County

The flotilla of pleasure boats that plies the 600-plus miles of Talbot County's coastline might fool visitors into thinking that maritime-related tourism is the county's most important product—but it's not. Although Talbot County has the longest shoreline of any county in the United States, agriculture still ranks first as the largest local commercial industry, a fact easily proven by a short drive away from the well-known haunts of captains and crews. Soybeans, corn, and wheat make up the bulk of the produce that serves as the backbone of Talbot's economy. All told, farms in the region gross more than $40 million a year. However, the waters—including the Tred Avon, Tuckahoe, Wye, Miles, and Choptank Rivers—produce their own riches, from seafood to dockage. This is a difficult place to visit on a tight budget, so be prepared.

Talbot County Scenic Loop

There's a 25-mile scenic loop from St. Michaels, ideal for drivers or bicyclists: Drive east on Route 33 to Bellevue Road, then make a left (south) on Bellevue to the ferry. Float across to Oxford, then take Route 333 (Almshouse Rd.) east, then north, connecting with Route 322 to Easton. Return on Route 33 to St. Michaels.

Information

An overview of all the towns in Talbot county and their attractions can be obtained from the **Talbot County Office of Tourism** (11 S. Harrison St., Easton, MD 21601, 410/770-8000, www.tourtalbot.org/visitorinformation).

CAMBRIDGE

Cambridge, the largest town in the county, is one of the oldest in the state, settled in 1684.

Tobacco built the local economy on the backs of slaves. As trading ships from Europe began to dock in Cambridge during the 1700s (the unusable harbor had been dredged out to create a deepwater port), seafood and muskrat pelts joined tobacco as the major exports. The industrial revolution brought lumber mills and flour mills to Cambridge, and in the late 1800s, oyster-packing became the major source of employment, second only to Baltimore. In 1911, Phillips Packing Company took over the oyster packing plant, and drove the town to new heights of prosperity, earning the name "Queen City." Phillips folded in the 1950s, and Cambridge was left to struggle.

Museums

The city of Cambridge merged two small museums focusing on different aspects of maritime history into a $10 million showplace maritime museum on the water. The former James B. Richardson Maritime Museum added its collections to The **Brannock Maritime Museum** (106 Hayward St., 410/228-6938, projected opening spring 2008) to create detailed displays on shipbuilding, oystering, and Dorchester County's role in American history. Call Dorchester County Tourism (41//228-1000 or 800/522-8687) for a progress update and visitor information.

The **Meredith House and Nield Museum** (902 LaGrange Ave. at Maryland Ave., 410/228-7953, 10 A.M.–3 P.M. Tues.–Sat. April–Nov., 10 A.M.–1 P.M. Tues.–Fri. and 11 A.M.–3 P.M. Sat. Dec.–March, $3 adults) is the 1760 Georgian home of a former Maryland Governor; period antiques and a doll and toy collection are on display. The museum features antique toys, agricultural and maritime artifacts, Native American handiwork, a blacksmith shop, and a colonial herb garden.

The **Harriet Tubman Museum and Learning Center** (424 Race St., Cambridge, 410/228-0401, tours by request) stocks a few items, but more significantly houses a learning center focusing on the life of Dorchester-born national heroine Harriet Tubman. Storyboards line the walls, illuminating the life of Tubman and other famous black Americans, the Underground Railroad, and other topics of interest. Admission is free, but donations are appreciated. **Hometown Tours** works out of the gift shop, and offers a tour of the county centered on the life and times of Ms. Tubman ($10 adults, $7 kids). Other tours—with an African American viewpoint—can be tailored to individual interests and may include historic buildings and churches.

Dorchester Arts Center (DAC)

This local art hot spot (120 High St., Cambridge, 410/228-7782, www.tourdorchester.org, 10 A.M.–2 P.M. Mon.–Sat., 1–4 P.M. Sun., free) offers classes in artistic disciplines and exhibits local work. The gift shop is inspired and well worth a stop. The location, in a stately Victorian, is another reason to visit High Street. DAC is redeveloping the historic Nathan Building at 321 High Street and plans to expand classes and gallery space to that location.

Cambridge Historic Homes

During Cambridge's wealthiest periods, **High Street** was *the* address, and a stroll from the long wharf up to Poplar Street provides the evidence. Several Maryland governors had homes on High, and the properties have been cherished and kept up over the years. Homes range in age from the late 18th century to the early 20th, most built 1850–1880. A few of note are the **home of Governor Charles Goldsborough** (200 High St.), built in 1790; it's one of the best-preserved federal-style houses on the Eastern Shore. The **Sulivane House** (205 High St.) was built in 1763 and was home to generations of Sulivanes, including Colonel Clement Sulivane, a Confederate solider who participated in the burning of Richmond. The **Bayly House** (207 High St.) was built in 1755 in Annapolis and barged across the bay in 1760—still in the Bayly family, the white-columned porches recall the old South. **Christ Episcopal Church,** on the corner of High and Church Streets, was built from stones shipped over as ballast—there's no natural building stone in the area. The grave-

© JOANNE MILLER

High Street mansion in Cambridge

yard was established before the Revolutionary War; Civil War era graves of both Confederate and Union boys lie next to one another. The Dorchester County Department of Tourism publishes an excellent free guide to historic homes in Cambridge, including those on High Street. Visitors can pick one up at the Arts Center. For an interesting contrast, you might want to walk up Water Street and stroll on Vue de Leau Street, one block away from High Street; these were the homes of local watermen.

Shopping

Cambridge has a dandy antiques center, **Packing House Antiques** (411A Dorchester Ave.), plus nearby **Bay County Antiques** (415 Dorchester Ave.). Both renovated warehouses (at the intersection of Dorchester and Washington Sts.) offer miles of aisles and multiple dealers. The 400–800 blocks of Race Street also feature a variety of shops.

Recreation

Boat tours are a popular way to see the area.

The **Cambridge Lady** (410/221-0776) is a classic wooden yacht that offers several tours, including "Michener's Chesapeake Tour," which visits Oxford and Cambridge by water and includes narration that brings the times and places of the novel to life. Combination walking and boat tours, a nautical history tour, and eco-tours are also offered, along with a cruise-and-dine option (you're ferried to a local restaurant) or dine-aboard buffets. Co-captains Frank and Sherri Herbert are locals who love the area and freely share their enthusiasm. The *Lady* sails daily May–October (Nov.–Apr., they head down to Florida). If a skipjack is more your style, the **Nathan of Dorchester** (410/228-7141, www.skipjack-nathan.org) is the boat for you. The *Nathan* is newish—built in 1994—but has all the fine features of traditional skipjacks. Trips include narration on the lives of Chesapeake Bay watermen. The *Nathan* sails most Saturdays May–October. Both boats are docked in Cambridge.

For sportfishing charters, the **Joint Venture** (311 Nathan Ave., Cambridge 410/228-7837), under Captain Ben Parks, provides a variety of bottom fishing, trolling, and casting day trips, from Tilghman Island to the Virginia line.

Accommodations

The (**Cambridge House** (112 High St., Cambridge, 410/221-7700 or 877/221-7799, www.cambridgehousebandb.com, $125–175), a bed-and-breakfast, is an elegant Queen Anne–style Victorian built for a wealthy sea captain. It was a peeling wreck when innkeeper Stuart Schefers took over in 1996—now, the meticulously renovated rooms are decorated in period antiques and all have fireplaces, private bath, air-conditioning, and TV. Stuart, a professional restaurateur, opened 37 restaurants in New York City before retiring to Cambridge. The breakfasts are spectacular, as you might expect.

Another bed-and-breakfast, the **Mill Street Inn** (114 Mill St., Cambridge, 410/901-9144, www.millstinn.com, $125–225) is in a beautifully refurbished Victorian that opened for business in 2006. The innkeepers, Skip and Jennie, are retired teachers and organic farmers who serve up a lovely breakfast and tea. Each of the three suites is beyond comfortable; prices reflect day of the week and season (midweek and off-season are always lowest). This is an adults-only, no-pets inn.

Luxury, thy name is (**Hyatt Regency Chesapeake Bay** (100 Heron Blvd., 410/901-1234, $170 and up). This painstakingly designed and landscaped spa resort is a feast for the eye (and stomach). Perched like a castle on the shores of the Choptank River, it offers an 18-hole, par-71 golf course (the River Marsh Golf Club, created by Keith Foster); a full-service, top-flight spa (the Stillwater); tennis courts; a small private beach with paddleboats; a marina (with a provisions store); an exercise facility with classes; and three swimming pools, one of which appears to merge with the river below it. Visitors pull up to the grand circular arrival court via a private entry road that winds through natural plantings and the golf course. Every room has a view—of the river, fountains, or the golf course—in this truly beautiful

place. Guests who choose not to dawdle in their airy and spacious rooms can mingle with others in the handsome glass-enclosed bar or Michener's Library, shoot a game of snooker, or just sit by the big outdoor fireplace at night and roast a s'more. Though the resort appears to be a playground for adults, families are equally welcome; Hyatt offers Camp Hyatt at Pirate's Cove, activities for children ages 4–12 (half-day sessions $28, full days $52).

Luxury has its price, as the room rates indicate. Use of the beach, pools and tennis courts is included with the room, but exercise classes, golf, and spa treatments are extra (expect to pay $100–200 for spa services).

Food

The (**Portside** (201 Trenton St., Cambridge, 410/228-9007, lunch and dinner Tues.–Sun., $5–20) is the sort of ultracasual place where locals come for a bite. The menu focuses on seafood as entrées, in sandwiches, and in baskets with fries. There's a good view of the boats plying the river below. Also recommended in Cambridge is **Snappers** (112 Commerce St., 410/228-0112, 11 A.M.–10 P.M. Mon.–Sat., 11 A.M.–9 P.M. Sun.), another local favorite for seafood.

For a more upscale, fine dining experience, you'll have plenty to choose from. The latest addition to Cambridge's best restaurants is the **Blue Point Provision Company** (100 Heron Blvd., in the Hyatt Chesapeake, 410/901-1234, dinner daily, $30). A seafood specialty eatery, it's located at the far end of the resort, looking out over the River Marsh Marina on the shores of the Choptank River. Panoramic water views and an outdoor patio make this an outstanding place to view the sunset over the Chesapeake. Reservations recommended.

The soaring ceiling and subtle lighting of (**Water's Edge Grill** (100 Heron Blvd., in the Hyatt Chesapeake, 410/901-1234, breakfast, lunch, and dinner daily, $10–35) reflect the lofty aims of the chefs at what is undoubtedly the most elegant restaurant in this part of the bay. Sophisticated variations on regional specialties such as crab cakes and roast duck are well prepared and beautifully presented.

Also in the Hyatt Chesapeake, the **Eagle's Nest Bar and Grille** (100 Heron Blvd., 410/901-1234, 11 A.M.–3:30 P.M. daily, $12) may be the most manly golf club restaurant and bar ever conceived. Large bronze sculptures of Chesapeake wildlife by William Turner stand guard over a long, dark-toned wood room with enormous windows and imposing wrought-iron chandeliers. It's open for beer, cocktails, and sandwiches.

Greater Dorchester County

Dorchester is largely rural and threaded by rivers, including the 68-mile Choptank, immortalized by authors James Michener *(Chesapeake)* and John Barth *(Tidewater Tales* and *Floating Opera).*

Tourism is breathing new life into the city and the county. In addition to time-honored boating recreation, **Sailwinds Park,** a $30 million waterfront multi-use facility for concerts, fairs, festivals, and trade shows, is under development in Cambridge; a beautifully designed Hyatt golf resort and spa has opened; a Holiday Inn Express has set down roots; and other major players in the hospitality industry will surely follow.

Spocott Windmill

Those interested in machines and history will want to stop by this structure on Route 343, six miles west of Cambridge in the vicinity of Lloyds. This is a rare post-style mill (it sits aloft a four-foot-diameter, 200-year-old stripped white oak tree like a lollipop on a stick). Though the interior is seldom open to the public, it's worth a look. At one time, 18 post windmills operated in Dorchester County—all were eventually destroyed by forces of nature. The Spocott was destroyed in the blizzard of 1880 and rebuilt in 1971, using the original millstones, interior stairs, and much of the original timber.

RECREATION
◖ Islands and Towns Tour

This 85-mile road trip begins and ends in Cambridge. The route makes a big loop around Dorchester County, swinging past several historic towns, crossing a large wildlife refuge and wandering into two island communities. None of these "attractions" are developed, in the tourist sense, so be prepared for some serene country vistas and great history. Since some of the route is on major highways, it's not recommended for cyclists. All distances are approximate.

Leave Cambridge heading east on U.S. 50, and turn left (north) on Route 16 (three miles east of town). Follow Route 16 five miles to the village of **East New Market,** settled in the mid-1600s. Most of the extant Colonial-era houses are along Route 16 (which veers to the left at Linkwood Rd.) and the intersection of Route 14 (Rte. 14 loops around to the town of **Secretary** and the Suicide Bridge Restaurant. The village that makes up the historic district is bounded on the south and east by Route 392 and on the west by Creamery Road. It features 75 buildings representing architecture from the 18th, 19th, and 20th centuries. The buildings are privately owned, and most look nearly new. For detailed information on some of the more prominent houses, contact **Dorchester County Tourism** (800/522-TOUR, www.tourdorchester.org) and ask for the *East New Market Brochure.*

Take Route 14 east and south out of town for five miles to Route 331, and follow it for six miles to **Vienna,** 0.5 mile below the intersection of U.S. 50. Settled about the same time as East New Market, Vienna's original name was "Vinnacokasimmon," after a native chief. It was also named Baltimore for a short period of time, at the request of the Calverts. Vienna prospered in the early years as a center for the tobacco trade and shipbuilding. As technology changed (and the river silted up), the town turned its focus away from industry and became a quiet residential village. It supports a B&B or two and a few antiques stores. As with East New Market, details on the town's architectural treasures (mostly on Water St. on the Nanticoke River, and on Church St. at the south end of Water St.) are in the brochure available from Dorchester County Tourism.

Leave Vienna and travel south on Crossroads Road six miles to Henry's Crossroads. Go right on Henry's Crossroads (west) to the end (two miles), and turn left (south) onto Griffith Neck Road, which turns into Bestpitch Ferry Road, to **Bucktown** (10 miles). Bucktown is the home of the former Brodess Plantation, birthplace of Harriet Tubman. Take Greenbrier Road three miles west to Maple Dam Road. Make a left (south) to Key Wallace Drive and the settlement of Seward.

Continue west on Key Wallace Drive through the top of **Blackwater National Wildlife Refuge** (three miles). As an alternative route, consider taking the refuge's driving tour, also great for cycling. Both routes dead-end on Church Creek Road.

Turn left on Church Creek/Golden Hill Road (south) until it dead-ends at Route 335/336, four miles. Turn right on Route 335/Hooper Island Road and follow it as far down into **Hooper Island** as you'd like (2–14 miles). You'll pass the diminutive Star of the Sea Chapel on the north side of the road; it was built before 1767 as a place of worship for local Roman Catholics. Hooper Island is actually a chain of islands named for the family that settled there in the late 1600s; Colonel Henry Hooper and his son, Brigadier General Henry Hooper, commanded local militias against the British during the Revolution. Nearly 75 years later, Ella Carroll—feminist, friend of Abraham Lincoln, and Northern spy—called the island home. Today, the dwellings are almost entirely made up of the homes of watermen, set among marshes—a surreal, floating landscape. Sandy's is a good place to stop for a snack and an opportunity to pick up a locally made souvenir.

church on Taylors Island

© JOANNE MILLER

Return on Route 335 to Smithville Road and make a left (north) for seven miles until it dead-ends at Taylors Island Road (Rte. 16). Make a left, and within a mile, you'll be in the community of **Taylors Island.** This quiet village was settled in the 1650s. Along with late-18th-century churches and schools, it boasts a British ship's cannon captured by local militia during the War of 1812.

Return on Taylors Island Road east to Church Creek (five miles). **Old Trinity Church** (1716 Taylors Island Rd.) is worth a look. The chapel was built between 1675 and 1690, then later refurbished to its original state. The floor tiles (laid with a mortar of burnt oyster shells), altar table, and exterior brick walls are all original. Fifteen high-backed, gated pews made of beeswax-rubbed heart of pine, finished with handmade H-hinges, are faithful representations of the period. The loft in back was for slaves and servants, who were locked in during the service. The church still maintains an active (voluntary) congregation; services are at 11 A.M. on Sunday. Call the rectory

(410/228-2940) to set up a tour of the church, or wander about the old graveyard. A church regular commented that the headstones reflect the leading preoccupations of many Eastern Shore dwellers: boats, booze, and broads. You'll find all kinds of history here.

Route 16 will take you east and north back to Cambridge (five miles).

Blackwater National Wildlife Refuge

Once a farm used by muskrat trappers for the fur trade, the refuge was established in 1933 to provide sanctuary for migrating waterfowl (2145 Key Wallace Dr., Cambridge, MD 21613, 410/228-2677; Fish and Wildlife Service, 800/344-WILD, www.fws.gov/blackwater, visitors center 8 A.M.–4 P.M. Mon.–Fri., 9 A.M.–5 P.M. Sat.–Sun. year-round). A daily permit is required: private vehicles cost $3 and pedestrian or bicyclists cost $1. Golden Eagle passes are accepted.

In the refuge, geese number approximately 35,000 and ducks exceed 15,000 at the peak of fall migration, usually in November. October–March is the best time to visit to see migratory birds, though many songbirds, reptiles, and mammals stay year-round. Blackwater is also a haven for three endangered or threatened species, the bald eagle (largest nesting population north of Florida), peregrine falcon, and Delmarva fox squirrel. The refuge is stunningly beautiful, particularly in the late afternoon when the setting sun reflects off the mirrored ponds and birds swoop to feed on the plentiful insects.

Blackwater may be seen in several different ways. The visitors center offers exhibits, naturalist talks, and films. From there, several walking trails, including a wheelchair-accessible loop, meander through different habitats. A wildlife drive along either a 6.5-mile loop or a 3.5-mile all-weather road winds along through ponds, woods, fields, and marshes; walking and biking on the wildlife drive are permitted. Cyclists may choose from a 20-mile loop or a 25-mile loop. Boaters may enter the refuge via one of the surrounding waterways April 1–September 30, but may not launch within the refuge (there is a public boat launch on Shorters Wharf Road on the southern boundary of the refuge).

Boat Tours

Let's say you were deeply influenced by *Showboat* in your youth—you'd probably like to checkout **Dorothy-Megan** (410/943-4775), run by the Choptank Riverboat Company in Hurlock. It's an 80-foot paddle-wheeler that offers sightseeing and lunch and dinner cruises late spring–October.

Sportfishing Charters

Sawyer Fishing Charters (1345 Hoopers Island Rd., Church Creek, 410/397-3743) will take you out into the bay to reel in the striped bass of your dreams. They offer full- and half-day trips, and special rates during the summer.

Bicycling

Dorchester County, like much of the Eastern Shore, is great biking territory. Along with the scenic loops in the Blackwater Refuge, an additional 32-mile back-road loop begins in Vienna. It covers part of the driving tour, but spends far more time on little-used roads. Take Crossroads Road south out of Vienna, and turn right (west) on Steels Neck Road. Continue to go straight when the road becomes New Bridge Road. It will dead-end at Ravenwood Road Turn left (south). Turn right at Drawbridge Road then left (west) on Decoursey Bridge Road. It dead-ends at Bucktown Road/Bestpitch Ferry Road Turn left (south). The turnoff for Greenbrier Road and Blackwater Refuge comes up about a mile down the road—if you take the short refuge loop on Key Wallace Dr., it will add another 12 miles to the trip. If you choose to continue south on Bucktown Road/Bestpitch Ferry Road, it will turn into Griffith Neck Road (east), and turn sharply north (you'll cross the drawbridge). Continue on Drawbridge Road north to Steels Neck Road, and make a right (east) to retrace your path to Vienna.

ACCOMMODATIONS

The Tavern House (111 Water St., Vienna, 410/376-3347, $70–80) was built on the Nanticoke River as a combination pub-and-inn to serve travelers during colonial times. Today, it offers three simply decorated bedrooms, all with shared bath; two of the bedrooms have fireplaces.

FOOD

Old Salty's (2560 Hoopers Island Rd., Hoopers Island, 410/397-3752, 11 A.M.–6 P.M. daily, sandwiches $4–8, entrées $6–18) is an inexpensive place to stop for a sandwich or an entrée. The crab sandwiches and fresh fish sandwiches are quite good. Old Salty's has gained quite a reputation with visitors over the past few years, and not just for the cheap snacks. A big room next to the restaurant sells craft items made by local people. How could you resist a gold-painted crab shell filled with cotton snow, a glittering miniature Christmas tree and bear, especially when the bear is hoisting a jug to his snout? I couldn't—it has a place of honor on my tree. The woven potholders are also irresistible; anything for sale there shames made-in-Taiwan, just-for-tourists merchandise.

Suicide Bridge Restaurant (6304 Suicide Bridge Rd., Hurlock, 410/943-4689, mid-April–Dec., lunch and dinner Tues.–Sun., sandwiches $8, entrées $12–32) is the most popular eatery around with both locals and visitors. It's about 10 miles out of Cambridge, on the Choptank River. Again, the focus is on seafood, baked, boiled, broiled, or fried, but they also have a complete beef/chicken/veal selection. The atmosphere is boating casual (*good* shorts and collared knit shirt).

INFORMATION

For brochures and information updates, contact the **Dorchester County Department of Tourism** (visitors center, Tailwinds Park, east end of Rte. 50 Bridge, 410/228-1000 or 800/522-8687, www.tourdorchester.org, 8:30 A.M.–5 P.M. daily). You can't miss the 100-foot-tall soaring "sails" of Tailwinds Park-it's become an eastern shore landmark, and the symbol of a town that is determined to make itself into a top tourist destination.

SUICIDE BRIDGE

In case you're wondering why they call the short span that crosses a tributary of the Choptank River "Suicide Bridge," here's the story. Apparently, this bit of wood and concrete has all the allure of San Francisco's Golden Gate Bridge. What it lacks is height, being only 10-15 feet above the water. That didn't stop the bridge's first victim, a postmaster from Hurlock, who shot himself and fell into the creek. The second victim, a local farmer, followed suit. The third victim either jumped off the bridge and struck his head on a piling or was a victim of foul play – it was never determined.

The original structure was built in 1888, then replaced in 1910 and once again in 1968. Less than six months after the newest bridge was built, a longtime employee of Continental Can in Hurlock chose to end his life rather than return to work from his vacation. He jumped off the bridge and drowned. Not long after that, another man who was born and raised within half a mile of the bridge and who had moved away for several years came back and shot himself – on Suicide Bridge.

But things may be looking up for the unfortunate span: One woman who had jumped into the icy waters recently changed her mind and began calling for help. She was rescued by Dave Nickerson, who lives next to the creek (and owns a nearby restaurant). Local resident Pete Moxey says, "I don't think the bridge is jinxed. Maybe it's just the name that brings them here." The only way to guarantee peace on Suicide Bridge may be to rename it – how about "Second Thoughts Bridge?"

If you're on the Eastern Shore, keep an eye out for the **Tidewater Times,** a little (3.5 by 5 inches) powerhouse of a monthly publication that has lots of great information and articles about the Eastern Shore, especially Talbot and Dorchester counties. You can also find the *Times* online at www.tidewatertimes.com.

Salisbury

Salisbury, the largest city on the Eastern Shore (granted, Ocean City's population waxes and wanes seasonally), began as a mill community in the center of dense woods in 1732. The Wicomico River provided critical water access to the Chesapeake, and Salisbury grew as the principal crossroads of the southern Delmarva Peninsula.

The town of Salisbury burned to the ground in 1860 and was entirely rebuilt. Today, the town continues to thrive as a center of commerce, and offers major historical and recreational activities for visitors (and the restaurants are good, too).

SIGHTS
◖ Ward Museum of Wildfowl Art

What was once necessity has become art, and nowhere is this better demonstrated than at the Ward Museum of Wildfowl Art (909 S. Schumaker Dr., Salisbury, 410/742-4988, www .wardmuseum.org, 10 A.M.–5 P.M. Mon.–Sat.,

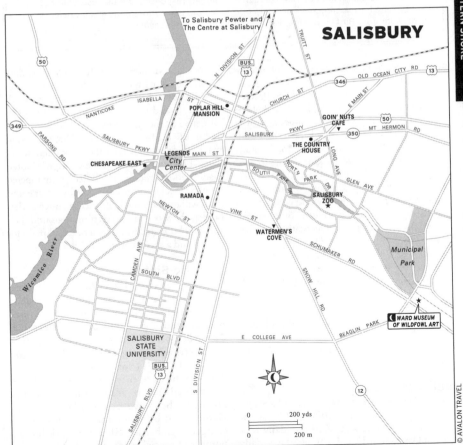

THE EASTERN SHORE

STOOL PIGEONS AND GUNNERS

In the 19th century, hunters gauged their success by the number of kills. The term "stool pigeon," which today alludes to someone who informs on his associates, originally referred to live passenger pigeons tethered to a tree-like post. Pigeons on the wing, being social creatures, would spiral down to land beside their brothers and be picked off by the hunter's guns. A good hunter with a repeating rifle could bring down 100 birds a day.

Once copious enough to darken the sky, the passenger pigeon population was endangered by the 1890s and extinct by 1914. Though it was too late for the gregarious passenger pigeon, Migratory Bird Laws were first passed in 1914, outlawing specific types of hunting. In 1918, the Migratory Bird Treaty prohibited commercial sale of game birds.

Chesapeake Bay Gunning Clubs, which started out in the 1850s, popularized the sport-hunting lifestyle, along with working companion dogs such as the Chesapeake Bay retriever and the Labrador and golden retrievers. Today, the clubs work actively to make sure the fate of the passenger pigeon isn't repeated. Through financial support and environmental lobbying, the clubs are largely responsible for the resurgence of waterfowl populations and habitat preservation on the Chesapeake.

noon–5 P.M. Sun., $9 adults, less for seniors and children). You will have to remind yourself that you are looking at carved and painted wood, not wild birds in flight. The work is extraordinary, as you might expect from the premier collection of wildfowl art in the world. The museum looks at the history and heritage of the art, from antique working decoys to contemporary carvings, and two additional galleries feature changing exhibits. Winners in all categories from the annual world competition are displayed, including Shootin' Stool (active decoys), Miniatures, and Decorative Lifesize. Among the winners of past Decorative Lifesize awards were "Road Kill Pheasant" (Winner, Best in the World—not only for the outrageously beautiful carving, but also for the sly humor), a pair of fighting cocks, and courting kestrels in midflight. Wow.

The exhibits have expanded to include jewelry and carved wood in a variety of diverse subjects, such as free-form sculptures, exotic plants, and other objects.

Salisbury Zoo

This little haven is a zoo hater's zoo (5 Park Dr., in Salisbury city park, 410/548-3188, www.salisburyzoo.org, 8 A.M.–7:30 P.M. daily Memorial Day–Labor Day, 8 A.M.–4:30 P.M. daily Labor Day–Memorial Day, free). Dr. Theodore Reed, Director Emeritus of the National Zoo, called it "one of the finest small zoos in North America," and so it is. Nearly 400 species—all native to the Americas—inhabit a compact and neatly landscaped 12 acres. One thing that makes this zoo unusual is the preponderance of natural habitats—cages are few. Bright colored macaws zoom around the tall trees, unhampered by wire; ducks and other waterfowl come and go at will on the stretch of Wicomico River that borders the zoo; prairie dogs tumble around their specially built enclosure. It's a peaceful place for a stroll and a special place for children.

Historic Sights

Salisbury has a major force for historical preservation in the Wicomico Historical Society (410/860-0447). The society maintains a small museum and store at **Pemberton Historical Park** (Pemberton Dr., 410/548-4900, www.pembertonpark.org), site of Pemberton Hall, built in 1741 for Colonel Isaac Handy. The grounds are threaded by 4.5 miles of self-guided nature trails, and the manor house may be toured 2–4 P.M. Sunday May–October and by appointment; a small fee is charged. Pemberton Historical Park hosts a number of special events during the year, notably the Colonial Fair (see the *Festivals and Events* section in this chapter). To get there from U.S. 50 east of Salisbury, turn left on Nanticoke Road, then take the first left on Pemberton Drive (south). Follow Pemberton Drive two miles; the park is on the left.

The historical society also publishes a walking tour of "Newtown"—now the oldest neighborhood in Salisbury—the area that was built immediately after the great fires of 1860 and 1886 destroyed much of the city (call 410/860-0447 for the brochure). One of the homes spared by the fires welcomes visitors: **Poplar Hill Mansion** (117 Elizabeth St., 410/749-1776, donations appreciated), built in 1799. It's open to the public for free tours 1–4 P.M. on the first and third Sunday of each month (tours arranged by appointment during other times, $3), and is a popular site for meetings and events.

The **Mason-Dixon Marker** lies north of Salisbury on the Delaware border, U.S. 13 just past Route 54 on the west side of the road. Charles Mason and Jeremiah Dixon surveyed the line between 1763 and 1767, and it was used as the formal dividing line between slave and free states. Maryland—below the Mason-Dixon Line—chose to be a free state, at least technically. One deciding factor was that the Emancipation Proclamation freed slaves only in those states that seceded from the Union. Therefore, slave owners in Maryland were not obligated by law to manumit their slaves.

SHOPPING

Between Division Street and Main Street, Salisbury has closed traffic and created a **pedestrian mall** (City Center) surrounded by pretty historic buildings. The area includes sophisticated women's clothing stores, several antique shops, among them **Parker Place Antiques,** and a few galleries, including the **Salisbury Art Institute and Gallery.** Also on Main, **Under the Rainbow** features a stunning collection of dolls. On Division Street, **Tyme for Tea** is a good place to stop for coffee and gaze at the Tiffany windows in Trinity Church across the street.

Several folks mentioned the **Country House** (805 E. Main St., Salisbury, 410/749-1959, www.thecountryhouse.com) as a great place to look for casual items for house and garden. The building is big—16,000 square feet—so you'll probably find more than you were looking for.

Salisbury Pewter (2611 N. Salisbury Blvd., Salisbury, 410/546-1188, www.salisburypewter .com) is the "home store" of the international company, and visitors have a chance to see the artisans at work while picking up some good buys. Pewter is a mixture of tin, copper, and antimony; during fabrication, the lead is removed, making the pewter safe for food. Those who work forming the flat pewter discs into cups and trays are called spinners—a 10-year apprenticeship is the norm—and the Salisbury Pewter trademark is applied by hand. Tiffany, the largest buyer, sells Salisbury pewter under its own trademark; the second biggest consumer of engraved pewter is the U.S. government. Check out the samples on display, and you'll see the names of several presidents.

The Centre at Salisbury, on U.S. 13 at the bypass (north of town on U.S. 13), fulfills all mall fantasies. It offers more than 90 stores and is anchored by **Boscov's, Hecht's,** and other major retailers.

An unusual shop, **Chesapeake East** (501 W. Main St., 410/546-1534) is definitely worth a stop. It's full of bright and amusing made-in-Salisbury ceramics and other local goods.

ACCOMMODATIONS

Salisbury tends to attract businesspeople, and therefore has a number of chain hotels. One of the most attractive is the **Ramada Inn** (300 S. Salisbury Blvd., 410/546-4400 or 888/800-7617, www.salisburyramada.com, $79–145). It's in a quiet south-of-downtown location and has a restaurant and indoor pool. A number of packages are available; one combines a stay with a round at local golf courses.

Another chain that offers a lot of amenities and some attractive packages is **Country Inn and Suites** (1804 Sweetbay Dr., Salisbury, 410/742-2688, www.countryinns.com,

$79–189). It features a fitness facility and indoor pool, and is southeast of downtown, not far from the University.

FOOD

Watermen's Cove (925 Snow Hill Rd., Salisbury, 410/546-1400, lunch and dinner daily, $8–26) is a cheery place and attracts a casual business lunch crowd. The menu features shrimp scampi, a seafood platter, and other seafood, chicken, and beef dishes, plus salads and sandwiches. Readers of *Metropolitan Magazine,* a Salisbury publication that serves the eastern Delmarva Peninsula, voted Watermen's Cove the best place for seafood five years in a row.

Goin' Nuts Café (947 Mt. Hermon Rd., Salisbury, 410/860-1164, lunch and dinner daily, $5–22) is a one-stop world food shop. It has a complete Italian menu, plus Thai seafood, quesadillas, bratwurst, Jamaican jerk chicken, Greek salad, Caribbean salad, broccoli tempura, and other vegetarian dishes.

◖ Legends (City Center on Main St., Salisbury, 410/749-7717, lunch Mon.–Fri., dinner Mon.–Sat., $15–22) is an exceptional fine dining restaurant—the best in town. Charcoal-grilled filet mignon, Louisiana pasta with andouille sausage, a variety of large salads (the chicken salad has half a roasted chicken, fresh corn, and pine nuts), and the usual fresh fish dishes grace the menu. Reservations are recommended.

Greater Wicomico County

This heavily traveled area of the state has a low number of permanent residents, except in Salisbury and Ocean City. The county is rich in waterways, which made it easy for colonial farmers to get their produce to market in the big cities. The area is still green with farms, though you're just as likely to see telephone pole farms (tall, sparse pines) as golf courses these days. The importance of water travel during colonial times was emphasized by the prevalence of ferries; one that survives today is the Whitehaven Ferry, on the very southern end of the county.

RECREATION
Whitehaven Loop

This 38-mile round-trip from Salisbury is ideal for a leisurely two-day bike trip or a one-day car trip. It travels along straight two-lane roads through marshes, open fields, and "telephone-pole farms"—groves of commercially grown tall pines.

Begin on U.S. 50 in Salisbury, heading east. Make a left on Nanticoke Road, then take the first left on Pemberton Drive (south). Follow Pemberton Drive as it angles sharply right, then left. You'll pass historic **Pemberton Hall**

(described in this chapter) on the left, and the **Rockawalkin Schoolhouse** near Rockawalkin Creek. Built in 1872, it's typical of one-room schoolhouses of the period. At one time, it housed 35 students in grades one through seven. It's open by appointment (call the Wicomico Historical Society, 410/860-0447).

Pemberton Drive ends at Route 349. Turn left (west) and, less than a mile, make the next left (south) on Route 352 (Whitehaven Rd.). This will take you all the way down to the **Whitehaven Ferry.**

To get some idea of how old the settlement of Whitehaven is, consider that one of the first residents was Colonel George Gale, whose first wife was George Washington's grandmother. The free ferry has been operating over the narrow stretch of the Wicomico River since 1692; it was once a link on the old colonial road between the thriving seaports of Vienna and Princess Anne. The ferry can take a car or several bicycles. It operates year-round, though hours change with the season (7 A.M.–6 P.M. Mar. 1–May 15, 6 A.M.–7:30 P.M. May 16–Sept. 15, 7 A.M.–6 P.M. Sept. 16–Oct.31, and 7 A.M.–5:30 P.M. Nov. 1–Feb. 28). It's part of the Maryland Highway System, and informa-

Old Menhaden fishing boat, Whitehaven

tion is available at 410/548-4872. Unless you're eating or staying in the area, take the ferry across to Whitehaven Ferry Road.

Whitehaven Ferry Road dead-ends on Polks Road. Turn left (east) and continue for about five miles to Loretto-Allen Road, then turn left (north). Cross Wicomico Creek and enter the village of Allen. At the stop sign, turn right (north) and go up Allen Road, which turns into South Camden Avenue. You'll return to Salisbury on this road, passing the outlying residential areas and the pretty campus of Salisbury State University.

Golf

The Salisbury area is home to a number of golf courses, including **Elks Golf Club** (401 Church Hill Ave., Salisbury, 410/749-2695), a nine-hole, par 72 course.

Green Hill (410/749-1605, www.greenhill .com) is the local country club, in operation since 1927. This beautiful 18-hole championship golf course, ranked #2 in the state by the *Washington Times*, is open for limited public play.

Nutters Crossing (30287 Southampton Bridge Rd., Salisbury, 800/615-4657) is another popular semi-private club. The **Ramada Inn** offers a number of golf packages that include play at any or all of eight local courses, including those mentioned above.

ACCOMMODATIONS

If a quiet country place on the Wicomico River is your style, try the **C Whitehaven Hotel Historic Bed & Breakfast** (2685 Whitehaven St., Whitehaven, 410/873-2000 or 877/809-8296, www.whitehaven.tripod.com, $110–150). This Victorian beauty was built in 1810 to service travelers on the Whitehaven ferry and steamship passengers who were working their way around the Eastern Shore. Over the years, the hotel sunk deeply into a state of dilapidation; saved from the wrecking ball in 1994 by a coalition of local residents and Wicomico Historical Properties, it won the Maryland State Preservation Award in 2005. The hotel offers seven rooms with private baths.

FOOD

It's difficult not to wax rhapsodic about the **C Red Roost** (off Rte. 352—follow the signs, 2670 Clara Rd. Whitehaven, 410/546-5443, dinner Mar.–Oct., platters $14–19, all-you-can-eat specials $15–35). In the late 1940s, the Roost was just that—a chicken house. Chickenmeister Frank Perdue stopped by to unload feed (Perdue lived in Salisbury until his death in 2005). After a series of high tides floated away the last of the poultry in the 1960s, the place was abandoned until Frank Palmer, a car dealer from Hyattsville, attempted to turn it into a campground. The 1970s oil embargo (and the fact that the Roost was out in the middle of nowhere) kept customers away in droves. Mr. Palmer decided to experiment in the restaurant business by steaming up a few crabs and local corn. Word spread, and in 1978, when the all-you-can-eat feast was instituted, the Red Roost became an official Eastern Shore experience. Alas, the all-you-can-eat menu is restricted to fried chicken, steamed crabs, BBQ ribs, steamed shrimp, or Alaskan snow crab legs (there are dinner platters on the menu, but why would you pass up this amazing opportunity to see just how much you can stuff down your gullet?). To loosen you up before the feast begins, the kitchen sends out platters of perfect fried chicken, corn on the cob, fried shrimp, clam strips, french fries, and homemade hushpuppies—all come with dinner. You will eat too much, guaranteed—especially if you're lubing up at the full bar. Then, if it's one of the entertainment nights (banjo, piano, Irish bands), you'll probably get up and dance and sing, too. Welcome to the Eats-tern Shore. If you can get there, go!

INFORMATION

Sandy Fulton at the **Wicomico County Convention & Visitors Bureau** (U.S. 13, Salisbury, MD, 21801, 410/548-4914 or 800/332-8687, www.wicomicotourism.org) is a real county booster and a good source of information.

Crisfield

The biggest (eight stoplights) and best-known town in Somerset County, Crisfield has long been a destination for anglers and seafood lovers. The first English settlers adopted the Native American name Annamessex for the little fishing village that was to become Somers Cove. When the railroad was extended to the harbor in 1867, the town was renamed for the man whose efforts made it all possible: John Woodland Crisfield. By 1910, the Crisfield Customs House (now a marine supplies store) boasted the largest registry of sailing vessels in the nation, and Crisfield was a boomtown. Nearby Marion may have been the strawberry capital of Maryland, but the seafood industry was always Crisfield's ace; that mainstay of 1950s Catholic Friday night dinners, Mrs. Paul's, was based in Crisfield, churning out fish stick after fish stick. Oysters were literally the foundation on which Crisfield was built: From the water tower on Eighth Street to the City Dock, the streets are laid atop billions of oyster shells. Though crabbing and commercial fishing has replaced the moribund oyster industry, Crisfield remains on top of it all.

SIGHTS
◖ Gov. J. Millard Tawes Historical Museum

The museum (Somers Cove Marina, at the end of 9th St., 410/968-2501, 9 A.M.–4:30 P.M. Mon.–Fri. and 10 A.M.–3 P.M. Sat.–Sun. Memorial Day–Oct., 9 A.M.–4:30 P.M. Mon.–Fri. Nov.–Memorial Day, $2.50) is named for a local resident and the 54th governor of Maryland. Governor Tawes was responsible for the creation of the Center for Public Broadcasting and the second span of the Chesapeake Bay Bridge, among other achievements. The museum features a well-put-together display on local marine life and its care and harvesting, as well as a section on the history of the area beginning with the native inhabitants. Rotating exhibits add interest; recently, the gallery exhibited "woolies," the embroidered renderings (usually depicting ships under full sail) of 19th-century sailors. One of the most interesting museum offerings is the **Port of Crisfield Escorted Walking Tour.** Guides take visitors through town, revealing bits of history (for instance, the fact that Charlie Adams Corner is named for an eccentric local who used to sell newspapers there) and illuminating hidden hideaways of commerce that the average visitor would miss. **Goode's Boat Yard** (GOOD-ez) has several examples of different watermen's craft in dry dock; a walk through the **Metompkin Soft Shell Crab processing plant** and **Metompkin Bay Oyster Co.** is like slipping into another era. Everything, from sorting to picking, is done by hand. Softshell crabs were the first aquaculture industry in the United States, and a mainstay of the economy here. This is an informative and fun introduction to Crisfield; the museum also offers this tour via trolley for $3.50. Another offering by the museum is the **Ward Brothers Heritage Tour,** which explores the workshop of the famous brothers who pioneered the art form of decoy carving and painting in the Jenkins Creek area. Call the museum for information on scheduled tours, and make a reservation.

In the early part of the 20th century, brothers Lem and Steve Ward, residents of Crisfield, carved some of the most sought-after duck decoys on the Chesapeake. The **Ward Brothers Workshop** (3195 Sackertown Rd.) has been restored and is open by appointment; it's part of the Crisfield Heritage Tour and may be booked through the visitors center by calling 410/968-2501.

SHOPPING

The last five blocks of Main Street leading to the City Dock in Crisfield are dotted with boutiques and gift shops. Two of note are **Jane's Accents** (907 W. Main, 410/968-0668), which carries new and consignment household items, and **This Is The Life** (529 W. Main St., 410/968-1577, www.thisisthelifeinc.net), a gift shop specializing in nautical, beach, and tropical theme items, plus work by local artists.

An out-of-town treasure, **Kings Creek Antiques & Design Center** (Rte. 13 and Perry Rd., Princess Anne, 410/651-2776, www.kingscreekantiques.com), is one of those warehouse-like multi-dealer shops that provide hours of amusement for those who love to look (and buy). You'll find lots of American/nautical antiques and varied collectibles.

RECREATION
Cedar Island Marsh Sanctuary

Covering nearly 3,000 acres of tidal marsh, ponds, and creeks, this sanctuary in Tangier Sound near Crisfield attracts millions of black ducks in winter. In the 1960s, the black duck was declining in numbers due to loss of habitat. Today, black duck populations are on the mend, and Cedar Island is one of Maryland's best places to see the birds. Other tidal wetland wildlife species are also attracted to the area;

barn owls use nest boxes placed in the marsh to raise their young, typically between April and September. Trapping is offered by yearly lease, and crabbing, as well as fishing for sea trout, rockfish, bluefish, and spot are additional activities enjoyed by visitors. The island can only be reached by boat. The **Crisfield Heritage Foundation** (3 9th St., at the Crisfield Historical Museum, Crisfield, 410/968-2501, 9 A.M.–5 P.M. Mon.–Sat., also Sun. in summer) offers guided kayak tours for individuals, children, and families, plus photography classes. Call for a tour schedule and reservations.

Jane's Island State Park

This really beautiful public space (office 410/968-1565) on 3,100 acres includes pristine beaches, wetlands, and abundant wildlife. Eight miles of sandy beaches invite nature walks, beachcombing, picnicking, and swimming. Fifteen miles of canoe/kayak trails offer protected paddling. There are two mile-long walking trails, one with 12 exercise stations. The mainland portion of the island is accessible by car, but part of the park is accessible only by boat.

The original inhabitants, a tribe of Native Americans, left artifacts and shell mounds on the island. The latecomer Europeans used high ground for farming, and a fish processing plant operated on the south end of the island from 1877 to 1908, when menhaden fishing (an endangered species) was outlawed in Maryland. Though the plant returned and processed other fish after World War I, the stock market crash of 1929 made it unprofitable. Its 50-foot brick chimney still remains.

The park has 104 campsites, 20 of which are waterfront. Five rustic mini-cabins are available during the warmer months, and four fully equipped, full-size cabins are available year-round. The cabins all have spectacular views of the sunset, so plan to book a year in advance (888/432-2267, http://reservations.dnr.state.md.us). There are also accommodations at the island's **Daugherty Creek Conference Center** (sleeps 16—the entire center must be rented). Transient berths with hookups are available for visitors who arrive by boat. Motorboats, canoes, and kayaks may be rented at the Eagle's Nest park store. A softball field, volleyball courts, horseshoe pit, and shuffleboard area are also available.

To get to the park, take Route 358 west from Route 413. For information and reservations, call the office number listed above.

Fishing

Tangier Sound is one of the best places on the East Coast to catch fish: trout, flounder, drum, croaker, rockfish, and perch are plentiful. Aspiring anglers with their own fishing licenses may rent 16-foot fiberglass boats by the hour, half day, and full day from **Croaker Boat Rentals** (Somers Cove Marina, 410/968-3644). Crocker also offers rods and reels and ring traps for crabbing.

Head boats are a big business in Crisfield; for a complete list, contact the tourism board (410/651-2968 or 800/521-9189, www.visit somerset.com/charter_boat_captains). Visitors who choose the head boat option don't need their own licenses, as the boat captain's license covers everyone on the boat. Two speedy party boats that take visitors out for bottom fishing are **Barbara Ann II** and **Barbara Ann III** (Somers Cove Marina, Pier N, 410/957-2562). Also out of Crisfield is the **Prime Time II** (800/791-1470).

Tours

Captain Larry Laird Jr. invites visitors aboard his Chesapeake Bay workboat on the waters around Crisfield for a **Learn-It Eco-Tour** (1021 W. Main St., Crisfield, 410/968-9870). Visitors can see and hear about wildlife above the water such as ducks, geese, and osprey, and below the water: terrapins, eels, and those fast-moving, elusive oysters. Tours depart daily during the summer. Call for hours and reservations.

ACCOMMODATIONS

The **Somers Cove Motel** (700 Norris Harbor Dr., Crisfield, 888/315-2378, www.crisfield .com/somerscove, $45–85 depending on season) is a basic motel owned by the Best Value chain. Barbecue grills are available to guests, and boat launch ramps are nearby.

Bea's B&B (10 S. Somerset Ave., Crisfield, 410/968-0423, $85–100), is a nice little Victorian that's been simply restored. Three rooms either share a bath or have individual baths. Rates include breakfast.

FOOD

In the film *Star Wars,* Luke was misdirected when he was told to beware the **Dockside.** This friendly, casual restaurant (1003 W. Main St., Crisfield, 410/968-2800, breakfast, lunch, and dinner daily, $6–14) is a good place for inexpensive meals. Lots of Crisfield watermen eat here.

Also recommended: the **Side Street Seafood Restaurant** (204 S. 10th St., Crisfield, 410/968-2442, lunch and dinner daily, $7–29), which has a nice outdoor dining area; and the **Watermen's Inn,** in an old blacksmith's shop (901 W. Main, Crisfield, 410/968-2119, http://crisfield.com/watermen, 11 A.M.–9 P.M. Wed.–Fri., 8 A.M.–9:30 P.M. Sat., 8 A.M.–8 P.M. Sun. in summer, Thurs.–Sun. in winter, $6–29).

Smith Island

Accessible only by boat, Smith Island was chartered by Captain John Smith in 1608 and settled by dissenters from St. Clements Island in 1657. Many of the former Catholics converted to Methodism, which is now the only religion officially practiced here. Smith Island is made up of three bodies of land; the two southernmost are inhabited, and the northern island is the **Martin National Wildlife Refuge.**

Current denizens of Smith Island live in three small communities: Tylerton, Rhodes Point (formerly Rogue's Point, after the local pirates), and Ewell, the island's largest town. **Tylerton** is accessible by packet (mail) boat from Crisfield, and among the residences are a post office, a one-room schoolhouse, a church, and a market. **Rhodes Point** is connected to Ewell by road through the salt marsh and a wooden bridge; the only boat repair facility on Smith Island is in this tiny community. **Ewell** is the "big city," the place where the ferry boats dock and most of the island's residents can be found. The majority of the 380 Smith Islanders descended from the original colonists, cattlemen who turned to fishing by necessity. Some visitors claim that the heavy southern Maryland accent you'll hear spoken locally is reminiscent of the Elizabethan/Cornwall dialect brought here in the 18th century. The isolation of the island is highlighted by the fact that phone service wasn't available on the island until 1940, and electricity was nonexistent until 1949.

RECREATION

If you've got energy to burn, you've come to the wrong place. Smith Island will remind you that at one nearly mythical time, life wasn't lived by the clock. A walk around the streets will take about 15 minutes. A bike ride will take five minutes (you can rent bikes for $5 an hour at the booth next to the ferry dock), or you can go in style with a golf cart for $10 an hour. During your tour, you can count the multitude of shy feral cats that live off the seafood bounty.

Boat-watching is a big activity here, as is sitting. Watching people sit in their living rooms is frowned upon.

Or you can shop: **Ruke's General Store** (corner of Jones Rd. and Smith Island Rd.) is a combination flea market jumble and country store, and **Bayside Inn** (4065 Smith Island Rd.) offers souvenirs, as well as hearty meals. Both are open daily, with irregular hours (if you live there and want something, you go to the owner's house; if you came in on the boat, both shops will probably be open).

When you're done shopping, you can learn something: The **Smith Island Center** (Jones Rd. and Smith Island Rd., 410/425-3351 or 800/521-9189, www.smithisland.org/museum .html, noon–4 P.M. daily Apr.–Oct., $2) is an information and heritage museum. The center was the focus of a design award in 2003 by the American Institute of Architects.

The **Martin Wildlife Refuge** is almost

crab shack on Smith Island

A VICTORY FOR TEMPERANCE?

In 1999, the Associated Press reported that a Smith Island shopkeeper's attempt to end a 300-year ban on alcohol sales on the island ended in failure. About a third of the island's 350 or so residents headed to the mainland to encourage the Somerset County liquor board to turn the liquor license down; the board voted 2-1 to deny.

The shopkeeper's request was opposed by longtime residents, many of whom are Methodists with a strong bent for temperance. The shopkeeper, who moved to Smith Island in 1997, maintained that times had changed since the island was settled in 1657, and that the sale of alcohol is a sign of progress. Some locals apparently feared the availability of alcohol would lead to fighting (those wild tourists!). The nearest police officer is a 40-minute boat ride away.

entirely salt marsh, broken up by a maze of tidal creeks and freshwater potholes. It's accessible by boat from Smith Island (the refuge is operated by the U.S. Fish and Wildlife Service, Blackwater National Wildlife Refuge, 2145 Key Wallace Dr., Cambridge, MD 21613-9536, 410/228-2692, http://northeast.fws.gov/md/mrn.htm). Visiting species change with the seasons; winter brings the heaviest populations of ducks (roughly 10,000), Canada geese (4,000), and tundra swans (1,500). Though it's possible to cruise by boat around the perimeter of the refuge, the interior is closed to the public.

ACCOMMODATIONS AND FOOD

Eating is another diversion. The **Bayside Inn** (410/425-2771) has a package deal with groups that arrive on the Tyler boats from Crisfield that includes transportation and lunch (lunch alone runs $11 for soup and a crab sandwich to $19 for the deluxe all-you-can-eat buffet). The season starts on Memorial Day and extends to October 15—the restaurant is open 11:15 A.M.–4 P.M. during that time, and it's closed the rest of the year. If you're diabetic, pack your own food—Smith Island cuisine is heavy on nonperishable ingredients, especially sugar. It's a prominent additive to everything from stewed tomatoes to corn fritters, but you won't go away hungry. The crab soup is quite good.

There are a few places to stay in Ewell, and one in nearby Tylerton. The **Chesapeake Sunrise B&B** (Chesapeake Bay Marina, next to the Bayside Inn, Ewell, 410/425-4220, www.smithisland.us/rooms, $95–124) also offers boat slips. **Fisherman's Rest** (20930 Somers Rd. Ewell, 410/425-2095 $100) is a small cottage that's popular with visitors. The **Ewell Tide B&B** ("Turn right at the dock, we're right up the street," Ewell, 410/425-2141, $95–105) offers simple accommodations with a beautiful view. If you really want to get away from it all ("it" being roads, cars, people, and noise), take the non-vehicular ferry **Captain Jason II** from Crisfield to Tylerton (it runs at 12:30 and 5:00 P.M., $25/person round-trip, leave your car at the adjacent J.P. Tawes & Bro. Hardware parking lot in Crisfield for $3 per overnight).

Tylerton, made up of 70 residents separated by water from the rest of Smith, is the remote place you didn't think existed anymore, the community Tom Horton celebrated in his *An Island Out of Time*. Surrounded on three sides by water, **The Inn of Silent Music** (2955 Tylerton Rd., 410/425-3541, www.innofsilentmusic.com, $110–130) offers stunning views, charming rooms decorated in an eclectic style, and good food. A full breakfast is included, and you may order dinner for an additional $25. Rooms all come with bath and refrigerator. The inn closes for the season mid-November and reopens mid-March.

GETTING THERE

From Memorial Day through October, you can reach Smith Island daily via passenger cruisers captained by Otis Tyler and Terry Laird (Crisfield Dock, Crisfield, 410/968-1118 or 410/425-5931, boats leave around 12:30 P.M.), and another by Captain Alan Tyler (Tawes Museum, 410/968-2220). Reservations are necessary; round-trip fares are around $24. All year long, the smaller mail boats *Captain Jason I* and *Captain Jason II* (Crisfield, 410/425-5931) also ferry passengers to the island. The big boats cruise in style—the trip takes about an hour, and the gentle movement of the boat is very relaxing.

The mail boats are speedier and choppier; the trip takes about 35 minutes.

Mail boats and the passenger cruisers mentioned above also sail to Tangier Island, Virginia, from Crisfield. Another vessel that offers transportation is the **Steven Thomas** (City Dock, May–Oct., 410/968-2338 or 800/863-2338). Tangier Island is about the same distance from Crisfield as Smith Island and offers the same amenities, though it's slightly more developed.

Greater Somerset County

It seems the farther south you travel on the Delmarva, the more things slow down. Driving through this rich farming region, you'll pass seemingly endless fields of sorghum and soy. Local Native Americans—Pokomoke, Annamessex, Minokan, Nessawattex, and Acqintica—lived comfortably in the area, and in 1677, the largest Native American town in Maryland, Askiminokonson, existed nearby at what is now the intersection of Route 364 and U.S. 13.

Princess Anne, the county seat of Somerset County, is a sunny, one-main-street municipality, with centuries of well-preserved architecture and a well-attended house and garden tour that focuses on the town's historic past. It's also the site of the University of Maryland Eastern Shore, a modern college campus that offers a diverse curriculum. It was founded in 1886 under the auspices of the Methodist Episcopal Church and Centenary Biblical Institute of Baltimore as a school of higher learning for black Americans; today, its student body has an international profile.

In mid-May, the fish are running, and autumn is hurricane season—and they do blow through here. Deal Island and the other local destinations all offer mellow getaways and a pace reminiscent of the Deep South.

SIGHTS
Princess Anne
Founded in 1733, this town was named in

honor of the 24-year-old daughter of King George II of England. Princess Anne is distinguished by many colonial-era, federal-style dwellings and mid-to-late-19th-century Victorian homes. One of these, the **Teackle Mansion** (11736 Mansion St., 410/651-2238, http://teackle.mansion.museum, 1–3 P.M. Wed., Sat., and Sun. Apr.–mid-Dec., 1–3 P.M. Sun. mid-Dec.–Mar., $6) is open for tours. Littleton and Elizabeth Teackle built the symmetrical and elegant mansion shortly after their marriage in 1800. Mr. Teackle had diverse interests as a merchant, statesman, and entrepreneur, but suffered from financial instability (possibly because of being named Little Teackle) and sold the mansion in 1839. The mansion was divided into rental properties over the years and was purchased by a local group of residents determined to preserve it in the 1950s. The Historic Princess Anne self-guided walking tour, which covers 37 other significant buildings, is available at the mansion or through the county's tourism board.

Accohannock Tribal Museum
The Accohannock (ah-co-HAH-nahk) tribe, one of the original populations on the Eastern Shore, maintains a museum in Marion, 14 miles north of Crisfield (Crisfield-Marion Rd., Marion Station). For hours of operation and more information, contact the tribe (410/623-2660, by appointment only). The museum building houses

artifacts collected and owned by the tribe, and is the site of classes in native arts and crafts. The tribe also hosts powwows and special events throughout the year, including Thanksgiving and Christmas dinners. The village (which is also the tribal home) provides easy access to Pocomoke Sound, either by canoe or pontoon boats; tours of the local bird sanctuary, wildlife refuge, and Pocomoke Sound are offered.

Deal Island

This three-mile-long spit of land is accessible by car at the end of Route 363. Ancestors of some of the current 350 inhabitants began to make a living from the sea here in 1675. **Arby's General Store** is a combination fisherman's supply store/restaurant you'll encounter when first crossing the bridge. The food is local and fresh, in spite of the sign that advertises the mouthwatering duo of bloodworms and cheese steak.

Two of the island's churches, **St. John's Methodist Episcopal** and **John Wesley United Methodist**, come complete with their own cemeteries. The epitaphs tell the story of life in a watermen's community. Graves are covered with concrete slabs; because of the high water table, they cannot be dug to the standard depth.

The island's 20-vessel skipjack contingent— the last of the 19th-century oyster fleet—is docked at the end of the road, in the village of **Wenona**. To see them, it's best to come late in the day, when they return from harvesting on the bay. There's a skipjack race every Labor Day weekend. Get the latest Deal Island news at www.dealislandmaryland.com.

ACCOMMODATIONS

◖ Waterloo Country Inn (28822 Mt. Vernon Rd., Princess Anne, 410/651-0883, $125–255 Apr. 1–Oct. 31, $125–225 off-season) is the place to go for a romantic getaway in elegant surroundings. Henry Waggaman, a wealthy local landowner, built the house in 1750 as a showplace residence. Like many properties that lie some distance from an urban center, the manor suffered years of neglect before being lovingly restored by Theresa and Erwin Kraemer, who emigrated from Switzerland in 1995.

They came upon the crumbling edifice while visiting friends in the area, fell in love with it, and took the necessary actions to refurbish it and turn it into a wonderful B&B. Rooms are tastefully decorated in the Victorian style.

Canoes are available for guest use, and the nearby waterways are a haven for migrating Canada geese and other waterfowl. Paddling along during the late afternoon is an almost surreal experience. The inn also has a swimming pool and bicycles for guests.

The Waterloo serves dinner by advance request—the menu is a sophisticated blend of American and Swiss entrées—and occasionally hosts special events. If you'd prefer peace and quiet, make sure your visit doesn't coincide with one of these. Breakfast is included with an overnight stay.

FOOD

Peaky's (30361 Mt. Vernon Rd., Princess Anne, 410/651-1950, lunch and dinner daily, lunch $7, dinner $14) is owned, as you might expect, by the Peacocks—Greg and Anne. It's the hot spot in the area; everybody seems to eat here all at once. The good news is there's plenty of room. The menu is classic American diner: grilled ham-and-cheese sandwiches, fried chicken, rack of pork ribs. The prices are classic, too, and the pies are homemade.

If you're looking for a quick, inexpensive sandwich or supplies for several days, go to **Lankford Sysco Food Services** at the intersection of Route 667 and U.S. 13. The company store there has a deli and a grocery/produce store. You may not need a 20-pound bag of ginger snaps, but even small items are priced reasonably.

Allegro Coffee & Tea Salon (11775 Somerset Ave., 6A, Princess Anne, 410/651-4520) is a homey stop for a quick cup and a leisurely browse among the gift items for sale.

SOMERSET COUNTY INFORMATION

Contact **Somerset County Tourism** (P.O. Box 243, Princess Anne, MD 21853, 410/651-2968 or 800/521-9189, www.visitsomerset.com).

Snow Hill

Snow Hill, the county seat of Worcester, was settled in 1642 and made its mark as a trading port for schooners and steamboats. Today, the sedate river town offers a quiet getaway with stately B&Bs, a fine small museum, a historic village built around a peat-fired furnace, and canoe trips on the mirror-like Pocomoke River.

SIGHTS
Julia A. Purnell Museum

This museum (208 W. Market St., 410/632-0515, www.purnellmuseum.com, 10 A.M.–4 P.M. Tues.–Sat. and 1–4 P.M. Sun. Apr.–Oct., adults $2) is named in honor of the mother of a local resident. At the age of 85, a fall confined Mrs. Purnell to a wheelchair; she took up folk art needlework and completed more than 1,000 pictures before her death in 1943—two months after her 100th birthday, and two years after she was inducted into the National Hobby Hall of Fame. Many of her pictures depict historic buildings and scenes from Snow Hill, and the museum continues to focus on local history. Tools, toys, machines, curios, and clothing are exhibited, along with their stories. Though many small museums fall into the dusty-cabinet category, this one makes the displays lively and colorful. In keeping with Mrs. Purnell's love of needlework, the museum holds the Delmarva Needle Art Show and Competition in September. If you're expecting grandma's embroidered linens, you're in for a surprise. Submissions include cross-stitch, embroidery, tatting, lace, quilting, and appliqué, all expertly done—and some so fantastically modern that the old techniques seem new again. One recent award winner was a portrait done in sepia-toned yarns that was indistinguishable from a photograph. This has to be seen to be appreciated.

Historic Homes of Snow Hill

While walking around the historic homes of Snow Hill (a walking tour brochure is available at the Purnell museum or from Worcester County Tourism), you might come across the **Mt. Zion One-Room School Museum** (Church and Ironshire Sts., www.octhebeach.com/museum/zion.html, $2), which was moved to Snow Hill from the countryside and opened to the public in 1964. The school contains 19th-century texts and furnishings. It's open 1–4 P.M. Tuesday–Saturday mid-June–September 7. One of the loveliest of the area's public historic homes is **Costen House** (206 Market St., 410/957-3110, 1–4 P.M. Wed.–Sat. May–Oct., $2), a Queen Anne Victorian with extensive gardens that once was home to the mayor of Pocomoke.

Furnace Town

This restored village (Old Furnace Rd., four miles north of Snow Hill 410/632-2032, www.furnacetown.com, 10 A.M.–5 P.M. daily Apr.–Oct., $4 adults) is built around an iron furnace once fueled by bog-ore; in the 1840s, the furnace was a feat of mechanical engineering unmatched in the state. During its nearly 80 years of operation, it was converted from the standard cold-blast method to the high-tech (for the 19th century) hot-blast method using an innovative system of recirculated heated air. Various artisans demonstrate 19th-century crafts in the village buildings and on the grounds.

The village includes a museum, woodworker's cottage, weaver's house, blacksmith shop, print shop, woodworkers shop, and the Old Nazareth Church. Off the main parking lot, the Nature Conservancy maintains an easy mile-long trail through the Pocomoke Forest and over the **Nassawango Cypress Swamp**. The preserve is open year-round, and Nassawango Creek is banked by centuries-old bald cypress and black gum trees. One way to appreciate the serene beauty of the area is by canoe, between Nassawango Road and Red House Road. This is a two-mile route, and canoes may be launched on Red House Road, or it can be reached from Snow Hill via the Pocomoke River—about three miles away. Canoes may be rented in Snow Hill.

To get to Furnace Town by car from Snow Hill, take Route 12 north five miles. Turn left (west) on Old Furnace Road, and proceed for one mile. Furnace Town is on the left. Furnace Town often holds special events, such as a 19th-century Christmas church service in December and the Worcester County Fair in August.

RECREATION

The Pocomoke is an exceptionally beautiful and uncrowded black-water river. The most fun way to see it is by canoe or kayak. The **Pocomoke River Canoe Co.** (312 N. Washington St., 410/632-3971 or 800/258-0905) rents both (and 14-foot aluminum boats) by the hour, day, or weekend. It also offers trips that include portage to the put-in and take-out sites.

ACCOMMODATIONS

The **River House Inn** (201 E. Market, Snow Hill, 410/632-2722, www.riverhouseinn.com) offers two deluxe cottages and two apartments

Furnace Town steam vents

in a separate building set on more than two acres of rolling lawns that lead down to the Pocomoke River. The Riverview Hideaways features two suites, both with mini-fridges and microwaves ($250 each); the River Cottage ($250) carriage barn has a microwave, fridge, and coffeemaker; the Ivy Cottage ($300) features all the comforts of home: fireplace, hot tub, TV, dining area, 1.5 baths, a full kitchen, and a bedroom upstairs. Larry and Susanne Knudsen have restored the house and outbuildings to their former Greek Revival glory, and they furnished everything in period style. The covered porches provide space for luxurious naps on hot summer afternoons, and the Adirondack chairs on the river's edge have armrests big enough for a wineglass.

The Mansion House Bed & Breakfast (4436 Bayside Rd., Public Landing, Snow Hill, 410/632-3189, www.mansionhousebnb.com, rooms $140–160, Sunset Cottage $150–300 per night or $1,000 per week) is on the National Register of Historic Places. The property overlooks a broad expanse of Chincoteague Bay with Assateague Island in the distance. This planter's residence was built around 1835 and has been carefully restored to its original charm, It's located in the village of Public Landing, about five miles from Snow Hill. The four guest rooms in the Mansion House all have private baths, fireplaces, and three feature a water view. Sunset cottage is two blocks from the main house, and has a view of Paw Paw Creek and the Chincoteague Bay.

FOOD

A few local recommendations are: **Palette** (104 W. Green St., 410/632-0055, dinner Tues.–Sat. $12–25) for fare with a French twist; **Take 2 Scoops** (111 Pearl St., 410/632-3933) for great homemade ice cream; **China Moon** (305 E. Market St., 410/632-0885, lunch and dinner daily, $6–17) for American Chinese; **Tavern on Green Street** (208 West Green St., 410/632-5451, lunch and dinner daily, $5–18) for pub food; and **My Sister's Place** (5610 B Market St., 410/632-1154, breakfast and lunch Mon.–Sat., $6–20) for sandwiches and light meals.

Berlin

Colonial travelers once looked forward to this stop on the old Philadelphia Post Road, mainly due to the Burleigh Inn. In fact, the village name is thought to be a contraction of Burleigh Inn, hence the emphasis on the first syllable (BUR-lin, as in "I was burlin' through town when I saw the police car"). The inn is no more, but this pretty little town has a wonderful hotel and a number of historic homes among its tree-lined streets. If you saw the film *Runaway Bride,* with Richard Gere and Julia Roberts, you got an eyeful of Berlin. Besides being Hollywood's version of a small midwestern town, it's a popular place to stop on the way to or from Ocean City.

SIGHTS
Calvin B. Taylor House Museum

One of Berlin's historic homes is open to the public (Main and Baker Sts., 410/641-1019, www.taylorhousemuseum.org). The Taylor House gives visitors an inside look at 19th-century decorative arts and features a collection of local memorabilia. It's open 1–4 P.M. Monday, Wednesday, Friday, and Saturday from Memorial Day to October. Donations are appreciated.

ACCOMMODATIONS

The **Atlantic Hotel** (2 N. Main St., 410/641-3589 or 800/814-7672, www.atlantichotel.com, standard $85–180, deluxe $115–215) is so modern and meticulous, you wouldn't know that it's been around since 1895. But much of that Victorian flavor is retained—the rooms are spacious, with all the amenities, and the hotel has an elevator, a rarity in vintage buildings. This is a pleasant, well-run hotel that also offers an apartment and cottage ($140–230). Room rates depend on season and day of the week; midweek winter rates are always lowest. Richard Gere himself slept at the Atlantic and

© JOANNE MILLER

Atlantic Hotel

the hotel staff found him "real nice and down-to-earth" and "good-looking in person, but shorter than I thought."

Merry Sherwood Plantation (8909 Worcester Hwy., Berlin, 410/641-2112 or 800/660-0358, www.merrysherwood.com, $100–175 mid-Oct.–mid-May, $125–200 mid-May–mid-Oct.) was built in 1859, the result of a union between a wealthy Philadelphian, Henry Johnson, and a local girl, Elizabeth Henry. There are five rooms with private baths, two rooms with a shared bath, and a honeymoon suite. Ms. Henry's father requested that a suitable house be built for his daughter on the property given as her dowry. The 8,500-square-foot Italianate/Greek Revival structure was designed for lavish parties, with enough bedrooms to put guests up for long periods of time. It's fitting, then, that it's become an elegant country inn. The building and grounds are popular for weddings and receptions, so call ahead to see if a room is available.

FOOD

The Atlantic hotel (2 N. Main St., 410/641-3589 or 800/814-7672, www.atlantic.hotel.com) has an excellent restaurant, **(Solstice,** with dinner entrées like butter-poached beef ribeye with roast potatoes and chimichurri brown butter ($26) and pan roast wild rockfish with roasted carrots, cauliflower, and salisfy in a red-wine bacon sauce ($25). Solstice serves a less formal menu for lunch, including pork and beans (smoky black bean soup with a spicy pork and butternut squash salad, $10) and a grilled angus chuck burger with smoked bacon, blue cheese pickled red onion and rocket greens on ciabatta ($10).

The **Globe Theater and Café** (12 Broad St., Berlin, 410/641-0784, www.globetheater.com), serves breakfast, lunch, and dinner daily in addition to hosting art displays and music events. Soups and sandwiches range $5–12, and dinner entrées range $19–28. It's open daily, and there are lots of specials. Brunch on Sunday is often accompanied by live music.

Ocean City

The biggest destination in Worcester County and Maryland's Eastern Shore is Ocean City, "Miami of the North"—so nicknamed because of the 10-mile strip of fancy resort hotels and condos that line the beach and bay. Yet it's not nearly as tacky as its southern namesake or even nearby Atlantic City, saved by a lack of casinos, limited development space, and an emphasis on the beach. And what a beach it is. A seemingly endless swath of soft beige sand extends along most of the peninsula, and the wide boardwalk itself is several miles long. In the summer, brightly colored umbrellas (for rent on the beach) provide shade and color in the white-hot sun, and at night, the boardwalk is merry with strolling couples, singles, and families. Getting around is easy; there are two main north–south streets (Philadelphia heading south and Baltimore heading north—both turn into Coastal Highway above 33rd St.). Addresses are sometimes indicated as "oceanside" (closer to the Atlantic), "oceanfront" (on the beach), or "bayside" (closer to Isle of Wight Bay).

For a spot with so many part-time residents and visitors, you'd expect everything from wax museums to shell collections—not here. A few attractions aimed at tourists have been around for a while and have somehow managed to escape the oily, worn funkiness of such places. Newer attractions are squeaky clean. The city refers to itself as "The East Coast's Number One Family Resort," and it's easy to see why.

There's enough to do in town to satisfy every taste and time limit. You could spend two weeks on the miniature golf courses alone, and several standard-size courses are within easy driving distance. The beaches of southern Delaware are all within an hour by auto. Atlantic fishing is a major pastime, as is horse racing. And Ocean City has its quirks: Along the boardwalk, there's an artist who makes sand sculptures by moonlight; his creations are there to greet beachgoers the next day. Incredibly detailed, the sculptures all have religious themes, often illustrating a quote from the Bible.

If you need refueling after all the sights and activities, Ocean City is famous for its "beach food": the ultimate munchie triumvirate of Thrasher's french fries, Dumser's ice cream, and Fisher's caramel corn. There are cheap places to eat and expensive places to eat, classic and avant-garde menus. You won't be bored, guaranteed.

SIGHTS
⟨ Ocean City Boardwalk
Stretching from the inlet north past 27th Street, the boardwalk functions as a chronological history of this fishing village/resort. During the day, trams run the full length of the boardwalk; tickets are $2.75–3 and include frequent stops. The oldest and most active part of the boardwalk is between the inlet on South First Street and Eighth Street. The inlet itself didn't exist until a 1933 storm removed a swath of land that connected Assateague Island with Ocean City. Locals liked the new bay access so much, they continued to dredge the inlet to keep it open.

In 1976, sculptor Peter Toth placed his 21st carving at the base of the inlet. The artist had vowed to create works that would honor Native Americans, one for each state. He dedicated the 30-foot-tall, 100-year-old oak carving to the local Choptanks, Nacotchtanks, Chapticons, and Nanticokes. The sculpture, dubbed the **Inlet Indian,** serves as his memorial to the first people.

At the beginning of the boardwalk, just beyond the inlet Indian, the Ocean City Life-Saving Station Museum sits on the location of a U.S. Coast Guard lifesaving station designated by the federal government in 1878. Surfmen patrolled the beach on foot and horseback, watching for foundering vessels. The station was in use until 1964, when a new station was built on the bayside.

A little farther north, Trimper's Rides began in 1902 with the installation of a steam-powered 45-animal carousel, and has been expanded since.

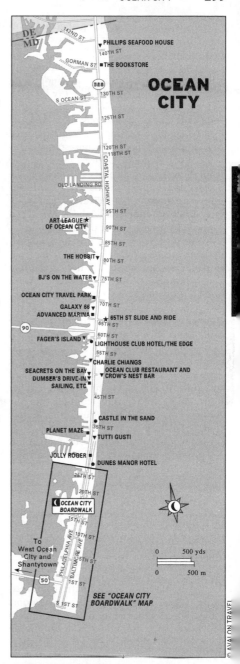

Grandparents now bring their grandchildren to ride their favorite steeds or sit on the carousel's rocking chair.

Taylor's Ocean Pier was completed in 1907, offering visitors a place for line fishing and trapshooting. Destroyed by fire in 1925, the city built a larger pier, complete with a frame building used as a convention hall and teen center. The building has been remodeled to hold souvenir shops and concessions.

In 1905, Rudolph Dolle, a candy-maker from New York, began his business on the boardwalk. He lived over the store and hand-pulled his most famous creation: salt-water taffy. **Dolle's Candyland** has been owned and operated by generations of the same family.

Women played a major role in the development of Ocean City as a resort destination. Lizzie Hearne turned her eight-room beach house off Dorchester Street into a hotel in 1905. A nearby cottage, the Belmont, was joined to the Hearne property, and the **Belmont-Hearn Hotel** is currently run by the fourth and fifth generations of the original family. The **Lankford Hotel** is another example. Several hotels still in operation a block from the boardwalk were also built around this time: Josephine Hastings converted her house and two adjacent cottages into the **Avelon Inn** (1st and N. Baltimore Sts.—note that S. 1st St. is on the inlet, and 1st St. is several blocks north). Ms. Hastings also built the **Atlantic House** (N. Baltimore between 5th and 6th Streets).

Two blocks west of the boardwalk, at 502 South Philadelphia Avenue, **Dumser's** has built a replica of its original pier building that stood on the boardwalk. Inside, a full-scale manufacturing plant is on view, and visitors can enjoy a sundae in the adjacent ice cream parlor.

The remainder of the boardwalk contains the usual compendium of souvenir shops and T-shirt emporiums, and a smattering of restaurants and fast-food places. Their doors blow open with the late spring winds and slam shut with the arrival of autumn. But Ocean City will continue on, with the boardwalk as its backbone.

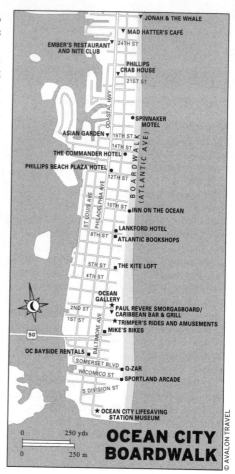

OCEAN CITY BOARDWALK

© AVALON TRAVEL

Amusement Parks

Probably the oldest ongoing attraction in Ocean City is **Trimper's Rides and Amusements** (Baltimore and 1st Sts. on the boardwalk and fishing pier, www.beach-net .com/trimpers), which has been around since the early 1900s. But the whirling rides, brightly lit games, and mechanical fortune-tellers are so well maintained that the only real reference to Coney Island is an antique Coney Island–style Herschel-Spellman merry-go-round, glittering with jewels and fantasy animals.

© JOANNE MILLER

Ocean City's finest

Daniel Trimper bought the massive carousel in 1902—the only other carousel similar to this one, incidentally at Coney Island, was destroyed by fire. There's plenty of neon, skill games, Ferris wheels, merry-go-rounds, and bumper rides—more than 100 in all—so kids won't be at all disappointed. It's open year-round—during the warm months, the hours are noon–midnight on weekends, 1 P.M.–midnight during the week. As the weather cools down, the hours become shorter and some rides shut down. Tickets may be purchased in blocks or by single ride.

Jolly Roger (30th St. and Coastal Hwy., 410/289-3477, www.jollyrogerpark.com, 9 A.M.–5 P.M. Apr.–Memorial Day, 9 A.M.–midnight Memorial Day–Labor Day, 9 A.M.–6 P.M. Labor Day–Oct. 9 and Oct. weekends, closed Nov.–Mar., not all amusements open at all hours) is the city's largest family entertainment center, with a water park, car racing, miniature golf, rides, games, and concessions. Rates are based on individual amusements.

One of the newer mini-amusement parks in town is **65th St. Slide & Ride** (bayside at 65th St., 410/524-5270, www.slidenride.com, 10 A.M.–6 P.M. May–June and Sept., later hours July–Aug., closed Oct.–Apr.), with water slides, miniature golf, batting cages, bumper boats, and more.

Planet Maze (33rd Street and Coastal Highway, 410/524-4386, wwwlplanetmaze.com) is open year-round, offering water play such as indoor and outdoor tubes and slides, tunnels, and a misty maze for hot days. There's a video arcade for the less active. It's open weekdays 10 A.M.–6 P.M. (until 9 P.M. weekends) and stays open until midnight Memorial Day–Labor Day. Winter hours vary, so call or visit the website to confirm.

There are two laser-tag places in town, both with high-tech arcades. **Laser Storm** (33rd St. and Coastal Hwy., part of Planet Maze) offers a "Stargate" arena. **Q-Zar** (401 S. Atlantic Ave./boardwalk, 410/289-2266, www.ocean-city.com/q-zar, 9 A.M.–2 A.M.) is right off the beach. Both are open year-round.

Frontier Town Western Theme Park (Rte.

KRAZY GOLF

Ocean City is Fantasy Island when it comes to miniature golf. Local course owners try to outdo each other with themes, exemplified by figures and settings made of chicken wire and plaster, enhanced by imagination and a creative sense of geography. Ice Land Golf, at the south end of the peninsula, is notable for oversized polar bears and frolicking penguins; Hawaiian Gardens relies on the tiki torch, as does the Polynesian section of the 136th Street triple course. The other two courses on the property are Pirate (masted ships, peg legs, and parrots) and Safari (elephants, lions, and giraffes). Viewed from the street, this one presents a very confused cultural picture.

While our imaginations are primed, it would be a fantasy violation to leave out Medieval Castle & Big Top Circus, and Dinosaurs! & Indoor Underwater. Somewhere, people are making big bucks creating giant clown heads and life-size rubber pterodactyls. Meanwhile, right here in Ocean City, visitors can spend many a lazy evening swinging miniature putters over a gargling sea monster, or aiming between the legs of a dancing suit of armor. If all else fails, return to the Garden of Eden. You can go home again.

- **Bamboo Golf:** 3rd Street and Philadelphia, 410/289-3374

- **Doughroller Bamboo Golf:** 41st Street and Philadelphia, 410/524-2476

- **Garden of Eden:** 19th Street and Philadelphia, 410/289-5495

- **Ice Land Golf:** 400 South Philadelphia Street, 410/289-0443

- **Jungle Golf:** 30th Street and Philadelphia, 410/289-4902

- **Maui Golf:** 57th Street and Philadelphia, 410/424-8804

- **Old Pro Golf Dinosaurs! & Indoor Underwater:** 68th Street, 410/524-2645

- **Old Pro Golf Lost Temple:** 23rd Street and Coastal Highway, 410/289-6501

- **Old Pro Golf Medieval Faire:** 28th Street, 410/289-9286

- **Old Pro Golf Pirate, Safari, & Polynesian:** 136th Street, 410/524-2645

And on the Delaware border above 145th Street:

- **Fen-Tiki Golf:** Fenwick Avenue and Coastal Highway, 302/537-9779

- **Golf Down Under:** Route 54 and Coastal Highway, 302/539-1199

611, West Ocean City, 410/641-0057, www.frontiertown.com, 10 A.M.–6 P.M. mid-June–Labor Day) has developed the Disney concept of Frontierland into an entire park. Wild West shows, gunfights, paddle boats, trail rides, Indian dancing—one admission covers it all.

Baja Amusements (12639 Ocean Gateway/U.S. 50, West Ocean City, 410/213-2252, www.bajaoc.com) offers a large go-kart track, just west of the city. It's open 9 A.M.–midnight during the warm months, and 9 A.M.–sunset October 1–November 15.

Sportland Arcade (506 S. Atlantic Ave./boardwalk at Wicomico Street, 410/289-4987) offers the latest electronic games, along with virtual reality theater. Up to 20 people can participate together, competing with each other to play out scenes. There's also a section of "Las Vegas–style" games with the opportunity to win tickets that can be converted to prizes. Call for hours.

Art Galleries

Ocean Gallery (2nd St. at the boardwalk, 410/289-5300, www.oceangallery.com) isn't really an art gallery, unless you're seriously looking for paint-by-numbers seascapes, those big rolling ocean pictures of the sort that decorate motels located several hundred miles from saltwater. The real art here is the building itself, which is made of nailed and pasted-together bits of wood, parts of torn paintings, signs, and other flotsam. Once in a while, an equally flamboyant art car encrusted with leftovers from the building's exterior is parked on the street outside.

The **Art League of Ocean City** (516 94th St., 410/524-9433, www.artleagueofoceancity .org, 11 A.M.–4 P.M. Tues.–Thurs. and 1–4 P.M. Fri.–Sun. year-round, free) is a community-oriented organization that sponsors classes, workshops, and a public art exhibit (no paint-by-numbers here). Meet the artists at a reception held the first Friday of each month (5–7 P.M.).

Museums
Ocean City Life-Saving Station Museum
(boardwalk at the inlet, 410/289-4991, www .ocmuseum.org, 10 A.M.–10 P.M. daily June–Sept., 10 A.M.–4 P.M. daily May and Oct., $3) is a fascinating small museum that preserves the history of the U.S. Life-Saving Service, telling the story of the heroes who were always at the ready to rescue passengers and crew from downed ships. Call for winter hours. The museum also focuses on Ocean City and its past. Exhibits change regularly; a recent one displayed delightfully kitschy shell-covered souvenirs from the town's past—jewel boxes and mermaids, mirrors and salt shakers. The museum's displays are both informative and charming; who could resist a collection of sand from around the world and dollhouse-sized models of local hotels and businesses? It's a fond look at a resort that's been functioning for more than a century. Don't let the big shark get you!

Wheels of Yesterday (12708 Ocean Gateway, West Ocean City, 410/213-7329, www .wheelsofyesterday.com, 9 A.M.–9 P.M. June–Sept., 9 A.M.–5 P.M. Oct.–May, $4) is a must-see for car buffs, especially those with an eye for classic models. The 1928 Lincoln Overland touring car used in Jack Benny's TV program during the 1950s is here, as is an 1830 rural mail delivery wagon and a 1934 racing car, all in prime condition. There's an early version of a recreational vehicle, and an intact 1950s service station.

ENTERTAINMENT
Nightlife
Ocean City has a major bar scene at night, sometimes featuring live music. The acknowledged premier spot in town, which many other night spots are modeled after, is **Seacrets** (49th St. and bayside, 410/524-4900, www .seacrets.com, lunch and dinner daily). It serves food and drinks on a year-round artificial beach that is so Jamaican in execution, you'd be hard-pressed to remember you're in Maryland after a couple of rum drinks. The owner was the first to bring in palm trees and keep them alive by heroic measures during the intemperate winters. Seacrets is definitely still the hippest place in town, and it features live entertainment nearly every night. Get ready to shuffle to reggae—don't worry, be irie, but don't call the bartender "Ay, mon."

The **Caribbean Bar & Grill** (2nd and boardwalk in the Plim Plaza Hotel, 410/289-6181) is definitely an imitation, but has the advantage of being on the boards and next to Revere's Smorgasbord, so you can either enjoy the Caribbean's pub menu or stagger off next door to ingest large quantities of food. Live entertainment on the weekends.

Fager's Island (60th on the bay, 410/ 524-5400, www.fagers.com, lunch and dinner daily) is also a popular restaurant, with Pacific Rim cuisine, half-price specials, and Sunday brunch. It's open year-round and has a variety of live entertainment (soul, rock, Top 40) and late-night action every night. Fager's has nine brews on draft and a tequila bar. Try to make it for the sunset; the restaurant pipes in Tchaikovsky's *1812 Overture* as the bay turns bright orange.

The **Ocean Club Restaurant & Crow's Nest Bar** (49th St. at the beach, 800/638-2100, www.clarionoc.com/nightlife, lunch and dinner daily) has a great view of the beach, but it's the live entertainment and dancing most nights that brings 'em in. The restaurant is all wood and arched windows, with a view of the "tropical" beach, and the open-air bar is on the second floor. Both facilities are attached to a resort hotel, the Clarion.

BJ's on the Water (75th St. at the bay,

410/524-7575, www.bjsonthewater.com) is another restaurant that offers entertainment nearly every night; bands range from blues to zydeco, hard rock to jazz.

SHOPPING
Antiques and Collectibles

The **Seaport Antique Village** (six miles west of Ocean City on Rte. 54, 302/436-8962) is actually in tax-free Delaware; it features 25 dealers and a variety of merchandise and is open daily year-round. **Ocean Downs Flea Market** (at Bally's racetrack, U.S. 50 and Rte. 589) takes place every weekend in September.

Malls

Shantytown, just west of the bridge on U.S. 50 in West Ocean City, is where the fishing boats depart from. It's an interesting little village made up of individual shops. Of course, Ocean City has a big **Factory Outlet** mall, with Bass, Ann Taylor, Haggar, Reebok, and so on. It's at U.S. 50 and Golf Course Road, 0.5 mile west of the U.S. 50 bridge in West Ocean City.

Books

The **Mason Collection** in Shantytown Village is a book lover's paradise, with thousands of used books for sale. **The Bookstore** (137th St. and Coastal Hwy.) specializes in mysteries, but features all sorts of new and used books. **Atlantic Bookshops** (701 N. Atlantic Ave., 410/289-1776) is the place to go for new and shiny volumes. It also has outlets in Rehoboth Beach and Bethany Beach, Delaware.

Specialty Shops

One of the most popular shops in Ocean City is **The Kite Loft** (5th St. at boardwalk, 410/289-7855, and 131st St. and Coastal Hwy., 410/250-4970, www.kiteloft.com). As you might expect, kites are a big pastime on the beach, and this shop has a wide variety.

RECREATION
Bicycles

Mikes Bikes (N. Division St. and Baltimore Ave., 410/289-5404) rents bikes year-round.

On the Water

Sailing, Etc. (46th St. at the bay, 410/723-1144) rents inline skates, windsurfers, parasails, sailboats, and kayaks and includes lessons on the use of each.

O.C. Bayside Rentals (Dorchester St. at the Olde Town Marina, 410/289-7112) is the place for jet boats and pontoon boats.

Advanced Marina (66th St. at the bay, 410/723-2124) is a complete marine store with fishing equipment and waverunners, water skis, and ski tubes for rent.

The **O.C. Fishing Center** (Rte. 50, West Ocean City, 800/322-3065, www.ocfishing.com) lists a number of charter boats available for anglers of all skill levels.

The **O.C. Rocket** (Talbot St. pier, 410/289-3500, www.talbotstreetpier.com/boat rides), a speedboat, conducts dolphin-, bird-, and whale-watching expeditions that sometimes include a cruise by Assateague Island to spot wild ponies.

NOT-SO-KRAZY GOLF

Worcester County has dozens of challenging courses, including:

- **Deer Run:** 8804 Logtown Road, Berlin, 410/629-0060 or 800/790-4465, www.golfdeerrun.com.
- **Nutters Crossing:** 30287 Southampton Bridge Road, Salisbury, 410/860-4653 or 800/615-4657, www.nutterscrossing.com
- **Ocean City Golf Club:** 11401 Country Club Drive, Berlin, 410/641-1779 or 800/442-3570, www.oceancitygolfclub.com
- **River Run:** Beauchamp Road off Route 589, Ocean City, 410/641-7200 or 800/733-7786, www.riverrungolf.com (designed by Gary Player).
- **Rum Pointe:** 7000 Rum Pointe Lane, Berlin, 410/629-1414 or 888/809-4653.

Golf

Here are a few of many choices, all open year-round: **Rum Pointe Seaside Golf Links** (700 Rum Pointe Ln., Berlin, 410/629-1414 or 888/809-4653, www.rumpointe.com); **Ocean City Golf Club** (11401 Country Club Dr., Berlin, 410/641-1779 or 800/422-3570, www.oceancitygolfclub); and **Eagle's Landing** (12367 Eagle's Nest Rd., West Ocean City, 410/213-7277 or 800/283-3846, www.eagles landinggolf.com).

Harness Racing

At **Ocean Downs** (Rtes. 50 and 589, officially in Berlin, but less than one mile west of Ocean City, 410/641-0600, www.oceandowns.com), the ponies race with tiny carts behind them during the summer months. Simulcast racing is available year-round if you just need to see horses run really fast. The track restaurant offers specials on Friday and Sunday.

ACCOMMODATIONS

Lodging in Ocean City can be broken down into five subsections: big hotels, small hotels, B&Bs and inns, condo rentals, camping, and, for the truly budget-minded, sleeping in doorways. The last is recommended for those traveling close to the bone, as it's difficult to get a roof over the old noggin for less than $130 a night in season (weekdays in winter are a different story). Rates run roughly $60 per night in the low season, up to $300 in the high season, regardless of the lodging you choose. Weekly stays are discounted.

To complicate matters, each lodging's "season"—and the higher prices associated with it—is slightly different. Many accommodations are on the boardwalk—the advantage being instant access to the beach, the disadvantages (below 8th St.) being crowds and noise, more during the day than at night. Quite a few apartments are on the main streets—Baltimore heading north and Philadelphia heading south, and the cross-streets. Prices are better, but traffic is heavy all the way up the peninsula during the day, somewhat less at night. The cross-streets are slightly better, but since the blocks are so narrow, the improvement is slight. Your best bet for a quiet night is the boardwalk above 8th Street or cross streets right off the boardwalk. The following listings represent what's available. Whatever accommodation you choose, you're never more than a short stroll to the beach.

Big Hotels

Many hotels have been in operation for decades, and like all big hotels, some portion is usually being renovated. These are the rooms to ask for; the older rooms are sometimes comically small, with mattresses that offer support equivalent to stale marshmallows.

The Commander Hotel (oceanfront at 14th and the boardwalk, Ocean City, 410/289-6166 or 888/289-6166, www.commanderhotel.com, mid-Mar.–mid-Nov.) was called the "Grand Lady" and "Jewel of the Boardwalk" when it was built in 1930 by Mrs. Minnie Lynch. Innovations included an elevator and a telephone switchboard. It's now owned by fourth-generation members of the Lynch family, and has been completely modernized over the years. For an indirect oceanview efficiency on the side of the building, rates range from a rock-bottom March–April $65 weekday to $209 for a weekend night. For an oceanfront view suite, rates for those time periods are $82–279. Weekly rates are slightly lower. Lowest rates are for efficiencies with one double bed and a small refrigerator. Higher rates reflect oceanfront views, large suites with a refrigerator and a microwave, two double beds, and a private balcony. Cabanas have private balconies, full-size refrigerators, two double beds, and microwaves; they're located in the back section of the building away from the ocean and run $69–252 per night, depending on the season. The Commander also rents two-bedroom apartments by the week that range $795–1,795, depending on the season. Parking is free (a major advantage), and the hotel features indoor and outdoor pools and a guest laundry. It also offers golf packages.

Phillips Beach Plaza Hotel (1301 Atlantic Ave./boardwalk, 410/289-9121 or 800/492-5834, www.phillipsbeachplaza.com, Mar.–Dec.) has its front entrance on a side street but is actually on the beach, near 13th Street. This is the place to indulge your Victorian fantasies, right down to the heavy ruby-colored velvet draperies and crystal chandeliers. The hotel features a cozy bar and fancy restaurant (below). Rooms range $45–170 per day (no ocean view or limited ocean view) and $55–185 (ocean view), depending on the season (high season is June 25–Aug. 22). The hotel also offers lodgings ranging from small efficiencies to three-bedroom apartments, all with full kitchens, from $65–275 per day, seasonally adjusted. Weekly rates are lower. Golf packages and three-day/two-night specials with breakfast and dinner are available.

The **Dunes Manor Hotel** (28th St., one block from the boardwalk, 410/289-1100 or 800/523-2888, www.dunesmanor.com, year-round) is a modern take on the Victorian theme—think Victoria in the tropics without half her luggage. The hotel was built in 1987 and features an indoor-outdoor pool, a fitness room, and a restaurant and lounge. Word has gotten out about the free afternoon tea 3–4 P.M., so the number of "guests" in the hotel seems to double during that hour. Parking is free for one car per room. All rooms have an oceanfront view and private balcony, and rates run $45–289 per day. High season is June 28–September 1. Two types of efficiency apartments are offered, with rates ranging $109–355 per day. Packages are available.

Castle in the Sand (oceanfront at 37th St., 410/289-6846 or 800/522-7263, www.castleinthesand.com, Feb.–Nov.) is close to the Ocean City Convention Center and boasts a wide array of lodgings, from standard hotel rooms to two-bedroom cottage apartments. A 25-meter Olympic-size pool is nestled among the hotel's buildings. Some rooms feature a glass wall to take in the ocean view, others have balconies. Not all rooms have an ocean view. Rates range $69–239 per day, $395–1,895 per week for rooms and suites. Efficiency apartments range $79–279 per day, $465–1,475 per week. The high season is roughly mid-June–late August. The Castle offers good packages, plus substantial discounts for seniors.

Small Hotels, B&Bs, and Inns

Keep in mind that the older, less expensive boardwalk hotels and basic motels are often booked far in advance by regulars who come back every year.

The **Lankford Hotel** (boardwalk at 8th St., 800/282-9709 for reservations only, www.lankfordhotel.com) is a sedate and slightly creaky three-story lodging right on the boardwalk. Built in 1924, it was one of the original boardwalk hotels and is still run by relatives of the builder, Mary Quillen. The hotel welcomes guests with reasonable rates—though if you're part of the party-all-night crowd, this may not be the place for you. The rooms have private baths and air-conditioning. An ocean view ($72–120) isn't much more than a side room ($66–114). Side suites of two rooms and a bath are ideal for families ($107–175).

The **Lankford Lodge,** just around the corner on 8th Street, 100 feet from the boardwalk, has rooms with private baths and air-conditioning. Rooms run $83–127, two-room suites (one bath) are $107–175. The Lankford Hotel and Lodge also offer apartments in nearby buildings.

The **Inn on the Ocean** (1001 Atlantic Ave., 410/289-8894 or 888/226-6223, www.innontheocean.com, year-round) is one of the prettiest renovated Victorian hotels on the beach. Attractively decorated rooms, all with private baths, air-conditioning, and breakfast, range $130–290, depending on the season (high season is roughly June–Sept.). Parking is available, along with bicycles, beach chairs, and umbrellas.

The **Spinnaker Motel** (18th St. at the boardwalk, 410/289-5444 or 800/638-3244, www.ocmotels.com, Mar.–Oct.) offers kitchenettes, cable TV, and two double beds in all units. Rates start out in May $45–115, go up in June to $155–185, peak in July–mid-August at $226, then slide down again to a low of $49–79 late September–October.

The ◗ **Lighthouse Club Hotel** (56th St. bayside, 410/524-5400 or 888/371-5400, www.fagers.com, year-round) is one of the most romantic places to stay in Ocean City. Built like an octagonal lighthouse (similar to the Thomas Point Lighthouse in the Chesapeake), the structure encloses 23 luxurious suites. Marble baths, hot tubs, Caribbean-style custom decor, wet bars, and refrigerators are in each suite (some have fireplaces); most have views of Isle of Wight Bay. Though "in town," the hotel is built on the wetlands of Fager's Island, and the feel is of being much more secluded than the location would suggest. Fager's Island restaurant is connected to the hotel by a footbridge, and guests receive passes for Ocean City Health & Racquet Club, a short drive away. When I stayed there, the weather was dark and sultry, but the building seemed like a safe haven in any storm, and the rooms are more like apartments. Ask about getaway specials throughout the year that include all meals. The lowest rates of the year are $99–139, in effect January 2–March 30. High-season rates (June 15–Oct. 4) range $224–305 per night. Breakfast is included, and the hotel offers specials throughout the year.

The Edge (60th St. on the bay, 410/524-5400, ext. 4021, or 888/371-5400, www.fagers.com, year-round) is the Fager empire's newest hotel, built for luxury. Twelve suites with panoramic water views, Jacuzzis, feather beds, and natural soaps and lotions are named according to decor: South Beach, Left Bank, The Jungle, and so on. Tariffs range $209–439 per night, depending on time of year.

Condos and Apartments

These are ideal for larger groups and longer stays. Some services, such as **Summer Beach Condos** (410/289-4669 or 800/678-5668, www.seagateoc.com), only handle rentals from a specific property (in this case, Seagate, a condo community three blocks from the beach). **Ocean City Weekly Rentals** (800/851-8909, www.ocwr.com) handles a number of properties for weekly, weekend, and midweek packages. **Holiday Real Estate** (800/638-2102, www.holidayoc.com) will send a rental catalog. They also handle multiple properties in the area.

The same people who manage the Lankford Hotel, mentioned above (800/282-9709, www

.lanfordhotel.com), also rent out the **Sea Robin Apartments** on Eighth Street in a two-story older home 100 feet away from the boardwalk on Baltimore Street, the main route through town. The Sea Robin includes two apartments: one two-bedroom ($269–378 per day, $788–1,080 per week) and one three-bedroom ($411–504 per day, $1040–1,613 per week). Both apartments feature living and dining rooms, bath, and kitchen.

The Commander Hotel rents apartments within the hotel and in separate buildings, as do Phillips Beach Plaza, Dunes Manor, and Castle in the Sand. The **Sovereign Seas Condominiums** (two-bedroom/two-bath units half a block from the beach run $1,885 per week) are close to—and managed by—Castle in the Sand (410/289-6846 or 800/522-7263, www.castleinthesand.com). **Wagner Cottage** (one bedroom, one bath, $1,495 per week) is one of Castle in the Sand's cottage apartments and townhouses in the vicinity of 37th Street; all are rented by the week.

Camping

Ocean City Travel Park (105 70th St., 410/524-7601) is the only campground in Ocean City and is open year-round. It's one block from the beach and near the local bus service. It features all hookups, a laundry, and a camp store, and welcomes both RVs (no dump station) and tents.

Frontier Town (Rte. 611 and Stephen Decatur Hwy., 410/641-0880 or 800/228-5590), the Western theme park mentioned above, has all facilities for RVs and tents, and is open April–mid-October.

Additional camping is available at Assateague National Park and Assateague State Park.

FOOD
Cafés and Light Fare
Mad Hatter's Cafe (25th St. between Baltimore and Philadelphia Aves., 410/289-6267) serves deli fare (including vegetarian items) to eat in or take out—they also offer free delivery. Prices average $9.

Beach Food

For the best sand-and-sea cuisine, look to Ocean City's holy triumvirate: Dumser's, Thrasher's, and Fisher's.

Dumser's Drive-In (49th St. and Coastal Hwy., 410/524-1588) has been around since 1939. The restaurant is justifiably famous for its homemade ice cream, serving up big milkshakes, floats, sodas, sundaes, and cones. For lunch and dinner, there's a malt-shop menu with sandwiches and subs (average $8).

Thrasher's, with several locations on the boardwalk, is known for its french fries. Other beach eats, like corn dogs on a stick, are also available (under $5).

Fisher's, also on the boardwalk in several locations, is the place for caramel corn and sweets (under $5).

There's an outlet for everything these days. The **Jerky Outlet** (12842 U.S. 50, just over the bridge in West Ocean City, 410/213-1830) features Polish sausage, as well as a plethora of dried meats and a deli.

Buffets

The **Paul Revere Smorgasbord** (2nd St. and boardwalk, 410/524-1776) is a cherished hangout for the college crowd and families on a budget. The all-you-can-eat colonial feast Friday–Saturday is $9.99 for adults, less for kids, and even cheaper if you get there between 4 and 4:30 P.M. There's plenty of meat, plenty of fish, and lots of carbs—gourmet it's not, but you'll be fortified for several busy days.

Though it can't match the prices at Paul Revere's, **Embers Restaurant & Nite Club** (24th St. and Coastal Hwy., 410/289-3322) is a huge place with an all-you-can-eat seafood buffet with prime rib bar and breakfast buffet plus à la carte dishes ($12–30). It's open 2–11 P.M. March–October.

Jonah & the Whale Seafood Buffet (boardwalk and 26th St., 410/524-2722) is another big place with an all-you-can-eat seafood buffet, including a raw bar, dessert and salad bars, and a prime rib carving station. Prices are similar to Embers. It's open 4–9 P.M. mid-May–mid-September and offers early-bird specials.

Asian

Charlie Chiangs (5401 Coastal Hwy., 410/723-4600) advertises Hunan and Szechwan cuisine, but the menu concentrates on Mandarin-style favorites—General Tso's chicken, kung pao trio (chicken, beef, and shrimp), and O.C. specialties such as golden softshell crabs. It's open for lunch and dinner every day, and entrées average $14.

The Rice House (Rtes. 50 and 611, Teal Marsh Shopping Center, West Ocean City, 410/213-8388) serves a full Chinese menu ($9) in addition to sushi. It's open for lunch and dinner daily.

Asian Garden (1509 Philadelphia Ave., 410/289-7423) covers a lot of bases. Its menu features Chinese, Nepalese, and Indian dishes. It's open for dinner daily, and entrées average $11.

Italian

Tutti Gusti (3324 Coastal Hwy., 410/289-3318, www.ocean-city.com/tuttigusti, dinner Wed.–Mon.) gets my vote for the best food in town. Whole roasted garlic and olive oil accompanies fresh bread, and the housemade pappardelle pasta bathed in fresh Bolognese tomato sauce is excellent. It features a full range of Italian specialties and desserts. Entrées range $14–24. Tutti Gusti is open during the summer high season (until Oct. 15) and plans to stay open all year. Several patrons recommend the "weapons grade" martini. Reservations are a good idea.

O.C. Traditional

The restaurant most people associate with Ocean City is **Phillips Crab House** (21st and Coastal Hwy., 410/289-6821, lunch and dinner April–Oct.). Other locations are Phillips by the Sea (boardwalk and 13th St. in Phillips Beach Plaza Hotel, 410/289-9121, lunch and dinner Mar.–Dec.) and Phillips Seafood House (141st St. and Coastal Hwy., 410/250-1200, lunch and dinner Feb.–Nov.). You'll see the Phillips name a lot in Maryland. The restaurants employ so many people that the company imports help from overseas and provides inexpensive housing for them in Ocean City. The empire started with A. E. Phillips, a waterman from Fishing Creek on Hooper's Island. His grandson Brice moved to Ocean City in 1956 and opened a fresh crab takeout on 21st and Coastal Highway. It's still in operation, filling a corner of the larger restaurant, which is decorated in what the employees call "early Shirley," Shirley being Mrs. Phillips: carousel horses and Victorian stained-glass windows. Phillips serves a full menu (entrées average $18), but it's known for the buffet. It features snow crab, steamed blue crab, raw clams and oysters, cooked shrimp, and lots more, for around $30. You might want to wash it all down with an Eastern Shore Lemonade: citron vodka, triple sec, sour mix, and 7-Up.

You'll find many more locals than tourists at the **Hobbit** (101 81st St., 410/524-8100, dinner daily $26). It's the kind of dark wood/oak tables/big plates place that has kept people coming back for decades.

Crab Alley Restaurant and Seafood Market (9703 Golf Course Rd. and Sunset Ave., West Ocean City, 410/213-7800, lunch and dinner daily year-round, $12–30) is another eatery that's popular with locals. It's off the beaten path—on the west side, a few blocks south of Route 50. Though the restaurant serves a typical seafood menu, the ultra-fresh fare is brought in by local watermen.

Nouvelle Cuisine

◖ **Galaxy 66 Bar & Grille** (6601 Coastal Hwy., 410/723-6762, lunch and dinner daily year-round, $16–36) could be set in a major city; its sharply designed blue-and-gold, astronomically correct interior looks as if it's been plucked out of New York or San Francisco. The food tastes as good as it looks, and the wine list is sophisticated—in fact, it won a *Wine Spectator* Award of Excellence.

GETTING AROUND

The most common way to get to Ocean City is by car, though the area is serviced by a municipal airport three miles west (12724 Airport Rd., Berlin, 410/213-2471). Taxi service and car rentals are available at the airport.

Ocean City has wisely instituted a public transportation system that operates along the Coastal Highway January–late September, 24 hours a day. **The BUS** runs every 10 minutes 6 A.M.–noon and every 5–7 minutes noon–3 A.M., and every 20 minutes 3–6 A.M. May–September. You can catch it every other block from South First to 141st Streets on Philadelphia Avenue (which becomes the Coastal Highway as it proceeds north) and Baltimore Avenue. Two dollars (exact change) buys unlimited use within a 24-hour period. Call 410/723-1606 for more information. A handicapped bus is also available 7 A.M.–11 P.M., daily; call 410/723-1606 24 hours in advance of pickup time.

INFORMATION

Ocean City does a good job with promotion. For an information packet, contact the **Ocean City Department of Tourism** (4001 Coastal Hwy., Ocean City, MD 21842, 800/626-2326, www.ococean.com).

Assateague Island

Assateague is a 33-mile-long sandy barrier island, originally created by glacial movements at the end of the last ice age, and continually recreated by wave and wind action. Before 1933, Assateague was connected to Ocean City, part of the peninsula that extended from Fenwick Island in Delaware. During that year, a powerful storm removed a shallow sand spit, and might have replaced it if it weren't for human efforts to deepen and widen the subsequent channel.

It's doubtful that the island was a place of permanent habitation by the local Assateague Indians, though the first European to report on it in 1524, Giovanni da Verrazano, found it "very beautiful." He promptly kidnapped an Indian boy who was attempting to hide, but gave up on a young girl of 18 "because of the loud shrieks she uttered as we attempted to lead her away." Welcome to the New World.

Over the years, small settlements grew on the island, but most faded away before 1900. As early as 1935, the federal government surveyed the island as a possible park, but no action was taken. Developers began building dwellings on the island in the 1950s, leveling the dunes for road access. Thanks to the lack of impediments, another storm literally floated the houses away in 1962.

At that point, the government did step in. Today, the island consists of three major public areas: Assateague Island National Seashore, managed by the National Park Service (the entire island, open year-round); Assateague State Park, managed by the Maryland Department of Natural Resources (the northern end); and Chincoteague National Wildlife Refuge, managed by the U.S. Fish and Wildlife Service (the southern end). There is no access from the northern end of the island to the southern end: the Maryland side is accessed via Route 611 on the mainland, the Virginia side by Route 175. The 680-acre State Park offers swimming, surf fishing, surf boarding, bathhouses with hot showers, a bait and tackle shop, camping, and a snack bar. Because of the wildlife population, pets are not permitted on most of the island.

Chincoteague Island does not allow camping in the wildlife refuge, though it's an excellent birding and wildlife spotting area. Some hunting is allowed on the Virginia side during September. The refuge was purchased with duck stamp revenues in 1943 to provide a protected environment for migrating waterfowl. The **Chincoteague Refuge Visitor Center** off Maddox Boulevard (follow signs from Route 175) offers guided walks and programs; a tour bus is available. Contact the refuge manager (Chincoteague National Wildlife Refuge, P.O. Box 62, Chincoteague, VA 23336, 757/336-6122) for more information.

Many visitors come to see the island's large herds of wild horses. The origin of the sturdy little animals has been disputed, though it's agreed that they roamed the island as early as the 17th century. Some say a Spanish or English ship floundered off the southern end of the island and the animals swam ashore; others claim that the horses are descended from domesticated stock that was grazed on the island (a handy way for local planters to avoid mainland taxes and fencing requirements). Today, a fence separates the herds across the state line. The Maryland herd is protected by the state and roams freely throughout the park, though they stay well away from groups of people on foot. The Chincoteague Volunteer Fire Company owns the Virginia herd; each year, horses are rounded up and many of the foals are sold at the Pony Penning and auction, held on the last Wednesday–Thursday In July. The funds support the fire company, and the animals are prized for their strength and longevity.

RECREATION
Water Sports
Assateague State Park provides lifeguards throughout the summer on its **swimming** beaches. Both visitors centers present **surf fishing** demonstrations during the summer; no saltwater license is required. Fishing is prohibited on lifeguarded beaches, and an after-hours fishing permit is required on the Virginia end of the island. **Crabbing, clamming, and shell collecting** are popular pastimes; clamming is especially good on Maryland's bay side. **Canoes** may be rented from a concession at the end of Bayside Drive on the Maryland side. The bay is quite shallow, and canoeists and boaters may not land anywhere on the island's Virginia end other than Fishing Point September 1–March 14.

Hiking and Biking
On the Maryland side, hikers may use several short self-guided nature trails, or trek on the beach to Ocean City or south on the off-road vehicle (ORV) trail to the Virginia border. Cyclists can enjoy three miles of paved bike paths along Bayberry Drive; bike rentals are available from a concession at the end of Bayside Drive. In Virginia, 15 miles of trails wind through marshes and forests, and include a path to the

Assateague Lighthouse. Hikers may also enjoy miles of undisturbed beach north of the Toms Cove Visitor Center. Half the trails are paved for cyclists, and a bike path leads from the town of Chincoteague to the refuge. In fact, bicycling is encouraged in the refuge during the busy summer weekends.

Off-Road Vehicles

ORV zones are posted and maps are available at the visitors centers and refuge headquarters. The National Seashore (410/641-3030) requires permits and strict specifications for ORVs. You can also contact the Assateague Island National Seashore (7206 National Seashore Ln., Berlin, MD 21811) for information.

Camping

The Maryland side features the **Barrier Island Visitor Center,** maintained by the Assateague Island National Seashore. A live touch tank, exhibits, guided walks, and other programs are available to visitors. This is also the place to inquire about backcountry camping: two oceanside sites and four bayside camps are backpack- and canoe-accessible. They have chemical toilets but no drinking water, and are free with a parking and backcountry use permit. The nearest is four miles from parking. For more information, stop by the visitors center or contact Assateague Island National Seashore (7206 National Seashore Ln., Berlin, MD 21811, 410/641-1441, www.nps.gov/asis).

In addition, the State Park offers two car campgrounds, Oceanside and Bayside, which are equipped with chemical toilets, drinking water, and cold showers. There is a dump station but no hookups, and a few sites are for tents only. Some are open year-round. Reservations are necessary; Reserve America (877/444-6777, www.recreation.gov) takes reservations up to six months in advance of the date you want to camp April 15–October 15. The State Park campground can accommodate any size camping unit, but may be closed during the winter. Reservations for a full week may be made only during the summer. For more information and reservations, contact Assateague State Park (7307 Stephen Decatur Hwy., Berlin, MD 21811, 410/641-2120).

Chincoteague Island does not allow camping in the wildlife refuge.

INFORMATION

Worchester County covers a lot of ground, from scenic Snow Hill to the sandy reaches of Assateague and Ocean City. For comprehensive information, contact **Worcester County Tourism** (104 West Market St., Snow Hill, MD 21863, 410/632-3110 or 800/852-0335, www .visitworchester.org). Ocean City's tourist site is also a good source for most of the county.

UPPER DELAWARE

The top half of Delaware—consisting of New Castle and upper Kent counties—seems fated to be either ignored or flambéed by the press and the world at large. Yes, Wilmington used to have problems (long since quelled), and Delawareans have rightfully had it up to here with people saying "Dela-WHERE?" In spite of it all, the area continues to offer a trove of cultural treasures and American history for willing seekers.

The Brandywine Valley forms most of New Castle County's topography and boasts the lion's share of Delaware's scenic properties, thanks to its du Pont heritage. The entire valley is rich with horse properties and stately homes.

Though the Philadelphia-Wilmington corridor can truly be called a megalopolis, there are plenty of pockets of green west of the Delaware River, including two public parks bequeathed by... who else? On the "Maryland side" of New Castle County, the University of Delaware anchors the lively town of Newark, a hot spot for late-night music and entertainment. The area's many shopping malls lure visitors with the promise of tax-free purchases.

As one of the wealthiest cities in the nation—thanks to the clustering of Fortune 500 companies—Wilmington is experiencing a renaissance reminiscent of resurgences in Pittsburgh and Baltimore. The Riverfront Development Corporation (RDC) is a state-funded organization that's transforming Wilmington's Christina riverfront into a center for arts, entertainment, dining, and shopping. The area is becoming a destination, with attractions that include changing events and exhibitions.

© JOANNE MILLER

HIGHLIGHTS

◖ Hagley Museum/Eleutherian Mills:
The origin of the du Pont fortune, this former
black-powder mill is set in a serene narrow gorge.
Also on the grounds are the Hagley Museum and
Library, the Du Pont family home, barn, and business office – all in the setting of natural greenery
and formal gardens (page 317).

◖ Winterthur: Perhaps the best-known
property in the du Pont constellation,
Winterthur (WIN-tur-toor) continues the family fascination with horticulture combined with
American decorative arts. The vast grounds
and multiple buildings filled with his family's
treasures are a must-see (page 321).

◖ Delaware History Museum: This innovative museum, housed in a storefront in
downtown Wilmington, is one of the most
pleasant ways to combine education and fun
in town. Set in a renovated 1940s Woolworth's,
it's packed with cleverly presented information
about the first state. Nostalgic memorabilia,
artifacts, art, and scale-model historic scenes
are interspersed with audiovisual displays and
computer games (page 327).

◖ Delaware Art Museum: This museum is
distinguished by outstanding holdings in works
by American illustrators, paintings and sculpture
by American fine artists and a world-class collection of paintings by the English group known
as the Pre-Raphaelites (page 330).

◖ New Castle Historic Homes: The entire town of old New Castle is a treasure, and
the best way to appreciate it is to tour the
town's historic homes: all authentic, all from
different eras and classes (page 337).

◖ Fort Delaware State Park: An island
paradise – for the birds! (This is a major stop
on the flyway.) A superbly maintained park
on Pea Patch Island, the fort was originally
built in 1819 for the protection of Wilmington
and Philadelphia, then served as a prison for
Confederate soldiers during the course of the
Civil War (page 341).

LOOK FOR ◖ TO FIND RECOMMENDED SIGHTS,
ACTIVITIES, DINING, AND LODGING.

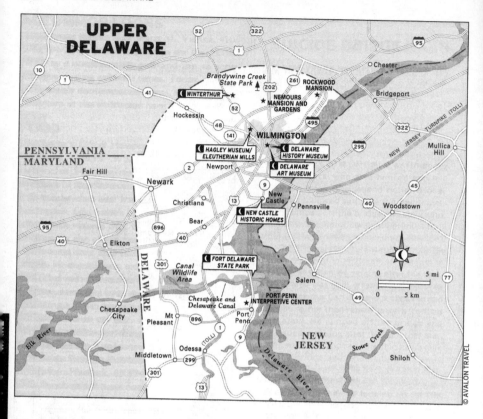

The Delaware Theatre Company pioneered the revitalization of this area when it built a marvelous 400-seat theater along the riverfront in 1985. Development on the Christina River is evolving into a world-class draw, equal to the area's restaurants and hostelries. It's happening now—don't miss it.

South of Wilmington, delightful New Castle and quiet Odessa (over the county line in Kent County) offer visitors contemporary history lessons—these long-standing villages are still inhabited today. However, the real draw in upper Kent County is the stunning country set aside for public use. The state and national parks and wildlife areas are beyond compare, bursting with life from both the sky—the area is a major flyway—and the salty reaches of Delaware Bay. The verdant fields that patch-

work the byways lull visitors into the beautiful calm that is upper Delaware.

HISTORY

Wilmington (along with the rest of Delaware and nearby Pennsylvania and New Jersey) got its start when the *Kalmar Nyckel* arrived from Sweden in 1638, filled with the Swedish, Finnish, Dutch, and German settlers who built Fort Christina, surrounding the first two log cabins in the New World (a Finnish form of architecture). By 1700, mills had been built along the swift-flowing Brandywine River. In 1731, Thomas Willing laid out "Willingtown" between the Christina and Brandywine Rivers. The crown chartered the town as Wilmington in 1739, in honor of Spencer Compton, Earl of Wilmington. The site was laid out as a series of "farmlets." In 1802, the du Pont family arrived and began the gunpowder factory on the outskirts of town. Since then, the du Ponts have been major players not only in Delaware, but across the nation. The Brandywine Valley—named for the river that flows from Pennsylvania to the sea—contains numerous testaments to their wealth and taste.

The town of Wilmington did not see much development until 1816, when the Industrial Revolution revved up the local economy. The Mexican War, the opening of the West, the building of the Transcontinental Railroad, the Civil War, the Spanish-American War, two world wars, and the Great Depression brought booms and busts. Today, the city's economy is based on credit-card banking and the chemical/pharmaceutical industries.

ORIENTATION

Delaware's famous "bulge" at the top of the state—a result of territorial wrangling between William Penn and Lord Baltimore—also houses one of the wealthiest and prettiest areas in the state: the Brandywine Valley. The western border is largely rural, except for development around the University of Delaware in Newark and the I-95 corridor. The eastern part from Philadelphia to Wilmington is nearly solid development, with one suburban town bleeding into another for miles.

Below the Chesapeake and Ohio Canal, the land again opens out into a rural landscape. From here all the way south, the terrain is as flat as an ironed pancake. The shore on the east side, indented with dozens of bays, is marked by small villages and enclaves of watermen; including New Castle, a charming colonial village that was once the capital of Delaware. Below New Castle, two of the state's loveliest parks welcome visitors. The land away from the shore is dotted with small towns separated by acres of farmland in shades of green, yellow, and brown.

The main route from northern Delaware to the central and southern reaches of the state is U.S. 13, also known as the DuPont Highway—and by many other more foul names by drivers

---

THE OCCUPATION OF WILMINGTON

After World War II, Wilmington experienced a great general flight from the city center, roughly the loss of 15,000 denizens over two decades. Since those who left tended to be more well off, the tax drain was enormous, and Wilmington began to unravel around the edges. After the assassination of the great humanitarian leader Martin Luther King Jr. on April 4, 1968, race riots broke out in several sections of town. Entire blocks were consumed by flames, and the mayor called in the National Guard and declared martial law. The city was occupied for nine months under restrictive curfews – far longer than necessary, according to many residents. Wilmington took years to heal. A long-hoped-for revival has sprung to life only in the last decade or so, and shows every sign of instilling new optimism in the once demoralized town.

---

who hoped to make the trip south in a hurry. It won't happen. U.S. 13 is downright festive with traffic lights, and travelers are never at a loss for roadside businesses of all types.

PLANNING YOUR TIME

Northern and Central Delaware have all kinds of different experiences to enjoy, depending on your interests. If learning about American decorating, architecture and gardening are on your checklist, the du Pont properties surrounding Wilmington are must-sees. Plan on three days: one each for **Hagley Museum/Eleutherian Mills** and the **Nemours Mansion and Gardens,** and the other for **Winterthur.** Plan to overnight in Wilmington, or, if this is a special trip, at the **the Inn at Montchanin Village.**

Wilmington packs quite a few surprises. The **Delaware History Museum** will delight people of all ages, and the **Delaware Art Museum**'s collection of illustrations and pre-Raphaelite art is an essential stop for lovers of fine art.

New Castle features interesting history, attractive lodgings, and good eateries in a charming setting—perfect for a weekend. But if you plan to stay one or two extra days, include a trip aboard the *Three Forts Ferry* and be sure to spend time at **Fort Delaware** for a picnic or event.

No road trip to the country—especially in December—would be complete without a stop at the village of **Odessa** to view the locals' special decorations.

FESTIVALS AND EVENTS

From June through September, Wilmington is home to a number of ethnic celebrations, including the Greek Festival, St. Anthony's Italian Festival, St. Hedwig's Polish Festival, and the Caribbean Festival. Since contact numbers tend to change annually, contact the Greater Wilmington Convention & Visitors Bureau for updates (in-state: 302/652-4088, elsewhere: 800/489-6664, www.visitwilmingtonde.com).

The **Wilmington International Exhibition of Photography,** often held on the university grounds in Newark in January or February, has been an annual event since the early 1930s. It's sponsored by the Delaware Photographic Society (www.delawarephotographicsociety.org/wiep).

February brings the annual **Delaware Antiquarian Book Show/Sale** to the Wilmington campus of the University of Delaware. It's a good place to scout for rare first editions.

In April, the tiny town of Delaware City holds a **Town-Wide Yard Sale** for shoppers who just can't resist a bargain.

Peek behind the scenes at **Wilmington Garden Day** (www.gardenday.org), an annual May tour of private gardens.

The second Saturday in June is **Separation Day** (www.newcastlecity.net/visitors/events) in old New Castle, when the town celebrates Delaware's separation from Pennsylvania with a fair and fireworks.

Each September since 1907, the artists' community of Arden has held its annual **Arden Fair** (www.ardenclub.com/ardenfair.htm).

During November and December, **Yuletide**

at **Winterthur** (800/448-3883, www.winterthur.org) fulfills the fussiest decorating fantasy.

INFORMATION

The Greater Wilmington Convention & Visitors Bureau (100 West 10th St., Ste. 20, Wilmington, DE 19801, in-state: 302/652-4088, elsewhere: 800/489-6664, www.visitwilmingtonde.com) serves northern Delaware. General information is also available at the **I-95 Visitor Information Center** (302/737-4059), south of Wilmington in the middle of I-95 between Route 896 (exit 1) and Route 273 (exit 3—there is no exit 2). The center can also help with hotel and motel reservations. For more information on Odessa/Upper Kent County and central Delaware, contact the **Kent County & Greater Dover, Delaware Convention and Visitors Bureau** (435 North DuPont Hwy., Dover, DE 19903, 302/734-1736 or 800/233-5368, www.visitdover.com).

GETTING THERE
By Air

The closest major airport to Northern Delaware is Philadelphia International Airport (PHL, about 30 miles north of Wilmington). Philadelphia handles flight traffic from all major carriers, and all major car rental companies are represented. The New Castle Airport traffic includes commuter airlines and limited flights from one carrier, Delta.

By Train

Wilmington is one of Amtrak's key stations (code: WIL, 100 South French St. Wilmington, DE 19801, 800/872-7245, www.amtrack.com). The Acela Express, Cardinal/Hoosier State, Carolinian/Piedmont, Crescent, Regional, Silver Service/Palmetto, and Vermonter all pass through here. There is also a minor pickup point in Newark (code: NRK, 429 S. College Ave.).

By Bus

Greyhound has a stop in Wilmington (101 N. French St., Wilmington, 302/655-6111). Information and tickets may be purchased online at www.greyhound.com or by calling 800/231-2222.

By Car

Cars are by far the easiest method of transportation in the state. The main north–south routes are: U.S. 13 (plenty of stoplights in the northern part of the state) and Route 1; east–west: I-95, U.S. 40, Routes 2 and 9 in the north, and I-301 near Odessa.

GETTING AROUND

DART First State Transit serves all three Delaware counties from the main transit stations in Wilmington and Dover, and also offers inter-county transit. Information is available at 910/652-3278 (New Castle County), 800/553-3278 (Kent and Sussex Counties), 800/652-3278 (from area codes 215, 267, 410, 443, 484, 609, 610, and 856), 302/652-3278 (all other locations), or www.dartfirststate.com Fares are $1 and up, depending on destination.

Wilmington and the surrounding area are serviced by WAVE (910/343-0106 www.wave transit.com), which runs the buses ($1 adult, exact fare required) and the free downtown trolley.

The Brandywine Valley

Embraced by Wilmington and the Pennsylvania and Maryland borders (and beyond, if you count Longwood Gardens in Kennett Square, just over the Pennsylvania border, and the Historic Homes of Odessa, south of New Castle), the Brandywine Valley is du Pont land; the famous name is everywhere. Former du Pont properties gifted or sold to the state offer the ultimate opportunity to see how the upper 1 percent lives. The du Ponts live elsewhere, but their generosity is local—the properties they've bequeathed to the public are rich in history, landscape lore, and just plain what-money-can-buy. Fortunately for the hordes of visitors that swarm over du Pont land every year, individual family members were blessed with superb taste, a refined interest in horticulture, and a generous hand. Every one of the properties open to the public is a gem for one reason or another. This is an extremely wealthy area; the back roads reveal subtly landscaped estates and grazing pleasure horses around every turn. Near the Maryland border to the west, miles of rural environs are dotted with villages and larger towns, such as Newark, along with a cheerful compendium of malls and roadside businesses.

SIGHTS

Hagley Museum/ Eleutherian Mills

Of the du Pont properties in Delaware, Hagley (302/658-2400, www.hagley.lib.de.us) is my favorite. It describes the origins of the du Pont fortune and has little of the rampant conspicuous consumption found at the other properties. The site is on Route 141, just north of the intersection of Route 100, on the east side of the road; it's open 9:30 A.M.–4:30 P.M. daily early March–December 31. From January–early March, the site is open 9:30 A.M.–4:30 P.M. on weekends and offers one guided tour each weekday at 1:30 P.M. (Henry Clay Mill opens at 1 P.M. for ticket sales). Admission is $11. The Belin House Restaurant (which may be visited without admission) is open 11:30 A.M.–4 P.M. daily early March–November 30, plus weekends in December.

The setting is serene, blooming with natural and planned beauty. Deep in a narrow gorge, the Brandywine River flows through the property, dropping 160 feet on its journey to the coastal plain. In the early spring, the mist on the river makes the fiery purples and pinks of the rhododendrons and azaleas even brighter. Just the place for a black-powder factory.

The powder yards are only one part of the property, though all facets of the business are included: rolling mills, machine shops, storehouses and drying tables, and the workers' village. Also on the grounds are the Hagley Museum and Library, the du Pont family home, barn, and business office—all in a setting of natural greenery and formal gardens.

BOOM!

Explosive black powder, composed of 75 percent saltpeter (potassium nitrate), 12.5 percent sulfur, and 12.5 percent charcoal, originated in China centuries ago. É. I. du Pont imported most of his materials: Naturally occurring saltpeter was brought from the Bengal region of India; sulfur was imported from Sicily, until sources were found in Louisiana and Mexico; and charcoal was produced onsite from burnt willow branches. Purity was important. Sulfur was boiled into a liquid, then vaporized and condensed. Saltpeter was boiled in kettles with water and a little glue, poured into cooling vats, and crystallized. It was then washed several times, dried, and pulverized.

All the ingredients were ground and sifted separately, then mixed with water proportionately. Water cooled and diluted the mixture, as it needed to be thoroughly mixed. Initially, a dangerous hours-long mortar/pestle process was used; in later years, the mixture was rolled in a circular trough under massive stone wheels, called a rolling mill.

After mixing and drying, the powder was pressed into cakes, then broken into chips, which were sieved and separated according to size and need: Cannon powder was large, while guns and fireworks required a much finer grain. The sorted powders were dried on racks, and then certain grades were glazed with graphite for easier pouring.

From 1822 on, DuPont workers used rolling mills instead of the mortar/pestle process, which made the process somewhat safer. Considering that one ounce of black powder could send an object a distance of 20 yards, and each rolling mill processed 600 pounds of powder at once, it's no surprise that nothing but wooden nails were used to construct the rolling mill rooms, and workers were routinely inspected for metal objects – a dropped belt buckle and a single spark could, and did, blow wheel and workers to their final reward.

Tours start at the Henry Clay Mill, originally built in 1814 as a cotton-spinning mill. The DuPont Company acquired the mill in 1884 and converted it to the production of powder containers. Today, visitors view exhibits, dioramas, and models that give the history of the site, as well as two special exhibitions on the second floor, installed in 2002 to celebrate the company's 200th anniversary. They include hands-on science projects, a real space suit, one of Jeff Gordon's NASCAR racers, and more. The small stone building next to the mill, a former cotton picking house, is now a gift shop called the Hagley Store. The property is 230 acres, so visitors may either walk or take vans that leave every few minutes from the Henry Clay Mill and make regular stops along the road. Each of the buildings has a costumed interpreter, all of them extremely well informed.

On Blacksmith Hill, the remaining buildings of one of several workers' communities contains a blacksmith shop (not open to the public), a carriage house, and a springhouse; the Gibbons House, a restored foreman's house; and the Brandywine Manufacturers' Sunday School, where workers' children received a serviceable if limited education. The Belin House, former home of the company's bookkeepers, is now a seasonal restaurant.

The Hagley Yard—the black-powder factory—is on the main road near the river. An exhibit of working models in the millwright shop illustrates the powder-making process. The Eagle Roll Mill, with its multiple "rooms" featuring massive eight-ton rolling wheels and five-foot-thick walls, faces the river, where blowouts—powder explosions—could do the least damage. In the 120-year period that powder was processed here, the yard experienced 288 explosions and 258 fatalities—dangerous business. The yard area also contains a press house with a hydraulic press used to compact the powder; dry tables to dry it; and a graining mill, where powder was ground, sifted, and sorted according to size. Using artifacts, the yard traces America's expansion from small, water-powered mills through the Industrial Revolution. Upstream from Hagley Yard are the remains of the Birkenhead Mills, the oldest roll mills in the yard, and their reconstructed water wheel. The engine house at the farthest end of the yard features a working 1870s steam engine, used to supplement waterpower. In contrast to the yard's utilitarian stone buildings, three remarkable native trees stand on the grounds: a 300-year-old, 85-foot bald cypress and a 121-foot butternut (the second largest in Delaware) among the rolling mills, and a 200-year-old, 135-foot green ash near the quarry.

The du Pont family home—Eleutherian Mills—overlooks the powder works. Built in 1803, the home still contains many of the original furnishings. The second floor reflects the earlier generations of du Ponts, while the first floor remains much as Éleuthère du Pont's great-granddaughter, Louise du Pont Crowninshield, left it. Nearby, the first office used by the DuPont Company is still set up for business; the barn displays carriages, wagons, and weathervanes. The front yard of the house is a restored 19th-century French garden ,as planted by Éleuthère du Pont, and the backyard of the house, which faces the creek, is a classical "ruins" garden planted by Ms. Crowninshield. The Hagley Library, a modern center for research in business and technological history, is open to the public 8:30 A.M.–4:30 P.M. Monday–Friday, as well as the second Saturday of every month.

The **Delaware Toy & Miniature Museum** (302/427-8697, www.thomes.net/toys, 10 A.M.–4 P.M. Tues.–Sat., noon–4 P.M. Sun., $6), just inside the entrance to the Hagley Museum on Route 141, is one of only three such museums in the United States. It's a mélange of antique and contemporary dollhouses, miniatures, furniture, dolls, toys, trains, lead soldiers, boats, and planes of both European and American origins. In addition to 100+ furnished dollhouses, the museum features a permanent collection of more than 700 miniature vases dating from 700 B.C. Works by Tiffany, Fabergé, and Satsuma are on display, as well as carved crystal, jade, and amethyst pieces. Though the museum mainly focuses on dollhouse miniatures, it also offers several special exhibits throughout the year, such as "A Century of Dolls" and "Trains of Yesteryear." One advantage of visiting this museum early in your stay is that it frequently offers discount tickets to Hagley.

Nemours Mansion and Gardens

For Alfred I. du Pont, price was no object. The wealthy heir built a 102-room Louis XVI–style château in 1909–1910 and named it after the town in North-Central France that Mr. du Pont's great-great-grandfather, Pierre-Samuel du Pont de Nemours, represented as a member of the French Estates General in 1789. The mansion began major renovations in 2005 and is expected to reopen in 2008.

To get to Nemours mansion, take exit 8 (Rte. 202) on I-95 and head north to Route 141. Make a right (west) on Route 141 to Children's Drive, and go left on Children's Drive at the second traffic light, then another left on Rockland Rd. The parking lot is approximately .12 mile on the right. Follow the signs to mansion parking and the reception center. Guided tours are given at 9 A.M., 11 A.M., 1 P.M., and 3 P.M. Tuesday–Saturday, and 11 A.M., 1 P.M., and 3 P.M. on Sunday May–December. Holiday tours are available from mid-November until after Christmas. Tour groups are limited in size, so visitors are strongly encouraged to make reservations: Call 302/651-6912 during regular business hours, or write to Nemours Mansion and Gardens (P.O. Box 109, Wilmington, DE 19899, sjelinek@nemours.org). Visitors must be at least 12 years of age, and no food is allowed on the premises, though the hospital cafeteria is open to visitors. The tour involves climbing several staircases. Admission is $12.

The mansion contains furniture, Oriental rugs, tapestries, and paintings dating back to the 15th century. Three hundred acres of gardens surround the mansion and extend for .33 mile along the main vista from the house. The gardens are classic French style, very formal,

DU PONT DYNASTY

Du Pont Family Home, Eleutherian Mills

In the mid-1700s, Louis XV was king of France, and Pierre-Samuel du Pont was a relatively unknown writer of plays. Pierre's mother arranged for his introduction to a group of wealthy capitalists, and he was immediately impressed by the power of the new merchant middle class. He abandoned his plays and began to compose pamphlets on the fashionable topic of bourgeois economics. One of these pamphlets found its way to Jacques Turgot, a financier and capitalist leader, who became his mentor. Du Pont was given the job of editing Turgot's new *Journal of Agriculture, Commerce, and Finance*. At 26, Pierre married his childhood sweetheart, and by 1770 had fathered two sons. Du Pont asked Jacques Turgot to act as godfather to his second child; Turgot requested that the boy be named in honor of Liberty and Peace: Éleuthère Irénée.

Pierre was involved in negotiations that led to the peace treaty of 1783 between France's new ally, the United States, and her archenemy, Britain. In return for his service, he was rewarded with nobility. He chose a coat of arms emblazoned with ostrich feathers, a lion, an eagle, and the motto "By Uprightness I Stand."

and exceedingly beautiful—especially if you like cherubs.

Mr. du Pont put the considerable unspent portion of his fortune into a trust. His will stated, "It has been my firm conviction throughout life that it is the duty of everyone in the world to do what is within his power to alleviate human suffering. It is, therefore, natural that I should desire, after having made provision for the immediate members of my family and others whom I have seen fit to remember, that the remaining portion of my estate be utilized for charitable needs." His widow, Jessie Ball

Pierre's new status proved to be a handicap during the French Revolution. He and his son Éleuthère, royalists to the end, were constantly in and out of jail. Finally, with the help of a friendly government official, Pierre pleaded senility and managed to get himself and his family exported to the New World, along with millions of francs of investment money. The family traveled to America under the noble banner of du Pont de Nemours aboard the *American Eagle*. The journey was rough – the family survived at one point on a soup made from rats.

Upon arrival, the du Ponts immediately established themselves in New Jersey and went into business in New York City. Because of his prior negotiations, Pierre had a powerful political connection in the New World: Vice President Thomas Jefferson. The family used the investment capital from France to go into a number of businesses. After a long search, É. I. purchased land along the Brandywine River in Wilmington and established his black powder mill there on April 27, 1802. He was so successful (and unscrupulous, by some accounts) that he financed many of the other du Pont undertakings – while managing to avoid paying off his French creditors.

Pierre du Pont longed to return to France, and did so. He remained there until Napoleon's return to Paris, at which point the elder du Pont sailed speedily back to the New World, where he died and was buried in the family plot near Wilmington. Meanwhile, É. I. rescued his older brother, Victor, from numerous failed schemes and bought his way into a variety of businesses and banks. Never too busy for family life, É. I. and his wife, Sophie, had seven children along the way.

On March 19, 1818, five powder rooms at the factory near the family's home exploded (the ruins are still visible at Eleutherian Mills), killing 36 workers and permanently wounding É. I.'s wife. However, É. I. rebuilt and continued to expand his businesses and political connections (Victor was already a member of Delaware's House of Representatives in 1815). É. I. du Pont died of a heart attack in 1863, in the same city – and in the same hotel – as his brother had seven years prior. He was buried to the right of Victor and their father, Pierre, in the family plot on Buck Road in Greenville.

More than seven generations of du Ponts have been born in the New World, and the family's wealth has increased exponentially. Black powder was a source of profit for many years, but the family's wealth expanded into banking, chemicals, and other industries – family members are major shareholders or own large blocks in more than 100 national corporations. With little fanfare, the du Ponts have become the wealthiest family in America.

The fifth and final du Pont resident of Eleutherian Mills, Louise du Pont, visited the home often as a guest of her grandparents. She married shipping magnate F. B. Crowninshield in 1920, and in 1923, Mrs. Crowninshield's father gave her Eleutherian Mills under the condition that she spend part of each year there. So, after renovating the home, the Crowninshields and their staff of nine – personal maid, parlor maid, chambermaid, cook, kitchen helper, waitress, laundress, and two chauffeurs – traveled to Delaware during the spring and fall of each year, spending winter in Florida and summer in Massachusetts. Eleutherian Mills, the seat of the family fortune, opened to the public after her death.

du Pont, was given control of the trust, and with her brother Edward proceeded to establish a number of medical facilities in Delaware and Florida. One of the best known is on the Nemours premises: the A. I. du Pont Institute, a hospital facility that specializes in children's medicine.

◖ Winterthur

Perhaps the best-known property in the du Pont constellation, Winterthur (WIN-tur-toor, 800/448-3883, TTY 302/888-4907, www .winterthur.org, open 9 A.M.–5 P.M. Mon.– Sat., noon–5 P.M. Sun.) illustrates the family's fascination with horticulture combined with

American decorative arts. Winterthur is on Route 52, six miles northwest of Wilmington. Tours are available for all tastes and budgets, including introduction tours, one- and two-hour decorative arts tours, and a garden walk (visitors must be escorted in the main house). Admission starts at $15 adults and goes up depending on which tour you choose.

The site was originally the home of Evelina Gabrielle du Pont (Éleuthère's daughter) and her husband, James Bidermann, who named Winterthur after the Bidermann ancestral home in Switzerland. The original house on the site was a fairly modest three-story Greek revival built in 1839; it was enlarged and renovated several times before passing into the hands of Henry Francis du Pont, great-nephew of the Bidermanns, in 1927.

Like his ancestors before him, Henry du Pont appreciated and collected fine European furniture and antiques. After World War I, a new wave of nationalistic sentiment caused collectors to look with a fresh eye at American objects. That great arbiter of taste, the Metropolitan Museum of Art in New York, opened an American Wing in 1924, and America's wealthy collectors followed suit. Henry Ford announced his plans to build a museum celebrating American ingenuity; John D. Rockefeller reconstructed the colonial capital, Williamsburg; and Henry Francis du Pont started collecting American furniture with moneyed enthusiasm.

Henry du Pont's collection quickly surpassed personal decorating needs and grew to museum size. He moved the best of his items to Winterthur, doubled the size of the existing house, and converted his home to a showplace for what many consider the most important assemblage of early American decorative arts in the world. In 1951, the du Pont family created a nonprofit institution to manage Winterthur and opened it to the public.

The public part of the museum consists of two buildings, one with 175 period rooms and another with three exhibition galleries. The period rooms contain more than 89,000 objects made or used in America between 1640 and 1860, including silver tankards made by Paul Revere and a 66-piece dinner service made for George Washington. The exhibition galleries feature both interactive displays focusing on American decorative arts and changing exhibitions. There's also a Touch-It Room, featuring a child-size period room, and a small general store with activities geared toward children. Don't miss the Campbell Collection of soup tureens in the "Glass Corridor" near the gallery wing.

The Louise du Pont Crowninshield Research Building, attached to the main house, holds the Winterthur Library, a research center for the study of American decorative and fine arts. The collection of more than 500,000 books, manuscripts, and visual images is open to the public (8:30 A.M.–4:30 P.M. Mon.–Fri.) Visitors may copy individual pages, but borrowing books is limited to Winterthur staff and decorative arts students of the University of Delaware. A variety of short- and long-term fellowships, which support undergraduate and postdoctoral study, exhibition, and publication research, are available and may include on-site housing. For details, contact the Advanced Studies Division (302/888-4649).

Winterthur's buildings are surrounded by 966 acres, 60 of which are part of Henry du Pont's naturalistic landscaping. Miles of surfaced paths and woodland trails crisscross the estate, and visitors are welcome to stroll the gardens or ride the tram. The garden starts to get interesting in February, when snowdrops, crocuses, and other early spring flowers announce themselves on the March Bank, followed by the huge, saucer-shaped plantings of flowers in Magnolia Bend in April. In May, eight-acre Azalea Woods is in full bloom, as is the Peony Garden. The Enchanted Woods, a special three-acre garden, was installed in 2001. The gardens continue to produce well into the fall. The paths are open 9 A.M.–dusk Monday–Saturday, noon–dusk Sunday.

Informal dining is available on the premises: the Cappuccino Café is near the museum entrance the main building, and the slightly fancier Garden Cafeteria (10 A.M.–4 P.M.) is in the visitors center. There are two museum stores: Books and inexpensive items are in the visitor pavilion, and another shop on the grounds at Clenny Run offers more expensive, high-quality reproductions and decorative items (it's a great store).

Delaware Museum of Natural History

The original designers of this small museum (4840 Kennett Pike/Rte. 52, 302/658-9111, 9:30 A.M.–4:30 P.M. Mon.–Sat., noon–4:30 P.M. Sun., $6) were artists in the finest sense of the word. The visual beauty of the dark interior is dreamlike: half-domed dioramas glow like jewels against a curved wall; a few feet away, a five-foot-diameter clear globe surrounds a star-like object, each of its hundreds of projections ending in a different exotic shell. The museum rightfully prides itself on its collections of shells (the 10th largest in the country), a re-creation of a section of the Great Barrier Reef set into the floor (visitors must walk across it, akin to walking on water), and a children's interactive room. The H. Lawrence du Pont (that name again!) Discovery Room offers science-related activities for children of all ages, including a Discovery Box Station, with a series of single-themed, self-contained kits containing fossils, shells, and skeletons, magnifying glasses, scales, and activity cards. Little ones will love the large Puzzler, where they can match magnetic animals to their habitats. Every member of the family will appreciate the care taken with displays. You seldom think of a natural history museum in the same terms as fine art, but these displays break all the rules.

A relative newcomer to the Brandywine Valley, the museum opened in 1972; it's also the only place in Delaware with *real* dinosaur skeletons. In addition to its regularly changing exhibits—a recent one looked at sounds that dinosaurs might have made—it's home to a set of animal models by artist Carl Akley. The models were created as scale references for an exhibit at the Museum of Natural History in New York. They depict a herd of elephants—bulls, cows, and babies—in perfect, enchanting miniature.

Rockwood Mansion

A 19th-century country estate, Rockwood (610 Shipley Rd., Wilmington, 302/761-4340, mansion tours: on the hour 10 A.M.–3 P.M. Tues.–Sun., $5; park: 6 A.M.–10 P.M. daily, free), was built in the Rural Gothic style. The mansion, conservatory, and assorted outbuildings sit on 72 acres of wooded trails. The main building is lavishly decorated with 17th- through 19th-century pieces, and tours of the house include the interactive history displays of Bringhurst Gallery. Rockwood mansion has been intermittently under renovation for some time, though the grounds continue to be open to the public for walking and cycling; be sure to call for current hours and tour availability. The Butler's Pantry tearoom (8 A.M.–3 P.M. Tues.–Sun.) offers light refreshments. Rockwood is the site of an enormously popular Ice Cream Festival in July, which usually includes a performance by the Delaware Symphony Orchestra. During the winter holiday season, tall trees on the estate are wrapped with more than 900,000 lights, and the mansion stays open in the evening.

SHOPPING

Each of the **du Pont properties** features shops stocked well with tempting merchandise.

Antiques and More

The villages of **Centreville, Greenville,** and **Hockessin** all offer a bevy of antique shops (at last count, Centreville alone had seven). The villages in this upscale area also have boutiques and art and craft shops.

Malls

For your last (or first) chance to shop tax-free, try the **Christiana Mall** (Rte. 7 and I-95, exit 4 south, 302/731-9815, near Newark) It includes a Macy's, Lord & Taylor, J.C. Penney, 19 food outlets, and more than 130 mall stores.

RECREATION
Parks

The du Ponts turned over their 850-acre dairy farm to the state for conversion into a park in 1965. **Brandywine Creek State Park** (41 Adams Dam Rd., Wilmington, 302/577-3534, www.destateparks.com/bcsp, open 8 A.M.–sunset daily) was one of the first parks in America to be purchased with Land and Water Conservation Funds. The park is three miles north of Wilmington at the intersection of Routes 100 and 92. A $3–6 entrance fee is charged per vehicle.

Two nature preserves are located in the park: Tulip Tree Woods, a stand of 190-year-old tulip poplars; and Freshwater Marsh, a conservation area for Muhlenberg bog turtles. In addition, the park features an active bluebird population program and a variety of habitats for year-round wildlife observation. The park maintains 12 miles of hiking trails and several open fields for both summer and winter use. The Brandywine Creek offers a site for fishing, canoeing, and tubing.

Bellevue State Park (800 Carr Rd., Wilmington, 302/761-6963, www.destateparks.com/bvsp, 8 A.M.–sunset daily, $3–6 entrance fee per vehicle) offers another sterling opportunity to sample a former du Pont property. Once the country estate of William H. du Pont Jr., the 271-acre park is home to a mansion (no tours), two indoor and eight outdoor clay tennis courts, stables, a band shell, gardens, and a 1.33-mile fitness track.

Equestrian facilities are for boarding horses and riding lessons only—no trail rides (302/798-2407). The tennis courts are open to the public, and a pro is on duty for lessons (call 302/798-6686 for reservations). All facilities are run by private concessionaires and require additional fees.

The fitness track, as well as the walking and biking trails that wind through the entire estate, are free. The band shell offers evening concerts June through August, and each season brings different recreational activities, such as hayrides in autumn and ice-skating in winter.

Bellevue State Park is in north Wilmington on Carr Road, the frontage road off I-95. Take exit 9 (Marsh Rd.), then turn left on Carr.

ACCOMMODATIONS

National hotel chains are available all along the I-95 corridor and in Wilmington. If you'd rather stay somewhere cozier, most of the Brandywine Valley's B&Bs are over the state line in Pennsylvania, around Kennett Square and Chadd's Ford. However, there is one outstanding country option in Delaware: the Inn at Montchanin Village.

The Inn at Montchanin Village

Once a crossroads settlement for employees of the nearby DuPont powder mills and factories on the Brandywine River (**The Inn at Montchanin Village** (Rte. 100 and Kirk Rd., Montchanin, 302/888-2133 or 800/269-2473 for reservations, www.montchanin.com, rooms $179–229, suites $269–399) became a stop of the Wilmington & Northern Railroad between 1870 and 1910, but faded into memory when the economy of the area shifted. Now, the remaining 11 buildings have been renovated into luxury accommodations linked by winding paths, a first-class restaurant, a fitness center, and beautifully tended gardens. The setting is bucolic and peaceful, surrounded by farms and avenues of old trees.

All 28 guestrooms and suites have been restored with the sophisticated traveler in mind. The suites are more like condominiums—each sitting room has a bar and refrigerator, a large tiled bath, and private garden. This is a lovely place to get away from the city overnight or longer. Prices are high, but worth it.

FOOD
Brandywine Valley East

(**Harry's Savoy Grill** (2020 Naaman's Rd./Rte. 92, Wilmington, 302/475-3000, www.harrys-savoy.com, lunch Mon.–Fri., dinner daily, brunch Sun., $12–20) is a deservedly popular restaurant north of I-95, near the Pennsylvania border. In spite of its hectic location in the middle of a tangle of roadways and development, this old favorite offers a broad menu of quality American fare (Caesar salad, crab cakes, pasta, steaks, burgers, etc.) in a cozy atmosphere. The food and service are both excellent, and there's a full bar on the premises.

Also recommended: **Stanley's Tavern** (2038 Foulk Rd. near Harry's, 302/475-1887, www

.stanleystavern.com, lunch and dinner daily, $9), a casual sports bar with beer and great sandwiches, plus some dandy daily specials.

Central Valley

◖ **Krazy Kat's Restaurant** (Inn at Montchanin Village, Rte. 100 and Kirk Rd., Montchanin, 302/888-4200, lunch Mon.–Fri., dinner daily) has wacky decor but serious, Mobil four-star/AAA four-diamond dining. The contemporary decor is feline-based: Portraits of cats in full formal dress reflect the leopards leaping on place settings. The food is fresh and sophisticated—this is definitely a destination restaurant. It has received *Wine Spectator*'s Award of Excellence every year since 1996. Lunch averages $13 for an entrée, less for salads and sandwiches; dinner is around $27 for an entrée. Venison chops, grilled ostrich, and sesame seed–crusted yellowfin tuna are typical menu items.

◖ **Buckley's Tavern** (5812 Kennett Pike, Centreville, 302/656-9776, www.buckleystavern .net, lunch Mon.–Sat. and dinner daily, $8–25) is another enormously popular local place that lives up to its reputation. The all American menu is served in pleasing portions by cheerful staff, and dining on the deck outside is a real treat in good weather. Buckley's is in a small shopping enclave with unpretentious antique and secondhand shops that are fun to stroll through.

Brandywine Valley West

Newark (pronounced as two separate words, NEW ARK) is the seat of the main campus of the University of Delaware. It's a good rest stop between Wilmington and Baltimore, and a handy place to pick up Fighting Blue Hen T-shirts. There are a couple of restaurants of note in town. Warning! The main street (named, oddly, Main Street) is parking ticket hell for the unwary. The meters run 8 A.M.–1 A.M. and gobble a quarter every 15 minutes. The **Iron Hill Brewery** (147 E. Main St., 302/266-9000, www.ironhillbrewery.com, lunch and dinner Mon.–Sat., brunch and dinner Sun., $9–22) has its own free parking lot in back, good-to-excellent brewpub food, and tasty beers. The atmosphere is upscale but comfortable. It's definitely a first choice, if quality is high on your list.

The **Deerpark Tavern** (108 W. Main St., 302/ 369-9414, www.deerparktavern.com, lunch and dinner daily, brunch Sun., $9–16) is the place to go if you want some college-style action (students and teachers), gallons of on-tap, high-volume chitchat, and a menu that has improved somewhat over the years to match the ambiance. The building has history: Edgar Allan Poe is reputed to have hung out here, and the cast-metal ceilings are plenty authentic, but you might have a problem getting your shoes unstuck from the floor to take a tour.

Nightlife: Newark has a booming (sorry about that) late-night music scene catering to the college crowd. **The Stone Balloon** (115 E. Main St., 302/368-2000, www.stoneballoon .com) features live rock music, and the **East End Café** (270 East Main St., 302/738-0880, www.eastend-cafe.com) offers a wide variety of alternative music, and a long list of imported and domestic beers by the bottle.

Wilmington

In 1997, The *Wilmington News Journal* reported that "for many years, despite Wilmington's slogan as 'A place to be somebody,' it really has been a place from which to go somewhere else. But things have turned around." And so they have.

The riots of 1968 and subsequent National Guard occupation changed the face of the city for the worse, but Wilmington's recovery has been significant. The city is riding the crest of its own wave, much like Baltimore in the 1970s and Pittsburgh in the 1950s. Wilmington is a stew of ultra-wealthy international corporations, such as DuPont, AstraZeneca, MBNA, Bank One, First Union Bank, and Wachovia; elegant homes built for the elite; and crowded,

UPPER DELAWARE

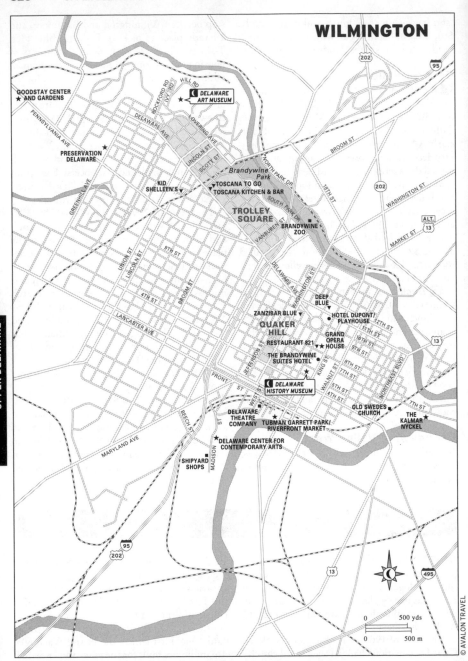

WILMINGTON

202

95

GOODSTAY CENTER
AND GARDENS ★

PENNSYLVANIA AVE

ROCKFORD RD
IVY RD
HILL RD

LOVERING AVE

DELAWARE AVE

☾ DELAWARE
ART MUSEUM

BROOM ST

202

PRESERVATION ★
DELAWARE

GREENHILL AVE

LINCOLN ST

SCOTT ST

NORTH PARK DR

Brandywine Park

14TH ST

WASHINGTON ST

ALT.
13

MARKET ST

KID
SHELLEEN'S ▼

★ TOSCANA TO GO
■ TOSCANA KITCHEN & BAR

SOUTH PARK DR

UNION ST

9TH ST

**TROLLEY
SQUARE**

VANBUREN ST

★ BRANDYWINE
ZOO

DELAWARE AVE

WASHINGTON ST

LINCOLN ST

BROOM ST

4TH ST

LANCASTER AVE

DEEP
BLUE ●

ZANZIBAR BLUE ▼

**QUAKER
HILL**

RESTAURANT 821 ★

THE BRANDYWINE ●
SUITES HOTEL

JEFFERSON ST

WEST ST

FRONT ST

KING ST

WALNUT ST

● HOTEL DUPONT/
PLAYHOUSE

12TH ST

11TH ST

GRAND
OPERA ★
HOUSE

10TH ST

9TH ST

8TH ST

7TH ST

5TH ST

4TH ST

NORTHEAST BLVD

13

☾ DELAWARE
HISTORY MUSEUM

OLD SWEDES
CHURCH ★

7TH ST

THE
KALMAR
NYCKEL ★

■ DELAWARE
THEATRE
COMPANY

★ TUBMAN GARRETT PARK/
RIVERFRONT MARKET

MARYLAND AVE

BEECH ST

MADISON ST

★ DELAWARE CENTER FOR
CONTEMPORARY ARTS

■ SHIPYARD
SHOPS

95
202

13

495

☾

0   500 yds
0   500 m

© AVALON TRAVEL

litter-strewn slums. It took a mighty strong love of place to stay when run-down neighborhoods turned dangerous and began to eat up block after block of a once livable small city—especially when the economic means existed to flee to the suburbs. Many made that move. Those who stayed and those who have returned have been rallying—especially since 1990—to bring back Wilmington. In large measure, they have succeeded; although, as anyone who lives here will admit, there's still a distance to go before the race is won.

Indications for success are obvious. Wilmington's smaller size works for it. This city, like Baltimore, has good bones: a foundation of beautiful architecture, strong business and cultural support, and, most important, people who are working to revive and revise their hometown. The 1970s restoration of the glorious Grand Opera House, built in 1871 by the Masons, got downtown revitalization rolling. The Amtrak Station was refurbished and is the ninth busiest in the nation, with more than 70 trains daily. Downtown neighborhoods have become highly desirable for young families. Tall office buildings that stood vacant as a result of corporate downsizing have been converted into luxury apartments, and people are moving to downtown. Top-quality restaurants have opened and are thriving. A new 221-seat art-film theater that opened in the Nemours Building in 2002 has since needed to add extra showings to its schedule.

The Wilmington Renaissance Corporation, an amalgam of local businesses and citizen groups, is hard at work redeveloping the historic Ships Tavern District at the lower end of Market Street. The project is creating street-level boutique shops and upper-floor apartments in 19th-century buildings. New townhouses and condos are being built across the river from the train station. And the Riverfront Development Commission has led the way for public and private funds that have rebuilt the Riverfront, a project that includes the Shipyard Shops, the Riverfront Market, the Riverwalk, water taxis, and restaurants and museums.

Wilmington's downtown center is quite safe during the day and in the evenings, when events are being held. Police and safety patrol are present, and a network of surveillance cameras has been installed. As in all cities of any size in the northeast United States, there are neighborhoods that should be generally avoided unless you have family, friends, or (legal) business there.

SIGHTS
◖ Delaware History Museum

Don't let the storefront facade of this innovative museum fool you—it's one of the best things to see and do in downtown Wilmington. The center (505 Market St. Mall, 302/656-0637, www.hsd.org/dhm, 11 A.M.–4 P.M. Tues.–Fri., 10 A.M.–4 P.M. Sat., $4 adults) is set in a renovated 1940s Woolworth's packed with cleverly presented information about the first state. Nostalgic memorabilia, artifacts, art, and scale-model historic scenes are interspersed with audiovisual displays and computer games.

For instance—do you have a future in the poultry industry? In the "Distinctively Delaware" exhibit, visitors are invited to play a computer game in which they invest in chickens; depending on the type of chicken, cost of feed, market demand, and other factors, either your investment will lay an egg or you'll advance in the corporate hierarchy of the Terrifically Big Cluck Company (pa-GAWK!). Other computer setups help visitors learn about transportation using real figures from history, including a colonial widow who made a go of her husband's plantation. Visitors are asked to help figure out how she did it by trying different ways of transporting her grain to market.

In the "Made in Delaware" exhibit, you'll learn the origins of Teflon, Tyvek, Gore-Tex (originally made as electrical ribbon cable, stretched to a thin layer), and polyester (there's a powder-blue leisure suit to die for). You'll see adults glued to the screens, while the kids are equally fascinated. Children may also enjoy Grandma's Attic, a discovery room with vintage dress-up clothes, an old-fashioned marketplace, and historic games and toys. The museum features changing exhibits and has an

UPPER DELAWARE

excellent gift shop. The whole place can occupy you for hours.

Next door is Old Town Hall, another part of the museum. This Georgian-style building served as the center of Wilmington government and social activity beginning in 1801, and it now showcases changing exhibits. The Historical Society of Delaware operates the museum and town hall, as well as the Read House in New Castle.

Quaker Hill: Wilmington's First Neighborhood

In 1735, Willingtown consisted of 15 or 20 houses perched on the low banks of the Christina River. In May of that year, William and Elizabeth Shipley, Quakers from Ridley Township in Pennsylvania, moved to Willingtown. While still in Pennsylvania, Elizabeth dreamed of a forested hill above a river where they would settle—when she saw the rise above the Christina, she recognized it as the manifestation of her dream. The Shipleys built a one-story brick house near what are now 4th and Shipley Streets, and the first Friends worship meeting was held in the Shipley home. By 1748, a new, larger structure had been built, followed by a third Meeting House in 1816. The latter still stands today as an active community center on West Street between 4th and 5th Streets. The grounds contain more than 3,000 graves (often layered on top of one another to save space), including that of John Dickinson, a signer of the Declaration of Independence; and Thomas Garrett, the famous Underground Railroad stationmaster.

The 19th century saw great change in the small community. Now called Wilmington, the city became an industrial center, with factories lining the Christina River. Quaker Hill continued to appeal to both workers and owners. As the economy boomed, many of the 18th-century structures were replaced. In the late 19th century, Quaker Hill became a predominantly working-class neighborhood, though a few prominent people, including the mayor, continued to live there.

A few homes from the 1700s can still be found. On West Street, between 7th and 8th

TAVERN REVIVAL

In the late 18th century, the 200 block of Market Street, near the Christina River in Wilmington, boasted a dozen or more taverns that served the thirsty sailors and stevedores who worked the docks a block away. The entire area, known as the Ships Tavern District, fell into disarray and remained there until early 2002. Investors saved several historic three-story buildings on the west side of the street from demolition – the early-19th-century structures had trees growing through their roofs – and rehabbed them into shops, apartments, and parking.

Streets, look for numbers 701 and 703. They were built in 1745 and 1760, respectively, by Joseph Woodward and his son, Mordecai—two Quaker rope makers whose business was on the grounds.

The Cathedral of St. Peter, on the corner of West and 6th Streets, was built in 1816. The first Catholic church in the city, it was probably designed by Pierre Bauduy, architect of the town hall. The church features several examples of stained-glass work from different periods. Six clerestory windows, and the windows above the altar and in the choir loft, are of particular interest. They appear to be from the Munich school, dating from approximately 1900; the intricate detail in the windows suggest they are the work of Franz Xavier Zettler, master glass painter to the Royal Court of Bavaria between 1870 and 1910, or possibly his pupil Franz Mayer. Their work is frequently seen in Baltimore and New York.

A block west on 6th Street (600 Washington St.), local ironworker Enoch Strotsenburg built an elegant home in 1798. It was later expanded by other owners and also used as a funeral home. A block south on Washington Street, 501 West 5th Street was built by Joshua Heald, founder and president of the Wilmington and Western Railroad, in 1860.

Back on West Street, numbers 501 and

503 occupy the site of the first house built on Quaker Hill in 1738 by Thomas West. His great-great-grandson built the current homes on the site. The Quaker Meeting House and cemetery are on the next block toward the river. The 500 block of West 4th Street, which can be seen clearly from the corner of 4th and West, was built around 1894–1895, and is now a nearly intact block of Victorian rowhouses and semidetached homes. Across 4th Street on West is one of the oldest remaining buildings on Quaker Hill. Built in 1750, the basement of the house at 310 West Street is believed to have been part of the Underground Railroad in the mid-1800s. Built between 1851 and 1865, 304 and 308 West Street were part of lumber merchant Joshua Simmons's family enclave that included 300 and 309 West Street, since demolished. In 1871, 222 West St. was the home of David Woolman, owner of Wilmington Water Works. Later, the building became a Protestant mission. The oldest building in this block, 200 West St., was originally the home and butcher shop of Patrick Taylor in 1855.

During the 20th century, Quaker Hill went into decline, as the suburbs attracted many residents from the area. The housing stock deteriorated, and in 1971, an urban renewal project cleared the land south of 4th Street, removing the remaining 18th-century structures. The remaining buildings were designated a National Register Historic Landmark in 1978.

The *Kalmar Nyckel*

Formerly known as "the 7th Street folly," this reproduction of the tall ship that brought the first settlers to Wilmington is now everybody's darling—and it's precisely for that reason that visitors may not be able to see the ship at all when they're in town (Kalmar Nyckel Shipyard, 1124 E. 7th St., Wilmington, 302/429-7447, www.kalmarnyckel.org, 10 A.M.–4 P.M. weekends). Unlike static ship displays, the *Kalmar Nyckel* is fully Coast Guard–certified to carry passengers, and she is Delaware's seagoing Ambassador of Good Will. Visitors can book a cruise on the ship while she's in port by contacting the shipyard by phone or online.

Originally the brainchild of a group of history buffs, volunteers, and hobbyists in 1985, the project floundered at first, due to lack of direction and funding until 1990. Then, thanks to the influence of new members of the board of directors and a loan from the Wilmington Riverfront Development Corp., the ship became a reality. The *Kalmar Nyckel* is a beauty—a 240-ton, triple-masted merchant vessel, authentic down to the carvings and 10 cannons aboard. Her mainmast rises higher than a 10-story building, and carries 7,600 square feet of sails.

Seventh Street, accessed through a rough-looking neighborhood, is home of the modest digs of the Kalmar Nyckel Foundation and shipyard. The shipyard will eventually be linked to other attractions on the Christina River, including the original landing place ("The Rocks," now Fort Christina State Park), Old Swedes Church, and the Hendrickson House. In the good-weather months you're likely to see the ship on the Christina and the Delaware Rivers—or in Norfolk, Washington, Philadelphia, Baltimore, New York, or Boston at sailing events. She's also in demand by Hollywood. Make sure to call ahead.

Old Swedes Church

Constructed in 1699 to hold Swedish Lutheran services (606 Church St., 302/652-5629, www.oldswedes.org, 10 A.M.–4 P.M. Wed.–Sat.). A tour of the church and Hendrickson House Museum costs $2, the nation's oldest standing church building continues to hold Episcopal services. The museum also houses a number of historically significant objects, including the oldest known pulpit in the United States. The graveyard predates the church by 60 years and is the final resting place of the early settlers as well as Revolutionary War soldiers and Thomas Bayard, Secretary of State under President Grover Cleveland. The Hendrickson House, built in 1690 in Chester, Pennsylvania, was brought to Wilmington in 1958 and restored on the church grounds; furniture and everyday objects from the 1700s are on display.

◖ Delaware Art Museum

A recent $24 million expansion and renovation resulted in an outstanding new venue for viewing fine art and illustration (2301 Kentmere Pkwy., Wilmington, 302/571-9590 or 866/232.3714, www.delart.org, 10 A.M.–4 P.M. Tues.–Sat., 1–5 P.M. Sun., $10 adults, free admission every Sun.). The Delaware Art Museum is distinguished by outstanding holdings in three areas: works by American illustrators, paintings and sculpture by American fine artists from 1840 to the present, and a world-class collection of paintings and decorative arts by the English group known as the Pre-Raphaelites.

The Brandywine Valley was home to America's most beloved illustrators at the dawn of the 20th century, when illustration meant fine art reproduced in popular magazines and books. Howard Pyle, a Wilmington resident, worked and taught extensively in the area. In 1912, the desire to keep 48 treasured works by Howard Pyle in Wilmington led to the founding of the Delaware Art Museum organization. Today, paintings and drawings by Pyle and his students, N. C. Wyeth, Frank Schoonover, and Maxfield Parrish, among others, are regularly exhibited. The work is delightful and of exceptional quality.

The museum's 19th- and 20th-century American art collections capture the best work of U.S. artists of all periods and styles, including contemporary works by Grace Hartigan and Claes Oldenburg. However, the Delaware Art Museum is perhaps best known for its unique 19th-century collection of Pre-Raphaelite art by English artists such as Dante Gabriel Rossetti and Marie Spartali Stillman. The collection, second only to that of the Victoria & Albert Museum in Britain, was bequeathed to the museum in 1935 by Samuel Bancroft Jr., a wealthy Wilmington industrialist. The romantic paintings and objects represent a reaction to the increasing mechanization of the late 19th century.

The museum also features changing exhibits—a recent one illuminated the works of glassblower Dale Chihuly—and an excellent café and gift shop.

Delaware Center for the Contemporary Arts

In the mid-1970s, the Delaware Center for the Contemporary Arts (DCCA, 200 S. Madison St., Wilmington, 302/656-6466, 10 A.M.–5 P.M. Tues., Thurs., Fri., and Sat., noon–5 P.M. Wed. and Sun., $5 adults) was started in an unpainted, abandoned warehouse on French Street. In 1984, urban redevelopment forced the relocation of the DCCA to the historic Waterworks complex on the Brandywine River. But it soon outgrew that space, so in 2000, the organization moved from its improved but painfully small space of 2,200 square feet to the 33,000-square-foot historic Harlan & Hollingsworth Car Shop II in the heart of the rejuvenated riverfront. The DCCA, a non-collecting museum, showcases the work of regionally, nationally, and inter-

THE PRE-RAPHAELITES

The Pre-Raphaelites were a group of English artists who, in reaction to the increasing industrialization and social upheaval of the world in the mid-19th century, developed a lush, sensual style based on the works of the Italian Renaissance before the period dominated by the painter Raphael. The group, consisting of Dante Gabriel Rossetti – who often used Jane Morris, the wife of his friend, designer William Morris, as a model – Edward Burne-Jones, John Everett Millais, Ford Madox Brown, and others, began painting around 1848.

Their works are characterized by rich colors, contrasts, sinuous rounded designs, and an almost medieval use of symbolism. Though the pictures appear romantic and decorative today, many were controversial at the time of their creation for both subject matter and presentation. A full-lipped and seductive Mary Magdalene, for instance, drew criticism for its questionable representation of a sacred Christian figure.

nationally recognized contemporary artists. It is also a venue for dialogue, promoting discussion with its programming, exhibitions, gallery talks, receptions, and symposia.

The DCCA has close ties to the community. Through Contemporary Connections, a model program, a professional artist works in a classroom with a teacher to develop an art project that connects students to core curriculum subjects. Recently, artist George Apostos worked with a ninth-grade math class using algebraic formulas to create a permanent ceramic-tile wall mural based on tessellation (that's patterning based on small squares, but you knew that). The DCCA's Visual Arts Residency Programs also touches the community. As part of the Art and Community Residency, artists make a full-time commitment to a community group to create works of art relevant to the participants' lives. In 2002, printmaker and sculptor Jennifer Schmidt worked with women and children from YWCA Home-Life Management Center to create books and collages that illustrated individual histories and identities.

Annually, the DCCA has more than 30 exhibitions of cutting-edge contemporary art in all media. Private tours can be arranged. The building houses seven galleries and 26 artists' studios, a high-tech auditorium, and a gift shop featuring one-of-a-kind handmade items.

Goodstay Gardens

PARKS AND GARDENS
Goodstay Gardens
The simple rock cottage that would become Goodstay was built around 1740 (2600 Pennsylvania Ave., 302/573-4468). The surrounding gardens are open dawn–dusk, and the Lincoln Collection inside the building has complicated hours (noon–4 P.M. Tues. Oct.–May, 10 A.M.–4 P.M. February 12/Lincoln's Birthday, noon–4 P.M. Sun. and 10 A.M.–4 P.M. Mon. of President's Day weekend, free). Over the years, the cottage was expanded and remodeled into a country mansion complete with formal Tudor gardens, now part of the University of Delaware campus. In 1853, it became the boyhood home of Howard Pyle, who later wrote in *Woman's Home Companion*, "Nowhere do I find a single place (except it be in those early childhood days) whereupon I may set my finger and say: 'Here my fortunes began.'" Famed for his book and magazine illustrations and writing, Pyle went on to teach Charles Dana Gibson, Ethel P. B. Leach, and N. C. Wyeth.

In 1868, the house was purchased by the du Pont family and remained with them until they gifted it to the university in 1968. The mansion serves as a meeting place for various groups, and the upper floors contain the Lincoln Collection, three rooms of pictures, memorabilia, and a library of books and documents pertaining to the celebrated president. Though many of the artifacts are reproductions, the collection includes a Ford's Theatre playbill from the night of Lincoln's assassination, the shawl worn by Lincoln during a visit to General McClellan during the Civil War, and several notes and documents with Lincoln's signature. Arrangements to visit during off hours may be made by calling 302/573-4468.

The Goodstay Tudor garden, one of the oldest in Delaware, includes a magnificent magnolia walk leading to a circular pool in which a statue of Venus is reflected. The magnolias are best in April; early May is lilac time. Howard Pyle commented, "It was such a garden as you will hardly find outside of a story book.... I cannot remember anything but bloom and beauty, air filled with the odor of growing things, the birds singing in the shady trees." The garden is made of several "rooms" that offer floral displays year-round. This idyllic place is far removed from the bustle of the nearby city.

Marian Coffin Gardens at Gibraltar

An estate owned by the Sharp branch of the du Ponts (Greenhill Ave., 302/651-9617, dawn–dusk, free), Gibraltar features restored gardens designed by Marian Coffin, circa 1918. H. Rodney Sharp, who was largely responsible for the preservation of Odessa (see "Central Delaware"), married Isabella du Pont, sister of Pierre S. du Pont, and bought the "country" estate in 1909. Marble terraces are joined by a grand staircase, surrounded by shrubs, perennials, annuals, sculpture, garden ornaments, ironwork, a fountain, and a reflecting pool. None of the Sharp heirs wanted to take on the renovation necessary to reclaim the estate for personal use. H. Rodney Sharp III, grandson of the original owners, said the restoration would not only cost millions, but would require a full staff to maintain. "You'd have to be a real aficionado of that kind of living," he said. "There are better things to spend your money on than living in a house with a huge staff." After five years of negotiation, the property came under the auspices of Preservation Delaware. As with most du Pont properties, the garden is considered the best feature of the estate, though there's some talk of turning the house into a hotel and restaurant.

Delaware Center for Horticulture

A nonprofit organization housed in a former city maintenance building (1810 N. Dupont St., 302/658-6262, www.dehort.org, 9 A.M.–5 P.M. Mon.–Fri., plus Sat. during the summer, free), the center is focused on the greening of Wilmington. Members of the center work with citizens' groups to turn vacant lots into community gardens, plant trees on weed-strewn thoroughfares, and promote urban gardening skills; a program to prepare young people for work in the horticultural trades is one of its offerings. An annual Harvest Festival showcases the achievements of neighborhood groups throughout the city. At the center, visitors will find exhibits and workshops on urban gardening, as well as a seasonal garden-themed art exhibit. A rare plant auction and spring and fall plant sales are held annually. The center also puts together group tours to explore private and public gardens in the city. The grounds surrounding the modern building are planted as demonstration gardens that showcase urban planting/landscaping ideas and design.

Brandywine Park and Zoo

In this pleasant, tree-shaded, 180-acre urban park, the **Brandywine Zoo** (1001 North Park Dr., 302/571-7747, www.brandywinezoo.org, 10 A.M.–4 P.M. daily, adults $5 June–Sept.,

river otters, Brandywine Zoo

$4 otherwise) is the main attraction. The zoo, which remains small and intimate, was begun in 1905. Its animals—llamas, condors, and bobcats, with a tiger and a variety of monkeys thrown in for exotica—come largely from the western hemisphere. The hands-down most popular exhibit includes the zoo's rambunctious pair of river otters, Jester and Delta, beloved by visitors and zoo personnel alike. Possessing the camera savvy of supermodels, they offer shutterbugs a variety of comely poses in between frantic dips and frolics in the pool. The keepers say that Jester and Delta's favorite activities are "destroying and climbing on anything they can, as well as stealing stuff when we aren't looking."

ENTERTAINMENT AND NIGHTLIFE
The Bar Scene
Kid Shelleen's (14th and Scott Sts., 302/658-4600, www.kidshelleens.com, lunch and dinner daily, brunch Sun., $6–19) is the hip spot to have a beer and hang out. The service and the food can both be uneven, but the place gets really hopping with local thirtysomethings in the evening. The restaurant features a full bar with an assortment of draft beers, plus a pizza/burger/pasta/salad menu with a few fancy entrées such as enchiladas, blackened salmon, and London broil with caramelized onions. Live bands play Wednesday and Friday nights from 9 P.M. to midnight, and there's a DJ and dancing on Thursday and Saturday nights.

Musical Performances
The beautifully restored **Grand Opera House** (818 N. Market St., box office: 302/652-5577), hosts a year-round program of concerts, pop music, entertainers, and dance shows. It's home to **Opera Delaware** (302/658-8063, www.operade.org) and features performances by the **Delaware Symphony Orchestra** (818 N. Market St., 302/652-5577, www.desymphony.org). The symphony also offers a music series in southern Delaware, small ensemble performances at Winterthur, and chamber concerts in the Hotel du Pont's Gold Ballroom.

Live Theater
The **Delaware Theatre Company** supports a six-play season on the Christina Riverfront (200 Water St., 302/594-1100, www.delawaretheatre.org) and **Candlelight Music Dinner Theatre** (2208 Millers Rd., 302/475-2313, www.new candlelighttheatre.com) presents year-round musicals, revues, and comedies north of the city in the community of Arden. The **DuPont Theatre** in the Hotel du Pont (11th and Market Sts., Wilmington, 302/656-4401, www.play housetheatre.com) presents touring companies of Broadway shows and New York–bound productions throughout the year. The **Three Little Bakers Dinner Theatre** (3540 Three Little Bakers Blvd., Wilmington, 302/368-1616, www.tlbinc.com) is located north of I-95 and presents new and classic shows and revues. In addition to musicals, TLB presents a wide variety of celebrity shows and concerts.

SHOPPING
Trolley Square
The neighborhood bordered by Kentmere Parkway, Lovering Avenue, Delaware Avenue, and I-95 is a particularly pleasant place to have a cup of coffee and wander about (www.visittrolley square.com). More than 80 shops, restaurants and galleries are in the area, including **My Thai** (21A Trolley Sq., Gilpin Ave., Wilmington, 302/428-1040), a shop featuring handwoven silk, accessories, jewelry, handicrafts, and gifts from Thailand; and **Sandy Hollow Herb Company** (1715 Delaware Ave., 302/654-2911), which displays art among its herbal offerings.

Wilmington Farmers Market
Open May through November (8th and Orange Sts., Wilmington), this farmers market offers the biggest selection of Delaware-grown produce. Market days are Wednesday, Friday, and Saturday from 8 A.M. to noon.

The Shipyard Shops
On the riverfront, Shipyard Shops (900 South Madison St., Wilmington, 302/425-5000) features tax-free shopping at outlets such as L.L. Bean and Coldwater Creek.

Govatos Chocolates

Founded in 1894 by John Govatos, a Greek immigrant, the confectionary shop paid for the passage of three of John's brothers to America. Renamed in 1898, Govatos Chocolates and Luncheonette introduced Wilmington to the latest rage, the ice cream soda. Sometime around 1918, the business moved to its present location (800 Market St. Mall, Wilmington, 302/652-5252; there's another branch in the Talleyville Shopping Center on Concord Pike). Obviously, it's been successful, and one mouthful of a Govatos chocolate-covered caramel will tell you why. The candy store is also a casual restaurant, open for sandwiches and light snacks 8 A.M.–3 P.M. Monday–Friday.

ACCOMMODATIONS

There are a number of moderately priced **chain hotels** in downtown Wilmington, including Courtyard by Marriott, the Sheraton Suites, and Economy Inn. The least expensive housing option close to Wilmington is the **Goldey-Beacom College** dorm (4701 Limestone Rd., 302/998-881)4. Single and double rooms are available June 15–August 15 and run $20–40. Since the college books conventions over the summer, the rooms may not be available—be sure to call and plan ahead.

The Brandywine Suites Hotel

This well-kept lodging managed by Clarion/Choice Hotels caters to businesspeople and families (707 N. King St., 302/656-9300 or 800/756-0070, www.brandywinesuites.com, $129–149). It's downtown, on a major thoroughfare just behind the Grand Opera House and town center, with easy access to the Riverfront and other attractions on the river. The hotel's 49 rooms are all suites: big, pleasant, and spotless, surrounding a light-filled atrium. The hotel offers complimentary van transportation to a nearby full-service health club and nearby attractions. Parking is available in the lot across the street, and a restaurant off the main lobby offers a complimentary continental breakfast.

Hotel DuPont

Wilmington's finest (11th and Market Sts., 302/594-3100 or 800/441-8019, www.dupont.com/hotel, standard $139–389, one-bedroom suite $359–650, two-bedroom suite $509–750) is renowned for its luxurious accommodations, fine service, and dining. In fact, it's Delaware's only Mobil four-star/AAA four-diamond–rated hotel. All guestrooms have separate sitting areas and bathrooms big enough to accommodate a family of five (all at once). The hotel offers 24-hour room service and a business center. The parking garage is half a block away, and the valet parking is much appreciated—especially in this central downtown location, which resembles nothing so much as a ghost town after dark. (This is likely to change as the area becomes more gentrified.)

The hotel features a lounge and classic French restaurant on the premises: the Green Room (open for breakfast, lunch, and dinner, dinner entrées $25–40) is a four-star/four-diamond eatery. There's also a 1,230-seat theater that showcases Broadway musicals. The DuPont shrieks "luxe," and the prices reflect it; however, it does offer weekend and romantic escape packages that are comparatively good deals.

FOOD
Delis and Food Courts

Toscana To Go (1402 N. DuPont St., Trolley Sq., 302/655-8600, www.toscanatogo.com, 7 A.M.–9 P.M. daily, until 10 P.M. Fri.–Sat., $6–15) is the takeout arm of Toscana Kitchen. Items are usually high quality and vary in price. The chef prepares 25 soups, salads, sandwiches, and pastas every day. The desserts are especially good.

The **Riverfront Market** (next to Tubman-Garrett Park, 302/322-9500, 9 A.M.–6 P.M. Mon.–Fri., 9 A.M.–4 P.M. Sat.) is an upscale food court with Thai, sushi, pasta, and ice cream booths, plus purveyors of fresh produce and ingredients, all in a historic restored warehouse.

Fine Dining

⬛ Restaurant 821 (821 N. Market St., 302/652-8821, www.restaurant821.com, lunch

Mon.–Fri., dinner Mon.–Sat.,), offers $30–75 prix fixe dinner menus with such delicacies as Atlantic salmon with basil whipped potatoes, and baby clam with preserved lemon and tomato brodetto. The menu changes frequently and centers on fresh produce, some of which is grown on the restaurant's own farm in New Jersey. Tasting menu entrees include "One Fish, Two Fish, Three Fish…" (tomato and black olive–braised swordfish with green olive pesto; Perona Farms smoked swordfish with Meyer lemon vinaigrette; grilled swordfish chop, potato, and red onion confit, $24) and "Bucket of Quail with Two Carbs" (country fried quail, buttermilk biscuit with sawmill gravy, skillet corn bread, and a sunny-side-up quail egg, $29).

Toscana Kitchen + Bar (1412 Dupont St., 302/654-8001, www.toscanakitchen.com, lunch Mon.–Fri., dinner Mon.–Sun., $15–21) was the first restaurant started by local celebrity chef/owner Dan Butler, and it remains extremely popular. Butler started out as a dishwasher at the Hotel DuPont and worked his way up the kitchen prep lines to open Toscana at age 30. The menu is upscale Italian, and the crowd is dressy and hip. The roasted butternut squash ravioli in butter and sage sauce is a perennial favorite.

Seafood

This brings us to Dan Butler's other restaurant, **Deep Blue** 111 W. 11th St., 302/777-2040, www.deepbluebarandgrill.com, lunch Mon.–Fri., dinner Mon.–Sat., $12–39), a major risk that's paid off handsomely. The restaurant was a gamble because of its downtown location (no-person's land after 5 P.M.) and the concentration on a very different type of menu: fresh seafood. But Deep Blue has become the place the sophisticated suits meet after work,

and the sleek decor is a fitting background for well-prepared fish and shellfish dishes (plus free-range chicken or beef tenderloin for those in a landlubber mood). Nearby parking is complimentary.

Harry's Seafood Grill (101 S. Market St. on the waterfront, Wilmington, 302/777-1500, www.harrys-savoy.com/seafood, lunch Mon.–Sat., dinner daily, $10–30), an extension of the original Harry's out on Naaman Road, is one of the city's go-to places for fresh seafood. The kitchen serves raw oysters and several varieties of ceviche (fresh fish marinated in lime and lemon juice), lobster, and boiled, baked and broiled seafood (never fear, you can also get a good burger here). *Wine Enthusiast* magazine named Harry's Savoy Grill and Harry's Seafood Grill among the best restaurants in the country for impeccable service, outstanding food, alluring decor, and distinctive wine programs.

INFORMATION

The Greater Wilmington Convention & Visitors Bureau (100 West 10th St., Ste. 20, Wilmington, DE 19801, in-state: 302/652-4088, elsewhere: 800/489-6664, www.visitwilmingtonde.com) serves the Brandywine Valley and all of northern Delaware. General information is also available at the **I-95 Visitor Information Center** (302/737-4059), south of Wilmington in the middle of I-95 between Route 896 (exit 1) and Route 273 (exit 3—there is no exit 2). The center can also help with hotel and motel reservations.

The **Riverfront Development Corporation of Delaware** (Chase Center on the Riverfront, 800 South Madison St., Wilmington, DE 19801, 302/425-4890, www.riverfrontwilm.com) is responsible for much of Wilmington's renaissance and also offers information on town activities.

New Castle and Environs

Once the capital and largest city in Delaware, New Castle is now a carefully preserved historic site. William Penn himself ordered the building of the town. The courthouse was Delaware's first, and New Castle served as an immigration port until Philadelphia eclipsed it. It was also a noted transport center: Packet boats from Philadelphia transferred their cargo in New Castle to stagecoaches bound for Frenchtown, Maryland. Andrew Jackson, Stonewall Jackson, Davy Crockett, Osceola, and Black Hawk all passed through New Castle on their way to Washington, D.C.

Since 1804, New Castle has been preserved to reflect its long heritage. Public historic homes are a short stroll from each other along rippling sidewalks raised by the roots of ancient trees. In the summer, these trees provide welcome shade; and in the autumn, a dizzying display of color. Your car tires will shudder in amazement on a few of the cobblestone streets. But historic New Castle is more than a museum—it's a living town, with cafés, restaurants, and shops interspersed with residential areas. The town meets the Delaware River in a green and peaceful riverfront park frequented by joggers and strollers. It's a wonderful place to sit and watch the massive cargo ships move north on the Delaware River toward Wilmington and Philadelphia.

Central Delaware—"lower, slower Delaware"—traditionally starts south of the Chesapeake & Delaware Canal on the border of Kent County. New Castle is a good base for exploring Fort Delaware and the northern greenways. Central Delaware seems to be drenched in perpetual golden light, reflecting off the endless stretch of wheat-covered farms and the waving sea grasses of the marshes. It's a region of quiet towns and fishing villages—the county's long coastline is pocketed with dozens of small, scenic watermen's villages, and the back roads are a feast for the eyes.

WHEN A BEACH IS NOT A BEACH

Many of the villages named "beach" in upper and central Delaware are fishing ports or residential areas with limited recreational opportunities for visitors. Beaches on the Delaware River north of Prime Hook tend to be gravel-covered and rough, as opposed to the fine sand beaches of Lewes, Rehoboth, Bethany, and Fenwick Island – they're also considerably more deserted, which has advantages and disadvantages (auto break-ins, etc.). The coastal areas are fun to explore, but if you're seeking sun and sand, use this information as a rough guide.

Slaughter Beach has a dune crossing (a designated area where people can cross over the dunes to the beach, in order to prevent erosion), a picnic pavilion, and bathing area, but no other facilities – most of the area is residential. **Broadkill Beach** also has a dune crossing and a little store, plus a residential area. The beaches

of Bowers are separated by an ocean inlet and can be reached by two different roads: **North Bowers Beach** has a tiny maritime museum on Marin and Williams Streets, which is open weekends June-August; **South Bowers Beach** has a small, sandy beach on the bay. **Kitts Hummock, Primehook Beach,** and **Pickering Beach** are largely residential with limited parking. Bay View Beach, Big Stone Beach, Fowler Beach, and Bennetts Pier are fishing villages with few or no tourist facilities.

Woodland Beach features a boat launch, small beach, and fishing pier with pretty coast views. Woodland Beach, Augustine Beach, and Collins Beach all used to have boardwalks or amusement piers that were popular in the late 19th century – the hurricane and tidal wave of 1878 destroyed piers, buildings, roads, and tourist facilities, putting many of these resorts underwater. Facilities for visitors are limited.

There's plenty of history in central Delaware, captured in museums and shaped in architecture, but there's also living history—farmers and anglers making a living from the land as they have since the first European settlers pulled their own plows and Native Americans laid nets in the water. It is a sweet, bright country, where, in the autumn, the calling geese can be heard for miles.

SIGHTS
The New Castle
Court House Museum
The Court House (211 Delaware St., 302/323-4453, 10 A.M.–3:30 P.M. Tues.–Sat., 1:30–4:40 P.M. Sun., donations accepted) harkens back to the time when New Castle was the state's colonial capital, though its history extends far beyond that era. A Swedish colony had settled near Wilmington in 1638; in order to isolate the population and control river traffic, Dutch governor Peter Stuyvesant established Fort Casimir in 1651, later renamed New Amstel (New Castle). Ownership of the site was

New Castle Court House cupola

continually disputed by the Swedes, Dutch, and English, and the final dispute involved Lord Baltimore and William Penn over the boundaries of Maryland and Pennsylvania. In 1682, the Duke of York awarded Penn the "three lower counties of Pennsylvania" (Delaware), making him the largest landowner on both continents. New Castle was Penn's first landing site in the New World. The cupola on the courthouse is the point from which the 12-mile radius was measured that ensured Penn his freshwater port. When Delaware finally broke away from Pennsylvania in 1704, New Castle, then the largest city, was named capital of the new colony. The courthouse contains paintings and artifacts that illuminate the town's multinational history; tour guides also provide insight.

◖ New Castle Historic Homes
Two historic homes built for two different residents of New Castle are the **Dutch House** (32 E. 3rd St., 302/322-9168, www.newcastle history.org) and the **Amstel House Museum** (4th and Delaware Sts., 302/322-2794). Both homes are open 11 A.M.–4 P.M. Wednesday–Saturday and 1–4 P.M. Sunday April–December. Each charges a separate admission fee of about $4, or you can pay $7 for both. The Dutch house was built in the early 1700s and is one of the oldest in Delaware. It's typical of early colonial housing, with a double fireplace and a hip (some call it "gabled") roof. The illustrated bible from 1714 and large carved Kas ("Kasht" in Dutch—a cupboard where most of the family goods were stored) are authentic to the period. The Amstel House, 1738, was likely the home of Governor Van Dyke and the most elegant house in town when it was built. The structure seems cramped and cottagelike now, but few homes can boast a hearth honoring the attendance of George Washington at the governor's daughter's wedding in 1784. The Staffordshire china and the Venetian blinds on the windows were appropriate for a wealthy family of the time. The home is artfully decorated with period antiques, right down to the *klumpen* (wooden shoes).

The most "recent" of New Castle's public

historic homes is the **George Read II House and Gardens** (42 The Strand, 302/322-8411, 10 A.M.–4 P.M. Tues.–Sat. and noon–4 P.M. Sun. Mar.–Dec., weekdays by appointment Jan.–Feb., $5). Built in 1801 by the profligate son of a notable politician, the home is as elegant and modern as Mr. Read's extensive credit would allow. Read, an attorney, hoped to follow in his influential father's footsteps, so he built a place to entertain his future friends. The kitchen had the latest steam system, including a "Rumford Roaster" powered by wood fires. Unfortunately, his dreams never materialized, and he died in bankruptcy. The house is, however, a real beauty, furnished to the period. The Victorian-style gardens around the house were added by William Cooper, who grew up next door and bought the house in 1846.

Other Historic Sites

The **Old Library Museum** (40 E. 3rd St., 302/ 322-2794, 1–4 P.M. Sat.–Sun. Mar.–Dec.,

free) was designed with a series of skylights and light-sinks (glass floors) by Philadelphia architect Frank Furness in 1892. The unusual building no longer houses a library, but it does specialize in displays on the history of New Castle.

While strolling through town, you'll pass **Immanuel Church** (100 Harmony St., on the green, 302/328-2413), the oldest Anglican parish in Delaware (1689), and the **Presbyterian Church** (25 E. 3rd St., behind the George Read House, 302/328-3279), founded in 1657 by a Dutch Reformed congregation. These points of historical and architectural interest are open most of the time. On some evenings, you can catch choir practice—heavenly song wafts out of brightly lit stained glass windows, just as it has for hundreds of years.

The **New Castle Historical Society** (2 E. 4t St., 302/322-2794) has additional information on the city's history.

ACCOMMODATIONS

The Armitage Inn (2 the Strand, 302/328-6618, armitageinn@earthlink.net, $105–150) is surely the prettiest place to stay in New Castle. One of the oldest homes in town, the inn has some portions built in the 1600s. Once referred to as the Van Leuvenigh House, after its original owner, the inn faces the riverfront park, and some of the rooms look out over the Delaware River. Each of the five lavishly decorated guestrooms is equipped with a private bath, cable television, a telephone, and air-conditioning. Innkeeper Stephen Marks could have another career as a chef if he so desired, judging from the wonderful breakfast served in the morning.

At least two of the homes downtown, across from the old marketplace, have been restored as bed-and-breakfasts. One is the **William Penn Guest House** (ca. 1682, 206 Delaware St., 302/328-7736, $85–105). The four rooms can be set up as either two private rooms with baths or four rooms with two shared baths. Rates include a continental breakfast.

Also recommended: the **Terry House**

EXEMPLARY VERTUES

A twilight stroll through the cemetery at Immanuel Church in New Castle is a treat during the early fall, when the crickets still sing lazily to one another. While checking out the odd funerary furniture – two pieces look like a chaise lounge and table, ready for someone to plop down with a steamy novel and a cold drink – stop by the grave of Jane, the wife of William Read, one of New Castle's earliest settlers. It's instructive to learn the desirable character traits of a woman in MDCCXXXII:

> Many were her Exemplary Vertues Her temper meak and carriage obliging Strict chastity prudent oeconomy Piety without ostentation And hospitality without crudgeing....

Sounds like Martha Stewart (though the "prudent oeconomy" may be contested).

THE WILD GREEN ROAD/NORTH

The greenway that runs along the Delaware River from New Castle in New Castle County to Cape Henlopen in Sussex County is a prime feeding stopover for migratory shorebirds and other species; its importance is such that it was designated as the first reserve in the Western Hemisphere Shorebird Reserve Network. This system of easily accessible preserves is rife with local and migrating species.

Famed for its population of shorebirds, the area hosts sandpipers, plovers, avocets, stilts, oystercatchers, and four types of sandpiper (the red knot, sanderling, ruddy turnstone, and semipalmated), among hundreds of other avian species. Shorebird migration is distinguished by two characteristics: the distance traveled (19,000 miles round-trip for the red knot, from Argentina to the Hudson Bay), and the fact that they seldom stop for food, so each stop is crucial. The Delaware Bay is one "staging area," due to its abundance of horseshoe crab eggs in late May and June. Shorebirds bent on doubling their body weight swarm the shoreline; a 50-gram sanderling will eat one crab egg every five seconds for 14 hours each day; the birds reach only the top layer of eggs, leaving the deeper ones to hatch later.

From spring through fall, flocks of bird species probe the mudflats for the food that means survival during their long journey. Birders and other naturalists can enjoy frequent sightings by driving south from New Castle on Route 9 and taking advantage of these viewing areas: **Battery Park Trail,** which begins in New Castle, is a 1.25-mile ramble that runs along Army Creek and Gambacorta Marsh. Continu-ing along Route 9 to Delaware City, you'll pass through a major industrial complex keep an eye out for trucks. The largest landholder is Star Enterprises, which has devoted 1,700 acres to a freshwater wildlife preserve, **Dragon Run.** In addition to migratory birds, this is a good place to spot muskrats and amphibians.

In Delaware City, take the ferry to Fort Delaware and **Pea Patch Island,** a notorious hangout for ibis, herons, and egrets. On the way to Port Penn, you'll pass through the largest freshwater marsh in the state, **Thousand Acre Marsh.**

Reedy Island Quarantine Station in Port Penn was the Delaware River's main quarantine detention center until 1936. It can be seen from the Wetlands Trail in the **Augustine Wildlife Area.**

Continuing south on Route 9 past the Odessa turnoff, you'll come to Taylor's Bridge; its main characteristic is the Reedy Island Rear Range Light, a 135-foot cast-iron light tower created in the mid-1800s. As sailors cruised the waters of the Delaware Bay, they timed the unique pattern of flashes from each range light to aid navigation. Blackbird Creek, near Taylor's Bridge, is a research site for the Delaware National Estuarine Research Reserve, and is not open to the public.

Woodland Beach Wildlife Area, a 4,794-acre preserve, is a popular site for fishing, crabbing, and birding. A bird-watching tower is located nearby, with a good opportunity to see huge flocks of snow and Canada geese and other waterfowl. The town of Woodland Beach is a short detour east on Route 6.

Bed and Breakfast (130 Delaware St., 302/322-2505, www.terryhouse.com, $90–110), which features four spacious guestrooms with private baths, queen-size beds, and modern amenities in a lovely three-story 1860 Federal townhouse. The rooms offer a view of Battery Park or Market Square, the Court House, and the Delaware River during the winter months. Rates include a full country or continental breakfast.

FOOD

Jessop's Tavern (114 Delaware St., 302/322-6111, www.jessopstavern.com, lunch and dinner Mon.–Sat., $8–18) is the best place to eat in downtown New Castle, as well as the most popular. It serves a modified pub menu with a few old favorites, such as shepherd's pie and prime rib, plus hearty and fresh soups, sandwiches, and salads. Get in early for dinner, especially on weekends, or call for reservations.

The constant heavy traffic on U.S. 13 (DuPont Pkwy.) south of the U.S. 40 intersection might make it easy to miss two restaurants worthy of note. The **Lynnhaven Inn** (154 N. DuPont Pkwy., 302/328-2041, lunch and dinner Mon.–Fri., dinner only Sat.–Sun., $12–20) could be mistaken for just another fast-food place, until you walk into the elegant foyer. The candlelit dining room could be a million miles away from the rumbling trucks outside. A well-kept favorite of residents for years, the inn serves a variety of seafood and meat for dinner, with lighter fare for lunch.

Though the food quality can be uneven, **Air Transport Command** (143 N. DuPont Hwy., 302/328-3527, lunch and dinner daily, $8–27) should be on everyone's fun list. The name says it all: Air Transport Command is set up like a World War II field station, complete with vintage trucks and blown-out walls. The Andrews Sisters wail over the intercom, and vintage armed forces memorabilia lines the walls. The menu is American.

Also recommended: **Casablanca Restaurant** (4010 N. DuPont Hwy., 302/652-5344, dinner Tues.–Sun., $20), for its exotic Moroccan atmosphere and food. Low tables, belly dancers, and contagious music heighten the gustatory pleasures of well-prepared chicken, couscous, lamb, and other specialties.

INFORMATION

New Castle is served by the **City of New Castle** (302/322-9801, www.newcastlecity.org). The Greater Wilmington Convention & Visitors Bureau (100 West 10th St., Ste. 20, Wilmington, DE 19801, in-state: 302/652-4088, elsewhere: 800/489-6664, www.visitwilmingtonde.com) serves northern Delaware, including New Castle. General information is also available at the **I-95 Visitor Information Center** (302/737-4059), south of Wilmington in the middle of I-95 between Route 896 (exit 1) and Route 273 (exit 3—there is no exit 2). The center can also help with hotel and motel reservations.

Odessa and Upper Kent County

It's easy to slip past Odessa on U.S. 13 without a glance down Main Street. However, those interested in architecture, American decorative arts, and living history would miss out by failing to stop. Odessa is a beautifully preserved small town in a scenic rural area 23 miles south of Wilmington. Several of its properties—officially called the Historic Houses of Odessa—were owned by Winterthur Museum and are now owned by the Historic Odessa Foundation.

Historic Houses of Odessa

Reservations are not necessary at this complex (Main St., 302/378-4119, www.historicodessa.org, 10 A.M.–4:30 P.M. Thu.–Sun. Mar.–Dec., adults $10, seniors and students $8), but the last tour leaves at 3 P.M. daily. Historic house tours start at the bank, built in 1853 as the First National Bank of Odessa. Today, the bank houses a visitors center and the Historic Odessa Foundation offices. Three of the homes, the Corbit-Sharp House (ca. 1772), the Wilson-Warner House (ca. 1769), and the Brick Hotel Gallery (ca. 1822), are open to the public by guided tour. The buildings are all furnished with exquisite period furniture and porcelain (including French pieces owned by the du Ponts), and the household items are regularly rotated. The Brick Hotel Gallery features history exhibits. A recent one included Belter furniture: Pineapples, cherries, and all other manner of carved fruit erupted from table bases and chair arms, resulting in the weighty household appurtenances that were the height of Victorian fashion.

Before European settlement, Lenni Lenape named the little port Appoquinimie, for which Appoquinimink Creek (ah-po-KWIN-a-mehnk) was named. In 1731, a man named Cantwell built a toll bridge over the creek, and travelers renamed the little settlement Cantwell's Bridge. The town was named

THE PARLOR AS THEATER

Victorian fascination with the study and control of nature found full expression in the parlors of American homes with the revival of rococo-style furniture. Henry Belter, a native of Germany who immigrated to New York and set up a furniture-crafting business in 1850, became the best-known proponent of the style.

Belter and his many imitators built furniture from hand-carved rosewood, with curved pieces made from a series of 7 to 21 thin wood veneers. New technology in the manipulation of sheets of laminated wood created rounded chair backs and sinuous table legs in stark contrast to the plain, functional styles of the past.

Deceptively fragile-looking openwork provided the base for massive marble tabletops; delicate parlor chairs were engineered to support the weight of the heftiest tea sipper.

Belter furniture, made 1840-1860 and sold for premium prices, was an updated version of the French Louis XIV style. Realistically carved fruit and leaf motifs, a variety of woodland animals, figures from mythology, and sensuous curves crowded together on table legs and chair arms. A parlor filled with the dark, heavy pieces – often upholstered in fine needlepoint – became a formal setting for guests dressed in voluminous satin and velvet, a place to see and be seen.

Odessa in 1855 in the hope that the tiny port would flourish like its Russian namesake, in spite of the fact that the railroad had bypassed the town by three miles. For a time, the name brought luck—but when a viral disease, "the yellows," destroyed the local peach crop in the 1890s, the port declined and the town fell asleep. The du Pont family had used a property in Odessa as a retreat, and they understood the value of the 200 years of colonial, Federal, and Victorian architecture in the town. Winterthur Museum acquired the buildings, opening them to the public and using them as living laboratories for students of American Studies at the University of Delaware and other institutions. Tours sometimes include a special tea or hearth-cooked meal based on current exhibits (call for a schedule). One specialty is Appoquinimink cakes, a forerunner of a modern tortilla; settlers modified the flour-and-water cakes eaten by the Lenni Lenape and used them as a base for both sweet and savory dishes.

Many homes in Odessa continue to be privately owned, but they are sometimes opened to the public during Christmas in Odessa, an extremely popular event held annually on the first Saturday in December (reservations are advised). Christmas is always a special time at the historic houses. Each year, the buildings are decorated according to a theme. In 2007, the holiday exhibit featured 30–40 trees; each was inspired by a classic from children's literature.

RECREATION
Delaware River & Bay Authority (DRBA) Three Forts Ferry

A great opportunity for a boat ride, a visit to historic military installations from three different eras, or just a picnic, the Three Forts Ferry runs between Fort Mott in New Jersey, Fort Delaware State Park on Pea Patch Island, and Delaware City in Delaware from April through October. Boats run 10 A.M.–5:45 P.M. on weekends, holidays, and Wednesday–Sunday from mid-June through the end of July. Tickets cost $5 for adults and $4 for children 2–12. The ferry leaves on the hour and half hour from the end of Clinton Street in Delaware City, a charming village with some unique shops (look for signs from Rte. 9). Battery Park in Delaware City, right next to the boat dock, offers a beautiful view of the river.

Fort Delaware State Park

This superbly maintained park on Pea Patch Island in the Delaware River was originally built in 1819 for the protection of Wilmington and Philadelphia (P.O. Box 170, Delaware City, DE

19706, 302/834-7941, www.destateparks.com/fdsp, open 10 A.M.–6 P.M. Sat.–Sun. last weekend in Apr.–Sept., Wed.–Sun. mid-June–first weekend in Sept., $6 adults, $4 children 2–12 for seasonal programs). It was rebuilt in 1859 and served as a prison for 33,000 captured Confederate soldiers over the course of the Civil War. The prison was unusual not only for its size, but also for the unique perspective of the man who ran it. General Albin F. Schoeph, a native Austrian freedom fighter, had lived in the United States for more than a decade and served as an engineer in the U.S. War Department when he was tapped to oversee prison operations in 1863. Educated in Vienna, Schoeph was familiar with germ theory and insisted on several innovations that saved the lives of his prisoners: smallpox inoculations, flush toilets, regular bathing, and the use of disinfectants in the two hospitals on the island. Dysentery was the biggest killer of the Civil War: Of 600,000 military deaths, two-thirds were from disease, but on Pea Patch Island, the death rate due to disease was 7.9 percent. The prisoners "were for saving," according to the warden.

Fort Delaware was known as a "country club" prison. It was very much like a city—the grocery store sold beer, the staff was evangelical, and visitors were allowed. Prisoners came from every walk of life: officers and foreign nationals shared quarters with deserters, murderers, and thieves. Occasionally, a "political prisoner"—captured and held to interfere with pro-Confederate political processes—would be a guest at Pea Patch. F. R. Lubbock, governor of Texas, and Jefferson Davis's personal secretary, Burton Harrison, both did time in the prison.

The fort today consists of the main star-shaped brick building surrounded by a "wet ditch" (moat), a few additional buildings, and a 1855 New Columbia Rodman Cannon, with a range of four miles. The cannon is fired daily at 3 P.M.—don't miss this! Actually, you can't, because the cannon is loud enough to stop and restart your heart. Inside the fort, costumed interpreters (including General Schoeph) talk about day-to-day life in the prison. Many visitors bring a picnic lunch (grills are available) and spend the day on the pleasant, parklike island. No overnight facilities are available.

Because of its large waterfowl population, Fort Delaware is a birder destination. The fort also has many special events throughout the year; two popular activities are the Halloween Ghost Tour in October and the Garrison Weekend in August.

Fort Delaware State Park is reached via a half-mile boat ride. Unless there are special programs and reenactments scheduled, admission to the park is free.

Fort DuPont, DE, and Fort Mott State Park, NJ

One of two other stops on the Three Fort Ferry, Fort DuPont (same contact information as Fort Delaware) was named for Rear Admiral Samuel Francis du Pont, who served in both the Mexican-American War and the Civil War. The fort was actively used as a military base from the Civil War through World War II. The park features 322 acres along the scenic Delaware River and the Chesapeake and Delaware Canal. Open year-round, it offers ample opportunities for picnicking, fishing, and hiking. A self-guided trail is available for exploring the site's rich historic past. For more active visitors, the park provides both tennis and basketball courts.

Fort Mott (ca. 1896), across the river at Finns Point in Salem County, New Jersey, was erected in anticipation of the Spanish-American war. Century-old gun emplacements, shot rooms and other structures may be toured daily, and the Friends of Fort Mott (P.O. Box 278, Salem, NJ 08079, 856/878-0267) also plan activities. A museum and gift shop are on the premises.

Port Penn and the Augustine Wildlife Area

Port Penn is a tiny fishing village about four miles south of Fort Delaware on Route 9, and is the home of the Port Penn Interpretive Center (Market and Liberty Streets, 302/836-2533, Memorial Day–Labor Day, Weds. –Fri. 11 A.M.–4 P.M., weekends and holidays 1–5 P.M., free). The center is a one-room schoolhouse/folk museum

UPPER DELAWARE GREENWAYS

A greenway is a natural area of unbroken vegetation where recreation and conservation are the primary goals. The following greenways are either completed or under construction:

In 1990, the Delaware Nature Society began a **Stream Corridor Greenways** protection program as a means of improving water quality and protecting animal migration corridors along waterways in Northern Delaware and Chester County, Pennsylvania. Riparian landowners are contacted and encouraged to become stewards of the greenway corridor by managing their lands in an environmentally sensitive manner.

The **Upper Christina River Greenway,** a joint project of the Christina Conservancy and the Delaware Nature Society, strives to improve water quality through education of private landowners in the upper reaches of the Christina River in northwestern Castle County, Delaware; Cecil County, Maryland; and Chester County, Pennsylvania.

The **White Clay/Middle Run (Northern Delaware Greenway – West Link)** begins at the western terminus of the Mill Creek Greenway near the Middle Run Natural Area northeast of Newark. Several trails have been constructed throughout the Middle Run Natural Area County Park that continue westward to the Possum Hill Area of White Clay Creek State Park. The Hopkins Trail, a multi-use trail, continues over the "Land Bridge" in White Clay Creek State Park linking the Mason-Dixon trail, the White Clay Creek Preserve, the city of Newark and University of Delaware, and the Fairhill Natural Area near Elkton, Maryland.

New Castle County Department of Parks & Recreation, Christina River Development Corporation, City of Wilmington, Christina Conservancy, Delaware Department of Natural Resources, and Kalmar Nyckel Foundation are all contributing to protection of the **Lower Christina River Greenway.** These efforts include creating pathways and revitalizing the Christina Riverfront in Wilmington.

Brandywine Nature Trail, Marketplace Trail, Swedes Landing Trail, the Historic Trail, the Brandywine Riverwalk, and the Christina Riverwalk are six **Wilmington Walkways** and driving tours that give visitors the opportunity to enjoy the historic, cultural, and architectural amenities of Wilmington's past and present, ranging from serene, pastoral settings to active recreational areas. Bicycle routes have been designated and marked on Kennett Pike, Route 141, Faulkland Road, Route 9 to New Castle, and Route 7.

The 6,000-foot-long **Elsmere** pathway goes through the town park to link Centerville Road with Du Pont Road on the north side of the railroad tracks.

The urban trail, **Northern Delaware Greenway – East Link,** spans 10 miles of northern New Castle County from Fox Point State Park on the Delaware River to Brandywine Creek State Park. It connects with Wilmington Walkways and links together residential communities, schools, businesses, parks, and cultural sites. Eventually, the Northern Delaware Greenway will stretch across New Castle County and will connect with greenways in Middle Run Natural Area and White Clay Creek State Park near Newark. Fox Point State Park is the northern end of the Coastal Heritage Greenway.

The path of the **East Coast Greenway** in Delaware is still under construction. It's planned as an 80 percent offroad route for cyclists, hikers, and other users – a more urban alternative to the Appalachian Trail. When completed, the East Coast Greenway will connect existing and planned trails with new corridors using waterfronts, park paths, rail trails, canal towpaths, and parkway corridors.

A greenway corridor and trail development from Beck's Pond to Lums Pond State Park, New Castle County, the **Pencader Hundred** will include a new regional park near Glasgow, former Frenchtown Railroad lands, suburban streets through the Mansion Farms area, and a new district park.

Mill Creek Hundred trail winds through a combination of public lands, suburban streets, and lands held by community associations in the Mill Creek and Pike Creek areas of New Castle County. A trail crosses the wooded open space behind the North Pointe Town homes on Stoney Batter Road, extending to Delcastle Recreation Area.

that celebrates the lives of the watermen, hunters, fishers, and farmers who populate the area. This is the place to learn about muskrats (also known as bog bunnies) which have been trapped in the area for meat and fur from well before European settlement—the museum explores the lives of the versatile little rodents. The drive from Fort Delaware, over a curving bridge through the open marshland of the Augustine Wildlife Area, is idyllic. (Because traffic is light, especially midweek, it would also be an excellent choice for bicyclists.) In mid-September, Port Penn holds a Wetland Folk Festival with food (crab cakes!), storytelling, living history programs, and music. Call the Port Penn Interpretive Center or Delaware State Parks activities (www.destateparks .com/activities) for dates and times. Self-guided walking tours are available featuring the historic homes of Port Penn, as well as the scenic marshlands surrounding the town.

FOOD

Crabby Dick's (30 Clinton St., Delaware City, 302/832-5100, www.crabby-dicks.com, Wed.–Sun. Oct.–Apr., daily Memorial Day–Labor Day, lunch and dinner, $8–30) has taken over the Olde Canal Inn. Dick's serves burgers, salads, and sandwiches, along with crab cakes and steamed clams. The shop also features dozens of "crabby" items, such as T-shirts and mugs.

Kelly's Tavern (at the end of Market St., Port Penn, 302/834-9221, $6) is a good place to stop for a beer and a burger. It doesn't have a sign, just a neon beer light in the window (there's a phone booth on the street in front). Several people have raved about the crab cakes, but mine were not picked—all the tiny bits of cartilage and shell removed—as well as they could have been. Maybe the pickers were picnicking that day.

LOWER DELAWARE

Lower and slower? Not necessarily! Dover, Delaware's capital, dozes contentedly in the middle of the state, surrounded by farms and forests. It's the only semi-urbanized area in central Delaware, blooming in the midst of a fertile farming and fruit-growing region. The silence can be deceptive, however: Dover and Harrington ring with the pounding of horse hooves, the squealing of racecars, and the clanging of slot machines, and Dover is also home to an exceptional Air Force museum, art collection, and more. In addition, the area offers plenty of outdoor recreation, including Bombay Hook, one of the most beautiful wildlife refuges in America.

For lovers of sea and sand, the southern shore *is* Delaware. Cape Henlopen and Delaware Seashore draw the largest number of visitors in the state, surpassing all other attractions. Each resort town is unique: Lewes, Rehoboth Beach, Dewey Beach, Bethany Beach, and Fenwick Island all attract aficionados for different reasons. However, southern Delaware has far more to offer than just its beaches. Quiet, historic towns in the state's interior—like Laurel, Seaford, and Blades, once known for shipbuilding—provide quaint respite from grit and glare. Prime Hook National Wildlife Refuge, one of the busiest stops on the Atlantic flyway, affords a glimpse into a rare ecological system.

Southern Delaware is also a major agricultural area: It contains the largest population of broiler chickens on the Delmarva Peninsula. More evident, though, are the bountiful fruits and vegetables the region produces. In

© JOANNE MILLER

HIGHLIGHTS

◖ **Sewell C. Biggs Museum of American Art:** In the state capital of Dover, this marvelous 14-gallery collection strongly emphasizes art from Delaware and the Delaware River Valley, including many world-famous illustrators and painters, such as portraitist Charles Willson Peale (page 352).

◖ **Delaware Agricultural Museum and Village:** The rural basis of central Delaware is celebrated in this comprehensive museum, which offers a number of farm buildings to explore, equipment remarkable for its size, decoration, and/or weirdness of function, and farm-related professional art exhibits and special events (page 352).

◖ **The Air Mobility Command Museum:** One of the most unusual assemblages anywhere lives inside the main hangar. Restored airplanes from all phases of military use and history glimmer brightly among exhibits, while outside, more airplanes invite visitors to explore America's aviation and military past up close (page 352).

◖ **Bombay Hook National Wildlife Refuge:** One of the most important links on the Atlantic flyway, Bombay Hook encompasses more than 16,000 acres of brackish marsh, freshwater pools, brush, timbered swamp, farms, and grassy upland. It's also home to hundreds of indigenous species of birds, mammals, reptiles and amphibians (page 357).

◖ **Cape Henlopen State Park:** Site of a former lighthouse and World War II military base, Cape Henlopen became a 543-acre recreational area in 1964. Today, piney dunes and ocean-lapped sand beckon campers and beach lovers from the entire eastern seaboard (though, fortunately, not all at once). You can take the Cape May, New Jersey, ferry from here (page 365).

◖ **Rehoboth Beach Boardwalk:** Sixteen blocks of pure beachiness, including shops, food concessions, sand sculptures, rides, and games make this summer destination one of the Eastern Shore's hot spots (page 370).

◖ **Delaware Seashore State Park:** Perhaps the narrowest state park in existence, this 2,825-acre site covers the slim strip of land that separates the Atlantic Ocean from Rehoboth Bay between Dewey Beach and Bethany Beach on Route 1. This park offers all manner of recreation, from lolling on the beach to rowing on the Bay (page 375).

◖ **River Towns and Highlights Tour:** Though the beaches are the destination for many visitors to lower Delaware, the inland areas offer special charm. On this tour, visitors will see Laurel – the wealthiest town in the state around 1900 – the old Woodland Ferry, and the shipbuilding towns of Bethel and Seaford, among other sights (page 379).

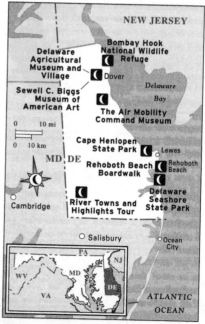

LOOK FOR ◖ TO FIND RECOMMENDED SIGHTS, ACTIVITIES, DINING, AND LODGING.

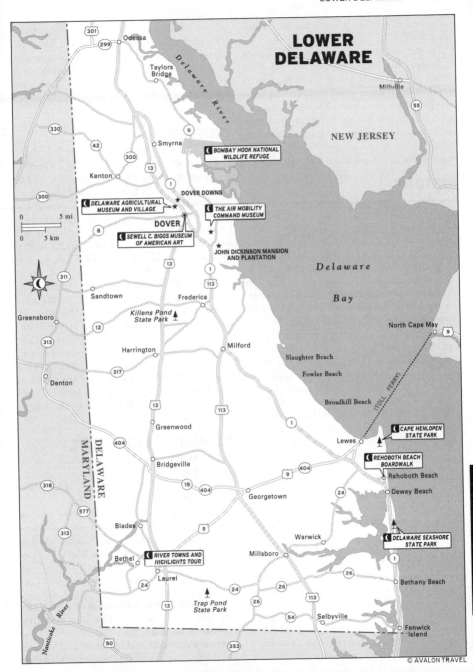

LOWER DELAWARE

NEW JERSEY

MARYLAND

DELAWARE

Delaware River

Delaware

Bay

BOMBAY HOOK NATIONAL WILDLIFE REFUGE

DELAWARE AGRICULTURAL MUSEUM AND VILLAGE

DOVER

THE AIR MOBILITY COMMAND MUSEUM

SEWELL C. BIGGS MUSEUM OF AMERICAN ART

JOHN DICKINSON MANSION AND PLANTATION

CAPE HENLOPEN STATE PARK

REHOBOTH BEACH BOARDWALK

DELAWARE SEASHORE STATE PARK

RIVER TOWNS AND HIGHLIGHTS TOUR

Odessa
Taylors Bridge
Millville
Smyrna
Kenton
DOVER DOWNS
Sandtown
Frederica
Killens Pond State Park
Greensboro
Harrington
Milford
North Cape May
Slaughter Beach
Fowler Beach
Broadkill Beach
Denton
(TOLL FERRY)
Greenwood
Lewes
Bridgeville
Rehoboth Beach
Georgetown
Dewey Beach
Blades
Warwick
Bethel
Millsboro
Laurel
Trap Pond State Park
Bethany Beach
Selbyville
Fenwick Island

0   5 mi
0   5 km

Nanticoke River

© AVALON TRAVEL

the summer, interior villages burst with roadside stands.

All year, antiques hunters can find a surfeit of choices and equally choice scenery along the back roads. Though beach towns tend to be seasonal, the tourist "year" is expanding from May well into November. The least crowded times to visit are during the spring and after Labor Day. The beaches are spectacularly uncrowded then, and, especially in the fall, the water and weather are warm and welcoming.

HISTORY

Founded in 1683 and laid out in 1717 by the order of William Penn, Dover has been the capital of Delaware since 1777. Not only was city distant from the dangers of seafaring warlords (unlike New Castle), but it was also the center of agriculture, which was—and continues to be—the source of the state's wealth. The rich farmland of central Delaware is fed by numerous streams and waterways. Though the first people and many early colonists made their living from the Delaware Bay and River by fishing and birding, the interior absorbed the expanding populations of Pennsylvania to the north and Maryland to the west, and the region remains the state's political power base.

Many of Delaware's citizens aligned with the British during the Revolution, but the majority of landowners voted for independence: The Delaware quarter, stamped with the likeness of Caesar Rodney, a Delaware Superior Court Judge and member of the Continental Congress, portrays his famous ride from the Dover area to Philadelphia to cast the deciding vote.

Plentiful waterways provided a convenient way to transport grain and other produce to the big markets of Philadelphia and Baltimore. Seaford, which now appears landlocked in the middle of the Delmarva Peninsula, was actually the heart of a ship-building industry. The "worthless sand" of the state's southern beaches meant little to the land-hungry early colonists.

Delaware remained a slave state during the Civil War, though it sided with the north (only states that declared themselves independent of the Union were required to divest themselves

of slave labor). After the Civil War, many farms struggled to continue without free labor. Industry, often financed by the du Pont family, revived the economy. As the automobile made distance travel possible and more Americans enjoyed leisure time, the sands of southern Delaware became the state's golden treasure.

ORIENTATION

U.S. 13 divides the state neatly in half down to Dover, where it splits, with U.S .13 veering westward to the river towns and U.S. 113 sidling east to the beaches. From Dover, Rte. 1 parallels the coast. The interior of central and southern Delaware—with the exception of Dover, and, to a lesser degree, Harrington and Milford—is rural. The area contains several outstanding public parks and wildlife refuges: Bombay Hook, Killens Pond State Park, Prime Hook, and Delaware Seashore State Park. The east–west roads, with the exception of Route 9, are all two lanes: Routes 8, 317, 404, 24, and 26. The beaches, all bathed by the Atlantic Ocean, are bastions of sugary sand. The towns of Lewes (LOO es), Rehoboth Beach, Dewey Beach, Bethany Beach, and Fenwick Island on the Maryland border are the local population centers, each with a personality of its own—Rehoboth Beach being the largest and most developed.

PLANNING YOUR TIME

Lower Delaware could easily absorb all your vacation time. Whether you're here for the gambling, shopping, birding, beaches, or nightlife, you can find it all here.

Many visitors to **Dover** come for the gaming and ponies, and depending on your predilection, several days and nights can be spent at **Dover Downs** or the **Midway Slots** in Harrington. If you have more than a couple of days in the area, however, there are several interesting sites to visit for local color and history: **Sewell C. Biggs Museum of American Art** (one–three hours), **The Air Mobility Command Museum** (one–two hours) and the **Delaware Agricultural Museum and Village** (two hours), and the **John Dickinson Mansion** and **Plantation** (two hours) are entertaining and give great insight into the area and its people. The **Amish Country Auto/Bike Tour** (one hour–all day) is a pleasant way to see the countryside. For shopping, don't miss **Spence's Bazaar** (two hours–all day). And no visit to Dover would be complete without dining at **The Blue Coat Inn** or **Sambo's Tavern.**

For nature lovers, **Bombay Hook Wildlife Refuge, Killens Pond** and **Prime Hook Wildlife Refuge** are absolutely beautiful year-round. Each will take at least one day to visit, depending on transportation and activities.

Moving south to the charming town of **Lewes**, the **Shipcarpenter Square Historical Complex** (one–two hours) offers an opportunity to see the architectural history of lower Delaware. The town itself is stroll-worthy for the shops and eateries. **Cape Henlopen State Park** has everything a beach lover could want and more (one–three days). Don't miss a stop at **Nassau Valley Vineyards** to sample the local wines.

Rehoboth Beach and Dewey Beach are synonymous with summer in this part of the world. The **Boardwalk** (one hour–all day), though not as grand as Ocean City's, is filled with the whoops of kids at **Funland** and redolent with eau-de-beach: caramel popcorn and coconut-scented suntan oil. Eating here is an art form, especially at **LaLa Land, Ristorante Zebra,** and **Big Fish Grill.** Of course, leave time for shopping at **The Outlets** (one day–one year).

One of the best parks for beach fans, **Delaware Seashore State Park** (one day–one week) is a must. **Bethany Beach** is the "quiet" resort, mainly for those who want beautiful beaches and peaceful stays. Inland, the **River Towns Highlights Tour** (two hours–all day) is a great way to enjoy the countryside. Make sure to include a gourmet visit to **Bon Appetit Restaurant** in Seaford as part of your itinerary.

INFORMATION
Southern Delaware Tourism (P.O. Box 240, Georgetown, DE 19947, 302/856-1818 or 800/357-1818, www.visitsoutherendelaware.com) provides a free vacation-planning guide. It can also provide information and contact numbers about individual towns, attractions, and areas. The state's official website, www.visitdelaware.com, is also a font of information.

FESTIVALS AND EVENTS
It's always best to check the county tourism agency's website for the dates and contact numbers of events, as many are run by volunteers who vary annually.

In April, **Delaware Book Fair and Authors Day** (http://heritage.delaware.gov/book_fair) celebrates those who write about the state at the Delaware Agricultural Museum and Village in Dover.

How much chocolate can you eat? In March, Rehoboth Beach hosts an annual **Chocolate Festival** (302/227-2772), and researchers are standing by to find out.

Fly high at the **Great Delaware Kite Festival** in Cape Henlopen State Park in mid-April.

Celebrate independence on the beach at the **Rehoboth Beach fireworks** (302/227-2772), the best in the area.

In August, the Rehoboth Beach–Dewey Beach Chamber of Commerce sponsors the annual **Sandcastle Contest** at Rehoboth Beach (800/441-1329, ext. 12).

Delaware's governor hauls the skeletons out of the closet for the **Governor's Fall Festival,** held in October at Woodburn, the Governor's mansion in Dover. Rehoboth Beach's annual **Sea Witch Halloween & Fiddler's Festival,** also in October, includes creative parades, contests, and lots of great fiddle music; costumed kids can trick-or-treat at many of the shops on Rehoboth's main street (800/441-1329).

The general revelry around **World Championship Punkin' Chunkin'** (302/856-1444, www.punkinchunkin.com), in Harbeson, is something a few locals would rather forget—but it's impossible to ignore giant squash flying over fields of stubble, powered by homemade catapults. Distance matters.

Caroling on the Green and a **Candlelight**

Tour of Homes are wonderful ways to spend the December holidays in Dover (www.dover museums.org/events2.htm). Lewes celebrates the holidays with a **Christmas parade, tree lighting, and caroling.**

GETTING THERE
By Air

Dover, located in central Delaware, is equidistant from Philadelphia International (PHL) and Baltimore International (BWI) Airports: about 70 miles. Points farther south are best served by BWI. Both airports handle flight traffic from all major carriers and offer cars from all the major rental companies.

By Train

Wilmington is one of Amtrak's (code: WIL, 100 South French St., Wilmington, DE 19801, 800/872-7245, www.amtrack.com) key stations: the Acela Express, Cardinal/ Hoosier State, Carolinian/Piedmont, Crescent, Regional, Silver Service/Palmetto, and Vermonter trains all pass through here. There are also minor stations or pickup points in Dover (code: DVR, Dunkin' Donuts, 470 South Dupont Hwy.) and Seaford (code: SAD, 1609 Middleford Rd.).

By Bus

Greyhound has a stop in Dover (Dunkin' Donuts, 470 S. DuPont Hwy.), but tickets are not sold at this location. Information and tickets by mail may be purchased online at www.grey hound.com or by calling 800/231-2222.

Trailways (800/343-9999, www.trailways .com) offers summer service only to Rehoboth, with two daily drop-offs at the Valero convenience store at 801 Rehoboth Ave.

By Car

Car travel is by far the easiest method of transportation in the state. The main routes are: north–south U.S. 13 and Route 1; east–west all two-lane roads, except U.S. 9; Routes 6 and 8 in the midlands; and Routes 14, 404, 20, 24, and 26 in the southernmost part of the state.

GETTING AROUND

DART First State Transit serves all three Delaware counties from the main transit stations in Dover, Lewes, Georgetown, and Rehoboth Beach, and also offers inter-county transit. Special Resort Service buses from upper Delaware to lower Delaware run late May–mid-September. For information, call 800/652-3278 (from area codes 215, 267, 410, 443, 484, 609, 610, and 856) or 302/652-3278 (from all other locations), or visit www.dart firststate.com. Fares are $1 and up, depending on your destination.

Resort Transit (Memorial Day weekend– mid-September daily 7 A.M.–1 A.M.) covers most routes in Lewes, Long Neck, Rehoboth Beach, Dewey Beach, Bethany Beach, South Bethany Beach, Fenwick Island, and Ocean City, Maryland. The Beach Bus (Memorial Day weekend–Labor Day weekend on Friday nights, Saturdays, and Sundays) stops at Christiana Mall, Smyrna Rest Stop, Scarborough Road Park & Ride in Dover, and Super Wal-Mart in Milford. The last stop is the Resort Transit Park & Ride lot, where you can connect with the Resort Transit bus service. Both can be reached by calling 302/226-2001 or 800/652-3278 or by visiting www.beachbus.com.

The Jolly Trolley serves Rehoboth Beach and Dewey Beach with stops around town May 25–Labor Day.

Dover

Dover aptly reflects the balance of power in Delaware—the populous urban north is no match for the political strength and conservatism of Delaware's farmers and rural dwellers. Dover is a shipping and canning center with varied light industries: Dover Air Force Base, a principal military air cargo terminal, is a major factor in the city's economy, as is Dover Downs, with auto and horse racing and a casino.

Several attractions are within walking distance of the Delaware State Visitor Center and Galleries (406 Federal St., 302/739-4266), in the middle of town. The visitors center offers all the information you could ever want about the state; behind the information desk is a store loaded with tempting Delaware souvenirs. The galleries, part of the visitors center, are open Monday–Friday 8:30 A.M.–4:30 P.M., Saturday 9 A.M.–5 P.M., and Sunday 1:30–4:30 P.M. Admission is free. Changing exhibits feature Delaware history and culture. One recent exhibit, "Fighting the Dragon," touched on all

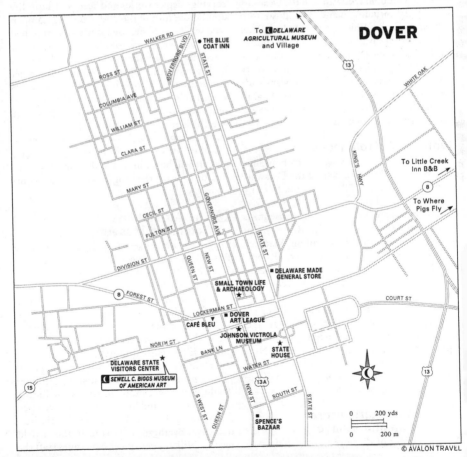

© AVALON TRAVEL

aspects of volunteer firefighting through the state's history.

SIGHTS
◖ Sewell C. Biggs Museum of American Art

This marvelous 14-gallery collection shares space with the visitors center (406 Federal St., Dover, 302/674-2111, www.biggsmuseum.org). The museum is open 10 A.M.–4 P.M. Wednesday–Friday, 9 A.M.–5 P.M. Saturday, and 1:30–4:30 P.M. Sunday. It's an excellent way to spend the afternoon, especially considering admission is free, though donations are accepted. The collection strongly emphasizes art from Delaware and the Delaware River Valley, including many of its illustrators; portraitist Charles Willson Peale, Hudson River School landscape painters Thomas Cole and Albert Bierstadt, and impressionist Robert Reid are also represented. The galleries contain a variety of sculptural pieces, porcelain, American-made silver, furniture, clocks, and an exhibit of paintings and book illustrations by Frank Schoonover from the golden age of publishing.

Johnson Victrola Museum

Turn off your iPod and visit this truly unique collection (3 S. New St., behind the Delaware Archaeology Museum, 302/739-4266, 10 A.M.–3:30 P.M. Tues.–Fri., 9 A.M.–5 P.M. Sat., free, donations accepted). The Victrola Museum is a tribute to Delawarean Eldridge Reeves Johnson, who founded the Victor Talking Machine Company in 1901—the first commercially produced sound recordings in history. The museum features a 1920s Victrola dealer's store, complete with a variety of talking machines and early records. Photographs and memorabilia of recording artists from the era are on display, and Victor recordings play on modern and antique equipment. The original oil painting of Nipper the dog listening to his master's voice from the horn of a Victrola—the original logo of the company—can be seen here.

◖ Delaware Agricultural Museum and Village

A wide variety of displays beyond old farm equipment makes this museum well worthwhile—but that's not to discount the equipment, much of which is remarkable for its size, decoration, or weirdness of function (U.S. 13 at State St., 866 N. DuPont Hwy., Dover, 302/734-1618, www.agriculturalmuseum .org, 10 A.M.–4 P.M. Nov.–Mar., 10 A.M.–4 P.M. Tues.–Sat. Apr.–Oct., Tues.–Sat., 1–4 P.M. Sun., $5). The museum offers a number of farm buildings to explore, as well as farm-related professional art exhibits and programs and special events that change regularly. One of the most amusing permanent offerings is a collection of woodcarvings by Jehu Camper. The rustic carvings depict stories and scenes of farm life around the turn of the 20th century. Camper, who was born in nearby Harrington and died in 1989, gave advice to others who might be interested in "whittlin'": "The first thing you do is get yourself a piece of wood… then get yourself some Band-Aids and a few cuss words and start in." The continually expanding museum is enjoyable for all ages. Tots go for the live chickens pecking around the chicken industry exhibit, as well as the playroom, where they can "drive" an Amish buggy to market. Seniors will be reminded of the time when agriculture, rather than big business, was a common way of life.

◖ The Air Mobility Command Museum

To get to this museum on Dover Air Force Base (U.S. 113, two miles south of Dover, 302/677-5938, www.arcmuseum.org, 9 A.M.–4 P.M. Tues.–Sun., free), visitors must check in through the fenced Route 9 entrance, half a mile from the intersection of Rte. 9 and U.S. 113 south of the base. When the base is on alert, the museum may not be open to the public. It's a highly unusual collection: Inside the main hangar, restored airplanes from all phases of military use and history glimmer brightly; outside, more airplanes, including racy jet fighters and huge transports, are open for exploring. Roaring jets stationed at the base maneuver overhead, then land in the airfield nearby. Military personnel sometimes staff the cockpits and answer questions about modern flying and the Air Force's air mobility command, which is in the business of moving soldiers and equipment all over the world.

The museum features an exhibit on WASPS, World War II women pilots who flew transport. These pilots were organized at the New Castle Air Base; 25,000 applied for the job, and 916 made it through training. Of these, 38 died in service. Because WASPS performed ferrying services, they were never military personnel, and the families of women who died were never compensated. WASPS were finally granted veteran status in 1979. The museum also features a number of rare and unusual aircraft: a C-47 Gooney Bird used in the D-Day troop drop, an O-2A used for rescue in Vietnam, and the last C-54M in existence, used to haul coal during the Berlin airlift.

They've also added a snappy new flight simulator, available to anyone 10 or older 10 A.M.–2 P.M. Wednesday–Saturday.

John Dickinson Mansion and Plantation

This plantation (340 Kitts Hummock Rd., off U.S. 113, six miles south of Dover, 302/739-3277, 10 A.M.–3:30 P.M. Tues.–Sat., 1:30–4:30 P.M. Sun., Jan.–Feb. closed Sun., free) is a reconstructed farm complex originally built in the mid-1700s by Samuel Dickinson. His son, John Dickinson, a framer and signer of the U.S. Constitution, grew up on the plantation and supported the farm through his work as a lawyer. His "Letters from a Pennsylvania Farmer," published in major newspapers of the day, stated his opposition to British taxation of the colonies.

The property contains a Georgian mansion, a log building similar to the original slave's quarters (Dickinson's slaves were manumitted-"freed by his hand"—in 1787), and all the outbuildings necessary to maintain a self-contained plantation lifestyle. Costumed interpreters guide visitors through plantation life during Revolutionary times. The oddly named St. Jones River borders the plantation; apparently, Mr. Jones, an early landowner, designated

the waterway as the "stream of Jones." Since all deeds and maps were hand-lettered in the early 1700s, the term was abbreviated to "str. of Jones," which eventually became St. Jones.

Dover State House

Simple and elegant, the state house (10 A.M.–4:30 P.M. Tues.–Sat., 1:30–4:30 P.M. Sun., free) was completed in 1792 as the Delaware Capitol building. It faces Dover's central green, a public area designated by William Penn in 1683. The interior of the building contains a courtroom and an exhibit on the building's history; on the ceiling, visitors can view the sunflower (base of the central chandelier) that is the symbol of Delaware's State Museums (though you may not find ladybugs—the state insect—anywhere).

Delaware Archeology Museum and the Museum of Small Town Life

Housed in the Old Presbyterian Church of Dover and built in 1790 (316 S. Governor's Ave., 302/739-4266, 10 A.M.–3:30 P.M. Tues.–Fri., 9 A.M.–5 P.M. Sun., free, donations accepted), the museum displays 11,000 years of human habitation in Delaware through pictures and artifacts such as arrowheads, ceramics, stone and bone tools, glass, and other objects from the 17th, 18th, 19th, and 20th centuries. The stained-glass windows in this former church are especially beautiful in the late afternoon. The Museum of Small Town Life (same hours), in a building next the church once used for Sunday school, focuses on the state's small towns and more recent history, with a re-creation of an old print shop and an antique letterbox from a country post office. Ask to hear the "Grand Harmonica," a set of glass goblets that ring to individual notes when touched.

Dover Downs

Dover's adult entertainment hub, the Downs (U.S. 13, 302/674-4600, www.doverdowns .com) features the "Monster Mile" of car racing challenges, a steeply banked (24 degree) track that hosts the NASCAR Winston Cup twice each year. When professionals aren't using the

LOWER DELAWARE GREENWAYS

A greenway is a natural area of unbroken vegetation where recreation and conservation are the primary goals. The following greenways are either completed, or in construction:

Smyrna Trails, a paved bicycle/pedestrian trail along Green's Branch in northern Smyrna, connects three major thoroughfares: Glenwood Avenue, Duck Creek Parkway, and North Main Street. The trail provides offroad access for pedestrians and cyclists to numerous residential and commercial areas, and will also provide access to two scenic overlooks of Duck Creek. This project represents the first phase of implementation of a town-wide system of trails.

The **St. Jones River Greenway Commission** was created as an umbrella organization to coordinate greenway efforts in the capital city of Dover, working to preserve and enhance the cultural, historic, and recreational resources of the area. As part of the overall plan, the city of Dover is planning a one-mile pathway from Silver Lake Park to the Legislative Complex; Kent County is creating a third landing at the midpoint of the St. Jones River at Lebanon Landing; and 431 acres along the St. Jones River are being protected as part of the National Estuarine Research Reserve system. In this preserve, an interpretive center and one-mile self-guided trail focus on the historical interaction of people and their environment.

For the **Murderkill River Greenway,** more than 2,028 acres and three miles of river corridor have been protected at Killens Pond State Park and the Murderkill River Nature Preserve stretching from Route 13 to Frederica. A 0.5-mile pathway runs from the park entrance on Route 384 to the U.S. 13 intersection. The pathway is part of State Bicycle Route 1 and links Lake Forest High School and Killens Pond State Park. A 3.5-mile canoe trail was established from U.S. 13 to the Coursey Pond spillway.

The **Mispillion Riverwalk,** in the city of Milford, connects the downtown business area, library, amphitheater, community theater, University of Delaware Milford Campus building, and recreational areas. Plans are under way to link the Riverwalk via a pedestrian bridge to a long established park on the river's north bank.

For the **Mispillion River Greenway,** The Nature Conservancy, Delaware Wildlands, and U.S. Fish & Wildlife Service have preserved 2,600 acres at Milford Neck. The greenway extends north from Abbotts Pond to Blairs Pond and will eventually connect the Milford chain of lakes.

The town of Milton has undertaken an ambitious plan to create Governor's Walk along the **Broadkill River,** commemorating the

---

track, racing wannabes can test their mettle by signing up for **Monster Racing Excitement,** 800/468-6946, www.monsterracing.com). For $89, a racing instructor will take you around the track four laps in a Winston Cup racing car or truck—for $379 and up, you can drive the Monster yourself. Stock car racing takes place late spring and late fall.

November through April brings on the ponies for harness racing and simulcasts. Contact Dover Downs (800/711-5882, www.dover downs.com) for entries and results.

Dover Downs' video lottery gaming terminals—better known as slots—are available every day. The casino is a mini–Las Vegas with a Sistine Chapel–like ceiling that gives the illusion of being outdoors on a fresh spring day. Otherwise, it's full of eau de gambling: the throaty pitch of possibility tempered by the sugary scent of exotic drinks. The former third element, cigarette smoke, is no longer allowed in public places. The slots draw a truly mixed crowd, a few of whom look like they should be saving their quarters in a coffee can rather than donating to a one-armed bandit—er, a video lottery gaming terminal. But Lady Luck may be electronically hovering over your Stampede, Piggy Bankin,' or Bonanza machine, who knows? Two restaurants, the Garden Café, which serves decent meals

birthplace of four Delaware governors and a Wyoming governor. The Nature Conservancy has begun a new effort to protect land both upstream and downstream of the town. In addition, Milton has made outstanding efforts to preserve its historic town center.

The **Lewes Greenway** Committee is building a network of protected open space and pedestrian and bicycle pathways that link parks, natural areas, and historic sites throughout the town.

On the **Nanticoke River,** the city of Seaford is planning a riverfront walkway, and the town of Blades is working to create open space and new recreational opportunities.

The center of the **Broad Creek Greenway** is in the heart of Laurel. The greenway begins at Records Pond and extends west to Riverfront Park, linking the downtown area and the river.

The Division of Parks & Recreation holds 66 acres paralleling the **Assawoman Canal:** A master plan includes a pathway with connections to residential developments along the canal, water access points, and other amenities. The town of Bethany Beach has planned a system of pathways for pedestrians and bicyclists that will provide recreation and transportation and link with the Assawoman Canal lands.

A new long-distance trail, the **American Discovery Trail (ADT)** (www.discoverytrail .org), is a continuous multi-use hiking path extending across the United States from one coast to another. The ADT eastern trailhead is in Cape Henlopen State Park. The route of the ADT through Delaware travels about 45 miles of sidewalks and rural roads, most with paved shoulders. The trail passes through Redden State Forest and the towns of Lewes, Milton, and Bridgeville, but it mostly follows open farmland. A principal goal of the ADT has been to connect as many of the National Trail System trails and local and regional trails as possible in order to complete a system of trails. Reaching across 15 states, the ADT connects six national scenic trails, 10 national historic trails, and 23 national recreational trails and leads to 14 national parks and 16 national forests.

The **Coastal Heritage Greenway** is the most comprehensive in the Greenway Program, spanning a corridor of open space along more than 90 miles of Delaware's coast between Fox Point State Park and the state line at Fenwick Island. Focus areas along the Coastal Heritage Greenway include: Fox Point, New Castle, Delaware City, and Port Penn in New Castle County; Woodland Beach Wildlife Area, Lower St. Jones River, and Milford Neck in Kent County; and the Cape Henlopen Focus Area in Sussex County.

---

for around $15, and the Festival Buffet, a bargain at $13.50 for lunch and $16.50 for dinner combined with a fine view of the track, are worthwhile places to stop for a meal.

Harrington

Most often recognized as home of the Delaware State Fair, the small town of Harrington has a few other sites of note. The **Harrington Railroad Museum** and **Harrington Museum** (110 Fleming St., 302/398-3698, 11 A.M.–3 P.M. Mon.–Fri., free) feature local history. There's a railroad car to explore and exhibits on train lore. The Harrington Museum is in an 18th century Episcopal Church with a glorious stained glass rose window. Exhibits include a glass hearse carriage (circa 1800) complete with funeral attire, a history of harness racing, and information on the local fire company, military veterans, traveling salesmen, and rural home life. Other fun items are a vintage soda fountain, Jehu Camper folk art carvings, and a wooden model of the town.

The **Messick Agricultural Museum** (325 Walt Messick Rd., Harrington, 302/398-3729, 7:30 A.M.–4:30 P.M., Mon.–Fri., farmer's hours, donations accepted) mostly displays the shiny green-and-gold equipment of the John Deere Company, plus a few antique tractors and bicycles. The museum is in the warehouse of a

THUNDER ROAD

Stock-car racing is one of America's fastest-growing spectator sports. Since 1991, attendance at races affiliated with NASCAR (National Association for Stock-Car Auto Racing) has grown by 70 percent. In 2003, 200,000 people attended the 45th annual Daytona 500 in Florida, and television polls showed that an additional 29.4 million viewers tuned into some part of the race. The Daytona 500 is part of the Winston Cup, a 33-race series — and one of many public races on tracks all over the East Coast.

Nearly half of all stock-car racing fans are women. Fans attribute the popularity of the sport to everything from the drama of "cautions" (track accidents) to the fact that fans have two things to get excited about: the personalities of the racers and their vehicles. One speedway promoter referred to this combination as "mechathletes" — perhaps in the future, the two will join permanently to form a *Robocop*-style competitor. Fans also spend a great deal of time inspecting and appreciating the mechanical accessories that are a necessity of the sport: the race cars, their tires and engines; the truck-like rigs that tow them; and the colorful custom buses that house the top drivers. In fact, most fans travel the stock-car circuit in their own mechanical mini-versions of home: before each race, the lots are full of motor homes, trucks, and travel trailers.

Stock-car racing was born on the dirt roads of southeastern America after the second World War. The predecessors of today's racers might have been back-country bootleggers hauling their wares to market in the first supercharged versions of street cars. Though many commercial racetracks are paved today, the slick clay soil of the Piedmont Plateau that stretches between the Appalachian Mountains to the Atlantic Ocean, from New York to Alabama, continues to provide some of the best racing dirt in the world. Both Delaware and Maryland have dirt tracks of varying sizes. Dover Downs International Speedway in Delaware hosts one of the Winston Cup races along with slot machines and harness horse racing.

The cars themselves, standard-issue street cars on the outside, are driven by 500-horsepower engines with a top speed of nearly 200 miles per hour. NASCAR rule makers continually come up with technical impediments to slow the cars down, and racing teams spend enormous amounts of time and money to circumvent them — secrecy is as tight as a war room, but leaks are common, as are private and public disagreements both on and off the raceway.

Race car driving is labor-intensive. NASCAR crews work 12-hour days, six days a week, then race on Sunday. On smaller tracks, local racers often have full-time jobs but spend their evenings in the garage. Most winnings are poured back into improving the vehicle. Anyone who opts for a career in racing needs sponsorship, and stock-car racing has been given an enormous boost by corporate sponsors. Large corporations have found that the loyalty of racing fans for their heroes extends to the products whose logos cover the cars. The first of these was R. J. Reynolds, the tobacco giant, which sponsors the Winston Cup, among other events.

Stock-car racers have reached nearly god-like popularity. Four-color images of NASCAR Winston Cup 2000 champion Bobby Labonte, 2003 Daytona 500 winner Michael Waltrip, and other road warriors grace T-shirts, baseball caps, trading cards, soft-drink machines, and a host of other items. If stock-car racing hasn't thundered into a town near you, it's only a matter of time.

farm-equipment company; stop by the Taylor and Messick office for admittance.

For fans of gaming, Harrington is also home to **Midway Slots,** Delaware State Fairgrounds, U.S. 13, 888/88-SLOTS (888/887-5687, www.midwayslots.com). Midway is right next door to one of the oldest harness racing venues in America, the **Harrington Raceway** (302/398-7223, www.harringtonraceway.com, May–July and mid-August–mid-Nov.), where the ponies run very fast with tiny carts (and people) behind them.

Barratt's Chapel and Museum

The "Cradle of Methodism," Barratt's Chapel (6362 Bay Rd. off U.S. 113, 302/335-5544, 2–4 P.M. Sat.–Sun. and by appointment, free) was the site of the organization of the Methodist Episcopal Church in the United States. In 1780, Phillip Barratt donated land to the Methodist Society. John Wesley ordained America's first two Methodist clergymen, Dr. Thomas Coke and Rev. Richard Whatcoat, and in 1784, they administered the first American Methodist services in Barratt's Chapel. The simple brick building with its traditional Georgian architecture is one of the oldest houses of worship still extant in America. The museum features artifacts from the founding of Methodism in Delaware and an archival collection of memorabilia. The complex is one mile north of Frederica.

SHOPPING

In addition to the bulk market mentioned in the Dover Amish Country Tour, **❰ Spence's Bazaar** (South and New Streets, Dover, 302/734-3441) is a fun place to browse for both food and junque. It's a combination produce market, auction, and flea market; the Amish community is well represented. The bazaar operates on Tuesday and Friday.

The **❰ Delaware Made General Store,** in the historic John Bullen House (214 S. State St., Dover, 302/736-1419, Mon.–Sat.), is a showcase of gifts from many talented Delaware craftspeople. The shop sells souvenirs, pottery, tinware, art, candy, jams, cards, antiques and collectibles, and much more.

Loockerman Street, between S. Queen and S. State Streets, features a stroll's worth of shops and cafés. One place of note is the **Dover Art League** (21 Loockerman St., 302/674-0402, www.doverart.org, 11 A.M.–5 P.M. Tues.–Fri.), a sales gallery that displays juried work of local artists.

RECREATION
❰ Bombay Hook National Wildlife Refuge

Established in 1935, Bombay Hook (2591 Whitehall Neck Rd., Smyrna, 302/653-6872, www.fws.gov/northeast/bombayhook, 8 A.M.–4 P.M. Mon.–Fri., 9 A.M. 5 P.M. Sat.–Sun., $5) is one of the most important links on the Atlantic flyway. The word "hook" is derived from the Dutch term for a stand of trees. More than 16,000 acres of brackish marsh, freshwater pools, brush, timbered swamp, farms, and grassy upland are home to 256 identified species of birds, 33 species of mammals, and 37 species of reptiles and amphibians. The visitors center features wildlife exhibitions and a number of ranger-led programs; a 12-mile auto tour loop starts at the center (this may be downloaded from the website). Along the auto route, five nature trails ranging from a .25 mile to one mile in length are available to hikers and photographers. If you intend to leave your car, insect repellent is a must! Throughout the warmer months, the marshes are filled with an equal number of biting insects and rainbow-hued wildflowers. During spring and fall migrations, the ponds are often crowded with thousands of egrets or Canada geese (Bombay Hook has the largest count in the United States); numerous other migratory species, such as bald eagles, take advantage of a safe stopover at the refuge. Late October is a peak season for shorebirds, warblers, reptiles, and amphibians. In April and May, both red and gray fox sightings are common. Along the autoroute, you'll notice cultivated farm fields. The refuge permits farmers to work the land in exchange for a designated portion planted with crops favored by the park's wildlife. To reach the refuge from Rte. 9, turn east on Whitehall

Neck Road; continue 2.3 miles to the visitors center. Visitors may rent a 2X sighting scope at the center. There are no overnight facilities.

The Allee House is one of the best-preserved early farmhouses in Delaware. Built by Abraham Allee in 1753, the property overlooks woodlands and broad fields in the Bombay Hook Refuge. The farmhouse, with quarters for servants and slaves, has remained unaltered in appearance. It has been closed for repairs for some time, but may be open at this writing; call the park for more information.

Killens Pond State Park

Centrally located in the heart of Kent County, Killens Pond State Park (5025 Killens Pond Rd., Felton, 302/284-4526, www.destateparks .com/kpsp) has something for everyone. The park's centerpiece is a 66-acre millpond, which was established in the late 1700s. Prior to the pond's creation, the Murderkill River and surrounding hardwood forest were sites of several Native American homes and hunting camps. Killens Pond became a state park in 1965. Killens Pond Water Park, a sort of super swimming pool, offers resort entertainment in a serene, natural setting.

Open year-round, the park's campground and cabins are popular retreats in every season. Playground equipment and picnic areas are available, and four pavilions can be reserved for larger group events. A number of recreational programs are conducted during the summer, and autumn hayrides—the best way to view vivid fall foliage—are available by reservation after Labor Day through mid-November.

Hiking, Running, Biking: Hiking trails and a cross-country running course wind through several different native plant and animal habitats. The Ice Storm Trail gives hikers a chance to observe the forest's recovery from the devastating ice storms that struck the area in 1994. A bike path from U.S. 13 to the main entrance provides a leisurely passage into and out of the park.

Playing Fields: Game courts and ball fields are available to those with team play in mind, and an 18-hole disc golf course challenges players as well.

Boating: Canoes, rowboats, and pedal boats can be rented during the summer. A narrated pontoon boat tour of the pond is offered on summer weekends and holidays. The Murderkill River Canoe Trail offers a challenge for more adventurous paddlers.

Fishing: The pond is home to largemouth bass, catfish, carp, perch, crappie, bluegill, and pickerel.

Swimming: Killens Pond Water Park is more than a pool. Its innovatively designed zero-depth entrance makes getting in and out easy, and it also features three lap lanes, along with interactive water features such as the Floating Lily Pad Fun Walk. Two 27-foot-high, 205-foot-long twisting and turning waterslides end in a specially designed splash pool. At the tot pool and tot lot, bubblers, ground water jets, small slides, and a poolside water play system give smaller visitors lots of fun on a warm summer's day. A swim shop and food concession are nearby.

Overnight Facilities: The park offers 59 campsites with water and electric hookups accommodating both tents and recreational vehicles, 17 primitive tent campsites, and 10 cabins. One of the cabins, the Pond View Cottage, is a deluxe model with extra amenities and a view of the pond. Campsites are on a first-come, first-served basis, but reservations for cabins are accepted up to 120 days prior to the date of arrival. From Memorial Day weekend to Labor Day weekend, the park takes reservations for full-week rentals only. The cabins sleep four and feature an efficiency kitchen with an eating area, bedroom, bath with shower, air-conditioning, and heat. A picnic table, grill, and porch are located outside. Subject to availability, cabin rentals include the use of a canoe and rowboats. For reservations, call the park office at 302/284-4526.

Prime Hook Wildlife Refuge

This refuge (11978 Turkle Pond Rd., Milton, 302/684-8419, www.fws.gov/northeast/prime hook, sunrise–sunset, free), transected by four state highways, was established in 1963 to preserve coastal wetland for migratory waterfowl.

THE WILD GREEN ROAD SOUTH

Directly off Route 9, **Bombay Hook National Wildlife Refuge** is one of the best places to view birds and other marshland wildlife. Three of the trails in the refuge have 30-foot observation towers, and visitors may rent high-power viewing scopes.

Port Mahon, a short detour east on Route 89 from Route 9, is a good spot to see shorebirds – however, the road is sometimes impassible due to flooding. Port Mahon once had a beautiful lighthouse and thriving fishing community, but the lighthouse burned down in 1984, and the buildings rotted away. As a startling example of beach erosion, the Port Mahon lighthouse once stood 200 feet inland; its pilings are now in the bay.

The northern section of **Little Creek Wildlife Area** adjoins Bombay Hook. Most of the property is managed for waterfowl, with hunting blinds, photographic blinds, an observation tower, and a boardwalk.

Take Bergold Lane from Route 9 and follow it to Kitts Hummock Road and the entrance to **St. Jones Reserve.** The 700-acre reserve features a one-mile nature trail that includes a 0.25-mile boardwalk across the marsh. Turn west on Kitts Hummock Road past the Dickinson Plantation, and take U.S. 113 south to Route 1. Turn east on Route 36, then north on Route 203, to reach **Slaughter Beach,** one of the best places to see horseshoe crabs. This beach is the former site of the Mispillion Lighthouse, the last wood-frame lighthouse in Delaware, destroyed by lightning in 2002. Route 203 will take you through the Cedar Creek section of the **Milford Neck Wildlife Area,** an excellent place to view shorebirds.

Return to the Route 36 intersection and follow Route 204 along the shore. Take Route 224 to return to Route 1. Several roads heading east from Route 1 lead into the Prime Hook and the seashore; Route 220 to Route 221 to Route 199 leads to Fowler Beach; Route 198 to Route 222 to Route 38 leads to Primehook Beach (Shorts Beach). The main entrance is via Route 16 to Broadkill Beach.

Waters within **Prime Hook National Wildlife Refuge** are open for canoeing and boating, and four hiking trials include a boardwalk trail over the marshes. At Broadkill Beach, turn south from Route 16 to South Bay Shore Drive to reach Beach Plum Preserve.

The northern half of **Beach Plum Island Nature Preserve,** a 129-acre barrier island, is open to the public. Roads within the area are open to offroad vehicles only, so plan to walk from the parking lot.

Return to Route 1 via Route 16 and head south toward Lewes (LOO-es). Route 1 becomes Route 9. Follow Route 9 (King's Highway) into Lewes, proceed east on Savannah Road, then south on Cape Henlopen Drive.

Former site of the famed Cape Henlopen Lighthouse, which blew down during a fierce storm in 1926, **Cape Henlopen State Park** offers several different environments in which to view wildlife and shorebirds.

Most of the 8,817-acre refuge is marshland, and water levels are manipulated through a system of dikes and water control structures to stimulate growth of plants used by wildlife. As in Bombay Hook (Central Delaware), the upland fields are managed under an agreement with local farmers who leave a portion of their crops in the field to provide supplemental food and cover.

All tidal waterways and enclosed ponds are open to **sportfishing, hunting** is permitted within season. Special regulations apply for all hunters: More information is available from the refuge headquarters (c/o Refuge Manager, Prime Hook National Wildlife Refuge, RD3, Box 195, Milton, DE 19968).

Canoeing and boating enthusiasts have more than 15 miles of streams and ditches to explore. Several boat-launching ramps are available (maps may be requested from the refuge headquarters or downloaded off the website). There are no canoe rental facilities available.

Two trails are open for **hiking, photography, and wildlife observation.** The **Mispillion**

Lighthouse, the oldest surviving wood lighthouse in Delaware, was originally located north of Prime Hook National Wildlife Refuge near Slaughter Beach off Rte. 36 on Lighthouse Road.

Amish Country Auto/Bike Tour

The Amish community around Dover is a fairly recent development. Unlike the colonial farms of eastern Pennsylvania, central Delaware's Amish families moved to the area from California and Indiana during the Great Depression when land prices were severely depressed. Old Order Amish, an ultraconservative branch of the Christian Mennonite sect, appear to have rejected—and perhaps transcended—the modern world. Amish distinguish themselves from the communities around them by conservative dress, the practice of traditional religious worship, adoption of strict codes of behavior, and disavowal of telephones, cars, electricity, government, advanced schooling, and many other "modern" aspects of life. Old Order Amish retain a visible and powerful presence throughout central Delaware.

All Amish and Mennonites trace their roots to the Anabaptist ("new birth") movement in Switzerland in 1525, an offshoot of the Protestant Reformation. Toward the end of the 17th century, the Anabaptist movement split over several issues, chiefly the practice of "shunning": social ostracism of community members for disobedience. Old Order Amish, a sect dwelling primarily in the Alsace region of France, chose to continue the practice. Anabaptists separated into two main camps, the Amish and the more liberal Mennonites. Since the original schism, each of the main branches has split many times. Almost obliterated in their European homeland, the Amish have flourished in the New World. One thing is true of all Amish—the religious basis of their lives demands that they be aware of the larger world, but not participants in it.

Amish who reside around Dover are unselfconscious and comfortable in their worldly surroundings. The area west of Dover consists of numerous Amish farms; buggies on back roads and steam-powered farm equipment are common. Conservatively dressed men in their black felt or straw hats, and women with long skirts and capped hair, pick up basketfuls of produce at local stores. The loop represented by this tour is only a small portion of the Amish community. Much of the farmland in eastern and southern Kent County is farmed by Amish or Mennonites, and is recognizable by the lack of motorized vehicles and phone and power lines.

This easy 16-mile round-trip tour starts in downtown Dover on the corner of Loockerman (LAHK-er-mehn) and Queen Streets. All distances are approximate. Loockerman becomes Forest Avenue/Route 8; follow the signs for Route 8 west out of town and stay on the road until the intersection of Rose Valley School Road, in less than five miles. **Byler's Country Store,** a bulk market, is on the corner, and you may see a buggy or two parked outside. Turn left (south) on Rose Valley School Road. Look for the Amish School with its his-and-hers outhouses. For a shorter trip, continue on Rose Valley School Road to Hazlettville Road and return to Dover, as below. Otherwise, look for the intersection of Yoder Drive (0.75 mile south of Rte. 8) and turn right onto it (west). Follow Yoder about two miles to Pearsons Corner Road and turn left (south). In a little over a mile, you'll come to the intersection of Hazlettville Road; turn left (east). Dover is about seven miles away; you'll pass **Eden Hill Farm,** a nursery with a you-pick pumpkin patch in the autumn. Once in Dover, make a left on Queen to return to the start.

As with anywhere else, don't trespass on private property, nor photograph people without permission. Many, though not all, Amish people consider a photograph in which they may be identified as a "graven image" or a sign of vanity, and therefore a violation of biblical precepts—not to mention a major invasion of privacy.

ACCOMMODATIONS

Rose Tower Bed & Breakfast (228 E. Camden-Wyoming Ave., Camden, 302/698-9033, $76–120) is a spacious home built in 1807

© JOANNE MILLER

a farm stand in Dover

and now listed on the National Register of Historic Places. Jane and Ed Folz have decorated the rooms in the style of the historic houses of Odessa. Though the house is on the main street of the old section of Camden, it's very quiet and peaceful, and the rose garden in bloom is a delight to behold. Each of the rooms has a private bath, and reservations are necessary.

Also recommended: **Little Creek Inn B&B** (2623 N. Little Creek Rd., Dover, 302/730-1300, www.littlecreekinn.com, $150–195). It has five rooms, all with baths (two have whirlpool tubs), plus down pillows and comforters, in an 1860 Italianate-style home with swimming pool. Rates include a full breakfast.

FOOD

The Blue Coat Inn (800 N. State St., 302/674-1776, lunch Mon.–Sat., dinner daily, Sun. brunch noon–2:30 P.M., lunch $8, dinner $24) is one of Dover's finest dining establishments and an old favorite of the town's cognoscenti. The view over Silver Lake at sun-

set is spellbinding. The setting is elegant, and the American menu features such favorites as chicken marsala, crab imperial, oyster sandwiches, and filet mignon.

Café Bleu (25 West Loockerman St., 302/678-9463, lunch 11 A.M.–2 P.M. Tues.–Fri., dinner by reservation only 5–9 P.M. Thurs.–Fri., $9) offers a gourmet lunch served by a chef classically trained in the French tradition (she once worked at Krazy Kats outside Wilmington). Everything is made from scratch; look for dishes such as savory sage sausage and mushroom strudel with port reduction ($9).

Where Pigs Fly (617 E. Loockerman St., Dover, 302/678-0586, www.wherepigsfly restaurant.com, lunch and dinner daily, $6–16) is a great place to get huge helpings of messy pulled pig barbecue. Hamburgers, hot dogs, sandwiches, and beef and chicken platters are also available.

Sambo's Tavern (293 Front St., Leipsic, 302/674-9724, 11 A.M.–10:30 P.M. Mon.–Sat., $13) has the best crab cakes in central Delaware. Am I prejudiced? You bet! In the constant search for creamy, crusty, crabby crab cakes, Sambo's wins, claws down. This comfortable roadhouse on the water is a local legend; the bar opens earlier than the restaurant and closes later. Since Sambo's is a tavern, no one under 21 is admitted. Seafood is served only in season—no frozen imports here.

INFORMATION

For more information on Dover, Kent County, and central Delaware, contact the **Kent County & Greater Dover, Delaware Convention and Visitors Bureau** (435 North DuPont Hwy., Dover, DE 19903, 302/734-1736 or 800/233-5368, www.visitdover.com).

Lewes

The charming town of Lewes provides a respite from the nearby sun-and-fun frenzy of Rehoboth. Many visitors to the area prefer to stay in this quiet town and visit the local small beach or larger beaches during the day. The town also features sophisticated restaurants, shopping, and a healthy dose of history. Lewes, "the first town in the first state," was the site of the original settlement in Delaware in 1631, named Zwaanendael (Valley of the Swans).

SIGHTS
The De Vries Monument
The plaque and modest monument on which it's mounted (Pilottown Rd., about a mile north of Savannah Rd. in the center of town) commemorate the Dutch West India colony that settled here in 1631, staying until cultural misunderstandings between the Dutch and resident Native Americans culminated in the extermination of the Europeans by the locals. Apparently, a tribesman had pried the metal shield off the front of the fort because he liked the unicorn symbol on it. When the Dutch traders complained, the chief had the "thief" killed and sent his head to the leader of the Dutchmen. The Dutch were aghast at the severity of the penalty, and dressed down the chief for his action. Deeply insulted that their kinsmen had made restitution with the thief's life and the gesture was not accepted, the thief's relatives massacred the encampment. Who could understand those hard-to-please Europeans?

The Zwaanendael Museum
This clever little collection (102 Kings

Zwaanendael Museum

Hwy. and Savannah Rd., 302/645-1148, 10 A.M.–4:30 P.M. Tues.–Sat., 1:30–4:30 P.M. Sun., free, donations welcome) tells the story of the early encampment and has a copy of the goofy-looking red unicorn that proved such a fatal attraction (the unicorn is the symbol of the town of Hoorn in the Netherlands, the origin of most of the early Dutch traders). The museum itself, built in 1931, is a striking replica of the Town Hall of Hoorn. In addition, it features changing exhibits on other historical aspects of the area. One such exhibit delved

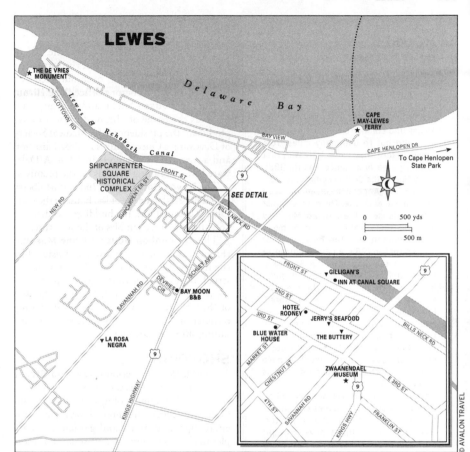

into the area's maritime connections, including information on slops (regulation British sailors clothing), long toggies (sailors in civilian clothing—getting a set of slops was imperative for new sailors), and Welsh wigs (worsted knit caps worn by sailors).

Shipcarpenter Square Historical Complex

The Lewes Historical Society (110 Shipcarpenter St., 302/645-7670, www.historiclewes .org) maintains a group of 12 restored buildings, many of which were moved from other areas. Self-guided tours originate at the Society

office. The buildings are open 11 A.M.–4 P.M. Saturday May–mid-June and late September– first week in October, 11 A.M.–4 P.M. Monday–Saturday mid-June–mid-September, and on Sundays mid-July–mid-August. Admission is $7 for all houses/museums, $2 for individual houses. A trolley tour is offered at 11:30 A.M. Tuesday–Thursday late June–late September. It costs $5 and leaves from the DART bus stop at Second and Market Streets.

One of the buildings open to the public is the **Burton-Ingram House** (Shipcarpenter and 3rd Sts.). It features hand-hewn timbers and cypress shingles (drawn from fallen trees in the

HOUSES IN MOTION

Uprooting entire buildings from their foundations and subsequently transporting them to a new location has long been practiced in Sussex County. More than 85 homes and commercial structures were built and put to use many miles from Lewes before they came to rest in that town. One early instance was the 1825 relocation of the Burton homestead from the town of Angola to Savannah Road near the canal bridge. The old Methodist Meeting House, at the corner of Mulberry and 3rd Streets, was moved three times.

So common was the movement of houses that in 1983, a pair of entrepreneurs created Shipcarpenter Square in Lewes, an 11-acre community of 38 buildings that were brought to the site from within a 40-mile radius and then restored. Lewes' second-largest enclave of "scooter houses" (moved dwellings) belongs to the Lewes Historical Society – seven of the eight buildings (the Ryves Holt House, on 2nd St., is in its original location) have been transported. The Doctor's Office is on its fifth site.

Early scooter houses were pulled by oxen on skids; today, homes can still be seen rolling down the road on tractor-trailers. Modern times have brought changes, though: It's often necessary to dismantle a building to allow passage under overhead utility wires.

Pocomoke cypress swamp that once covered the area), and a cellar made from ship's ballast stones. The **Rabbit's Ferry House** (3rd St.) is an early-18th-century farmhouse expanded with a second room in later years.

The **Thompson Country Store** (3rd St.) has many of its original appointments and has remained essentially the same as when it operated full-time from 1888 to 1962. The **Ellegood House** (behind the country store) contains the historical society's excellent gift shop, full of handcrafted items. Also behind the country

store, the **Early Plank House** is an example of a Swedish-type settler's cabin.

The Doctor's Office (near the Plank House) is a handsome Greek revival structure built around 1850. It has been outfitted as a late-19th-century doctor's office. The **Hiram R. Burton House** (2nd St. and Shipcarpenter Sq.) was the home of Hiram Burton, a Lewes physician, the president of the Medical Society of Delaware, a Queen Anne's Railroad director, and a member of Congress in 1904. A Delaware history reading room is on the premises.

The **Ryves Holt House** (2nd and Mulberry Sts.) is believed to be the oldest house in the state. Once a colonial inn, the building was dated to 1665 through core samples of the structure.

The **Cannonball House Marine Museum** (Front and Bank Sts.) is also administered by the historic society. So named because it was struck by a cannonball during the bombardment of Lewes by the British during the War of 1812, the museum houses an ever increasing number of nautical exhibits, including model sailing ships and artifacts.

SHOPPING

A two-block-long section of **Second Street** off Savannah Street is the shopping district in Lewes, with a number of upscale clothing, antique, and collectible shops. Blown glass, oriental rugs, and house and garden items are plentiful. A few shops are seasonal, but most are open year-round. Notable stops include **2nd St. Popcorn** (135 2nd St.), which features exquisite candied apples like old-fashioned red cinnamon, Heavenly Hash (chocolate, marshmallows, and walnuts), and gooey caramel; **Gerties Greengrocer** (119 2nd St.), which sells organic produce; **Books by the Bay** (103 2nd St.), which features publications with a local twist; and **King's Ice Cream** (210 2nd St.), the place for frozen treats.

A block away (114 3rd St.), **Preservation Forge,** an old-fashioned forge complete with blacksmith, sells metal items.

Food and Wine

The **Historic Lewes Farmer's Market** (302/

644-1436, www.historiclewesfarmersmarket
.org), featuring produce straight from the
farm to you, is held at 110 Shipcarpenter
Street or Shields Elementary (910 Shields
Ave.) 10 A.M.–noon on Saturdays from June
to September.

Here's something visitors don't expect to
find: "The First Winery in the First State,"
Nassau Valley Vineyards (36 Nassau Commons, 302/645-9463, www.nassauvalley.com).
The wines, made from local grapes, are quite
good. Winemaker Peg Raley was trained in
France and Spain, and she really knows her
stuff. See for yourself—the vineyard has a
tasting room (open 11 A.M.–5 P.M. Tues.–Sat.,
noon–5 P.M. Sun.). The vineyard is located just
off of Rte. 1 west of Lewes.

RECREATION

In addition to lolling about on the pretty public
beach on Cape Henlopen Drive, visitors can join
a sportfishing expedition aboard one of the many
party boats docked at **Anglers Fishing Center**
(Angler's Rd., 302/644-4533, www.anglers
fishingcenter.com). Contact **Fisherman's
Wharf** (at the drawbridge, 302/645-8862,
www.fishlewes.com) for dolphin- and whale-
watching cruises.

◖ Cape Henlopen State Park

In 1682, when the current lands of the state
of Delaware were granted to William Penn, he
proclaimed that Cape Henlopen and its natural resources were for the common usage of
the citizens of Lewes and Sussex County, thus
establishing one of the nation's first "public
lands." For more information, contact park
headquarters (42 Cape Henlopen Dr., Lewes,
DE 19958, 302/645-6852). For details on nature programs, call 302/645-8983.

Cape Henlopen's strategic location at the
mouth of the Delaware Bay contributed to
its importance in local shipping and military
history. The longlamented Henlopen Lighthouse no longer helps guide vessels through
the treacherous bay waters (it blew down in
a windstorm in the 1920s), but the two stone
breakwater barriers off the point of the Cape,

NEW LIFE FOR AN OLD LIGHT

In 2001, the oldest surviving wood lighthouse in Delaware, the **Mispillion Light,**
was teetering on the edge of destruction – the frail lighthouse was only a few
feet away from the encroaching bay.
Riprap, broken concrete slabs reinforced
with rebar, were piled atop the edges of
the beach in an attempt to hold back the
insistent power of erosion. The lack of
interest in preserving the old building,
located north of Prime Hook National
Wildlife Refuge near Slaughter Beach,
was evidenced by the decaying paint and
broken windows.

On the morning of May 2, 2002, a wild
storm moved across the bay and lightning struck the old lighthouse, burning the upper portion of the tower and
much of the building's interior, dashing
the hopes of a small group of citizens recently banded together to try to restore
the light.

In the nearby town of Lewes, John and
Sally Freeman purchased a building lot in
Shipcarpenter Square, a neighborhood
reserved for residences consisting of
relocated historic structures. A few days
after the storm, Sally saw a picture of the
damaged lighthouse in a local newspaper. By the end of the year, Mispillion was
gone: Lighthouse enthusiasts believed
the beacon was destroyed forever, another victim of neglect. But in July 2005,
a modern lantern that cost over $53,000
was placed atop a reconstructed and
expanded Mispillion River Lighthouse in
Shipcarpenter Square.

completed in 1869 and 1901, still form a safe
harbor for boats during rough seas.

In 1941, the U.S. Army established a military base at Cape Henlopen. Bunkers and gun
emplacements were camouflaged among the
dunes, and concrete observation towers (one
of Henlopen's notable sights) were built along
the coast to spot enemy ships. In 1964, the

World War II watchtowers at Cape Henlopen State Park

Department of Defense declared 543 acres of the cape lands as surplus property, and the State of Delaware established Cape Henlopen State Park.

In addition to expansive bay and ocean beaches, the 3,143-acre maritime park contains Gordon's Pond Wildlife Area, a unique saltwater impoundment. Along the coast, the Great Dune rises 80 feet above sea level; further inland, "walking dunes" slowly move across the pine forests. A broad salt marsh stretches along the park's western boundary. The variety of habitats within the park makes it a valuable home to many species of birds, reptiles, and mammals, including threatened shorebirds.

The park also features a picnic pavilion, a 19-pole disc golf course, and basketball courts. Winter hunting is permitted in some areas of the park—a hunting permit is required, and information can be obtained from the park office. Annual events, such as the Kite Festival and the Halloween Spook Trail, are family favorites. The park also conducts a number of entertaining recreational programs, including the annual Shoretalk series, outdoor concerts, seaside seining, and bird watching.

The **Seaside Nature Center** offers environmental education programs and recreational activities year-round, and it's a good place to stop for park information. Marine aquariums and displays enable visitors to meet ocean creatures face to face. An auditorium for audiovisual programs and a gift shop complete the attractions at this popular facility.

Hiking: Hiking trails and interpretive displays throughout the park help visitors learn about the area's natural features. In addition, several World War II–era bunkers provide scenic overlooks, and one of the concrete observation towers has been renovated to provide a panoramic view of the cape.

Fishing: A .25-mile-long pier provides convenient access to Delaware Bay. The bait and tackle concession at the pier offers fishing supplies and snack foods, and transportation along the pier is available for people with disabilities from April 1 to October 31. Surf fishing is a year-round activity along the park's ocean beaches. Dune crossings allow pedestrian and vehicle access to the designated fishing areas. A surf-fishing vehicle permit is required in order to drive onto the beach. Permits are available at the park office.

Swimming: Cape Henlopen's beaches attract thousands of visitors who enjoy ocean swimming and sunbathing. Two designated swimming beaches are guarded Memorial Day–Labor Day. The northern swimming area also features a modern bathhouse with showers, changing rooms, and a food concession. Umbrellas are available for rent during the summer.

Overnight Facilities: Pine-covered dunes surround 159 spacious sites, each with a water hookup. Camping is available March 1–November 30; call 877/987-2757 for reservations, or reserve online at http://delaware.reserve world.com.

Beach Plum Island Nature Preserve

A satellite of Cape Henlopen State Park, most of this 129-acre barrier island is protected to preserve habitat for native plant and animal species, but surf fishing and beachcombing are permitted along the Delaware Bay shore. The island is located north of the city of Lewes, with vehicle access from Broadkill Beach (open Mar.–mid-Dec.).

The Cape May-Lewes Ferry

A popular way to start off an engaging day trip, the ferry (800/643-3779, www.cape maylewesferry.com) leaves daily year-round from the dock on Cape Henlopen Drive. The 70-minute trip across Delaware Bay ends in the Victorian town of Cape May, New Jersey. Departure times vary depending on month and day. During the summer months, the ferry leaves Lewes at 7 A.M. and every 45 minutes thereafter, with extended hours on weekends and June–September. Foot passengers pay $3.50–7.50 round trip (free for children under 6), and a vehicle with a driver costs $20–24 round trip (additional passengers pay the same as foot passengers); larger vehicles pay propor-

tionately more. Bicycles are free. Call ahead for reservations. It's a good idea to arrive 30 minutes before departure.

ACCOMMODATIONS
Bed-and-Breakfasts

Some B&Bs limit their lodgings to guests over the age of six; check before making reservations. High season—Memorial Weekend–Labor Day—brings the highest rates. Prices have increased dramatically over the years, thanks to the increasing popularity of the area. Tariffs are reduced by 10–30 percent at other times of year. Make sure to check prices with your host, as different properties have different opinions on when high season actually happens. Some places also require a two-night minimum stay, particularly on weekends.

The **John Penrose Virden House** (217 2nd St., 302/644-0217, $110–215, cash and checks only) is a lovely, deep green Victorian that attracts guests from all over the world. Each of the three pleasant rooms has a full bath, and one is a deluxe suite with a private entrance. The house is half a block from Lewes' shopping district, restaurants, and beach.

The **Blue Water House** (407 E. Market St., 302/645-7832 or 800/493-2080, www.lewes beach.com/welcome2, $100–300, two-night minimum) brings a touch of the Caribbean with its brightly colored exterior and four guestrooms, all with private baths. It caters to families, with rooms large enough for cots, plus a variety of toys—boogie boards, bikes, towels, umbrellas, movies, and an open-air patio—to satisfy everyone. A hot breakfast is served in the morning.

Inns and Hotels

There's a **Sleep-Inn** on Hwy. 1 (800/753-3746) in addition to other chain hotels listed under Rehoboth Beach.

Open all year, the 〖 **Inn at Canal Square** (122 Market St., 302/644-3377 or 888/ 644-1911, innatcanalsquare@ce.net, $105–250, closed Dec. 18–26) offers the most modern lodgings in town, with 19 spacious suite rooms with full baths. All have a water view, and 17 rooms have private balconies. The inn also offers two luxury cottage suites at $500 or $600 per night, with a two-night minimum. A modest continental breakfast is served. The inn offers specials and packages, especially during the Lewes Jazz Festival, held the third weekend in October.

Hotel Rodney (142 2nd St. at Market, 302/645-6466 or 800/824-8754, www.zwaan endaelinn.com, $50–280), the former Zwaanendael Inn, was built in 1926 and renovated in 1989. The hotel, with 18 rooms and five suites, features all the modern conveniences, including a fitness center. The rooms have much more individual charm than a run-of-the-mill hotel, and they're close to everything in town. The hotels offers discounts for multiple-night stays, and there's a two-night minimum on weekends during high season.

FOOD

Located in the historic Trader mansion, **◖ The Buttery** (2nd and Savannah Sts., 302/645-7755, www.butteryrestaurant.com, lunch and dinner daily plus Sun. brunch, $10–36) is a classic American restaurant with a well-deserved reputation for fine dining. The bistro-like restaurant offers a $28 three-course prix fixe dinner 5–6:30 P.M. Monday–Sunday. Lunch entrées include a smoked salmon BLT with applewood smoked bacon, romaine, smoked salmon, and tomato on toasted rye with horseradish mayonnaise, served with creamy red bliss potato salad ($12). For dinner, try the spring vegetable biryani with tomato coconut curry, saffron basmati rice, crisp pappadums, and cucumber mint raita ($26).

◖ Gilligan's Waterfront Restaurant and Bar (134 Market St. at Front St., 302/644-7230, lunch and dinner Tues–Sun., $8–30) is one of the most popular places to eat in town—for good reason. The outside bar that fronts the channel is a meeting place for locals and visitors alike. The menu is American, featuring seafood, beef, and chicken.

A local critic's-choice winner for best upscale Italian, **La Rosa Negra** (1201 Savannah Rd., 302/645-1980, www.larosanegrarestaurant.com, dinner Mon.–Sat. year-round and Sun. June–Aug., $18) is packed during the evenings with those who appreciate fine seafood-filled ravioli and other Italian cuisine. The spectacular desserts are baked on the premises.

The former Rose & Crown Pub and Restaurant has morphed into **Jerry's Seafood** (108 2nd St., 302/645-6611, www.jerrys-seafood.com, lunch and dinner daily, $10–30), home of the crab bomb: That's 10 ounces of jumbo lump crab seasoned with Old Bay and baked ($32). Jerry's serves all manner of seafood and shrimp, if you'd prefer something like a garden salad topped with a mound of homemade chicken salad and fried oysters ($12).

Rehoboth Beach and Dewey Beach

If there were ever an archetypal beach town, Rehoboth is it: an endless boardwalk filled night and day with throngs of scantily clad humans, thrill rides, T-shirt booths, junk food, and miles of sugary sand, striped umbrellas, and roasting sunbathers. And the restaurants are top-notch! Rehoboth's distinction comes from its humble origin as a Methodist summer camp (Carey's Camp Meeting Ground is still in operation for revival meetings during the summer), its subsequent death, and its eventual resurrection. After World War II, Atlantic beach resorts took a hit as families found other forms of recreation. The once thriving community decayed. During the real-estate mania of the 1980s, farsighted investors, many of them gay, bought up property there. And Rehoboth came back better than ever. Though its reputation as a gay resort town kept some families away during the late '80s, that's no longer true. People of every hue, persuasion, spiritual leaning, and nuclear grouping shuffle along the bustling sidewalks.

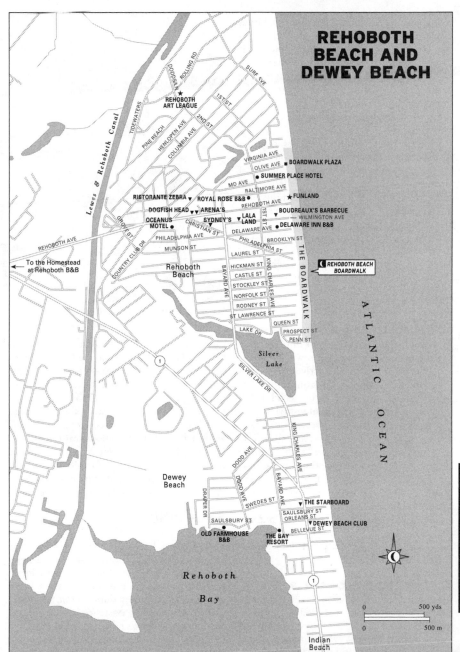

REHOBOTH BEACH AND DEWEY BEACH

ROLLING RD

DODDS ST

SURF AVE

1ST ST

2ND ST

★ REHOBOTH ART LEAGUE

PINE BEACH

HENLOPEN AVE

COLUMBIA AVE

TIDEWATERS

Lewes & Rehoboth Canal

VIRGINIA AVE

OLIVE AVE ■ BOARDWALK PLAZA

MD AVE ● SUMMER PLACE HOTEL

BALTIMORE AVE

RISTORANTE ZEBRA ▼ ▼ ROYAL ROSE B&B ★ FUNLAND

REHOBOTH AVE

DOGFISH HEAD ▼ ▼ ARENA'S 1ST ST

OCEANUS SYDNEY'S ● ▼ LALA ▼ BOUDREAUX'S BARBECUE
MOTEL ● LAND — WILMINGTON AVE

CHRISTIAN ST DELAWARE AVE ● DELAWARE INN B&B

GROVE ST

REHOBOTH AVE

PHILADELPHIA AVE BROOKLYN ST

COUNTRY CLUB DR

To the Homestead
at Rehoboth B&B ← MUNSON ST PHILADELPHIA ST

Rehoboth Beach LAUREL ST

HICKMAN ST

BAYARD AVE

KING CHARLES AVE

CASTLE ST

STOCKLEY ST ☾ REHOBOTH BEACH
BOARDWALK

NORFOLK ST

RODNEY ST

THE BOARDWALK

ST LAWRENCE ST

QUEEN ST

LAKE DR PROSPECT ST

PENN ST

ATLANTIC OCEAN

Silver
Lake

SILVER LAKE DR

KING CHARLES AVE

DODD AVE

Dewey
Beach

DRAPER DR

DODD AVE

SWEDES ST

BAYARD AVE

▼ THE STARBOARD

SAULSBURY ST
ORLEANS ST ▼ DEWEY BEACH CLUB

SAULSBURY ST

OLD FARMHOUSE
B&B ● ● THE BAY BELLEVUE ST
RESORT

Rehoboth
Bay

1

0   500 yds
0   500 m

Indian
Beach

SOUTH DELAWARE

© AVALON TRAVEL

Just south of Rehoboth Beach, the habitués of Dewey Beach play in a different scenario—the town has a reputation for high-time, hard-partying nightlife, which delights some visitors and disturbs more than a few residents. The bars are packed during summer nights, but the town immediately quiets down again when autumn winds blow. The beaches are a continuation of Rehoboth perfection.

The best time to visit the beaches is during the first two weeks of September (if you're looking for hot, sunny days and an active nightlife) and mid-September to late October if you prefer beach without the night action. At this time of year, most of the restaurants are open and the crowds have thinned to a trickle. The "permit parking only" restrictions on roads leading to Rehoboth and Dewey Beaches end around mid-September, making it easy to drive right up to the beach of your choice and hop out of the car for a few hours of working on your tan.

fun on the beach with piping plovers

SIGHTS
◖ Rehoboth Beach Boardwalk

This stroll on the beach extends from Virginia Avenue on the north end of town 16 blocks south to Penn Street. The active part—with shops and food concessions—runs from Olive Avenue in the north down to Laurel/Philadelphia Street in the south. **Funland** (rides and games, www.funlandrehoboth.com) is clustered at the terminus of the three main streets in town: Baltimore, Rehoboth, and Wilmington Avenues. On warm evenings, it's a pleasure to walk the hundreds of little gaming booths and rides and see the glowing faces of small children reflected in the bright lights. It's an old-fashioned style of family fun, but one that hasn't lost its sheen during the past century. Tickets cost 30 cents, and rides require 1–5 tickets each.

The Rehoboth Art League

An unexpected oasis of calm in a wealthy suburb of Rehoboth Beach (12 Dodds Ln., Henlopen Acres, 302/227-8408, www.rehobothartleague.org), the league was founded in 1938 to encourage interest and participation in cultural and artistic activities. Attractions include Corkran/Tubbs Gallery and the Marsh Homestead House (open 10 A.M.–4 P.M. Mon.–Sat. and noon–4 P.M. Sun. Apr.–Oct.). The league's buildings, including the 1743 Peter Marsh Homestead, sit on 3.5 heavily forested acres. The league offers concerts, lectures, classes, workshops, and art exhibitions year-round. The Corkran/Tubbs Gallery and Marsh Homestead house show exceptional art exhibits by league members. The grounds offer pleasant strolling, the art is all for sale, and there's no fee to enter.

SHOPPING
Outlets

Shop-a-rama! The malls that stretch between Lewes and Rehoboth Beach deserve special notice—not because they don't duplicate a lot of the outlet malls you can find anywhere (they do), but because they duplicate *all* of them: every outlet store in existence is there, plus a few more, and there's no sales tax in Delaware. Genius! The outlets consist of three major shopping centers interspersed with several

INSPIRATION

In the last years of the 20th century, Wilmington resident Howard Pyle often illustrated stories and nonfiction work for *Harper's Monthly*, and he was celebrated for his ability to bring historic subjects to life. Pyle's talent was no accident: He researched each illustration meticulously, making sure that the garments worn by a colonial tradesman – and the tack on his horse – were historically accurate. Pyle founded the Brandywine school of painting, noted for its dreamy, luminous backgrounds portraying "natural" sites and glowing, surreal figures. His teaching is readily evident in the work of his student, Maxfield Parrish.

Another of Pyle's famous students, N. C. Wyeth, found fame for his book illustrations. *Treasure Island* is one of several Wyeth-illustrated books that bring big prices from collectors.

In the early 1900s, Ethel Pennewill Brown became the most successful American illustrator of her day at a time when a woman earning a living as an artist was a rarity. In her early 20s, she overcame social, financial, and geographic barriers to attend the prestigious Art Students League of New York. She then studied with Howard Pyle at his studio in Wilmington. Ethel Brown was one of Pyle's first female students.

Later, she went to France and studied and exhibited in Paris. Brown appreciated the modern style of Matisse and Picasso, but preferred a more realistic style, similar to that of another American expatriate, Mary Cassatt of Pittsburgh.

While a student, Brown worked as an illustrator. As her popularity grew, her work appeared in major magazines in the early 1920s, such as *Good Housekeeping, Harper's Bazaar,* and *Harper's Monthly.* She also illustrated books, notably the Betty Baird series and works by Louisa May Alcott.

At the age of 45, Brown married fellow Delaware artist William Leach, and the couple settled in Frederica. She then turned from illustration to serious painting. Ethel P. B. Leach played a pivotal role in the creation of the Rehoboth Art League in Rehoboth Beach, and generously encouraged the work of other artists throughout her life. Her paintings include landscapes of Delaware and numerous portraits.

---

minor ones on "mall mile" (Rte. 1). Contact the outlets (302/226-9223, www.shoprehoboth .com) for a map of who's where.

One unique store tucked between chain outlets is **Peppers** (Tanger Factory Outlets/ Outlet #3, 800/988-3473, www.peppers.com). If you're a serious peppermeister or just looking for an unusual gift, this is the place. Proprietor Luther "Chip" Hearn and his sister, Randi, have gathered the largest collection of fiery condiments in the world—more than 3,000 sauces and 50 salsas—and added a few prize-winning combinations of their own. The sauces sold at Peppers are all rated for heat factor, and a few—such as Pure Cap and Dave's Gourmet Insanity Sauce, Private Reserve—are so hot that customers must sign a waiver before purchasing them. Peppers also has a salsa bar where you can taste before you buy. Offerings include hot-pepper jelly beans and a collection of "pepperwear" aprons and cooking accessories. The brightly colored store started out as a hobby, an adjunct to the Hearns' popular Starboard Restaurant and Bar in Dewey Beach. They have a catalog for shoppers who just can't get enough of that endorphin rush.

Rehoboth Avenue

For pure beach-mania overload, Reho Avenue is a must-see. You'll pass more ocean-themed shops, seashell stores, and saltwater taffy places than you ever thought possible. But the real draw is the parade of people, from nattily dressed ladies with poodles to teenage punks, from deeply tanned bikini-wearers (male and female) to the paler folks in pastel plaid.

ACCOMMODATIONS

Rehoboth has dozens of places to stay, fitting every taste and budget. The lowest rates on the

CHRISTMAS IN JULY

While you're on beach leave during the warm months of the year, it's a good time to think about Christmas – shopping, that is. The outlets, especially with their lack of sales tax, make shopping for everyone on your list a sea breeze. Many of the shops will ship bigger items, and your beach lodging may help you forward any cartons to your home via its UPS connection.

The secret to shopping in July is planning. Like Santa, you have to make a list and check it twice, including everybody's sizes and preferences (getting a map listing the available stores in the outlets is a good idea). Not only do you avoid the Christmas crowds, you have the fun of adding shopping to your sunshine holiday activities. Just make sure you shake out the sand before you tie the shiny red bow.

scale are midweek, midwinter (often in Dec. only). Here are a few:

Bed-and-Breakfasts

Most of the restful lodgings noted below are all close to the center of town, but a few blocks away from the beach. Some B&Bs limit their lodgings to guests over the age of six; check before making reservations. High season—Memorial Weekend–Labor Day—brings the highest rates. Tariffs are reduced by 10–30 percent at other times of year. Be sure to confirm prices with your host, as different properties have different opinions on when high season actually happens. Some places also require a two-night minimum stay, particularly on weekends.

The **Delaware Inn Bed and Breakfast** (55 Delaware Ave., Rehoboth, 302/227-6031 or 800/246-5244, www.delawareinn.com, $80–190) has been in operation since the late 1920s and features single rooms with private or shared baths. Open year-round, the inn provides off-street parking, which is at a premium this close to the beach. Two-or-three-

night minimums are required, and prices are lowest in December.

The **Royal Rose** (41 Baltimore Ave., Rehoboth, 302/226-2535, www.royalroseinn.com, $70–190) is a 1920s beach cottage converted into seven rooms, each with a private bath and breakfast included. It features a sun deck and a hot tub and is 1.5 blocks from the beach and boardwalk. The Rose offers one parking space per room—again, a real bonus.

The Homestead at Rehoboth (35060 Warrington Rd., Rehoboth, 302/226-7625, www.homesteadatrehoboth.com, $80–125, adults only, small pets OK) is about three miles from the beach, but it offers a different and peaceful getaway from the beach hubbub. It also features a couple of acres for walking your pet, if need be, and all the rooms in this country Victorian come with a private bath and include breakfast.

The **Old Farmhouse Bed and Breakfast** (204 Saulsbury St., Dewey Beach, 302/227-2359, www.oldfarmhousebnb.com, $169–199) sits on Rehoboth Bay; it was built in 1832 and moved from the town of Millsboro in 1956. Looking out the window from the upper floor, you'd swear you were on a boat. This is the closest you can come to being on the water in complete comfort. The house has a view of Thompson's Island, a nature preserve and archaeological site that holds evidence of habitation from around 500 B.C. A paddleboat is available for guests a few feet from the back porch. Inevitably, the town of Dewey Beach has grown up around the once-remote site, and neighbors' parties are a rare but real nuisance. The Old Farmhouse is open May–October, and a two-night minimum is required on weekends. Rooms all have private baths.

Hotels and Motels

There are chain hotels such as Comfort Inn (800/228-5150), Hampton Inn (800/426-7866), and Econolodge (800/553-2666) out on Hwy. 1. Call their 800 numbers or check the chain websites for more information.

An occasional bit of paper chaos in the lobby of the **Summer Place Hotel** (30 Olive Ave. at 1st St., Rehoboth, 302/226-0766 or

800/815-3925, www.rehobothsummerplace.com, $45–155) may put some visitors off, but the rooms and condos are reasonably priced and in a convenient, quiet location. This small hotel is open year-round and also offers condos for $60–210, with price breaks for weeklong stays.

The **Oceanus Motel** (6 2nd St., Rehoboth, 302/227-8200 or 800/852-5011, www.oceanus motel.com, $89–179) is just off Rehoboth Avenue, two blocks from the beach. A two-night minimum is required in season. Rooms feature private baths and refrigerators; some have microwaves. The Oceanus is open from mid-March to the first week in November.

In Rehoboth, the attractive **Boardwalk Plaza** (boardwalk at the end of Olive Ave., 302/227-7169 or 800/332-3224, www.board walkplaza.com, $79–539) features a variety of rooms, efficiencies, and apartments. Open all year, the hotel—complete with sundeck, heated indoor-outdoor pool, restaurant, pub, and grand Victorian decor—is one of the fanciest in town.

A good value, especially for families, **The Bay Resort** (126 Bellvue St. at Bayard St., Dewey Beach, 302/227-6400 or 800/922-9240, www.bayresort.com, Apr.–Oct., $59–229) is off the beaten path in Dewey, but still within a few blocks of the beaches and nightlife. The resort requires a two-night minimum stay in season. All rooms are efficiencies and some overlook Rehoboth Bay.

FOOD
Fast Food
Boudreaux's Barbecue (17 Wilmington Ave., 302/226-3010) is nothing more than a walk-up window midway between the boardwalk and 1st Street on Wilmington Avenue, but it's a handy place for southern-style snacks ($9).

Grotto Pizza (36 Rehoboth Ave., 302/227-3278), and just about everywhere else in southern Delaware, has good pizza by the slice or pie ($10).

Breakfast/Lunch
Java Beach Café (167 Rehoboth Ave., Rehoboth Beach, 302/226-3377, 7 A.M.–10 P.M. daily, $7) is a reliable source for coffee, pastries, sandwiches (including fried-egg), and salads.

Arena's (149 Rehoboth Ave., Rehoboth, 302/227-1272, 11 A.M.–1 A.M. daily) has great build-your-own sandwiches and microbrews. It features quiet indoor-outdoor dining during the day and becomes a hopping bar at night, with live music on Saturdays.

Local Favorites
◖ **LaLa Land** (22 Wilmington Ave., Rehoboth, 302/227-3887, www.lalalandrestaurant .com, dinner Thurs.–Sun. April–mid-May and late Sept.–Oct., daily in summer, $29) has captured a couple of "Best of Delaware" Awards from *Delaware Today* magazine, and was noted by *Wine Spectator* magazine for its wine list. The menu features vegetarian, fish, and rack-of-lamb entrées, among others. The signature soup, golden lump crab velouté with dry sherry and saffron, crowned with crab strudel ($10), is a reliable winner.

◖ **Ristorante Zebra** (32 Lake Ave., 302/226-1160, dinner daily in summer, $17) receives raves for its friendly atmosphere and excellent pasta dishes (the homemade pasta with mushrooms and truffle oil stands out). The Italian menu has been a favorite of diners for many years, and the prices are reasonable.

Victoria's Restaurant (Boardwalk Plaza Hotel, Olive Ave. on the boardwalk, Rehoboth, 302/227-0615, www.boardwalkplaza.com, breakfast, lunch, and dinner daily, $10–32) features regional American cuisine in lush Victorian surroundings combined with ocean views. Portions are on the small side, so if you're a big eater, this wouldn't be to your liking. The attached walnut-lined pub is a popular spot and offers a more streamlined (and less expensive) menu.

◖ **Big Fish Grill** (4117 Hwy. 1, Rehoboth Beach, 302/227-9007, www.bigfishgrill.com, dinner Memorial Day–July 1 and Labor Day–Memorial Day, lunch and dinner on weekends July 1–Labor Day, dinner daily July 1–Labor Day, $29) has become the fresh-fish hot spot in Rehoboth, often with a wait for the tables. It features the usual seafood house menu, with the addition of meat and chicken dishes; you can also buy fresh fish in the attached seafood store.

The **Eden Restaurant** (23 Baltimore Ave., Rehoboth, 302/227-3330, dinner Mon.–Sat., $24–30), headed up by chef Jaime Wilson, has become one of Rehoboth's top special-occasion dinner spots. The menu includes pan-seared day boat scallops served with an applewood smoked bacon/Swiss chard/lump crab tart and spiced lobster broth ($30).

Dewey Beach Club (1205 Rte. 1, Dewey Beach, 302/227-0669, dinner daily, $15) is open year-round and features pub food with lunch and dinner specials.

Nightlife

Rehoboth has several free newspapers with event listings, all available at most newsstands.

Sydney's Blues & Jazz Restaurant (25 Christian St., Rehoboth Beach, 302/227-1339, Thurs., Fri.,and Sat. in the off-season, Tues.–Sun. May–Oct.) is the local club for live blues, jazz, and R&B. The kitchen also serves a Cre-ole menu, like Cajun but not as spicy: lots of seafood smothered with tomatoes and onions, and brown-sugar-glazed pork chops with sweet potatoes. Dinner is served nightly and prices average $20.

Dogfish Head Brewing & Eats (320 Rehoboth Ave., Rehoboth Beach, 302/226-2739, www.dogfish.com, lunch and dinner daily, $18) ferments its own ales and serves them up with organic wood-grilled pizzas, seafood, and steaks. Dogfish Head also has a craft brewery in Milton (6 Cannery Village Center, 302/684-1000 or 888/836-4347, open 10 A.M.–4 P.M. Mon.–Fri.) Tours are given on Thursdays 1–3 P.M.

The Starboard (corner of Salisbury St. and Rte. 1, Dewey Beach, 302/227-4600, http://thestarboard.com, 7 A.M.–1 A.M. daily during the warm months and 24/7 on weekends, $6–25) has a Bloody Mary smorgasbord where you can make your own, as well as an extensive Cajun/pub menu. The restaurant host a big blowout party in September to close down for the winter.

Bethany Beach and Fenwick Island

South of Dewey Beach, Delaware Seashore State Park is one of the prettiest beach parks in the land, bordered on one side by the Atlantic and on the other by Rehoboth Bay. The state's quieter resorts are south of Delaware Seashore State Park: Bethany Beach is a tiny version of Rehoboth, a small enclave of mostly residential dwellings with a fairly sedate, two-block city shopping area. Fenwick Island is joined at the hip with Ocean City, Maryland; so much so that the boundaries between the states collide and disappear. As it passes through Fenwick, Rte. 1 is festooned with beach shops and hotels, all threatening to blend into one another.

SIGHTS
Fenwick Island Lighthouse
The beautifully preserved, 89-foot Fenwick Island Light, off Route 54, Fenwick Island, looms over the low commercial buildings that surround it; the tower was built in 1852, when farmland covered the area. In 1869, one of the duties of the assistant lighthouse keeper—paid the grand sum of $660 a year—was to stay up all night to replenish whale oil that might smoke and obscure the light. The lighthouse is on the Transpeninsular line, the east–west boundary between Pennsylvania's "three lower counties" and Maryland, from which Mason and Dixon sighted their eponymous border in 1750. The Fenwick Island light was decommissioned during World War II.

Though visitors can't go up into the tower for insurance reasons, the entranceway to the lighthouse and the small museum within are open most days in the summer (free, donations appreciated). For more information, contact Friends of the Fenwick Island Light-

© JOANNE MILLER

Fenwick Island Lighthouse

house by calling the director, Mr. Cropper, at 302/539-4115.

DiscoverSea Museum

This informative collection (708 Ocean Hwy. above Sea Shell City, Fenwick Island, 302/539-9366 or 888/743-5524) was created through the efforts of one man, professional diver Dale Clifton. The museum is open 11 A.M.–8 P.M. daily June–August, September–May weekends only 11 A.M.–3:30 P.M. Admission is free. Dale has hundreds of underwater hours to his credit—he worked on the raising of the *Atocha*, featured in Georgetown—and has dedicated his life to revealing the romance and history of treasure ships. All materials in the museum were recovered by Dale himself from pre-1860 Delmarva Peninsula shipwrecks. The china, jewelry, pottery, buttons, shoes, weapons, and reams of other found objects represent only about a tenth of his collection. Visitors quickly understand that Dale's concept of "treasure" means not only gold and silver—there's plenty of that—but also items that were dear to the

hearts of those who died beneath the waves: a pocket watch from 1541, a doll's face, a tiny "moon" cannon that would fire on the hour. DiscoverSea features a combination of classic display cases and high technology, and the displays are changed twice each month. Visitors get a personalized tour tailored to their interests, though the younger set are mostly fascinated by "Crabby," the blue crab who marches around one of the aquarium cases waving his arms frantically (he may be waving hello, or he may be filtering oxygen-heavy water through his gills; probably both).

SHOPPING

Bethany Beach town center, at Atlantic and Garfield Streets, features a small mall and several shops selling clothing, books, candy, and jewelry. The **Inland Drive** on Route 26 west from Bethany Beach to Dagsboro, then south on Route 20, then east on Route 54 to Fenwick Island, passes a bulk store and a number of collectible, antique, and art shops, especially on the first leg through Ocean View and Millville. The drive is especially scenic and passes through farmland and ocean marshes. In Selbyville, turn west on Route 54 to visit the **Route 54 Flea Market** and **Magee's Maize Maze** and farm store.

RECREATION

Bethany has a beautiful beach and a short boardwalk with a few shops on it, but no rides or games. Fenwick's beaches are often private or fronted by major hotels.

◖ Delaware Seashore State Park

This 2,825-acre state park covers the narrow strip of land that separates the Atlantic Ocean from Rehoboth Bay between Dewey Beach and Bethany Beach on Route 1. A barrier island, the sandy spit was largely inaccessible until 1939, when the federal government built two iron and stone jetties, stabilizing Indian River Inlet and permitting a road to be built. Information and maps may be requested from Delaware Seashore State Park (Inlet 850, Rehoboth Beach, DE 19971,

DELMARVA'S SIREN CUSS

The Delmarva Peninsula is the site of several hundred shipwrecks. Besides those caused by storms, rough waters, and rocks, there have been manmade causes. A good living could be made in the salvage industry as a "moon cusser," a pirate who cursed the full moon because it put him out of business. On the blackest nights, moon cussers would lead a lantern-laden donkey along the ridges near rocky shoals or light tin drums afire, simulating the lights that burned to guide ships up the coast into the Delaware River. The false lights would bring the ships too close to the shore, running them aground. After the crew and passengers were safely rescued and brought ashore by the local surfmen, the moon cussers would raid the ship, taking whatever valuables they could find.

302/227-2800, www.destateparks.com/dssp). There is a day-use fee to enter the park during the summer (through Labor Day) and on spring and fall weekends.

Swimming: Areas on both the ocean and bay are lifeguarded from Memorial Day to Labor Day. Two of the larger public areas, Tower Road Ocean Beach and Southeast Day Area, feature bathhouses, umbrella and raft rental, a picnic area, and food concessions—the day area even has a designated surfing beach. Swimming outside the guarded areas is discouraged, as is crossing the fragile dune system at any point other than clearly designated dune crossings.

Surf fishing: Vehicles may be driven on designated beaches with a permit (available from the park office). The Indian River Marina sells bait and tackle; a boat ramp and charter boats are also available.

Hiking: Near the park office on Indian River Inlet, a 1.5-mile nature trail leads to Burton's Island.

Camping and cottages: On the south side of the inlet near the Southeast Day Area, the park offers a small campground with hookups and tent sites (call 302/539-7202 for campground information). The park also offers charming beach cottages ($175/day, $875/week off-season, $1,750/week in season). Reservations may be made online at www.destateparks.com/dssp or by calling 877/987-2757.

The **Indian River Inlet Lifesaving Station Museum** (Rte. 1, one mile north of Indian River Inlet, 302/227-0478) features an interesting small exhibit chronicling the history and duties of the men who risked their lives to save shipwrecked sailors during the late 19th century. These surfmen lived sometimes tedious lives in primitive conditions waiting for the cry, "Ship ashore." They then launched their wooden boats into the stormy sea and set out to rescue crew and passengers from vessels torn by the Atlantic's rocky coast. The restored stationhouse—the only one left standing in its original location on the East Coast—is next to the museum. Both are open 10 A.M.–5 P.M. Tuesday–Sunday, with reduced hours in winter. Admission is $4.

Magee's Maize Maze

Who says corn can't be fun? Magee's Farm (Rte. 54, Selbyville, 302/436-5578) morphs into a gigantic cornfield maze that appears every summer in different shapes, like a football-field-size chicken or a fire engine. Participants have said that it's a lot harder than you'd think to find your way around, but it's great fun. The maze is open 10 A.M.–6 P.M. Tuesday–Sunday July–September, weather permitting. There's also a petting zoo, picnic area, and straw bale maze. Admission is $8 for adults, $6 for children.

Thunder Lagoon Water Park

Wet fun for the family, the park (Rte. 1 at Rte. 54, 302/539-4027, www.vikinggolfamusements.com) offers a pair of 25-foot twister slides, a kiddie pool, a 3,000-square-foot activity area, and other features for those who prefer their water less salty. Prices range $9–15.

ACCOMMODATIONS

The **Blue Surf Motel** (oceanfront at Garfield Parkway, 302/539-7531, Apr.–mid-Sept., $60–260) is a pleasant, functionally modern lodging alternative in Bethany Beach. Each of the rooms has a balcony and small kitchen; some face the ocean. The Blue Surf's high season is late June–late August, with lower prices during the off-season. Book as far in advance as possible, since many of the motel's patrons return here year after year.

The **Addy Sea** (99 Ocean View Pkwy. and N. Atlantic Ave., Bethany Beach, 302/539-3707 or 800/418-6764, www.addysea .com, $100–400, depending on day and season, discounts for longer stays and off-season) offers secluded charm. Fronting the quiet beach, this three-story Victorian was built in 1901 as a home for the wealthy family of a pastor of the Church of Christ. One of their contemporary descendants, Martha Jean Addy, manages the historical museum downtown. The family sold the house—since 1974, it has been run year-round as an inn. True to its past, several rooms on each floor share one shower/bath, though each room has a small toilet (sometimes in the closet!) and sink. Decor is a mix of authentic and faux period pieces. The measured pace of time in the town and inn seems to make the hours slow down. A continental breakfast is served in the parlor in the morning, sometimes to the accompaniment of stories of ghost sightings during the early days of the inn.

Food

Bethany Beach has a number of upscale restaurants in town. One of the local favorites is **The Parkway** (in the Antal Building, 114 Garfield Pkwy., 302/537-7500, www.parkwaydana.com, dinner daily June–Sept., reduced hours the rest of the year, $27), which serves an American menu in a casual setting.

If a bowl of inexpensive, good, homemade chicken soup is what you're after, drive out Route 26 to Ocean View and look for the **Ocean View Family Restaurant** (42 Atlantic Ave., 302/539-4864, breakfast, lunch, and dinner daily, $5–20). This family-run, family-style diner isn't fancy, but the food is good and the prices are great.

Greater Sussex County

The beaches of Sussex County are the destinations for most travelers. But for a break from surf and sand, go west. A couple of Delaware's most popular parks, plus a scattering of small-town attractions, await the adventurous.

SIGHTS
Governor Ross Mansion and Plantation

This lovely Italian villa–style mansion (N. Pine Street, Seaford, 302/628-9500) was built in 1854, as the Delaware governor was finishing his term in office. The furnished mansion, grounds, and outbuildings, including the slave quarters, are open to the public 1–4 P.M. on the fourth Sunday of each month, and at other times by appointment. Admission is $2. Governor Ross, a slaveholder, was a Southern sympathizer; branded a traitor, he was forced to spend the Civil War years traveling in Europe after President Lincoln issued a warrant for his arrest. Governor Ross brought the railroad to southern Delaware, installing a station on his 1,400-acre plantation, but the family went bankrupt within a few generations.

Millsboro

A former mill town, Millsboro is now the center of Delaware's broiler chicken industry, a fact celebrated in June by the annual Delmarva chicken festival, featuring the world's largest frying pan, among other oddities. The area's tree-shaded farmlands are also home to the Nanticoke Indian tribe, whose villages used to cover the area from one coast of the Delmarva Peninsula to the other.

THE NANTICOKE POWWOW

In pre-contact days, the Algonquian word *pauwau* referred to the healing and curing ceremonies conducted by Indian spiritual leaders to drive sickness and negative energy away. Nanticoke see powwows not only as tools to preserve their heritage, but also as devices to cure misconceptions about the beliefs and values of the first people. The Nanticoke powwow began in 1921, in an attempt by tribal elders to hold on to the vestiges of native culture that were slipping away. World War II halted the festivities for a few years, but the powwow was revived and has grown bigger than ever.

Every year in mid-September, the Nanticoke tribe of southern Delaware holds its powwow weekend west of Rehoboth Beach near the Nanticoke Indian Museum outside Millsboro. The powwow, set in a cool and peaceful grove, is open to everyone, and word of the friendly reception to other Native Americans and non-Indians has spread, increasing the size of the get-together every year.

Dancing, which is the major activity, is primarily for Nanticoke tribal members and visitors from other tribes across the nation. On Saturday, the festivities start at noon with the "Grand Entry": all dancers follow behind U.S. and tribal flags. The entry is followed by an invocation to the Great Spirit, lighting of the peace pipe, and herbal purification. For the next few hours, dancers perform traditional and specialty dances, followed by an hour of storytelling until 4:30; the dancing then continues until 7 P.M. On Sunday, a Christian church service with singing takes place 11 A.M.–noon, and the dancing continues 2–5 P.M. Both days, booths around the dance area featuring handmade goods, fry bread, Indian tacos, and more are open 10 A.M.–8 P.M. Though some seating is provided for the elderly and infirm, visitors are expected to bring their own folding chairs.

The **Nanticoke Indian Museum** (Rtes. 24 and 5, 12 miles west of the Rte. 1 intersection, 302/945-7022, 10:00 A.M.–4:00 P.M. Fri.–Sat. in April and Tues.–Sat. May–Oct., donations appreciated) tells the history of the Nanticoke through displays and written information. The museum was converted from the former Indian school by members of the tribe in the early 1980s, and it features a research library with information on the Nanticoke and other Native American peoples. In September of each year, the tribe holds an exceptional powwow that's open to all.

Georgetown

The **Delaware Technical & Community College** (Rte. 18 just west of U.S. 113) has two exhibits in the library building that may interest visitors. The first is **Treasures of the Sea** (302/856-5700), a museum-like exhibit created by a group of Delmarvans who invested in the raising of the Spanish treasure ship *Nuestra Señora de Atocha*. The exhibit is open 10 A.M.–4 P.M. Monday–Tuesday, noon–4 Friday P.M., and 9 A.M.–1 P.M. Saturday. Admission is $2. The ship, a seagoing fortress with 20 cannons, went down in a hurricane in 1622. The exhibit tells the story of Spanish shipping in the Indies and the process of finding shipwrecks. The *Atocha* yielded gold, silver, and more than 300 uncut emeralds; some of the gold and jewelry is on display, in addition to a video and artifacts from the raised vessel.

The grounds of the college also feature the **Trees of the States Arboretum,** a self-guided walking tour of 51 trees representing 50 states, plus the District of Columbia. Florida's sabal palm is there, along with California's sequoia and Maryland's wye oak. The grounds are open during college hours. Call 302/856-5400 for information.

SHOPPING

Stop by **Bargain Bill's, the Shore's Largest Flea Market** (U.S. 13 and Rte. 9E, Laurel, 302/875-9958). This covered and open market sprawls over several acres and operates 8 A.M.–4 P.M. Friday and 8 A.M.–5 P.M. weekends year-round. Friday is a fairly slow day, but the weekends are bursting with people, particularly in the summer. You can find anything here, and usually for the price you want to pay. If you're still in a shopping mood after Bill's, consider a side trip: Drive to **O'Neal's Horse Jewelry** (109 N. Central Ave., Laurel, 302/875-4444) for that diamond-encrusted horseshoe you've always dreamed of. No, it's not for your horse—it's for you.

RESULTS! RETURN DAY IN SUSSEX COUNTY

Since 1792, citizens have been returning to the county seat of Georgetown two days after each major election to hear election results and bury the hatchet, accepting both wins and losses. By 1888, "Return Day" drew several thousand people in a carnival-like atmosphere that included attendees "dressed in costumes which were used in primitive times, and others purposely arraying themselves in an outlandish manner to give more zest to the spirit of the occasion," according to Thomas Scharf in *The History of Delaware*. People decorated their horses, oxen, and wagons, as well as themselves.

The advent of radio in the early part of this century quieted down the festivities, but Return Day was revived by that rarest of animals, a donkephant – members of local Democratic and Republican parties worked together to revive the custom in the early 1950s. Today, Return Day is a legal half-holiday for Sussex County, and voters from all over make a special trip to Georgetown for the roasted ox sandwiches, arts and crafts vendors, and parade that seats winners and losers together in decorated carriages and convertibles. The leaders of the local political parties actually do bury a hatchet – until the next major election.

RECREATION
Trap Pond State Park

A popular destination for Delawareans, Trap Pond (Rte. 449 east of Laurel, 302/875-5153, www.destateparks.com/tpsp) is a freshwater swamp featuring the northernmost natural stand of bald cypress trees in the United States. The park is laced with hiking trails, and fishing and boating in the swamp are major activities. Rowboats, pedal boats, and canoes may be rented from a concession near the park office; a park interpreter narrates pontoon boat tours on weekends and holidays during the summer months. There is a guarded swimming area and bathhouse nearby. Picnic sites, volleyball courts, and horseshoe pits are available for those who prefer drier fun.

Camping: The park offers 152 campsites for both tents and RVs; half are equipped with water and electric hookups. Call 302/875-2392 for campground information and 877/987-2757 for reservations, or reserve online.

◖ River Towns and Highlights Tour

This tour begins in Laurel and ends a few miles north in Seaford. The distance traveled is approximately 17 miles, with a 13-mile return to Laurel via Route 13A. The route is very flat and could easily be biked as well as driven (though U.S. 13 can get very busy with car traffic). Keep in mind that several of the sights along the route have very limited "open" hours.

One mile east of Laurel off Route 24, **Old Christ Church** (Chapman's Pond Rd.), built in 1771, is one of the few churches to survive unaltered from America's pre-Revolutionary past. Stepping inside has been likened to "entering 18th-century England." It's open 1–4 P.M. on Sundays and July 4.

Before exploring the elegant neighborhoods of Laurel—it was the wealthiest town in the state around 1900—you might want to stop by **Bargain Bill's, The Shore's Largest Flea Market** (U.S. 13 and Rte. 9E, Laurel) or **O'Neal's Horse Jewelry** (109 N. Central Ave. Laurel), both listed in the *Shopping* section.

Explore the streets in the older part of Laurel

RIVER TOWNS

Location, location, location. Some may be puzzled that Seaford, Bethel, and Laurel – so far inland – prospered from the water transport of agricultural and forestry products, then made new fortunes in the shipbuilding industry. But location is everything: Seaford is on the Nanticoke River, and Bethel and Laurel are both on Broad Creek. When the Nanticoke Tribe inhabited this region, Laurel was known as "the wading place," the last crossing before Broad Creek widened and met the Nanticoke River on its way west to the Chesapeake Bay. These small towns, in the center of Delmarva Peninsula's great agricultural area, profited from the sending of goods west to the bay, Baltimore, and the Atlantic seaboard beyond. Bethel, famous for shipbuilding, became an enclave of Victorians built for sea captains by ships' carpenters.

Up until World War I, Bethel, Laurel, and Seaford experienced intermittent economic booms that resulted in a number of grand homes. Laurel has more than 800 buildings listed on the National Register, and the entire town of Bethel is listed. Though now the towns afford a quiet grace, they continue to retain the charm of small-town America. In fact, Seaford ranked 28th in the second edition of *The Best 100 Small Towns in America*.

The ferry, which can carry two or three cars, is free. When you get to the other side of the narrow but deep river, take time to enjoy a picnic in tiny Woodland Park next to the ferry.

Drive from Woodland a short distance, then turn right onto Route 78 toward Seaford. Proceed 3.6 miles to Gethsemane United Methodist Church (referred to locally as "the burnt church"), then turn right onto Route 20 east. You will drive through the country on Route 20, then enter the town of Seaford. You'll pass the Nylon Capitol Shopping Center on your left. Seaford is the site of the world's first nylon plant—in fact, the DuPont Highway, aka U.S. 13, was built by the du Ponts in order to transport supplies and materials to Wilmington. There will be a sign on the right side of the road that says "Library." You'll need to make a bit of a loop to get to the other side of the road. Go across the bridge and make the first right as soon as you reach the foot of the bridge onto Pine Street. Turn right when you reach the first road to your right (6th St.). Take this road until you reach Cedar Street (6th St. dead-ends on Cedar). Make a right onto Cedar. This will take you under the bridge. Follow Cedar around. At the first intersection, make a right onto Oak Street, then a left back onto Pine Street. Continue half a mile to the Governor Ross Mansion and Plantation. You will see an orange Victorian cottage on the right. Turn toward the cottage and park; take an hour or so to visit the mansion and grounds before returning on Route 13A.

Golf and Biking

Sea Dogs of Bethany Beach (888/371-7888) offers golf getaways all over the Delmarva Peninsula, complete with accommodations and green fees.

Biking Inn-to-Inn takes participants on a four-day, three-night biking and bed-and-breakfast tour from Laurel to Lewes and back. Call Ambassador Travel (800/845-9939) for more information.

ACCOMMODATIONS

Holiday Inn Express has a branch in Seaford (210 Rte. 13/N. Dual Hwy., 302/629-2000).

around Route 24. This street intersects Route 492 in the western part of town. Follow Route 492 through the country to Route 493, where you'll cross Broad Creek into **Bethel**. Once a busy shipbuilding center, this quiet community of seafarers' homes is listed on the National Register of Historic Places. Continue on Route 493 to Route 78. Turn left onto Route 78. You'll see signs for the Woodland Ferry. Travel to the end of Route 78, and you'll be at the ferry crossing.

The **Woodland Ferry** is a bit of old Delaware that still remains. The drive to the ferry (which crosses the Nanticoke River) is a scenic one.

Ask for a room on the back side of the hotel for a view of Williams Pond.

Spring Garden Bed and Breakfast (10905 Delaware Ave. Extended, Laurel, 302/875-7015 or 800/797-4909, $85–110) takes care of quite a few guests who visit nearby Trap Pond. The innkeepers are heavily involved in local ecotourism and a good resource for information on the topic. This 18th-century country manor was once a working farm and sea captain's home. Four spacious rooms either share a bath or have private baths; a suite is lso available. All are complemented by a full breakfast in the morning. Next door, the property's old barn houses antiques and artist's workshops. Though the B&B is easy to get to, lack of street signage makes it difficult to find; call for exact directions when making your reservation.

Becky's Country Inn (401 Main St., 302/ 732-3953, $65–100) is in the hamlet of Dagsboro, off the beaten path—perfect if you're biking the back roads or making the inland drive. This cute little 1850 farmhouse has three rooms with private baths, all of which open onto a deck. Be prepared, however: The inn faces the main road through Dagsboro, and the agricultural trucks may be noisy in the morning.

FOOD

Smith's Family Restaurant (115 E. Market St., Georgetown, 302/855-0305, breakfast, lunch, and dinner Mon.–Sat., $5–20) is an excellent stop for lunch. It's a casual, inexpensive, home-cooking-style place. While you're there, drive around the town's central circle and check out the historic homes on the surrounding streets. Many were built in the early 1800s, after the county seat was moved to Georgetown from Lewes.

The (C) **Bon Appetit Restaurant** (312 High St., Seaford, 302/629-3700, www.bon appetitseaford.com, lunch Tues.–Fri., dinner Tues.–Sat., lunch $10, dinner $21)is one of those unexpected places lucky travelers run across. The place is well known in the area for its gourmet nouveau French menu, featuring items such as the antipasti sandwich for lunch (grilled eggplant, provolone cheese, basil, and tomato on garlic French bread, $8.25) and for dinner, salmon chimichuri ($21.95). Highly recommended.

Britts Dutch Inn (1012 S. Central Ave., Laurel, 302/875-7158, breakfast and lunch Mon.–Sat., $8) on the other hand, is the kind of down-home place where people stop by for a cup of coffee and a tuna sandwich.

The **Old Mill Crab House and Restaurant** (Rte. 54 and Waller Rd., Delmar, 302/846-2808, www.oldmillcrabhouse.com, dinner daily Mar.–Nov., $19) is a big favorite of locals. It specializes in Eastern Shore delights like ribs with crab cakes and fried shrimp.

BACKGROUND

The Land

GEOGRAPHY
Maryland

Maryland covers 10,460 square miles across three vastly different types of terrain. From east to west, bordering the Atlantic Ocean, the Tidewater consists of flat, sandy marshland surrounding the Chesapeake Bay. The land then rises into the rocky, fertile Piedmont Plateau, culminating in the ancient rounded mountaintops and piney forests of the Appalachians. At its narrowest point, between Garrett and Washington Counties in the west, it's less than two miles wide. The highest point in the state—also in the west—is 3,360-foot Backbone Mountain.

The most notable geographic feature of Maryland is the Atlantic Coastal Plain, formed by glacial advance and retreat, invasion and flooding by the Atlantic Ocean and Susquehanna River. From Baltimore south to Washington, D.C., the soil is made up of silts and clay; Southern Maryland is a combination of sand, silt, and clay; all of the southeastern shore and Atlantic shore is composed of homogenous silt, clay, shell beds, sand, and gravel. The Atlantic shore was once connected to Baltimore by land—a grass-covered, sandy valley consisting of layers of sediment, which reached from the region of Queenstown across to Annapolis. As the waters rose at the end of the last ice age,

© JOANNE MILLER

the Susquehanna filled the valley and met the ocean, creating the Chesapeake Bay.

The Piedmont Plateau is a region of lowlands and gentle hills. The area is extremely fertile; the terrain, covering the hills like velvet in a jewel box, boasts some of the best farmland in the country. The northern section of the plateau has remained productive due, in large part, to the soil conservation methods practiced by Mennonite and Amish settlers who have dwelled there in large numbers since moving west from Philadelphia during the early days of the colonies.

South Mountain, on the southern state border near Gettysburg, marks the end of the Piedmont Plateau and the beginning of the Appalachians. Of all the mountain ranges of Appalachia, South Mountain is the oldest. Structurally, it's a continuation of the Blue Ridge Mountains in Virginia.

The Appalachian Mountains, reaching up into the far northeast, tumble down through Pennsylvania into western Maryland. The Appalachians are a product of glacial carving, eons of ice scraping away neatly horizontal layers of rock, though the smooth, rounded, wooded hills near Deep Creek Lake are due more to steady erosion. In the northwest section of Maryland, south of Pittsburgh, the coal-mining valleys that contain the Youghiogheny (yock-a-GAY-nee) and Allegheny Rivers are deep, layered fissures marking the edge of the Appalachian Plateau.

Delaware

Delaware's tiny patch of rolling hills in the Brandywine Valley, part of the Piedmont region in the extreme north, provides the only variation in the state's terrain. The highest point in Delaware is there: 442 feet. From that dizzying elevation, a low, gently undulating plain slopes down to the Atlantic Ocean. The lowland is part of the Atlantic coastal plain; a northeast-southwest fall line separates the two regions. Most of Delaware is characterized by two types of soils built on clay accumulation (ultisols): humults, with a high organic carbon content, found in northern and central areas;

and aqualts, with a higher clay content, found in coastal and southern areas.

For all of Delaware's early peoples, wealth came on the water, and the state has more than its share. The Delaware Bay provided food and transportation for generations of Native Americans and the settlers who came after them. The Atlantic Ocean enabled speedy access to Europe.

Among the state's most prominent geographic features are salt and freshwater marshes, both inland and along Delaware Bay. Most of Delaware's rivers, such as the Christina and its tributary Brandywine Creek, as well as the Murderkill, Mispillion, Broadkill, Leipsic, and Smyrna, are relatively short waterways that flow eastward into Delaware Bay. Two larger rivers in the southern part of the state, the Nanticoke and Pocomoke, flow southwest through eastern Maryland into the Chesapeake Bay. Pocomoke Swamp, in southern Delaware, is the northernmost cypress swamp in North America. All ponds and lakes in Delaware are captured water—there are no natural springs. Groundwater is held in permeable marine deposits atop crystalline bedrock.

The Chesapeake & Delaware Canal, an artificial waterway, links the Delaware Bay to the Chesapeake Bay (its western terminus is Chesapeake City, Maryland) as well as the Delaware River and the port of Wilmington (the eastern terminus is just south of Delaware City). It's one of the busiest canals in America, accommodating most oceangoing vessels and smaller craft.

CLIMATE

The climates of Maryland and Delaware vary as much as the geography. In the eastern part of Maryland, the buffering effects of the Chesapeake Bay and Atlantic Ocean create a moderate, insular climate. Mild winters (with an average of 8 to 10 inches of short-lived snow) and summers of high humidity with generally warm days and nights are the norm. Temperatures are rarely excessive, though humidity certainly can be.

The climate of the western half of the state

matches that of the interior of the continent, with cold air masses in winter from central Canada and the western United States bringing low temperatures and snow. In summer, winds from the southwest and the Gulf of Mexico bring hot, humid air and rain through the lower elevations of the western counties, making the area as warm—and sometimes as humid—as the east. Rainfall averages two to four inches a month, with the greatest precipitation in July and August.

In Delaware, expect long, warm, humid summers and relatively mild winters. Wilmington temperatures dip down to freezing in January and average 75°F in July. There is some snow in the northern part of the state, less in the south; the average is 15 inches a year. Meteorologists characterize the climate as humid-continental. The Atlantic Ocean and Chesapeake Bay combine to temper storms coming in from the Gulf of Mexico and continental weather systems from the west. Rainfall averages 44 inches a year.

Flora

Most of Maryland and Delaware has been cultivated since European settlement. Tobacco was the first crop, primarily in Maryland, but because it demanded so much from the land, its cultivation decreased when market prices dropped after the American Revolution. Farmers began planting their fields with more renewable crops, such as wheat, soy, and market vegetables.

Fortunately, cultivated fields encouraged wildflower growth. Many varieties sparkle like jewels set in golden field grasses, and they're often gathered for household bouquets. Native flora may be in short supply, but the many estate gardens and tree plantings—some maintained since colonial times—are truly spectacular. Many urban areas celebrate spring under the blooms of cherry and other decorative trees, including the 40-foot-tall Princess Paulownia, awash in royal purple flowers.

TREES
In Maryland, about a third of the land remains forested, though old-growth stands are rare. Due to the state's varied terrain, trees characteristic of eastern hardwood forests—seven species of oak, four species of hickory, five types of red and yellow maple, and beech—are common, while the extreme west of the state extends into the northern and southern evergreen zones, with nine types of conifers, including white pine and spruce. Trees that

grow easily and in large numbers without cultivation are the tulip poplar, yellow locust, yellow birch, pignut hickory, white oak (the state tree), and white ash. Crape myrtle and varieties of magnolia are found in the southern parts of the Atlantic Coastal Plain, where wild trees often remain shrub-size due to the sandy soil. Disease has depleted native species of elm and chestnut, though dogwood, hackberry, and sycamore continue to thrive.

Forest covers roughly 622 square miles in Delaware. Oak, beech, walnut, maple, and dogwood are the prevalent species in northern Delaware. In the south, loblolly and Virginia pines are mixed with sweet and black gums, oaks, maples, yellow poplars, and hollies. Wild persimmons are an important food source for wildlife. Both Maryland and Delaware claim the country's northernmost stand of bald cypress—but Delaware wins by a few miles.

SHRUBS AND FLOWERS
In the spring, through the summer, and into early fall, Maryland is festooned with wildflowers. Azalea, rhododendron, redbud, mountain laurel, and honeysuckle are common in shady areas. Sunny fields boast red wild bergamot, wild valerian, monument plant, wild rose, daisy, tiger lily, goldenrod, and black-eyed Susan, the state flower.

Under the forest canopy, spring brings delicate wood violets to bloom alongside Indian

© JOANNE MILLER

harvesting beans for the winter

pipe, spring beauty, Jack-in-the-pulpit, wild grapevine, Turks cap lily, trillium, Dutchman's breeches, and yellow lady's slipper. Several types of ferns thrive along streams and rivers, among them bracken, New York fern, lady fern, and Christmas fern.

Along the shorelines, wildflowers hide among native grasses like redhead grass, wild celery, eelgrass, and Widgeon grass. One unusual wild find along the beaches is yucca, a flowering succulent normally associated with desert regions.

Delaware's freshwater marshes are living wildflower garlands throughout spring, summer, and fall. Red bergamot, wild valerian, wild geranium, chicory, wild rose, daisy, goldenrod, wild iris, and dozens of other roadside species brighten up native grasses and tint the edges of fields. Shade is the ideal foil for jack-in-the-pulpit, trillium, trout lily, and wood anemone. Moist areas shelter flowerless plants such as royal, cinnamon, New York, sensitive, and marsh ferns.

In the northern part of the state, azalea, rhododendron, redbud, mountain laurel, and magnolia are present as cultivars and naturalized plantings. The public du Pont properties are especially notable for their beautiful gardens. Many sections of Wilmington are dreamy pink with flowering cherry in the spring.

In both states, freshwater native grasses such as cattail, pond lily, bulrushes, and smartweed, plus well-adapted sea grasses like cordgrass, wave along the state's shorelines, sometimes supplanted by the ivory plumes of phragmites, a nuisance plant introduced from Eurasia.

Fauna

Mammals

Central Maryland is largely urban and suburban, which leaves little room for larger mammals common to the northern and southeastern regions of the United States. Raccoons, which have adapted to suburban intrusion, are an exception. However, the forests and fields of the Delmarva Peninsula and southern and western Maryland continue to support a variety of wildlife. White-tailed deer, once severely overhunted and devastated by heavy deforestation, are slowly returning. Black bears and wildcats, though not considered endangered, are rarely seen in their western mountain habitats. Other animals common to North American forests, such as foxes, beavers, mink, raccoon, opossums, woodchucks, striped skunks, gray and black squirrels, and wild rabbit have adapted and now thrive in all areas with a bit of meadow. Muskrats, beavers, marsh rabbits, and otters inhabit the marshes. The endangered Delmarva fox squirrel, a victim of habitat encroachment, is on the way back.

With few exceptions, Delaware is marsh or open farmland with a few wild forested areas, so large mammals are rare to nonexistent. Deer and small game—river otters, raccoons, opossums, red and gray foxes, striped skunks, gray and black squirrels, marsh rabbits, and muskrats—are present in the more rural areas of the state. A number of species of bats, including the little brown myotis, silver-haired bat, eastern pipistrel, big brown bat, red bat, and hoary bat, inhabit the state year-round. Harbor seals form nursery colonies on the shore.

Birds

Though habitat encroachment may challenge larger mammals, it's a windfall for species *Aves*. Maryland is bird-watching heaven. Birders in Charles County, in the central part of the state, have spotted more than 321 varieties of birds—nearly every county provides a bird-watching checklist. A walk on any trail in the state will provide a glimpse of several winged beauties,

including the rare indigo bunting and the Baltimore oriole (both spotted on Wye Island, Eastern Shore).

Delaware is on the Atlantic migratory bird flyway, and the marshy Delaware Bay shore is a refuge for both migrating and local birds. Canada geese, wood ducks, and tundra swans gather in massive flocks on the edges of ponds and lakes (and in public and private parks, much to the annoyance of groundskeepers and owners) during migratory seasons. Some have found Delaware so inviting that they've established year-round residency, as at Hagley Mills.

Perching birds: Ravens, orioles, and bluebirds are found everywhere in Maryland. The brown-headed nuthatch is found in extreme southern areas, while mockingbirds, hawks, and crows are numerous throughout the coastal plain. Purple martins, the largest of American swallows, are valued for their voracious appetite for insects; refuges and farmers around the Chesapeake Bay encourage the birds to nest by building martin "hotels." The cardinal, Carolina wren, and tufted titmouse are often spotted in the Piedmont Plateau. Thrushes, chestnut-sided warblers, and many species of northern birds are commonly seen in the mountainous areas. Nocturnal birds, including the screech, great horned, and barred owls, roam the skies in lightly wooded areas and suburbs year-round. Ground-nesting birds such as the bobwhite quail, Hungarian partridge, woodcock, wild turkey, and ring-necked pheasant are common in the woodlands.

Shore and water birds: These are perhaps the most symbolic of Maryland's and Delaware's bird populations. More than 40 varieties of ducks have been observed. Year-round varieties include the canvasback, red-breasted merganser, black head mallard, black duck, and wood duck. Canada geese gather by the thousands on the edges of ponds and lakes during migratory season, as do tundra swans.

A shorebird, the killdeer, with its long legs and black double necklace, wades alongside the endangered piping plover (easily identifiable by the *peep peep* of its call), willits, avocets, seagulls, terns, and dozens of varieties of sandpipers on the shorelines. Ospreys, peregrine falcons, eagles, and other raptors take to the skies along the Chesapeake and Delaware shores and nest on telephone poles and park structures. The great blue heron, a three-foot-tall wading bird, can be found nesting in trees in Chesapeake marshes.

In Delaware, on the inland marshes and Pea Patch Island, great blue herons, egrets, cranes, and other wading birds ply the shallow waters. Along the shore, loons, grebes, gannets, pelicans, and cormorants take to the air.

Reptiles

Eight varieties of nonpoisonous snakes inhabit Maryland: corn, yellow, rat, brown, king, striped water, water pilot, and scarlet. The two poisonous types are the timber rattlesnake in the mountain counties and the copperhead in the wetter areas. Delaware has more than a dozen varieties of nonpoisonous snakes, including rough green, northern black racer, black rat, eastern king, eastern garter, and eastern milk.

Several varieties of turtles, including the diamondback terrapin, eastern box turtle, snapping turtle, mud turtle, musk turtle (stinkpot), and eastern painted turtle, sun themselves along freshwater ponds. The flesh of the now-common diamondback terrapin was so popular around the turn of the 20th century that the animal was nearly hunted into extinction.

Amphibians

Frogs, newts, and salamanders inhabit the banks of streams, rivers, and catch basins of Maryland and Delaware. Common amphibians are the spotted salamander, purplish-black with yellow or orange spots; the marbled salamander, black with white or gray patches; the eastern tiger salamander, similar in marking to the marbled, but with bright yellow, irregular spots; and the red-spotted newt, which spends part of its life strolling forest floors after rainstorms (they're also called "efts" during this stage, when they turn bright scarlet or orange).

Freshwater Fish

Fish species in Chesapeake Bay overshadow those of all other localities in the state. Perch, blue fish, striped bass (the state fish, also known as stripers or rockfish), and some 200 other varieties of finned fish are found there. Lower sections of the Chesapeake's tributaries are breeding grounds for herring and shad in the early spring. (Predicting when the shad will run has become a pseudo-religion among a certain set of anglers.) Formerly, because of pollution, only the spring breeders and catfish could be found on the Potomac River below the Falls; now the area is making a comeback.

Maryland's rivers and man-made lakes above and below the Great Falls of the Potomac contain such freshwater fish as largemouth and smallmouth bass, white perch, and varieties of sunfish and catfish. Northern pike have been introduced with some success into Tridelphia and Pretty Boy Lakes. Trout, occasionally seeded in selected up-country waters, make their way into smaller streams. In Delaware, black crappie, white crappie, rock bass, white bass, walleye pike, pickerel, trout, muskellunge, sunfish, bluegill, pumpkinseed, and perch are all found in freshwater streams, lakes, and impoundments.

Saltwater Fish and Invertebrates

From Lewes in southern Delaware, the Atlantic is full of tuna, bluefish, dolphins, and occasionally marlins. Dolphins can be spotted from the shore, and whale-watching boats leave from all the major resort towns. Numerous ocean-based species, including mako, blue, great hammerhead, tiger sharks, and smaller coastal species such as the finetooth shark and porbeagle, are common.

Offshore from Ocean City, Maryland, dolphins occasionally come into the bay, sometimes with disastrous results. The National Fisheries Service warns against feeding or attempting to swim with the wild animals, as dozens of bites have been reported, and the animals are often injured by boat propellers.

Shellfish such as clams and blue crabs—the symbol of the Chesapeake—are abundant, but

BEAUTIFUL SWIMMERS

Callinectes sapidus, the scientific name for Chesapeake Bay's blue crab, means "beautiful swimmer/tasty" – one of the most apt descriptions in the lexicon. The crustacean is equipped with paddle-like back legs that help propel it through the water on its endless quest for food. The blue's propensity to eat just about anything in its path has been a true saving grace: The Chesapeake Bay was one of the world's most productive ecosystems up until the 1960s. Disappearance of underwater grasses from great areas of the bottom of the shallow bay, combined with toxic wastes, added to the decline of the bay's fish and shellfish populations. The blue crab, however, is genetically primed to survive, rising and falling in the moving currents until it finds feeding grounds.

The blue crab is hatched in deep water near the mouth of the bay and produces a million eggs for every crab that reaches maturity. Like most marine creatures, the crab thrives in a narrow range of salinity, whereas the bay has a very wide range, from freshwater to Atlantic salt tides. The saltwater, being heavier, sinks to the bottom and flows in, while the fresh water flows out over it. The crab larvae are programmed by nature to rise and drop in the water and thus ride currents that take them to shallow, grassy feeding grounds.

A crab's life is one of continual expansion and release, from its first summer days as a plankton-sized zoea to its maturity 12 to 18 months later, and beyond. As the crab increases in size, it needs to molt, or shed its old hard shell. The crab pumps water into its body to enlarge its new soft shell and within a few hours, the shell hardens (one of the primary reasons soft-shell, or molted, crabs are raised by aquaculture).

Upon reaching maturity, the male crab attracts a female by strutting about, waving his claws and walking on tiptoes (the origin of stiletto heels, no doubt). The lucky female backs underneath the male, who cradles her between his walking legs until she molts, at which time they mate. After the female's shell hardens again, the male releases her; he will remain in the bay until fall, while she journeys out to spawning areas near the mouth of the Chesapeake to lay her eggs in early winter.

The death of underwater grasses presents a problem: This is where the growing crabs hide to reach maturity. The lack of oxygen in the water, a product of algae growth, sometimes creates a phenomenon known as a "crab war," when crabs are driven up onto the land, fleeing the "dead" water. In spite of these hazards, the crab harvest increases and decreases without identifiable reasons. Because of this phenomenon, crabs are not considered in jeopardy. However, scientists, watermen, and the millions of others who dwell on the bay are keeping a sharp lookout for signs of trouble with their beautiful swimmers.

are always threatened by the effects of population growth around the Bay. Oysters have experienced a severe downturn in recent years.

The horseshoe crab, closely related to the spider, is the symbol of Delaware. Shellfish, hermit crabs, and other small varieties of crustaceans are found on the shore.

Insects

Though the ladybug is the Delaware state insect, the common mosquito wins the prize for sheer numbers and annoyance factor. Maryland and Delaware's wonderful state parks and resource areas are most seductive in summer, when the little buzzers are at their peak. Bring plenty of insect repellent, and go boldly into that marsh or lake.

ENVIRONMENTAL CONCERNS

Prior to the arrival of Europeans, most of Maryland was covered with old-growth forest, and the Chesapeake teemed with oysters, crabs, and fish. Around 1676, an anonymous settler wrote: "The abundance of oysters is incredible. There are whole banks of them, so that the ships must avoid them. A sloop, which was to land us at Kingscreek, struck an oyster bed, where we had to wait about two hours for the tide." A chart of the James River, published by the Dutch, shows seventeen "reefs." None exist today. Oysters, which filter and clean the water of the bay while feeding, used to be so plentiful that they accomplished in a few days what takes the current oyster population a year.

In Maryland and Delaware, agricultural techniques, domestic livestock, and the runoff produced by both have changed the face of the land for the worse. Marshes were drained for planting, which reduced the land's ability to filter storm water into the watersheds. By the late 1800s, hunting and habitat overuse severely depleted or wiped out the once thriving population of game animals, and pollution assaulted the marshes from the lowest levels of the ecosystem to the top predators. At one point, two thousand skipjacks and other boats dredged Chesapeake Bay and creek beds for oysters; a dozen railroad cars filled with shellfish left Baltimore daily to points as far west as San Francisco.

The conservation movement and changes in the local economy—chiefly a reduced market for commercial game meat—began to reverse the damage at about the same time. Wildlife and waterfowl have increased greatly in the past century. The waters of Chesapeake Bay, however, continue to inspire efforts to reduce pollution and sedimentation.

The bay presents a graphic illustration of the chain of life. In the early 1980s, fishermen were the first to spot bright green mats spreading over the Potomac. The green was algae, tiny primitive plants, and they symptomized trouble. Algae populations had exploded, thanks to an abundance of food: nutrient runoff (nitrogen and phosphorus) from farm fertilizers, waterside factories, sewage treatment plants, and automobiles. Minnows, small fish, and microscopic water animals were unable to consume all the algae, and the remainder sunk to the bottom of the bay. Bottom bacteria gorged on the bonanza, meanwhile robbing the water of oxygen, a condition known as anoxia. Other creatures that normally lived in these depleted zones were either forced to leave or suffocated. Fish and shellfish weren't the only victims.

Algae shaded and choked submerged sea grasses (often called SAV, for submerged aquatic vegetation), the "breeding farms" of the bay. In 1997, pollution was also blamed for an outbreak of pfiesteria, a flesh eating microbe, which in turn was blamed for huge fish kills all over the bay, as well as skin problems reported by human swimmers. Though the pfiesteria threat has diminished, scientists remain watchful.

Numerous groups have banded together to monitor and improve the health of the bay and Delaware marshlands, including the Chesapeake Bay Trust, the state of Maryland (which issues special "Treasure the Chesapeake" license plates and offers a tax-form donation choice), and scientists from Maryland, Virginia, Washington, D.C., Delaware, and the Environmental Protection Agency. The turning point came in 1983, when sewage-treatment plants were put in place in cities around the bay and on major tributaries. The largest of these installations is the Blue Plains plant (aka the Craphouse Taj Mahal) on the Potomac River. Industrial wastes has proven a more difficult problem, as it does not flush out with the tides but settles to the bottom. The worst spot is in the James River, where the Allied Chemical Company dumped quantities of an ant-and-roach poison, Kepone. It's expected to stay in the water for many decades. Richard Lacouture, a scientist with the Estuarine Research Center in Calvert County, says, "The bay isn't all that fragile. It has an amazing capacity to resist change. But that's not to say we haven't pushed it over the edge. We can never hope to see the bay that John Smith saw, or even the oystermen of the last century."

One success story has been the comeback of rockfish, or striped bass, the prime sport fish of the northern Atlantic Coast. Ninety percent of the coast's rockfish are hatched in the Chesapeake's tributaries. The population was almost wiped out by the early 1980s, and Maryland imposed a total ban on angling for rockfish, naming it an endangered species. The ban was an economic disaster—7,500 workers lost their jobs on the East Coast—but the drastic effort was successful. In 1989, the rockfish count

CRABS CROON, FULL MOON, MAY AND JUNE

Has there ever been a sight or sound more romantic than the scuttling of thousands of tiny tank-like creatures, as they assail the moonlit beaches of central Delaware, dragging their males behind them? It all begins in the depths of the Atlantic Ocean and Delaware Bay each March, when the water begins to warm. Horseshoe crabs – which aren't really crabs at all, but related to spiders and scorpions – are stirred by the warming waters into a spawning frenzy that culminates in the appearance of millions of the creatures on the beaches of Delaware during May and June.

Females, which can grow up to two feet long and weigh up to 10 pounds, clamber onto the beaches with the much smaller males clinging to their spiky tails. The females dig shallow nests and lay up to 20,000 small, olive-green eggs, then drag their males over the eggs to fertilize them. Together, they cover the eggs with sand and head back to the water. After two weeks, the crablets scuttle to the water themselves, to feed on worms, clams, and dead fish, and spend the next nine or 10 years molting to maturity and their own chance to mate in the moonlight.

Delaware Bay is home to the largest population in the world of the four remaining species of this trilobite-like creature. Though some may find the armored shuffler frightening (though the long, hard tail, the telson, is only used to maneuver into more favorable positions), horseshoe crabs are not prone to aggressive behavior of any kind. In fact, the peaceful little beasts that resemble wind-up toys are responsible for three Nobel Prizes in medical research. Much of our knowledge about the human eye was based on studies of the crab's compound eye; the crab's pure chitin shell has led to chitin-coated sutures and burn dressings that promote healing with less pain; and its copper-based blue blood contains a clotting agent called lysate that attaches to bacterial toxins. Modern pharmaceutical firms test their products for purity with lysate drawn from crab's blood – the crabs are captured, bled, and released.

Unfortunately, the commercial demand for horseshoe crabs has increased, as they are the preferred bait for the eels and conchs popular in European and Asian markets. Coupled with the fact that horseshoe crab eggs are the main food of many of the western hemisphere's migrating birds, this caused the decline of the crab population, which prompted the Atlantic States Marine Fisheries Commission to develop a management plan to ensure an enduring population of the ancient sea dweller. At midnight, by the light of the full June moon, it will continue to look like the rocks are dancing.

jumped sharply and restrictions were eased, though the fish is still heavily monitored.

Oysters, once so plentiful in Chesapeake Bay, are being wiped out by pollution and two parasitic diseases, MSX and dermo. In efforts to study and combat these ailments, citizens have joined scientists through volunteer programs that count and check oyster sites.

Recent years have seen significant declines in the number of horseshoe crabs and shorebirds. The usual suspects are pesticides in bird wintering grounds, overharvesting of horseshoe crabs for bait and scientific purposes, and loss of coastal wetlands along migration routes. New regulations in Delaware, New Jersey, and Maryland have reduced the legal harvest of horseshoe crabs.

The greatest environmental concern in Delaware has been preservation of wetlands. The Coastal Zone Act, passed in 1971, took a major step toward balancing development with the natural environment by throwing a protective net around the coastal marshes. However, economic interests continue to challenge the act. The state has few natural resources to exploit: Mineral resources are located in the north, with kaolin the most significant, followed by construction granite, gravels, and clay (used to make bricks and tiles). No hydroelectric power has been developed in Delaware.

To learn more about citizens' programs, contact the Chesapeake Bay Foundation's Philip Merrill Environmental Center (6 Herndon Ave., Annapolis, MD 21403, 410/268-8816, www.cbf.org) and the Delaware Department of Natural Resources and Environmental Control (89 Kings Hwy., Dover, DE 19901, 302/739-4403). For information on the bay and Delaware marshes in general, visit the U.S. Fish and Wildlife Service online at www.fws.gov.

History

First People

Early hunter-gatherers ranged across this part of North America between 9,000 and 12,000 years ago. Later tribal units came almost entirely from the Algonquian language–speaking family: the Piscataway and Yoacomocos (Wicomocos) on the western shore, and the Nanticokes, Wicomesse, Choptanks, Arseek, Cuscarawaoc, Pocomoke-Assateague, and Nause (reputedly formidable sorcerers and poisoners) on the Eastern Shore.

Lenni Lenape, called "Delaware" by European settlers because of their encampments on the Delaware River, were the state's original inhabitants, along with the Nanticoke, Pocomoke-Assateague, and Nause. Lenni Lenape were actually an Algonquian-speaking confederacy made up of three major tribes: the Munsee, Unalachtigo, and Unami. Tribal units would cultivate land near the rivers during the spring and summer, then depart to gather syrup and hunt during the winter, returning to the old encampments in the spring. They didn't farm, because foraging was excellent. Broadly speaking, both group leadership and territory were ill-defined, and political organization was kept on a small scale. Algonquian groups were among the first native North Americans to suffer destruction at the hands of Europeans; many cultures were destroyed before the 18th century.

In 1609, Henry Hudson, an Englishman in the employ of the Dutch West India Company, sailed into Delaware Bay and noted the favorable conditions. In 1631, a small group of Dutch West India traders established a tobacco-growing and whaling industry at Zwaanendael (Lewes). They were there less than a year before the local Indians became frustrated with the settlers' apparent lack of cultural understanding and wiped out the entire camp.

Giovanni da Verrazano is thought to have visited the Atlantic coast near Chincoteague Bay in 1524. In 1526, Spanish explorers sailed into Chesapeake Bay and called it Santa Maria, a name that appears on a 1556 map. In 1608, Captain John Smith sailed into the Chesapeake and explored the eastern shoreline, finally choosing to settle in Virginia.

Lord Calvert Sees the Light

In 1580, George Calvert was born into a wealthy landowning family in Yorkshire, England. He served several terms in the House of Commons, then became Secretary of State and member of the Privy Council under King James I. He was knighted for exemplary service in 1619.

As Sir George was building his career, the Anglican Church was the official church of England; Henry VIII had broken with the Roman Catholic Church nearly a century earlier because of objections to his multiple marriages. Catholics were under perpetual suspicion of disloyalty to the crown, unable to hold public office or hear Mass in public, and they were fined for failing to attend Anglican services—an important source of income for the crown at the time.

At the age of 44, at the height of his political power, George Calvert announced that he had become a Roman Catholic, and subsequently resigned his public office. Unable to lure him back into service, King James awarded him a barony in the Irish peerage. George Calvert became the first Lord Baltimore, which included

COLONIAL HOMES

Many examples of early Maryland architectural styles – catslides, telescopes, and plantation clusters – still exist around the state. Their enduring style was based on colonial practicality.

By 1657, the population of Maryland had reached approximately 10,000, largely farmers. The earliest homes, built as one large room, were often divided in two by a plank wall. The larger room was used to conduct plantation business, and the smaller was for the family to withdraw to (hence its name: the withdrawing or drawing room). The house was often made of wood at the front and back and brick at the ends, with double chimneys at either end – the space between them was bricked up and made into a "pent closet" for dry storage. A common way to expand the house was to add two or more "cell" rooms to the back, giving the rear half of the roof a longer distance to run than the front – called a "catslide house."

The fanciest homes were built on the same basic principles, but perhaps 1.5 or two stories instead of one. A house might have had a "stair case," a small, one-room-sized, two-story enclosure to contain the stairs, which give the floor plan a squat T shape; and the gambrel roof would have been covered with cedar shingles instead of thatch. Sometimes the freestanding upper parts of the chimneys were set in a "diamond stack," catercorner to the lower halves. Houses were not always enlarged; rather, a small house might have a larger one right beside it, and a larger one right beside that, so the row of houses looked like it could telescope into itself – a "telescope house."

A plantation consisted of a manor house and several outbuildings. On the Western Shore, plantation houses of the wealthy were made entirely of brick. On the Eastern Shore, homes were built of wood. Every plantation in Maryland was legally required to have a name. Some, like Littleham and Tilghman's Hope, reflected the owner's name, while others were fanciful: Penny Come Quick, Duck Pye, Coffin, Dear Bought, The Remains of My Lord's Gracious Grant Well Meaning.

A tidewater plantation house often consisted of a central block, 2.5 stories high, containing a main hall, library, study, withdrawing room, lady's parlor, bedrooms, and an attic for storage. At either side of the main building, a narrow passage one story high (called a hypen) connected the main house with two buildings at either end. One of these 1.5-story buildings was the kitchen, with rooms above for the cook and house servants. The other building was often used as a chapel for private services for Roman Catholics, and a schoolroom for the owner's children. The main house had two "front" doors – one that faced the road as an entryway, and the other, the "private" or "garden front" door that opened onto the gardens.

Plantations were entirely self-contained. Hidden from the main house by trees or hedges, a wind- or water-powered gristmill provided flour, and a group of log cabins were divided into sections for men's work (smokehouse, smithy, shoemaker, carpentry shop, cooperage, saw pit) and women's work (vegetable/herb garden, springhouse, icehouse, weaving-and-spinning house, storehouse, laundry, soap-making house, dovecote, chicken run, and orchards).

---

a grant of land on the Avalon Peninsula, Newfoundland. Eager to explore his new real-estate opportunities, Calvert journeyed there with his family and 40 others in 1628, and in his letters to King James wrote, "From the middlest of October to the middlest of May, there is a sad fare of wynter upon all this land." The next year, the colony moved en masse to Jamestown, Virginia. Meanwhile, in late 1631, a trapper named William Claiborne established a fur-trading post, the first permanent European settlement in Maryland, on Kent Island (off the Eastern Shore opposite Annapolis).

In Search of Fairer Climes

Lord Baltimore explored the Chesapeake, then

returned to England to request a new grant of land on the bay. His patron, James I, had died, but James's son, Charles I, granted Baltimore an enormous charter that included the Potomac River in its entirety, all of modern Maryland and Delaware, and a large strip of southern Pennsylvania, including much of Philadelphia (the northern boundary, the 40th parallel, runs roughly through the middle of today's Fairmount Park).

In addition, Lord Baltimore had near royal rights over the territory, with the ability to make laws, create and summon militia, carry out judicial proceedings, and confer land grants and titles. Unlike the Virginia colony, Lord Baltimore's settlements were given the right to trade with countries other than England in return for one fifth of all gold and silver discovered in the new colony, plus an annual quitrent (similar to a lease payment) of two Indian arrows. He certainly knew how to make a deal.

George Calvert was determined to create something unknown in the Old World: a land of religious tolerance for all people—including non-Christians—nearly 50 years before William Penn founded Pennsylvania on similar principles. Calvert's ambitions were seen as a model of enlightened self-interest: the more people drawn to this land, the greater profits for him. The new land was to be named after King Charles's wife, Henrietta Maria—*Terra Mariae,* Mary's Land.

In 1638, the New Sweden Company built a fort and trading post in the vicinity of modern Wilmington, but Lord Baltimore did nothing to remove them. The Dutch attempted to claim the Delaware River and its territories; they sent Peter Stuyvesant to oust the Swedes and claim the land as part of Nieuw Netherland. Lord Baltimore didn't protest the presence of either the Swedes or the Dutch, and died before action could be taken; the charter was awarded to his 27-year-old heir, Cecil (Cecilius) Calvert, who promptly turned the day-to-day process of colonization over to his younger brothers Leonard and George.

The First Colonists

The Calverts set generous terms for new colonists: Every adult journeying to Maryland would be granted 100 acres of land, and every child under 16 would receive 50 acres. If a new colonist brought servants provisioned with tools, clothes, and food, the colonist was also awarded 100 acres for each retainer. If he transported five men, he was to receive 1,000 acres (a manor) and could sit in judgment over local civil offenses, among other rights. For every grant of land, the grantee was to swear an oath of fealty to the proprietor, Cecil Calvert, and pay an annual sum of up to 20 pounds.

Men who indentured themselves were to receive 50 acres of land, an ox, a gun, two hoes, a new suit of woolen cloth, stockings, shoes, and hat upon conclusion of the term of service—usually four to seven years. Indentured women received a suit of clothes and three barrels of Indian corn (unequal wages are nothing new).

Though Lord Baltimore intended to offer a place of refuge to Catholics, the majority of the first group of more than 200 settlers to the new land were Protestant. This initial expedition left England in 1633 in two ships, the 360-ton *Ark* and the much smaller *Dove.* Cecil stayed home in England, and Leonard and George accompanied the first settlers and served as governor and deputy governor in Cecil's stead.

The passage was far from smooth. Anti-Catholic feelings still ran high, and a British naval vessel intercepted the ships, claiming the true nature of the expedition was to send reinforcements to Catholic Spain. Released a month later, the ships were separated by a fierce storm. The *Ark* headed for Barbados, where it was later joined by the *Dove.* The ships landed on St. Clement's Island, Maryland, on March 25, 1634, and celebrated Catholic Mass. Leonard Calvert negotiated with members of the local Piscataway and Yoacomoco tribes; in exchange for 30 square miles of land, Calvert gave the Indians hatchets, axes, hoes, and cloth (Leonard inherited the Calvert deal-making gene). The new settlement was named St. Mary's. The Yoacomoco welcomed the newcomers and traded freely with them; as with all successful European settlements in the New World, the natives' help and instruction were the key to survival. Farming, the production of tobacco as a profit-making crop, the plantation system, and the abundance of the countryside brought relative prosperity and growth to the early colony.

The Swedes camped out in northern Delaware surrendered the territory to the Dutch, but the Dutch refused to move until the British bested them in a European-based trade war. Dutch influence remains in the names of rivers; "kill" is the Dutch term for waterway. The Dutch turned the colony over to the British in 1664, and Delaware officially became part of Maryland. Unfortunately, Charles Calvert, the heir of Cecil Lord Calvert, failed to inherit his father's and grandfather's negotiating skills. By 1670, a joint Maryland-Virginia commission—surveyed by Edmund Scarbourge, a Virginian—"accidentally" shaved 23 square miles off Maryland's territory. It was only the beginning.

William's Weak Bottome

In England in 1680, the rebel Quaker son of an aristocratic family, William Penn, agreed to exchange a debt owed his family by King Charles for land in the New World. He planned to name it for his father: Pennsylvania, or "Penn's woods." Penn was determined to have access to the Atlantic Ocean, even though his land grant clearly placed him out of reach, above the point where the Delaware River met Delaware Bay. In fact, New Castle, Lord Baltimore's settlement, was considered the mouth of the bay, and was 20 miles south of Penn's legal border.

Penn persuaded the Duke of York to issue him a grant to New Castle plus a circle of territory 12 miles in radius (hence the odd bulge at the top of the state), plus a piece of land from this circle down to Cape Henlopen—almost all of the current state of Delaware. Penn was well aware that his claim to the territory was fictitious; he commented on "the weak bottome of their Grant—the Duke of York never having had a grant from the king"; he sailed to the New World and met with Lord Baltimore several times, trying to persuade him to deliver New Castle into his hands. Both men

returned to England to plead their case. The king favored Penn: In 1682, Delaware came under the proprietorship of William Penn, but was administered separately from Pennsylvania as a distinct entity called the "three counties of Delaware" or "the three lower counties." At that time, the counties were named New Castle, St. Jones (now Kent County), and Whorekill (Sussex County—no need to question the name change). Further shady dealings involving faulty placement of Cape Henlopen on a map annexed another section of Maryland for Delaware.

By 1720, the Five Nations Iroquois League, a confederation of Iroquois-speaking tribes based in northern New York and Ontario, Canada, dominated much of the remaining Lenni Lenape homeland by war or treaty. As European settlers moved in, the majority of the Lenni Lenape and other indigenous tribes moved west, away from the colonies, eventually establishing villages in eastern Ohio. Today, small Nanticoke colonies exist in Kent and Sussex Counties.

Maryland Goes West

As Annapolis thrived and became known as "the Athens of America," nearby arable land became less available; pioneers began to push inland up the Potomac and toward the mountains. Some were free and poor: failed Tidewater tobacco farmers or former indentured servants who had worked their time; but most were part of a new flood of immigrants. Germans from the Rhineland and the Palatine came to America at the urging of William Penn, and moved west into Maryland and south into Delaware from the port of Philadelphia. Scotch-Irish of Ulster Province also landed at Philadelphia, made their way to the Susquehanna, and turned south into Maryland. In 1729, a tobacco port on the Patapsco River was named after the colony's founder, Baltimore. Georgetown was established as a shipping port for tobacco. Hagerstown was settled in 1737, Frederick (named for the Prince of Wales) in 1745.

In 1750, Cumberland, in the Allegheny

Mountains, was a storehouse and trading post for the Ohio Company, a group of wealthy Virginia planters (including a young British Army officer, George Washington) and London merchants who wished to keep the Ohio Valley away from the French. French and English forces were expanding into Pennsylvania's rich Ohio Valley, forming alliances with Indian tribes and setting up encampments. As territorial hostilities heated up, young Washington published his journal—a chronicle of a soldier's life on the frontier—in the Annapolis *Maryland Gazette*. His words not only established him as a leader, but also garnered support in Annapolis for the French and Indian War.

The French Challenge

The British sent George Washington to northern Pennsylvania to demand an end to French interference in the Ohio Valley; he was politely rebuffed, then barely escaped assassination. Cumberland became a fort and an embarkation point for British troops. General Edward Braddock, fresh from England, marched from Cumberland with volunteers to rout the French from their encampment at Fort Duquesne (doo-KAIN) in what is now downtown Pittsburgh. Braddock was guilty of the same error that has felled American troops in other wars: He had no idea how to fight guerrilla-style. When warned of an ambush by French-allied Hurons, he replied, "These savages may, indeed, be a formidable enemy to your raw American militia, but upon the King's regular and disciplined troops, sir, it is impossible they should make an impression." The general struggled alongside his troops in the thick of the fighting; he and two-thirds of his men died in the mêlée. The French controlled the west for the next three years, and their Indian allies began to raid and destroy outlying settlements.

Fort Cumberland was left with a skeleton garrison, and the few forces that remained withdrew to Fort Frederick at Big Pool. In 1757, British troops found Fort Duquesne abandoned and in ruins. The Battle of Quebec finally ended French domination of North America. After the treaty, old boundary disputes among Pennsylvania, Delaware, and Maryland were again addressed through the creation of the Mason-Dixon Line.

Pontiac's Rebellion

Not long after the French and Indian War, numerous Indian tribes in the northeast rose up under the Ottawa chief Pontiac, driving away the few European settlers who had returned to the western territory. One early pioneer and founder of Oldtown, Thomas Cresap, packed up his family and went east of Conoccocheague Creek (ca-NO-ca-cheek) near Williamsport, Maryland. With his older sons and some neighbors, Cresap began to raid Indian villages. His oldest son died during one of the skirmishes, as did a black volunteer, Nemesis, who is memorialized at Negro Mountain in Somerset County, Pennsylvania. The western frontier of Maryland remained free of European habitation until a treaty was signed with the Iroquois Confederation in 1768.

Throwing Off the Homeland

In 1765, 12 Frederick County justices repudiated the British Stamp Act, the colony's first official act of rebellion against the British. Marylanders had their own "tea party" in 1774 in Chestertown when the tea-carrying ship *Geddes* was burned in the city's harbor. On July 3, 1776, the state disavowed allegiance to the king; four months later, Maryland was the first of the former colonies to adopt a state constitution.

State representatives signed their own Declaration of Independence first, then sent Charles Carroll, Samuel Chase, Thomas Stone, and William Paca to Philadelphia to sign the declaration composed by the Continental Congress. During the Revolutionary War, no fighting took place in the state, but Maryland troops distinguished themselves in battle throughout the colonies.

Though there were plenty of loyalists among Delaware's colonial inhabitants, the settlers proved to be fervent supporters of colonial autonomy. Three weeks before the signing of the Declaration of Independence, Delaware's assembly voted to separate not only from the

MASON AND DIXON

British surveyors and astronomers Charles Mason and Jeremiah Dixon sailed from Britain to Philadelphia in 1763, expressly hired by the British crown to settle the boundary disputes that plagued Delaware, Maryland, and Pennsylvania. After comparing old deeds and hearing testimony, they decided that the north wall of a house on the south side of Cedar Street (now South Street) in Philadelphia was the proper southern limit of the city. Maryland's northern boundary was to follow a line parallel to the southern limit of Philadelphia and 15 miles south of it. So as to avoid the Delaware "bulge," they moved due west for 31 miles and set up a marker, the Stargazers' Stone (in Chester County, Pennsylvania), which set the Maryland boundary. A Transpeninsular Marker near the site of the Fenwick Island Lighthouse indicated the southern boundary between Pennsylvania's "three lower counties" and Maryland. In April 1765, Mason and Dixon began to move west. Sighting was done from horizon to horizon, and as each mile was measured off, workmen piled up a rough heap of stones – later to be replaced with milestones that carried an "M" on the southern side, a "P" on the northern. Crown stones marked every fifth mile, with the Penn coat of arms on the north and Lord Baltimore's on the south. By November 1766, Mason and Dixon entered hostile Six Nation Iroquois territory to the west. The party was allowed to continue with an Indian deputation, but when they reached the Monongahela River, a party of native guides and workmen refused to go on into Shawnee territory. Two weeks later, the chief Iroquois delegate announced that he would go no further, and advised the British surveyors to follow his example. They took his advice and marked the end of the Pennsylvania border.

British, but also from Pennsylvania. Caesar Rodney, a resident of New Castle, rode through the night to Philadelphia and cast the deciding vote for independence.

In the winter of 1776, Congress sent a delegation to Montreal to sound out French Canadians as allies in the American cause. Though not a delegate to the Continental Congress, Charles Carroll had attended its sessions as an unattached observer. He was asked to join the mission, along with his cousin, the priest John Carroll—Congress was hoping to impress the Catholic French Canadians with token Catholics. In a sterling example of "what goes around comes around," the French refused to help, citing the lack of freedom of American Catholics.

In August 1777, the British fleet was sighted in the approaches to Chesapeake Bay. There was a strong pro-British following in parts of the Eastern Shore, and Annapolis and Baltimore both girded for an invasion. Instead, the ships sailed up the Delaware River and landed troops below Philadelphia, the colonial capital. After George Washington was defeated at Brandywine Creek in Pennsylvania, Philadelphia and Wilmington were taken. The nearby colonial capital of Delaware, New Castle, was threatened, and the government was moved to the safer inland location of Dover, where it remained. The Revolutionary War dragged on until 1787, when both sides agreed to allow the colonies to form their own nation.

Washington nicknamed Maryland the "Old Line State" in honor of her valiant troops of the Continental Line. Delaware was the first state to ratify the U.S. Constitution in 1787, thus earning the sobriquet "The First State." This is a point of pride for Delawareans; you'll often see the phrase "Delaware First" on businesses and license plates, as well as on the back of the 1999 state quarter (the first one issued), which bears the image of Caesar Rodney on horseback. Delaware troops in the Continental Army were nicknamed "Blue Hen's Chickens" for the tenacious fighting cocks they brought with them from Kent County, all from the brood of a single blue hen. Today, the name lives on in the University of Delaware football team (Go Blues!). Maryland became the seventh state to ratify the new constitution. Two years later, the state conveyed 69.5 square miles to house the seat of government for the District of Columbia: Washington, D.C.

Expansion

Baltimore, incorporated in 1797, grew rapidly as a port and shipbuilding and industrial center, overshadowing Annapolis in commerce and attaining a population of 26,500 (more than Boston) in 1800. Maryland's early years of statehood were spent in developing the state's resources.

Delaware's booming (no pun intended) chemical industry was born in 1802 when a French immigrant, Éleuthère Irénée du Pont, established a black powder mill near Wilmington. The site is now a public park, Hagley Mills. By the mid-19th century, the Delaware landscape had been made over. In northern Delaware, industry had expanded from simple tanning, grain milling, and paper making to sophisticated gunpowder and textile manufacturing.

Britain and France had been at war since 1793, and Britain was infamous for impressing (seizing and forcing into labor) American sailors. In 1812, America declared war on Great Britain. England planned to cut the country in half at Chesapeake Bay; Maryland and federal forces were routed at the battle of Bladensburg, and British troops went on to burn Washington. Baltimore was spared capture, thanks to an intrepid stand at Fort McHenry against a 25-hour-long bombardment. While watching from a British treaty ship, Francis Scott Key penned a poem, "The Bombardment of Fort McHenry"; his publisher changed the title to a snappier "The Star-Spangled Banner." In 1815, the final battle of the war—Andrew Jackson's victory over British forces—took place in New Orleans, two weeks after a peace treaty had been signed.

Following the war, development of swift clipper ships and steam locomotives multiplied trade possibilities. New routes such as the National Road (U.S. 40), the Chesapeake and Delaware Canal (across the Delmarva Peninsula), the Chesapeake and Ohio Canal (along the Potomac River to the coalfields of Cumberland and western Maryland), the Philadelphia, Wilmington, and Baltimore Railroad, and the Baltimore and Ohio (B&O) Railroad increased access from lands west of the Appalachians into Chesapeake ports. The B&O, begun in 1828, was the first U.S. passenger railroad. First Citizen Charles Carroll laid the cornerstone of the train depot in Baltimore, shortly before his death.

Entrepreneurs and citizens alike benefited from improved turnpikes, canals, and railroads. By 1856, railroad lines wound through both states, bringing the economic boom to agriculture-based businesses throughout Maryland and Delaware.

Slavery and the Dred Scott Decision

Mid-19th-century America experienced a heated battle over states' rights, particularly over the right of a state to declare slave ownership legal or illegal. In 1857, Dred Scott, a Missouri slave, claimed that he had become a free man when his master transported him temporarily into a free state. The case went all the way to the U.S. Supreme Court and was heard before Chief Justice Roger Taney, a resident of Frederick, Maryland—and a slaveholder.

Five of the nine justices who served on the court supported slavery and slaveholding rights in the territories. The court ruled that all laws restricting the free movement of property—including, shamefully, human property—were unconstitutional; that no black person in the United States enjoyed "any rights which the White man was bound to respect." In principle, the Dred Scott decision meant that all the states and unincorporated territories were open to slavery. It undercut the makeshift solution of popular sovereignty (the right of each area to take its own position on slavery) in the territories. Rather than solving the sectional crisis, the court heightened tension. Several southern slaveholding states seceded. Without an active declaration of war, Union troops fired on Fort

© JOANNE MILLER

Confederate Soldiers Memorial in Frederick

Sumter, South Carolina, in 1861; the conflict had begun.

Civil War

New Castle County, where Wilmington is located, grew in response to urban-industrial developments in nearby Philadelphia; Kent and Sussex Counties to the south remained rural and culturally a part of the American South. This duality extended to the divided role Delaware played in the Civil War. The state's original constitution in 1776 forbade the further importation of slaves, and abolition bills narrowly failed in the 1790s and 1847. Less than 2,000 slaves and about 20,000 free blacks were part of the total population of 112,000 in 1860. Though technically a slave state (slaveholding was legal and binding), Delaware did not secede; the majority of Delawareans took a moderate stance and supported the Union with labor and troops.

Maryland had almost equal numbers of slaves and free blacks. Marylanders were also divided over the issue of slavery—southern

Maryland and the Eastern Shore favored the South, while northern and western Maryland were pro-Union—and Maryland soldiers fought on both sides during the Civil War. When neighboring Virginia seceded, Maryland's presence within the Union became vital to the defense of Washington, D.C., and President Lincoln prevented secession by imposing military rule. Raids across the Potomac by Confederate cavalry were a constant threat. Fierce battles fought on Maryland soil included South Mountain and Antietam (both in 1862) and Monocacy (1864).

After the Civil War, however, black rights were vigorously opposed. In 1873, blacks were effectively disenfranchised by poll taxes and corrupt politics. In 1897, the poll tax was replaced by a literacy test.

Economic growth continued: manufacturing expanded rapidly and eventually emerged as the mainstay of Maryland's economy. Thousands of Greek, German, Italian, Russian, Polish, and other immigrants, together with newly freed blacks migrating from rural counties, flocked to take jobs in Baltimore's textile factories and other industries. In Delaware, wealth and power were concentrated in Wilmington; tax laws instituted in 1899 encouraged corporations to locate their headquarters there. By 1920, the city contained almost half of Delaware's population.

Modern Times

In 1904, Baltimore was devastated by fire, but the city recovered to grow rapidly as World Wars I and II increased demand for its industrial products. The area was buffered from the worst effects of the Great Depression in the late 1920s, thanks to its strong industrial base. As the fruits of American industry has diminished in importance from the late 1950s to the present, Baltimore has turned increasingly to tourism. In the rest of the state, agriculture and aquaculture remain the mainstays of rural areas, while central Maryland enjoys a prosperity fueled by jobs in U.S. government–related research and services.

Delaware's economic growth was fueled in

© JOANNE MILLER

Revolutionary War and Civil War Cemetery in Cambridge

the 1980s by the passage of laws favorable to banking and corporate interests. By the 1990s, more than 183,000 corporations had headquarters in the state, largely in the Wilmington area.

The state's more liberal urbanized north and conservative rural south continued to battle over the state's social services and other public sector issues. As a result of legislative conflict between the northern and southern factions, state unemployment insurance was withdrawn at the height of the Great Depression in 1934. Legislative districts that had long benefited the rural south were not redrawn until the 1960s in favor of the more populous Wilmington suburbs.

In 1968, the assassination of the great humanitarian leader Dr. Martin Luther King Jr. ignited a long-burning fuse. Blacks rioted in the streets of Wilmington. The National Guard was called in, and the city was placed under martial law. Today, Wilmington is peaceful, though it continues to be highly segregated.

Modern Maryland and Delaware face problems common to much of the United States—rapid development, suburban crowding, and economic growth versus environmental preservation. Wilmington is directing much of its wealth into a revitalized downtown area with tourist attractions that will rival those of Baltimore.

The fabulous beaches of southern Delaware and Ocean City, Maryland, remain destinations for thousands of visitors each year, and deservedly so. The last 30 years have seen a revitalization of the once run-down, sleepy beach areas.

Government

MARYLAND

Modern state government in Maryland is based on the Constitution of 1867. The Maryland legislature consists of a General Assembly made up of a House and Senate. The governor serves a four-year term. Acting as a liaison between the executive and the legislature is the Board of Public Works—an agency composed of the governor, the controller of the treasury, and the treasurer. The executive branch is headed by the governor, who oversees 12 departments; the secretaries of the departments form the state cabinet.

The highest tribunal in the state is the Court of Appeals, a convention retained from the Constitution of 1776. The court judges are appointed by the governor to serve a brief term, and then may be elected for a 10-year term. The governor designates the chief judge. A constitutional convention meeting in 1967 further modernized the government, as voters reacted negatively to changing the public election of many executive officials to appointment status.

Since the 19th century, commissioners serving both the legislative and executive functions have governed Maryland's counties. However, Montgomery, Prince George's, and Baltimore Counties have adopted charter governments with specialized departments and officers to perform functions once exercised by the boards of commissioners. In addition, more than 50 incorporated towns and cities hold charters.

Several times during Maryland's history, political machines dominated state politics, and each was swept away by reformers; unfortunately, government seems to attract those with questionable motives. Spiro T. Agnew, former governor of Maryland, was elected U.S. vice president in 1968 and 1972. In 1973, however, he resigned the office during an investigation of charges of graft while he was serving as a Maryland official. Governor Marvin Mandel, Agnew's successor, was indicted on similar charges in 1975, then convicted in 1978 on charges of mail fraud and racketeering, and sentenced to jail. Forced by Maryland law to resign, Mandel resumed office for the 45 remaining hours of his term after the overturn on appeal (later reversed) of his conviction. Today, the overriding issues concerning Maryland government are tax revenues and racial politics.

DELAWARE

Delaware continues to abide by a constitution created in 1897. An earlier version was presented to the people of Delaware, who voted it down; the current constitution was adopted without a popular vote. Since Delaware consists of only three counties, the state government fills many of the functions normally served by local leadership, though incorporated towns handle their own tax issues, and individual counties largely manage tourism.

State government consists of three bodies: executive, legislative, and judicial. As head of the executive branch, a governor is elected for four years and a maximum of two terms. The legislature (General Assembly) consists of a 21-member Senate and a 41-member House of Representatives; senators serve four-year terms

---

BIG D OR LITTLE D?

It's a proofreader's nightmare. É. I. du Pont, founder of the Du Pont dynasty, always signed his name with a small "d" out of deference to his father, Pierre-Samuel du Pont de Nemours. The tradition has continued, and when using names of individual members of the Du Pont family, the small "d" is still used. However, when discussing the family as a whole, or any of the DuPont companies, the big "D" is correct usage.

and representatives serve two-year terms. The governor has veto power, although a three-fifths vote in each house will override it.

The judiciary consists of a supreme court, superior courts, courts of common pleas, family courts for juveniles, and a court of chancery for corporate matters. The Republican Party has dominated the state's politics in recent years, though registered Republicans and Democrats are evenly matched.

Economy

MARYLAND

Although Maryland's economic activity is varied, it centers principally on manufacturing, which employs more than a quarter of a million people. Since the end of the Revolution, the center of manufacturing has been Baltimore. Montgomery, Prince George's, and Washington Counties follow in importance. The leading manufactured products are metals, chiefly steel; food and related products; electrical machinery; transportation equipment; and chemical and allied products.

Maryland ranks in the lowest 15 of the 50 states in total land under cultivation and value of agricultural products sold. At one time, less than 0.1 percent of the population derived income from dairy and poultry products; that's changed in recent years with the growth of the chicken market. In western and southern Maryland and the Eastern Shore, a dense network of small farms produces greenhouse vegetables, corn, melon, and fruit for private use and local consumers, and there's a limited commercial soybean and tobacco market.

Fishing and forestry are important resources. Virginia and Maryland share the major fishing grounds, but more than half of the processing is in Maryland. Annapolis, Somerset, and Dorchester Counties on the Eastern Shore

© JOANNE MILLER

crab steamers

have more than half of the seafood processing plants. Almost 90 percent of seafood income comes from clams, crabs, and oysters. Two-thirds of forestry production is in sawn timber, and the remaining third consists of pulpwood, poles, and piling.

The existence of Washington, D.C., has greatly stimulated the economy of the surrounding areas of Maryland, including Prince George's and Montgomery Counties, which are considered part of the district's metropolitan area. Many federal institutions and agencies contribute markedly to the state's economic life, and the Washington-Baltimore "corridor" is responsible for more than half of the economic productivity of Maryland. The government—on the local, state, and federal levels—employs more than 300,000 Marylanders.

The Port of Baltimore boasts the fourth largest foreign export trade in the United States and has been central to Maryland's economy since the mid-18th century. The Baltimore area has always offered excellent deep-water harbor facilities. The increased use of container shipping has led to modernization and has enhanced the port's ability to move bulk cargo. Ships can reach the port by way of both the southern end of Chesapeake Bay and the western end of the Chesapeake and Delaware Canal.

DELAWARE

Industry is Delaware's mainstay. Wilmington has been the state's industrial center since the colonial period, though space and price considerations have caused industries to spread downstate. Top-grossing industries include chemicals, food processing, primary metals, machinery, printing and publishing, leather goods, fabricated metals, transportation equipment, and textiles. If the vision of a smoking, chugging juggernaut comes to mind, it's useful to remember that a considerable amount of the output of these industries isn't produced in Wilmington—the income is based on the fact that the city is home to the corporate headquarters of industrial companies.

Prior to 1900, Delaware was known as the "Peach State," but repeated blights wiped out most of the orchards. Peach growing was replaced by the chicken industry; poultry plays such a large part in Delaware's current economics that it's hard to believe it started by accident. In 1923, Cecile Steele, a resident of Ocean View, received 500 chickens instead of the 50 she ordered. She raised the birds to eating size and sold them in one large lot. Prior to that time, chickens were eaten when their egg-laying days were over, and stewing was the primary cooking option. The new "broilers" caught on, and now more than half of Delaware's agricultural income comes from the production of broiler chickens. The remainder is spread out among various items, including soybeans, greenhouse products, milk, and corn.

Education

MARYLAND

In 17th-century plantation society, hired tutors or churchmen usually taught privileged children, and the gentry sent sons to study in England or on the Continent. Only benevolent societies or generous teachers served poor youngsters.

The first signs of public interest in tax-supported education began in 1694, when the assembly taxed specific export items, ruling that the proceeds were to be used for schools. Twenty years later, the law required the establishment of a school in every county, supported by taxation on imported blacks and Irish Catholic servants. The law met with indifferent success.

One of Maryland's leading colonial institutions was King William's school, founded in Annapolis in 1694. The school flourished because of the generosity of leading citizens and support from taxation. This academy—later known as St. John's College—lasted until the time of the Revolution, when, with Washington College, it formed the first state university.

Public education began in earnest in the years following the Revolution; a county received grants of money from the legislature if that county's citizens would provide the building and teachers. In 1826, the legislature voted to establish public schools throughout the state. Though schools in the cities flourished, education in the rest of the state lagged behind. Finally, in 1864, the creation of a State Board of Education and the appointment of a superintendent of public education inaugurated the modern system. Racial segregation was gradually eliminated in schools following the U.S. Supreme Court decision of 1954.

Today, Maryland boasts dozens of sites of higher learning. Johns Hopkins University in Baltimore and the University of Maryland College Park have gained worldwide recognition as centers of learning and research; the Peabody Institute in Baltimore enjoys an international reputation in the arts.

A major state library, Enoch Pratt in Baltimore, contains a large circulating library and special collections of rare books, manuscripts, and Marylandia. Among its precious collections are the papers and works of Edgar Allan Poe and H. L. Mencken. The nearby Peabody Library is distinctive for its rare books and musical publications.

DELAWARE

The oldest school in Delaware is the Wilmington Friends School, founded by Quakers in the early colonial days. The state established a public education system in 1829, but funding was erratic and the quality of teaching uneven, and blacks were excluded. This was partially remedied in 1907, when compulsory education was instituted. It took nearly 20 more years and considerable voter pressure (and outright financing by Pierre du Pont) for an administrative and taxation system capable of supporting modern educational facilities to be created. Du Pont insisted that relatively poor areas should not be forced to put up with inferior schools simply because of poverty. Schools were desegregated in 1954, and in 1978, court-ordered busing mixed students from white suburban schools with those of the predominantly black schools of Wilmington.

The University of Delaware at Newark (pronounced as two words: NEW ARK), which evolved from an academy in existence since 1743, and Delaware State College, in Dover, are the two public four-year institutions of higher learning in the state.

People and Culture

MARYLAND

Historically, Marylanders have been seafarers and fishermen. Once completely dependent on a rural economy, the state now ranks 40th in farm acreage; Maryland south of Prince George's County and western Maryland beyond Frederick still exhibit a rural aspect, but these areas are not heavily populated. Much of the state is now urban, such as the densely populated "Washington gateway" that runs from Baltimore to Washington, D.C. More than half of the state's residents are concentrated in the metropolitan Baltimore area, and almost a third live in the suburban Washington, D.C., region.

Howard County, a southwestern suburb of Baltimore, is experiencing the greatest population growth, though the counties that surround Baltimore and the Washington gateway—Calvert, Charles, Carroll, and Frederick—are all expanding. Queen Anne's County, across the Bay Bridge, is also targeted for growth.

Generally, where Marylanders choose to live results from their age group. Families tend to live in the suburban areas that make up the Washington gateway; rural areas such as the

Eastern Shore and southern and western Maryland have an older population; and the urban areas of Baltimore and Annapolis largely consist of young adults. With marriage, young white couples usually depart to the suburbs, while young black couples tend to remain in the cities.

Race relations remain a concern, particularly between blacks and whites. Relations were severely strained by the 1954 U.S. Supreme Court decision to end segregation, and widespread rioting occurred in the 1960s, mostly in Baltimore. Today, the city presents an interesting contrast to the picture many people have of a large urban black population: Baltimore boasts some of the wealthiest black neighborhoods in America.

Ethnography

Maryland has always had a large black population. During the slavery era, Baltimore contained the largest free black population of all the northeastern slaveholding states and was second only to New Orleans during this time. Today, blacks constitute about 22 percent of the total population of the state. Non-white settlements are sharply localized. Baltimore contains the largest non-white population, while Garrett County has the smallest. Old slavery areas in southern Maryland and the Eastern Shore have seen a shift of blacks to cities. Chinese, Japanese, Filipinos, and displaced Indo-Chinese have also become a population segment in Maryland, and they generally remain in urban areas.

Scotch-Irish, fleeing English persecution, and Palatine Germans, seeking relief from religious intolerance, were among the first non-English European nationalities to move to the Piedmont Plateau in the early 18th century. The Germans belonged to Pietistic faiths, such as Lutheranism, or were Mennonite, Amish, or Moravian.

Religion

The quest for religious freedom led to Maryland's founding and played a crucial role in the state's history. George Calvert desired to found

Amish farm

a place where Roman Catholics could worship freely—Catholicism had been repressed in England since the early 16th century, following the founding of the Anglican Church, and came heavily under fire with the Protestant movement of the mid-16th century in Britain and on the Continent. The Roman Catholic Church, first and largest of the Christian churches, attached great significance to the infallibility and worldwide ministry of the pope and his representatives, priests—beliefs that directly challenged the sovereignty of kings and the Protestant belief that man had a direct line to God. Though they succeeded in planting the seeds of Catholicism and liberal religious freedom in America, the Calvert family was frustrated by the ongoing politics and power plays of the Protestant Reformation.

In the mid-17th century, the more extreme Protestants within the Church of England were called Puritans. They thought the English Reformation had not gone far enough and wanted to purify their national church by eliminating every shred of Catholic influence. A Puritan group settled south of Baltimore and worked successfully to unseat the Calverts and return control of the colony to England.

Though Puritans are no longer visible as such, another group of conservative Protestants remains highly visible in areas of the Eastern Shore and southern Maryland: Old Order Amish. The Amish have adopted a highly stylized, conservative style of dress (the predominant clothing color is black; married men are bearded; women's hair is always covered), along with a carefully maintained separation from "worldly" things like automobiles and computers. Amish farms are easily identified, especially during the fall harvest: Sheaves of wheat in the old-fashioned X shape are laid neatly in the field, picked up slowly and steadily by straw-hatted farmers pitchforking the sheaves high up into the air on top of a horse-drawn wagon.

The Society of Friends, commonly called Quakers, was also part of the Protestant movement, though its members were nearly as reviled as Catholics, due to their firm belief that they owed allegiance to no one but God. Groups of believers moved south and west from Pennsylvania into Maryland during the colonial era. Quakers were instrumental in developing the Underground Railroad before the Civil War to transport slaves north from Virginia. One of the oldest—and still active—colonial-era meeting houses still exists outside Easton (see Talbot County in the Eastern Shore chapter).

Christianity, Buddhism, Judaism, and all other belief systems coexist peacefully in Maryland today. Though the first Calverts never lived to see it, religious tolerance is the rule, much as they had planned; religion no longer plays as divisive a role as it has in the past.

DELAWARE

Delaware has a population density well above the national average, due mainly to its geographical position: The northern section of the state is part of the megalopolis between Philadelphia and Baltimore/Washington, D.C. Most of Delaware's residents live in this urban region and outlying suburbs.

Ethnography

The 19th century saw major migration into the Wilmington area by Germans and Irish, followed by Italians, Poles, and pan-European Jews. The early 20th century brought Greeks and Ukrainians. Today, Asians and Hispanics are the fastest-growing groups of new settlers.

At the time of the American Revolution, blacks made up a fifth of the total population. In 1990, the population was about 80 percent white and 17 percent black.

The ethnic mix of southern Delaware has changed little over the years. Consisting of primarily German and Scotch-Irish peoples, the area received an influx of Germanic Amish and Mennonite settlers during the Great Depression of the 1930s. Today, an enclave of one of Delmarva's indigenous tribes, the Nanticoke, has been established in southern Delaware near the town of Millsboro.

Religion

Roman Catholics make up the single largest denomination in Delaware, though all Protestants taken together—Methodists, Presbyterians, and Episcopalians—outnumber them. The state also has significant numbers of Jews and Orthodox Christians.

LANGUAGE

English is the prevalent language in Maryland and Delaware. However, you will find small traditional communities, such as Smith Island, whose members are reputed to speak a variation of Elizabethan English. Some claim it's more rural southern than historic speech, but it's all in the ear of the beholder.

ESSENTIALS

Getting There

BY AIR

Baltimore-Washington International (BWI, 410/859-7111 or 800/435-9294), 10 miles south of Baltimore and 30 miles north of Washington, D.C., is Maryland's major airport, with international traffic from 31 foreign and domestic carriers. US Airways has a hub there and operates flights daily to and from all major U.S. cities, as well as commuter flights to many Maryland destinations. Washington National Airport (DCA, 703/661-2700) and Washington Dulles International Airport (IAD, 703/419-8000) in Virginia also serve Maryland.

Smaller airports connect travelers with every region. St. Mary's County Airport is in south-ern Maryland, and Greater Cumberland Regional Airport, Washington County Regional Airport (Hagerstown), and Frederick Municipal Airport serve western Maryland. Cambridge Airport, Easton Municipal Airport, Ocean City Municipal Airport, and Salisbury-Wicomico County Regional Airport serve the Eastern Shore.

Philadelphia International Airport (PHL, 215/937-6937) is the closest full-service airport to Delaware. Wilmington is about 45 minutes from Philadelphia and 1.5 hours from Baltimore by car; add another hour if your destination is Dover. The state also has a network of public and private airports, most of which

can accommodate commercial and corporate aircraft. Limited commercial airline service is available through the New Castle County Airport (302/571-6300), located on U.S. 13 just south of Wilmington. There are 12 other public airports in Delaware. For further information, call the Delaware Department of Transportation (302/739-3264).

BY RAIL

Amtrak has eight rail stations in the Maryland area, including Washington's Union Station, Baltimore's Penn Station, and West Virginia's Harpers Ferry Station. Amtrak's Capitol Limited stops in Pittsburgh; Connellsville, Pennsylvania; Cumberland, Maryland; Martinsburg, West Virginia; Harpers Ferry, West Virginia; Rockville, Maryland; Washington, D.C.; Baltimore; Philadelphia; and New York City. Amtrak may be reached by calling 800/USA-RAIL (800/872-7245). The Amtrak line connects directly to the Maryland Area Rail Commuter (MARC) system, a Monday–Friday commuter service with 75 trains on three lines in the Baltimore-Washington corridor, eight Maryland counties, and northeastern West Virginia. Call 800/325-RAIL (800/325-7245) for routes and schedules.

Amtrak serves Wilmington on the Northeast Corridor Line with 76 trains a day. Two trains per day also run to Newark. This is the easiest way to get to Wilmington from New York, Philadelphia, or Washington, D.C., along with stops in between.

BY BUS

Greyhound offers dozens of connecting routes from all over the United States and within the state. Call 800/822-2662 for specific departure times and destinations; schedules and prices are available over the phone.

Greyhound, Carolina Coach Trailways, and Peter Pan Trailways serve Wilmington and Delaware. For information, call the Wilmington Transportation Center (302/652-7391). Salem County Transit (SCOT) provides bus service between Salem County, New Jersey, and Wilmington. Contact SCOT through New Jersey Transit (215/569-3752).

© JOANNE MILLER

skipjack on the water

BY CAR

There is one official toll road in Maryland, I-95, a four-lane that runs from the northeastern border of Delaware through Baltimore to the Washington, D.C., Beltway. It also goes through the Fort McHenry Tunnel.

U.S. 40, one to four lanes built on the old colonial toll road, parallels I-95 from Delaware to Baltimore, then heads west alongside I-70 from Baltimore to Hancock (where I-70 turns north to Pennsylvania) and I-68 from Hancock to the western Maryland border and beyond. The latter two are high-speed roads that vary between two and four lanes; U.S. 40 rambles alongside like a distracted mule tethered to a wagon. Another major route is U.S. 50, which runs east–west from Annapolis over the Bay Bridge with two to four lanes, turns south, and then turns east to Ocean City. I-83 is the main high-speed route from Baltimore to Pennsylvania; I-270 performs that function from Washington, D.C., to Frederick. I-495/I-95 loops around Washington, D.C., and I-695 circles the city of Baltimore and crosses the Francis Scott Key Bridge ($1). I-895 is a short stretch south of Baltimore through the Baltimore Harbor Tunnel ($1). For online information on the latest toll rates and access to maps, visit www.mdot.state.md.us.

In Delaware, the main access roads north–south are U.S. 113 and U.S. 13, which switch between four-lane and two-lane stoplight roads. In the northern part of the state, I-95 is the high-speed access road.

BY WATER

Maryland is a boater's paradise, and most of the state's counties are accessible by boat along the Potomac River, Chesapeake Bay, and the Atlantic Ocean. Every town on the water has a marina; for information on pleasure-boating facilities, call the Marine Trade Association (410/269-0741). The Port of Baltimore has hosted a number of impressive luxury liners, including the *Queen Elizabeth II.* It's a port of call for 15 cruise ships with destinations in the Caribbean and Europe. Call the Port of Baltimore (410/385-4454) for more information.

The Cape May–Lewes Ferry (800/64-FERRY or 800/643-3779) operates vehicle and passenger service daily from Cape May, New Jersey, to Lewes, Delaware, though schedules vary by season. The crossing takes one hour and 15 minutes.

Getting Around

INTERSTATE AND INTRASTATE RAIL TRANSIT

MARC commuter trains run Monday–Friday on three lines: The Brunswick Line runs between Martinsburg, West Virginia, and Washington, D.C.; the Camden Line connects Baltimore's Inner Harbor and Washington, D.C., and the Penn Line links Perryville, midtown Baltimore, and Washington, D.C. (800/325-RAIL or 800/325-7725).

Washington Metro Rapid Transit (202/637-7000) features five **subway** lines that travel from downtown Washington to Maryland and Virginia. Baltimore Metro (410/539-5000) operates between the city and the northwestern suburb of Owings Mills, with links to an aboveground light rail system between northern Anne Arundel County and Timonium in Baltimore County.

SEPTA runs commuter trains Monday–Saturday between Wilmington and Philadelphia, as well as Wilmington and Newark.

INTERCITY BUS TRANSIT

The Maryland Transit Authority (MTA, 410/539-5000, www.mtamaryland.com) runs 75 bus lines in the city of Baltimore and throughout the state. Call or visit the website for schedules and routes. The Washington Metropolitan Area Transit Authority (202/637-7000) operates Metrobus (Metro) in Washington, D.C., and the surrounding Maryland suburbs.

PUBLIC TRANSIT

The website for the American Public Transportation Association (APTA, www.apta.com) offers the latest information on public transportation in the United States.

Greater Wilmington, Dover, and Sussex Counties all have municipal bus systems. For detailed information and route maps, contact DTC (400 S. Madison St., Wilmington, DE 19801, 800/652-DART or 800/652-3278). Paratransit services are available for disabled, elderly, and special-needs customers; call 800/553-3278 for more information.

BY CAR

Hundreds of little Maryland kids must be traumatized every year when asked to draw an outline of their state in school. What mnemonic device can one possibly use? Seagull with a broken wing? A lumpy rendition of the letters "TL?" Just as the outline fails to fit a mold, so does the state. Car travel is the best way to appreciate Maryland's rural beauty and to visit some of its less accessible attractions. Proximity is one advantage of travel in Maryland: in each of the state's divisions as laid out in this book, visitors have the choice of spending less than three hours point-to-point on the road—or far longer, depending on chosen routes.

The highway speed limit in Maryland is 65 mph unless posted otherwise. Children under three must ride in approved safety seats, and drivers and front-seat passengers must wear seat belts.

Historically, the Chesapeake Bay and its tributaries allowed the simultaneous development of cheap water transport and complicated land transport. Bridges of every description are scattered throughout the state. Major projects joined the state's many smaller ones; the completion in 1952 of the four-mile Chesapeake Bay Bridge facilitated travel from the Eastern Shore to the Western Shore. The completion of the Baltimore Harbor Bridge (1957), Fort McHenry Tunnel (1985), and the Francis Scott Key Bridge across the Patapsco River (1977) helped to move traffic around Baltimore. Along with bridges and tunnels, the state maintains an active ferry system, serviced by the Maryland State Highway Administration. A map of ferry services is available by calling 800/252-8776, or by visiting www.mdot.state.md.us.

In Delaware, U.S. 13 and U.S. 113 are the major routes—consequently, progress can sometimes be agonizingly slow, especially between Wilmington and New Castle. U.S. 40 (the National Road) runs through the top of the state and crosses over to New Jersey. Delaware is full of lovely two-laners. Considering that the drive from the northern border to the southernmost point, Fenwick Island, takes around three hours, it would behoove the interested visitor to wander off on a few of them. It's hard to get lost, thanks to a simple and well-maintained road and signage system and accurate maps, available from the state tourism board (800/441-8846).

Visas and Officialdom

Overseas visitors need a passport and a visa to enter the United States. This means (except for diplomats, students, or refugees) a nonimmigrant visitor's visa. You must obtain this in advance at a U.S. consulate or embassy abroad. Residents of western European and Commonwealth countries usually receive these readily; residents of other countries may have to provide the consulate with proof of "sufficient personal funds" before the visa is issued.

Upon your arrival in the United States, an immigration inspector will decide on the time validity of your visa—the maximum duration of a temporary visitor's visa (B-1 or B-2) is six months. If your U.S. visa has expired, you can still enter the country (for a stay of 29 days or shorter) with a transit visa, but you may be required to show proof of onward travel, such as an airplane ticket or ship travel voucher.

Recreation

Maryland and Delaware's recreation areas make the great outdoors available to all, whether you're inclined to backpack the 185-mile Chesapeake and Ohio Canal trail, stroll through a historic home, go clamming, or glide in a silent canoe over ink-colored water. National parks offer a mix of activities, from active recreation to historic house tours, while state parks are more oriented toward outdoor activities. A chapter location is given for those parks detailed in this book.

PARKS
National Parks
In Maryland, the National Park Service maintains and administers five historical sites and museums. Fort McHenry National Monument and Historic Shrine (see *Baltimore* chapter) is the birthplace of our national anthem and the scene of a historic naval assault during the War of 1812. Antietam National Battlefield and Monocacy National Battlefield (see *Western Maryland* chapter) were the setting for significant Civil War battles; Antietam National Cemetery, near the battlefield, is the result of one of the bloodiest battles in our history.

Other National Park sites were created to retain the history of everyday life. Hampton National Historic Site is an elegant mansion set in 62 acres of parkland. Thomas Stone National Historic Site (see *Southern Maryland* chapter) is the home of one of the colony's early movers and shakers.

The National Park Service is also responsible for a number of outdoor recreation sites. Greenbelt Park (see *Central Maryland* chapter) offers 12 miles of trails and overnight camping. Catoctin Mountain Park (see *Western Maryland* chapter) is another popular venue in the forested mountains north of Frederick.

Assateague Island National Seashore (see *Eastern Shore* chapter) and Chesapeake and Ohio Canal National Historical Park (see *Western Maryland* chapter) are among two of the best-known national parks. Assateague, a barrier island on the Atlantic Ocean, is home to a famous wild pony herd. The C&O Canal offers a 184.5-mile towpath to hike or bike.

State Forests and Parks
Maryland has invested more than 280,000 acres in public land, so there's a state forest or park within a 40-minute drive of any point in the state. Most of the state's 54 parks are open year-round, with most facilities (snack bars, swimming pools, and boat rentals) available from Memorial Day weekend to Labor Day. All state park day-use areas are open year-round, 8 A.M.–sunset, unless posted otherwise. All of Maryland's forests and parks are "trash-free"—

there are no trash receptacles in picnic or beach areas, and visitors are expected to pack out their own trash, a system that works surprisingly well. Because the terrain varies from park to park, the system offers a wide variety of outdoor activities, from picnicking, swimming, boating, hiking, and camping to whitewater rafting and mountain biking. (Boats must have current state registration.) In icy weather, many parks offer winter sports: boating, fishing, skating, sledding, cross-country skiing, and snowmobile trails. A number of parks also feature historical events and family-oriented activities throughout the year.

Maryland boasts a number of unusual state parks. St. Clement's Island (see *Southern Maryland* chapter) off St. Mary's County, offers pristine beaches accessible only by boat. Sideling Hill Exhibit Center, six miles west of Hancock (see *Western Maryland* chapter) and Calvert Cliffs State Park (see *Southern Maryland* chapter) offer unique natural geological features. Sideling Hill is on a mile-long, 340-foot-high section of exposed rock layers millions of years old; the Calvert Cliffs are made of 15-million-year-old fossils.

For general information on all Maryland state parks, call the State Forest and Park Service (877/620-8367) or visit its website (www.dnr.state.md.us).

Delaware features 14 state parks, so a park is within two hours of any point in the state. The parks offer a surprising variety of natural areas: ocean beaches, inland ponds, forests, rolling hills, and piedmont streams. Pea Patch is an island with Civil War significance (see *Upper Delaware* chapter); Cape Henlopen, Delaware Seashore, and Fenwick Island State Parks are all on the ocean; Killens Pond, Lums Pond, and Trap Pond State Parks are all freshwater impoundments (see *Lower Delaware* chapter). On top of all that, Killens Pond has a water park. The parks offer a number of activities, including camping, boat rentals, educational programs, hiking, surf fishing, sunbathing, clamming, crabbing, surfing, and swimming.

Delaware State Parks are largely self-funded and rely on user fees for about 75 percent of their operating and maintenance budget. Fees vary from park to park. Daily entrance fees are in effect on weekends in May, daily from Memorial Day to Labor Day, and weekends in September and October; season passes are available. For more Information, contact the Delaware Division of Parks and Recreation (302/739-4702, www.destateparks.com).

In 1994, the Delaware State Parks established the Carry In Carry Out Trash-Free Parks Program. Trash cans were removed from most areas, and visitors now take their trash with them when they leave, reducing the strain on limited resources and increasing the beauty of the parks.

Wildlife Management Areas and Refuges

Not all of Maryland's wild land is designated as state parkland. The State Forest and Park Service maintains 21 wildlife management areas for the purpose of conserving wildlife for sightseers and hunters. Though no facilities are offered, almost all of these areas are open to the public and accessible to hikers, horseback riders, snowmobilers, riders of all-terrain vehicles, and cross-country skiers. For information on management areas, call 877/620-8367 or visit www.dnr.state.md.us/publiclands.

Delaware's Bombay Hook National Wildlife Refuge and Prime Hook National Wildlife Refuge are bayfront areas administered by the U.S. Fish & Wildlife Service expressly for the preservation of native flora and fauna. Both provide ample opportunities for naturalists, bird-watchers, photographers, and casual observers to enjoy the unique beauty of Delaware's coastline. For further information, contact the U.S. Fish & Wildlife Service (Bombay Hook NWR, 2591 Whitehall Neck Rd., Smyrna, DE 19977, 302/653-9345).

Greenways

Delaware's Greenway and Trail Program, administered by the Division of Parks and Recreation, is a statewide initiative to preserve and protect corridors of open space. A greenway is a natural area of unbroken vegetation where recreation and conservation are the primary goals. Greenways wind along rivers and streams, skirt wetlands, and cross barrier beaches, hilltops, abandoned rail lines, fields, and forests. Some greenways are publicly owned; others are private. Some are for recreation, with biking and hiking trails; others protect a scenic view or wildlife habitat.

In spring 1996, Delaware's extensive Greenway and Trail Program was awarded the American Greenways DuPont Government Award, established by the DuPont Company in partnership with the National Geographic Society and the Conservation Fund to recognize businesses, nonprofit organizations, and government agencies that have been successful in creating greenways. Today, the state continues to add and enhance greenways, keeping urban areas green and the countryside open. Projects are detailed in individual destination chapters.

BOATING AND SAILING

The State of Maryland offers many opportunities for those who bring their own vessels. You can launch in fresh or saltwater and see hundreds of different plants and animals along Maryland's 4,360 miles of tidal shorelines. Some 17,000 miles of waterways, including 42 rivers, flow into the 1,726 square miles of the Chesapeake Bay. There are 623 square miles of inland water areas and 31 miles of Atlantic Ocean coastline.

All commercial or recreational power boats must be registered in Maryland if equipped with any kind of primary or auxiliary mechanical propulsion and used principally in Maryland. Boats registered with the U.S. Coast Guard are exempt. Licensing fees include excise tax equal to 5 percent of the purchase price of the vessel, motor, and accessories (excluding the trailer) or the current fair market value; a $5 title fee; and a $29 registration fee (vessels 16 feet in length or less, propelled by a motor of 7.5 horsepower or less, are exempt from the fee). The registration is valid for the calendar year in which it's issued plus the subsequent year. Boat registration is handled by the Maryland Department of Natural Resources Service Centers (Annapolis Metropolitan Area, 580 Taylor Ave., Annapolis, MD 21401, 410/260-3220; Central Maryland, 2 Bond St., Bel Air, MD 21014, 410/836-4550; Dundalk Service Center, 7701 Wise Ave., Baltimore, MD 21222, 410/284-1654; Eastern Maryland, 201 Baptist St. #22, Salisbury, MD 21801, 410/543-6700; East Central Maryland, 120 Broadway Ave., Centreville, MD 21617, 410/819-4100; Southern Maryland, 6904 Hallowing Point Rd., Prince Frederick, MD 20678, 410/535-3382; Western Maryland, 3 Pershing St., Rm. 103, Cumberland, MD 21502, 301/777-2134). You can download forms from www.dnr.state .md.us/boating/registration.

Central Maryland is all about the Chesapeake, and the bay is all about sailing (though there are also plenty of motor yachts on the water). Every town on the bay has a marina, and visitors who don't bring their own vessels can rent passenger space on a bewildering range of boat designs for anywhere from an hour to several days. The Chesapeake is also the home of boat-and-breakfasts—a sail combined with an overnight. Some of the most popular stops for pleasure boating enthusiasts (and best places to sightsee) are Solomons Island (see *Southern Maryland* chapter), Annapolis (see *Central Maryland* chapter), Rock Hall and Chestertown (see *Northern Maryland* chapter), and St. Michaels (see *Eastern Shore* chapter).

In Delaware, boat rentals are available at some state parks: Lums Pond, Killens Pond, Trap Pond, and Fenwick Island State Parks during the summer, as well as on weekends in May and September (weather permitting). A variety of vessels are available: rowboats, $6 per hour or $25 for an eight-hour period; canoes, $7 per hour; sailboats, $15 per hour; paddle boats, $7 per half hour or $9 per hour; water bikes, $6 per half hour or $8 per hour; and kayaks, $7 per hour/one person or $9 per hour/tandem.

The Indian River Marina (302/227-3071), part of Delaware National Seashore, is a state-owned facility that permits dockage for fees ranging from $25 per day to $3,360 per year.

CANOEING AND KAYAKING

The Potomac River is only partially navigable for small craft; certain areas, such as the river around Big Pool, are considered safe. A good place for information on the river is the Chesapeake & Ohio Canal National Historic Park. Maryland's other large rivers, among them the Susquehanna, Patapsco, Patuxent, and Pokomoke, are almost entirely navigable (the Pokomoke seems made for quiet paddling). Hundreds of smaller streams throughout the state provide adventure for canoeing enthusiasts, and Deep Creek Lake and Rocky Gap State Park (both in western Maryland) are indicative of the state's few but fine lakes. Many commercial riverside liveries rent canoes and kayaks. Exploring the marshy shoreline of the Chesapeake in a sea kayak is a particularly good way to see waterfowl and wildlife, particularly during seasonal migrations. While rounding a marsh on the Manokin River, not far from Princess Anne in Somerset County, I came upon 150 Canada geese taking a break on the water.

CRABBING AND CLAMMING

No license is required for those who love to play in the mud: Crabbing and clamming are available to anyone who wants to bait a trap or dig a hole anywhere along the marshes. Assawoman Bay and Isle of Wight Bay, both east of Ocean City, are popular spots. Blue crab, soft shells, conch, lobster, oysters, and clams are available for the taking at public beach areas in Delaware from May to December. The Division of Fish and Wildlife (301/739-3441, www.nmfs.gov) has regulations regarding minimum size, daily limits, and locations of approved areas; no license is required. The shores of Indian River and Rehoboth Bay are also popular locations.

CYCLING

Maryland comes close to paradise as a destination for road cyclists of all abilities. The state is laced with paved two-lane roads, and outside the Washington-Baltimore corridor, the roads see little traffic. Western Maryland offers hilly terrain and breathtaking farmland, lake, and stream views; southern Maryland and the Eastern Shore are both flat as a crab cake and provide the road cyclist with a wide variety of scenery, from fields of golden wheat to whispering marsh grasses. The water is never very far away. Southern Maryland and Kent County both publish bicycle-touring information from their respective tourism offices.

In Delaware, multi-use trails are available for biking in most state parks. This information can be found in the park map legends. Outside the park system, Delaware has many bicycle-friendly routes. The state publishes maps and information; contact the DELDOT Division of Planning (Bicycle/Pedestrian Coordinator, P.O. Box 778, Dover, DE 19903, 302/739-BIKE or 302/739-2453). For a free brochure of the Southern Delaware Heritage Trail, which includes historic towns, greenways, parks, rivers, shops, and lodging, call 800/357-1818.

FISHING

Fishing—freshwater, bay, and surf—is a consuming activity in Maryland. Freshwater species, often supplemented by state breeding programs, inhabit thousands of lakes, rivers, ponds, and streams. Nearly all of the state parks offer fishing opportunities. Choptank River Fishing Pier in Cambridge on the Eastern Shore (410/820-1668) offers two public piers. Surf fishing is available at Sandy Point State Park at the base of the Bay Bridge below Annapolis (see *Central Maryland* chapter), and Assateague State Park (see *Eastern Shore* chapter) has miles of ocean frontage.

Fishing is strictly controlled by the Maryland Department of Natural Resources. Licenses are required for anyone over the age of 16. Freshwater licenses cost roughly $12 for residents and $24 for nonresidents, and a trout stamp (allowing an angler to fish in catch-and-return trout management areas and to possess trout taken from nontidal waters) is an additional $7. A freshwater license allows an individual to fish in the fresh waters of Maryland from January 1 through December 31; a five-day nontidal license ($7) allows residents and non-residents to fish in the freshwaters of Maryland for five consecutive fishing days. Sportfishing (bay and surf) licenses run $11 for residents and $16 for nonresidents; a five-day Bay Sport license is available for $8. Head boats (fishing boats that charge by the head) include a boat license charge in their fees, so no additional license is required. For more information or to submit license applications, contact any DNR Service Center (in Annapolis, Cumberland, or Centreville) or the Maryland Department of Natural Resources (Licensing and Registration Service, 580 Taylor Ave., Tawes State Office Building/C-1, Annapolis, MD 21401, 410/260-8200). The DNR has an informative website, www.dnr.state.md.us/service/license.htm, and applications are available online.

In Delaware, anyone between 16 and 65 years of age is required to have a license to fish in tidal and/or nontidal waters—lakes, ponds, impoundments, and streams—in Delaware. A license may be obtained from the Delaware office of the Division of Fish and Wildlife (89 Kings Hwy., P.O. Box 1401, Dover, DE 19903, 302/739-3441, www.dnrec.state.de.us/fw/index.htm) or from more than 100 license agents (mostly sporting goods and hardware stores) throughout the state. All funds derived from the issuance of fishing licenses are dedicated to the purpose of matching and securing federal money allotted to Delaware under the provisions of the Federal Aid in Sport Fish Restoration Act. Together, these funds support projects for restoration, conservation, management, and enhancement of sport fish and the provisions for public use and benefit from these resources.

The state's freshwater species include four varieties of bass, two types of crappie, and two varieties each of pike, pickerel, salmon, muskellunge, sunfish, bluegill, perch, and pumpkinseed. Delaware's freshwater trout program is a self-supporting put-and-take fishery in selected streams in northern New Castle County. The fees paid for trout stamps are used to purchase trout from commercial hatcheries. Rainbow, brown, and/or brook trout are stocked in selected streams within two weeks of the spring opening date and for an additional period of time into the season. No fishing is permitted in any designated trout stream within two weeks of the opening day of spring trout season, which is the first Saturday in April. Trout stamps are available from license agents.

Most of Delaware's bay communities have beaches suitable for surf fishing, with proper state licensing. State park fishing beaches are available at Cape Henlopen, Fenwick Island, and Delaware Seashore; surf-fishing licenses are $55 for Delaware residents and $110 for nonresidents. Atlantic croaker, Atlantic sturgeon, bluefish, black sea bass, red drum, and scup are a few of the fish commonly caught.

Delaware State Parks also allow the use of licensed beach vehicles in strictly limited areas. Surf fishing vehicle permits are issued for the calendar year. These permits allow four-wheeled vehicle access to designated areas for the purpose of surf fishing. The permits cost $55 for residents and $110 for nonresidents.

Lewes is a center for sportfishing. Migratory oceanic species such as bluefin tuna, bigeye tuna, yellowfin tuna, true albacore, blackfin tuna, swordfish, billfish, and certain shark species, when caught in waters outside Delaware's jurisdiction (ocean waters farther than three miles offshore), are subject to federal regulations. For further information on federal regulations, call the National Marine Fisheries Service (301/713-2347 or 508/281-9260). A 24-hour information line is also available (301/713-1279 or 508/281-9305).

GOLF

Both states boast hundreds of public golf courses, with a heavy concentration on the Eastern Shore and Delaware near the beaches, and in Central and Western Maryland. Individual destination chapters list courses, facilities, and contact information.

HIKING

The 2,167-mile Appalachian Trail—the longest continuous footpath in the world—runs through Maryland, stretching from the Maryland-Virginia border through South Mountain State

Park (see *Western Maryland* chapter) to Washington Monument State Park (the trail passes next to the monument). The trail continues north through Greenbrier State Park up to Blue Ridge Summit in Pennsylvania and beyond. The trail is open to hikers and backpackers, and the Maryland portion is saturated with Civil War history. The Appalachian Trail Conference (ATC, P.O. Box 807, Harpers Ferry, VA 25425, 304/535-6331, www.atconf.org) is an umbrella organization that coordinates and oversees some 30 groups that maintain sections of the trail from Maine to Georgia. The organization publishes maps, a newsletter, and other information about the trail, and operates a store in Harpers Ferry, Virginia (799 Washington St.).

The American Discovery Trail (ADT, P.O. Box 20155, Washington, DC 20041-2155, 703/753-0149 or 800/663-2387, www.discovery trail.org), is a new breed of national trail: part city, part small town, part forest, part mountains, and part desert. Its 6,300 miles of connected multi-use trails stretch from Cape Henlopen State Park, Delaware, to Pt. Reyes National Seashore, California. The ADT incorporates trails designed for hiking and bicycle and equestrian use. The Maryland portion passes through the Eastern Shore over the Bay Bridge through Annapolis to Washington, D.C.

Though it lacks the length of the Appalachian Trail and ADT, the C&O Canal towpath (see *Western Maryland* chapter) is exceptional for hiking and biking. It begins in Washington, D.C., and follows the Potomac River to Cumberland, more than 100 miles to the east. Sights along the way include a French and Indian War site near Big Pool, Fort Frederick, considered the best-preserved pre–Revolutionary War stone fort in America. The C&O Canal is one of nine National Recreation Trails in Maryland designated for hikers, bikers, and backpackers by the rails-to-trails movement, which converts unused railroad corridors and canal paths to multi-use trails. For the most part, the towpath isn't paved, but it's an easy and level road.

Gunpowder Falls State Park (410/592-2897) north of Baltimore offers numerous scenic areas and over 100 miles of hiking trails. The park maintains the North Central rails-to-trails route for hikers, bikers, and equestrians; it extends 21 miles from Ashland to the Maryland-Pennsylvania border.

Ten of Delaware's state parks contain more than 80 miles of scenic trails. Delaware has also come up with an ingenious and fun hiking program called the Trail Challenge. Hikers who take the Trail Challenge cover almost 40 miles in 15 designated state park trails in a 12-month period. Those who complete the challenge win the Golden Boot Award, a distinctive patch, and a certificate. Hikers can acquire a Trail Challenge card through any Delaware State Park Office, or from Cultural and Recreational Services (89 Kings Hwy., Dover, 302/739-4143). Participants locate the trail punch station along each trail, and use the coded punch to mark the appropriate space on the card. If you miss the marker at any park, the park office can help out. State park trails in the Trail Challenge program are in Brandywine Creek, Fort Delaware/Port Penn, Lums Pond, White Clay Creek (all New Castle County); Killens Pond (Kent County); and Cape Henlopen, Delaware Seashore, Holts Landing, and Trap Pond (Sussex County).

HUNTING

The Maryland Department of Natural Resources also administers the state's hunting program through its Wildlife & Heritage Division (410/260-8540). Hunting is a time-honored tradition in Maryland, and related expenditures add millions of dollars to the state's coffers—about 95 percent of Maryland's state budget for wildlife programs comes from these sources. Revenues from hunting licenses and federal excise taxes on hunting equipment provide for the scientific investigation, protection, and management of wildlife. In a blazing example of enlightened self-interest, the hunting community is often the first to support and appreciate wildlife resources and the ecological principles upon which scientific wildlife management is based. Hunting promotes a personal desire to restore and improve wildlife habitat.

Among the game seasons available to hunters are migratory game bird, waterfowl, furbearers, forest game, upland game, deer (antlerless and antlered), and sika deer. All hunters must have licenses, and hunting licenses are valid from the date of issue to July 31, except the three-day nonresident license; the state offers a variety of licenses based on type of game and other factors. A Resident Basic License (about $30) allows you to hunt or trap all legal game in season except deer and waterfowl. A Harvest Information Program (HIP) permit is required to hunt all migratory game birds. Deer and waterfowl stamps may also be required for use with these licenses. Nonresidents (from outside the state) are required to present a valid ID and pay a fee of $90–150. This license allows nonresidents to hunt all legal game except waterfowl and deer during bow and muzzleloader seasons. Bow and Muzzleloader Stamps, as well as Waterfowl Stamps, may be purchased for use with this license. A license is also required for nonresidents to trap in Maryland. For more information, contact the DNR Wildlife & Heritage Division (Permits Coordinator, 580 Taylor Ave., E-1, Annapolis, MD 21401, 410/260-8200, www .dnr.state.md.us/service/license.htm). Applications are available online.

Stamps are similar to stamps in a passport: They allow a licensed hunter to approach a certain type of game or use a specified weapon. Among the stamps currently available for an extra charge are the Maryland Migratory Waterfowl Stamp, Federal Migratory Bird Hunting and Conservation Stamp, Deer Stamp, Bow Stamp, and Muzzleloader Stamp. Licenses and stamps are available by applying in person at any DNR Sport License Agent. Call any DNR Licensing and Registration Service Center (Annapolis Service Center, 580 Taylor Ave., P.O. Box 1869, Annapolis, MD 21404-1869, 410/260-3220; Western Service Center, 3 Pershing St., Rm. 103, Cumberland, MD 21502, 301/777-2134; East Central Service Center, 120 Broadway Ave., Rm. 207, Centreville, MD 21617, 410/758-5252) for the location of an agent near you, or visit the DNR online at www.dnr.state.md.us/service/netag2.html.

Federal Migratory Bird Hunting and Conservation Stamps are available at post offices and National Wildlife Refuges, or by calling 800/ STAMP24 (800/782-6724).

The Delaware Division of Fish and Wildlife also administers hunting in the two national refuges and several private tracts. A state license is required for all hunters; nonresident deer hunters must also purchase a permit, and all waterfowl hunters need state and federal duck stamps. Contract the DFW for current seasons and regulations.

SWIMMING, SURFING, AND PERSONAL WATERCRAFT

Freshwater swimming is available at dozens of parks around Maryland, among them Swallow Falls State Park (waters rush through a canyon over boulders—very popular and scenic), Rocky Gap (lake with beaches), and Cunningham Falls State Park (lake and streams) in the west. Several state parks offer public Olympic-sized swimming pools, as do larger municipalities. Point Lookout (see *Southern Maryland* chapter) and Sandy Point State Park (see *Central Maryland* chapter) offer bay beaches, as does Janes Island State Park (see *Eastern Shore* chapter). Assateague Island State Park on the Eastern Shore features ocean beaches for swimming and surfing.

Ocean City has its own surfing culture (the city has erected a statue in memory of a young local surfer). Though the waves will never rival Hawaii's, there are still plenty of good rides. Personal watercraft (also known as Jet-Skis) rentals are popular here, most often for use on the calmer waters of Assawoman Bay, on the west side of the peninsula. Personal watercraft are also used frequently on Deep Creek Lake in western Maryland. Equipment rentals are available in all areas.

Delaware's beach dunes are a fragile and constantly endangered ecostructure. Except for designated crossing areas, people, pets, and vehicles are to keep off dunes. Foot or vehicular traffic quickly kills the fragile dune grasses that stabilize the shifting sand.

Fourteen miles of ocean beaches at Cape

Henlopen, Delaware Seashore, and Fenwick Island State Parks offer guarded swimming and surfing away from the crowds of resort beaches. Delaware's beaches offer slightly calmer waves due to proximity to Delaware Bay, but swimming and wave-hopping will never go out of style. The ponds at Killens Pond, Trap Pond, and Lums Pond State Parks offer warm sand and beautiful scenery in a bucolic setting. The Water Park at Killens Pond State Park gives visitors a chance to slide down the tallest water slides in Kent County.

WINTER SPORTS
Because of Maryland's comparatively mild winters, most cold-weather activity takes place in the western part of the state.

Maryland's only downhill ski area, Wisp, is just north of Deep Creek Lake. Several additional downhill ski areas are just across the Pennsylvania border in the Laurel Highlands

south of Pittsburgh (Seven Springs, Hidden Valley, and Laurel Ridge State Park), and north of Hagerstown (Blue Knob State Park).

Herrington Manor State Park, not far from Wisp, offers cross-country skiing and snow-shoeing, with equipment rental. Nearby New Germany State Park also opens cross-country trails, and both parks have winter rental cabins. Ice fishing is also permitted (see *Western Maryland* chapter).

Deep Creek Lake State Park offers six miles of snowmobile trails in winter, and many other parks offer limited snowmobile trails.

Snowmobiles are permitted on designated state park trails with proper registration ($14 fee covers two years). Snowmobiles owned by nonresidents and covered by a valid registration in another county or state are exempt from this requirement. Registration does not grant permission for operation on any highway or on private property.

Conduct and Customs

CARRIAGES
Though it won't happen as often as in Pennsylvania, you'll occasionally come upon Amish families traveling by horse-drawn carriage. They don't drive on the interstates or highways, but they do use two-lane roads, so you're liable to encounter them anywhere in the state.

Carriages are impossible to miss; all carry red reflector triangles. In general, etiquette calls for automobile drivers to slow as they approach until a clear path for passing is available; then pass slowly—just fast enough to get around—and accelerate away, also slowly. You don't want to spook the horses; even though they're accustomed to cars, it's entirely possible to startle them.

ELECTRICAL APPLIANCES
The electrical current is the same as in the rest of the United States. It functions on 110 volts, 60 cycles of alternating current (AC). Appliances requiring the normal European voltage of 220 will not work.

LEGAL GAMBLING
Delaware has slots (video lottery terminals similar to Las Vegas's one-armed bandits) and simulcast racing only, no table games. Slot machines are only permitted in areas that had existing horse racing facilities when the law was passed to allow gambling. There are three slots locations: Dover Downs International Speedway and Slots (U.S. 13, one mile north of Dover, 302/674-4600), also home to two annual NASCAR races and harness racing; Midway Slots and Simulcast at the Delaware State Fair Grounds (U.S. 13, Harrington, 888/88-SLOTS or 888/887-5687) shows harness racing; and Delaware Park Racetrack and Slots (777 Delaware Park Blvd., Wilmington, 302/994-2521) presents thoroughbred racing.

LIQUOR LAWS
In Maryland, wine, liquor, and beer are served in bars, taverns, and most restaurants, but they are not available for takeout. All types of liquor

are sold in grocery and liquor stores. Though the state has a dozen wineries, distribution is tightly controlled and the selection in stores may be limited—the best way to sample it is to visit the winery (they're almost all located in north-central Maryland).

In Delaware, wine, liquor, and beer are served in bars, taverns, and most restaurants, but are not available for takeout. Beer and alcohol are sold only in privately owned liquor stores, not in groceries or convenience stores. Beer and alcohol are not sold on Sundays, and Delaware has an open container law (you can't drink on the street like you can in New Orleans). You have to be 21 to drink in both states.

POLICE

The interstates are regularly patrolled, and main highways also get a fair share of police pass-throughs. Baltimore is a major American city whose police force and meter readers are on par with those of similar-sized municipalities. Suburbs along the entire Baltimore–Washington, D.C., corridor are regularly patrolled. One thing to remember: Even in the smallest town, a good portion of municipal income is derived from parking fines, and the days of $2 parking tickets are behind us. Though Maryland's rural areas seem far removed from the hustle and bustle, they are eminently civilized; houses are dotted throughout the landscape. Small towns may seem quite spread out, but the jurisdictions cover a lot of territory; law enforcement is often represented by part-time police or volunteers, who are occasionally overeager to nab out-of-staters, speeders, and other scofflaws. When nearing a town of any size, slow down and be careful.

Wilmington has a large municipal police force, including beat cops, who cover the downtown area on foot. Most of the city is totally carefree, but some neighborhoods are iffy, and others downright dangerous. Make sure you know where you're going, particularly at night; the downtown area used to look like a ghost town after dark, but that's changing.

TIME ZONES, BUSINESS HOURS, AND SALES TAX

Maryland and Delaware are in the Eastern Standard Time zone. In the larger cities, merchants keep longer hours and days, but elsewhere, food, clothing, and general-goods stores are normally open Mon.–Sat. 10 A.M.–6 P.M. Many shops close on Sunday, and those that cater primarily to tourists often shorten their hours (or close entirely, like Rehoboth Beach and Ocean City) during the winter months. Hotels, inns, and bed-and-breakfasts are generally open daily year-round. Some restaurants are open daily, but most close one day a week, often Sunday, Monday, or Tuesday. Many restaurants open early, around 6 A.M., and stop serving at 10 P.M.

Maryland state sales tax is 5 percent. Restaurants and hotels usually charge a premium tax over the state tax, totaling an average of 11 percent. Delaware has NO sales tax, but does require a hotel tax of 8 percent.

TIPPING

On a restaurant bill, a 15 percent tip is standard; leave 20 percent or more to reward outstanding service. Taxi drivers typically receive 15 percent of the total bill, and airport porters and bellhops about $1 per bag. It's customary to leave $5 per person in a hotel room for an exceptionally clean room.

WEIGHTS AND MEASURES

The United States does not use the metric system. Instead, the country measures distance in inches, feet, yards, and miles (see the conversion table at the back of this book). In the United States, dry weights are measured in ounces and pounds, and liquid weights in ounces, pints, quarts, and gallons. Temperature is measured using the Fahrenheit, not the Celsius, scale.

WORSHIP MEETINGS

If you have an interest in attending services in an unfamiliar religious tradition, use the following general guidelines. Methodist, Lutheran, and Catholic churches are open to visitors. In order to participate in the sharing of bread and wine at a Catholic church, however, you must be a baptized Catholic and recently confessed. Since the Catholic mass is highly ritualized, it's a good idea to sit in the back, so you won't end up standing when everyone else kneels, etc. Quakers welcome everyone to their worship meetings and are quite tolerant in general. Mennonites are a measure *more* welcoming—missionary work plays a significant part in their beliefs. Old Order Amish meetings are closed to everyone except members (unless you know someone in the community).

Tips for Travelers

Though urban areas pose the usual threats to visitors traveling alone, seniors, students, and gay and lesbian travelers will find few difficulties along the road in either Maryland or Delaware. City dwellers are ethnically mixed, but the rural population tends to be of white, western European origin. In spite of this, locals are generally blasé about those who appear "different" (Washington, D.C., brings in plenty of international visitors). Helpful and friendly people can be found everywhere in the state.

ACCESS FOR TRAVELERS WITH DISABILITIES

Tourism-oriented Baltimore offers advantages and facilities for travelers with challenges, including wheelchair access and services for hearing- and vision-impaired visitors. Outside the city's boundaries, however, access and services are limited. Several state parks in Maryland offer handicapped-accessible facilities; a complete list is available on the Maryland DNR website (www.dnr.state.md.us/accessforall). The **Maryland Relay Service** (MRS, www.mdrelay.org) is a free statewide phone service that links standard voice telephones with text-telephone (TTY) users. The access number is 771 in Maryland, 800/201-7165 for the voice line, or 800/669-0865 TTY.

The Delaware Relay Service (access 711 or 800/232-5460 TTY) links standard telephones with text-telephone users.

The Society for Accessible Travel and Hospitality (212/447-7284, www.sath.org, annual membership fees: $45 adults, $30 seniors and students) offers a wealth of travel resources for all types of disabilities and informed recommendations on destinations.

TRAVELING WITH CHILDREN

All trips around the bay and in Delaware are highly adaptable for the entire family, depending on age. Small children can enjoy three to four hours with the play-crazy charms of Port Discovery, three hours at the aquarium, and another two hours at the zoo in Baltimore. A beach vacation combined with camping in the Twin Beaches (Chesapeake Beach and North Beach) area of Southern Maryland or in the Delaware Beaches or Ocean City is another good choice, permitting little ones to spend a few hours each day building sandcastles on the beach and splashing in the water. All of the above destinations offer lodging specials to families.

Older children may enjoy a vacation that combines a higher level of activity—cycling or hiking or miniature golf—with camping or a beach visit. Ocean City and Rehoboth Beach are likely to interest them, as are Delaware Seashore State Park in Delaware and Point Lookout and Deep Creek lake in Maryland.

WOMEN TRAVELING ALONE

As you might expect, I travel alone a lot to research this book and others. I've been to every corner of Maryland and Delaware and have never encountered a problem, but I always follow a few simple rules, especially in urban areas. Every city has "no-fly" zones that no stranger should venture into—but fortunately, most tourist attractions are in highly populated areas.

If I'm out at night on foot, I always stick to well-lighted areas with lots of people. When the destination is more than a block or two from my lodging, I take a taxi—even if I have my own vehicle (you may have to park quite a distance from your destination).

Lone travelers often find staying at a B&B a comfortable choice; the innkeepers can recommend restaurants and give directions. Lunch out isn't a problem, but if eating alone in a fancy restaurant for dinner isn't on your menu, take a book and go when the restaurant opens at 5 or 5:30 P.M. (they may have early bird specials!), or buy a sandwich and enjoy an evening at your lodging. If you fancy a drink, hotel bars are usually good choices.

During the day, the worst you might encounter is an aggressive panhandler or an ever vigilant pickpocket (they love crowded tourist areas and beaches). I usually carry $20 in cash in my wallet, plus one credit card and another bill somewhere on my person, but I use credit cards for just about everything. Make sure you have a copy of your cards (front and back) at your lodging in case you need to make that call.

In rural areas, none of these warnings apply, and most people are extremely friendly and helpful. One last thing: Never travel with anything you can't stand to lose or replace.

SENIOR TRAVELERS

Elders and those with impaired mobility would most enjoy easy access to a variety of sites in a small area—Baltimore is the top choice, with its wealth of public transportation, multitude of interests, and good restaurants. Wilmington and the Brandywine Valley are more spread out, but the du Pont properties all offer some kind of motorized tour. Driving tours and fishing on party boats are additional suggestions.

GAY AND LESBIAN TRAVELERS

In the big cities, there's very little prejudice against same-sex couples and families. Baltimore and Wilmington have large gay and lesbian populations, as does Rehoboth Beach. Rural areas really aren't that different; most innkeepers, hoteliers, and restaurateurs welcome everyone's business. If you'd prefer more specialized recommendations, Orbitz, one of the biggest travel providers on the internet has its own specialty service (www.orbitz.com/gaytravel). The Gay and Lesbian travel center (www.gayjourney.com) is an excellent resource. Another service, Gaymart (gaymart.com/5persorg/6city/targ) lists accommodations and more by state (unfortunately, Maryland isn't listed there—yet).

Several B&Bs listed in this book welcome gay and lesbian travelers: the William Page Inn Bed & Breakfast, Annapolis; Celie's Waterfront Inn, Mount Vernon Hotel, and the Admiral Fell Inn, Baltimore; and the Robert Morris Inn, Oxford.

Health and Safety

Falling ill in a strange place can happen to anyone, but fear shouldn't prevent visitors from enjoying the charms of Maryland and Delaware. Travelers who take regular medication should bring along enough to cover their expected stay, though most prescriptions are readily available throughout the state.

Baltimore, Ocean City, Frederick, Wilmington, Dover, the Rehoboth area, and towns in the Washington, D.C., gateway all have excellent hospitals, pharmacies, and emergency medical services, extensive police services, and fire stations. Firefighters are frequently trained in emergency medical procedures. Any of these services are only minutes away by phone (dial 911 in case of emergency, and the appropriate agency will respond, whether with a police offer or an ambulance for transport to a hospital). Hospitals often require some form of assurance of payment upon admittance, usually medical insurance billable in the United States, cash, or credit cards.

Police and fire services are free to everyone. Street crime is more common in the urban ar-

LYME DISEASE LOOKOUT

During years with mild winters, insect populations that are normally depleted by cold explode in the spring and summer. One of the most unpleasant is the deer tick, a tiny (pinhead-sized) black bloodsucker that can cause health problems a million times bigger than itself.

When a deer tick has managed to burrow into a host (that's some unlucky mammal, possibly you) for more than 15 hours, during the blood extraction process he will expel bacteria into the host's bloodstream. The bacteria, which can be one or a combination of hundreds of strains, may result in Lyme disease. Most people don't even realize that a tick is attached to them, as there's no pain or itching, and the tick drops off by itself in about three days.

Lyme disease manifests in several ways. Most victims experience flu-like symptoms – headache, nausea, muscle or joint pain – about three days after the initial infection. It's easy to mistake this for a bout of food poisoning, as it usually lasts less than 12 hours, then disappears. During the next few days, only about a third of all victims experience a telltale "bull's-eye rash," a red center with a red circle around it that can occur anyplace on the body (and sometimes in several places). About three weeks after the initial infection, victims begin to develop arthritis symptoms, usually on one side. The pain is constant, sometimes moves from joint to joint, and may appear to be muscle or tendon strain that just doesn't go away. This is accompanied by severe fatigue and, as time passes, depression, mental confusion, forgetfulness, and other rashes. It doesn't get better by itself.

Lyme disease is supposedly completely treatable with antibiotics, and the sooner treatment begins after infection, the more effective and complete the recovery. However, the disease is often ignored and frequently misdiagnosed; to complicate matters, medical experts disagree on length and type of treatment. There are blood and urine tests that vary greatly in effectiveness – at best, the most effective test can only identify a few different strains of the many possible strains of bacteria.

If you even suspect you've been infected, insist on immediate treatment. Keep the tick if you have it (it can be tested), but keep in mind that a percentage of people who are infected don't register on a blood test or have a bull's-eye rash. Experts recommend 21 to 90 days of doxycycline, 100 mg two to three times per day (30 days is the average, and most victims don't experience a relapse after this dose and duration). Chronic Lyme disease – usually misdiagnosed or untreated for months or years after an initial infection – requires more intensive and longer therapy. Some people report relief from the use of traditional Chinese medicine (herbs), acupuncture, and energy-movement touch therapies such as Jin Shin Jyutsu.

The best offense is a good defense. When hiking in wooded areas with long grasses (a favorite tick hangout), wear long pants – preferably light in color – tucked into your socks. Long-sleeved, cuffed shirts are also good, but always check exposed skin by sight and by running your hand over your skin (you may not see them, but you can feel them). Don't forget to check your face and hair. Not all ticks are dangerous, just as not all mosquitoes carry malaria – but when it comes to Lyme disease, it's better to be safe than sorry.

For additional information on Lyme disease, go to www.lymealliance.org.

---

eas—pickpocket theft, car break-ins, and muggings are the crimes most reported by visitors. Baltimore makes major efforts to educate and protect travelers. The usual rules apply: Leave the 24-karat dog collar at home, and don't use large-denomination paper money as origami or stroll aimlessly in questionable neighborhoods—leave that to the police decoys. With the excep-

tion of Wilmington, Delaware is supremely safe for visitors. Wilmington suffers from the usual woes of a big city, but crime against visitors is still a non-issue. Even so, the old rules apply: Know where you're going and how to get back, and leave the Hope diamond in the safe.

Crime against visitors in smaller cities is virtually unknown, and the villages and rural areas are quite safe. Occasional vandalism on parked cars in state park parking lots has been reported, however, so make sure everything is in the trunk and out of sight.

As the town size decreases, so does the number of health and safety services. Cities with populations of more than 1,000 are minimally equipped with small police and firefighting forces, and a clinic that will handle emergency health problems. In villages and rural areas of less than 1,000, these services are provided by visiting medical personnel and volunteer police and firefighters. The dangers of snakebite, bear or wildcat maulings, tick bites, and other wildlife-encounter indignities are negligible outside the more isolated hiking trails. Use the emergency procedures outlined below to get help.

Highway Patrol cars are frequently seen on the interstates and highways of more than two lanes, but are seldom seen on the millions of miles of two-lane roads that net the two states—a boon to those who trifle with speed limits, but a problem for those who are lost or have suffered a car breakdown. Fortunately, there's usually some kind of dwelling within walking distance if an emergency occurs. People are remarkably helpful, but respect their privacy. Knock on the door, then step away so they can get a good look at you. Be prepared to ask your questions through the door, and request that they call the emergency service for you. Sometimes, you'll be invited in for coffee and cake.

Emergency Services

In any of the larger cities and towns, police and medical emergency services can be reached by dialing 911 (there is no charge for the call if you make it from a public phone). Much of the state is rural and the towns and villages may be far between, however, so a 911 call may not get a response. In that case, call the operator (dial "0") for the number of a local clinic and park or police authorities. State parks are usually staffed full-time during the day, and an office on the premises will dispatch necessary help.

In addition, many police departments monitor CB Emergency Channel 9, in case you're on the road and have citizens band radio.

Information and Services

MONEY
Currency

U.S. paper currency is all the same size, and most of the bills are the same color, too. If you're not acquainted with it, you would be well advised to familiarize yourself with the common denominations to avoid making expensive mistakes. Paper currency (bills) comes in denominations of $1, $2 (uncommon), $5, $10, $20, $50, and $100. Bills larger than $100 are not in common usage. There are presently two different editions of $5, $10, $20, $50, and $100 bills in circulation. They both bear portraits of the same people, but older bills have "little heads"—smaller portraits—and new bills have "big heads with a ghost"—a shadow portrait on the right-hand side that shows when held up to the light. Newer versions of bills feature colored ink and other anti-counterfeiting measures.

Coins in circulation come in denominations of one cent (called a penny, it's 1/100 of $1), five cents (a nickel), 10 cents (a dime), 25 cents (a quarter), 50 cents (a half-dollar, rarely used), and $1 (called a Sacajawea dollar, gold in color, rarely used). Quarters released since 1999 feature various designs on the back that honor the 50 states.

ATMs

Maryland generally participates in all the benefits and conveniences of modern life, including automated teller machines (ATMs) and instant credit-card approval. However, a vast majority of Maryland is rural, and you will find that many of the state's smaller settlements and villages don't have banks or ATMs and won't accept payment by personal check. For this reason, you should carry a reasonable

HORSEMAN ON THE QUARTER

When the U.S. government decided to issue quarters with a design chosen by each state on the back, Delaware was, naturally, first. But a lot of people were confused by the charging horseman chosen as the First State's symbol, and the name "Caesar Rodney" stamped below the image didn't help (many thought it was Paul Revere – oops, different state). Actually, Mr. Rodney was instrumental in making the First State first. Unfortunately, there are no true representations of Rodney – his face was apparently deformed by disease or injury, and he never allowed his image to be captured for posterity.

Caesar Rodney inherited his father's large Delaware estate and served as a member of the colonial legislature for 17 years, rising to the position of Speaker of the Assembly. He was an organizer of the Continental Congress, on which he served for two years.

On July 2, 1776, gathered delegates to the Continental Congress were locked in controversy as to whether to create the United States and break with Britain or remain loyal. As the vote neared, key Delaware players Thomas McKean and George Read stood on opposite sides of the issue; McKean favored independence and Read didn't. Though desperately ill and unable to attend the initial debates in Philadelphia, Caesar Rodney rode from his home in Sussex Country through "thunder and rain," as the legend goes, all the way to the City of Brotherly Love to cast the deciding vote for independence and statehood. As a result of his speedy return to Congress, the Delaware delegation was able to vote two to one for the adoption of the Declaration of Independence, thus making adoption by the 13 colonies unanimous. Rodney signed the Declaration and was commander of the Delaware militia when British troops marched through Delaware and occupied Wilmington in late 1777. He was elected president (governor) of Delaware the following year, serving until 1781. He died three years later.

To impress your friends while showing off your state quarter collection, you might want to reel off the original 13 colonies in order of statehood: Delaware, Pennsylvania, New Jersey, Georgia, Connecticut, Massachusetts, Maryland, South Carolina, New Hampshire, Virginia, New York, North Carolina, and Rhode Island. By the War of 1812, Vermont and Kentucky had been admitted to the Union, and the flag that inspired Francis Scott Key was emblazoned with 15 stars.

amount of cash (enough for a room and food) when heading to the hinterlands. A rule of thumb: If a town has a stoplight, it probably has a bank branch and possibly an ATM. Almost all ATMs are equipped to handle Cirrus and other bank cash-transfer requests.

COMMUNICATIONS AND MEDIA
Newspapers

Maryland has been a journalism pioneer since the colonial period. Beginning in 1727 with the *Maryland Gazette* of Annapolis, newspapers and printing developed rapidly during the Revolution. Today, more than 50 towns publish newspapers, some full of local merchants' ads and the latest high-school basket-ball victories. The newspaper with the greatest readership and influence in the state is the *Baltimore Sun,* established in 1837. Circulation for its daily and evening editions exceeds 170,000 each, and the paper's Sunday readership is more than 300,000. Also widely read is the award-winning *Washington Post.* Both Washington, D.C., and Baltimore also boast wide selections of specialized, alternative, and free papers.

Delaware has several local newspapers and two daily newspapers: the *Delaware State News,* published in the state capital of Dover, and the *News-Journal,* published in Wilmington. Newspapers and broadcast media are limited to local news, with the exception of a public television channel based in Wilmington.

Magazines

Baltimore is a glossy "city" monthly magazine that focuses on local food, fads, and fashion. The articles are well written and fun, and the restaurant review section in the back of each issue is informative. Call 800/365-2808 for subscription information, or check the magazine out online at www.baltimoremag.com.

Tidewater Times was established in 1952 as a specialized monthly magazine aimed at visitors, prospective land buyers, and others for whom the Eastern Shore had special allure. The articles are quite good. For rate or subscription information, contact the paper directly (P.O. Box 1141, Easton, MD 21601, 410/226-0422, www.tidewatertimes.com).

Mid-Atlantic is published 10 times a year, with three annual guides. It's a slick and well-illustrated contemporary magazine that covers the entire region. For subscription information, call 800/777-0999.

Radio and Television

Radio and television are dominated by the centers of mass media in the area, Baltimore and Washington, D.C.

MAPS AND TOURIST INFORMATION
Maps and Directions

Maryland and Delaware mark roads and streets well, with few exceptions—it's a lot harder to get lost here than in, say, Pennsylvania. Maryland Tourism sends a Maryland Transportation Services map along with its information packet, and other maps, such as *Scenic Routes,* are available. The map the state provides is not perfect: A few of the back roads that were marked "paved" weren't. An auto club map (AAA), though not quite as detailed, proved to be quite accurate. If you're planning on car-touring in any of the rural counties, a local map is highly recommended—they can often be acquired through the county tourism office before your trip, or at a gas station while on the road.

Tourist Information

The **Maryland Office of Tourism** (217 E. Redwood St., Baltimore, MD 21298, 800/462-9443, www.mdisfun.org) is stocked with brochures on every part of the state, and you can talk with a friendly and knowledgeable volunteer if you have questions. The "starter" book, *Destination Maryland,* outlines the state's attractions. Several websites offer information for visitors: www.maryland.com and http://delmarweb.com/maryland/travel.html are two good ones.

The Department of Natural Resources (580 Taylor Ave., E-3, Annapolis, MD 21401, 410/974-3771 or 800/830-3974, www.dnr.state.md.us/index.html) publishes a free *Maryland State Forests and Parks Guide* that includes general information on all state park and forest facilities, plus individual phone numbers for more detailed maps and reservations.

The **Delaware Tourism Office** (99 Kings Hwy., P.O. Box 1401, Dover, DE 19903, 302/739-4271 or 866/284-7483, www.visitdelaware.com) can send out a comprehensive travel packet and answer your general questions. Call the office directly or visit one of the many walking information centers: Delaware Memorial Bridge (I-295), Greater Wilmington Convention & Visitors Bureau Center (100 S. 10 St., Ste. 20, Wilmington), I-95 Visitor Center (I-95, between Exit 1 and Exit 3), or the New Castle Court House (Delaware Street, Old New Castle). Three regional offices serve different parts of the state: Northern Delaware information is found at Greater Wilmington Convention & Visitors Bureau (302/652-4088 or 800/422-1181); Central Delaware, Kent County Convention & Visitors Bureau (302/734-1736 or 800/233-5368), and southern Delaware, Sussex County Convention & Tourism Commission (302/856-1818 or 800/357-1818).

International visitors may want to contact the **Delaware Council for International Visitors** (910 Gilpin Ave., P.O. Box 831, Wilmington, DE 19899, 302/656-9928) with additional questions. Each county has its own tourism office (listed under each county).

State Park information is available from the **Delaware Division of Parks and Recreation** (302/739-4702, www.destateparks.com).

RESOURCES

Suggested Reading

ARTS AND CRAFTS

Bethke, R. and J. Camper. *Americana Crafted: Jehu Camper, Delaware Whittler.* Jackson, MS: University Press of Mississippi, 1995. All about whittlin' and the constructed wooden folk art of Jehu Camper. Delaware Art Museum. *American Illustration Collection of the Delaware Art Museum.* Wilmington, DE: Delaware Art Museum, 1991. A broad and varied look at the work of local illustrators.

Delaware Art Museum. *Wondrous Strange.* Wilmington, DE: Bulfinch Press, 1998. This illustrated book showcases the work of Delaware's best-known illustrators and painters— Howard Pyle, N. C. Wyeth, Andrew Wyeth, and James Wyeth.

Fenimore, D., R. Trent, and E. Fowble. *Eye for Excellence: Masterworks from Winterthur.* Winterthur, DE: Winterthur Museum Press, 1997. When only the best will do.

DESCRIPTION AND TRAVEL

Chase, H., ed. *In Their Footsteps.* New York: Henry Holt and Co., 1992. Chase, the editor of *American Visions* magazine, compiled this book of black heritage sites all over the United States.

Corddry, M. and E. Corddry. *City on the Sand: Ocean City and the People Who Built It.* Centreville, MD: Tidewater Publishing, 1991. An illustrated history of the resort.

Gallagher, C., ed. *Antietam: Essays on the 1862 Maryland Campaign.* Kent, OH: Kent State University Press, 1989. This well-received series of short pieces from different sources covers Civil War history in depth. Gallagher also edited another series of essays in 1999 *(The Antietam Campaign),* published by University of North Carolina Press.

Hanna, J. *Tales from Delaware Bay.* Salisbury, MD: Cherokee Books, 2000. Crabbing, boating, and life on the water—watermen tell the stories of their lives in their own words.

High, Mike, *The C&O Canal Companion.* Baltimore, MD: Johns Hopkins University Press, 1997. A definitive and well-written guide to C&O Canal National Historical Park history, points of interest, and recreation.

Horton, T. *An Island Out of Time.* New York: Vintage Books, 1997. Tom Horton, an environmental writer for the *Baltimore Sun,* moved his family to Smith Island for two years. This is an affectionate memoir of their stay.

Sherwood, J. *Maryland's Vanishing Lives.* Baltimore, MD: Johns Hopkins University Press, 1995. These short essays profile people who are unique to the Tidewater by virtue of their occupations, such as a bridge operator and a teacher in a one-room school. With the growth of the region, many of these jobs are disappearing, and with them a way of life.

Simon, D. and E. Burns. *The Corner: A Year in the Life of an Inner-City Neighborhood.* New York: Broadway Books, 2000. Guess which inner city? If the bucolic countryside has lost its charm, try this rough-edged true tale of Baltimore's seamier side. HBO based a TV special on this book.

Turner, W. *Chesapeake Boyhood: Memoirs of a Farm Boy.* Baltimore, MD: Johns Hopkins University Press, 1997. It was a different world in the 1940s and '50s, and this good storyteller spins a warm and entertaining tale of life on a Tidewater farm.

Warner, W. *Beautiful Swimmers.* New York: Little Brown/Back Bay Books, 1999. A lovely "little" book that's an excellent companion to travels in Talbot County. The title refers, of course, to blue crabs.

FICTION

Barth, J, and M. Johnston. *Tidewater Tales.* Baltimore, MD: Johns Hopkins University Press, 1997. Maryland's most famous contemporary author, John Barth has based a number of his novels on his life on the Chesapeake. This fictional family drama unfolds in a series of stories about the Tidewater.

Cherry, L. *Flute's Journey—the Life of a Wood Thrush.* New York: Harcourt Brace & Co, 1999. An entertaining and educational book for children about the challenges facing wildlife in modern times. Flute, a wood thrush, faces habitat loss and food shortages in his search to start his own family. The book is based on an endangered old-growth forest in Maryland that Ms. Cherry, working with others, managed to save.

Michener, J. *Chesapeake.* New York: Fawcett Books, 1990. The classic story of history on the bay, starting from pre-colonial times. It's big, and it slows down a bit here and there, but Michener did his homework, so it's a good read for history and adventure buffs.

FOOD

Junior League of Baltimore. *Hunt to Harbor: A Maryland Cookbook.* Baltimore, MD: Perry Publishing, 1996. This is the real thing, Hon—straight from the horsey set's mouth. It features all sorts of general recipes, plus "Ethnic Festival Menus."

Shields, J. *Chesapeake Bay Cooking with John Shields.* New York: Broadway Books, 1998. This is the companion book to John Shields' popular TV program of the same name. You'll find ham pâté and beaten biscuits, in addition to pan-fried chicken and seafood galore.

HISTORY

Bready, J. *Baseball in Baltimore: The First 100 Years.* Baltimore, MD: Johns Hopkins University Press, 1998. Covering 1859 to 1954 (when Baltimore returned to the major leagues), Bready unearths enough diamond trivia to satisfy the most ardent fan. Did you know that one Baltimore franchise won three Negro League titles?

Dickens, C. *American Notes.* New York: St. Martin's Press, 1985. Charles Dickens' record of his travels across the United States, 1840–1842.

Fetzer, D., B. Mowday, and L. Jennings. *Unlikely Allies: Fort Delaware's Prison Community in the Civil War.* Mechanicsburg, PA: Stackpole Books, 2000. This "how to run a prison right" guide takes a look at Pea Patch Island during the conflict. Dale Fetzer is one of the park's living history guides—he not only researched his subject, but also plays the part of the enlightened prison commandant several days a week.

McElvey, K. *Early Black Dorchester, 1775–1870.* This scholarly research paper is a private publication and may be ordered by calling 800/521-0600 and asking for #9133192, 1998. The paper is an excellent reference source for anyone interested in Harriet Tubman and the lives of slaves in the colonies.

Rouse, P. *The Great Wagon Road: From Philadelphia to the South.* New York: McGraw-Hill, 1973. A kaleidoscopic picture of colonial times, when it was, as Rouse quotes, "a great life for dogs and men, but... hell on women and steers."

Shivers, F. *Maryland Wits and Baltimore Bards: A Literary History.* Baltimore, MD: Johns Hopkins University Press, 1998. The gang's all here. Contemporary authors John Barth and Adrienne Rich put in a word or two as Mr. Shivers chronicles the state's literary luminaries—among them E. A. Poe and F. Scott Fitzgerald.

Weslager, C. *The Delaware Indians: A History.* Piscataway, NJ: Rutgers University Press, 1990. Despite the author's odd choice to reference the Lenni Lenape by the tribe's European name, Weslager's book is generally perceived as quite accurate. Until we see a history written by tribe members, this will have to do.

MARYLAND-DELAWARE PERSONAGES

Banks, R. *Cloudsplitter.* New York: HarperCollins, 1999. A best-selling fictional account of John Brown's life, written from the point of view of his atheist son and companion, Owen (several of Brown's sons and daughters followed him to Maryland for the Harpers Ferry rebellion).

Bradford, S. *Harriet: The Moses of Her People.* Applewood Books, 1994. This inspiring classic was written while Harriet Tubman was alive. Her vision of freedom is shown from her own deeply spiritual perspective.

Colby, G. *Du Pont Dynasty: Behind the Nylon Curtain.* New York: Lyle Stuart, 1984. This is a muckraking look at the history and dealings of the Dupont clan—you can be sure that Mr. Colby never did lunch in Delaware again after this book.

Oates, S. *A Woman of Valor: Clara Barton and the Civil War.* New York: Free Press, 1995. Though this book covers only Ms. Barton's Civil War years, it uses many quotes from her personal correspondence to bring the era to life.

Olds, B. *Raising Holy Hell.* New York: Penguin, 1997. Another account of John Brown's life, this time told through a pastiche of journal excerpts, news articles, and popular contemporary songs.

Internet Resources

Most of these websites will link to many other points of interest:

HISTORY

The Chesapeake Bay Bolide
http://woodshole.er.usgs.gov/epubs/bolide

The U.S. Geological Survey explores the bolide (big crash from a celestial object faster than a speeding bullet—no kidding, that's the definition) that created the Chesapeake Bay.

Library of Congress
www.memory.loc.gov

Wonderful site from the Library of Congress with selected Civil War photographs.

MEDIA

Baltimore Sun
www.sunspot.net

The award-winning newspaper online.

Chesapeake Bay Magazine
www.cbmmag.net
Glossy and full of interesting articles of Maryland life.

IN AND AROUND CHESAPEAKE BAY

BayDreaming.com
www.baydreaming.com
Features an excellent list of marinas and boating facilities, plus tips on fishing and general information on the bay.

The Bay Guide
www.thebayguide.com
A site by boaters for boaters.

U.S. Department of Fish and Wildlife, Maryland
www.fws.gov/northeast/md.htm

TheChesapeakeBay.com
www.thechesapeakebay.com
Calendar for bay events and general articles on the Chesapeake.

Chesapeake Bay Gateways Network
www.baygateways.net
Offers links to all the public access parks around the bay, plus additional information, articles, and a calendar.

CONSERVATION ORGANIZATIONS

Chesapeake Bay Foundation
www.cbf.org
The largest and best known.

Alliance for the Chesapeake Bay
www.acb-online.org
The ACB offers guided trips, as well as online information.

GENERAL INFORMATION

Maryland

Visit Maryland
www.mdisfun.org
Maryland's official tourism website.

Maryland's State Forest and Park Service
www.dnr.state.md.us
Information on all state parks, camping, and more, plus links to boating and fishing license information and forms.

Delaware

Visit Delaware
www.visitdelaware.com
Delaware's official tourism website.

Delaware State Parks
www.destateparks.com/index.asp
Guide to state parks, greenways, and trails, plus camping information and trail updates.

TOWNS AND PLACES OF INTEREST

Maryland

Baltimore
www.baltimore.org

Annapolis
www.visit-annapolis.org

Montgomery County
www.cvbmontco.com

Southern Maryland
www.somd.com
A good general website for the region.

Calvert County
www.co.cal.md.us

Solomons Island
http://sba.solomons.md.us
The village and surrounding area.

Western Maryland
www.visitwesternmaryland.com

Havre de Grace
www.hdgtourism.com

Chestertown
www.chestertown.co

St. Michael's
www.stmichaelsmd.org

Salisbury
www.salisburymd.com

Ocean City
www.oc0cean.com

Delaware

Wilmington
www.visitwilmingtonde.com
Site for the city of Wilmington and the surrounding Brandywine Valley.

Southern Delaware
www.beach-fun.com
Rehoboth Beach and Dewey Beach share this website for fun in the sun in southern Delaware.

Index

www.moon.com

For helpful advice on planning a trip, visit www.moon.com
for the **TRAVEL PLANNER** and get access to useful travel
strategies and valuable information about great places to
visit. When you travel with Moon, expect an experience that is
uncommon and truly unique.

 HANDBOOKS | METRO | OUTDOORS | LIVING ABROAD

MAP SYMBOLS

▭▭▭	Expressway	C	Highlight	✗	Airfield	⚲	Golf Course
▭▭▭	Primary Road	○	City/Town	✈	Airport	P	Parking Area
▭▭▭	Secondary Road	◉	State Capital	▲	Mountain	▰	Archaeological Site
▭▭▭	Unpaved Road	⊛	National Capital	✦	Unique Natural Feature	⛪	Church
-------	Trail	★	Point of Interest			⛽	Gas Station
·············	Ferry	•	Accommodation	⚑	Waterfall		Glacier
＋＋＋	Railroad	▼	Restaurant/Bar	▲	Park		Mangrove
▭▭▭	Pedestrian Walkway	▪	Other Location	⊓	Trailhead		Reef
▣▣▣	Stairs	▲	Campground	✗	Skiing Area		Swamp

CONVERSION TABLES

°C = (°F - 32) / 1.8
°F = (°C x 1.8) + 32
1 inch = 2.54 centimeters (cm)
1 foot = 0.304 meters (m)
1 yard = 0.914 meters
1 mile = 1.6093 kilometers (km)
1 km = 0.6214 miles
1 fathom = 1.8288 m
1 chain = 20.1168 m
1 furlong = 201.168 m
1 acre = 0.4047 hectares
1 sq km = 100 hectares
1 sq mile = 2.59 square km
1 ounce = 28.35 grams
1 pound = 0.4536 kilograms
1 short ton = 0.90718 metric ton
1 short ton = 2,000 pounds
1 long ton = 1.016 metric tons
1 long ton = 2,240 pounds
1 metric ton = 1,000 kilograms
1 quart = 0.94635 liters
1 US gallon = 3.7854 liters
1 Imperial gallon = 4.5459 liters
1 nautical mile = 1.852 km

MOON MARYLAND & DELAWARE
Avalon Travel
a member of the Perseus Books Group
1700 Fourth Street
Berkeley, CA 94710, USA
www.moon.com

Editor: Shaharazade Husain
Series Manager: Kathryn Ettinger
Copy Editor: Mia Lipman
Graphics Coordinator: Stefano Boni
Production Coordinator: Darren Alessi
Cover Designer: Stefano Boni
Map Editor: Kevin Anglin
Cartographers: Kat Bennett, Chris Markiewicz
Indexer: Deana Shields

ISBN-10: 1-56691-830-8
ISBN-13: 978-1-56691-830-5
ISSN: 1531-5592

Printing History
1st Edition – 2001
3rd Edition – May 2008
5 4 3 2 1

Some photos and illustrations are used by permission and are the property of the original copyright owners.

Front cover photo: Bethany Beach, Delaware
© John Hartman/Stock Connection/drr.net
Title page photo: © Joanne Miller
Interior color photos: © Joanne Miller

Printed in the United States by RR Donnelley

KEEPING CURRENT

If you have a favorite gem you'd like to see included in the next edition, or see anything that needs updating, clarification, or correction, please drop us a line. Send your comments via email to feedback@moon.com, or use the address above.